ROUTLEDGE HANDBOOK OF SUSTAINABLE PRODUCT DESIGN

As a cultivated form of invention, product design is a deeply human phenomenon that enables us to shape, modify and alter the world around us – for better or worse. The recent emergence of the sustainability imperative in product design compels us to recalibrate the parameters of good design in an unsustainable age. Written by designers, for designers, the *Routledge Handbook of Sustainable Product Design* presents the first systematic overview of the burgeoning field of sustainable product design. Brimming with intelligent viewpoints, critical propositions, practical examples and rich theoretical analyses, this book provides an essential point of reference for scholars and practitioners at the intersection of product design and sustainability. The book takes readers to the depth of our engagements with the designed world to advance the social and ecological purpose of product design as a critical twenty-first-century practice. Comprising 35 chapters across 6 thematic parts, the book's contributors include the most significant international thinkers in this dynamic and evolving field.

Jonathan Chapman is Professor of Sustainable Design and Director of Design Research at the University of Brighton, UK. His research shapes future design paradigms for longer-lasting materials, products and user experiences – an approach he defines as 'emotionally durable design'. He has developed this research with over 100 global businesses and governmental bodies – from Sony, Puma, The Body Shop and Philips to the House of Lords and the United Nations – advancing the social and ecological relevance of their products, technologies and systems. Professor Chapman's work in sustainable product design has generated international media attention from publications such as *The New York Times*, *The Guardian*, *The Independent*, CNN International and BBC Radio 4. *New Scientist* described him as 'a mover and shaker' and a 'new breed of sustainable design thinker'.

'Brimming with intelligent viewpoints, critical propositions, practical examples and rich theoretical analyses, this book provides an essential point of reference for scholars and practitioners at the intersection of product design and sustainability.'

– John Thackara, Founder, Doors of Perception

'To profoundly understand something, you need to study it from all possible angles. This impressive volume does exactly this. With contributions by leading scholars from a diverse range of backgrounds, it brings us the multidisciplinary perspective on sustainable product design that designers, academics, and – ultimately – the world so desperately need.'

– Paul Hekkert, Professor, Department of Industrial Design, Delft University of Technology

'The case against mindless design has never been made more effectively. Chapman brings together an amazing assembly of contemporary design researchers to discuss one of our greatest challenges: making the world safe for future inhabitants. Whatever you are designing, you may want to keep this book close to remind you of all the exciting new possibilities for sustainable design.'

– Conny Bakker, Associate Professor, Design for Sustainability / Circular Product Design, TU Delft

'Product design is at a crossroads with product designers now a fractured constituency. The difference can be viewed in three ways: retaining the historically established focus on the object, be it so often bonded to the unsustainable; redeeming the object by attempting to make it "sustainable"; or lastly, abandoning, eliminating or dematerialising it. This collection of essays gives the discerning reader the opportunity to make an informed decision on the most appropriate path design and designing should take.'

– Tony Fry, Director, Studio at the Edge of the World

'An utmost intriguing and extensive multi-angled journey through the constructed world we live in. Design lies at the core of the errors in our system and can only be solved by rethinking it all from the start. This handbook makes clear how we can realise this necessary transformation towards intelligent products with healthy upcyclable materials. When we understand where we come from and are aware of the beneficial alternatives for today's tomorrow, we can define our future positively.'

– Michael Braungart, CEO EPEA Internationale Umweltforschung, Co-founder Cradle to Cradle

'Chapman offers an authoritative view on sustainable product design through the collective understanding of key protagonists in the field. Sometimes they agree, sometimes they don't, but the breadth of writing and analysis of key concerns frames the social and ecological agency of design and its role in our material future. It will become essential reading for anyone working in product design and its associated practices.'

– Matt Malpass, University of the Arts London: Central Saint Martins

'Drawing from his experience exploring our emotional relationship with objects, Jonathan Chapman gathers and frames a vital and plural collection of texts on sustainability from the key thinkers in the field. Chapman and his co-authors ably illustrate that the problem is a political one, confounded by our conflicting notions of progress, and reliant upon the psychological frailties of consumer behavior and the appetite for organizational change.'

– Tim Parsons, Chair of Designed Objects Programs, The School of the Art Institute of Chicago

ROUTLEDGE HANDBOOK OF SUSTAINABLE PRODUCT DESIGN

Edited by Jonathan Chapman

Routledge
Taylor & Francis Group

LONDON AND NEW YORK

FIDM Library
55 Stockton Street
San Francisco, CA 94108

First published 2017
by Routledge
2 Park Square, Milton Park, Abingdon, Oxon OX14 4RN

and by Routledge
711 Third Avenue, New York, NY 10017

Routledge is an imprint of the Taylor & Francis Group, an informa business

© 2017 selection and editorial matter, Jonathan Chapman; individual
chapters, the contributors

The right of Jonathan Chapman to be identified as the author of the
editorial material, and of the authors for their individual chapters, has been
asserted in accordance with sections 77 and 78 of the Copyright, Designs
and Patents Act 1988.

All rights reserved. No part of this book may be reprinted or reproduced or
utilized in any form or by any electronic, mechanical, or other means, now
known or hereafter invented, including photocopying and recording, or in
any information storage or retrieval system, without permission in writing
from the publishers.

Trademark notice: Product or corporate names may be trademarks or
registered trademarks, and are used only for identification and explanation
without intent to infringe.

British Library Cataloguing in Publication Data
A catalogue record for this book is available from the British Library

Library of Congress Cataloging in Publication Data
Names: Chapman, Jonathan, 1974- editor.
Title: The Routledge handbook of sustainable product design / edited by
Jonathan Chapman.
Description: New York : Routledge, 2017. | Includes bibliographical
references and index.
Identifiers: LCCN 2016044175| ISBN 9781138910171 (hb : alk. paper) |
ISBN 9781315693309 (ebook)
Subjects: LCSH: Product design--Environmental aspects. | Sustainable
design.
Classification: LCC TS171.4 .R685 2017 | DDC 658.5/752--dc23
LC record available at https://lccn.loc.gov/2016044175

ISBN: 978-1-138-91017-1 (hbk)
ISBN: 978-1-315-69330-9 (ebk)

Typeset in Bembo
by HWA Text and Data Management, London

To Ming Ming and Jasper

CONTENTS

List of figures   xi
List of tables   xv
List of contributors   xvi

Introduction   1
Jonathan Chapman

PART I
The made world   7

1 A brief history of (un)sustainable design   11
   Damon Taylor

2 The half-life of a sustainable emotion: searching for meaning in
   product usage   25
   Gerald C. Cupchik

3 A renaissance of animism: a meditation on the relationship between
   things and their makers   41
   Michael Leube

4 The object of nightingales: design values for a meaningful material
   culture   53
   Stuart Walker

5 Challenges of the cultural differentiation of technology   69
   Petran Kockelkoren

Contents

6 Sustainable product design: an oxymoron?   83
Clive Dilnot

PART II
Agents of change   **97**

7 Sustainable thinking   101
Aaris Sherin

8 Engaging designers in sustainability   112
Vicky Lofthouse

9 Design for sustainable behaviour   127
Debra Lilley and Garrath T. Wilson

10 Mending broken promises in sustainable design   145
Alex Lobos

11 Sharing, materialism, and design for sustainability   160
Russell Belk

12 A journey of two designers   173
Yorick Benjamin

PART III
Materials and processes   **193**

13 Conflict minerals and the politics of stuff   197
Colin Fitzpatrick

14 Materially yours   206
Elvin Karana, Elisa Giaccardi and Valentina Rognoli

15 Mediating matters   222
Nick Gant

16 Print to repair: 3D printing and product repair   236
Miles Park

17 Unmaking waste   250
Robert Crocker

PART IV
User experience 267

18 Emotional sustainability 271
Deana McDonagh

19 Pleasant experiences and sustainable design 282
Juan Carlos Ortíz Nicolás

20 Surprising longevity 298
Silvia Grimaldi

21 Design for sustainable use using principles of behaviour change 316
Casper Boks and Johannes Zachrisson Daae

22 Hacking the probe-head: manipulations for social sustainability 335
Otto von Busch

23 Transitions in sociotechnical conditions that afford usership:
sustainable who? 349
Cameron Tonkinwise

PART V
Systems and services 359

24 Product service systems and the future of design 363
Tracy Bhamra and Ricardo J. Hernandez

25 A consumer's perspective on the circular economy 374
Ruth Mugge

26 Designing circular possessions 391
Weston Baxter and Peter Childs

27 Which way to turn? Product longevity and business dilemmas in
the circular economy 405
Tim Cooper

28 How about dinner? Concepts and methods in designing for
sustainable lifestyles 423
Annelise de Jong and Ramia Mazé

29 The Sustainable Energy for All Design Scenario 443
Carlo Vezzoli and Elisa Bacchetti

Contents

PART VI
Design futures   465

30 From good to the greater good   469
    Anna Pohlmeyer and Pieter Desmet

31 Plans and speculated actions: design, behaviour and complexity in
    sustainable futures   487
    Dan Lockton and Veronica Ranner

32 From product design to relational design: adding 'jeong' to the
    metadesigner's vocabulary   502
    John Wood

33 Products of the open design context   514
    Paul Micklethwaite

34 Promoting sustainability through mindful design   527
    Kristina Niedderer

35 Design for social innovation and new product contexts   540
    Nicola Morelli

    Index   555

FIGURES

2.1	Stone tool from the Sinai Desert at least 500,000 years old	26
2.2	Leather sofa chair, Link, designed by Matthijs van Dijk for the Dutch design agency KVD	28
4.1	Three facets of human meaning and their interrelationships	57
4.2	Beliefs, values and actions	59
8.1	The spectrum in which designers can engage with sustainability	114
8.2	SenseoUp one-cup coffee machine, Philips Design, 2015	114
8.3	Nest Thermostat, by NEST, 2015	118
9.1	Design for sustainable behaviour design process	128
9.2	Matching methods with factors	130
9.3	Axis of influence	132
9.4	Required intervention obtrusiveness	135
10.1	A model for effective sustainability in product design is based on three parts laid simultaneously across a product's lifecycle	148
10.2	Broom chair	150
10.3	Detail of chair's recycling symbol	150
10.4	Project Ara Spiral 2 prototype	152
10.5	Acute washer concept with floating frame allows for reduced proportions without worrying about excessive vibration	155
10.6	Washer can be accessed as a top loader (increasing convenience) and run as a front loader (reducing water consumption)	156
12.1	Overview human health, ecosystem quality and resources analysis of the two shelter designs	180
12.2	Potential impacts to human health are significantly different in the two designs	180
12.3	D4S Shelter for TfL incorporating SD strategies of product longevity reuse, colocation, future proofing and back-to-grid solar and renewable resources	181
12.4	Shelters install in 15 minutes minimizing disruption and environmental impact	186
12.5	Maxi shelter for approximately 16 users	187
12.6	Mini cantilever design: a compact design for low footfall sites and for narrow pavements	189

12.7	Midi, the square base design allows installation in 90° increments for weather protection	189
14.1	Coffee cups designed with waste coffee grounds by Lou Io	210
14.2	543 Broadway Chair designed by Gaetano Pesce	211
14.3	The Happy Misfit Armchair, designed by Rutger de Regt from Handmade Industrials	211
14.4	Brass Watering Can which develops patina over time, designed by Lee West	213
14.5	*Underskog* designed by Kristine Bjaadal	213
14.6	*Propolis* made of insects by Marlène Huissoud	215
14.7	Xylinum Cones by Jannis Huelsen with Stefan Schwabe for Science Gallery/Dublin	216
14.8	Yoga set by Joseph Guerra and Sina Sonrab	217
14.9	Soft Light by Simon Frambach	218
15.1	Coffee cups and coffee machine made from waste coffee, by Adam Fairweather	229
15.2	Gumdrop Bin made from waste chewing gum, by Anna Bullus	229
15.3	New Balance 'Farmer's Market' trainers (2012)	231
15.4	Flip-Flopsam and Jetsam (2011): flip-flops made from plastic beach waste embossed with a map relating to the source of material	231
16.1	The Ultimaker Original is offered as a DIY kit that can be upgraded	240
16.2	Redesigned bread maker latch printed in laser-sintered stainless steel	243
16.3	3D print files for replacement and customisable knob for the OP-1 music synthesizer	243
18.1	The four key life stages and their relation to material consumption	276
18.2	Alternative to buttons, metal bar and hoop as clothes fastener	279
18.3	Example of a silicon wrap on the packaging for enhanced functionality	279
19.1	The Rubik's cube	286
19.2	A tool that aims to communicate how people experience inspiration	288
19.3	A Polaroid camera that enhances a significant experience	291
20.1	Passport design sketches from the competition held by the National Police Directorate of Norway	299
20.2	Knotted Chair by Marcel Wanders	306
20.3	*Waterproof Lamp* by Hector Serrano	307
20.4	*Spineless Lamps* by Frederik Roijé	307
20.5	*Grand Central Chair* by David Rockwell	308
20.6	*Soft Urn* by Hella Jongerius	309
20.7	*Nipple Chair* by Dunne and Raby	310
20.8	*Gauge* by Jim Rokos	311
20.9	*On-Edge Lamp* by Silvia Grimaldi	313
21.1	Timeline for the development of Design for Sustainable Behaviour as a research field	318
21.2	Control–obtrusiveness landscape	319
21.3	Ideas for design interventions plotted into the control–obtrusiveness landscape	322
21.4	Finding out how different personas would react to various control–obtrusiveness combinations	323
21.5	Reasons for using too much detergent	327
21.6	Research process	328
21.7	The ★Roll design solution developed in response to case study data and insight	329
21.8	Mapping 'forceful/subtle' and 'user in control/product in control' scenarios	331

23.1	Models of transition to more sustainable futures	352
24.1	Main categories and subcategories of product service systems	367
25.1	Circular economy butterfly diagram	376
25.2	Modular components of the Fairphone 2	377
25.3	My television screen	379
25.4	My Tube Light	379
25.5	My Aalto vase	380
25.6	My bear sculpture	381
25.7	Hierarchy of product attachment	382
25.8	Personalization strategy: Pop Light by Bernabeifreeman	383
25.9	Growing, designed by Marc Benito Padró (2014)	384
26.1	Framework for psychological ownership-based attachment to possessions	394
26.2	Four common paths for developing attachment or psychological ownership	397
26.3	Common paths for detachment and absolving psychological ownership	401
28.1	The position of practice theory within social theory	426
28.2	Positioning social practices	427
28.3	Static! Erratic Radio prototype and household study	429
28.4	Storyboard, documenting cooking practices and socio-cultural 'doings'	434
28.5	Blog procedure for the food waste study	435
29.1	The paradigm shift from non-renewable/centralized to renewable/distributed energy generation systems	445
29.2	A schematic representation of distributed renewable energy generation	445
29.3	Vision 1: Energy for all in daily life	448
29.4	Screenshots from the video *Energy for all in daily life* by Korapan Vanitkoopalangkul	449
29.5	Screenshots from the video *Energy for all in daily life* by Korapan Vanitkoopalangkul	449
29.6	Vision 2: Energize your business without investment cost	451
29.7	Screenshots from the video *Energize your business without investment cost* by Korapan Vanitkoopalangkul	453
29.8	Screenshots from the video Energize your business without investment cost by Korapan Vanitkoopalangkul	453
29.9	Vision 3: 'Pay × use' your daily life products and energy	454
29.10	Screenshots from the video *Pay × use* for your daily life products and energy, by Korapan Vanitkoopalangkul	455
29.11	Screenshots from the video *Pay × use* for your daily life products and energy, by Korapan Vanitkoopalangkul	455
29.12	Vision 4: 'Start-up your business' paying per period for equipment and energy	457
29.13	Screenshots from the video *Start-up your business* paying per period for equipment and energy, by Korapan Vanitkoopalangkul	459
29.14	Screenshots from the video *Start-up your business* paying per period for equipment and energy, by Korapan Vanitkoopalangkul	459
29.15	Screen shot from the tool: Sustainable Design Orienting Scenario for Sustainable Product-Service System applied to Distributed Renewable Energy	460
29.16	Screenshots from the video *Energy for all in daily life*, by Korapan Vanitkoopalangkul (screenshot of main video)	461
29.17	Screenshots from the video *Energy for all in daily life*, by Korapan Vanitkoopalangkul (screenshot of sub-video 1)	461

29.18 Screenshots from the video *Energy for all in daily life*, by Korapan
       Vanitkoopalangkul (screenshot of sub-video 2)   462
29.19 Screenshots from the video *Energy for all in daily life*, by Korapan
       Vanitkoopalangkul (screenshot of sub-video 3)   462
30.1   Positive design framework   472
30.2   Bits 'n' Bytes by Marije Vogelzang   474
30.3   Kitchen Safe by David Krippendorf: a time-locking container, designed to
       support self-control   477
30.4   Classroom layouts for individual, teacher-centred learning and teamwork,
       respectively   479
31.1   The Design with Intent toolkit cards   493
31.2   Design students at Carnegie Mellon University trying out an early version of
       the consequence questions together with the Design with Intent toolkit cards 496
33.1   The Double Diamond representation of the design process   523
34.1   Safety feature   532
34.2   Mindful design mechanisms   533
34.3   *Keymoment*   535
34.4   Keymoment – have a break   536
35.1   Two perspectives of change   545
35.2   The Life 2.0 ecosystem   549

TABLES

2.1	Complementary processes extended to design product relations	31
2.2	Complementary relationships with design objects	34
4.1	Characteristics of ethical and meaningful design decision-making	66
7.1	Steps for developing a design strategy	105
12.1	Sustainable design features of the Maxi shelter	187
16.1	General advantages for 3D printing replacement parts	241
16.2	Environmental advantages for 3D printing replacement parts	245
18.1	Four seasons of life	275
26.1	Affordance principles aiding in the creation of psychological ownership	396
30.1	Differences and similarities of well-being ingredients	481
32.1	Revision of the usual distinctions between 'theory' and 'practice'	506
32.2	Relative benefit/loss chart for different types of coupling	511
34.1	Basic design mechanisms for enabling behaviour change	530

CONTRIBUTORS

Elisa Bacchetti is currently a PhD student at the Politecnico di Milano, Design Department, with a topic related to System Design for Sustainable Energy for All (SD4SEA). She has been lecturing on this issue in South Africa, Uganda and Botswana. She has a managing role in the LeNSes (EU funded, 2013–2016 Edulink II programme) and the LeNSin (EU funded, 2015–2018 Erasmus+ programme) projects, both coordinated by Politecnico di Milano.

Weston Baxter is a doctoral candidate in the Dyson School of Design Engineering at Imperial College London. His research focuses on understanding and designing for consumer behaviour within the circular economy.

Russell Belk is York University Distinguished Research Professor and Kraft Foods Canada Chair in Marketing, Schulich School of Business, York University. He has approximately 600 publications. His research tends to be qualitative, visual and cultural. It involves the extended self, meanings of possessions, collecting, gift-giving, sharing, digital consumption and materialism.

Yorick Benjamin is Director of Sustainable Design at Falmouth University and the company 'Natural Shelter'. He explores context within whole systems to unlock innovation through the smallest of details. His clients include the European Environment Agency, United Nations Environment Programme-IE, the European Foundation the British Standards Institute, Transport for London, Clear Channel and The Body Shop International.

Tracy Bhamra is Professor of Sustainable Design and Pro Vice-Chancellor (Enterprise) at Loughborough University. In 2003 she established the Sustainable Design Research Group at Loughborough University that undertakes world-leading research in areas such as design for sustainable behaviour, methods and tools for sustainable design, sustainable product service system design and sustainable design education.

Casper Boks is Professor in Sustainable Design and Head of the Department of Product Design, NTNU Norwegian University of Science and Technology. His research interests include sustainable product innovation and education in general, and currently focus on design for sustainable behaviour, and organizational, managerial and stakeholder conditions for successful implementation of sustainable product innovation.

Peter Childs is Head of the Dyson School of Design Engineering and the Professorial Lead in Engineering Design at Imperial College London. His general interests include creativity tools, product and system design, fluid flow and heat transfer. He is a director of Q-Bot Ltd and Creative Director at ICeni Labs.

Tim Cooper is Professor of Sustainable Design and Consumption at Nottingham Trent University and Co-Director of the EPSRC-funded Centre for Industrial Energy, Materials and Products. Contributing editor of *Longer Lasting Products* (Gower, 2010), his research interests are multidisciplinary and embrace sustainable design, consumer behaviour, public policy and environmental values.

Robert Crocker is a researcher whose interests lie in the history of consumerism and its relationship to design. He is the author of *Somebody Else's Problem: Consumerism, Design and Sustainability* (Greenleaf, 2016), and co-editor of *Subverting Consumerism: Reuse in an Accelerated World* (Routledge, 2016). He is working on a history of the idea of the Circular Economy.

Gerald C. Cupchik studied with Bob Zajonc at the University of Michigan (BA), received his Masters (1970) and PhD (1972) at the University of Wisconsin with Howard Leventhal before doing postdoctoral study with Daniel Berlyne (1972–74) at the University of Toronto where he has been a professor of psychology since 1974. He has collaborated with scholars from many fields emphasizing the complementary use of quantitative and qualitative research methods to study responses to art, design, literature, and film. He was president of APA Division 10, the International Association for Empirical Aesthetics, and the International Society for the Empirical Study of Literature, and received the Rudolf Arnheim Award in 2010 from the APA.

Annelise de Jong is Senior Researcher at the Interactive Institute Swedish ICT. She has worked as Assistant Professor in the Industrial Design faculty at TU Delft, in the Applied Ergonomics and Design Department, where she also obtained a PhD in Industrial Design.

Pieter Desmet is Chair of the Design for Experience research group and programme director of the Design for Interaction master's program at the Faculty of Industrial Design Engineering at TU Delft. His main research interests are in the fields of design, emotion and subjective well-being.

Clive Dilnot is Professor of Design Studies at Parsons School of Design, The New School in New York City. Recent work includes the co-authored *Design and the Question of History (2014),* the edited volumes *The John Heskett Reader: History, Design, Economics* (2016) and *Design and the Creation of Value* (2017). He is preparing a four volume series of collected papers, *Rethinking Design (On History, On Ethics, On Knowledge, On Configuration*; 2018).

Colin Fitzpatrick is a Senior Lecturer in the Department of Electronic and Computer Engineering at the University of Limerick, Ireland. He teaches and researches extensively on Eco Design, Product Lifetime Extension, Reuse, Conflict Minerals, Circular Economy, WEEE and Electricity Demand Management as they relate to the electronics sector.

Nick Gant is a design researcher with material specialism at the University of Brighton, UK. Nick's practice-based research has been utilized by iconic brands, charitable organizations and NGOs providing expertise on material design, transformation and application to enhance the performance, value and meaning of objects, products and spaces.

Elisa Giaccardi is Professor and Chair of Interactive Media Design at Delft University of Technology, where she leads the Connected Everyday Lab. From her pioneering work in meta-design and participatory technology to the non-human in the Internet of Things and multi-situated materials, her design research reflects an ongoing concern with design as a shared process of cultivation and management of opportunity spaces.

Silvia Grimaldi is a Course Leader of the BA (Hons) Spatial Design at London College of Communication, University of the Arts London. She is currently researching the role of narrative in users' interpretation of product experience. Other research focuses on emotional design, in particular investigating the role of surprise in eliciting product emotions.

Ricardo J. Hernandez is Lecturer in Design and Innovation at Lancaster University. He holds an MSc and MRes in Industrial Engineering and completed his PhD in Design of Sustainable Product-Service Systems at Loughborough University in 2012. His PhD explored how design can support small and medium sized enterprises to make a transition towards sustainable operations using the PSS concept.

Elvin Karana is Associate Professor at Industrial Design Engineering, TU Delft. She leads research projects focusing on design for material experiences, demonstrating the applicability of this thinking in design research and design practice. Elvin is the main editor of *Materials Experience: Fundamentals of Materials and Design* (2014, Elsevier).

Petran Kockelkoren studied philosophy at the University of Groningen in the Netherlands. He got his PhD in 1992 on the topic of 'a hermeneutics of nature'. Central to his thesis was the concept of 'technical mediation', that is the idea that technology does not per se alienate our perceptions of nature but may contribute to a 'mediated' reading of meanings in nature. From 2001 to 2011 he was professor in art and technology at the Department of Philosophy in the Faculty of Behavioral Sciences of the University of Twente, Enschede. From 2003 to 2007 he was simultaneously appointed professor in art and technology at ArtEZ Institute of the Arts, Dutch Vocational University Arnhem/Enschede. He is the author of several books on the subject of the artistic domestication of technology and on mediated vision.

Michael Leube is an Anthropologist (BA from the University of California at Berkeley, MA from the University of Vienna, and PhD from the University of Zagreb). At the Salzburg University of Applied Sciences and other universities worldwide, he researches and teaches on the sustainable interface between anthropology and design.

Debra Lilley is a Senior Lecturer in Industrial/Product Design at Loughborough Design School. Debra completed the first UK PhD in Design for Sustainable Behaviour and has extensive knowledge and experience of applying user-centred sustainable design methods and tools to generate behavioural insights to drive design development of less resource intensive products.

Alex Lobos focuses on sustainability, emotional attachment and user-centred design. He is an Associate Professor of Industrial Design and Miller Professor for International Education at Rochester Institute of Technology in upstate New York. Alex holds a MFA from the University of Notre Dame and a BID from Universidad Rafael Landivar.

Dan Lockton is a designer and researcher interested in human behaviour, understanding and sustainability. He joined Carnegie Mellon University's School of Design in 2016. Dan is author of *Design with Intent* (O'Reilly), based on his PhD at Brunel University, and was previously a visiting tutor at the Royal College of Art.

Vicky Lofthouse is a Senior Lecturer in Industrial Design and heads the Sustainable Design Research Group in the Design School at Loughborough University. She has been a practicing researcher/consultant in the field since 1998. Her current research explores the implementation of sustainable design in professional industrial design practice.

Ramia Maze is Professor of New Frontiers in Design at Aalto University, Finland. Previously in Sweden, she worked at Konstfack College of Arts Crafts and Design, at KTH Royal Institute of Technology and as a Senior Researcher and project leader at the Interactive Institute. Her PhD is in Interaction Design.

Deana McDonagh is Professor of Industrial Design in the School of Art & Design at the University of Illinois (Urbana-Champaign) and faculty at the Beckman Institute of Advanced Science and Technology. Prior to joining the University of Illinois she was a Reader in User-Centred Design at Loughborough University, UK. She is an Empathic Design Research Strategist who focuses on enhancing quality of life for all through more intuitive and meaningful products, leading to emotional sustainability. She is a Research Fellow at Coventry University (UK) and Director of Research for Herbst Produkt design consultancy (USA).

Paul Micklethwaite is Course Director of MA Sustainable Design at Kingston University, London. He is interested in the impact of the sustainability agenda on theories and practices of design, and modes of design practice which are explicitly social. He is co-author of *Design for Sustainable Change* (AVA Academia, 2011).

Nicola Morelli is Professor at Aalborg University in Denmark. He has previously worked at RMIT University, in Australia and Politecnico di Milano, Italy. He teaches on the Service Systems Design Masters at Aalborg University, and coordinates several research projects on service design, with a special focus on public services social innovation and sustainability and service design methodologies.

Ruth Mugge is Associate Professor of Consumer Research at the Faculty of Industrial Design Engineering at TU Delft. Her research focuses on understanding consumer response to product design to help designers create successful, sustainable products. She has published her research in various design and sustainability journals.

Kristina Niedderer is Professor of Design and Craft at the University of Wolverhampton. Apprenticed as a goldsmith and silversmith in Germany, she subsequently trained as a designer and design researcher in the UK. Niedderer is Secretary for Special Interest Groups of the Design Research Society and she leads the European project 'Designing for People with Dementia'.

Juan Carlos Ortíz Nicolás is Assistant Professor at the Autonomous University of Ciudad Juarez. He undertook his PhD in User Experience at Imperial College London. His research develops better understandings of the relations between people and the products they own and the artefacts they create. He is editing a book on *Design and Affection* to be published in Mexico. Juan Carlos has delivered lectures in interaction design and user experience at postgraduate level in the Netherlands, Japan, the United Kingdom, Panama and Colombia.

Miles Park is a Senior Lecturer in Industrial Design at the University of New South Wales, Australia. He leads the graduation year design studio, and contributes to other technology and design theory courses. His research includes product lifespans and repair, e-waste, design and digital prototyping, and is co-chair of IDEN (Industrial Design Educators Network).

Anna Pohlmeyer is Assistant Professor at the Faculty of Industrial Design Engineering, TU Delft, and co-director of the Delft Institute of Positive Design. With a background in psychology, engineering, and design, her research focuses on experience design and design-mediated subjective well-being.

Veronica Ranner is a designer, artist and researcher interested in networked cycles, emerging bio-technologies and bio-fabrication, systems design and new roles for designers. She is currently pursuing an AHRC funded PhD at the Royal College of Art, examining the burgeoning domain of the bio-digital – a converging knowledge space where computational thinking meets biological matter.

Valentina Rognoli is Assistant Professor at the School of Design, Politecnico di Milano, Italy. In 2004, she completed her PhD with a thesis titled 'Expressive-Sensorial Atlas of Materials for Design'. She is part of Madec, a research centre of material design culture, collaborating with *Polifactory*, the makerspace of Politecnico di Milano and she is one of the founders of Experience and Interaction Research Lab. Her research and education interests include materials education, Materials Driven Design MDD method, materials for interactions, emerging materials experiences and DIY materials.

Aaris Sherin is an Associate Professor at St. John's University in Queens, New York. She is the author of a number of books including her most recent publications *Sustainable Thinking: Ethical Approaches to Design and Design Management* (Bloomsbury, 2013) and *Modernism Reimagined: The Art and Design of Elaine Lustig Cohen* (RIT Press, 2014). In her research Sherin addresses complex issues including the environment, creative thinking and innovative problem solving methodologies that can occur across media and disciplines.

Damon Taylor is a design theorist and philosopher who writes on the relationship between the made environment and the politics of action. He is Senior Lecturer in Design at the University of Brighton, where he teaches design and craft history and theory, (un)sustainable design, socially useful design, and design systemics.

Cameron Tonkinwise is the Director of Design Studies and Doctoral Studies at Carnegie Mellon University's School of Design. Cameron has a background in philosophy of technology and his research and teaching focus on service design for systems of shared use and transition design.

Carlo Vezzoli has 20 years' experience on researching and teaching Design for Sustainability (DfS). He is Professor of Design for Sustainability at the Design Department of the Politecnico di Milano and founder of the *Learning Network on Sustainability* (LeNS), a worldwide network of more than 50 top universities from all continents aiming at diffusing DfS with an open and copyleft ethos (www.lens-international.org).

Otto von Busch is based at Parsons School of Design, The New School, where he explores the emergence of a new *hacktivist* role in fashion, where the designer engages participants to reform fashion from a phenomenon of dictations, anxiety and fear, into a collective experience of empowerment and liberation.

Stuart Walker is Chair of Design for Sustainability and Director of the Imagination Lancaster Research Centre at Lancaster University. He is also Visiting Professor at Kingston University, UK and Emeritus Professor at the University of Calgary, Canada. His books include *Sustainable by Design*, *The Spirit of Design*, *The Handbook of Design for Sustainability*, *Designing Sustainability* and *Design for Life*. His propositional designs have been exhibited in Italy, Canada, Australia, at the Design Museum, London and Brantwood, John Ruskin's former home in Cumbria.

Garrath T. Wilson is a Lecturer in Industrial/Product Design at Loughborough Design School. Combining professional design practice and research experience with a PhD in Design for Sustainable Behaviour, Garrath is interested in understanding and developing the role that design can take in reducing domestic energy consumption.

John Wood is Emeritus Professor of Design at Goldsmiths, University of London. His book *Designing for Micro-utopias: Thinking beyond the Possible* (Ashgate, 2007) outlines a basis for re-designing paradigms. As a Director of Creative Publics he applies his 'metadesign' approach within an organizational and industrial context.

Johannes Zachrisson Daae is a product designer educated at NTNU and TU Delft, and holds a PhD in Design for Sustainable Behaviour from NTNU. He currently works as Eco Designer at Bergfald Environmental Consultants and has a research position, as Associate Professor, at Oslo and Akershus University College.

INTRODUCTION

Jonathan Chapman

Sustainable product design is an essential discipline for the twenty-first century, located at the nexus of our most critical social, ecological and economic concerns.

Professionals and researchers alike engage with this burgeoning field, working as agents of change, with significant influence over the way in which the material world is realised. To date, this influence has largely been used as a means to pursue greater levels of economic growth, with little or no consideration of the associated social or ecological impacts. In the context of sustainable product design, the social, ecological *and* economic, are valued equally.

Serially produced, model after model, products are a constantly emerging synthesis of technological, social, cultural and economic agendas. Each product represents a moment, a piece of punctuation, on the longer narrative of our development and evolution. Far more than mere slick, shiny gizmos, products say a great deal about the collective values, aspirations and development of the society from which they emerge.

Product designers do not work in a bubble – few disciplines do – and must connect and engage with countless other specialists including digital marketing, electrical engineering and brand management, for example. That being said, it is the site of product design where meaningful syntheses are forged between disparate disciplinary agendas. Through this synthesis, new values, meanings and possibilities emerge. These emergent properties are the product designer's gift to the world.

The 35 chapters within this book argue for the development of products, materials, systems and services that are: circular not linear; fixable and repairable; fairer to all people across the supply chain; experientially rich; energy and resource efficient; and, physically and emotionally durable. Collectively, these agendas give shape and purpose to the notion of sustainable product design. Importantly though, this does not define sustainable product design in a closed or conclusive way. It would be counter-productive to do so at the outset of a book which explores, expands and adds specificity to the field. Rather, this book recalibrates the parameters of good product design in an unsustainable age. In doing so, it defines the field in a way that is fit for purpose in tackling the thorny problems of the twenty-first century.

Context and rationale

The closer you look into the hidden story of our designed goods, the more bizarre and distorted it becomes. Over the past century, the product design profession has unknowingly made the transition from *world maker*, to *world breaker*. Today's dominant model of product design and manufacture is still largely based on a linear system, with inbuilt ecological destruction at either end. This outdated system is driven by the flawed economic premise that equates product throughput with commercial success, regardless of the social or ecological consequences.

In terms of electronic products, we generate 40 tonnes of waste, to produce just 1 tonne of products. Of that 1 tonne, 98 per cent are discarded within just 6 months of purchase. Landfill sites aren't graveyards as people often claim – they're orphanages. The majority of products that end up here still function perfectly, in a utilitarian sense. In a world smothered in people and products, it must be questioned what – beyond a conventional understanding of functionality – is all this meaningful stuff really for, and why does it transform into meaningless rubbish so quickly?

It is well established that less than one sixth of all e-waste is properly recycled – despite it being stacked in neat, categorised stockpiles. This waste contains high levels of lead compounds, as well as mercury, cadmium, chromium. Other conflict minerals such as cassiterite, wolframite and coltan are in there too, due to their importance in the manufacture of electronic products. Fuelled by an unquenchable thirst for innovation, we stride forth in pursuit of faster, lighter, stronger futures. In doing so, we leave a trail of unwanted products behind us – toasters, flat screen TVs, potato peelers, tennis shoes, wardrobes and a host of other newly orphaned products, scar the rear view. This wasteful process is exacerbated by our deployment of material goods, as a means to mediate our constantly changing identities, as once loved products fall out of favour all too quickly.

Most people would decline the offer of a 500kg smartphone. Something so ridiculous, and so unfeasibly heavy could never form a part of your well-considered material world. It may surprise you to know then, that the majority of us already own such a product. The smartphone you cherish, and no doubt have with you right now, weighs 500kg. Let me explain. Put it on the scales and it will come out somewhere near 200g, give or take a gram or two. But product weight only tells a fraction of the whole product story. The true weight of the product is only revealed if we take into account all the resources needed to bring this product into the world. If we calculate the per-unit weight of the whole product story (including resource extraction, material processing, component manufacture, product fabrication, shipping, distribution, retail, use and eventual disposal) it weighs about half a tonne. Numbers can be a little abstract, so to put this into some kind of context, the average horse weighs about 500kg. So, sustainable product design is not about the 200g smartphone, it's about the whole 500kg. It's about the whole horse!

The materials we specify in products don't come out of the ground ready-formed, and often require complex processing, refinement and conversion to afford them the properties we require. The process of converting mined-matter into precious resource consumes vast amounts of energy, and often involves several other compounds in order for correct alchemy to occur. Most of these materials take several centuries to fully degrade – one reason why there are more Lego people in the world today, than actual people. Many materials are made up of several other materials, in composite, and complex component parts consume resources from an even wider pool. For example, a thumbnail-sized microchip contains almost all elements in the periodic table – a highly complex assemblage of physical and human resources. Furthermore, this conversion and processing of materials frequently takes place in parts of the world where workers rights are sorely compromised, lack fairness and are ambiguously defined at a policy level.

Even precious elements like gold are surprisingly commonplace in electronic products, largely due to their excellent conductive capabilities. For example, in terms of e-waste, there is more gold in a tonne of phones than there is in a tonne of rocks from a gold mine – a mind-boggling idea that shifts focus from waste management, to resource management. Despite this, the rock-bound gold is still considered more economically viable to extract than its phone-bound counterpart. This kind of waste is a design flaw. With rising resource costs, and mounting levels of legislation-driven producer responsibility, situations such as these must change – this book tells us how.

Aims of the book

The *Routledge Handbook of Sustainable Product Design* provides an essential point of reference for anyone working at the intersection of product design, sustainability and human behaviour. The book brings together previously disconnected bodies of scholarship to compile a rich repertoire of creative tools, methods and frameworks, for designers and design researchers to more effectively engage the sustainable product design space. The ultimate aim of this book, therefore, is to advance design research and business thinking, while reinvigorating the culture of social and ecological critique, so essential to the field of product design.

This book presents the first systematic overview of the burgeoning field of sustainable product design, brimming with intelligent viewpoints, controversial propositions, practical examples and theoretical analyses. Unified through the lens of product design, the divergent arguments within this book fuse sources from early social and philosophical writings to contemporary theories in cultural studies, anthropology, engineering, design and ecology. Through this approach, the book reframes design as both a prospective and transformative activity, to mount a sustainable revolution in product design.

The book features fresh thinking, from over 40 acclaimed researchers, to give context, meaning and purpose to this relatively new and emerging field. Their chapters draw into focus the critical role of product design in tackling complex twenty-first-century global issues. Collectively, the contributions in this book provide a timely review of the key literature in sustainable product design, and its neighbouring fields. Through this, each chapter provides an original point of entry into the complex and fascinating world of sustainable product design. In this way, the book has been shaped around the needs of a wide community of readers. Though predominately targeting the product design community this is a book for all learners, academics, professionals and students alike. The book will be of particular interest to postgraduate students and design researchers in the following fields: product design, industrial design, furniture design, experience design, interaction design, design anthropology and design management.

At times, the voices in this book agree, forming a fairly unanimous consensus. At other times, they clash, grate and collide awkwardly against one another – such is the contentious nature of the sustainable product design debate. This dynamism is important to the vitality of the field, and embracing difference of this nature is a key lesson in the path to sustainable product design. After all, in ecology we speak of the importance of diversity all the time. Yet, when it comes to research, we seem to forget these essential lessons from nature, in the blind pursuit of singular truths, and mass answers.

Scope of the book

This book takes us beyond the field's preoccupation with energy and manufacturing, to also engage the underlying psychological phenomena that foster cycles of desire, consumption, user experience and waste. By bringing together these two often separated approaches (the physical and the experiential), the book takes a 360° view of sustainable product design. It engages the discipline through two complementary lenses: the world of matter and energy, and the world of human experience. Through this fusion, the chapters within this anthology create a meaningful synthesis between two frequently opposing worlds.

Product design is a growing and dynamic field, connected to a surprisingly vast number of neighbouring fields at its periphery. A day in the life of a product designer, involves a great many collaborative encounters, with a great many individuals – stylists working with materials innovators, product engineers working with brand consultants and ergonomists working with user experience designers, to name but a few. It is an incredibly far-reaching field, and spills outwards into practically all disciplines – whether it's anthropology, developmental psychology and consumer studies, or material science, pharmacy and economics, they all connect to the multifaceted role of product design in important ways. In fact, I challenge you to name a discipline, which does not connect to the process of product design, in some way.

Design has a particularly broad epistemological base, and draws together a great many forms of knowledge – economic, scientific, social, medical and cultural, for example. There are times, in fact, when it becomes difficult to pinpoint exactly what, and who, a product designer is! Yet, if we strip away the titles, and the disciplinary jargon, we see quite a different collaborative picture. What we see at this moment, are groups of purposeful individuals exchanging skills, passions and knowledge to explore better ways of creating the material world around us. A good product designer knows this, and thrives in the role of catalyst, and broker of knowledge, among networks of other creative individuals.

As a cultivated form of invention, product design is a deeply human phenomenon that enables us to shape, modify and alter the world around us, for better or worse. The desire to enhance the parameters of life has always lurked within us as a species. In this way, it is perfectly natural to imagine how current situations, can be transformed into *preferred* ones. In many ways, product design is exactly this kind of process, and has been for many decades. What has changed in recent years, however, is what we mean by terms like *preferred*. Let me give you an example. To an ecological activist, these terms would refer to significantly reduced levels of consumption, entirely restructured economic systems and a rewriting of the script to which capitalism performs. To an account manager, the term *preferred* may very well relate to increased profit margins, innovative angles on taxation or a more relaxed legislative operating environment, for example.

Of course, design has always been about change, and making things better. In the context of sustainable product design, *better* helps us to aspire to new and innovative means of striking that elusive balance between social, environmental and economic wellbeing, in a continually changing world. In doing so, sustainable product design can be seen as the prospective and transformative activity that it is. Both individually, and as an aggregate package, the chapters in this book support this position, by providing the insight, knowledge and inspiration needed to drive social, economic and ecological progress.

The book's structure

The book is a whole and complete experience, but one which is made up of essential component parts. While the book has a clear agenda and purpose, each individual chapter within it, approaches this from a very different angle. Consequently, different readers will be drawn towards different authors, topics and arguments. This is an important learning experience for the reader, because it helps you to find your place within the vast sustainable product design debate. After all, it would be unrealistic for each of us to develop specialism within every single aspect of the topic – the field is simply too great. In contrast, the approach I encourage is to have a general understanding of the whole context of sustainable product design, but to also be aware of the specific areas within that, where you especially fit, and where your skills and capabilities are particularly valuable, impactful and potentially transformative.

The contributors to this book are proficient and excellent writers, as well as researchers. Each of their chapters has a readerly style, supported by robust theoretical foundations, and clearly framed arguments. As well as providing rich resources, each chapter also provides a helpful gateway into the literature associated with that particular topic. Readers of this book can select individual chapters as starting points for their research journey, then read outwards from there, using the the references as pathways into other research and scholarly domains. Much of this associated literature will also be found within other chapters of this book. However you choose to engage with this text, your journey through this book should be a positive and empowering one.

The 35 chapters within this book have been arranged across 6 themed parts, designed to take you on a clearly structured journey through the sustainable product design terrain. The key stages of this journey are as follows:

- Part I – The made world
  Examining the interactions between product design, the natural world and the underlying psychological phenomena that drive consumption and waste of consumer goods.
- Part II – Agents of change
  Reframing product designers as agents of social, ecological and economic change, supported by creative tools and methods that optimise the positive roles that material things play in our lives.
- Part III – Materials and processes
  Uncovering the ecological and sociopolitical dimension of materials and resources, to redefine their role as powerful mediators of product performance, perceived value and experience.
- Part IV – User experience
  Focusing on the use-phase of products, to define more resource efficient encounters with the material world, through the design of longer-lasting products, materials and user experiences.
- Part V – Systems and services
  Revealing system-level principles and tools that reconfigure the activity designing products and services in a way that is fit for purpose in delivering the circular economy vision.
- Part VI – Design futures
  Shaping new and emerging directions in sustainable product design, to highlight the ever-expanding role of the product designer in tackling complex twenty-first-century problems.

Despite reading being considered a fairly linear process, the book as a whole has been designed so that it does not need to be read from start to finish. It is a rare scholar indeed who picks up an edited volume of this scale, and reads it sequentially from cover to cover. More commonly, individuals will read portions that feel most relevant to their particular focus on the topic. A handbook such as this is something that researchers come back to, time and time again. As different research projects come and go, so too do the changing requirements for knowledge and understanding. This book aims to provide such a resource over the years to come.

PART I

The made world

Human destruction of the natural world is a crisis of behaviour and not one simply of energy and material alone. The made world is the way it is, because of the thinking, values and understandings that underpin its formation. As a cultivated form of invention, product design is a deeply human phenomenon that enables us to shape, modify and alter the world around us – for better or worse. The recent emergence of the sustainability imperative in product design compels us to recalibrate the parameters of *good design* in an unsustainable age.

This opening part of the book takes us beyond the field's preoccupation with materials, manufacturing and distribution, to engage the underlying cultural and psychological phenomena that foster cycles of desire, consumption, experience and waste. Each of the six chapters engages the core theme of design, and its relation to the made world. Their collective aim is to reframe the underlying behavioural phenomena that shape patterns of design, consumption and waste. In doing so, they show the complexity of the territory, while highlighting key opportunities for sustainable product design research and intervention. The contributors writing in this section draw together previously disconnected scholarship in behavioural psychology, anthropology, sustainability and design history, culture and theory. In doing so, they reimagine the role and purpose of design as a transformative process, driving human flourishing, prosperity and wellbeing. Their chapters may be summarized as follows:

1 A brief history of (un)sustainable design – *Damon Taylor*
   This chapter examines the emergence of the paradigm of sustainability in the practice of product design over the last half-century; arguing that the changing relation of design to issues of sustainability can be understood as an emergent 'environmentality', which shapes designed response.
2 The half-life of a sustainable emotion: searching for meaning in product usage – *Gerald C. Cupchik*
   The roots of product attachment can be found in the experiential structures of our interactions with material things. This chapter explores these roots, asking why users hold on to certain products that are beyond their prime, while discarding and replacing other products so frequently?

3 A renaissance of animism: a meditation on the relationship between things and their makers – *Michael Leube*
   Designers speak of the *spirit* of good design, yet it escapes definition, description and often evades discussion. This chapter reviews *animistic* epistemologies to further clarify the term and to enable a more inclusive and relational discourse for product design theory.
4 The object of nightingales: design values for a meaningful material culture – *Stuart Walker*
   Dominant commercial and political interpretations of progress and growth run in conflict with human values. This chapter reconsiders product design values that are congruent with age-old understandings of human meaning as well as with contemporary notions of sustainability.
5 Challenges of the cultural differentiation of technology – *Petran Kockelkoren*
   The ubiquitous dissemination of technologies has led to one universal consumer society revolving around the products of a handful of multinationals. The universalizing tendency of technology is over, making way for culturally differentiated forms of technological intimacy.
6 Sustainable product design: an oxymoron? – *Clive Dilnot*
   The origin, logic, direction and operative power of 'sustainability' and 'product design' are often deeply opposed. This chapter uncovers the limitations of the term 'sustainable product design' to propose a new language and direction for this expanded field of practice.

As these chapters collectively argue, the process of consumption is motivated by complex drivers, and is about far more than just the mindless purchasing of newer, shinier *stuff*. Rather, it is a journey towards the ideal or desired self that through cyclical loops of desire and disappointment becomes an endless process of consumption and waste. As we inefficiently fumble our way through countless embraces with material experiences – from skyscrapers to saltshakers – we temporarily connect with a longer-standing struggle to understand complex existential phenomena such as time, mortality, identity, meaning and utopia, for example. In the context of sustainable product design, this scenario raises critical questions, surrounding the greater role, meaning and purpose of products in our lives.

Our ecological impacts have been shaped over decades by the choices we make as an industry, the values we share as a society and the dreams we pursue as individuals. Ever increasing rates of consumption married with diminishing levels of societal and personal wellbeing expose the folly of this progress illusion. Furthermore, while the designed world continues to develop in technological and scientific complexity, the underlying human condition has changed relatively little. And so today, we find ourselves as primitive beings, transplanted into progressively abstract and technologically complex environments that are, arguably, beyond our nature as a species.

The made world may be understood as an inevitable consequence of the human condition, in which we have progressively found ways to modify and enhance the world around us. The urban spaces we roam, buildings we inhabit, products we use and garments we wear, collectively represent our intellectual capacity to imagine a better world that is beyond our current level of experience. Whether faster processing speeds, taller structures, smarter textiles or smaller components, we apply science, technology and design to realize our visions, and make them liveable. Take the running shoe, for example. Dissect such a product, and you will learn something of its construction, of the way it functions and of the basic relational properties of the materials and processes that make it, as a system, perform. Yet, the information revealed through this technical exercise would be limited, as it tells us nothing of the origin, direction, drive, intention and future of the design vision that underpins the development of this product. Now, dissect 20 generations of running shoes, one per season dating back 5 years, and you will learn significantly more. You will reveal the incremental adaption that this product has undergone. You will see clearly the direction of this evolution, and from this understand the values, goals and aspirations of the design culture from which it emerged.

1

A BRIEF HISTORY OF (UN)SUSTAINABLE DESIGN

Damon Taylor

Abstract

This chapter examines the emergence of the paradigm of sustainability in the practice of product design over the last half-century. It begins by acknowledging the difficulty in attempting to write any such history, while suggesting that it is by discussing the discourse of sustainability in design that any coherency can be achieved. The analysis centres upon three strands: international conventions and reports from bodies such as the UN are used as an index of the shifting nature of how the problem of sustainability has been understood; the response of the 'design world' to such changes is charted; and, the manner in which this has happened against a developing consumer culture is then mapped against these coordinates. It is argued that the changing relation of design and the wider culture to issues of sustainability can be understood as an emergent 'environmentality', a certain form of subjectivity that determines how such issues can be conceived of, which thus shapes the nature of any designed response. Three phases of this developing mindset are then identified: the 'greening' of design; 'ecodesign'; and sustainable approaches. Each of these paradigms are then critically examined to demonstrate how design, as a field of activity, has responded to the shifting definition of the problem as the model we now recognize as 'sustainability' has developed.

Keywords: sustainability, green consumerism, ecodesign, environmentality

Introduction

Until relatively recently, nobody outside of forest management talked very much about sustainability (Caradonna, 2014). Now, the idea that the design of any product should consider its environmental impact and the extent to which it should be sustainable have become commonly recognized parameters of design. It is difficult, therefore, to believe that sustainability has only been a recognizable concern in product design for less than twenty years. Yet in attempting to write the history of this development, to chart how this has come about, there are clear difficulties. Not least is that there is no agreed model for how this should be done. As the design historian Kjetil Fallan has observed, 'the history of sustainable design

11

remains to be written'. His suggestion is that one way to do this would be to examine 'how sustainability has been envisioned and visualized in the history of design since the 1960s, and how these visions have varied between different (sub)discourses and arenas and changed over time' (Fallan, 2015, p15). This seems a good way to approach the subject, since to come at it head-on may give something of a false impression. If the method was to chart the actual material design interventions themselves, to examine the actual products, then what might start to emerge is the appearance of a smooth progression from the carefree, polluting and resource-heavy product design of the 1960s, through to the increasingly efficient devices and dematerialized Product-Service Systems of the present day. It would be perfectly possible to do this: improvements in recycling could be demonstrated; appliances could be shown to use less energy and work more effectively; transport systems could be shown to be green, clean and ever improving. But this would be a distortion.

Yes, the above advances have been taking place, but this has been against a backdrop whereby, at least until very recently, such innovations actually represent very small interventions in a process that seems in reality to be going in the other direction. In order to chart the way in which an idea of sustainability, what might be called a discourse (Foucault, 2001; Dryzek, 2005), a way of talking and thinking about the problem, has come to change how product design is practised and conceived of, it may be necessary to examine the bigger picture. While it is beyond the scope of this short chapter to take on Fallan's larger project, the modest goal of this chapter is to chart the way in which three strands in the history of the last half-century have become interwoven. Throughout, the 'official' response to growing concerns about the way in which we are living is altering and damaging our natural environment, in the form of international conventions and reports from bodies such as the UN, is used as an index of the shifting nature of how the problem has been understood. Against this is placed the response of the 'design world', that is the practices of industry and the operations of the market, as positioned in relation to the often more radical commentary offered by those who reflect upon the practice of design. Finally, these themes are examined against the backdrop of a popular culture of making and using that could be described as the *rise and rise* of consumer culture. The final purpose of this is to lay out the development, or more properly the *descent* (Agamben, 2008), in the meaning of lineage, of a particular way of conceiving of the environment. The purpose of this is then to show how this has given rise to a certain way of seeing the world, a particular form of subjectivity, the effect of which it is argued can be seen in our relationship to the designed products that we make and use.

Design and the environment

Product design as a category is hard to define, given that it can refer to the design of appliances, furniture, lighting, signage, or even these days, elements of services or systems. As a practice it can be said to refer to the creation of objects that originate as design proposals in the form of sketches, drawings and models, through a process of prototyping, production, distribution and marketing (Slack, 2006). Historically speaking, what is described as product design developed to facilitate the creation of material objects to be sold in the marketplace and used by consumers. Trying to understand how product design could then be described as in any way becoming 'sustainable' is perhaps more troublesome. As the design historian Jonathan Woodham has observed, one of the key problems that the design profession has faced in adopting a more responsible role has been 'its intrinsic economic dependence on business, manufacturing industry and the retail sector' (Woodham, 1997, p230). Modernism, even at its most ideological in the early days after the Russian revolution, was intended to pursue a socialist design agenda through the optimization of function (Kiaer, 2008). The sense was that through greater refinement of the design and making process ever-better goods could be created for use; that a grammar of design could be elaborated and through this design would constantly improve, function would be optimized and design and the objects it helped create would be constantly made better (Heskett, 1980). What has been crucial to the form that product design has taken, however, is the extent to which this approach to the conception and making of things has been determined by its role in not just imagining how they might manifest on a physical level, but in bringing them to market and ensuring that designed products come to be interwoven within the lives of those who consume them. As Victor Margolin notes, as long as there has been anything that could recognizably be called design, it has been firmly 'embedded in consumer culture' (Margolin, 1998, p83). This has therefore been a defining feature of how design as a practice and a profession has been able to respond to the environmental crisis that has become increasingly apparent in the last half-century.

It was in the 1960s that the developed West discovered that it was living in an environment. It seems to have been an issue of scale. With regard to nationalism Benedict Anderson (1990) famously called the nation an imagined community, in that it existed once the conditions were such that individuals could perceive (or imagine) themselves to be part of a nation through shared experiences such as reading the daily newspaper. In the same way, it required a certain level of interconnectedness in the form of access to the media and communication technologies for people to be able to conceive of themselves as being part of something of the scale of an overarching and all-encompassing environment. Much is made of the photographs taken of the earth from space in the late 1960s and early 1970s and the effect that these had upon human consciousness, as people realized that the earth was a fragile, finite planet (Roloston, 2015). Yet it was the developing mass media of the time that made it possible for most people to see such images at all. The awareness of earth's unitary nature was not derived from the photographs alone, but was also dependent upon being able to experience them, and this was an effect of communication technology, of the emergence of a certain infrastructure of perception at this time.

Initial popular insight that something was wrong with humanity's relationship to nature began with growing concern about issues such as pollution and environmental degradation (Isenhour, 2015). Books such as Rachel Carson's *Silent Spring* (1962), which suggested that the use of pesticides could destroy North America's bird population, and large-scale pollution incidents such as the Torrey Canyon oil spill off Cornwall in 1967, represented some of the first stirrings of a public realization that there may be some drawbacks to the otherwise overridingly positive narrative of technological advancement that held sway at the time. Publications such as Paul and Anne Ehrlich's *The Population Bomb* (1968) and Garrett Hardin's *The Tragedy of the Commons* (1968) discussed the way in which the natural environment was being degraded. The suggestion was that as population grew, particularly in what was then called the 'third world', so resources would come under stress (Adams, 2001). At the same time a developing counter-culture introduced a more mystical element based on the idea that there was a spiritual dimension to humanity's relationship to the earth that was being strained by the technological bent of capitalist progress (Farrell, 1997). What unified such disparate strands was a growing sense that what had been hailed as ultimate and unassailable 'progress', the upward ascent of humanity through ingenuity, was no longer unquestionable.

In 1972 the Club of Rome published a report that seemed to give scientific weight to this assessment. In this analysis, conducted by a team of systems analysts led by Jay Wright Forrester, and using the startlingly modern new technology of computer modelling, the authors suggested that the 'carrying capacity' of the earth (the level at which the environment can absorb demands upon it) was not going to be able to sustain the rate of growth seen at that time. In *Limits to Growth*, the authors presented a stark conclusion: things could not continue as they were (Meadows *et al.*, 1972).

If at this point we are to look for the reaction of the design world (if there can be said to be any such thing), it might be most accurate to say that there was not one. In industrial design in the 1960s in the USA and Europe the major drive behind attempts to reform the role of designers in industry was the desire for legitimacy. For bodies such as the Industrial Design Society of America and the Council of Industrial Design in the UK, the main pressure was to attempt to have manufacturers take design seriously in the production process (Woodham, 1997). There were, of course, some outliers who spoke up to suggest that there needed to be an ecologically responsible design practice, but these were far from being typical (ibid.). In the 1969 book *Operating Manual for Spaceship Earth*, Richard Buckminster Fuller wrote of the need to understand earth's resources as finite, to see the planet as a closed system, as with a spaceship. A couple of years later Victor Papanek published *Design for the Real World* (1971) in which he argued for a political design practice that could cope with the challenge to the planet's capacity to sustain life. Thus it would be false to say that nobody was discussing how design could and should change in response to the circumstances. However, as Margolin has observed, 'this remained very much a marginal position and despite their later influence, at the time of their publication they had no significant impact on the practice of industrial design at the time' (Margolin, 1998, p84). This does not mean that such interventions can be ignored, however. What is interesting is the way in which such concerns were framed. Both Fuller and Papanek were hooking into a sense that the expansionary nature of capitalist progress, with its continual need for growth, was both a practical problem and a conceptual one. That is, on a material level more people, more manufacturing and more consumption would need ever-greater resources, and this was in the end not sustainable. This then meant that the very imaginative basis of such progress was in doubt: if things cannot grow forever, then where is this so called 'progress' taking us?

In 1973 Schumacher's *Small is Beautiful: A Study of Economics as if People Mattered* and Ivan Illich's *Tools for Conviviality* were published. Both of these suggested that a central problem of expansionary capitalism was that it had grown too far and that the scale of capitalism had become too huge for people; they argued for the benefits of small-scale production and a more human-centred approach. Thus it can be seen that in the analysis of the time the late 1960s and early 1970s were being characterized as a period in which the benefits of capitalism and production for consumption that had been expanding largely unchallenged since the end of the nineteenth century were coming to be seen as a threat to the systems upon which human civilization depends. While this can be understood as a rational analysis of the problem, it can also be seen as an imaginative response, in that any critique depended upon a wider sense of what was perceived to be in play, and what was at stake.

Environmentality

The increased productive capacity of industrialization has allowed for the development of large-scale populations. This has brought practical pressures to bear in terms of resources, but it has also necessitated shifts in how such 'masses' are to be controlled and how power relations arise. The philosopher Michel Foucault has discussed how governments govern in such situations. He argues that rather than seeing power as something that is exerted from above in such a situation, rather, in Foucault's terms, it can be understood as something that is present in every interchange, as a structuring logic. For him this is the result of the development of populations, of large bodies of people that are beyond the simple physical control of the state. In this way he suggests that the way power works can be seen as control through the 'conduct of conducts', a 'management of possibilities' (Foucault, 2001, p341). He calls this 'governmentality', whereby a form of governance, the method of control, is played out as a certain type of mentality, a particular kind of subjectivity: a way of seeing the world. In terms of government this is then more about a state that keeps their citizens under observation than any form of physical coercion, to the point where individuals internalize the rules and come to see the ways things are as 'natural' (Foucault, 1991; Dean, 2007). So, this is a model of control that is not just about formal state control (though it includes this), instead it is about the range of strategies that have emerged to allow a dominant world-view to persist, whereby the way the problem is continuously framed in a certain way, so people conceive of it in this manner, and, crucially, any response is then framed and understood in these terms. This approach can then be applied to the way in which human subjects relate to the world they inhabit, since as Arun Agrawal observes, 'much can then be learned from asking *how* "socially situated actors" come to "care about, act in relation to and think about their actions in terms of something they identify as 'the environment''' (Agrawal, 2005, p162).

In terms of the developing awareness that there was a 'problem' with the environment, so a very particular 'environmentality' can be seen to have been emerging in the late 1960s. That is, the issue was seen to be that the earth had been 'discovered' to be a finite place, not least through mediagenic images such as the 'Blue Marble' photographs of the planet hanging alone in space, but also through the phenomenon of large numbers of people experiencing such a sensation together through the mass-media. Thus the first stirrings of this phase of globalization, of not just materially increased global flows of trade, but the understanding of life existing at a global level, began to constitute an environmentality that could conceive of the degradation of the natural environment in such terms. Because at this time the issue seemed to be one of too many people putting pressure on the simple physical limit of Spaceship Earth, so this formed the imaginative sphere in which any response would take place.

The first major international gathering held to discuss sustainability at a global scale was the UN Conference on the Human Environment, held in Stockholm in 1972. This led to the establishment of the UN Environment Programme (UNEP) as well as the creation of many environmental protection agencies at the national level. However, there was still little wider perception that the natural world was under any significant threat. Since the Second World War, if most people had thought of environmental destruction at all it was not in terms of the slow decay of natural processes, it was more likely to be in the form of nuclear annihilation (Walker, 1994). Within public consciousness, this appeared to be the primary threat to life on earth at that time. People were generally not scared about the gradual decline of the natural environment over a large timescale, but the high-speed cataclysm of nuclear destruction. Certainly this was the case throughout the 1960s and 1970s, as the evidence seemed to suggest this was really what there was to worry about. If this pertained in the 1980s, then in the minds of the public, a new worry was to be added to the register of concern. In May 1985 scientists from the British Antarctic Survey reported that there appeared to be a 'hole' in the ozone layer. The data suggested that chloroflourocarbons (CFCs), gases used in refrigerators and aerosols, were primarily to blame. As Jonathan Shanklin of the British Antarctic Survey said: 'There was a scary side of the ozone hole, linked to skin cancers and cataracts and so on, which immediately engaged the public' (Hanwerk, 2010). The discovery of the hole in the ozone layer thus resulted in perhaps the one unmitigated success of environmental policy of the last thirty years, The Montreal Protocol of 1987, which outlawed the use of CFCs. With the ozone hole the health dangers appeared immediate. It was also possible to create substitutes for CFCs with little added cost, and so there was no real impact on the consumption habits and lifestyles of consumers.

What is thus striking about this first real intimation of the scale of the problem being beyond one defined by a simple population/resources calculation, is that it seemed that human ingenuity, in the form of technology, as regulated by international law, would be able to remedy such difficulties. What this did not do was challenge the dominant environmentality of the time, which could be said to have been located firmly within a narrative of technological progress based in a paradigm of economic development. Yes, it seemed to suggest that such development would need to be conducted in a careful and regulated manner, but there was at this time little sense that it could not go on indefinitely. However, as Schumacher observed, economics does not stand on its own feet – it must derive from meta-economics, a world-view that suggests what is and is not possible, or even conceivable. He notes that if economists do not take notice of this they fall into 'a similar kind of error to that of certain medieval theologians who tried to settle questions of physics by means of biblical quotations' (Schumacher, 1973, p38). That is to say, the old model of reality tends to set the parameters of the response.

Green consumers

In 1983 the World Commission on Environment and Development (WCED) was convened by the UN. Chaired by the Norwegian Prime Minister, Gro Harlem Brundtland, the WCED was created to address growing concern over the 'accelerating deterioration of the human environment and natural resources and the consequences of that deterioration for economic and social development'. In 1987 they produced the report *Our Common Future* (usually referred to as the Brundtland Report) that popularized probably the most well-known definition of sustainability: 'Development that meets the needs of current generations without compromising the ability of future generations to meet their own needs' (WCED, 1987, p45). Notice that this definition couches the problem in terms not simply of the sustaining of human life; rather it talks about sustainable *development*. In this way the international response, at the level of governmentality at least, was at this time framed in terms of being able to maintain 'development'. In this context what was meant was, of course, economic development in the form of growth. At one level it is easy to see why this should be. At Stockholm and in following debates those in the developing world argued strongly that any response could not simply end development, as the already industrialized West would have gained from an approach that favoured them, at the expense of those who had not experienced the fruits of such a process. However, this drive for 'equity' in any international response was then seized upon by those who had a vested interest in the continuation of the paradigm of development to allow not just for developing nations to catch up, but so that consumers in the West could continue their lifestyle without too much disruption.

By the early 1990s the sense that consumers were the heart of the problem was being directly reflected in the official discourse of environmental concern. The World Conservation Union's 1991 publication *Caring for the Earth* stated that a 'concerted effort is needed to reduce energy and resource consumption by upper income countries' (IUCN, 1991, p44). A year later the UN Conference on the Environment and Development held in Rio, often referred to as 'The Earth Summit', confirmed this noting as they did that while poverty can certainly be understood as a cause of particular types of environmental stress 'the major cause of continued deterioration of the global environment is the unsustainable pattern of consumption and production, particularly in industrialized countries' (UN, 1992, §4.3). It was therefore gradually becoming apparent that it was industrial production itself, and the concomitant consumption that it necessitates, that was the problem. Yet the response of both governments and industry (and therefore industrial design) was to institute what could be called 'ecological modernization' policies, which were essentially based on the assumption that the crisis could be averted by innovation in the supply chain and alterations within the accepted scope of industrial design (Isenhour, 2015).

If the twentieth century had begun with an intense esoteric debate as to the form designed goods should ideally take, then by the 1980s the practices of modern industry and the lifestyles of those who consumed its products appeared to have answered these questions (Foster, 2002; Cannell, 2009). The discussion about what constituted design as a way of giving form to the objects we use had essentially been answered by the rise of consumer design: the forming of objects to serve a particular market.

Against this backdrop the growing popular awareness of environmental problems and the rise of green parties across Europe meant that there was a 'sudden profusion of greenery within the media and advertising in the mid-to-late 1980s' (Madge, 1997, p45). As Andrew Dobson notes, at this time there was a 'veritable explosion of the popularity of green lifestyle changes' in Britain and the developed West (Dobson, 1998, p543). Manufacturers and retailers thus responded to this change enthusiastically as major players in the market began to stock their shelves with 'environmentally friendly' goods. As Dobson notes, this was not because they actually subscribed to any radical agenda of change, but because in such a context 'green' rapidly became the colour of 'capitalist energy and enterprise' (ibid.).

One of the central principles of consumer culture is that it is sold to us on the understanding that as consumers it is free will that drives us; that we make conscious decisions about the way we interact with things. As Don Slater observes, in such circumstances consumption is largely understood to be conducted through 'the exercise of free personal choice' in the marketplace (Slater, 1997, p8). Therefore we are encouraged to believe that we are surrounded by things that we have chosen of our own volition, rather than seeing such conditions as being the outcome of certain economic and cultural conditions that are themselves the product of broader power relations. In consumerism the flows of culture become personalized and internalized; we find ourselves in particular relationship to the things we use, which then have the appearance of having been deliberately chosen. However, as Michael Maniates has argued, 'the rise of fundamentally unsustainable consumer cultures has actually been facilitated by 'choice editing', the restriction of what can be chosen from, or even imagined as a choice' (Maniates, 2010, p123).

In the early 1990s, the philosopher Anthony Giddens argued that a requirement of consumerism is that individuals identify themselves through the adoption of a lifestyle (Giddens, 1991), a gathering together of objects and behaviours that express who we are, or want to be. A central stimulus to the development of design in the late 1980s and early 1990s, therefore, both as a body of goods and as a practice, was the drive towards the acquisition of goods in an effort to display the correct taste, and in doing so to take on the appearance of being the right sort of consumer. In such circumstances it is therefore understandable that getting the environment onto the design agenda at all was a major challenge in itself. It should be remembered that at this time there was no consensus that this was actually an issue of any real import, and it did not seem to be in the interests of producers to engage with it. It was not, therefore, necessarily beneficial to designers if they emphasized it in their practice.

For those within the design profession who did attempt to engage with environmental concerns the task was to begin to establish the broad parameters of what a green design practice might look like (Madge, 1997). With the publication of Brundtland and the introduction of international conventions such as that which outlawed CFCs, and the concomitant pressure on national governments, combined with a growing green consumer consciousness, so a picture of the landscape of what 'green' design might look like began to be established. It was to be concerned with making 'green' consumer goods, in that what was to be fundamental was that the development of this 'environmentally conscious' design agenda coincided with a developing interest in the design field of knowing the consumer and their motivations. The techniques of advertising and market research were being applied to industrial design and product innovation, and research began to move from the product to the consumer or 'user' (Almquist and Lupton, 2010). In such a circumstance it is perhaps inevitable that green design should come to be predicated on the rise of the green consumer: that the power to change things lay with individuals, that any form of green design would need to concentrate on what people consumed and how they consumed it (Cohen, 2005; Isenhour, 2015).

Exhibitions at this time, such as 'The Green Designer' held by the UK Design Council in 1986, were arguably intended to demonstrate that 'green' design was not 'anti-industry', that design could be seen as a motive force that was succeeding in greening industry. While from a position of retrospect it is easy to look down on the motives of those acting in this way, what must be understood is the extent to which the terms of the debate were being set by the conditions of the time. As Richard Welford notes, the dominant ideology of such 'corporate environmentalism' is a form of eco-modernism expressed as a form of 'eco-efficiency' (Welford, 1997, p16), whereby the issue is deemed to be one of the efficient use of resources and the deployment of technology. This thus appeared to be well within the remit of design, as a practice that had emerged to address just such issues as this. In this way even as 'green' (which is in the end, just a colour) rose in importance and 'green' design started to be taken seriously, so the form that any response could take was shaped by how those at the time saw the world. What then was inherent in what might be called the 'lifestyle' strategies is that they operate in such a way as to suggest that change is not 'political' in the sense of governance, but that it resides at the level of individual consumer choice.

Ecodesign

1991 saw three publications that sought to further the green design agenda: Paul Burrall's *Green Design*, Dorothy Mackenzie's *Green Design: Design for the Environment* and Brenda and Robert Vale's *Green Architecture: Design for a Sustainable Future*. Yet there was a growing sense that the 'greening' of consumption through design had been something of a triumph of style over substance. In 1989 Friends of the Earth had produced a publication called *Beyond Green Consumerism*, and in 1990 there was a conference at the Design Museum called 'Green Design: Beyond the Bandwagon'. This was illustrative of a general sense that companies were using a nod to environmental concerns to 'greenwash' their products. In design circles, therefore, throughout the 1990s the trend was away from a green agenda that seemed tainted with implications of marketing gloss, towards the development of an approach that was coming to be called 'ecodesign' (Madge, 1997). What was significant in the shift of nomenclature was that it represented much more than just a rebranding exercise on the part of those who argued for a new approach to design. The shift to 'eco-' symbolized an increased interest on the part of designers in the adoption of a more holistic approach to the issues, which perhaps represents the first stirrings of an attitude that suggests that what design can contribute may extend beyond the limited nature of efficiency alone.

In March 1991, under the aegis of the European Union's Eureka Programme, an international group of designers met in Amsterdam to discuss ecodesign. They focused on 'principles and methods as well as prevention by design' (Madge, 1997). That is to say the design profession had really started to work out a response which depended upon looking at whole structures of production and consumption, one that moved beyond a simple resources and pollution paradigm. In this conception there was still space for a product focused approach, which was concerned with making existing products more resource efficient, more recyclable and the like. What differentiated this new model, however, was the increasing emphasis on the new fields of *results* focused design strategies (attempting to produce the same outcome in different ways), and *needs* focused approaches (that actually began to question the need fulfilled by the object, service, or system) (Fletcher and Goggin, 2001, p16). The development of this approach was then predicated upon the creation of a new toolkit for designers and analysts. A great deal of the work that went on depended on the employment of methods such as life cycle analysis (LCA) and other life cycle modelling approaches, which charted material use and energy flows from 'cradle to grave' in the making, use and disposal of products. Other techniques that were developed as part of the ecodesign agenda in the 1990s included processes such as environmental impact assessment (EIA), which was intended to allow for the assessment of the environmental impact of a proposed project or development, taking into account inter-related environmental and socio-economic effect.

One concrete result of this change of emphasis on the part of the design profession was that appliance manufacturers began to provide products such as washing machines with energy and resource saving programmes (Woodham, 1997). This intervention was adopted because it had been discovered that with a typical washing machine, 95 per cent of its total environmental impact arises out of the use phase of the lifecycle (Fletcher and Goggin, 2001). Yet it is difficult not to conclude that these manufacturers adopted such innovations mainly because they knew it would make their products more saleable, and at this stage there was little suggestion that things would need to change in any fundamental manner. The message was simple: yes, there is a problem, but the practices of modern design can deal with this by making products better. One way in which products were being 'improved' in this way was by making them recyclable.

It was in the 1990s that the need to recycle began to impinge on public consciousness. Though recycling is certainly far from new (the poet Baudelaire was fascinated by the rag-pickers of Paris in the mid-nineteenth century, the Salvation Army sent out squads to recycle the cast-offs of Victorian society in the 1890s and 'mend and make do' was a rallying cry in the UK during the Second World War), it was certainly re-discovered in a big way at this time. Recycling seemed to have a dual effectiveness, in that on the product level it removed individual objects from the waste stream, at the same time as it provided raw materials. However, the case of bottled water illustrates how just as consumers were reassured by the recyclability of what they used, so this very quality simply added to its appeal, thus meaning that more was consumed in the process.

In 1975 the first polyethylene terephthalate (PET) disposable plastic bottle was introduced. Created by DuPont the PET bottle, which is used extensively to contain water and other soft drinks, allowed beverage manufacturers to shift from refillable glass to single-use disposable containers. Prior to this the business had depended upon glass reusable containers, which were returned to the retailer by the consumer for a small deposit. The manufacturer then brought the bottles back to the plant, washed and refilled them. At the time, this was an expensive and time-consuming practice. With disposable containers, since each bottle is used only once and then put into the refuse, after purchase it can be treated as the consumer's property and thus their problem. This means that the potential for profit on the part of the producers is enormous. For the price of one reusable bottle anywhere between twenty to forty single-use containers can be produced (Rogers, 2005). The masterstroke, however, was to make these bottles 'recyclable'. This meant that just as consumption rose, so the customer could be reassured that, even as what they were doing was glaringly more wasteful than before, it could be understood as acceptable because the product they were using was 'recyclable'. The Executive Director of the trade association, Petcore Europe, has called PET recycling 'a success story'. Yet since the 1990s the consumption of single-use water bottles has 'exploded' (Robbins *et al.*, 2014, p266). So when actual consumer behaviour and its effects are examined, it is clear that for all the improvements in production methods, in the developed West such gains have been grossly outweighed by an overall growth in market demand and consumption at a per capita level (Cohen, 2005).

In design terms at least, it can be said that 'eco' turned 'green' into a scientific paradigm where the science of the product as an object is dominant and its wider context is sidelined or obscured, even as it is apparently taken into account. The use of ecological models to analyse technological or industrial systems does make it possible to contain 'the complexities of an environmental approach to design within limits by defining the boundaries of a system' (Madge, 1997, p49). But this is actually the problem – it gives the illusion of scientific 'knowability'. This approach is technocentric and it 'embodies a belief in objective, value-free, scientific evidence' (ibid.). It depends upon models of closed systems that do not take into account the sheer complexity of the social problem being addressed. Despite their apparently scientific nature, such interventions can actually be seen to be vehicles for value judgment and ideology: they shape our ability to formulate what we think, and what we think we can do; they act to reinforce a certain environmentality in design. A characteristic of business approaches to environmental problems is that they do what is absolutely necessary, while what they do is given 'an extraordinary profile' (Welford, 1997, p33). In ecodesign there was a tendency to over-emphasize pollution and resource use during production as the main objects of environmental concern that design could tackle, this then had the effect of obscuring more paradigm-destabilizing questions concerned with the viability of consumption as a way of life. That is to say, the reliance of ecodesign on tropes of efficiency and scientific intervention overshadowed the importance of human choices and actions (Fletcher and Goggin, 2001, p15).

Sustainable futures

In 1990 the Intergovernmental Panel on Climate Change (IPCC), which had been convened by the UN General Assembly in 1988, reported that they were 'not quite sure if human activities were producing global warming'. By December 1995 they concluded that 'the balance of evidence suggests a discernible human influence on global climate change' (Rowell, 1996, p149). If pollution and resource depletion suggested that we needed to think about our relationship to making and using things, the growing awareness of anthropogenic climate change seems to have moved the problem onto an altogether larger scale.

It was from the late 1990s that the term 'sustainable design' began to gain currency (Madge, 1997; Margolin, 1998; Fletcher and Goggin, 2001). It has now come to be the dominant way of thinking about the problem of how to keep making and using things without destroying the planet (Margolin, 1998; Walker, 2006; Ehrenfield, 2008). As Jeremy Caradonna (2014) has observed, one key feature of the difference between environmentalism and the discourse of sustainability is the optimism of the latter, that concentrating on sustainability means to imply that things can be 'sustained' if only they were to be designed to be so. In conceptualizing the problem in this way, so design has come more to the fore and actually started to be in a position to make more of an impact than previous approaches have. The publication of books such as *Eternally Yours* by Ed van Hinte and John Kirkpatrick for the Netherlands Design Institute (2004), McDonough and Braungart's *Cradle to Cradle: Rethinking the Way We Make Things* (2002), and Jonathan Chapman's *Emotionally Durable Design: Objects, Experiences and Empathy* (2005) started to move the debate away from design being able to mitigate the problems of mass-production, and began to offer alternative roles that design could have in actually planning-out the destructive capacity of manufacture by thinking about people's relationship to the designed things they use. As McDonough and Braungart (2002) argue, for example, it may be possible to transition from a model based on eco-efficiency to one centred upon what they term as 'eco-effectiveness'. If the intended effect of eco-efficiency is the elimination or reduction of the negative effect created by unsustainable designed products and processes, then what is described as eco-effectiveness could be said to be intended to constitute a new approach to design that includes economic, social and cultural change. In order to do this many commentators argue that an approach to design must be developed that is capable of completing the process identified by Fletcher and Goggin (2001) whereby the emphasis moves from the design of material products, to a situation in which designers work on more complex systems and social structures. Thus in such a conception the idea of sustainability suggests a change in the role of design, including an inevitable move to approaches based on an understanding of complex systems theories and the 'dematerialization' of products, in that the need for physical artefacts is partially replaced with more systemic approaches. This will then involve a shift 'from hardware to software, from ownership to service, and will involve concepts such as dematerialization and a shift from physiological to psychological needs' (Madge, 1997, p52). Andrew Blauveldt argues that a truly sustainable design will be a form of relational design, in which the concentration will be on systemic structures beyond the simple object, and whereby 'the role of the designer is closer to that of an editor or a programmer, not an author but an enabler, while the consumer is recast as a more creative agent (in the guise of the designer, DIY-er, hacker, or "prosumer")' thus blurring the boundaries between production and consumption (Blauveldt, 2008, p9). Yet, this does to some degree seem to echo the rhetoric of green consumption.

Indeed, sustainable design has not been accepted as a universal good. As Tony Fry has argued, in design the concept of sustainability tends to suggest what could be done in material terms if the political issues were to be resolved. Such a 'business as usual' approach, in Fry's terms, ignores the fact that the futurity enshrined in the concept of the sustainable ties 'sustainability' to 'sustainable development' (2008). This can then simply be said to be the maintenance of consumer capitalism, that in this case what is being sustained is the dominance of the market. As Heiskanen et al. (2000) observe, those who argue for an approach that emphasizes approaches such as dematerialization still tend to take 'an engineering and mainstream economic approach to society'. That is to say they assemble a great deal of evidence that 'current levels of well-being could be achieved with radically lower natural resource use'. This is then to see 'dematerialization as an optimization problem, which can be solved through systems design and the right incentives'. However, this neglects the social (or indeed political) dimension, and ignores the question of whether 'social systems can be optimized that way, and who has the power to do so?' It is also a naïve use of systems theory in that the optimization of one subsystem may mean the destabilization of another (Heiskanen et al., 2000, p1). Herman E. Daly argues that sustainable development can actually be seen as a transitional state, a 'cultural adaptation' which has had to be made by society 'as it becomes aware of the emerging necessity of nongrowth'. That is to say, that believing that 'growth is still possible and desirable if only we label it "sustainable" or color it "green" will just delay the inevitable transition and make it more painful' (Daly, 1998, p286). As Welford notes, academics also must accept some of the blame. So often we concentrate on the outliers, we try to make generalizations about the 'greening of industry' without taking sufficient account of the wider cultural context of the organization (Welford, 1997, p35).

Conclusions

We all act as though there is still so much time. Given how serious the problem appears to be, it seems strange that more is not being done to address the question of how we might live such that we do not destroy the environment that we depend upon to survive. As has been argued in this chapter, the problem may be something to do with how we understand the nature of any 'environmental crisis' of which we are a part. It could then be that consumer culture itself has a structural logic that has meant that things have played out as they have. As Bill McKibben has argued, because of the perceived rate of technological change in the culture of the developed world, whereby new products seem to assail us daily and material 'progress' appears ready to overwhelm us with the new, so there is a tendency to think that time itself has speeded up – which of course, it has not. Concurrently, there is the distorted sense that there is another timescale of nature, one that is older, slower and not of 'our' making. As McKibben observes: 'we imagine that the earth must work on some other timescale' (McKibben, 2003, p7). In this sense the environmentality with which we must now deal seems to be working at two speeds; and this has happened because of the requirement that we reconcile our knowledge of the environmental crisis we inhabit with the need to live a social life in consumer culture.

Throughout most of the twentieth century design has served to make products more efficient and more desirable. Efficiency is a neo-classical concept dependent upon the idea of optimization; it suggests that the things we use can be optimized on a functional level. Yet we also want the things we use to be meaningful, and it has in the large part been the mechanisms of consumer culture that have operated to do this. The gradual realization that we cannot keep consuming at this rate forever has thus caused a profound disturbance in the continuum of consumer culture. One of the central reasons that greening and eco efficiency have been the dominant paradigms is because they do not actually require any radical change. They have also gained dominance because it has been difficult for those involved in industrial production to imagine a response beyond this (Welford, 1997). Now it seems that there is a gradual realization that the problems we face are of a scale that is way beyond the level of individual choice, that sustainable consumerism is a chimera. Because of this the design of products, the things we use to allow us to function and to make our lives mean something, will thus need to transform, to go beyond simplistic notions of sustainability, if it is to survive as a practice and fulfil its potential in the making of a new way of living.

References

Adams, W. M. (2001) *Green Development: Environment and Sustainability in the Third World*, Routledge, London

Agamben, G. (2009) *The Signature of All Things: On Method*, Urzone, Brooklyn

Agrawal, A. (2005) Environmentality: Community, Intimate Government, and the Making of Environmental Subjects in Kumaon, India, *Current Anthropology*, vol 46, no 2, pp.161–315

Almquist, J. and Lupton, J. (2010) Affording Meaning: Design-Oriented Research from the Humanities and Social Sciences, *Design Issues*, vol 26, no 1, pp. 3–14

Anderson, B. (1990) *Imagined Communities*, Verso, London

Blauveldt, A. (2008) *Toward Relational Design*, Design Observer, Yale, US, pp. 1–21

Buckminster Fuller, R. ([1969]2008), *Operating Manual for Spaceship Earth*, Lars Muller, Zurich

Burrall, P. (1991) *Green Design: Issues in Design*, The Design Council, London

Cannell, M. (2009) Design Loves a Depression, *New York Times*, www.nytimes.com/2009/01/04/weekinreview/04cannell.html (accessed 22 February 2016)

Caradonna, J. L. (2014) *Sustainability: A History*, Oxford University Press, New York

Carson, R. (1962) *Silent Spring*, Houghton Mifflin, New York

Chapman, J. (2005) *Emotionally Durable Design: Objects, Experiences and Empathy*, Earthscan, London

Cohen, M. J. (2005), Sustainable Consumption in National Context: An Introduction to the Special Issue, *Sustainability: Science, Practice, and Policy*, vol 1, no 1, pp. 1–7

Daly, H. (1998) *Ecological Economics and Sustainable Development, Selected Essays of Herman Daly*, Edward Elgar, Cheltenham

Dean, M. (2007) *Governing Societies*, Open University Press, Maidenhead

Dobson, A. (1998) *Justice and the Environment: Conceptions of Environmental Sustainability and Dimensions of Social Justice*, Oxford University Press, Maidenhead

Drexhage, J. and Murphy, D. (2010) *Sustainable Development: From Brundtland to Rio 2012*, UN, New York

Dryzek, J. S. (2005) *The Politics of the Earth: Environmental Discourses*, Oxford University Press, Oxford

Dryzek, J. and Schlosberg, D. (eds) (1998) *Debating the Earth: The Environmental Politics Reader*, Oxford University Press, Oxford

Ehrenfield, J. (2008) *Sustainability by Design: A Subversive Strategy for Transforming Our Consumer Culture*, Yale University Press, New Haven, CT

Ehrlich, P. and Ehrlich, A. (1968) *The Population Bomb*, Ballantine Books, New York

Fallan, K. (2015) Our Common Future: Joining Forces for Histories of Sustainable Design *Ecnoscienza: Italian Journal of Science and Technology Studies* vol 5, no 2, pp. 15–32

Farrell, J. (1997) *The Spirit of the Sixties: Making Postwar Radicalism*, Routledge, London

Fletcher, K. and Goggin, P. (2001) The Dominant Stances on Ecodesign: A Critique, *Design Issues*, vol 17, no 3, pp. 15–25

Foster, J. (ed.) (1997) *Valuing Nature? Ethics, Economics and the Environment*, Taylor & Francis, London

Foster, H. (2002) *Design and Crime (and Other Diatribes)* Verso, London

Foucault, M. (1991) Questions of Method, in G. Burchell et al. (eds), *The Foucault Effect: Studies in Governmentality*, University of Chicago Press, Chicago, IL, pp. 73–86

Foucault, M. (2001) The Subject and Power, in his *The Essential Works 1954–1984*, vol. 3: *Power*, Allen Lane, London

Fry, T. (2008) *Design Futuring: Sustainability, Ethics, and New Practice*, Berg Publishers, New York

Giddens, A. (1991) *Modernity and Self Identity: Self and Society in the Late Modern Age*, Polity, London

Hanwerk, B. (2010) Whatever Happened to the Ozone Hole, *National Geographic*, http://news.nationalgeographic.com/news/2010/05/100505-science-environment-ozone-hole-25-years (accessed 21 February 2016)

Hardin, G. (1968) The Tragedy of the Commons, *Science*, New Series, vol 162, no 3859, pp. 1243–1248

Heiskanen, E., Jalas, M. and Kärnä, A. (2000) *The Dematerialization Potential of Services and IT: Futures Studies Methods Perspectives*, paper presented at The Quest for the Futures Seminar: Workshop on Futures Studies in Environmental Management, Finland Futures Research Centre, Helsinki School of Economics, Organization and Management, Turku, June 13–15

Heskett, J. (1980) *Industrial Design*, Thames and Hudson, London

Illich, I. ([1973]2001) *Tools for Conviviality*, Marion Boyars, London

Isenhour, C. (2015) Sustainable Consumption and Its Discontents, in H. Kopina and E. Shoreman-Ouimet (eds), *Sustainability: Key Issues*, Routledge, Abingdon

IUCN (1991) *Caring for the Earth*, IUCN, Gland, Switzerland

Kiaer, C. (2005) *Imagine No Possessions; The Socialist Objects of Russian Constructivism*, MIT, Cambridge, MA

McDonough, W. and Braungart, M. (2010) *Cradle to Cradle: Remaking the Way We Make Things*, Macmillan, New York

McKibben, B. (2003) *Worried? Us?*, Granta 83, Cambridge, Autumn, pp. 7–12

Mackenzie, D. (1991) *Green Design: Design for the Environment*, Laurence King Publishing, London

Madge, P. (1997) Ecological Design: A New Critique, *Design Issues*, vol 13, no 2, pp. 44–54

Maniates, M. (2010) Editing Out Unsustainable Behaviour, in The Worldwatch Institute (ed.), *2010 The State of the World, Transforming Cultures from Consumerism to Sustainability*, Earthscan, London

Margolin, V. (1998) Design for a Sustainable World, *Design Issues*, vol 14, no 2, pp. 83–92

Meadows, D. H., Meadows, D. L., Randers, J. and Behrens III, W. W. (1972) *Limits to Growth: A Report for the Club of Rome's Project on the Predicament of Mankind*, Universe Books, New York

Papanek, V. (1971) *Design for the Real World: Human Ecology and Social Change*, Pantheon Books, New York

Robbins, P., Hintz, J. and Moore, S. A. (2014) *Environment and Society: A Critical Introduction*, 2nd edn, John Wiley and Sons, Hoboken, NJ

Rogers, H. (2005) A Brief History of Plastic, www.brooklynrail.org/2005/05/express/a-brief-history-of-plastic (accessed 12 February 2016)

Roloston, H. (2015) Environmental Ethics for Tomorrow: Sustaining the Biosphere, in H. Kopnina and E. Shoreman-Ouimet (eds), *Sustainability*, Routledge, Abingdon, pp. 347–359

Rowell, A. (1996) *Green Backlash: Global Subversion of the Environment Movement*, Taylor & Francis, London

Schumacher, E. F. (1973) *Small is Beautiful: Economics as if People Mattered*, Blond & Briggs, London

Slack, L. (2006) *What is Product Design?* Rotovision, Zurich

Slater, D. (1997) *Consumer Culture and Modernity*, Polity Press, Cambridge

United Nations (1992) *Agenda 21 - Changing Consumption Patterns*, Section 4.1

Vale, B. and Vale, R. (1996) *Green Architecture Design for a Sustainable Future*, Thames & Hudson, London

Van Hinte, E. and Kirkpatrick, J. (2004) *Eternally Yours, Time in Design: Product Value Sustenance*, 010, Rotterdam

Walker, M. (1994) *The Cold War and the Making of the Modern World*, Vintage, London

Walker, S. (1996) *Sustainable By Design: Explorations in Theory and Practice*, Earthscan, London

Ward, C. (2012) *Talking Green*, Five Leaves Publications, Nottingham

WCED (1987) *Our Common Future: Report of the World Commission On Environment and Development* ['the Brundtland Report'], Oxford University Press, Oxford

Welford, R. (ed.) (1997) *Hijacking Environmentalism: Corporate Responses to Sustainable Development*, Earthscan Publications, London

Woodham, J. (1997) *Twentieth Century Design*, Oxford University Press, Oxford

2

THE HALF-LIFE OF A SUSTAINABLE EMOTION

Searching for meaning in product usage

Gerald C. Cupchik

Abstract

This chapter examines two complementary questions. First, why do users hold on to products that are deteriorating and well beyond their prime? Second, why do users change products frequently when it is not necessary to do so, based on the state of their technology? The roots of product attachment can be found in the very structure of design products in which, like artworks, the concrete form (i.e. style) metaphorically shapes our experience of their function (i.e. subject matter). Optimal engagement with a design product balances the top-down appraisal of its function and bottom-up sensorily rich experience of its usage in context. Feelings of pleasure or excitement accompany the appraisal process whereas, emotions such as happiness, transform design products into 'transitional objects' of attachment that are rich in personal meaning. Overly rapid updating of products reflects the impact of surface changes on 'other-directed' consumers. The 'half-life' concept implies that we never really emotionally *let go* of utilitarian objects to which we are attached. Achieving a mindful and sustainable attitude means that we are able to decentre and shift between a top-down appraisal of devices in relation to our needs and a bottom-up appreciation of the roots of our emotional attachments to things in our life-worlds.

Keywords: Emotion, top-down, bottom-up, sustainable emotion, product attachment

Introduction

This chapter addresses complementary questions that are relevant for both users and designers of industrial products. On the one hand, why do people hold on to products when, logically, it is time to move on and replace them with ones that are technically 'up to date'? On the other hand, why do some people change products more frequently than is needed given the rate of technological developments? The first question has to do with forming attachments whereby useful *devices* are transformed into personally meaningful *objects* blending function and aesthetics in a social context. My sense is that this attachment process extends back to pre-historic times when a stone tool just 'felt right' in the user's hand. Every time I hold a stone tool from the Sinai desert that is 500,000 to 1,000,000 years old, I vicariously share a comforting experience of 'good fit' with the person who produced it through a knapping process and then used it (see Figure 2.1). The half-life of emotional attachment implies that people never really completely let go of products-as-objects which have become part of their lives, holding on to them in nostalgic ways past their primes (of both consumers and objects).

The second question concerns the impact of rapidly changing industry-driven surface refinements that attract people. A need for social acceptance and surface aesthetic changes would appear to be the culprits in this narrative of *conspicuous display* as a twenty-first century variation on Thorsten Veblen's (1899) notion of 'conspicuous consumption.' The sustainability problem is therefore shared by consumers and producers who are challenged to optimize the balance of instrumental value and mere possession. Consumers need to appreciate the core utilitarian values of products that become embedded in their daily lives. The half-life of a sustainable design product reflects its instrumental value during an era of intense corporate competition. Designers need to balance function or purpose and aesthetics, enhancing consumer awareness of significant design changes rather than distracting them with surface cosmetics. In the end, it is a question of establishing healthier producer-consumer relationships.

I approach the sustainability problem as a psychologist interested in the interaction between aesthetics and emotion (see Cupchik, 2016). My goal is to provide 'a language with which to address salient issues of emotional durability' (Chapman, 2009, p30). Can aesthetics help us understand the dynamics that transform a design *product* into a personally meaningful *object*? My positive answer is that relations between function and form in design products are analogous to those between subject matter and style in paintings (Cupchik, 2003). Both form and style provide evocative metaphorical contexts within which function and subject matter are experienced, respectively. The lines of a racing car connotatively imply speed just as the *tachiste* (i.e. scalloped) brush stroke in an Impressionist painting creates an expressive atmosphere inviting viewers to complete the image (Cupchik et al., 2009). The expressive effects of form and style that invite emotional engagement with products and artworks alike are fundamental to the development of object attachment.

Figure 2.1 Stone tool from the Sinai Desert at least 500,000 years old

Source: photograph by Sara Loftus

At a micro level of analysis, the dynamics underlying sustainability (balancing holding-on and letting go) involve top-down and bottom-up processes in a complementary manner. Top-down processes are cognitively based and focus on instrumental appraisals of design products in relation to the needs and goals of the user. Objective appraisal skills should enable users to determine when it is logically 'time to change.' In contrast, bottom-up judgments are affect and memory driven, transforming tools and devices into 'transitional objects' (Winnicott, 1965, 1971) of attachment that are part of a person's identity. The expressive and metaphorical qualities of design figure prominently in this process, providing a context for experience. As we all know, these emotional attachments cloud our decisions as to when it is indeed time to let go. Optimally, people balance top-down judgments about products that solve problems with their bottom-up experiences of using them in personally meaningful situations.

At a macro level, we benefit from considering corporate decision-making processes underlying the shift from a context of design to that of production. At the outset in a creative context, innovative design involves an effort to produce a tool or device that is both functional and beautiful. The successful outcome serves as a paradigm or ideal case which others might seek to emulate. Once an original design product becomes a commodity, business realities necessitate reducing the costs of production and increasing turn over by encouraging consumers to purchase the latest model. Changing surface qualities to attract attention might lead to short term gain and accelerate faddism through the medium of branding. However, deeper changes in the underlying functional paradigm that are properly understood by consumers will optimize decisions about *holding on* and *letting go*. In the end, the goal is to balance logic and emotion both for producers and users.

Complementary relations between function and form in design products

The power of iconic design products can be traced to relations between function and form that are inherently metaphorical. In essence, the function of the successful design object disappears and is reinforced by an experience of the visual (i.e. sensory) form. Thus, when a sofa-chair is designed to bring people together, the configuration can both echo and express its function (see Figure 2.2). Its designer, Matthijs van Dijk, states:

> The metaphor is, in my opinion, about 'connection'. This product emphasizes the connection between the different users which will result in their behaviour. Their behaviour will tell something about their social capabilities, their social status. This artificial human connection is literally accomplished by the physical connection of the three hassocks. The metaphor thus expresses the relationship between the psychological domain and the physical, structural, domain and can both be described as 'being connected'.
>
> *(Cupchik, 2003, p25)*

The underlying dynamics are not unique to design products but are shared by literary and artistic works in which there is a resonance between semantic and syntactic domains that are qualitatively different. The function (purpose), word, or subject matter domains are semantic and can be summarized propositionally or by algorithms. In contrast, the form, sound, or visual style domains embody sensory qualities, which are uniquely (i.e. syntactically) ordered and subject to Gestalt principles related to coherence and *good form*.

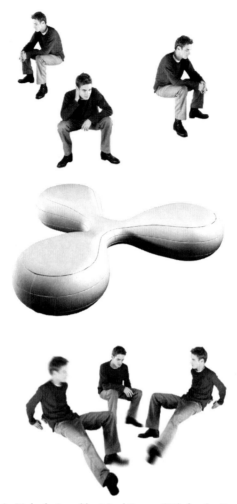

Figure 2.2 Leather sofa chair, Link, designed by Matthijs van Dijk for the Dutch design agency KVD

DESIGN			**LITERATURE**		**ART**
FUNCTION	(PURPOSE)	=	WORDS	=	SUBJECT MATTER
FORM	(DESIGN)		SOUND		VISUAL STYLE

In his analysis of metaphors in *The Philosophy of Rhetoric*, I. A. Richards ([1936]1965) described the 'interanimation' or mutual influence of words. The power of metaphors to draw our attention and have effects lies in *differences* between the two referents which create an experience of *tension*. Richards explored the implications of 'what happens in the mind when we put together – in a sudden and striking fashion – two things belonging to very different orders of experience. The most important happening – in addition to a general confused reverberation and strain – are the mind's efforts to connect them' (ibid., pp124–125). By way of extension to design products, a dynamic tension is initiated by the surface differences between its function and form that we unconsciously attempt to reconcile.

The functional value of utilitarian design products lies in the *top-down* efficiency and elegance with which tasks are undertaken. In contrast, the power of metaphors in language, art and design are shaped by the *bottom-up* modifying influence of form on function, sound on word, and visual style on subject matter. Tversky (1977) described a process of *dynamic asymmetry* caused by *relative salience*. In geometric figures, or design objects for that matter, relative salience is governed by *goodness of form*, a Gestalt quality pertaining to orderliness. For our purposes, the *salient* quality of the *form* is transferred to the *function,* and not vice-versa, in an effort to achieve *unity-in-diversity* of the total image at an 'optimal level of abstraction' (ibid., p348). This can also be discussed in terms of relations between parts (i.e. qualities of the form) and wholes (i.e. the functional design object). Ortony (1979) similarly emphasized *salience imbalance* to explain the effects of metaphors and their non-reversibility. Thus, in a successful metaphor, salient qualities of the part become attached to the non-salient properties of the whole. For our purposes here, the look, feel, and sound (i.e. sensory qualities) of industrial design products resonate with their function thereby making salient the experiential foundations of their functions.

Black (1962, 1993) offers an *interactive* account of *resonant* verbal metaphors as systems whereby recipients cooperate 'in perceiving what lies *behind* the words used' (Black, 1993, p26). By way of extension to the product domain, designers intuit Black's 'strong creativity thesis' which holds that 'some metaphors are what might be called *cognitive instruments*, indispensable for perceiving connections that, once perceived, are then truly present' (ibid., p37). In a similar manner, Hausman maintains that 'metaphors create integrated wholes' (Hausman, 1989, p45) and 'help constitute what may be called the *world*' (ibid., p83) by lending 'intelligibility to that on which attention focuses' (ibid., p121). The emphasis is therefore on *spontaneity* and *freedom* that enables creative people to generate meaningful metaphors which can modify worlds of experience. Hausman demonstrated that an interaction between the subject matter of a painting and its formal-expressive qualities (i.e. its style) 'generates and sustains tensions' (ibid., p180). Thus, in the painting *Young Woman with a Water Jug* by Vermeer, there is a dynamic interaction between the expressive sense of space created by his treatment of light and the young woman who is its major focus.

Successful design objects stimulate relational thinking, which is required when images are to be experienced and understood as part of a unified event in a particular context. The metaphorical effects embedded in design objects represent a case of *conjunctive ambiguity* wherein 'several fields are connected though remaining intact' (Kris, 1952, p248). For Kris, 'Metaphor serves as a stimulus to functional regression because the primary process itself is metaphoric and imagistic' (ibid., p258). According to Arnheim (1971), people are naturally disposed to resolve this ambiguity such that the liberated tension energizes the process. He argues that 'expression is an inherent characteristic of perceptual patterns' (ibid., p433) and metaphor can 'make the reader penetrate the concrete shell of the world of things by combination of objects that have little in common but the underlying pattern' (ibid., pp435–436). Thus, visual metaphors possess *physiognomic* (i.e. spontaneously expressive) sensory qualities that resonate with personal meanings (Straus, 1958). The co-presence of novelty and familiarity are a source of tension and absorption which stimulate a broad range of conscious and unconscious cognitive processes in an effort to resolve ambiguity.

My central argument, following Tversky's (1977) concept of *asymmetric similarities*, is that the form a design product *implicitly* and *spontaneously* shapes the *unified metaphoric experience* of the product as a whole, and not vice-versa. It does so because form is relatively more *concrete* on the continuum upward from sensory to verbal and then symbolic information. Designers intuitively create original metaphors that reflect a point of view which prompts recipients to adopt an appropriate perspective in their 'effort after meaning' (Bartlett, 1932) related to the product. The underlying sensory and stylistic structure stimulates resonances with the intended function of successful design products. The unified and meaningful experience of a design object will reflect the extent to which the function of the object becomes embedded in its form. In other words, when a person looks at a successful design product, there will be an immediate and spontaneous experience of unity; the sensory experience (visual, tactile, auditory, taste, and so on) gives a direct meaning to the function of the work thereby providing a basis for object attachment. Potential users who can place the design product in an appropriate context will *spontaneously experience the unity of the metaphor* and the product will become 'real' for them.

Complementary relations between top-down actions and bottom-up reactions to design objects

This section addresses complementary relations between *top-down* (i.e. purposive) and *bottom-up* (i.e. experiential) engagement with industrial design products. Purposive involvement is logically driven and accompanied by feelings that lie on *valence* (pleasant–unpleasant) and *arousal* (i.e. excitation) dimensions that are inherently quantitative. In contrast, experiential absorption is more closely allied with the metaphorical processes just discussed and provides a basis for emotionally grounded episodic and syncretic memories that govern attachment. As one might expect, logic facilitates decisions to let go (discard) of a design object and move on (purchase a new one), whereas emotion inhibits those decisions. Of course, the actual history of product engagement reflects a blend of facilitative and inhibitory processes. Let's consider these countervailing processes in greater detail.

Top-down actions and functional relations

The instrumental application of a design object is embedded logically in its design. This is a top-down process in that the sequence of operations (actions) needed to manipulate this device (tool) are formally, serially and hierarchically defined. The skilful execution of these operations will enable users to adapt to the challenges posed by situations or realize goals and fulfil needs. From a psychological viewpoint, design objects offer *sensory-motor affordances* so that the manipulation of a device in a particular manner will alter the environment. Monitoring feedback from these external outcomes is key to appraising successful execution of the process. With practice, the process of execution becomes automatic so that users need not attend to the sequence of individual actions.

From an affective perspective (Cupchik, 2016), the use of an industrial design object is accompanied by *transient feelings* associated with degrees of pleasure (i.e. valence) and arousal (i.e. excitation). This follows from the proposition that *feelings are the shadow of cognition*. In other words, usage of the device is predicated on an optimal level of cognitive activation to energize the process and foster attention to the ongoing task at hand. The manipulation of a design object will lead to different degrees of pleasure or frustration that are consequent to the ease or difficulty with which a given device is used. This is quite apart from the reward value of the completed task in relation to challenges and needs. Automaticity of task execution and level of frustration are inversely related. Obviously, the more difficult it is to use the device, the greater the level of frustration. The reverse is, of course, also true so that ease of use can provide a sense of pleasure. This is consistent with what is referred to as *effectance motivation* – the desire to experience mastery over the environment (White, 1959) – in this case through the efficient manipulation of a tool or device.

Table 2.1 Complementary processes extended to design product relations

Top-down processing	Bottom-up processing
Minds	Hearts
Objective	Subjective
Action	Reaction
Adaptation	Effort after meaning
Appraisal	Interpretation
Instrumental	Experience/expression
Sensory-motor	Motor-sensory
Feedback loop	Feed-forward loop
Matching	Coherence
Outcome	Process
Feelings	Emotions
Transient	Enduring
State relevance	Transitional object
Outer directed	Inner directed
Adopting	Attaching

In sum, tool usage is associated with top-down processing whereby a person first appraises a situation and then monitors the ongoing usage of a problem-solving device. The adaptation process is facilitated by optimal levels of arousal in conjunction with automaticity in the skilled usage of the tool. Arousal levels may increase substantially when the user encounters frustration either due to inefficient design or a lack of practiced skill or necessary talent. The success (or lack thereof) with which this process unfolds determines the levels of pleasure (or psychological and sometimes even literal pain) that the person experiences. While the *feelings* that accompany usage of design objects are *transitory*, they may serve as an *affective tag*, which determines whether the person desires further engagement with the device. In accordance with opponent process theory (Solomon and Corbit, 1974), the aversive feelings associated with failure to competently use a device are particularly potent. Discomfort working with a device can assume broader social meaning to the extent that social comparison processes are engaged. Thus, if someone feels embarrassed by publically demonstrating incompetence, uncomfortable feelings in social situations can readily morph into emotions such as fear or anger which might render a person phobic regarding further engagement with the product.

Bottom-up reactions and emotional experiences

My earlier account of bottom-up processes related to metaphor and design is recapitulated when it comes to emotional experiences (Cupchik, 2016). With reference to design objects, the idea was proposed that the form of a successful design product provides an experiential context that resonates implicitly with its function and shapes our experience of it. This is analogous to my belief that emotional experiences involve feed-forward loops whereby encounters with personally meaningful situations reawaken past episodic memories that rekindle the experiences. An experience involves observing, encountering or undergoing something in a coherent life episode. It refers to uniquely meaningful, salient, and coherent mental events with both cognitive and affective qualities. This is where top-down and bottom-up processes differ. Top-down efficient automaticity is the opposite of having an experience because there is no conscious component. We focus outward on the outcomes, the product. Bottom-up experiences of products *in situations* are reminiscent of the *deautomatization* (Shklovsky, [1917]1988) process that accompanies aesthetic experience – a reawakening of attention to the process itself.

This idea directed our study on *being moved* by industrial design products (Cupchik and Hilscher, 2008). We found that, the more integrated the expressive and instrumental properties, the more our design experts were *moved* by the product. *Personal connection* characterized many experiences of the design objects they chose. They ascribed human qualities to it, reported sharing a physical, emotional and/or intellectual interaction with it involving positive and/or negative emotions, and spoke at length about their experiences which had social meaning in that it had been given to them by someone special, reminded them of someone significant, or facilitated their socializing with others (ibid., pp248–251).

Following from the principles of *emotional phase theory* (Cupchik, 2016), attachment to a design object and the experience of related emotions (such as happiness) are shaped by a variety of factors. The object assumes symbolic social value given the situations in which it was acquired and used. So the meaning of the design object is embedded in a social situation that includes the user and significant others to whom the person is connected. Attachment to the object is therefore a product of engagement that is fundamentally *motor-sensory*. In other words, manipulating the design object in a coherent manner in social situations yields a variety of sensory experiences that become part of a *unified syncretic experience*. The person shapes the experience through acts of manipulation which are stored in episodic memory with strong sensory and proprioceptive elements. Subsequent encounters or thoughts about the design object rekindle these memories in a kind of feed-forward loop. Thus, emotional experiences which are consequent to engagement with design objects encompass the person, the interpreted situation and relevant others in a unified whole. Accordingly, experiences of happiness or surprise provide emotional *glue* that unifies our enduring relationships with design objects. This process gives our favourite design products a life of their own. When design products are turned into *objects* to which we are *emotionally attached* and have enduring *relationships*, letting go for rational reasons becomes a problem all of its own. This lies at the heart of the 'half-life' construct.

In reality, our relations to design objects balance logical *actions* and emotional *reactions*. The key to holding on or letting go at the appropriate time requires a level of reflective self-awareness. This transcendent act is crucial for getting us out of a rut and making the right decision. I recall very clearly many years ago when the owner of the garage in a small French Canadian town near Montreal gently told my father that it was time for him to let go of his beloved Dodge Dart which did not have many miles on it but was twenty years old. 'Dave, it's time to give it a rest …' I am not sure how my father arrived at his decision to actually let go. I can only feel that moment in the distant past.

Exploring the depths of emotional engagement

A cognitive science viewpoint

Donald Norman's book *Emotional Design* (Norman, 2004) provides an intuitively engaging account of the ways that cognition, affect and emotion influence our relations with design products. 'Emotion is always passing judgments, presenting you with immediate information about the world: here is potential danger, there is potential comfort; this is nice, that bad' (ibid., p10). The 'cognitive system interprets and makes sense of the world' (ibid., p11) – it assigns meaning. Affect refers to a value oriented 'judgmental system, whether conscious or subconscious' (ibid.) and emotion 'is the conscious experience of affect, complete with attribution of its cause and identification of its object' (ibid.). Implicitly following in the American tradition of Positive Psychology, Norman proposes that 'positive emotions are critical to learning, curiosity, and creative thought' (ibid., p19) and so the role of aesthetics in product design should 'make people feel good, which in turn makes them think more creatively' (ibid.) by attending to opportunities. This idea runs counter to the German Romantic view that underlying emotional *struggles* stimulate creative thought and this may represent one way in which design and artistic processes can be differentiated. Design activities are meant to enhance flow, where artistic activities are meant to embody meaning, sometimes painful, that resonates with both the artist's and beholder's lives.

Norman distinguishes between Visceral, Behavioral, and Reflective levels of processing. The Visceral level of response is described as 'bottom-up,' whereas the Reflective level is 'top-down.' 'Bottom-up' processes are 'driven by perception whereas top-down are driven by thought' (ibid., p25). In 'bottom-up' processing, sensory judgments of the environment, based on seeing, hearing, or feeling, influence the affect system which passes judgment and releases chemical neurotransmitters which can 'bias the brain to focus upon the problem and avoid distractions' (ibid., p26). Since the 'visceral level is pre-consciousness, pre-thought ... appearance matters and first impressions are formed' so 'Visceral design is about the initial impact of a product, about its appearance, touch, and feel' (ibid., pp36–37).

Emotions 'are responsive to immediate events [and] last for relatively short periods, minutes or hours, [and] change behavior over a relatively short term' (ibid., p32). The 'top-down Reflective level is 'very sensitive to experiences, training, and education' (ibid., p33) but can also include 'actual negative experiences' (ibid., p36) in using the product itself. Arguing from a cognitive rather than a psychodynamic viewpoint, Norman states that, since 'the power of emotion fades with time, the negative affect generated by our memories doesn't overcome the positive affect generated by the sight of the instruments themselves' (ibid.). He concludes that 'the highest levels of feeling, emotions, and cognition reside' (ibid., p38) at the Reflective level. At the lower Visceral level, 'there is only affect, but without interpretation or consciousness' (ibid.) which are associated with Reflective reasoning. By implication, Visceral design is concerned with appearances, Behavioural design is associated with pleasure and effectiveness of use, and Reflective design impacts self-image, personal satisfaction, and memories (ibid., p39).

The realities of planned obsolescence

Lobos and Babbitt (2013) address the problem of attachment and sustainability in relation to electronic product design. The short product life cycles in this industry have a negative impact both on connections with users as well as the accumulation of environmental detritus. This is stimulated by planned obsolescence, which encourages potential users to buy the latest product quite apart from functionality and without regard for 'end-of-life management through reuse or recycling' (ibid., p20). They propose integrating emotional attachment into design which should begin in the classroom through embedding these considerations throughout the design curriculum, at all levels. Successful connection between users and products should enhance pleasure and user experience with the result that product lifespan is increased.

The origin of planned obsolescence as an economic strategy was traced to the Great Depression. Bernard London (1932) offered a psychological analysis to the effect that fear led people to use products longer than had been the custom before the Depression. Planned product lifespan emerged as a strategy to encourage turnover and economic development. Marketers began encouraging people to buy new products on a more regular basis. The process was facilitated by increased consumption after World War II and the desire for a more convenient lifestyle with products that were 'more efficient, less expensive and, in many cases, disposable' (ibid., p20). This can lead to decreased attachment because of (1) the false assumption that products have a short half-life, and (2) the ever-presence of newer technologies and appearances which may be merely cosmetic.

One way to foster sustainability is to increase engagement with Emotional Design so as to enhance connections between products and users related to enjoyable experiences. Lobos and Babbitt (2013) argue that 'emotional attachment can occur at multiple levels such as sentimental relevance, dependability, timelessness, usability, and graceful ageing' (ibid., p24). Regardless of the basis for connection, emotionality is seen as the key to enhancing the perception of product value. For example, a preference for Apple over PC products has been tied to a variety of factors including 'perceived product dependability, cost of investment and pleasure when using the product' (ibid., p24), factors that link functionality with emotional association. To increase product lifespan, designers should 'allow for emotional attachment as well as for technological adaptability' (ibid., p25). Perceived qualities, such as signs of wear which reflect the character of the product (e.g. in a leather bag) or the potential for positive changes over time such as material ageing (as in the case of the Fender electric guitar), contribute to such emotional connections.

Jonathan Chapman (2008) studied 'relationship behaviours' that a large sample of respondents had with their domestic electronic products and, from this, derived six 'experiential frames' (see also Chapman, 2009, p33). These six experiential frames can be reduced to three complementary pairs within superordinate categories (the percentages in parentheses reflect

Table 2.2 Complementary relationships with design objects

Orienting to design objects: new (decontextualized) versus old (contextualized)	Perceptions of design objects: surface versus depth	Reactions to design objects: connection versus disconnection
Fiction: users are delighted or even enchanted by the object as it is not yet fully understood or know by the user; these are often recently purchased objects that are still being explored and discovered by the user (7%) *Narrative*: users share a unique personal history with the object; this often relates to when, how and from whom the object was acquired (24%)	*Surface*: the object is physically ageing well, and developing a tangible character through time, use and sometimes misuse (23%) *Consciousness*: the object is perceived as autonomous and in possession of its own free will; it is quirky, often temperamental and interaction is an acquired skill that can be fully acquired only with practice (7%)	*Attachment*: users feel a strong emotional connection to the object, due to the service it provides, the information it contains and the meaning it conveys (16%) *Detachment*: users feel no emotional connection to the object, have low expectations and thus perceive it in a favourable way due to a lack of emotional demand or expectation (this also suggests that attachment may actually be counterproductive, as it elevates the level of expectation within the user to a point that is often unattainable) (23%)

the relative frequency or salience of these themes). My goal is not to engage in a critique of the six themes represented here but, rather, to resonate with them and search for higher order categories within which they can be subsumed as complementary pairs.

At first sight, the themes of Fiction and Narrative might seem redundant to someone in the humanities. The underlying distinction would appear to contrast initial encounters with the design object, as such, based on its *fictional novelty* and appearance (7%) with the *narrative social context* within which the design object was first acquired (24%). This is reflected in the relative importance of these themes which is heavily weighted in favour of the context of acquisition. These themes also underscore the value of focusing on relationships of consumers with products – how they enter the person's life and transform from isolated *products* into personal *objects*.

The second thematic pairing reflects relations between *surface* and *depth* and a shift in how the design product is perceived. This transformation over time suggests that we are all *psycho-animists* at heart by which I mean that we retain a sensory appreciation of the transforming *surface* (i.e. *material*) qualities (23%) that constitute products which take on 'character' as they age through our interaction with them (my beloved leather shoulder bag comes immediately to mind). With time, these *products* transform into *transitional objects* to which (like good 'primitive' animists) we attribute *conscious* agency (7%). However, not unlike the teddy bears of our childhood (I confess to having 'unintentionally' ripped off an arm at the age of three ... sorry), we attribute quasi-human qualities to these devices (i.e. *machines*). As a consequence, this interaction between human and machine has many of the characteristics of social relationships. The Greek gods have indeed become human and can sometimes terrorize us ... not that I want to seem paranoid about my computer but you 'know' what I mean.

The third thematic pairing touches upon the most fundamental existential dimension of social relations; *connection* (16%) versus *disconnection* (23%). Chapman's treatment of the *connection* process encompasses 'service,' 'information,' and 'meaning.' I propose that there is much to be gained by contrasting *appraisal* of potential 'service' and 'information' with *interpretation* that is tied to the 'meaning' of the product for the person given the contexts within which it was received and used. Accordingly, people can feel *connected* to products that (1) fit their personal needs and goals or (2) are socially meaningful given the context of acquisition or usage. On the other hand, people can feel *disconnected* to products that (1) do not meet their 'expectations' or, I would add, (2) have an aversive social meaning (e.g. given to the person by an ex-boyfriend or ex-girlfriend). Chapman's point that *attachment* can be 'counterproductive' given 'the level of expectation ... that is often unattainable' (see Table 2.1) would refer specifically to disconfirmed appraisals. While the product may have looked good at first, efforts at using it proved to be frustrating either because the learning curve was too challenging or it did not fit with the person's needs.

Chapman (2009) segues into a psychodynamic and existential approach to product attachment when he relates it to a journey involving 'the ideal (or desired) self that, through cyclical loops of desire and disappointment, becomes a seemingly endless process of serial destruction' (ibid., p34). From a reader's ironic perspective, I am not sure whether the word 'destruction' refers to the product (that one hurls against the wall) or to the person whose self-esteem is destroyed through repeated failed attempts to master the product. This might seem like a stretch but I see this as referring to repeated attempts to pass one's first driver's road test. On the other hand, without the assistance of the University of Toronto IT team that is 'dedicated' to professors, I might have hurled a few laptops myself before being consumed with guilt and self-hatred!

While I have made light of the strong version of his hypothesis, Chapman touches upon some fundamental issues when it comes to object attachment in relation to the self. First, following Erich Fromm (1979), objects in general (and not just design products) 'provide an archaic means of possession by enabling the consumer to *incorporate* the meanings that are signified to them by a given object' (Chapman, 2009, p34). In this context, 'possessions are symbols of what we are, what we have been, and what we want to become' (ibid.). Thus, beyond their functionality, products 'provide important signs and indicators in human relationships' (ibid.). In a world filled with consumerism, 'adoration rapidly mutates into a resentment of a past that is now outdated and obsolete' (ibid., p34). At the industrial level, Chapman argues for a holistic form of '*emotionally durable design*' (ibid., p36) that increases 'the resilience of relationships between consumer and product' (ibid.).

The transformation of mere products into symbolically laden objects of possession reaches back to Upper Palaeolithic times more than 40,000 years ago and relates to the fundamental issues of being and meaning. Gamble (1999) has argued that the Upper Palaeolithic period was defined by a shift from routinized actions performed in the 'landscape of habit' to a 'social landscape' in which 'individuals as creative agents' (ibid., p269) embody meaning in symbolic artefacts that might be shared with clan members. 'Embodiment is therefore the mainspring for the symbolic force that resonates throughout any language structured by metaphor and more broadly applies to all aspects of materiality' (Gamble, 2007, p68). Malafouris (2007) views an image from the Chauvet Cave as 'a historically situated component of human perceptual and cognitive architecture' (ibid., p289) that relates to 'the coming-into-being of modern human cognition' (ibid., p290) and behavioural modernity. For Malafouris, 'the symbolic usage of material culture precedes symbolic thinking' (ibid., p293). Thus, the 'skillful interactive engagement' (ibid., p295) with a material means offers a new form of 'tactile' or 'visual thinking' (ibid., p298) which yields 'an object *for* perception and contemplation' (ibid., p299). Malafouris (ibid.) ties the 'emerging self' to the 'poetic' act of material engagement that links mind and brain.

Whether we are talking in terms of 40,000 years ago or today, our active engagement in the creation or utilization of useful tools affirms our sense of agency and of self. It makes our world 'real' for us and for others. What is different between Upper Palaeolithic time and the twenty-first century are the number of degrees of separation between us and the product that has turned into a 'transitional object' of attachment. During those early times, the person may have produced the simple tool or received it from someone else. But now, of course, there are many layers of agency between the designer and the end user. However, we invest meaning and life in objects (in a social sense of relationship) just as our ancestors did long ago. *Civilization* does not cure us from this inherent desire to interpret our world as filled with meaning and, dare I say, being. It may be that, the greater the degrees of separation from the product, the more we are susceptible to illusions and idealizations about it.

Holding on and letting go: the half-life of emotional attachment

Imagination has two complementary aspects, instrumental and expressive, that should be optimally balanced for both designers and consumers. For designers, instrumental imagination begins with the idea of what a tool or device needs to do in the light of all those that preceded it. Originality involves proposing a new approach that saves steps and uses materials in a more efficient manner. Expressive imagination embodies the function in a sensory-based material form that metaphorically captures its purpose. While the consumer has some idea about what a product can do, upon first encounter, the aesthetics of its form rapidly shapes the anticipated experience of using it. Even as I write, the 'Apple Watch is coming' on 24 April 2015, and its image on Google is sufficient to whet the average techy's appetite: one watch, with all the presumed apps, and three price points depending on the metal of the casing; aluminium, stainless steel or gold. We the consumers are a living laboratory for a successful advertising campaign in which expressive form 'trumps' (irony intended) familiar functions.

The notion of a 'half-life' implies that, while our attachment may weaken over time, we never really completely abandon it. The primacy of emotional attachment follows from Heinz Werner's ([1948]1957) Organismic Gestalt theory which examines the shift from syncretic (focused on perceptual and immediate experience) to abstract thinking based on logical inference in relation to child and cultural development. He describes the child and earlier forms of society as embedded in the 'field' or situation, which is experienced physiognomically (i.e. expressively). The person is dominated by 'vital drives, on the one hand, and by the concrete signals of the milieu on the other' (ibid., p194). Thinking is affectively dominated with a blending of imagination, perception, emotion and motor action in a 'concrete collective situation' (ibid., p228). With time, there is increased differentiation, articulation and organization of thought that is pragmatically and instrumentally based on 'geometric-technical' information. In this more abstract context, 'parts of a unit are detached from the whole, and separate qualities – color, form, etc. – are experienced in isolation' (ibid., p234) and related to adaptive behaviour to master a world using 'mediating devices' (ibid., p193). This ability to objectively assess contingencies in challenging situations fits very nicely with our use of design products as adults in the twenty-first century.

Our attachment to design products is the result of top-down and bottom-up processes. Top-down processes reflect the success with which we master the (sensorimotor) principles underlying the use of a tool or device. Success will result in *feelings* of pleasure and excitement, whereas failure will result in frustration and/or boredom. *Emotional* attachment reflects the (motor-sensory) experience one has actually using the product in concrete situations. In this context, imagination, sensation, emotion and meaning combine syncretically to bind the person to the product so that, over time, it becomes a 'transitional object'. The half-life of the design product and the half-life of emotional attachment become synchronized, and intertwined. For example, the ageing of leather in a favourite briefcase or shoulder bag acquires a softness that becomes associated with the many experiences that a person has had with it in personally meaningful situations. It is only when it begins to actually fall apart, because the handle breaks under the weight of books over the years or the seams of the leather become too frayed to be stitched together again, that the asynchrony awakens the person to a need for change and perhaps even upgrading. Accordingly, people hold on to objects that they should let go because of bottom-up emotional dynamics that are consistent with the general process of 'transitional object' attachment.

The shift from early to modern society (and the same applies to childhood) is marked by a dissociation of top-down and bottom-up processes. This reflects the increasing complexity of both tools and devices as well as social structure which also impacts identity formation. Hall and Khan (2003) examine technological adaptation curves accounting for the process of diffusion whereby the purchase of products (such as mobile phones) spreads throughout a society in accordance with the number of users. Diffusion rates reflect individual decisions regarding the value of adopting a new technology given limited amounts of information about it. Generally speaking, early adopters are people with top-down knowledge enabling them to quickly recognize the value of a new technology. Just between us, they are the same people who buy shares in these companies when they are still in the bargain basement domain.

Hall and Khan address the 'S' curve which characterizes an accelerating rate of diffusion once involvement arrives at a critical mass. They describe a rational model relating perceived value of the product to rate of change in its cost. An alternative sociologically based model has to do with the rate at which consumers are informed about the technology by their neighbours (and through media, social or otherwise). Once the market is saturated, the rate of diffusion decreases which results in the 'S' curve. Of course, the rational and sociological models are not mutually exclusive. This rate of diffusion model can help account for the second sustainability question addressed in this chapter which concerns *why people let go of* (i.e. *change*) objects when they don't really have to do so.

My answer to this question has to do with the rate of change in a particular product domain relative to the rate of change in the person. During a period of rapid social and technological change, the decision-making mind is affected by an Other-Directed disposition to be influenced by opinion makers so as to find social acceptance (Riesman et al., 1950). In this context, there is dissociation between intellect and emotion. Transient or surface feelings, associated with a need to fit it in, make the person susceptible to new product trends. I conjecture that the 'S' curve reflects a process of what might be called *affective diffusion* whereby consumers are swept up by *feelings of excitement* and anticipated *pleasure* that are consequent to purchasing a popular new product. The collective hysteria that makes people want to be part of the technological in-crowd might be responsible for the accelerated development of a critical mass associated with the 'S' curve. In other words, people let go of things all too readily when they are dominated by surface feelings that reflect a desire for the 'ideal self' to fit in with what is perceived to be the latest in modern technology.

Conclusion

I began this chapter by describing relations between function and form in design products that is analogous to that between subject matter and style in art and literary works. This argument drew attention to the asymmetrical bottom-up impact that form has on the overall experience of a product. In essence, the concrete sensory and structural properties of form modify the meaning attributed to a product and its function. This happens in the same way that visual stylistic properties modify (i.e. lend atmosphere) to our experience of haystacks or train stations in Impressionist paintings by Monet. Of course, design products are best understood in the context of usage and, for this reason, I drew a contrast between top-down rational principles that underlie function and bottom-up sensory (i.e. syncretic) and unconscious factors that shape our experiences when using these devices. The critical point is that emotional attachment happens when design products turn into 'transitional objects' through the bottom-up synchronization of motor-sensory based experiences with competent mastery of the product and its function.

This analysis provides a tentative answer to the two complementary questions relating to sustainable product design. First, a person will become overly attached to a design 'object' when its sensory qualities become attached to episodic memories by an autonomous 'inner-directed' person (Riesman et al., 1950). In other words, the object is immersed in the person's world and it becomes difficult to imagine it as separate and, hence, expendable or replaceable. To 'cure' the problem, so to speak, the 'object' has to turn back into a 'product' and this requires that the person adopt a top-down perspective wherein its properties can be logically appraised. Second, a person will all too readily let go of products and purchase new ones based on surface differences when their sense of self is 'other-directed' and they are influenced by perceived social trends.

I would suggest that optimization in the area of sustainable products requires a transcendent perspective for consumers. On the one hand, they should recognize the legitimacy of attachment to products that fit meaningfully into their lived-worlds. On the other hand, they need to be able to switch perspectives and understand the instrumental problem solving aspect of their lives, which can benefit from an upgrade, so to speak. Producers clearly have a role to play in helping people balance their hearts and minds, appreciating the value of technological developments while retaining the meaningful experience of developing a relationship with their devices. In this sense, not all that much has changed since Upper Palaeolithic times because tools can also be our friends as long as they do the job that is needed for adaptation.

References

Arnheim, R. (1971) *Art and Visual Perception*, University of California Press, Berkeley, CA

Bartlett, F. C. (1932) *Remembering: A Study in Experimental and Social Psychology*, Cambridge University Press, Cambridge

Black, M. (1962) *Models and Metaphors,* Cornell University Press, Ithaca, NY

Black, M. (1993) More about Metaphor, in A. Ortony (ed.), *Metaphor and Thought*, Cambridge University Press, New York, pp. 19–41

Chapman, J. (2008) Emotionally Durable Design: Sustaining Relationships Between Users and Domestic Electronic Products, unpublished doctoral dissertation

Chapman, J. (2009) Design for (Emotional) Durability, *Design Issues*, vol 5, no 4, pp. 29–35

Cupchik, G. C. (2003) The 'Interanimation' of Worlds: Creative Metaphors in Art and Design, *The Design Journal*, vol 6, no 2, pp. 14–28

Cupchik, G. C. (2016) *The Aesthetics of Emotion: Up the Down Staircase of the Mind-Body*, Cambridge University Press, Cambridge

Cupchik, G. C. and Hilscher, M. C. (2008) Phenomenology and the Design Experience, in P. P. M. Hekkert and R. Schifferstein (eds), *Product Experience,* Elsevier, Amsterdam, pp. 241–255

Cupchik, G. C., Vartanian, O., Crawley, A. and Mikulis, D. J. (2009) Viewing Artworks: Contributions of Cognitive Control and Perceptual Facilitation to Aesthetic Experience, *Brain and Cognition*, vol 70, no 1, pp. 84–91

Fromm, E. (1979) *To Have or To Be*, Abacus, London

Gamble, C. (1999) *The Palaeolithic Societies of Europe*, Cambridge University Press, Cambridge

Gamble, C. (2007) *Origins and Revolutions: Human Identity in Earliest Prehistory*, Cambridge University Press, Cambridge

Hall, B. H. and Khan, B. (2003) *Adoption of New Technology*, Working Paper Series, NBER, Cambridge, MA

Hausman, C. R. (1989) *Metaphor and Art*, Cambridge University Press, New York

Kris, E. (1952) *Psychoanalytic Explorations in Art*, International Universities Press, New York

Lobos, A. and Babbitt, C. W. (2003) Integrating Emotional Attachment and Sustainability in Electronic Product Design, *Challenges*, vol 4, pp. 19–33

London, B. (1932) *Ending the Depression through Planned Obsolescence*, pamphlet [no publisher listed], available at https://en.wikipedia.org/w/index.php?title=File:London_(1932)_Ending_the_depression_through_planned_obsolescence.pdf&page=8

Malafouris, L. (2007) Before and Beyond Representation: Towards an Enactive Conception of the Palaeolithic Image, in C. Renfrew and I. Morley (eds), *Image and Imagination: A Global History of Figurative Representation*, McDonald Institute Monographs, Cambridge, pp. 289–302

Norman, D. A. (2004) *Emotional Design: Why We Love (or Hate) Everyday Things*, Basic Books, New York

Ortony, A. (1979) Beyond Literal Similarity, *Psychological Review,* vol 86, no 3, pp. 161–180

Richards, I. A. ([1936]1965) *The Philosophy of Rhetoric*, Oxford University Press, New York

Riesman, D., Denney, R. and Glazer, N. (1950) *The Lonely Crowd: The Changing American Character*, Yale University Press, New Haven, CT

Shklovsky, V. ([1917]1988) Art As Technique, in D. Lodge (ed.), *Modern Criticism and Theory*, Longman, New York, pp. 16–30

Solomon, R. L. and Corbit, J. D. (1974) An Opponent-Process Theory of Motivation: I. Temporal Dynamics of Affect, *Psychological Review*, vol 81, no 2, pp. 119–145

reaction of the same people to Apple's launch of Siri (Speech Interpretation and Recognition Interface) as part of the iPhone 4S back in 2011. Talking to inanimate objects is nothing new and humans have likely done it since the beginning of our species but that communication has just transmuted to a dialogue. As our tools' communication improves, users move in a little closer to listen and respond. We already pinch, tap, touch, hold and talk to our devices and it seems that ironically, Modernity has returned to *animism*.

Anthropologist Alfred Gell calls the spell that speaking, beeping and flashing objects have on us the 'enchantment of technology.' He writes that this is 'the power that technical processes have of casting a spell over us so that we see the real world in an enchanted form' (Gell, 1992, p44). When the animated objects around us become interconnected – as in the phenomenon dubbed *internet of things* – our living rooms turn into living entities and we into modern shamans staring in disbelief. Indeed, it has become more normalized to be *animistic*, as the things around us are gaining 'souls'. Of course things have still not literally been animated but the distinction between life and death has become a little trickier, and more complex to manage. As Arthur C. Clark famously stated in his second law, it gets harder to distinguish between technology and magic, the more advanced a civilization is. Our phones communicating with our cars, thermostats, washing machines and us, has become a present scenario; the relationship we have with everyday objects is changing with what might be described as a kind of *renaissance of animism*.

Diametrically opposed to such *enchantment*, stands Max Weber's *disenchantment* to describe a world void of magic, a world predictable and calculable. Weber's *Entzauberung der Welt*, first used in 1919 was a concept borrowed from Friedrich Schiller's poem *Die Götter Griechenlandes* of 1788. Both Weber and Schiller addressed the consequences an overly rational worldview dawning during the Enlightenment might have, and the resulting romantic longing to magical and unexplored times. They insinuated that while the European mindset had accepted that the things surrounding them were void of magic rationally, on a more archaic and basal cognitive level the human mind has not been able to keep up with the rapid technological advances brought by Industrialization. What is striking is that now, when there seems to be more 'magic' around us than ever before we seem to be extremely careless and wasteful with the things producing such magic. Perhaps the most satisfactory explanation for why we have become so careless with our magical artifacts comes from the seminal *The Theory of the Leisure Class*, where Thorsten Veblen combined economics and Darwinian theory to explain why we conspicuously consume (Veblen, [1899]2005). Once basic human needs are satisfied – the argument goes – it makes sense to advertise the ability to consume over and beyond our share of resources. The resulting runaway consumerism seems to follow some archaic patterns and when combined with *planned obsolescence* obviously has detrimental environmental consequences (Slade, 2007). Geographer and biologist Jared Diamond even speaks of *ecocide* (Diamond, 2005) when describing this destructive behavioral pattern.

One approach to avoiding ecological disaster is the optimistic work of McDonough and Braungart. They believe that the green movement does not have to be based on austerity and to the contrary can be one of abundance as long as the 'technical nutrients' are kept in a healthy cycle (McDonough and Braungart, 2010, 2013). Evolution as an innovative process is very wasteful, and experimentation tends to trump conservatism. Similarly, humans could enjoy a life of abundance as long as the design of our everyday things considers several lives instead of just one. Instead of doing 'less bad', designers should be encouraged to do 'more good', to *upcycle* rather than recycle (McDonough and Braungart, 2010, 2013). Although such considerations are indispensable for a needed design revolution, this chapter argues for greater emotional attachment to the products we already have. As the things around us become 'alive', is it not feasible to expect more emotionality and experience? It is argued here that that more emotional durability can be achieved not simply through more things 'alive' but by actually overcoming the false epistemology of Cartesian objectivism. In the words of Bruno Latour:

> If there is one thing to wonder about in the history of Modernism, it is not that there are still people 'mad enough to believe in animism', but that so many hard-headed thinkers have invented what should be called inanimism and have tied to this sheer impossibility their definition of what it is to be 'rational' and 'scientific'. It is inanimism that is the queer invention: an agency without agency constantly denied by practice.
>
> *(Latour, 2010, p10)*

Animism then and now

The British anthropologist Edward Tylor (1832–1917) first articulated the term *animism* calling it the 'idea of pervading life and will in nature' (Tylor, 1871). In his *Primitive Culture*, published in 1871, he clearly laid out the task of cultural anthropology to discover 'stages of development or evolution.' One of the most important *unilineal evolutionists* of the nineteenth century, Tylor believed in set stages that all societies passed through. In that tradition, analysis of cross-cultural data was based on the assumptions that (1) contemporary societies may be classified and ranked as more 'primitive' or more 'civilized', (2) there are a determinate number of stages between 'primitive' and 'civilized' (e.g. band, tribe, chiefdom, and state) and (3) all societies progress through these stages in the same sequence, but at different rates. It is extremely important to note here that *unilineal evolutionism* built its 'evolution' on Lamarckian not Darwinian premises. Specifically it was the *social Darwinism* of Herbert Spencer with its assumption that cultural evolutionism followed the same laws as natural selection. Hence, 'primitive societies' were like time machines illustrating the different stages of a universal human history (Koeb, 1996). Herbert Spencer, the author of the infamous phrase 'survival of the fittest' was actually far more influential on nineteenth century social theorists than Charles Darwin ever was and most social scientists accepting evolutionism of that time were technically 'Spencerists', not 'Darwinists'. Perhaps the most important distinction to Darwin was that Spencer always included a teleological principle, which he called a *persistence of force* ordained by the *Unknowable*. Thus, it is very easy to hear echoes of Spencer in the following quote from Tylor written in 1889: 'The social habits of Mankind follow each other like geological strata, universally in the same fashion without regards to the superficial differences of race or languages' (Altner, 1981). Unlike his contemporary Lewis Henry Morgan, who addressed such 'strata' in terms of technological advances, Tylor did the same for spiritual stages. The anthropology of the nineteenth century was a science largely based on library research and grand theories and it was not until the early twentieth century that scientists like Bronislaw Malinowski and Franz Boas pioneered field research by actually visiting the people they wrote about. Peoples foreign to the so called 'armchair anthropologists' of the nineteenth century had and did things Europeans did in prehistory and were thus seen as being stuck in the Neolithic. Indeed the term 'stone age people' has remained popular to this day in popular science. While *unilineal evolutionism* argued that similarity is due to homology, a competing *diffusionism* postulated the spread of items of culture from regions of innovation.

Tylor will forever be held responsible for the anthropological construct known as *animism*. According to him, this was the most primitive stage in belief systems, strongly suggested spiritual or supernatural perspectives and came before the development of organized religion. The *animist* stage of belief was followed by a polytheistic and final monotheistic stage. To Tylor, *animism* has no institution (e.g. a synagogue, mosque, or church), it does not have an unchangeable doctrine (e.g. a belief in a son of God), and it doesn't have sacred literature (e.g. the Hebrew Bible, the Quran, the New Testament). From the Latin anima ('breath, spirit, life') it became known as the belief in the possession of a spiritual essence or soul of non-human entities such as animals, plants or inanimate objects. Interestingly the vast majority of cultures do not have a term for such belief and even the described practitioners of *animism* do not use the term, suggesting that the phenomenon is little more than a European construct of the nineteenth century.

The concept is one of the oldest – if not *the* oldest – concept in anthropology and is generally presented as a human universal pushed to the background through the advent of *Modernism*. Although it is generally presented as something existing in all human cultures, the only thing truly universal is its presence in anthropology textbooks. *Animism* stands for traditionalism; for an outdated, even absurd practice no longer done. The term also became part of a larger construct of the notion of a time before and after bestowing souls onto material things, a time before and after Modernity. If all matter has spirit – the logic goes – then the Cartesian duality of mind and matter and that of society and nature becomes senseless. With that juxtaposition, *animism* actually becomes a violation of the Cartesian worldview. Since the social condition and technological accomplishments associated with Modernity are founded on the categorical distinction of nature and society, *animism* became associated with something antiquated, nothing more than an anthropological curiosity. With modern product design, however, such ideas seem to be alive and well.

In all fairness Tylor did not propose a clear-cut division between *animists* and *non-animists*. He did concede that the strange *animistic* rituals that we continue practicing are *survivals* of times past. Examples include the knocking on inanimate wood in order to expel any bad spirits that might interfere with future plans, or the widespread use of talismans and lucky charms. His definition of such survivals:

> processes, customs, and opinions, and so forth, which have been carried on by force of habit into a new state of society different from that in which they had their original home, and they thus remain as proofs and examples of an older condition of culture out of which a newer has been evolved.
>
> *(Tylor, 1871, p16)*

Tylor conceptualizes his famous *survivals* as cultural elements or complexes that although once making a certain sense within a specific context they are now anachronistic remnants. It is interesting to note that the concept is similar to the idea of the *meme*. In *The Selfish Gene*, Richard Dawkins first called ideas that for better or for worse become viral, *memes* and actually founded a new field of inquiry called *memetics* (Dawkins, 2006). *Survivals* are no longer in harmony with current cultural settings and are thus like *memes* of the past. To Tylor they were to be eliminated as he considered them to be merely harmful superstition. Similarly, Dawkins considers religious practices anachronistic and harmful to a scientific worldview.

If we really are Cartesianists, and have moved beyond a spirited world save for a few vestibules, when was that stance really adopted? Nineteenth-century positivism raised technology to Godly heights and with it created a semi-religious faith in techno-scientific progress and empirical methods. There was no room for a worldview that regarded all natural phenomena on par. Tylor and other *unilineal evolutionists* maintained that *animists* were somehow stunted and maintained a lower conception of the universe *and animism* became a failed epistemology or backward stage in the social development. The danger and far-reaching consequences of such ideas become apparent when considering that *unilineal evolutionism* is intrinsically related to *Modernization Theory* (Rostow, 1990) via the writings of the so-called *Neo-evolutionists* (White, 1954) and thus the idea that all civilizations imperatively have to move through the same stages of development are causally linked to world developmental politics. Therefore, it seems there are two problems with the original perception of *animism*. First, the belief system was wrongly defined, and second the so-called developed world, the West isn't really Cartesian. For modern product design, however there might lurk an opportunity rather than a problem since animistic tendencies could potentially lead to more product attachment and consumer satisfaction.

Mistaken epistemologies

Ever since Descartes's *Discourse on Method* (1637), modern Europeans have decided to think in terms of subject/object dualism but such a mode of classification was just that: a classification. To a large degree *Modernism* is actually based on objectifying nature, of doing away with any notion of a subject–subject based relationship. *Animism* – as defined in the nineteenth century – rejects Cartesian dualism and is now – truly like a *survival* of itself – anchored in the esoteric, non-scientific traditions. Recently, anthropologists and comparative-religion scholars have re-defined *animism* to mean something different (Bird-David, 1999; Descola, 2005, 2006, 2009; Harvey, 2006; Ingold, 2000). Thus, our relationships with the world, and the frontiers between human and nonhuman – even between living and non-living – are being reconsidered.

Until recently, the core of anthropological research was indigenous knowledge, seen as mistaken epistemologies, as un-scientific and irrational worldviews. Lately the tables are being turned and indigenous thought is used to critique modern epistemology, which is closely linked to Western *modernization theory*. Tim Ingold (2000), Nurit Bird-David (1999) and Philippe Descola (1994) have shown that not only ancient but also contemporary people with diverse systems of subsistence continue to approach their non-human environments through what is now being called a *relational* stance. Radically, such *posthumanism* has spawned discussions on building a new Modernity after the present world order (Hardt and Negri, 2009). Indeed *animism* is going through a thorough reassessment (Bird-David, 1999; Ingold, 2006; Descola, 2013). Guthrie, in an extensive and comprehensive discussion of animism and anthropomorphism, defines animism as humans 'attributing life to the nonliving' and anthropomorphism as 'attributing human characteristics to the nonhuman' (Guthrie, 1993, p52). *Animism* is now treated as an alternative, relational ontology allowing a rethinking of the problem of matter and agency and as a worldview that goes beyond human exeptionalism and superiority; one that embraces all non-humans.

For example, in Descola's writing, a new classification of the term hinging on two sets of variables is offered. Cultural groups perceive a basic similarity or a fundamental dissimilarity between humans and non-humans in terms of (1) interiority, which could include such categories as *intentionality*, *reflexivity* and *subjectivity*, and (2) *physicality*, which include substance, form or phenotype (Descola, 2009, p150). He writes:

> Either most existing entities are supposed to share a similar interiority whilst being different in body, and we have animism, as found among peoples of the

Amazonian basin, the Northern reaches of North America and Siberia and some parts of Southern Asia and Melanesia. Or humans alone experience the privilege of interiority whilst being connected to the non-human continuum by their materiality and we have naturalism – Europe from the classical age. Or some humans and non-humans share, within a given framework, the same physical and moral properties generated by a prototype, whilst being wholly distinguishable from other classes of the same type and we have totemism – chiefly to be found among Australia's Aborigines. Or all the world's elements are ontologically distinct from one another, thence the necessity to find stable correspondences between them and we have analogism – China, Renaissance Europe, West Africa, the indigenous peoples of the Andes and Central-America.

(Descola, 2015)

For Descola, *animism* is thus an articulation of one of four options. It is an understanding that all classes of beings (human and non-human) exchange signs, similar to the tenet of the field of *biosemiotics*, where everything that occurs in the universe is a semiotic event (Hoffmeyer, 1996; Barbieri, 2008; Wheeler, 2006). What emerges is a scientifically sophisticated *animism*, which understands all things as related in their nature as signaling entities, but different in their physical appearances or phenotype. Entities such as plants or even rocks may be approached as communicative subjects rather than the inert objects perceived by rationalists. And indeed smartphones and microwave ovens that beep and blink are signaling entities and if we respond to them in a purposeful manner then communication is complete. This new perception of *animism* is important because it overcomes the nineteenth century conundrum of animism as nemesis to *Modernity*. Here *animism* is something that could be shared by all peoples regardless of their technological advances, something that can lead to more emotional attachment to things, and in turn more sustainability. Thus, Graham Harvey has used the *new animism* as a way of more sound ecological harmony with all things (Harvey, 2005) since for humans it is likely easier to exploit and abuse a soulless entity. Tim Ingold, too has contributed much to a relativist understanding of the phenomenon labeled *animism*. He writes of the people we typically label *animists* of the Amazonian and the circumpolar North:

> First, we are dealing here not with a way of believing about the world but with a condition of being in it … The animacy of the lifeworld, in short, is not the result of an infusion of spirit into substance, or of agency into materiality, but is rather ontologically prior to their differentiation.
>
> *(Ingold, 2006, p10)*

Parliament of things

French philosopher, sociologist and *post-constructivist* Bruno Latour writes: 'There is no way to devise a successor to nature, if we do not tackle the tricky question of animism anew' (Latour, 2010, p9). His *parliament of things* is probably the most radical notion emerging in a discussion on a new *animism* (Latour, 1993). He argues that *Modernity* was never more than a mode or ideology of sorting and that *pensée sauvage* (primitive thinking) was not displaced by a dualistic *pensée modern* (modern thinking). Of course Latour writes in accordance with structural anthropologist Claude Lévi-Strauss, who thought the *savage mind* not to belong to primitive people but as a kind of mind untamed by rational domestication (Lévi-Strauss, 1962). Thus, we have actually 'never been modern' and the notion of modern people cleanly separating the world of subjects and objects might have been an illusion from the start (Latour, 2012). Modern, industrialized Westerners animate objects around them more than the so-called *animists* and in reality humans everywhere attach *animacy* and personhood to things. We talk to our cars and give them anthropomorphic forms. We have favorite trees, houses, cars and teddy bears. We curse at our computers, give our boats names and – at least children – sleep with inanimate forms resembling animals. According to Latour, such hypocrisy must be addressed by first accepting that the Cartesian dualism we are socialized to accept is phony in order to then recognize a new *parliament of things*. He writes:

> However, we do not have to create this Parliament out of whole cloth, by calling for yet another revolution. We simply have to ratify what we have always done, provided that we reconsider our past, provided that we understand retrospectively to what extent we have been modern, and provided that we rejoin the two halves of the symbol broken by Hobbes and Boyle as a sign of recognition. Half of our politics is constructed in science and technology. The other half of Nature is constructed in societies. Let us patch the two back together, and the political task can begin again.
>
> *(Latour, 1993)*

Truly, Latour did not invent this kind of 'anthropology of things' and it does have a considerable history. At the end of the 1800s Émile Durkheim, for example already used his term *social fact* to mean equally a thing and a structure. Marcel Mauss's *Gift* (1950) gave a solid foundation to this analytic of things and is enjoying a kind of rebirth in discussions of post-capitalistic economies. And thus also can be understood Daniel Miller's current analysis of material culture in such books as *A Theory of Shopping* (Miller, 1998). However, what sets Latour apart is his clear, persuasive approach. By creating symmetry between human and non-human entities, Latour sees society as humans assembled around things instead of vice versa. In this way, he breaks down the heavy barriers between the realms of nature and of culture that we have learned to accept just as between the subject and object. This *principle of symmetry*, when coupled with John Law's actor-network theory shows a highly complex world where humans and non-human things and animals interact freely. It is a world where the non-human actors are granted the same amount of agency as humans. Latour's analysis is a fascinating exploration of hybridity of different 'network-players'. Ignored by the rigorously divided chambers of science and politics, the *parliament of things* would finally lend a voice to the hybrids of Modernity. An example of such a hybrid – a network player that is both thing and structure – is the ghetto of most modern cities. But most importantly, Latour's model is the rejection of the basic distinction between nature and culture and with that a rejection of modernity itself. Modern society itself seems to have rested on a collective self-delusion from the start.

The savage mind

There is no before and after in history. A modern, rational mind never replaced a superstitious, primitive one just like the *conquistadores* of various eras and nations never found *savages* on lower evolutionist strata. In short, mistaken epistemologies aren't replaced. Rather, the human mind perceives and makes sense of the world on different levels of abstraction simultaneously and it is thus important to inject the above epistemological discussions with some biological considerations. Here, we won't satisfactorily answer the question if humans are naturally prone to *animism* or not but we can assume that the human species – like all living organisms – is a complex product of evolution. We are so good at reasoning on the basis of design from birth onward that it is very likely a genetically evolved adaptation (Wilson, 2011), and thus each one of us truly is a designer.

At the dawn of speciation, *Homo habilis* developed the first artifacts, *culture* was synonymous with *design* and the designer was Promethean. Ancestral Hominids have failed to evolve many defensive characteristics (Lorenz, 1964), but without a doubt they advanced to become the species most sophisticated at *niche construction* since we deliberately change most aspects of our environment (Odling-Schmee et al., 2003). The blueprint for the things we design – hand axes, houses and smartphones – are never genetically anchored but the potential to shape existing matter into new forms and in new ways likely is. Dennis Dutton believes all forms of design including art are innate. He speaks of the *art instinct* and argues that the production and acquisition of aesthetic objects has brought our ancestors a survival advantage (Dutton, 2009). Most importantly here, is the consideration that while the designer has to design for the circumstances of the twenty-first century, they should never forget that the end user has an archaic mind.

Tim Ingold has addressed what he has labeled the 'logic of inversion,' according to which 'the person, acting and perceiving within a nexus of intertwined relationships, is presumed to behave according to the directions of cultural models or cognitive schemata installed inside his or her head' (Ingold, 2006, p11). Thus a person is not able to experience the world the way it truly is but is 'sealed off by an outer boundary or shell that protects their inner constitution from the traffic of interactions with their surroundings' (ibid.). When accepting a Darwinian evolution of the brain itself, it becomes plausible that individuals experience life on several epistemological levels simultaneously. Thus, it becomes plausible that the most archaic level of the human brain has set the basic belief that all things are acting entities as a default position. From the research of paleoanthropology, primatology, archaeology and genetics we now know that the vast majority of our evolutionary history was tribal, nomadic and sustainable and thus radically different to life today (Diamond, 2005, 2012; Wilson, 2012). If we just paid attention, we would realize that we are often ill adjusted to the niche we have designed around ourselves for hundreds of thousands of years. Hominids living in small tribes of hunter-gatherers evolved a decision-making pattern for archaic – not modern – circumstances and if that pattern led to their survival then their descendants' – our – heads hold a similar pattern to solve challenges today. Since cultural evolution has been much faster than biological evolution, however, our mental algorithms are often inept for the travesties of modern life. Science writer Michael Shermer puts it this way:

> What may seem like irrational behavior today may have actually been rational 100,000 years ago. Without an evolutionary perspective, the assumptions of Homo economicus – that 'Economic Man' is rational, self-maximizing and efficient in making choices – make no sense.
>
> *(Shermer, 2008)*

Long before the systematic evolutionary study of the human psyche began (Barkow et al., 1992) an evolutionary foundation to human behavior was predicted by Charles Darwin in his *The Expression of the Emotions in Man and Animals* (Darwin, 1872). *Evolutionary psychology* now stands as an explanatory framework with the potential for understanding all psychological phenomena. The aim of this young discipline is to understand why humans do what they do and it has the following main tenets:

1 Our ancestors faced many dire challenges during our species' evolutionary history and natural selection designed our ancestors' neural circuits to solve them.
2 Only those ancestors that were able to solve problems passed their genes on and those genes were used to build more successful neural circuits.
3 Thus, our modern skulls literally house Stone Age minds.
4 Most of the activity in our minds is unconscious and hidden from us.
5 The mind is modular and different types of neural circuits are all specialized for solving different adaptive problems (Dunbar and Barrett, 2007).

Interesting for the discussion on whether or not humans have animist tendencies is the psychological phenomenon called *pareidolia*, which lets humans wrongly perceive a random visual or auditory stimulus as significant. Seeing animals or faces in clouds or the man in the moon, and hearing messages on Black Sabbath records when played in reverse are examples of this sub-category of *apophenia*, the perception of patterns within random data. *Faces in the Clouds: A New Theory of Religion*, a recent book actually sees *pareidolia* as part of *animism*, positing that this might be a fitting evolutionary explanation for the birth of religions (Guthrie, 2015). It seems that we might actually be wired to see life rather than no-life in things. In the (critical) words of Tim Ingold:

> Thus we have all evolved to be closet animists without of course realising it. Intuitive non-animists have been selected out, due to unfortunate encounters with things that turned out to be more alive than anticipated.
>
> *(Ingold, 2006, p11)*

Another fascinating line of research suggests that we attach more significance to 'original' artifacts than to copies as if the former somehow bestows a soul or spirit. Psychologist Brandy Frazier and colleagues have found that college students consistently preferred 'authentic' objects (paintings, signatures…) to imitations even when the two cannot visually be differentiated (Frazier et al., 2009). Similarly, in a 2008 study, Bruce Hood of Bristol University demonstrated that school age children were fooled into believing that an object can be 'copied' but always preferred the original one to the 'copied' one (Hood and Bloom, 2008). Hood and his team of scientists demonstrated in three separate studies that the destruction of a photograph of an object dear to the subjects produced significantly more electrodermal activity than the destruction of photographs of other control objects (Hood et al., 2010).

Designed animism

We can only speculate whether or not the first 'product designers' considered their creations to be *animate*. All organisms that were observed as coming to be – in the sense of being born – have always been observed as being animate and thus the first designers likely saw their creations in the same way. Describing the *animist* ontology Tim Ingold writes eloquently, '[O]ne is continually present as witness to that moment, always moving like the crest of a wave, at which the world is about to disclose itself for what it is' (Ingold, 2006, p12). Is it possible that we have become so removed from the creation of the objects around us that we have dropped all parent-like affection? Industrialization and in a sense industrial design have removed the production of things by one degree creating a system where things are mothered by things. Further research might address any correlation between the Cartesian dualism and the Industrial era.

The idea of 'designed animism' actually dates back to the 1970s when design theorists treated the impact of pervasive computing on the human experience and design as a discipline (Laurel, 2008). Recent approaches in design research have been steered towards purposely increasing emotional durability of products through design. Jonathan Chapman's research has shown that emotional bonds with consumer goods reduce the likelihood of such goods to be discarded (Chapman, 2005). Importantly, the writings of Donald Norman consider the often-overlooked factor of cognition on design. He writes of three levels of human processing – visceral, behavioral and reflective – requiring three types of design considerations. Our everyday things might also be longer-lasting by adding *animacy* (Norman, 2004). One type of design, interactive design, actually requires a level of *animistic* thinking for the user experience to be a positive one. As shown in a recent conference paper, *animism* can actually be used as an appropriate design metaphor for interactive design (van Allen et al., 2013). Not all types of design share such intrinsic relationships with *animism*, but all would arguably benefit from the ongoing discussion of a *new animism*.

Conclusions

Wake up to find out that you are the eyes of the world
– Robert Hunter

It is tempting to ridicule followers of the famous cargo cults of the Melanesian islanders for their use of *sympathetic magic*. But, it was easier for them to believe that the control towers, headsets, and runways were the cause of the cargo-carrying airplanes rather than an effect. 'Modern' people make the same kind of mistakes, when for example it is assumed that wearing certain outfits worn by celebrities one is in turn transmuted into a celebrity. Similar to the *cargo cults*, we talk of *animism* with disdain as if it's only about ignorant, primitive people with a fascination for stuff.

In the end we can ask if *animism* is a vice or a virtue. Is it something to be encouraged or renounced for society to work? The evolutionary process is not teleological and, as Popper remarked, 'the future is open'; he added, 'Thus it is our duty, not to prophesy evil, but, rather, to fight for a better world' (Popper, 1967). It is argued here that there can only be a better world with better design solutions. It is safe to say humans have a deeply ingrained fascination with stuff, which has become a serious concern when considering the resources required in making all such stuff. *Animism*, understood as a deeply rooted understanding of a world unfolding, alive with things could very well lead to a more sustainable future.

References

Altner, G. (1981) *Der Darwinismus: Die Geschichte einer Theorie*, Wissenschaftliche Buchgesellschaft, Darmstadt.

Altner, G. (1995) Darwins Lehrer und Anreger. In *Der Darwinismus: Die Geschichte einer Theorie*, Wissenschaftliche Buchgesellschaft, Darmstadt.

Barbieri, M. (2008) Biosemiotics: A New Understanding of Life. *Naturwissenschaften* 95.7: 577–599.

Barkow, J. (ed.). (1992) *The Adapted Mind: Evolutionary Psychology and the Generation of Culture*, Oxford University Press, Oxford.

Barrett, D. and Lycett, J. (2002) *Human Evolutionary Psychology*. Princeton University Press, Princeton, NJ.

Bird-David, N. (1999) 'Animism' Revisited: Personhood, Environment, and Relational Epistemology 1. *Current Anthropology* 40.S1: S67–S91.

Chapman, J. (2005) *Emotionally Durable Design: Objects, Experiences & Empathy*, Routledge, Oxon.

Clarke, A. C. (2013) *Profiles of the Future*. Hachette UK, London.

Darwin, C. (1872) *The Expression of the Emotions in Man and Animals*, London, John Murray, London.

Darwin, C, Ekman, P. and Prodger, P. (1998) *The Expression of the Emotions in Man and Animals*. Oxford University Press, New York.

Dawkins, R. (2006) *The Selfish Gene*. Oxford University Press, Oxford.

Descola, P. (1994) *Pourquoi les indiens d'Amazonie n'ont-ils pas domestiqué le pécari? Genéalogie des objets et anthropologie de l'objectivation*, La Découverte, Paris.

Descola, P. (2005) On Anthropological Knowledge. *Social Anthropology* 13.1: 65–73.

Descola, P. (2006) *Beyond Nature and Culture*. Oxford University Press, Oxford.

Descola, P. (2009) Human Natures. *Social Anthropology* 17.2: 145–157.

Descola, P. (2013) *Beyond Nature and Culture*. University of Chicago Press, Chicago, IL.

Descola, P. (2015) Who Owns Nature? Retrieved from www.laviedesidees.fr/spip.php?page=print&id_article=184 (accessed July 2015)

Diamond, J. (2005) *Collapse: How Societies Choose to Fail or Succeed*. Penguin, London.

Diamond, J. (2012) *The World until Yesterday: What Can We Learn from Traditional Societies*. Penguin, London.

Dutton, D. (2009) *The Art Instinct: Beauty, Pleasure, and Human Evolution*. Oxford University Press, Oxford.

Frazier, B. et al. (2009) Picasso Paintings, Moon Rocks, and Hand-written Beatles Lyrics: Adults' Evaluations of Authentic Objects. *Journal of Cognition and Culture* 9.1: 1–14.

Gell, A. (1992) The Technology of Enchantment and the Enchantment of Technology. In *Anthropology, Art and Aesthetics*, Clarendon Press, Oxford, 40–63.

Guthrie, S. (1993) *Faces in the Clouds: A New Theory of Religion*, Oxford University Press, Oxford.

Guthrie, S. (2015) *Faces in the Clouds*. Oxford University Press, Oxford.

Hardt, M. and Negri, A. (2009) *Empire*. Harvard University Press, Cambridge, MA.

Harvey, G. (2005) *Animism: Respecting the Living World*. Wakefield Press, Mile End, Australia.

Hoffmeyer, J. (1996) The Global Semiosphere. *Approaches to Semiotics* 126: 933–936.

Hood, B. and Bloom, P. (2008) Children Prefer Certain Individuals Over Perfect Duplicates. *Cognition* 106.1: 455–462.

Hood, B. et al. (2010) Implicit Voodoo: Electrodermal Activity Reveals a Susceptibility to Sympathetic Magic. *Journal of Cognition and Culture* 10.3: 391–399.

Ingold, T. (2000) *The Perception of the Environment: Essays on Livelihood, Dwelling and Skill*. Psychology Press, Brighton.

Ingold, T. (2006) Rethinking the Animate, Re-animating Thought. *Ethnos* 71.1: 9–20.

Koeb, H. (1996) Die Wiener Schule der Voelkerkunde als Antithese zum Evolutionismus, Master's thesis, Vienna University of Economics and Business, Vienna.

Latour, B. (1993) *We Have Never Been Modern* (trans. C. Porter), Harvard University Press, US.

Latour, B. (2010) *An Attempt at Writing a Compositionist Manifesto: New Literary History*. Johns Hopkins University Press, Baltimore, MD.

Latour, B. (2012) *We Have Never Been Modern*. Harvard University Press, Cambridge, MA.

Latour, B. and Weibel, P. (2005) *Making Things Public: Atmospheres of Democracy*, MIT Press, US.

Laurel, B. (2008) 'Designed Animism' in Digital Design Theory, Chronicle Books, US, 122–126.

Lévi-Strauss, C. (1962) *The Savage Mind, Librairie Plon*, Paris.

Lorenz, K. (1964) *Das sogenannte Böse. Borotha-Schoeler*, Methuen Publishing, London.

McDonough, W. and Braungart, M. (2010) *Cradle to Cradle: Remaking the Way We Make Things*. Macmillan, New York.

McDonough, W. and Braungart, M. (2013) *The Upcycle: Beyond Sustainability – Designing for Abundance*. Macmillan, New York.

Mauss, M. (1950) *The Gift*, Presses Universitaires de France, France.

Miller, D. (1998) *A Theory of Shopping*, Polity, UK.

Norman, D. (2004) *Emotional Design: Why We Love (or Hate) Everyday Things*. Basic Books, New York.

Odling-Smee, F. J., Laland, K. N. and Feldman, M. W. (2003) *Niche Construction: The Neglected Process in Evolution*. Princeton University Press, Princeton, NJ.

Popper, K. (1967) *The Myth of the Framework: Rational Changes in Science*. Springer Netherlands, Dordrecht.

Rostow, W. (1990) *The Stages of Economic Growth: A Non-Communist Manifesto*. Cambridge University Press, Cambridge.

Shermer, M. (2008) The Mind of the Market. *Scientific American* 298.2: 35–36.

Slade, G. (2007) *Made to Break: Technology and Obsolescence in America*. Harvard University Press, Cambridge, MA.

Tylor, E. (1871) *Primitive Culture: Researches into the Development of Mythology, Philosophy, Religion, Art, and Custom*, vol. 2. John Murray, London.

Van Allen, P. et al. (2013) *AniThings: Animism and Heterogeneous Multiplicity*. CHI'13 Extended Abstracts on Human Factors in Computing Systems. ACM, Paris.

Veblen, T. ([1899]2005) *The Theory of the Leisure Class: An Economic Study of Institutions*. Aakar Books, Delhi.

Wheeler, W. (2006) *The Whole Creature: Complexity, Biosemiotics and the Evolution of Culture*. Lawrence & Wishart, London.

White, L. (1954) *The Energy Theory of Cultural Development*, University of New Mexico Press, Albuquerque.

Wilson, D. S. (2011) *The Neighborhood Project: Using Evolution to Improve My City, One Block at a Time*. Little, Brown & Company, New York.

Wilson, E. O. (2012) *The Social Conquest of Earth*. W. W. Norton & Company, New York.

4

THE OBJECT OF NIGHTINGALES

Design values for a meaningful material culture

Stuart Walker

Abstract

This chapter considers design values that are congruent with age-old understandings of human meaning as well as with contemporary notions of sustainability. A critique of naturalistic materialism and its relationship to un-sustainable interpretations of progress and growth is followed by a consideration of practical, social and personal meaning and their relationship to human values. A basis for meaningful values emerges for ethical judgment and product design decision-making. The result is an understanding of design and production that aligns more closely with sustainable principles and with deeper understandings of human flourishing.

Keywords: sustainability, design, meaning, values, tradition

> ... such madness is given by the gods to allow us to achieve the greatest good fortune;
> and the proof will be disbelieved by the clever, believed by the wise.
>
> – *Plato*

One evening in 1942, deep inside a wood in the southeast of England, a BBC sound engineer was recording the song of the nightingale. Coincidentally, this was also the night of a British bombing raid on Mannheim and while the sound engineer was at work, 197 bombers flew overhead on their way to Germany. The recording begins with the song of the nightingale and continues as the drone of the aircraft slowly increases, becoming a deafening roar as they pass directly above, before steadily decreasing and eventually fading away; throughout the recording the nightingale sustains its song (Mason, 1988; RAF History, 2005). It is a poignant and thought-provoking piece. The high, trilling notes of the nightingale are natural and unaffected, and to the human ear, pure, aesthetic and sublime. By contrast, the ominous cacophony of the bombers is the sound of human-made war technologies – the manufactured machines of conflict and purposeful destruction. Significantly, we can clearly identify what the bombers are for; their purpose is combat, damage and discord. But we cannot say what the nightingale is for; we cannot think of nightingales in instrumental terms. The nightingale is not a means to some other end, it is an end in itself; it simply *is*.

Robert Louis Stevenson also wrote of the nightingale:

> a remembrance of those fortunate hours in which the bird has sung to us … fills us with such wonder when we turn the pages of the realist. There, to be sure, we find a picture of life in so far as it consists of mud and of old iron, cheap desires and cheap fears, that which we are ashamed to remember and that which we are careless whether we forget; but of the note of that time-devouring nightingale we hear no news.
>
> *(Stevenson, 1888, p231)*

The nightingale has a long history of symbolic associations with creativity, the muse, Nature's purity and, in Western spiritual tradition, virtue and goodness (Tucker, 1998). Here, these various symbolic associations come together in a consideration of creative design and its relationship to human values.

I begin with a critique of our current predicament within a dominant ideology of naturalistic materialism, which judging by its outcomes appears to be seriously flawed in terms of its ethical and environmental implications. This widespread ideology, combined with the sophisticated capabilities of scientific and technological advancement, a corporate aspiration of unbridled profit and growth, and an undefined, yet largely relativistic ethical position, has created a potent recipe for human exploitation and environmental destruction. I suggest that any meaningful notion of sustainability must be grounded in a firm foundation of those values that are common to all the great wisdom traditions, both religious and non-religious, as well as to contemporary progressive forms of spirituality,[1] and that through adherence to such values design can make a tangible, discernible and positive difference to the nature and effects of our material goods.

Naturalistic materialism and human values

Naturalistic materialism is an ideology strongly associated with the post-traditional understandings and philosophies of modernity and late- or post-modernity. These are epitomized by the philosophy of Nietzsche, who so emphatically dismissed traditional beliefs as mere 'idols', along with the moral values that accompanied them (Nietzsche, [1889]2003, pp61–81). Also known as naturalism, physicalism, or simply materialism, naturalistic materialism has become the overarching doctrine of the modern Western world – a world characterized by its emphasis on secularism, rationalism, and industrial capitalism. Naturalistic materialism is, nevertheless, a belief system and is no more provable than the traditional beliefs it has tended to depose. As the principal ideology of modernity, its critics have included Thoreau (1854) in the nineteenth century, Horkheimer and Adorno ([1947]2010) in the mid-twentieth century and Schumacher (1973) in the later twentieth century. It is related to forms of modern secular humanism in which human interests and values are based on reason, scientific investigation and experience, and where human fulfilment must be found within the physical world; the physical universe being regarded as the totality of existence, with no place for traditional religious beliefs or notions of ultimate reality, whether theistic or non-theistic.

Thus, naturalistic materialism is an ideology that is linked to the physical sciences (Hick, 2002), indeed it is often seen as the only belief system that is compatible with them (Taylor,

2007, p28). It is also an ideology that seeks to mould the natural environment and human society to suit human purposes and is characteristically interventionist, functionalist and grounded in instrumental reason (ibid., p246). Scientific investigations and analyses of the physical world lead to understandings of physical principles, and such investigations are regarded as being value-free; being concerned only with the investigation, analysis and understanding of physical phenomena and the physical world.

However, physical principles can be, and frequently are, exploited and utilized for human purposes – and these kinds of activities are *not* value-free. The application of scientific principles to achieve human intention has an instrumental basis and, by the very fact that it is thought to be worth doing, a value judgement is made. Hence, when such applications are developed, either in academia or in corporate research facilities, the question of human values enters the scene. In academia the value may be to demonstrate usefulness and potential functional and/or economic benefit sometime in the future. In the corporate setting the relationship to economic potential will likely be more direct and more immediate. Yet, within the ideology of naturalistic materialism, which as we have seen holds that the value-free physical universe constitutes the whole of existence, the basis for a set of ethical values against which we can gauge the goodness or rightness of these judgements is by no means clear, apart from the claim that such actions are contributing to progress, which in and of itself may be meaningless and without value (ibid., pp716–717; Tillich, 1952, pp105–111). Public policy only consolidates such a direction by addressing its decision-making to purely material needs (Mathews, 2006, p90), which become increasingly relative. Within such an ideology, there is a danger that values become based merely on a foundation of ever-shifting societal mores and norms. Here, each incremental change might seem like a small and reasonable step forward but over time such steps can, cumulatively, take us down a path that is both socially exploitative and environmentally and, therefore, potentially self- destructive. In many respects, and despite, or indeed because of, the many and varied material benefits brought about by contemporary technologies, there can be little doubt that this is the road on which we now find ourselves. Traditional sources of meaning and value may have been abandoned, but nothing has replaced them, leading to what Beattie (2007, p134) has termed 'valueless' values and a proliferation of meaningless choices. Moreover, there is a certain ambiguity and confusion among some who reject the notion of absolute standards of morality. Arguing for a more pluralistic, and inevitably more relativistic, notion of morality, they also appeal to 'basic moral principles' while offering little justification for such principles or adequately distinguishing them from the 'absolute' moral standards they choose to reject. Apart from this internal contradiction, such a morality confines itself to knowledge and reason (Holloway, 2000, pp16, 151–157), which as we shall see, not only presents a more limited view than that afforded by the world's wisdom traditions, it also opens up the possibility of moralities that are patently immoral; Nietzsche, for example, dismissed traditional 'basic moral principles' such as equality and being kind to one another as mere moral pretensions (MacQuarrie, 1967, p233).

It is important to recognize too that the ideology of naturalistic materialism cannot rule out humanity's traditional understandings of reality. Just because science reports only on findings concerning the physical universe, it does not follow that the physical universe is the totality of existence. Nevertheless, this illogical conclusion is one that has become prevalent. It is a conclusion that is also unscientific; critique, therefore, is not aimed at science but at the scientistic ideology that we have built from its findings (Smith, 2005, p1). Here, Cottingham usefully distinguishes between notions of naturalistic materialism that are essentially methodological and those that are ontological. Methodologically, naturalistic materialism represents an attempt to explain the totality of existence via physical phenomena, with no reference to notions of a transcendent reality; as such it represents a set of investigative and exploratory aspirations. Ontologically, however, naturalistic materialism claims that the physical, phenomenal universe is the totality of existence – a claim that clearly lies beyond the realm of science (Cottingham, 2005, pp109–110). This still-prevalent ontological interpretation, with its ill-defined and questionable value system, is inextricably linked to industrialism and technological conceptions of progress, both of which are precariously dependent on energy resources, especially hydrocarbons. In turn, such developments are catalysts of urbanization, and the promulgation of globalized, growth-based consumer society. It is, therefore, an ideology that not only constricts humanity's notions of meaning and reality, it is also indelibly tied to stripping the planet of its resources at unsustainable rates while simultaneously eradicating the complex interdependencies of biodiversity on which all life depends. However, while it remains a widespread ideology, it is also one that we seem to be slowly freeing ourselves from (Smith, 2005, pp1–2), with many contemporary theorists regarding moral values as falling outside naturalistic explanation (Cottingham, 2005, p110). In moving beyond naturalistic materialism we have the opportunity to reassess our values. This can include the retrieval of understandings that have become increasingly marginalized in 'advanced' societies, but which, for thousands of years, had provided substantive foundations for living that were both meaningful and in balance with the cycles of Nature. Recognizing the significance of these foundations, together with the serious deficits, as well as the benefits, of contemporary approaches will, potentially, allow us to deal more effectively with the social and environmental challenges of our time.

Meaning and its relationship to values

A firmer basis for human values – and their relationship to human endeavour – emerges when we include traditional understandings of meaning. In this regard, there are three incontrovertible elements of the human condition. First, we exist within a natural environment that we utilize to our own ends. Second, human nature is such that we generally choose to live in social groupings. Third, we are individual beings with a distinct sense of selfhood. Corresponding to these three aspects of being human are levels of meaning that can be referred to respectively as *practical meaning*, *social meaning* and *personal* (or inner) *meaning* (Walker, 2011, pp185–210). This analysis extends Hick's (1989, pp129–171) proposition of natural, ethical and religious meanings so as to include not only religion but also contemporary, non-religious or atheistic forms of spirituality; the latter embracing interpretations of humanism that reach beyond the ontological doctrine of naturalistic materialism to acknowledge an ineffable, quasi-transcendent notion of the unity or one-ness of reality (Comte-Sponville, 2007, pp168–169). Such interpretations are not far removed from the more humanistic aspects of Buddhism, especially Zen Buddhism (Hick, 2004). These contemporary forms of spirituality can be entirely secular, or they can include elements of traditional religion, and they often provide a strong basis for inner growth, personal ethics, and for addressing today's important environmental and social concerns (King, 2009, p14). Hence, these three major facets of human meaning span physiological aspects of being human, social relationships, and personal values and spiritual growth, both religious and atheistic. These, along with their interrelationships, are summarized in Figure 4.1 and can be described as follows:

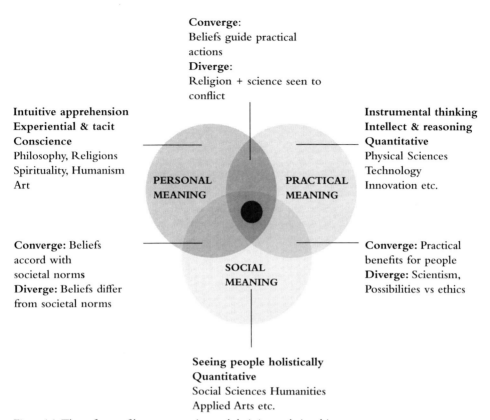

Converge:
Beliefs guide practical actions
Diverge:
Religion + science seen to conflict

Intuitive apprehension
Experiential & tacit
Conscience
Philosophy, Religions
Spirituality, Humanism
Art

Instrumental thinking
Intellect & reasoning
Quantitative
Physical Sciences
Technology
Innovation etc.

PERSONAL MEANING

PRACTICAL MEANING

Converge: Beliefs
accord with
societal norms
Diverge: Beliefs differ
from societal norms

SOCIAL MEANING

Converge: Practical
benefits for people
Diverge: Scientism,
Possibilities vs ethics

Seeing people holistically
Quantitative
Social Sciences Humanities
Applied Arts etc.

Figure 4.1 Three facets of human meaning and their interrelationships

- **Practical meaning:** The natural environment provides us with food, water, shelter, warmth and materials – all of which help satisfy our practical needs and wants. Appropriate interpretation of the natural environment and physical phenomena in order to satisfy these needs and wants, as well as a recognition of the consequences of our actions, give practical meaning to our decisions and actions. Practical meaning is characterized by: that which is sense-based and provable; instrumental thinking; intellect and reasoning; quantitative methods; evidence-based methods; analytical thinking; logic and efficiency. It is perhaps best represented today by disciplines such as the physical sciences, mathematics, engineering, and by technology and innovation.
- **Social meaning:** Our interactions and dealings with other people are mediated by concerns such as justice, peace, charity, compassion and the moral compass that informs our social relationships. Our decisions and actions, in relation to ethical principles, moral codes, and social mores and conventions, give social meaning to our lives. Hence, important aspects of social meaning include seeing people as individuals; asking what is good, right and fair (i.e. values/morals); empathy and compassion towards *the other*; and greater emphasis on qualitative rather than quantitative considerations. Social meaning is represented by disciplines such as social sciences, politics, law, philosophy, economics, as well as the applied arts such as design and fashion.
- **Personal meaning:** The interior life and addressing perennial questions about *being* itself, life's purpose and ultimate value cannot be pursued through rationalization or proved via empirical methods. These areas of human concern encompass what might be

termed the inner search and they can influence our actions in the world. Our attention to these age-old questions can give a personal sense of meaning to our lives through attention to spiritual growth and the development of an inner sense of that which is right and good i.e. a core sense of ethics and values, which Needleman (1989, pvi) has referred to as that which is permanent in us, irrespective of sociocultural particularities. The characteristic modes for developing this sense of personal meaning include reflection, intuitive apprehension, direct experience, and tacit ways of knowing that lie beyond the capacity of the senses and proof. Such modes transcend thoughts, judgements, knowledge, ideas and concepts and are more concerned with silence, listening and experiencing. They can also include aspects of the active life, especially 'good' works, and fidelity to tradition. Individual striving towards a personal sense of meaning is represented by the world's great theistic and non-theistic religions, philosophies and practices as well as by contemporary atheistic spiritualities. We could also include certain artistic practices and modes of expression in the fine arts, poetry, music and literature.

The interrelationships among the above categories can be described as follows:

- **Practical meaning and social meaning:** These converge when we develop practical benefits for people in ways that are safe, healthy, just, and considered right and good. However, they can diverge when, for example, empirical methods developed in the physical sciences are inappropriately used in the humanities – this leads to scientism and can be dehumanizing. They can also diverge when practical possibilities clash with ethical norms or with diverse ideas of what is right and good.
- **Social meaning and personal meaning:** These converge when personal beliefs, which provide the basis for one's values and ethical judgements, correspond with social conventions, moral codes, laws, and societal norms of fairness and justice. They diverge when questions of conscience and liberty of conscience arise, for example when religious or personal beliefs differ from societal norms and existing legislation.
- **Personal meaning and practical meaning:** Personal beliefs, which can include religious faith and/or spiritual convictions, are often a powerful motivator for developing practical solutions. When this occurs, 'higher' or 'inner' ideas find expression through techniques, skills and sense-based modes. Furthermore, the nature of these practical solutions will often differ qualitatively from similar initiatives where such beliefs are not a prime motivator. For example, provision of housing for the poor, when developed by faith groups, will often take a grass-roots approach that involves volunteerism and community and adopts self-build techniques, whereas a non-faith based approach might be the development of a large scale affordable housing project built by local government. However, personal meaning and practical meaning can frequently diverge because they represent very different ways of encountering the world; personal meaning based on inner conviction and beyond proof contrasts with practical meaning, which is both sense-based and provable. As a consequence, spiritual and religious understandings and scientific understandings are often perceived to be opposed and in conflict – even though, as is clear from the preceding distinctions, this is something of a false dichotomy.
- **The personal, the social and the practical:** The inner life, the social life and the active pragmatic life are, of course, simply different aspects of a single life. They provide us with a basis for doing the right thing and constructing what might be termed a meaningful life, and for making a meaningful contribution to society.

Meaning, values and design

We have seen from the above that the inner or reflective life and our sense of personal meaning can provide a basis for our beliefs and worldview – ranging from religious to secular humanist. It is these aspects of meaning-seeking and spiritual growth that have traditionally provided humanity with its understandings of virtue (Cottingham, 2005, p140); that is, its notions of what is good, right and true. In turn, this personal sense of ethical values can qualitatively affect our practical actions in the world, as illustrated in Figure 4.2.

Design is, of course, a practical activity which, when linked to mass-production, can have significant and far-reaching consequences. Much contemporary design has become completely bound up with consumerism, transient products and waste – a point raised in the 1970s by Papanek (1971). And because so many of these products are now based on rapidly developing digital technologies, design has become an accessory, firstly, in endorsing the environmentally unsustainable dogma of progress, which in practice means technological progress and, secondly, in supporting growth, which in practice means financial growth and the pursuit of ever-increasing profits. An almost pathological quest for the next technological advancement is driven by a desire for competitive advantage to ensure increased sales of mass-produced products which, in turn, create financial growth. These skewed priorities are systemically linked to human exploitation and environmental destruction – a state of affairs that Jackson (2009, p32) has termed the 'age of irresponsibility'. This is an inevitable

INNER LIFE
- contemplative, subjective, imaginative
- need not be developed
- basis of values

BASIC NEEDS
- active, objective, empirical
- have to be met
- values free?

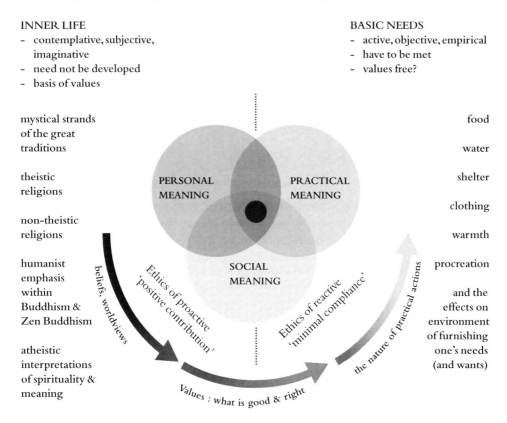

mystical strands of the great traditions

theistic religions

non-theistic religions

humanist emphasis within Buddhism & Zen Buddhism

atheistic interpretations of spirituality & meaning

food

water

shelter

clothing

warmth

procreation

and the effects on environment of furnishing one's needs (and wants)

PERSONAL MEANING

PRACTICAL MEANING

SOCIAL MEANING

beliefs, worldviews

Ethics of proactive 'positive contribution'

Ethics of reactive 'minimal compliance'

the nature of practical actions

Values : what is good & right

Morality and social norms, relationships, empathy, compassion, charity

Figure 4.2 Beliefs, values and actions

consequence of prioritizing growth in profits within a dominant ideology of naturalistic materialism in which instrumental, material benefits are lauded, ethical values are both vague and relativistic, and higher, more profound notions of human meaning are marginalized (Eagleton, 2009, p39).

To reform these practices, and particularly those associated with design decision-making, it becomes necessary to develop a clearer understanding of:

1 a basis for values;
2 values for meaningful design decision-making;
3 ethically questionable, unsustainable design practices;
4 ethical, sustainable design decision-making.

A basis for values

If, as discussed, the progress-and-growth system in which contemporary design exists fosters sentiments and decision-making that contribute to social injustice and environmental harm, then to formulate just sentiments and responsible design decision-making we must look to other sources for guidance. To this end, the world's major philosophical and spiritual traditions provide a rich foundation in understandings of virtue. However, it is important to recognize that there is a view within contemporary, economically developed cultures that has become increasingly disdainful and dismissive of these traditions. Here, the most prominent detractors are indicative of a pervasive current that prizes evidence-based research, with its accompanying requirements of facts and proof, over imagination, emotion, empathy and spiritual and cultural traditions. Yet, anthropologist Elizabeth Lindsey (2010) calls such traditions humanity's DNA, adding that today, we 'live in a society bloated with data, yet starved for wisdom'. Therefore, as we proceed it will be important to bear in mind that while it is all too easy to disparage more intuitive ways of knowing with mundane rationalisms (Lewis, 1947, p13), modes of living in which this has occurred are associated with staggering social inequities and unprecedented rates of environmental destruction.

It is important, also, to recognize that human values cannot simply be invented, nor can they be based on instinct or reached as a conclusion. Rather, our basic moral principles are grounded in a vast heritage of human experience and understanding, and as such they can be regarded as self-evident precepts and obligatory for their own sake (ibid., pp39–40). However, when this foundational heritage becomes marginalized in a world dominated by materialistic understandings, there is a danger that the anchor that holds a value system in place is cut free, allowing values to drift in whatever direction the wind blows. Yet, when we talk of sustainability, these traditions and their teachings are significant because they represent the source of congruence with Nature and of reciprocity with our fellow human beings.

While specific traditions and their cultural practices and accretions are not the concern of this present discussion, it will be worth noting some important features of these traditions, which lead to understandings of human values. We will then consider some of the fundamental values common to all the major traditions, which provide a basis for ethical decision-making.

Spiritual traditions and practices, and human values

Even though the world's major spiritual traditions are very diverse, there are two broad features that are common to them all. First, they all have what might be termed popular practices that serve everyday needs; these include various rituals, ceremonies and rites of passage. Second, there are more dedicated practices, disciplines and methods that are aimed at inner development, insight and transformation. An example from traditional Japanese spirituality is the systematic training method known as *koshinto* (Yamakage, 2006, p12). Similar methods are found in all the major traditions – from the *Rule of St. Benedict* and the fifteenth-century writings of Thomas à Kempis in Western Christianity to the *Middle Way* of Buddhism.

Why, one might ask, are such things still relevant? The reason these kinds of teachings, practices and disciplines remain important and are perhaps more relevant than ever is because they are concerned with a desire to reach beyond the ever-changing, frenetic distractions of the busy, active life – beyond the latest gadget, the ceaseless headlines, and the newest trend – to focus on more profound notions of meaning and to apprehend a deeper sense of reality. These traditions are concerned with self-discipline and self-examination, contemplation, silence and the interior life, and insights that extend beyond instrumental thinking and rationalizations. These ways of knowing, we are told, transcend conceptualizations, thoughts, knowledge, and words, and can lead to intuitive understandings and at least some apprehension of what has been referred to as the Real (Hick, 1989, p11), the ultimate reality or ground of being (Tillich, 1952, pp180–181), the Tao or Way of the Universe, and the interconnectedness and unity of all things (Comte-Sponville, 2007, p168). Such insights are experiential and cannot be attained through the senses or through intellectual reasoning. They lie beyond any particular religion or dogma but, whatever the tradition, they have led those who have followed such a path to similar conclusions about values and how we *ought* to live. Even though these values are found through delving deeper into self, fundamentally and somewhat paradoxically they transcend the ego, the self and selfishness; there are indispensable social as well as environmental (Nature, the universe) dimensions to such traditions. Emerging from these disciplines are teachings that advocate a course between deficiency and excess, as in Aristotle's *Ethics* (1106a) or the *Analects* of Confucius (6.29). Moreover, following this middle course is our ethical obligation – so as to ensure balance and harmony in ourselves, in our dealings with others and with the ways of Nature (Lewis, 1947, p18), and to attain any semblance of earthly happiness. Although there is no logically verifiable connection between these traditions and human values, they have for thousands of years and across all cultures provided the bedrock of ethical behaviour (Cottingham, 2005, p168).

A basis for judgement

To follow this path we must have a basis for making right judgements and, as classical Greek philosophy tells us, this is the role of education. True education is concerned with being taught to feel appropriate sentiments – 'to feel joy and grief at the right things', and to 'act according to the right principle', 'which is that which accords with prudence' (Aristotle, *Ethics*, 1103b, 1104b, 1144b). Thus, education is about learning to like those things that one *ought* to like, so that one's emotional responses are in line with virtue. Also, we should proceed with consideration and caution in regard to practical matters. In this regard, being frugal and acting with foresight in caring for resources and the economy become essential aspects of right judgement.

If one *ought* to feel joy or grief at the right things, and if there are certain kinds of activities and modes of conduct that one *ought* to engage in, and others to avoid, for one's endeavours to be meaningful and ethical then this implies that there are some objective standards against which one must judge one's behaviour. This is the principle of objective value (Lewis, 1947, p18). Here then, we have *subjective emotions*, which in and of themselves are not judgements, *facts*, which are value-free, and *objective value*, the belief that certain attitudes really are right or true while others are wrong or false. By becoming cognizant of these objective standards, via education, our emotional responses to external, factual phenomena have a reference point by which we can make right judgements, and thence act accordingly. For example, certain phenomena require a particular kind of emotional response, such as sympathy, delight or repulsion, and whether or not, as individuals, we are capable of feeling such emotions, knowledge of this requirement through education, can guide us to act in a certain way. This recognition of objective value allows our emotional responses to be linked to reason (i.e. our emotional response is reasonable when it aligns with what we *ought* to feel, and unreasonable otherwise; ibid., p19).

Irrespective of whether we are able to accept the above argument, let us look at the values that these traditions espouse so as to consider their relationship to sustainability. We will then be able to determine if, indeed, they have any relevance for contemporary design and for aligning the nature of our material culture with sustainable principles.

Values for meaningful design decision-making

The values and teachings of the various traditions are, of course, wide-ranging and diverse. Therefore, for illustrative purposes, we will focus on some of those that are especially relevant to design and sustainability.

In terms of social considerations, one of the longest-standing and widely accepted precepts found in virtually all cultures across time is the ethic of reciprocity known as the Golden Rule. The call to 'not do to others what you would not want them to do to you', as taught by Confucius (*Analects*, 15.23), is repeated in similar forms in the writings of Plato (*Crito*, 49c–d), Taoism (*Tao Te Ching*, 49), Hinduism (*Bhagavad Gita*, 12), Buddhism (*Dhammapada*, 10.130), Judaism (Leviticus, 19:18), Christianity (Matthew, 7:12) and Islam (*40 Hadith of an-Nawawi*, 13). The positive form of this ethic, 'do to others what you would have them do to you', tells us how we *ought* to act towards our fellow human beings.

Clearly, the inordinate economic and social inequities and human exploitation that are so prevalent today, both within and between nations are incompatible with this ethic. Furthermore, many of these inequities and exploitative practices are directly linked to products and product manufacturing. The social upheavals and poor conditions associated with product manufacturing, waste and pollution in many economically developing countries have received widespread publicity in recent years. However, forms of exploitation are also present in the ways products are designed and marketed, where people's susceptibilities are deliberately manipulated and preyed upon to secure sales, thereby contributing to corporate economic growth. One example of this is 'undercover marketing' where people are unaware that seemingly everyday occurrences are, in fact, staged marketing activities (Bakan, 2004, p134). Another is the common strategy of launching slightly 'improved' versions of essentially the same product at regular intervals, to stimulate desire and imbue notions of perceived obsolescence in relation to the previous model. Such approaches not only contravene the ethic of reciprocity, they are also fundamental to the environmental aspects of sustainability because they drive resource and energy use and generate waste.

Let us now look more specifically at the relationship of material goods to notions of meaning, so as to consider what value *should* be placed on them. The Chinese sage Lao Tzu not only advises against acquiring precious things, but also against putting ourselves in a position where we constantly see desirable things; such things come and go, but attention to them distracts us from what really matters (*Tao Te Ching*, 3) and what really matters is a recognition of the true self in relation to the Tao or the Real. Similarly, Buddhist teaching says that by hankering after transient things we fail to see life as it really is and forget life's true aim (*Dhammapada*, 16). The atheist existentialist Camus saw the mythic Sisyphus, forever pushing a rock up a mountain, and Kafka's K, attempting to reach The Castle, as two figures whose lives are taken up with the distractions and busyness of worldly affairs. For Camus, it is in the realization of the futility and absurdity of such worldly affairs that meaning is to be found (Camus, [1942]2005, pp115–116). By contrast, for the Christian existentialist Tillich, meaning is found in the acceptance of and struggle towards the heights, despite the day-to-day busyness and distractions; this, for Tillich, is 'the courage to be' (Tillich, 1952, pp171–190). So we see that, regardless of their nuances and differences, all these and many other traditional and philosophical sources suggest that a preoccupation with and craving for transient, worldly things is fundamentally lacking in meaning and detrimental to the human condition.

If this is indeed the case then the implications for design, and its relationship to sustainability, are critical. Not only is design a discipline that occupies itself with the definition of transient material things but, significantly, it tends to do so in ways that are deliberately intended to distract and arouse feelings of desire, craving and status. Marketing tends to only reinforce such feelings. The result is the constant production of fleeting enticements and contrivances that not only have little relationship to a meaningful life but which also divert us away from it. In the process, due to the sheer scale of contemporary product production and disposal, design is indirectly contributing to the rapid denudation of resources, the destruction of natural environments and the accumulation of climate changing emissions.

Clearly this raises significant and pressing issues with respect to design values – if we are to develop a material culture that is both meaningful and aligned with sustainable principles. Here, a meaningful material culture would be one that, in all its facets – its materials, its modes of production, its presence and use, and its ultimate disposal – conforms to, and serves to support, understandings of: human meaning and inner development; social relations and community wellbeing; and environmental stewardship. Therefore, recalling the basis of judgement described earlier, we will now consider some features of ethically questionable, unsustainable design practices, followed by an exploration of more ethical, sustainable design decision-making. However, it is important to note that such distinctions cannot be definitive. It is not so much a case of clear cut delineations but more a question of emphasis and tone, which can lead to important qualitative differences in the nature of manufactured artefacts.

Ethically questionable, unsustainable design practices

If we are to refrain from ethically questionable, unsustainable design practices, we *ought not* to be making design decisions that intentionally try to ensure material goods are:

- **Enticing:** through such commonly accepted practices as unnecessary styling changes, shiny surfaces and aesthetic perfection, and fashionable, exuberant or luxurious enclosures. Such practices stimulate emotions such as craving or vanity that conflict with more profound notions of personal meaning, fulfilment and happiness.
- **Transient:** by engaging in practices that lead to premature product obsolescence – through, for example, unnecessary aesthetic changes or the specification of delicate surfaces and materials that quickly lose their appeal through everyday use and wear.

- **Distracting:** by creating products that allow or encourage opportunities for interruption, endless diversion and amusement, that hinder reflection or are known to contribute to compulsive use behaviours.

Based on the arguments presented here, all the above factors can negatively affect human flourishing while having major detrimental effects on social equity and the natural environment because of their modes of production, use and disposal.

Ethical, sustainable design decision-making

To create a material culture that is supportive of higher notions of personal meaning and human potential, as well as being socially and environmentally responsible, we *ought* to be making design decisions that help ensure that our everyday material goods are:

- **Moderate:** by consciously avoiding excessive and/or distracting characteristics, features or modes of use. In his housing designs, Irish architect Dominic Stevens (2007, pp97–175) demonstrates that moderation need not compromise good design. His sensitively designed homes are modest, low cost, low energy buildings that often incorporate reused materials.
- **Relatively unimportant:** by recognizing the place functional goods *should* occupy in human endeavour if they are to comply with our most profound understandings of human meaning, and with ethical behaviours and environmental responsibility. This would mean that everyday products would have to occupy a far less dominant role than is the case today. To be in keeping with such a direction, their design would necessarily be more modest, recognizing their relatively minor place within human endeavours. One way of reducing the importance of possessions is through product sharing schemes, which already include car sharing and city bike programmes. In their explorations of sustainable living, Manzini and Jégou (2003, pp172–177) have developed more radical product sharing ideas, including kitchens, objects and clothing.
- **Useful tools:** by designing products to be functional, reliable and enduring but unassuming.
- **Congruent with meaning:** through their materials, modes of use, aesthetic definitions, symbolic references, and non-instrumental characteristics functional goods can, potentially, reinforce ideas of how we ought to act and behaviours that are congruent with environmental, ethical and meaningful ways of living. Conversely, products designed to encourage intense desire or envy would be incompatible with such ideas.
- **Warranted:** the relationship of transient things to obfuscation and distraction from more reflective, moderate modes of being has long been recognized in the major spiritual and philosophical traditions. In the past century these detrimental effects have become combined with the devastating social and environmental repercussions of growth-based globalized mass-production. Therefore, we can no longer simply ask how products might be designed in better, more responsible ways. We must also ask if the design and production of a product is even justified in the first place. Today, the design rationale for a new model of product is usually expressed in instrumental terms – it performs faster, it is thinner, it offers higher resolution. These very mundanities are the currency of aspirational marketing with minor technical and aesthetic changes being linked to success and status. However, the underlying reason for producing

yet another new model is invariably the generation of company profits and growth. When the source of our design decisions comes from a philosophical outlook that prioritizes materialism and worldly absorptions, the rationale and justification for design decisions will reflect this emphasis, and the product design itself will be a tangible manifestation of these practical, utilitarian values, with a corresponding lack of emphasis on other factors. Such validations are generally accepted and regarded as enough within the growth-based system in which design and manufacturing reside. However, given the corrosive effects that the global production of transient things, particularly short-lived technological products, can have on personal wellbeing (Power, 2000, p271; Carr, 2010, p119), social justice (Chan et al., 2008, pp24–26) and environmental stewardship (Jackson, 2009, pp32–33), there is a need to consider not only instrumental but also ethical justifications, as well as justifications that take into account deeper concerns related to spiritual or inner values. We must begin to ask if the production of yet another product is a good and right thing to do, and if the functional benefits or improvements, which are often minor, are warranted – now that we are aware of the cumulative effects of continuously producing, packaging, shipping, using and disposing of millions of such products. These questions are fundamentally related to notions of personal meaning and to sustainability; significant reductions in consumerism are essential for the furtherance of both.

- **Empathetic**: to help ensure that our material productions are more consistent with traditional understandings and ethical principles, we have to develop approaches that are far more empathetic to both people and place. It becomes important to be open to aspects that are often unconsidered or given short shrift in contemporary practice – aspects that can be intuitively apprehended but not necessarily supported by facts or intellectual reasoning. The architect Christopher Day (1998) recognizes these important facets of knowing when designing a new building for a particular site. His practice not only involves consensual, participatory methods, but he also spends time at the location being silent, listening, being open to first impressions – refraining from walking, talking, making value judgements or inferences, or even thinking – in order to apprehend something of the essence of the place.

The various characteristics of ethical and meaningful design decision-making are summarized in Table 4.1.

Conclusions

Not everyone is temperamentally inclined towards the interior quest (Armstrong, 1994, ppx–xi), and we may or may not be able to accept traditional understandings of inner apprehensions and ways of knowing as a basis for values. Nevertheless, it does seem that these traditions lead to values that are consistent both with human development and with contemporary understandings of social responsibility and environmental care. Crucially, the essential values these traditions advocate are fundamentally at odds with many of today's common practices in design – from built-in obsolescence and products of distraction, to incremental product releases that arouse feelings of dissatisfaction and stimulate consumption and waste.

The unremitting production and marketing of short-lived, unrepairable and often relatively trivial products is associated with gross social disparities and environmental destruction on a massive scale. In addition, according to the world's traditional sources of meaning, it is also destructive to our own wellbeing and happiness. For these reasons the ethical underpinnings of many of our contemporary, widely accepted practices are highly questionable. Morality and creativity have always been closely associated with the meaningful life – but in a globalized system of corporate profit-seeking that is driven by technological advancement and grounded in an ideology of naturalistic materialism with its facts, evidence and proofs, there is a danger that these more intuitive ways of knowing become drowned out by mundane rationalizations that offer only a narrow, meagre notion of human flourishing. To return again to Stevenson (1888), seeking for the nightingale and hearing him – which gives life its enchantment and grace – becomes overshadowed by 'cheap desires and cheap fears [and] that which we are ashamed to remember'.

Table 4.1 Characteristics of ethical and meaningful design decision-making

Importance	Characteristic	Descriptor
Essential	Ethic of reciprocity	Design decisions to reduce production costs are: in accord with good quality human work and do not depend on low wages, poor labour conditions or the elimination of jobs through automation. in accord with natural systems and do not degrade water quality, air quality or the environment.
To be promoted	Moderation	Intentional avoidance of excessive or diverting features and modes of use.
	Relative unimportance	Recognition of the relatively lowly place functional goods should occupy in our lives to be in accord with notions of human meaning and with ethical and environmental responsibilities.
	Congruence with meaning	Through their materials, use, aesthetics, symbolism and non-instrumental characteristics products can support ideas of how we ought to act and behaviours congruent with environmental, ethical and meaningful ways of living.
	Warranted	Is the design and manufacture of another product even justified given the corrosive effects that unprecedented levels of globalized production are having on nature, social wellbeing and personal contentedness?
	Empathy	Product concepts, production, use and disposal methods that are considerate of people and place.
	Usefulness	Products that are functional, reliable and enduring but unassuming.
	Elegance	Through attention to form, proportion, expression and detail, products that grace the world by their presence.
To be avoided	Enticing	Products designed to encourage consumption- through fashionable, colourful 'perfection', as well as branding and marketing that stimulate cravings and feelings of vanity.
	Transient	Practices that encourage perceived obsolescence - via regular model changes and aesthetic updates, use of delicate surfaces that quickly fade, and styles that rapidly become tired and outdated.
	Distracting	Products that encourage diversion or compulsive use behaviours, and that interrupt thoughts and hinder reflection.

Acknowledgements

This chapter is reprinted from *Designing Sustainability* by Stuart Walker (copyright © 2014), with kind permission of Routledge, Taylor & Francis Group, London.

Note

1 The term 'the great wisdom traditions' refers to those philosophical, religious and/or spiritual traditions that emerged from the so-called Axial Age. These include the Abrahamic religions, Buddhism, Hinduism, Taoism, Confucianism and the classical European philosophies of Plato, Socrates and Aristotle (Armstrong, 2002). Even though there is clearly much diversity among these traditions, all respond to humanity's deepest questions about the nature of reality, its values, its meaning, and its purpose (Smith, 1991). While acknowledging that their cosmologies and social conventions have been superseded, Smith maintains that their teachings about how we should live and about the nature of reality represent the essential wisdom of humanity. In addition, he indicates where these traditions speak with a more or less common voice:

- Ethical principles – how we ought to act (i.e. do not murder, steal, etc.).
- Virtue – how we ought to be, if we are to live authentic lives. This means not putting oneself above others (humility), giving due regard to the needs of others (charity), and truthfulness to the way things really are (veracity).
- A recognition that humanity's limited perspective allows only a partial, fragmented view of reality – one that leaves us unaware of its integrated nature. The great wisdom traditions represent humanity's most enduring and profound inferences and teachings about the meaning of, and our relationship to, this whole, which is considered *better* than any concept of it we may infer, indeed, it is regarded as perfection itself (Tao, Nirvana, Brahman, Allah, etc.). Moreover, this unity, this highest value, is beyond human capacity to fully grasp; at most, we perceive only fleeting glimpses (ibid.).

Lewis (1947), among others, expresses similar sentiments, arguing that these understandings of meaning and human values have never been surpassed and are as relevant today as ever.

References

Armstrong, K. (1994) *Visions of God: Four Medieval Mystics and their Writings*, Bantam Books, New York.

Armstrong, K. (2002) *Islam: A Short History*, Phoenix Press, London.

Bakan, J. (2004) *The Corporation: The Pathological Pursuit of Profit and Power*, Constable & Robinson, London.

Beattie, T. (2007) *The New Atheists: The Twilight of Reason & The War on Religion*, Darton, Longman & Todd, London.

Camus, A. ([1942]2005) *The Myth of Sisyphus*, Penguin Books, London.

Carr, N. (2010) *The Shallows: How the Internet is Changing the Way We Think, Read and Remember*, Atlantic Books, London.

Chan, J., de Haan, E., Nordbrand, S. and Torstensson, A. (2008) *Silenced to Deliver: Mobile phone manufacturing in China and the Philippines*, SOMO and SwedWatch, Stockholm, Sweden, available at www.germanwatch.org/corp/it-chph08.pdf (accessed 30 March 2011).

Comte-Sponville, A. (2007) *The Book of Atheist Spirituality: An Elegant Argument for Spirituality without God*, Bantam Books, London.

Cottingham, J. (2005) *The Spiritual Dimension: Religion, Philosophy and Human Value*, Cambridge University Press, Cambridge.

Day, C. (1998) Art and Spirit: Spirit and Place – Consensus Design, available at www.fantastic-machine.com/artandspirit/spirit-and-place/consensus.html (accessed 28 March 2011).

Eagleton, T. (2009) *Reason, Faith and Revolution: Reflections on the God Debate*, Yale University Press, New Haven, CT.

Hick, J. (1989) *An Interpretation of Religion: Human Responses to the Transcendent*. Yale University Press, New Haven, CT.

Hick, J. (2002) Science/Religion, talk given at King Edward VI Camp Hill School, Birmingham, March, available at www.johnhick.org.uk/jsite/index.php?option=com_content&view=article&id=52:sr& catid=37:articles&Itemid=58 (accessed 19 February 2011).

Hick, J. (2004) The Real and Its Personae and Impersonae, available at www.johnhick.org.uk/jsite/ index.php?option=com_content&view=article&id=57:thereal&catid=37:articles&Itemid=58 (accessed 19 February 2011).

Holloway, R. (2000) *Godless Morality*, Canongate, Edinburgh.

Horkheimer, M. and Adorno, T. W. ([1947]2010) The Culture Industry: Enlightenment as Mass-Deception, in V. B. Leitch (ed.), *The Norton Anthology of Theory and Criticism*, 2nd edn, W. W. Norton & Co., New York.

Jackson, T. (2009) *Prosperity without Growth: Economics for a Finite Planet*, Earthscan, London.

King, U. (2009) *The Search for Spirituality: Our Global Quest for Meaning and Fulfilment*, Canterbury Press, Norwich.

Lewis, C. S. (1947) *The Abolition of Man*, HarperCollins Publishers, New York.

Lindsey, E. (2010) Curating humanity's heritage, TEDWomen, December, available at www.ted.com/ talks/elizabeth_lindsey_curating_humanity_s_heritage.htm (posted February 2011, accessed 21 March 2011).

MacQuarrie, J. (ed.) (1967) *A Dictionary of Christian Ethics*, SCM Press, London.

Manzini, E. and Jégou, F. (2003) *Sustainable Everyday: Scenarios for Urban Life*, Edizioni Ambiente, Milan.

Mason, D. (1998) *Bomber Command – Recordings from the Second World War*, CD liner notes, Pavilion Records, Wadhurst.

Mathews, F. (2006) Beyond Modernity and Tradition: A Third Way for Development, *Ethics and the Environment*, vol 11, no 2, p90.

Needleman, J. (1989) Introduction, in *The Tao Te Ching*, (trans. G. Feng and J. English), Vintage Books, New York.

Nietzsche, F. ([1889]2003) *Twilight of the Idols and the Anti-Christ*, Penguin, London.

Papanek, V. (1971) *Design for the Real World – Human Ecology and Social Change*, Thames & Hudson, London.

Power, T. M. (2000) Trapped in Consumption: Modern Social Structure and the Entrenchment of the Device, in E. Higgs, A. Light and D. Strong (eds), *Technology and the Good Life*, University of Chicago Press, Chicago, IL, ch. 15.

RAF History (2005) Bomber Command: Campaign Diary May 1942, available at www.raf.mod.uk/ bombercommand/may42.html (accessed 18 March 2011).

Schumacher, E. F. (1973) *Small is Beautiful*, Sphere Books, London.

Smith, H. (1991) *The World's Religions*, revised edn, HarperSanFrancisco, New York.

Smith, H. (2005) Foreword, in W. Johnston (ed.), *The Cloud of Unknowing and the Book of Privy Counseling*, Image Books, Doubleday, New York.

Stevens, D. (2007) *Rural*, Mermaid Turbulence, Leitrim, Ireland.

Stevenson, R. L. (1888) The Lantern Bearers, in J. Treglown (ed.), *The Lantern Bearers and Other Essays*, Cooper Square Press, New York.

Taylor, C. (2007) *A Secular Age*, The Belknap Press of Harvard University Press, Cambridge, MA.

Thoreau, H. D. (1854) *Walden; or, Life in the Woods*, Ticknor & Fields, Boston, MA.

Tillich, P. (1952) *The Courage to Be*, 2nd edn, Yale University Press, New Haven, CT.

Tucker, S. (1998) ChristStory Nightingale Page, ChristStory Christian Bestiary, available at ww2. netnitco.net/users/legend01/nighting.htm (accessed 19 March 2011).

Walker, S. (2011) *The Spirit of Design: Objects, Environment and Meaning*, Earthscan for Routledge, Abingdon.

Yamakage, M. (2006) *The Essence of Shinto: Japan's Spiritual Heart*, Kodansha International, Tokyo.

5

CHALLENGES OF THE CULTURAL DIFFERENTIATION OF TECHNOLOGY

Petran Kockelkoren

Abstract

The modern philosophers of technology – Heidegger in Germany, Jacques Ellul in France and Lewis Mumford in the US – all contend that technology and media would uproot and alienate the modern subjects from their natural underpinnings. In this chapter I will scrutinize the opposite possibility. According to the philosophical anthropologist Helmuth Plessner, man is naturally artificial and constitutionally alienated. Human perceptions are inevitably mediated by language, images and instruments. Nevertheless the technical mediation of our perceptions prompts us to fine-tune our mediating apparatuses to the living environment. That may be done in many different ways. Here we encounter the tenacity of another mistaken tenet of the modern philosophy of technology: the notion that technology obeys universal laws and produces the one best way to go about. As a consequence, the ubiquitous dissemination of techniques would make the world everywhere the same: one universal consumer society revolving around the products of a handful of multinationals. Techniques have to be incorporated on the spot however. Sustainability depends on the local technological intimacy with nature, as will be shown. The cultural contexts were new products and apparatuses land procure their hybridization. The modern philosophers were misled by the mass-production and Fordism of their age. The idea of the universalizing tendencies of technology now reaches the end of its shelf life. How do we achieve a culturally differentiated technological intimacy with nature? Grassroots Design is our contemporary challenge.

Keywords: mediation, grassroots design, globalization, hackers, DIY

The embodiment of technology

If just a few decades ago a multinational of consumer electronics wanted to introduce a new product like a lady shave or a kitchen utensil on the international market, one usually started a try-out in a local test-group of selected users. After some intensive use in such a closed community the teething problems of the new device would be eliminated and the technology in question could then be distributed worldwide – or so one thought at least.

69

Apparently there was a widely shared consensus that a group of European or American users was somehow representative for African and Asian users as well. Behind this line of reasoning lies the modernistic idea that technology is always just a one-trick pony, whereby a technological device can function along one track only – that of the universal laws of nature implemented by engineers in resilient matter. Indeed, until recently technology was supposed to be universal, and it was only the outer appearance, its shell and the signs on the surface, that had to be different. Product design would consequently only pertain to the hull, not to the machinery and its programming inside. From a cultural point of view no greater mistake could be made. Thinking in this vein one must irrevocably come to the conclusion that the dissemination of technology around the globe must be a levelling force that in the long run reduces all cultural differences to nil. In this excessively streamlined scenario, only the names given to the products will differ in accordance with the language-groups addressed in the manuals and advertisements.

In the following chapter I will contradict this popular yet obsolete vision on the design of techniques: apparatuses, instruments, tools, gadgets and utensils. I will address the issue of cultural diversity on three different levels on which technical artefacts influence us. The first level is that of *semiotics*; signs on the hull, outer appearances or the images presented while the inner workings are obscured. The second is that of *mediation*; technologies have to be embedded in the cultures at the receiving end, where they have to be incorporated or literally embodied in our sensory equipment. Ever-new generations of technologies change our ways of seeing, hearing, smelling and touching. Technologies mediate our senses and disclose our environment in culturally differentiated ways. There is no universally valid one-best-way. Specific mediations depend on cultural context. So in addition to semiotics and mediation a third level must be addressed, and that is the level of *cultural diversification*. The processes of mediation take on different cultural flavours depending on the cultural context in which they operate. In the last resort we have to explore the confrontation of the undeniable globalizing and standardizing tendencies in product design with the thesis of the inevitable cultural diversification of technology (Van Eijk, 2007).

Of course you can design any given object in many different guises, depending on the target group. So you produce a radio, either for toddlers (like 'My First Sony', a radio cast in unbreakable plastic in primary colours) or for the elderly (a modestly coloured set with huge buttons indicating preference channels). Considering such a clichéd product design approach, you might just as well aim at the urban hip-hop subculture, designing a ghetto blaster with chrome *bling-bling*! You can accommodate these very different groups just by changing the outside appearance of the product, just using signs and symbols, whilst never entering the black box of the apparatus inside, which happens to work the same in all cases. You can design for the different groups just by changing the outside appearance using signs and symbols that are iconic for the different lifestyles in question. Of course we are referring each and every time to a postmodern variant of semiotics.

The postmodern variant of semiotics owes a lot to the Swiss linguist, Ferdinand de Saussure. He focused his attention on the indissoluble interconnectedness of language-signs. According to de Saussure, words derive their meaning from their position in a network of signs that mainly serve to define each other, relatively. Only in the last resort do they refer to an outside reality that is primarily disclosed as such by this interwoven web of signs. Roland Barthes also applied this view to the interpretation of cultural icons like the Citroën Déesse, the Tour de France as an epic event, soap-powder and other detergents (Barthes, 1957). In all cases a relatively inconspicuous thing, or event, is turned into a remarkable brand, simply by attaching storylines to it. The thing is not valued in itself but exclusively because of the pivotal role it plays in stringing together a set of stories people can identify themselves with. The thing is the empty 'X' in the middle, the peg to hang cultural identities on. The whole enterprise revolves in the symbolic sphere, never touching ground. A straight line leads us from this kind of ephemeral semiotics to the contemporary Creative Industries (Florida, 2002). There too, objects are not craved because of their intrinsic qualities but solely as representatives of a certain 'lifestyle' pretenders want to belong to. This explains why the radio of our example is obtainable in different versions, depending on characteristics like gender, race and age-groups the designers are peddling for. The creative differentiation of technological artefacts remains limited to semiotic inscriptions on their outer layers of skin. That is why I always resented the semiotic approach to product design.

The science of semiotics has a double parentage however, so one may cherish hope for the better. Charles Sanders Peirce is – besides de Saussure – an independent cofounder of the science of semiotics. Unlike de Saussure, he mainly took an interest in the embodied process of the expression and understanding of signs; a process of communication that he perceives as thoroughly incarnated in real-life exchanges. For Peirce 'indexicality' – sign language accompanied by ostentatious pointing at things in situations in which one is involved – forms his paradigm of *semiosis*. The semiotic triangle of signifier, signified and interpretant is not hovering on a linguistic meta-level but is always pragmatically embedded in behaviour and action. Peirce has a huge following as well. One of his adepts is the Danish professor Jesper Hoffmeyer, who propagates the theory of 'bio-semiotics' (Hoffmeyer, 2008).

For Hoffmeyer, semiosis is even an interspecies affair, working on all levels of expression and interpretation from bacteria to animal and human life. The expression of meaning on different levels of comprehension is an emergent property of all life. The theory of bio-semiosis allows us to leave the lofty plane of linguistics and to take a dive into the deeper recesses of the body and its exchanges with the living environment. It offers a promising approach towards an understanding of the embodiment of techniques and the subsequent mediation of the senses. To my regrets up to now no one has tried to employ this theory to product-design, to map criteria of adequate mediation in this respect. That remains to be done, but not especially by me. My curiosity was rather enrolled by a parallel development in philosophy, where more or less the same predicament was felt, and comparable solutions were sought for. I want to introduce the take on product design that was proposed by post-phenomenology.

Edmund Husserl was the patriarch of phenomenology. By academic education he was a mathematician and logician. That explains why his phenomenological method – in spite of his motto 'back to the thing itself!' – kept purely formal traits. According to Husserl, consciousness is not a passive faculty merely registering sense impressions. Rather, consciousness is characterized by intentional acts, by reaching outwardly, grasping objects of attention and turning them into meaningful phenomena. The meaning of things – their very appearance as objects – has to be constituted by a performing consciousness. Yet intentionality must not be mistaken for purposefulness. It is rather a technical term referring to the reciprocal implication of acts of consciousness and their correlative objects on many levels. Husserl was mainly interested in the formal structures of these multiple layered acts since he discerned in them the laws of logic and mathematics. His pupils soon took other routes to elaborate the phenomenological method.

Max Scheler argued that feelings and emotions must be understood as intentional acts in their own right instead of abrogating them as the jamming stations of reason and denying them all cognitive content. The phenomenologist who concerns us most is Maurice Merleau-Ponty who extended the phenomenological method to all sensory acts. In his view, consciousness is incarnated from the very start. In his phenomenological descriptions of acts of sense-perceptions we find the first elaborate examples of mediated intentionality. His justly famous example is that of the blind man groping his way along the alleyways with the help of his stick. The stick functions as an extension of his outstretched arm, and he literally 'feels his way' through the stick, which has been incorporated in his body-scheme. The span of his intentionality has been elongated towards the tip of his stick. The stick is an embodied part of his incarnated consciousness. In the same way, to bring this point home, we are all of us able to feel through the wooden spoon whether the boiling soup threatens to stick to the bottom of the pan.

Nowadays, a post-phenomenologist like Don Ihde actualizes the philosophy of mediation of Merleau-Ponty (Ihde, 1990, 2002). At the same time, and in league with the outlined post-phenomenological approach, Clark and Chalmers (1998) speak of the 'extended mind'. As a result of such *new-speak* we see our mind no longer as a calculating device enclosed within our skulls but as an intentional faculty that has been outsourced to all kinds of embodied products and equipment. The blind-man's stick and the wooden spoon have been replaced by ever more complex instruments and machineries. The dentist can feel his way through the miniature drill into the unseen cavities of your teeth. We are acquainted with the inside of our bodies by means of roentgen photography, PET scans and MRI imaging. We penetrate the secrets of far-off galaxies with the Hubble-telescope. Mediated imageries galore! The inside–outside division has gone haywire in the ensuing cultural clashes.

The introduction of ever-new technologies requires a cultural process of adaptation or the collective embodiment of mediating devices. Society has to open up channels for the exercise of brand-new perceptions. In *Technology: Art, Fairground and Theatre* (Kockelkoren, 2003) I explored the cultural pathologies that arise in circumstances like these. Think of nineteenth-century 'railway spine' (Schivelbusch, 1977), contemporary repetitive strain injury (RSI) and diseases like anorexia and bulimia (Watters, 2010). Our ways of looking, hearing and smelling are transformed during the process of the cultural domestication of new technologies, and the arts help us to cope with that process (Hughes, 1991). New techniques like the flight simulator, for instance, arise in scientific laboratories; they subsequently are transmitted to professional practices and in the wake of tinkering artists they finally filter down to fairgrounds, road shows and games where the general public may become acquainted with them.

The embodiment of technology may be articulated in terms of phenomenology as learning to insert oneself in the living tissue of the world (Merleau-Ponty), or as an inter-species exchange of signs like the bio-semioticists predicate. Both ways we descend the ladder of cultural coping-strategies from the lofty level of language into the deeper regions of incarnated communication. The first things we have to investigate are the possibilities and the limitations of such mediated perception. After we have accomplished that, we delve into the cultural diversity of mediation.

The impossibility to circumvent mediation

Media never represent reality just like that. Media often open up new registers of perception and therefore also require a new legible visual idiom and signification. What is more, the new media often absorb the old ones and perpetuate them in a new form: writing was converted into typesetting, which in turn was replaced by the typewriter and the word processor; the transfer of images passed via photography into film, TV, video and internet. This process has been called 'remediation', with the linguistic implication of a remedy or recovery from an illness (Bolter and Grusin, 2000). Artists are *par excellence* the ones able to develop remedies of this kind. Yet they encounter inevitably the limitations of this endeavour as well (Kockelkoren, 2007). In order to make this clear I will give a very brief outline of the history of optical instruments, starting with the nineteenth century stereoscope and ending with the Hubble-telescope.

In the nineteenth century the stereoscope was at the centre of heated epistemological discussions to which I would like to briefly introduce you because they reveal a great deal about media and the cultural self-inquiry that they make necessary. Stereoscopy yields a three-dimensional view of the world that is achieved by taking two photographs at the same time; the distance between the two lenses determines the effect of depth. Optimal 'realism' is achieved when the two lenses are the same distance apart as two human eyes with the nose between them. The further apart the lenses are, the more the depth seems to increase because from a much larger distance it is possible to see not only the front but also the side of an object. It is like looking through the eyes of a giant. In the nineteenth century it was particularly the photographers of landscapes and cityscapes who experimented with the giant's eye view for popular purposes. The frivolous experiment earned them a reprimand from the Christians: 'If God had wanted us to see reality like that, he would have set our eyes further apart' (Hankins and Silverman, 1995). Human proportions, reduced to the width of the nose, were proclaimed the norm and touchstone of the representation of reality. What deviated from that was called a 'distortion' of reality, on the one hand, or artistic freedom, on the other. The controversy was settled when the stereoscope, with an immensely increased distance between the lenses, acquired the status of an instrument of scientific research.

The moon is so far away from us, and the distance between our eyes is so infinitesimal by comparison, that we can only see the moon as a flat disc. But suppose that we were to occupy two points on a cosmic scale that enabled us to perceive the moon from two different angles at once – then we would see it is as a pock-marked sphere, suspended in space. It is difficult to do that from the earth, because the moon follows the earth's course and it always shows the same side to us. All the same, there is a slight fluctuation in the moon's orbit, known as *libration*, which causes the moon to show itself from a slightly different angle over time. If you take photographs separated by a certain interval of time and place them in a stereoscope, you suddenly see the moon in full three-dimensional glory, floating in space before your very eyes. This cosmic view was first achieved by Warren de la Rue in 1858 using the stereoscope. Bearing in mind the epistemological controversy that had arisen, he defended himself in the following words: 'We may well be satisfied to possess such a means of extending our knowledge respecting the moon, by thus availing ourselves of the giant eyes of science'. De la Rue referred with these words to Sir John Herschel, who added: 'lunar stereography entails a step out of and beyond nature' (Hankins and Silverman, 1995, p171).

Artists have prepared the way for the scientific application of the stereoscope and on the way called a philosophical controversy down upon their heads. Since then we have become clearer about what mediation is, for it was only through the experiments with the stereoscope that the yoke of the fixed standard of reality was shaken off. In this way, we can see that not only scientists and engineers but also artists open up the world, and our experience of it. It is their special task as artists to provide the changing perceptions with a repertoire of images and an audio language, so that the revealed worlds can be made legible and manageable. But that is a critical task. It is of the greatest importance to realize that the critical professional practice of the artist takes place in the media of sound, image and bodily movements. An example will throw light on the tensions that go with the embodiment of media. For closer inspection we turn to the world of the conversion of image into sound.

A striking discussion in this regard took place under the motto *Sonic Pulse* during the Dutch Electronic Art Festival (DEAF) in Rotterdam in November 2004 between two artists, each of whom locate their field of operations at the interface of visual and audio representations of scientific phenomena. Andrea Polli (US) played the sound recording of *Hurricane Bob* that traversed the east coast of North America (including New York) in 1991. To be able to do so, she had converted data stored at the time into sound by allocating sound qualifications to relevant parameters such as wind speed, temperature and air pressure. In Polli's sound-module the hurricane came to life, sighing and moaning. Polli explains her artistic motivations on the CD: 'The resulting turbulent and evocative compositions allow listeners to experience geographically scaled events on a human scale and gain a deeper understanding of the complex rhythms and melodies of nature'. Gavin Starks (UK) then proceeded to present a similar art project. He had converted the photograph of a distant nebula into sound. What makes a photo a photo? The so-called photographs of remote outer space have never been more than radiographically transmitted digital clouds of data, which are not visualized until they reach earth. The colours visible in the representation are only added to yield scientifically legible information. For instance, shifts in the red-blue spectrum indicate what is approaching or moving away from us. That also makes clear the distance separating the nebula in question from the postulated Big Bang. The cloud of data can be converted into sound just as well as into an image. That is what Gavin Starks did. Like Polli, he invited nature to sing her own song. But that immediately sparked off an important controversy between the two artists, and no wonder!

Polli's recordings in sound remained enigmatic. As a member of the audience, you were on tenterhooks because you thought that you had almost understood the language of nature before it slipped away again into chaos and crackling, while Gavin Starks' nature presented itself as a sort of over-harmonious New Age synthesizer symphony. Polli asked herself how Starks had qualified his parameters in audio terms – how much, in other words, his share was in the soundtrack of the stars. That question touched on a very sore point. In both cases – Polli and Starks - data were converted. In Starks' case a previous conversion had already been made because he started out from a photographic interpretation of data. One might suspect the scientists in question to have pimped their data in order to reach a large audience and to gain financial support for their costly research. But although meteorologists just might have better taste, Polli is open to similar objections. Her clouds of data are borrowed too from scientifically distinguished and measured parameters. Has the audience listened to nature, or to an artistic interpretation of a scientific representation? And should not these questions raised by art provoke the same doubts with regard to scientific representations? Were we discussing nature on her own terms or the aesthetics of scientific fields of inquiry? One is not obtainable without the other. The media dictate what may count as knowledge in the first place. Do we ever know what is really 'out there', beyond our media that we can never dispose of? It must be perfectly clear that it is impossible to jump over one's own shadow. In each and every form of mediation there is inevitably a cultural twist involved.

The German anthropologist and phenomenologist Helmuth Plessner gave voice to the irrevocable dilemmas of a mediated existence (Plessner, 1928; De Mul, 2014). According to him, human existence is marked by 'eccentricity': besides being immersed in action we are simultaneously the spectators of our ongoing actions. Between the two positions *immersion* and *spectatorship*, scores of mediators intervene, like language, images, instruments and tools. Because of these interventions, people may be described as 'naturally artificial'. What counts as reality in any cultural era is inevitably mediated in one way or another. There is no *natural benchmark*. Precisely that, the structural impermanence is a part of our biological constitution. Our dependence on perceptual mediations makes for a plurality in the cultural appropriations of technical devices. Although all humans share a common biological substrate, cultural diversity at the receptor-side of technologies inevitably leads to cultural diversification of perceptions and concomitant significations. There never will be a universal outcome, save by sheer force of the politics of multinationals. We have to investigate the cultural mechanisms that proliferate into evermore diversifications and the constraints exerted on them by standardization procedures.

The cultural embedding of technology

In primary school I was deeply impregnated with the idea that history is propelled by great thinkers: innovative scientists, elderly statesmen, stern judges and lawyers, for example. Culture was exclusively identified within this symbolic order, and the world of ideas was imprinted in coarse resilient matter by engineers. Technology was seen as *applied science*. But in the view propagated here – that of mediation as propelling force – the dominant view appears as a topsy-turvy rendering of reality. The technical instruments dictate the way nature is disclosed and submitted to formulas. Material mediations (products) call for significations and the bestowal of meaning and they do so within cultural constraints.

In 2004 I was given the opportunity of attending the first Shanghai Biennial for Media Art. Chinese art historians writing in the hefty catalogue were eager to take their turn at explaining how Chinese Media Art is not the same as American or European Media Art, as it is culturally embedded within a completely different aesthetic tradition. That tradition demonstrates a dynamic character through its ability to embody new media and transform them in accordance with its own principles (Fang and Xu, 2004). The concept of media art is represented in China by two characters: *ying* and *xiang*. *Ying* refers to every arbitrary pattern of dots, stripes or clouds, such as the pattern of shadows that the leaves of trees cast on a wall when there is a gust of wind. The character *xiang* also means a meaningful pattern, not only in the sense that you can read it, but also with the invitation to adopt it and follow its indications. Taken together, *ying–xiang* state that even in arbitrary white noise a message can be detected that shows the way. This is an appropriate metaphor for media art for the Chinese because it is applicable to the pixel-snow or white-noise on a TV screen. A slight tap to the antenna is enough to conjure up the image of a newsreader from the shimmering screen. This metaphor enables Western media art to be appropriated in China under a native sign. Western aesthetics is based on geometrical perspective, while Chinese aesthetics dispenses with a single vanishing or orientation point. Chinese art follows the tradition of the 'reading stones': stone surfaces whose veins and markings immediately evoke landscapes in our perception. To be able to look at the monitor screen in the same way, however, other than the usual qualities must be foregrounded in the device itself – the transmitter. What would be regarded as an unwelcome glitch in the West is a key to ultimate understanding for a philosophically schooled Chinese.

The Chinese example draws our attention to another revealing highlight as well: that of the genesis of cultural identity out of underlying mediations. What becomes discernible out of meaningful glitches is that tools and apparatuses do not only store knowledge, but in their turn have a backlash on the agent of knowledge-production itself. Not only is the perception of the world changed by mediation, but at the other end of the rope the perceiver is transformed as well. Knowledge is not only externalized, shouldn't be thought of as just 'embedded cognition' somewhere parked out there. There is a backlash on the tool handling subject as well. An extended concept of mediated cognition operates both ways: knowledge is *sedimented* in tools and tools coproduce the cognizant subject (Kockelkoren, 2003). The idea of agency is for example differently structured and communicated in a book, a film or a Facebook self-presentation. These different media refurbish the inventories of our so-called inner life, and the way we strive to put our lives in order. They even dictate what we may consider to be agency and subjectivity. As a consequence thinking subjects lose their vantage point in epistemology and are replaced by subjects who are rather products of their tools with their cultural twists.

In the west, agency is thought of as a core-quality, residing in a solid self that presides over its fate. In Chinese thought the figure-ground relation is reversed. The self emerges out of the vicissitudes of chance encounters. In the centre there is no hard core but a hole, an emptiness around which self-defining events are arranged. The western solid hardcore self was dependent on the mediations that underpinned the Cartesian era. Descartes saw the *camera obscura* as the outstanding model for the cognizant subject. Like the *camera obscura* the human eye casts representations in the shadowy recesses of the skull where the soul reads and acts on them by steering the body through the outside world represented on the inner screens.

As a matter of fact the *camera obscura* automatically produces the renaissance linear perspective. In this way a geometric grid was imposed on the perception of the world. In the same movement the distanced spectator was co-produced. This observing figure henceforward called 'the soul' by Descartes was by him projected inside the head and there situated at the helm in the pineal gland (Bailey, 1989). The Chinese were not exposed to these baroque subjectivations. Chinese aesthetics to the contrary takes its start from scholar stones and misty patterns. These orientations don't support the Cartesian subject still vigorous in the west. Subjectivation follows a different track in China; the incorporation of new media follows suit.

Optical devices are appropriated in many diverse forms. Film is obtainable in variants from Hollywood (US) to Bollywood (India), Nollywood (Nigeria) to Manga (Japan). The imported medium can be used following different semiotic codes (as in film) or appreciated on the basis of different qualities (a different foregrounding of qualities and attributes). The medium can also be the trigger for innovation in the act of appropriation. I learnt that when I visited the Centre of Product Design and Manufacturing in the Indian Institute of Science, Bangalore, in 2009. When I asked to see examples of cultural differentiation in technology, I was shown a range of electronic cooking implements that have become a part of the Indian kitchen, but have only vaguely similar counterparts in the European kitchen, if at all. I had not been looking for that, but it was so obvious. Technological differentiation is of course a grassroots phenomenon. It is precisely in places where technologies are submerged in everyday use, and transmitted from hand to hand, that you can expect to find innovative adaptations.

With only a few exceptions, commercial product design has turned a blind eye on the cultural diversification of technology up till now (Pacey, 1990; Feenberg, 1995). We can no longer afford to do so, but have to take the effects of mediation into account when we embark on a quest towards a sustainable society. At the root of sustainability lies the intimate rapport between technology and the specific 'genius loci'. Every attempt at the creation of a sustainable society has to start therefore with a clear understanding of the differentiation of technological cultures at grassroots' level.

Standardization versus differentiation

Of course, we have to put ourselves on guard against an essentialist vision on culture, as if entities as 'the' western culture encounter 'the' Chinese culture on the world stage. Cultures with their particular histories are part of a complex and cross-pollinating network, in a constant state of flux. We confronted a waning Cartesian modern worldview, typical of the west between 1600 and 1970 with a contemporary Chinese *mélange* of ancient aesthetics with new media. It's the media that provoke cultural clashes without precedent. This vision is at odds with the one presented by the famous critic of global culture, Samuel Huntington. In his influential book *The Clash of Civilizations* (1996) he divides cultures along religious and ideological lines and prognoses clashes on the frontiers of worldviews. He fails to take technical mediations into account as a force in cultural hybridization and development. In order to correct this fatal partiality I want to introduce the more risky frontier between the global culture of standardization and the local pockets of cultural hybridization due to specific modes of cultural incorporation of technologies. If formerly relatively quiet religious views suddenly rage on the world stage it's because they were able to incorporate new communication apparatuses and weaponry systems at a faster rate than previously established cultures; they did so by technical tinkering in niches fenced-in by religious enclosures and protected from inspection by ideological tall-talk. We have to expose the threats and possibilities of such niches. First we look into the mechanisms of standardization and then we finish with an inventory of technically driven differentiations.

There is, of course, certain reason to standardization. International agreements on weights and measures, currencies and power outlets avoid a lot of misunderstanding and inconvenience. But the principle that consumer electronics should support the worldwide dissemination of the American lifestyle and that branded food and drink must always and everywhere taste the same channels our senses within a heavily reduced spectrum of experience, behind which lie commercial interests. In itself technology is not partial to globalization but it becomes so by linking up with economic imperatives. There are many explanations of how such globalization came about; I offer one that focuses on the mediation effects of the means of transport invented and incorporated in the nineteenth century.

A motley crowd of professionals and occasional tourists travel the world with sovereign disdain as they make their phone calls, chat and shop and claim that the world is shrinking and becoming the same everywhere: McDonalds and KFC, Nike and Sony, Coca-Cola and Pepsi. Everywhere the same high-rise banks, real estate offices and multinationals. The historic inner cities, on the other hand, are all coming to resemble branches of Disneyland through City-Pimping, though each with its own old or new distinctive icon: the Eiffel Tower, the Kremlin, the Forbidden City of Beijing, the Sydney Opera House, Carnegie Hall, Gehry Los Angeles, Guggenheim Bilbao, the Pearl TV Tower in Shanghai or the Euromast of Rotterdam. All those icons of city and state figure as anchor points for the construction of cultural identities. As mere symbolic constructions they remain on the semiotic level of a global culture. How has this floating symbolic level been constructed, and how is it maintained?

To answer these questions we start with a precise diagnosis of how mobility corridors are construed. For this we can draw on Peter Peters, a Dutch philosopher who has developed a spot-on theory of passages (Peters, 2006). The next question to be raised is about the relation between the hectic inner world of transport tunnels and more peripheral or even external zones of relative calm where cultural differentiation is situated (Kockelkoren, 2014).

The world maps of flows of traffic are almost all misleading. After all, it is a mistake to accept the territorial notion of space just like that as the appropriate model for today's flows. Our calculations in a homogeneous space maintain the distance constant but make the duration of the journey variable, depending on the speed of travel, which depends in turn on the means of locomotion: by foot, bicycle, train, car, airplane. We feel the world growing smaller as we become able to travel the *same distance* in a shorter amount of time. Peter Peters objects to this way of seeing things. In his view, in our technological era we now find ourselves in a different time/space structure, which obliges us to account for travel in a different way. It is not that we cover fixed routes in a shorter or longer period of time. The reverse is the case: we create speed tunnels, corridors and passages through fast or slow technologies of travel. These passages are woven in the weft and warp of time and space. This leads to the emergence of landscapes divided into different speed zones. The political, economic and aesthetic layers of such landscapes are completely misrepresented if we impose a Cartesian/Newtonian grid upon them.

The great example of a gifted tunnel weaver is the nineteenth-century travel organizer Thomas Cook (1808–1892). Cook first travelled by train in 1841, when he was still a simple village carpenter. Ten years later he organized a visit to the world exposition in the Crystal Palace in London for 165,000 people, including the train journey, tickets for admission and accommodation. Ten years later, besides a round tour of Europe, starting with the world exposition in Paris, he organized trips to Egypt, Mecca and Medina. In 1872 he personally led the first journey around the world by steamer and post carriage. In the following year his timetable, the first international train timetable, was published. How did he manage all this?

Cook was quick to realize that travel is more than moving from one point to another in a homogeneous space. He had to give the space an attractive topography if he was to interest people in travel. Before long he created place myths, consisting of images and stories connected with places, from romantic Scotland to tragic Pompeii. He pinpointed the birthplaces of celebrities. Stratford-upon-Avon was declared the city of Shakespeare and has maintained its magnetism as a tourist attraction down to the present for that reason. He put city icons on the map: you had to see the Eiffel Tower and the Arc de Triomphe; otherwise you had not been in Paris and did not belong to the *beau monde*. But it is not enough to pinpoint attractions; they are only the beginning. Cook also designed the entire logistics of the experience. Anyone who travelled with Cook's firm would never feel lost. The passenger was surrounded by all kinds of services that added to the comfort and shortened the duration of the trip. Luggage was sent to the hotel in advance. Local agents and employees were stationed along all the routes to ensure that the journey through the travel corridor that had been opened up proceeded smoothly. Cook took care of the connections between one means of transport and another, deployed his personnel to assist during those transfers and settled agreements on the charges so that he could offer all-in vouchers for the entire journey.

Thomas Cook thus became the first architect of space/time corridors and even of the first passage around the world. A Cook passenger was a new sort of cosmopolitan who could find his way everywhere, knew the name for everything, but perhaps no longer had any real experience because he remained at all times and in all places, a spectator. The Cook tourist's photographs reproduce the iconographic attractions of Cook, not just passively, but also as an active reproductive agent of the Cook lifestyle. As a result of that alone, the world appears to these travellers in the same guise everywhere; this style is still very much alive, extending to the furthest corners of the world.

Today we live in and through technological culture. Cook immediately welcomed its guiding principles with open arms and built an empire on them. This empire has been solidified for many. Yet, for those without access to it, the international travel route resembles a global system of passages specially designed for climbing up the career ladder, a matrix of glamour illusions that in the end have given us nothing but economic crisis. The fortunate contenders deck themselves out with the insignia of cosmopolitism: Louis Vuitton handbags, Gucci sunglasses, Rolex watches, the lot. The elite opt for postmodern lifestyles based on superficial semiotic design. The successful entrepreneurs and stock exchange speculators jostle one another in the middle of the stream, while more alternative groups opt out, slow down and go in search of the remaining unpolluted and untouched corners of the world.

From the perspective of the technological mediation of experience it is impossible to claim that the mediations that have led to the creation of passage traffic are wrong and must be confronted with unmediated, 'pure' natural positions located at the as yet unspoiled periphery of the mainstream. The metaphor of core versus periphery, alienated versus rooted, false versus pure, makes no sense, simply because we are, as Plessner put it, *naturally artificial*. In short, the passages of accelerated space/time are technologically mediated and the passages of decelerated space/time are just as technologically mediated, though in a different way. I do not think that finding new roots in a pre-technological way of life is either possible or desirable. Even though it entails a certain artificiality, sensitive mediation is the new authentic and 'technopoëtics' the latest cry in engineering and design.

Philosophical and cultural anthropologists have by now achieved a broad consensus that human access to the world always proceeds via mediation. Cultural differentiation in grassroots movements is an inevitable by-product of the world of global passages. Neo-ethno-communities give form to their cultural identity on the global market by blending cultural tradition with technological innovation. In order to be recognized they have to enter their products on the international markets. In that way innovative products are removed from their specific cultural context and released into the mainstream flow. By that same action they are commodified. In terms of the philosophy of mediation, it is obvious that commodities mediate our perceptions and relations in a different way from tools and instruments embodied in everyday life. The process in the fast passages differs from that in the local workshops and households, not only in tempo but mainly in depth of engagement. Therefore we have to be prepared for clashes between cultural circles on different scales.

Future worlds: blade runners versus homeotechnology

The commodity culture cannot (continue to) exist without standardization. Standardization leads in the direction of increasing semiotization of goods and services. In this scenario, commodities gain token-value for cosmopolitan lifestyles while at the same time losing embodied content. There remain, however, pockets of resistance that grow and proliferate on the substrate of local embodiments of technologies – the adherents know how to find each other and lock power. In the past, like-minded individuals found one another in the political arena on the basis of a shared worldview or ideology. Such like-mindedness was based on a consensus of opinion through language. Opposed points of view were considered decisive for someone's engagement with those who shared the same views. Today, however, like-minded individuals meet via mail order businesses for T-shirts with provocative slogans or via the fan sites of rebellious rock bands. Communities of skateboarders, Hell's Angels (the Harley-Davidson) and break-dancers (the ghetto blaster) all arose from shared material mediations.

The worldview is no longer primarily based on the opposition Muslim/Christian or Liberal/Communist, but on a more expansive spectrum of material connections. Contrary to established opinion, online communities prove not to be confined to the virtual domain, but the members of such coalitions of shared interests meet one another in unregulated places and on unplanned occasions. They form neo-tribal groups that are based on Internet contact and are elusive for ideology hunters, because they share not ideas, but practices. International police and surveillance forces cannot get a grip on them, but in the meantime they disrupt the codes of commodification and standardization.

We have come to know two worlds: the universalist's world, based on the technologies of mobility, mass communication and surveillance, and beneath it the grassroots world of (neo)ethnological diversity, an archipelago of subcultures based on the differential appropriation of all kinds of devices. Unfortunately, the world is not so simple that it comes with a choice between two mutually exclusive options. The two worlds have completely merged. Because of the inherent frictions between levels in scale the world will never be uniformly the same, like the pessimist philosophers of technology fearfully prophesized.

If you had been able to survey the globe as a whole in 1492, the year that Columbus 'discovered' America, you would have seen an enormous diversity of kingdoms, religions and architecture, from the Temple of Heavenly Peace of the Emperor of China and the palace of the Oba of Benin in Africa to the Temple of the Sun of the Aztecs in Tenochtitlan (Levenson, 1991). If you had sailed around the world in a three-master in 1688, the era of Newton, you would not have been able to believe your eyes at the cultural diversity you would encounter, together with all the trade missions over the oceans between world empires (Wills, 2001). If you fly around the world nowadays, you see the same logos on the same high-rise buildings everywhere, yet I am convinced that this is only a temporary phase in cultural development. The world will become just as diverse as in the past. The overall image won't look like the picturesque survey at the advent of modernity though. Most probably we will create a world as depicted in the dystopian science fiction film *Blade Runner*, made by Ridley Scott in 1983.

The world of *Blade Runner* has been reduced to a single continuous metropolis. There is no greenery in sight. The buildings of the forces of command and their ubiquitous secret services extend in all directions so that the choice of an administrative centre is an arbitrary one. There is a permanent dusk. Larger than life projections can be seen between the buildings on gigantic screens or as holographs in the air; they are reassuring and promise happiness depending on your pattern of commodity-consumption. People and cyborgs inhabit the world; the latter are hybrid organisms-machines, combinations of wetware and software that are indistinguishable from real people. The cyborgs threaten rebellion because an expiry date was fixed when they were made, thereby preventing them from ever achieving a normal human lifespan. A *blade runner* is a policeman with the special task of tracking down and eliminating troublesome cyborgs. The most striking feature of the society, however, is the presence of neo-ethnic groups, the neo-tribal networks that hang out in the doorways, basements and taxi stations of the city. There is a level of global culture at the top of the towers, connected by hover taxis, where high tech dominates. And there is a bottom level, at which people tinker with discarded devices. They use bottom of the bucket technology to make new hybrids that they mainly deploy in the struggle for their existence.

Conclusions

The composition of society in *Blade Runner* is uncomfortably familiar today. Last year's newspapers regularly carried photographs of Syrian rebels welding and soldering their own systems of weapons together in devastated apartments because of the lack of imports. In the huge city-agglomerations of the global culture somewhere hidden in the interstices hacker-communities find their dwellings. By now hackers come in all shapes and sizes. There are the traditional software hackers and there are also the bio-art hackers who want to break into genetic modification protocols. Small wet labs are now springing up all over the world. The installation of an operational lab costs two thousand dollars and it can be accommodated in a handcart on wheels. They can be used for instance to make local species of antibiotics. Such endeavours go under the name of 'do it yourself' (DIY) technology – a movement that is gaining worldwide momentum (Van Boheemen, 2014). The adherents exchange via Internet blueprints and recipes for delicate tools and instruments made out of scrap materials. Making inventions available by means of an 'open source' policy is the norm. The actions of such neo-tribes – with shared codes of honour and rituals connected with their favourite toys – led to the formation of a new concept: 'tactical media'. Media are used tactically if they are deployed to achieve the opposite of what the designers of commodities intended. The tactical use of media and the hacker-collectives who explore them tend to be criminalized by the agents of the global surveillance network, but in order to gain the right perspective we have to raise a pertinent question: by what sort of values and criteria the hackers should ultimately be guided?

Let us follow the guidance of the German philosopher Peter Sloterdijk. He distinguishes between *allotechnology* and *homeotechnology*. As we saw in the example of the controversy between Andrea Polli and Gavin Starks, not all mediations are the same when it comes to treating nature properly with regard to its growth and self-regulation. Allotechnology is technology that confronts nature in a reductive and objectifying way in order to force it into a universalistic corset. Allotechnology produces de-contextualized commodities. Homeotechnology, to the contrary, is technology that is analogous to nature and works in the same direction as natural processes. In that case, Sloterdijk speaks of *biomimicry* and *biomimetic technologies* (Sloterdijk, 2004). There is no hope of gaining a sustainable society without taking heed of biomimetic tinkering within technologically differentiated cultural contexts.

If we take Sloterdijk's distinction as a guide, it should be clear that although both fast and slow passages are technologically mediated (that is not where the difference lies), we have to work towards a rehabilitation and promotion of grassroots differentiations of techniques. The fast, global ones are a good deal less biomimetic than the slow, regional ones. The tinkerers of weapons and communication-media of terrorist-groups are heading for a *Blade Runner* society under a fundamentalist canopy. As a counter-attack on the frontier of sustainability we will at any rate have to teach ourselves homeotechnologies and not allotechnologies. Product designers have to know where to find their allies (Spuybroek, 2011; Wendrich, 2014). They are scarce in the world of creative industries with their brands and icons. But both local cultures and sub-cultural hacker-communities work in the direction of rooted technological differentiation. The world will never be the same!

References

Bailey, Lee W. (1989) Skull's Darkroom: The *Camera Obscura* and Subjectivity, in Paul T. Durbin (ed.), *Philosophy of Technology*, Kluwer Academic Publishers, Dordrecht, pp. 63–79

Barthes, Roland (1957) *Mythologies*, Editions du Seuil, Paris

Bolter, Jay David and Grusin, Richard (2000) *Remediation, Understanding New Media*, MIT Press, Cambridge, MA

Clark, Andy and Chalmers, David (1998) The Extended Mind, *Analysis*, vol. 58, no.1, pp. 7–19

De Mul, Jos (ed.) (2014) *Plessner's Philosophical Anthropology, Perspectives and Prospects*, University Press, Amsterdam

Fang Zengxian and Xu Jiang (eds) (2004) *Techniques of the Visible*, Fine Art Publishers, Shanghai

Feenberg, Andrew (1995) *Alternative Modernity, the Technical Turn in Philosophy and Social Theory*, University of California Press, Berkeley, CA

Florida, Richard (2002) *The Rise of the Creative Class*, Basic Books, New York

Hankins, T. and Silverman, R. J. (1995) *Instruments and the Imagination*, Princeton Legacy Library, Princeton, NJ, pp. 148–177

Hoffmeyer, Jesper (2008) *Biosemiotics, an Examination into the Signs of Life and the Life of Signs*. University of Scranton Press, Scranton, PA

Hughes, Robert (1991) *The Shock of the New, Art and the Century of Change*, Thames & Hudson, New York

Huntington, Samuel (1996) *The Clash of Civilizations and the remaking of World Order*, Simon & Schuster, New York

Ihde, Don (1990) *Technology and the Lifeworld*, Indiana University Press, Bloomington, IN

Ihde, Don (2002) *Bodies in Technology*, University of Minnesota Press, Minneapolis, MN

Kockelkoren, Petran (2003) *Technology: Art, Fairground and Theatre*, NAi Publishers, Rotterdam

Kockelkoren, Petran (ed.) (2007) *Mediated Vision*, ArtEZ/Veenman Publishers, Arnhem

Kockelkoren, Petran (2014) Manifesto: the Art of Globalization, in Vroegop/Schoonveld (ed.), *Entre Otros*, VOF Kantoor van de Wereld, Groningen, pp. 5–25

Levenson, Jay A. (ed.) (1991) *Circa 1492*, Exhibition Catalogue National Gallery of Art, Washington, DC

Pacey Arnold (1990) *Technology in World Civilization, a Thousand Year History*, MIT Press, Cambridge, MA

Peters, Peter (2006) *Time, Innovation and Mobilities*, Routledge, London

Plessner, Helmuth (1928) *Die Stufen des Organischen und der Mensch*, Walter de Gruyter, Berlin

Schivelbusch, Wolfgang (1977) *The Railway Journey, the Industrialization of Time and Space in the 19th Century*, University of California Press, Berkeley, CA

Sloterdijk, Peter (2004) *Sphären III: Schäume*, Suhrkamp, Frankfurt

Spuybroek, Lars (2011) *The Sympathy of Things, Ruskin and the Ecology of Design*, V2_Publishing, Rotterdam

Van Boheemen, Pieter (2014) Blog posts, De Waag Society, Institute for Art, Science and Technology, Amsterdam, available at www.waag.org/nl/users/pieter-van-boheemen

Van Eijk, Daan (Ed.) (2007) *Cultural Diversity and Design*, University of Technology Delft

Watters, Ethan (2010) *Crazy Like Us, the Globalization of the American Psyche*, Free Press, New York

Wendrich, R. E. (2014) Hybrid Design Tools for Design and Engineering, in J. G. Michopoulos, C. J. J. Paredis, D. W. Rosen and J. M. Vance (eds), *Advances in Computers and Information in Engineering Research*, vol. 1, ASME, New York, pp. 215–238

Wills, John E. (2001) *1688, a Global History*, Granta Books, London

6

SUSTAINABLE PRODUCT DESIGN

An oxymoron?

Clive Dilnot

Abstract

In one of his writings the economist John Maynard Keynes famously comments on the tendency of practical businessmen to ignore economics. This is all very well, he notes, but these same businessmen are usually blithely unaware that their actions are nonetheless guided by (often defunct) economic ideas. Unawareness does not make the latter without effect. On the contrary, precisely as a result of being assimilated without thought these ideas are often far too powerful. Handbooks are practical things. But Keynes' lesson is that concepts may be no less practical than recipes for action. Product design, a notoriously practical discipline, in the main *assimilates* rather than *reflects* on its guiding concepts. These enter into practice almost below the level of thought, as scarcely questioned axioms. This remains true even though, especially at the pedagogical level, there has been a revolution, both in those doing product design (above all the entry of women into a field that as late as 40 years ago was almost entirely male) and – if far less focused – on the sense of what 'product' might be. Nonetheless, and this comes out particularly in the subject of this book, the relation between 'product design' and 'sustainability' or 'sustainment' remains un-thought, a matter of assumption not reflection, as this chapter argues. Above all there is lack of reflection on the manner in which the two active concepts or categories not only interact with one another but perhaps inhibit each other. The assumption that through virtuous intention it must be possible to render product design sustainable cuts out careful reflection on the tensions actually present in this relation; tensions that in fact inhibit and delimit practice. In this context there might therefore be *practical* value in raising what appears to be at first sight merely theoretical questions. It may be that through such questions it becomes possible to grasp the outlines of a practice that is able to overcome the tensions that in practice not only delimit and weaken the contribution of (even 'sustainable') product design to sustainment but more widely restrict and weaken the practice of designing things.

Keywords: sustainment, product design, capitalism, post-industrial economy, learning, making

Achieving political justice may require that we first arrive at an understanding of making and unmaking.

– *Elaine Scarry,* The Body in Pain

I: Introduction

The practical problems of categories

It says nothing about the intent of those who daily struggle with the tensions involved in this conundrum that the phrase that is the substantive title of this book and describes its intent is nonetheless an oxymoron. Speaking at best to what appears to be a necessary hybrid condition – the 'greening' of products as one of the prior conditions for a more sustainable economy – the term 'sustainable product design' nonetheless fails to acknowledge the force of its moments. Only thought superficially can these two concepts be considered commensurate. In origin, logic, direction and operative power 'sustainability' and 'product design' are deeply opposed – historically, economically and not least ethically. Given that the formulation is intended as little more than a slogan through which to organize virtuous practice these observations might be thought scarcely to matter. After all, ad-hoc responses may well, and as we know, often do, find ways through structural limits. However, the incommensurability involved here has practical, and not merely conceptual, consequences. The natural inclination to wish to link these terms and in so doing set the practice of product design in a more sustainable direction, overlooks the tensions involved, in the end to the demerit of practice. To too easily assume that 'product design' can be made sustainable is to fail to perceive the *resistance* to sustainment inherent in the category itself, and thus also in the practices it determines. Conversely, to make sustainment merely adjectival to 'product design' is to run the risk of domesticating it, to the extent of weakening the aspiration to induce or create an economy of sustainment (without which nothing 'sustainable' is possible).

Can 'product design' be sustainable?

That the purported relation runs counter to the logic of both terms – and yet does not issue in a third that might arise above this split – has more to do with the historical identity and consequent economic and ethical limits and possibilities of each than might initially be supposed. Despite the hope embodied in the slogan, 'product design' as historically understood cannot be made sustainable without developing beyond its identity and logic as such (to anticipate: 'Sustainable Product Design' would no longer be 'Product Design'). The reasons are historical. Born out of, and owing its phenomenal existence to, the maturing of industrial capitalism, 'product design' as a field, as a discipline, is *essentially* and not merely superficially, indissoluble from it. As a category and as a practice 'product design' makes sense *only* within the industrial epoch, just as it makes full sense too only as a crucial moment of industrial and especially capitalist value-creation. Its limits as a subaltern field (product design is created *by industry* for its purposes, it is *not* the creation of designers), as well as its professional possibilities (those that emerge from the quasi-autonomy its practitioners as professionals secure) are bound by that economy and that history. Yet today we are already in transition from the industrial economy, as in the sense that the industrial is no longer, as it was for the two centuries after 1775, formative in the global economy.[1] On the other side, while we are emphatically still *in* capitalism – that is, in an economy where the good is defined *only* by accumulation and by the possession of and access to goods and services (and where value is measured *only* in quantitative terms)[2] – it is becoming increasingly clear that in its modes of accumulation and appropriation, in the manner of how it comprehends growth and cost, in its principle of organization – that capitalism in these forms is radically incommensurate with sustainment. Even more strongly, in relation to the latter, the truth is that, historically and economically, 'product design', as a category and in the main as a practice, belongs to those forces which, as Heidegger put it (in what is perhaps the single most concentrated statement we have on the unsustainability of what-is) 'press toward a guarantee of the stability of a constant form of using things up' (Heidegger, 2003, pp103–104). Heidegger's pithy statement gets to the heart of the problems we face. An economy and a social fabric dependent for its (social and economic) stability on 'using things up' is the epitome of unsustainability. In relation to product design, the blunt truth is that, as an industrial category and practice it cannot but be aligned with this condition – indeed its professional origins (especially in the US) were here, in what, in the 1920s, was called, with mordant anticipation, 'consumer engineering'.

'Sustainment': a post-industrial and a post-capitalist category?

On the other side, or conversely, 'sustainment', considered as anything more than a fig-leaf, that is a realizable possibility and practice, is not only objectively and structurally other to capitalism *per se*, its entire necessity is bound up with the transition, beginning in the 1970s, to a 'post-industrial' economy. Strictly speaking – as the dates of origination of the green political parties tell us – sustainment only becomes possible to think as a practical (i.e. *political*) possibility (a possibility realizable in the world) once the formative force of industrialization begins to ebb (and, at the same time, as the consequences of industrialization begin to make themselves felt on a global scale). Put another way, in the same manner that product design belongs to the industrial epoch, 'sustainment', as a category, a possibility, a mode of acting in the world (at its widest a mode of how we 'event' our being-in-the-world; how we manifest ourselves and thus *make* the world) *belongs* to the world that is now emerging, i.e. the world-as-artificial, to what is loosely termed the Anthropocene (whose most manifest symptom to date is climate change) but which is more accurately defined as the world in which a passage has occurred where the horizon, medium and prime condition of existence for humans has shifted from nature to artifice;[3] a world that objectively opens up simultaneously both new dangers but also new possibilities for thought and action – possibilities that could not be thought or realized within the frameworks of the previous epochs.

'Sustainable product design': a category too naïve for the tasks it has to accomplish?

It is from this perspective that we can understand 'sustainable product design' as not only a hybrid, but as a transitional concept. The central problem is not here however (transitional strategies are indeed required, an entire pedagogy is now based on them) but in the potential naïvety with which, as such, the slogan understands the relations it is necessarily involved with. There is a long history of professional design's deliberate innocence when it comes to economics and politics. Design, and particularly product design, has often put itself forward, if not as the saviour, then at least as essential to business. At the same time a studied indifference to economics (and on the other side to politics) has allowed it to present itself as a kind of neutral practice, acting at best on the side of the putative user whilst solving practical and commodity problems. The aspiration to solving universal needs is by no means to be sneered at. This is after all the basis of all ethical and social action. Acting, 'without guarantee', as Gillian Rose would put it, 'for the good of all, taking the risk of the universal concerns' (Rose, 1996, p62) is the fundamental structure of all worthwhile political activity. The question for 'product design' and especially 'sustainable product design' is rather what it is that the slogan does *not* think, even unwittingly, the moment it is simply accepted without reflection? Of course, against this questioning it can be argued that since there are still products, indeed a global proliferation of them, the continuance of 'product design' is *per se* justified, all the more so that many of these products are radically disproportionate in their relation between their perishability as items of use vis-à-vis the resources they exhume and the baleful environmental and social consequences they induce (their *real* costs, as against their putative or nominal economic costs). Yet if that might well be turned as argument for why (sustainable) product design is required – 'sustainable product design' as the configurative means to re-attune these relations – we still need to ask the extent to which the maintenance of the category *as such* (i.e. as product design) is justified. The alternate case is that despite this important, indeed essential, practical mission it is nonetheless calling for the maintenance of the dominant category ('product design') and the impossibility of the relation ('sustainable product design') that makes it all but impossible to see clearly what is happening today – and therefore to plot actions adequate to the conditions we now face.

Three Problems

Three issues need examination here. The first is the question of history and specifically the history of 'product design' as a category, and through that the history of the surprisingly difficult relationship of persons and things, at least in thought, a relation that makes adequate praxis far more difficult and limiting than it might at first appear. A second is the condition of the world-as-artificial and the serious question as to whether 'product design' is any longer viable in such a world. A third, and which we can now begin again from, concerns the idea of 'sustainable product design' as a transitional category, and the further question of the relative neutrality, if not false innocence, of product design vis-à-vis the economy and more broadly of sustainment and capitalism.

II: Sustainment and capitalism: the difficult relation

'Sustainment' and the decay of the industrial epoch

Retrospectively, it is not difficult to see that the rise, from the 1970s, of green politics and hence of 'sustainment' as both a necessity and a (political) possibility, is a direct product of both the decay of the industrial as the formative condition of the global economy (which opened the possibility of another economy and technology, even if it was not then quite clear what that could be) and of increasing worries about the costs and consequences of economic growth on the industrial and capitalist model. It is hard now to appreciate how 'late' these concerns were. Of course one can trace back, across the nineteenth and early twentieth centuries, a whole lineage of figures that questioned the consequences and implications of the capitalist/industrial model. Ruskin and Morris in England for example, or in some respects more interestingly, the writings of the geographer and anarchist Kropotkin in Russia around 1900 or the later hints in some of Rosa Luxemborg's writings – the latter breaking in some respects with the otherwise valorization of industrialization in orthodox Marxism. Yet despite these concerns, as late as the 1960s one looks in vain for the impact of a text like E. J. Mishan's *The Costs of Economic Growth* (published in 1961), perhaps the first book in economics proper to call into question the paradigm of unbridled and continuous economic growth. At that point, to quote a famous political saying of the time the 'white heat of the technological revolution' still dominated. Yet only a decade later perceptions had begun to change. However problematically the infamous 1972 report of the Club of Rome is now viewed, it placed on the table concerns of resource depletion and the implications of an essentially extractive economy. Meanwhile, the sharp rise of concerns in relation to pollution, the destruction of the natural environments (both in the general, and the particular) and the overall sense of the baleful consequences of unrestricted industrial production (i.e., industry being allowed to 'externalize' its costs onto the natural and social worlds we inhabit) led to the formation, across the decade, of a number of green parties both in Australasia and Europe. Even more significantly in the longer run, in this decade too the consequences of the unrestricted rise of 'greenhouse gases' were beginning to pull into view. As early as 1973, in his book *Legitimation Crisis*, the social theorist Jurgen Habermas put the point with exemplary brevity. Even on 'optimistic assumptions' Habermas notes, 'one absolute limitation on growth can be stated ... namely the limit of the environment's ability to absorb heat from energy consumption' (Habermas, 1976, p42).

Sustainment, growth, capitalism: an impossible triad?

The green politics that arose in the 1970s and indeed the various strategies and ways of attempting to think sustainment encompassed a wide range of political and economic views. There was a natural tendency to seek for ameliorative measures, as well as to test the possibility of 'sustainable' strategies in practice (hence precisely circumlocutions such as 'sustainable product design'). Yet if this is understandable, the urge towards 'environmentalism', and the rendering sustainable or 'green' of what-is neglected, in some ways deliberately (and this was particularly true of the failed project of 'green capitalism'), the deeper structural issues at work here. In an important rider to the observation given above, Habermas catches what is politically and economically at stake in what we now colloquially call 'climate change' or 'global warming'. Continuing his point that the environment's ability to absorb heat from energy consumption provides one absolute limitation on growth, he goes on to point out that while this limitation 'holds true for all social systems',[4] it causes particular problems for capitalist societies:

> because they cannot follow imperatives of growth limitation without abandoning their principle of organization; a shift from unplanned nature-like capitalist growth to qualitative growth would require that production be planned in terms of use values. The development of productive forces cannot however be uncoupled from the production of exchange values without violating the logic of the system.
>
> *(Habermas, 1976, pp42–43)*

The limitation is crucial. The ideals of 'green capitalism' notwithstanding, *structurally* capitalist societies operate *only* on the principle of unrestricted and unfettered growth. For capitalism to succeed, for its dynamism of creation and destruction (Schumpeter) to continue, growth cannot be delimited nor, ultimately, can the absolute preponderance of 'exchange values' over 'use-value' be put at risk.[5] That capitalism has freed itself from the limits of industrial production does not evade this fact, indeed it exacerbates it. As the latter has opened entirely new zones of operation – for example the opening of every moment of human life and exchange to the market – so the degree to which the private interests of capital are self-presented as the *only* objectively viable and permissible system of economic organization is all the more assertively assured. Conversely, despite green politics and the almost half-century since Habermas delivered those lines, violation of the logic of the system has in many ways become increasingly impossible to envision, let alone realize. In this context, all that is encompassed as the side-effects of Heidegger's notion of the (social) 'guarantee of the stability of a constant form of using things up' only grows in account and consequence – and is now realized at scales beyond those that Heidegger anticipated, even in his most pessimistic moments.

The social guarantee of 'using-things up' as an intractable problem for 'sustainable product design'

The intensified *socially guaranteed* availability of 'using things-up' poses intractable practical as well as conceptual problems.

For product design it wraps the product (and therefore also its design) all the more completely within the ambience of where early 'consumer engineering' (the US in the early 1920s) wished to place it (i.e. within the sphere of that which is 'used-up' and not merely 'used'). As the cycle of circulation intensifies under the logic of 'using things up' so the tension between the economic impulse for the constant renewal of the product and the desire of 'sustainable product design' to extend product-life and reduce temporal intensity comes into increasing conflict.

For sustainment, this guarantee not only effectively constitutes the *objective* basis of the subjective impulse to consume (and hence drives towards unsustainment and thus, again in Heidegger's language, 'drives the earth beyond the developed sphere of its possibility into such things which are no longer a possibility and are thus the impossible'; Heidegger, 2003, p109) it makes it difficult if not impossible – politically, economically – to realize the sustainably necessary impulse to reduce or re-direct consumption. In such circumstances 'sustainability' either collapses into irrelevance (while maintaining a vestigial, more or less symbolic, existence on the margins of production – something akin to the role that the crafts play today) or (and this is what, in effect, will be argued here) it is forced to reconfigure its practice as the *economic* opposition to this most dangerous of Faustian bargains. But at that point practice goes beyond 'sustainment' and 'sustainable product design' it becomes the project of designing and making an-other economy, and indeed of designing and making, as we will see later, new modes of making itself.

A yet further problem in sustainment-capital relations: capital's limitations on its own problem-solving capacities

If, on this plane, the problems of 'product design', 'sustainable product design' and 'sustainment' meet over the structural intractability of socially promised 'using-up', there is a still further problem in the relation of sustainability and capitalism that must be noted. The emphasis that Habermas places in the quotations given above on '*logic of the system*' is because of the weight he gives to the force that social and economic principles of organization (in our case those of capitalism, especially as it is now the only global economic system) exert on the organization of the social system. For the question of sustainment, and of avoiding social and environmental catastrophe, where this matters particularly is in terms of the range of possible actions and imperatives that a system will accept as viable for it, above all in terms of solving steering problems.[6] Limitations placed on problem-solving capacities by the social system are neither arbitrary nor merely contingent. This becomes sharply evident – and of acute *practical* relevance to this question – when Habermas turns to the question of social and systemic crises. Crises occur at a societal level says Habermas, when a 'social system allows for fewer possibilities for problem-solving than are necessary for the adequate realisation of steering problems' (Habermas, 1976, p. 23). The linkage here is that the principle of organisation that secures a society and defines its (in our case, essentially economic) identity delimits the possibilities for systemic problem solving to those 'solutions' congruent with its primary modes of organisation. To put this slightly differently; what Habermas is telling us is that the social principle of organisation of society (in our instance, capitalism) will always *necessarily* place limits on the capacity of that society to learn as well as to be able to respond, with flexibility, to unforeseen problems. This means, for us, that capital will tend to rule out of court those solutions that break with, or which go beyond, its principles. It is almost unnecessary to add that today this is exactly what we see in the conventional responses of both governments and most private companies, to climate change.

An instance: the Paris conference on climate change, 2015

A classic example was seen at the last Paris summit on climate change. John Thackara caught the tensions involved in a post-conference blog:

> Take, for example, COP21 [the UNFCC 2015 conference on climate change]. For many people I met, the outcomes of the climate summit in Paris were grounds for anger: A reference to 'environmentally and socially sound technologies' was stripped out; aviation and shipping were simply removed from the agenda; and, although a warming limit of 1.5°C degrees is mentioned as a desired destination, the actual outcomes in the text lead us on a 3°C of warming pathway. What most worries many policy experts I met is that 1.5°C number; it opens the way, they say, for the so-called 'overshoot scenario'. This describes a moment a few years ahead when, as the impacts of climate change intensify, panicked governments will feel compelled to deploy geo-engineering fixes and so-called negative emissions technologies. As explained by Fred Pearce in Yale e360, 'the real game, many believe, is to unleash the forces of capitalism in the name of fighting climate change'. Foxes mobilized to save the rabbit? Sure. Quite apart from their vast costs, and the fact that they are unlikely to work, post-overshoot techno-fixes would almost certainly entail land grabs, social injustice and a massive loss of biodiversity – as is happening, right now, with biofuel production.
>
> *(Thackara, 2016[7])*

Sustainment as an absolute threat to capitalism: the implications for 'sustainable product design' and summary of to where we have now arrived

What occurred at the 2015 Paris conference was, in effect, a demonstration of the rule that, from the side of what-is, solutions to the 'steering problems' of climate change *must* come from within the existing logic of the system. Conversely, solutions to problems that lie outside those principles of organisation (i.e. which explicitly or tacitly embody or imply or require or demand a transformation in the principles of organisation or which offer a different logic valuation) *must* be ruled out of court. From the viewpoint of the governments gathered in Paris to adopt any other strategy (i.e. to adopt sustainment in its full logic, as Tony Fry would say, as 'sovereign') is to risk weakening system identity and bringing the system (and with it its principles of organisation) into question. The truth is – and Republicans/conservatives in many ways understand this more directly than do Liberals – sustainment, enacted at scale, threatens the core principles on which capitalism depends. To put this slightly differently, and to summarize where we have got to so far: what has to be understood very clearly today is that to call for sustainment as the necessary underlying sovereign principle of the economy (as against, say, private accumulation no matter what the cost) is *objectively* to issue a direct challenge to the principle of unplanned and unfettered market-forces. It is to place another value ('use value' in its most urgent twenty-first century form[8]) *before* exchange value (represented in our times by the economy of debt and rents and, most dangerously for the mass of the world's population, by the intensified and morally and politically un-checked impulse towards the monetization of the world – including of course, to the maximum, that of nature and so far resistant moments of human experience). To call for sustainment is therefore, *by definition*, to place capitalism in doubt; or, better, it is, in effect, to declare structurally the necessity of a post-capitalist economy. That is why no call for sustainment has any value unless it is explicitly understood as being linked to the creation of an-other economy. But once this is realized then the critical comment made earlier about sustainability being shunted into irrelevance or being forced to reconfigure its practice as the economic opposition to the Faustian bargain our culture and economy has made with 'using-up', can now be given a more affirmative thrust. Sustainability *is* precisely this. It is nothing other, at base, than economics, but – and this is the essential qualifier – its 'economics' is substantive and material. Economics is here not 'about' accumulation but about how we materially re-conceive the distributive politics, the underlying axioms of justice and the *materiality* of our relations with the world. 'Sustainable product design' can therefore be understood as the re-configurative practice whereby, and through which, what-is in terms of our relationships with things (using this term now at its broadest to encompass, given today the world-as-artificial, this totality) is re-cast in terms of distribution, justice and material relations.

III: Rethinking design

Steering crises and the necessity of learning

To begin to think what we might call the 'expanded field of practice' of sustainable product design we need to return for a moment to the Paris conference. All that has been said so far shows that we should not be in the slightest surprised at the opposition (by government as well as business) to sustainment thought at anything other than the micro-scale. Indeed, as we see in daily manifestations and not merely in Paris, there is almost no limit to how far this opposition will go. The last ten years have already shown that capitalism would rather run the risk of repeated crises than put at risk its own system identity (and thus its enduring short- and long-term principle of growth). In other words, *even at the risk of denuding the capacity of the system as a whole to learn and to respond to (potentially catastrophic environmental) steering problems* it is prepared to forgo sustainment as a possible solution to those problems. This last, and especially the proposition italicized above, is perhaps the most dangerous aspect of this whole crisis. If we turn back again to Habermas's formulations in *Legitimation Crisis* and look at his theorems on crises we begin to see some of the implications – and dangers – of the situation. In Habermas's view social systemic crises (as for us, for example, the crisis of climate change) are tests of a system's flexibility. If the system can learn – that is, if it can *allow itself* to learn – and if it can do so in such a way that, through a certain adroitness in decision and action, it can respond to system problems and preserve sufficient goal values, then it can survive the crisis. If it cannot, it will collapse. The two relatively recent examples that confirm this are the contrasting fates of the two largest Marxist states between 1978 and 1991. One (China) adaptively 'learnt', and survives, at least economically (in the short term) comparatively well. The other (the USSR) proved incapable of responding adroitly to accumulating systemic problems and collapsed. The crucial point, in both cases, is the capacity of systems to allow themselves, or to be forced by circumstance, to learn. The danger of the present situation in regard to dealing with climate change is that at the economic level (and indeed within the body-politic) the system effectively *refuses* to learn. In so doing, the system may well be putting its own longer-term (or even medium-term) economic and political survival in doubt. But in that the system believes in, and ensures, maximum flexibility towards (at least short-term) accumulation, this may matter (for it) less than we imagine.[9] What is of sharper occasion for us (and by 'us' I mean here the total population of *all* living things on earth) is that in the context of climate change 'systemic collapse' means very probably not merely the collapse of a governing political or economic system but wholesale social and ecological collapse. Denuding the capacity of the system to learn has thus significant *human* consequence. Conversely, for sustainment, learning, or the capacity to learn, is of maximum account. We know already that sustainment cannot simply 'happen', that it *is* learning. Sustainment is *learning* because sustainment is the learning of how we can collectively, systemically as well as in particular moments, negotiate incommensurable relations – above all, of course, the ultimate incommensurabilty of human and natural systems. Sustainment is a *systemic learning process* whose prime concern is with developing (learning, teaching) – *through reconfiguration* – the capacity of the systems we depend upon (economic, technological, symbolic, biological and quasi-biological) to respond sustainably (animated by the axioms of justice)[10] to the acute steering problems we face. More specifically, (and bringing us closer to design) sustainment is the act of *making* the system (re-)*learn* to become sustainable. But in fact we need also to turn this around. Sustainment is perhaps first and best described, especially in the context of design, as the act of (re-)learning *how to make*.

(Re-)learning how to make/the re-making of 'Civilisation'

What is at stake here, in this idea of our collective (re-)learning of how to make is caught in a beautiful line from Elaine Scarry. In her still unsurpassed study of making and unmaking she notes at one point that, 'the on-going work of civilization is not ... making *x* or *y* ... but *making making* itself, "remaking making", rescuing, repairing, and restoring it to its proper path each time it threatens to collapse into, or become conflated with, its opposite' (Scarry, 1985, p249). The civilizational project (one should read this term without, for the moment, the arrogating connotations of 'Civilization' capitalized) is not a mistake. Given the absolute dependency of the human on the world (re-)made (in however minute or all-but-absolute ways)[11] then sensitivity to modes of making and their sustainability across time[12] is an essential work of culture.[13] As we are increasingly forced to concede, that this sensitivity is all the more required today is because human action not only makes, it also (violently and destructively) un-makes. This is most obviously the case in war and violence; in the capacity for destructiveness (and self-destruction) that has been forever a force for desolation (one of the Four Horsemen of the Apocalypse) and which over the last century and more has threatened to become a pathological condition.[14] But of even more direct relevance to sustainment are the un-making actions of making itself. Making is irretrievable from un-making. Under the slogan 'creative destruction', the Austrian economist Joseph Schumpeter famously celebrated this as an integral part of capitalism's dynamic ('the problem that is usually being visualized is how capitalism administers existing structures, whereas the relevant problem is how it creates and destroys them'; Schumpeter, 1942, p84). Marx's entire work is an exploration of what is made and *un-made* in industrial capitalism.[15] The most obvious instances of the latter are the expropriation, exploitation and violence foisted on natural beings (including human beings) as a result of economic demands. But un-making is not confined to the natural world. The *making* of the Caribbean as a nexus of sugar-producing islands was accomplished only by the un-making, first of their indigenous populations, and second of the lives of the slaves brought to those islands. The truth, difficult for us though it may be for us to face, is that barbarism (the un-making of the human), greed (the unmaking of economic life)[16] and desolation (the un-making of nature)[17] are endemic to the acts of making human life. The paradox that arises from this condition is that, to the extent that the world-made becomes, as today, the effective totality of what-is, so the world also becomes increasingly at risk of becoming the world radically un-made.[18] In this context Scarry's 'civilizational act' of re-making making takes on new resonance. Or, rather, it also *reverses*. It *was* the ongoing task of civilization to 'rescue' making, up until the point at which the made-world becomes *world* (i.e. becomes a totality of the made; becomes, in short, the world as artificial, the world at once threatened by extreme danger and yet which also now contains objectively, genuinely Edenic possibilities). At this point a reversal happens. It is *now* the ongoing task of making-rescued (that is, of making rescued from un-making; sustainable-making rescued from unsustainment) to *re-make civilization*, to seek to prevent a disintegrating civilization from becoming desolation, from creating the conditions of inhumanity. This means that the two moments or projects, that of the re-making of making and that of sustainment, now become one. Sustainment *is* the 'civilizational act' of *making* the fundamental conditions of existence sustainable such that the ongoing human making of the world, *as against its un-making*, continues to be possible; it *is* the project of *using the remaking of making to re-make civilization*. Equally, 'making' now becomes understood as the project of *designing* (a new) making *against* (existing) un-making. And now a second reversal of Scarry occurs. Whereas she correctly pointed out that (historically) 'the ongoing work of civilization is not … making *x* or *y* … but [re-]*making making* itself', today under the conditions of the wholesale artificiality of the world 'remaking making' *only* occurs through how we remake *x* and *y*. '*x* and *y*' are not the ends of making, rather they stand for the way that 'making' as making must realize itself in the world. In other words, in sustainment (as we know) we re-make making *and* we exemplify that re-making in what we make.

Re-working 'product design'

This has brought us back, by circuitous route, to the question of 'product design'. There is temptation, in the last formulation, to think that after all, a practice animated by good intent might 'save' product-design as the latter is re-thought in terms of the re-making of making and its realization in the world. The mistake however would be to imagine that the frameworks sketched above can be lightly brushed aside. They cannot. The category 'product design' already delimits the condition of the thing to be re-made. Indeed, the very problem of the category of 'product design' is that it repeats and enacts a much older categorical division in knowledge (more, admittedly, than in practice) between, essentially, persons and things (and between persons, things and the environments to which things are our mediators). 'Product design' is essentially a category that exists at the long end of a process in knowledge that has gradually de-realized the thing, dissolving the substantive relations with persons, bodies and worlds, into the word or the category, and in the case of capitalism in particular, into the role of the commodity. 'Product' is precisely the name of the *reduction* of the complex, and multi-dimensional thing, that which 'gathers', and which in its role as that which necessarily engages matters of human concern, gathers, contains and negotiates, 'complex assemblies of contradictory issues', into a non-thing whose *primary* identity is singular: to act as an object of exchange-value. To be sure 'product-design' is invented as that practice which, by adding what we might call a depth-veneer of retrospective use-value, restores to the product some semblance of the depth of relations that the process of reduction of *thing* to *product* has removed. There is, in the history of product design, very few examples of this being undertaken in ways that are genuinely restorative of the resonant potential of things and of their capacity to act as prospective resolutions and negotiations of 'matters of concern'. The question here is not so much of the skills of the designer as the way in which a priori-categorization works to delimit, *in advance*, so many of the dimensions of practice. What this last discussion, linked to all the forgoing, suggests is that the practice of 'sustainable product design' is indeed necessary, but now as the dissolution, not of the thing – which on the contrary requires recovery – but of the limits of the categories deployed. 'Sustainable product design' is the designing and realizing of 'products' that break with the limitations of products and hence with the historic *limitations* of the category, norms and practices of product design itself. It means the creation of things as the exemplification of modes of sustainable making (the Scarry project reversed as it were) and the recovery of the capacity of things to engage and negotiate, at once propositionally and in realization, 'matters of concern' (i.e. matters of substantive human and sustainable concern). What is involved here is re-inversion. Traditionally, making is the 'umbrella' category within which the reductive specialist arena 'product design' emerges. But as industrialization and the economy of the commodity encompasses making and subordinates it to production, so minor category in inversion becomes domination. What making is, or what making can be, becomes delimited by or subordinated to 'product design'. (And if not, it becomes excluded, pushed out of practice). This is why 'sustainable product design' is the act of re-inverting making. It is the making-designing of things (as 'products') that exceed the category of 'product design' and in so doing exemplify other (more sustainable) modes of making and exemplify too, the possibility of an economy other than one grounded on exchange value and of social stability grounded on 'using-up'. In this sense, in that in the world of the artificial, mediation is, in a real sense, all we have, then making for sustainment is the recovery (and exploration) of what mediation might be. This means that in sustainment things face two ways, first to humans, who cannot be as such without things,[19] and second to the

93

worlds, artificial, social, 'natural', that we inhabit and must mediate and interact with. Yet it cannot be stressed too highly that this is not a mediation with the world-as-artificial that is somehow separate from this world. Sustainment means making the artificial, *as a totality*, sustainable. The artificial is sustainable when it sustains, adequately (meaning as well as we can reasonably achieve) the hospitable mediation of humans, non-humans and artificial and natural systems. 'Sustainable product design' necessarily has this as its ambition (it could have no other). To achieve it recovers, from and beyond the concept of product design, the possibilities of the thing as that which is potentially capable of exploring this four-fold mediation.

Notes

1 Of course there is still industrial production (China) and the idea of the de-materialization of the economy is one of the defining illusions of our time. But, beginning around 1975 the industrial ceased to the formative force in the world economy. That position is now ceded to consumption and above all to finance. The world economy is today essentially rent-seeking.

2 This is the point that we live not only in relation to a market economy but within a globalized market society.

3 Historically we can date this to the period *c*.1945–2005. In this period, which begins with the double event of the onset of all-but global destructive capacity worked through a war whose reach of technology and production sets industrialization for the first time as a global phenomenon, and which ends with the generalized acknowledgment of human-induced climate change, 'nature' loses its status as horizon to the effective emergent totality of artificial systems, at once technological, infrastructural, cognitive-representational and including of course the effective make-over of 'nature' as artifice or quasi-artifice. The result is that we now *inhabit*, post *c*.2005, a world that is, in effect, artificial. This world brings new dangers, but also qualitatively new possibilities of thought and action – possibilities other, that is, than the mere extrapolation of what-is (which belongs to the industrial epoch, *not* to the epoch we are now entering). In that sense 'Silicon Valley' is not part of the emerging world. As the evidence of Apple would show, the Californian digital world is essentially late-modern. It belongs to a world already past, even as it claims the future.

4 A 'sustainable' economy or society would face the same problem and limitation.

5 To take one, not so small, instance. Industrial production historically depended for its margins on the externalization of costs. Profit was secured not only by the gap in value between what (mental and physical) labour produced and the cost of producing that thing, but by the gap between costs that had to be borne by the enterprise and those that could be externalized – onto nature (pollution) onto society as a whole (say, the health consequences of pollution) and/ or onto future generations (say, climate change). The *internalization* of costs – which is what sustainment demands – would therefore produce a systemic crisis of profitability. Unless private interests were to receive actual or effective compensation for their 'losses' they will be oppose tooth and nail this principle – which is precisely, today, what we see in the opposition to even beginning to deal seriously with climate change.

6 Considered systemically, the crisis of unsustainment is a 'steering problem,' i.e., a problem of managing, globally, the direction or trajectory of the world economy in its relation to the social and natural worlds.

7 Recovered from @johnthackara, January 2016, www.doorsofperception.com/infrastructure-design/are-positive-stories-enough/. COP21 means the 21st 'Conference of Parties' since the first Rio 'Earth Summit' in 1982. UNFCC is the United Nations Framework on Climate Change. 'Yale e360' is Yale Environment 360 is an online magazine offering opinion, analysis, reporting and debate on global environmental issues (see. http://e360.yale.edu).

8 This is use-value not in its limited sense of 'function' but as a relation 'use' being, here, as Giorgio Agamben puts it in an important essay, 'a relationship with something that cannot be appropriated; it refers things insofar as they cannot become objects of possession.' See 'In Praise of Profanations' in Agamben (2007, p83).

9 The highest end of the financial markets have already realized, following Rothschild's famous dictum, that *all* crises can be worked for profit.

10 Lacking these, sustainment could well become terror, or what comes to the same thing, the saving of the few at the expense of the many.

11 On this see the superb study of Australian aboriginal economics by Noel Butlin, *Economics and the Dreamtime: A Hypothetical History* (1994).

12 See, with care, Stanley Diamond's *Collapse: How Societies Choose To Fail or Succeed* (2005).

13 This is despite, but sometimes because of, the fact that such work takes place almost *below* overt recognition of it.

14 Julia Kristeva describes this condition: 'We, as civilizations, we know not only that we are mortal ... we also know that we can inflict death upon ourselves. Auschwitz and Hiroshima have revealed that the "malady of death", as Marguerite Duras might say, informs our most concealed inner recesses. If military and economic realms, as well as political and social bonds, are governed by a passion for death, the latter has been revealed to rule even the once noble kingdom of the spirit. A tremendous crisis has emerged ... never has the power of destructive forces appeared as unquestionable and unavoidable as now, within and without society and the individual' (Kristeva, 1989, p221).

15 To see a reading of Marx from this perspective see chapter 4 of Scarry (1985).

16 I commented on greed or accumulation as the marker and agent of the destruction of economic life at the time of financial crisis (see Dilnot, 2008, 2009).

17 To which we should add instrumentalism as the unmaking of technology (and through that of making in general. Instrumentalism drives the separation of subject and object, act and consequence on which the unsustainable rests). Without exaggeration we can call the four agents named here the contemporary versions of the medieval 'four horseman of the apocalypse' (war, pestilence, famine and death).

18 More stolidly, and in some ways more sobering, is the recognition that from now on, as humans, we are *only* in un-sustainment; that is, we will perpetually face the danger of creating a lethal 'own goal' of species destruction. 'Humanity is at risk from a series of dangers of our own making.' This is the astronomer Stephen Hawking's view of how a combination of climate change, nuclear war and genetically modified viruses could potentially eradicate the human species in the next 100 years (noted from BBC news, 19 January 2016).

19 A paragraph in Roberto Eposito's *Persons and Things* (2013, p136) is relevant here. Quoting Latour, Esposito notes: 'Yes, the human, as we now understand, cannot be grasped and saved unless the other part of itself, the share of things, is restored to it.' He adds: 'Not only are objects intermingled with human elements, solidified and made interchangeable for others, people in their turn are traversed by information, codes and flows arising from the continuous use of technical objects. In perceptual and cognitive terms, neither the psychological nor the physiological features of humans are independent of their manipulation of things, to the point that humans have been defined as *artifacts of their artifacts*' (ibid.). The two quotations are, respectively, from Latour (1993, p136) and Kingdom (1993, p3).

References

Agamben, G. (2007) *Profanations*, Zone Books, London

Butlin, N. (1994) *Economics and the Dreamtime: A Hypothetical History*, Cambridge University Press, Cambridge

Diamond, S. (2005) *Collapse: How Societies Choose To Fail or Succeed*, Viking, London

Dilnot, C. (2008) The Triumph of Greed, *New Statesman*, 8 December, pp37–39

Dilnot, C. (2009) The Triumph – and Costs – of Greed (Part I), *Real-World Economics Review*, 49, 12 March, pp42–61

Eposito, R. (2013) *Persons and Things*, Polity, Cambridge

Habermas, J. (1976) *Legitimation Crisis*, Heinemann Educational Books, London

Heidegger, M. (2003) Overcoming Metaphysics, in J. Stambaugh (ed.), *The End of Philosophy*, University of Chicago Press, Chicago, IL

Keynes, J. M. (1936) *The General Theory of Employment, Interest and Money*, Macmillan, London

Kingdom, J. (1993) *Self-Made Man and His Undoing*, Simon & Schuster, New York

Kristeva, J. (1989) *Black Sun*, Columbia University Press, New York

Latour, B. (1993) *We Have Never Been Modern*, Harvard University Press, Cambridge, MA

Mishan, E. J. (1961) *The Costs of Economic Growth*, Penguin, Harmondsworth

Rose, G. (1996) *Mourning Becomes the Law*, Cambridge University Press, Cambridge

Scarry, E. (1985) *The Body in Pain*, Oxford University Press, Oxford

Schumpeter, J. (1942) *Capitalism, Socialism and Democracy*, Harper, New York

Thackara, J. (2016) Are positive stories enough? Blog post, 13 January, retrieved from www.doorsofperception.com/infrastructure-design/are-positive-stories-enough.

PART II

Agents of change

Product design is an opportunist, adaptive process of continual development, innovation and emergence. This persistent evolution responds to shifts in social, cultural, technological and economic norms and trends, and is unrelenting in its forward thrusting. Despite this seemingly progressive character, product design's recent transition from a 'world-making', to a 'world-breaking' enterprise has put it in a position of flux, in which urgent re-examination of the potential of the product designer, as an agent of positive change, continues to gather in intensity.

Comprising six chapters, the contributors writing in this second part draw together previously disconnected scholarship in consumer studies, environmental management, social innovation and design thinking. In doing so, they identify new and radical forms of sustainable product design intervention; reframing product designers as agents of social, ecological and economic change. Their chapters may be summarized as follows:

7   Sustainable thinking – *Aaris Sherin*
    This chapter introduces 'sustainable thinking', an extension of 'design thinking' that supports designers in navigating the realities of creating market-ready socially and environmentally transformative products, spaces and experiences.

8   Engaging designers in sustainability – *Vicky Lofthouse*
    Designers have an immense influence on the modern world but are not currently widely engaged in the sustainability debate. This chapter introduces ways that product designers can become more fully engaged in sustainable design, across a broader spectrum of activities.

9   Design for sustainable behaviour – *Debra Lilley and Garrath Wilson*
    Sustainable product design cannot reach its full potential without targeting user behaviour. This chapter shows how an increased design focus on the behavioural dimensions of the use-phase powerfully alters user interaction with products to leverage sustainable use patterns.

10 Mending broken promises in sustainable design – *Alex Lobos*
    For sustainable product design to yield the ecological and social benefits it promises, designers must develop a more multi-layered approach, engaging at the levels of: materials and processes; service systems; user experience; and, circular economy.

11   Sharing, materialism, and design for sustainability – *Russell Belk*
     This chapter examines positive and negative takes on sharing and materialism. Although sharing enhances resource efficiency, much of the 'sharing economy' isn't sharing, but selling access through rental; such 'sharewashing' provides a pro-social label for exploitative aims.
12   A journey of two designers – *Yorick Benjamin*
     Sustainable product design appeals to our need to 'do good' but twists our design mind into uncertainty and anxiety. This chapter follows two designers' quests to develop an everyday product, while attempting to integrate a variety of theoretical models along the way.

During the past 60 years alone we have stripped the world of a quarter of its topsoil and a third of its forest cover. In total, one third of all the planets resources have been consumed within the past five decades. Little of what could be referred to as *wilderness* remains. Within the last century and a half, we have mined, logged, trawled, drilled, scorched, levelled and poisoned the earth, to the point of total collapse. Impact assessment tools such as life cycle analysis (LCA) often come in at this stage; providing designers with a formative assessment of the environmental burden of both the manufacture and use of a given product. Anything that provides a more granular picture of the impacts associated with the various stages of a product's development must surely be a good thing. However, despite the scope of literature addressing LCA methodologies it is still commonly understood that LCA can be a problematic process, and many LCAs often reaching contradictory conclusions about similar, or sometimes identical products. Though useful in developing comparative analyses in product design development, LCA tools are often referred to as hazardous, because they may lead to a false sense of control.

Duped by the illusion of progress consumers continue to spend money they don't have on things they don't need and the wheels of conventional capitalism rotate with a familiar ease. This continual making and remaking of the world, ensures that the consumer appetite for fresh material experiences is sustained. Anxious to keep-up, consumers scramble to update their wardrobes, replace their trainers, refit their kitchens and trade in their phones. However, the much sought after experience of being up to date is a fleeting one. It should come as no surprise then that landfill sites, and waste recycling facilities, are packed with stratum upon stratum of durable goods that slowly compact and surrender working order beneath a substantial volume of similar scrap. Even waste that does find its way to recycling and sorting centres frequently ends up in international stockpiles as the economic systems that support recycling and disassembly fail to support them.

When new things are acquired, older things must be ejected from one's material empire, to make room, so to speak – out with the old, in with the new. This has led to the development of an increasingly 'disposable' character in material culture and design. Just over a century ago, disposability referred to small, low cost products such as the Gillette disposable razor or paper napkins, whereas today – largely through the efforts of industrial strategy and advertising – it is culturally permissible to throw anything away from TV sets and vacuum cleaners to automobiles and an entire fitted bathroom.

One doesn't need to be an ardent environmentalist to see that there is little or no logic to the way we relate to our environment. We clear carbon absorptive forests, to grow methane producing meat, and level vast areas of bio diverse wilderness with ecologically inert urban sprawl, riddled with mazes of oil-dependent highways. Through our drive toward a faster, lighter, brighter and more technologically advanced world, humans have wreaked havoc throughout all natural systems that support life on earth. If product design lays the basis for the formation of materials, objects, services and systems, then the product designer's influence over the sustainability of production and consumption is nothing short of pivotal.

7

SUSTAINABLE THINKING

Aaris Sherin

Abstract

As an extension of design thinking, sustainable thinking offers practitioners an opportunity to focus on environmentally and socially conscious outputs while combining strategies traditionally used in business with the creative flexibility and problem-solving long associated with the creative process. Whether one is designing complex systems and experiences or discrete objects, sustainable outputs must meet the needs of consumers and be economically viable. This chapter explores the challenges faced by designers working sustainably and examines areas where specific interventions and strategies can improve the ethical and environmental performance of products. By acknowledging the difficulties designers face, it is possible to identify particular areas of strength and to acknowledge where further improvements are needed. The chapter concludes with a list of touch points for sustainable practice. These provide an overview of the constraints and opportunities designers often face as they navigate the realities of creating market-ready socially and environmentally sensitive design solutions.

Keywords: strategy, sustainability, design thinking, methodology, change agent

Sustainable thinking

Social and environmental consciousness is reshaping the way design is practiced. In addition to being able to solve problems with clearly stated objectives, there is a need for professionals who are able to identify appropriate outcomes in less defined, and more ambiguous situations. Working at the intersections between client and end user, between governments and their citizens and between ideas and realized experiences, allows designers to give voice to the needs of multiple constituencies. Designers now work with diverse stakeholders and are as comfortable identifying objectives that give a company a competitive advantage as they are creating desirable and attractive physical forms or objects. They are transformers and change agents, and these new roles come with greater responsibility. As an extension of design thinking, sustainable thinking offers practitioners an opportunity to focus on developing sustainable outputs while combining strategies traditionally used in business with the creative flexibility and problem-solving long associated with the creative process. These methodologies provide additional resources to help designers navigate the realities of creating viable socially and environmentally sensitive design solutions.

This chapter is divided into three parts. The first part provides context about some of the most common challenges faced by designers looking to create sustainable products and experiences. The next part examines how interventions including the creation and implementation of project-specific strategies, acknowledgement of divergent behaviour motivators and the use of certifications and fair pricing can improve designers' abilities to produce effective outputs. Finally, the chapter concludes with a list of touch points for sustainable product design.

Ultimately, sustainable thinking requires a holistic, multifaceted approach to problem solving, robust assessment criteria and transparent messaging to consumers and stakeholders. By combining strategy, pragmatism and iterative creative processes, designers can develop memorable and relevant sustainable products and experiences.

Context and early adopters

Early product designers created visually compelling and practical three-dimensional forms while communication designers used visuals and text to entice consumers to purchase these same products. The needs of the client came first and little thought was given to the people who would eventually use designed objects. As the use of design expanded in the first half of the twentieth century some designers became troubled by the role they played in an increasingly commercialized world. In 1964, 22 visual communication designers signed a manifesto called *First Things First* which challenged designers to put their skills to worthwhile use (International Council of Design, 2014). Not long after, industrial designer Victor Papanek wrote *Design for the Real World* where he argued that designers had an obligation to work for the greater good and not just the financial well-being of their clients (Papanek, 1985). In his follow-up book, *The Green Imperative* Papanek focused primarily on environmental issues and he questioned, 'whether designers, architects, and engineers can be held personally responsible and legally liable for creating tools, objects, appliances, and buildings that bring about environmental deterioration' (ibid., p9). At the time, Papanek's ideas were considered too unorthodox for many colleagues but today the underlying principles described in his work have largely been accepted even though designers continue to struggle to balance the profit motive with our obligations to end users and the environment in which we live.

Aligning environmental concerns with business strategy

Toward the end of the 1990s and into the early 2000s, media outlets and governments began to focus on issues like climate change and it became crucial to align the ideas put forth by environmentalists and activists with the needs of market-driven companies and governmental organizations. Third-party certifications and oversight organizations were established to provide some assurance that companies complied with a specific set of standards. Corporate sustainability reports (CSR) and corporate responsibility reports started to augment more traditional annual reports and chief sustainability officers were given status previously reserved for business leaders and upper management (Sherin, 2008). Profit and ethics began to be seen as synergistic, rather than in conflict, as had previously been the case.

In 2007, Valerie Casey (formerly of IDEO, frog and Pentagram) founded the Designers Accord and began a five-year project to specifically address the intersection between business practices, sustainability and design. Casey developed standards and tools for both design firms and companies interested in creating positive environmental and social impact. Her guidelines included a pledge to initiate dialog with clients about environmental and social impacts and sustainable alternatives, educating employees, considering a firms own environmental footprint and working to advance the understanding of environmental and social issues from a design perspective (Casey, 2008). As a viable organization, Designer's Accord ended at the conclusion of Casey's 5-year mandate, but many of the principles originally put forth by Casey and other early adopters of sustainable design practices have since been endorsed by, and/or folded into, the standards of professional design organizations (Casey, 2016).

Unlike Casey, who advocated for increased engagement with the business community (Casey, 2008), some environmentalists still believe more stringent regulations are the only way to ensure that large multinational companies play by a standard set of rules. Regardless of which side of the debate you fall, the conversation about what constitutes progress and how responsibility should be shared is still evolving and contemporary designers have an opportunity to continue the dialog initiated by Victor Papenek and the signatories of *First Things First.*

Challenges and opportunities

While practitioners agree on many of the basic tenants of sustainability, how they go about realizing specific goals and the areas which they focus their attention are quite different. One size does *not* fit all and designers need the space to explore and to test new ideas. When we evaluate the merits of environmentally and socially conscious products, systems and experiences, we should be rigorous in our critique. Assessment is vital to promote continued improvement. However, even as products undergo thorough testing and evaluation it is important not to fall into the trap of being too prescriptive in our standards. Few products not created by nature can claim to be truly sustainable. Acknowledging progress is as important as evaluating where a product, material or experience falls short. Even small steps are meaningful. When a baby first learns to walk we don't criticize their steps as ungainly. By measuring intent and impact, as well as more concrete aspects of environmental performance, we can develop broader standards for evaluating sustainable products.

Certainly not everyone agrees with the need for more inclusive standards and measures by which to evaluate sustainable products. Environmentalists have long advocated for more stringent reforms to energy policy and corporate regulations. They are not wrong. In the face of unprecedented resource depletion and ever-rising levels of CO_2 a complete overhaul of environmental regulations may be humanity's only hope. However, while it is accurate this position is also unrealistic. And we quickly come up against the *people versus progress* debate. Is air-conditioning a luxury or a human right? Does every member of a growing worldwide middle class deserve the right to own and operate a motor vehicle? And if the answer is no, then who gets to make those choices and where do lines get drawn? In relatively temperate climates it is easy to say air-conditioning is a luxury rather than a necessity and in countries with robust public transportation systems, voluntarily giving up the right to own a motor vehicle is not only tenable, it may have additional positive impacts on quality of life, such as lowering costs and increasing individuals level of fitness. But then there is the rest of the world's population, many of who live in climates where the temperature exceeds 30 degrees

Celsius for months on end, or in cities where a lack of robust public transportation systems reduces the populations' ability to efficiently travel even small distances. If it is possible to understand the urgent need felt by militant environmentalists and climate protesters one also has to consider the rights of people who want to improve their situation today and don't believe they can afford to worry about a distant future.

Empathy is defined as the ability to understand and share the feelings of another (Merriam-Webster, 2015) and empathy is needed at all sides of the climate debate. It is also a key reason why the term sustainable should be used rather than eco-or eco-friendly. Products labelled 'eco-' may be better for the environment but by preferencing the environment we risk ignoring the reality faced by many of the 7.3 billion people sharing those limited resources on this planet. For design to be truly sustainable we have to be sensitive to the impacts that materials extraction, the manufacturing processes and waste disposal have on the environment. We also need to take into account the people who produce and who use a product or service. Finally, the products we develop need to be economically viable. Without this trifecta of achievements a product cannot be truly sustainable though it may still make important progress towards better environmental performance. The next section of the chapter will focus on specific areas where designers can develop successful interventions. Strategy, pricing, certifications, transparency and behavioural motivators will be discussed.

Design strategy

Design strategy refers to a plan of action based on vision, a set of defined goals and objectives and specific criteria for measuring success. Whether working on the redesign of a product or a design-led community engagement, all design incorporates some degree of strategy. Sometimes strategy will be developed as part of an articulated process, which begins with research and later moves on to more iterative creative approaches. At other times strategy becomes the primary focus of a design intervention. Strategy is now its own sub-specialization within the field of design. When working with large teams, strategy is often determined only after collaboration with professionals who have expertise in ethnography, business, social science and marketing.

Design is most successful when creative strategies complement an organization's overall vision and mission. How involved a designer is in analytics, planning and project management will depend on their skills and the organizational structure of the company they work for, or with. In some instances design objectives will be focused exclusively on creative outputs but when a designer is involved more broadly in business strategy she will need to be able to tie creative endeavours into existing corporate strategy. When developing objectives it is useful to consider technical parameters, budgetary guidelines and an organization's existing market position. In addition to establishing realistic goals and objectives, a strategist can help identify who should be part of the problem-solving process and define the specifics about each individual's role. Successful strategies are flexible enough to respond to changes in external market forces such as regulatory intervention, fluctuations in the economy, new distribution channels and evolving consumer preferences.

Design thinking

Tim Brown, CEO and president of IDEO popularized an iterative human-centred approach to problem solving in his book, *Change by Design* (Brown, 2009). At IDEO, design thinking,

Table 7.1 Steps for developing a design strategy

Mission:
What we do /the client does

Vision:
Who we (or the client) want to be
Audience and competitive analysis
Unmet needs

Review:
Internal and External factors impacting design

Create:
Goals and objectives

Evaluate:
What is ideal
What is most important
What is realistic in a given timeframe and with available resources

Develop:
An actionable plan for implementation
Synthesize into appropriate output

Design strategy should:
Be aligned with the client's/company's mission and brand values
Position the client/company in a distinct or unique way against competitors
Put the brand/product in a position of trust with the audience/consumers
Create actionable objectives with a clear plan for implementation

Design strategy can be used to:
Plan how design elements can be used to meet existing business goals
Create a plan of action that leads to a design solution
Help to position a client more effectively in their competitive landscape
Transition objectives into a guiding focus for design-related work
Translate brand vision/mission into actionable design-related goals and objectives
Help steer decision-making
Focus a brand or client towards social and environmentally responsible outputs
Align design deliverables with lifestyle and ethical values of the client or consumer

Source: first published in *Sustainable Thinking: Ethical Approaches to Design and Design Management* (Sherin, 2013)

as the process was known, was used to develop customized interventions and solutions regardless of whether the end result produced objects, experiences or new business strategies. Brown's focus on flexible incremental creative processes wasn't new but its applicability to a wide range of economic sectors and non-visual or object orientated outputs was. In the early 2000s IDEO and competitors like frog became known for their ability to use principles of creativity to solve complex problems. Inventing a new form factor for an organ transplant carrying case, developing systems to improve efficiencies at hospitals and helping companies leverage scale and move into new markets are all now acceptable outputs for design. In the years since Tim Brown introduced the principles of design thinking to a general audience they have been enthusiastically embraced for their flexibility and ability to leverage disruptive change.

Both design thinking and sustainability require a mixture of cognitive, creative and practical interventions. By explicitly linking these competences, sustainable thinking combines strategies borrowed from business with iterative creative processes and the technical skills to develop human-centred and environmentally preferable solutions. In addition to solving predefined problems, sustainable thinking (like design thinking) can be used to identify opportunities for innovation and work in areas where problems are more complex and, as such, less clearly defined.

Best practices

Continual improvements in technology and production processes can make it difficult to keep up with the pace of progress. The term 'best practices' refers to a practical way of describing decisions, which have been made at a specific moment in time while also accepting the reality that external forces may quickly render these same practices obsolete. Rather than adhering to a fixed or absolute set of criteria, designers and the clients they work with would do well to embrace constant improvement and commit to the *best practices* for the moment. In short, the principle allows designers to recognize and plan for change.

The need for *constant improvement* is particularly important as designers react to external changes in consumer preferences and other market forces. Best practices can be included in a broadly defined strategy, which focuses on how to respond to market pressures or changing external contexts. Instead of creating a set of absolute standards or a checklist it is often better to develop short-term objectives which include built-in opportunities for revision and reassessment.

Transparency

Consumers in Europe, North America, Japan and many other industrialized countries are familiar with environmental certifications and labelling. The function of independent third-party and/or government-sponsored certifications is twofold. First, they hold manufacturers to a specific set of standards. These include the need for continued improvements in performance as in the case of the standards used by the International Organization for Standardization (ISO), or they may target materials extraction and production processes such as the ones developed by the Forest Stewardship Council (FSC). Similarly, governmental standards such as the ones established by the European Council of Agricultural Ministers outline production standards in a particular industry (in this case organic farming) within a geographic location. In addition to providing clear guidelines for producers of goods and services, certifications also offer assurance to consumers. This second function can be particularly helpful for people who are confused by non-binding labels such as the recycled mark or the use of terminology like *eco* and *eco-friendly*, all of which are freely used in advertising but are not governed or overseen by any particular body. Certification helps level the playing field and provides a guarantee that the same assessment criteria are being used in multiple situations.

Contradictions in labelling

Whether it makes sense to use certifications or particular labelling will depend on the type of product being developed and the specifics of the market. Even when no appropriate labelling system exists, designers and the companies they work with should try to be as transparent as possible. This means providing information about the entire supply chain of the product from sourcing of materials through to consumer use and eventual disposal.

Using best practices principles can be helpful when determining how to convey applicable information in sectors where certifications are lacking or inappropriate. For transparency to be robust and meaningful it has to be current. Regularly updating information about new aspects of materials sourcing and/or production techniques is often necessary. Independent third-party certifications and transparent messaging do require extra time, energy and in the case of certifications can come with additional costs. Despite the extra work involved they often remain one of the only ways to combat the unfortunate practice of *greenwashing* and misrepresentations made by unscrupulous companies.

The decision of whether or not to overtly label a product as environmentally preferable or ethically produced is more complicated than it may seem. Sometimes environmental labelling (including certifications) won't appeal to a particular audience. In other cases labelling isn't aligned with a brand's image or core strengths. True success will be achieved when the entire category of values-based products is eliminated and all products become sustainable but we are nowhere near achieving that reality. In the meantime, designers, marketing professionals and strategists will have to carefully navigate the world of labelling and messaging. Contradictions are an unfortunate consequence of life. We can agree on the importance of clear messaging and labelling but doing so is only useful if it is relevant in the market where the product is going to be sold.

Fair pricing

Products produced by companies interested in highlighting their environmental and social attributes often command higher prices. In some cases paying a living wage to workers or using specific production practices or preferable materials actually does mean products have to cost more. But this isn't always the case (S. Aplin, interview with author, 9 September 2010). If customers are willing to pay more for products made by companies who share their values there is a temptation to charge more for these products even if there are no increased costs associated with manufacturing and distribution. Since products with environmental benefits so often cost more, consumers may ultimately think all values-driven purchases will be more expensive. This perception inhibits full market penetration and keeps cost-conscious consumers from purchasing sustainable products even though it does allow some companies to profit in the short-term. Regardless of whether or not products are labelled according to their environmental attributes it's important to avoid profiteering by taking advantage of consumers who have committed to making values-based purchases. To do so only increases distrust and scepticism and undermines the work done by individuals and companies who are committed to fairly reflecting the manufacturing costs at the point of purchase.

Behaviour motivators

Whether employed as government officials, CEOs of a company or workers paid by the hour, people have different values and are often motivated by different triggers. Diversity is considered an attribute when it gives rise to unique cultural practices, cuisines and handicrafts but it rarely helps when people try to agree on larger issues. Differences in regional values and cultural norms often exacerbate environmental problems and create barriers to the adoption of comprehensive standards on workers' rights and the environment. People from countries with strong central governments might say it is the government's responsibility to provide clear directives for businesses and citizens alike. Conversely, in a country committed to free market economics, the focus might be on innovation with preference for solutions originating in the private sector. Just as different triggers drive governments, people and the companies they work for adopt socially and environmentally conscious practices for different reasons. The barriers to ethically driven decision-making are diverse. To stimulate change one has to understand and acknowledge which values are most important to an individual and/or an organization.

Jamie Cloud, founder of the Cloud Institute for Sustainability Education, developed a list of sustainable motivators in the early 2000s. They have been used to help business leaders, schools and governmental organizations understand the differences in individual's interests and to explore the varied and complex reasons why particular companies or individuals may choose to align themselves with social and environmental values. Cloud's organizational motivators include managing brand reputation and value, protecting the right to operate, developing ongoing relationships with customers, pioneering new markets, and finally the ability to attract employees (J. Cloud, interview with author, 15 November 2007, cited in Sherin, 2008, p26). Further examination of each of these areas is useful as it further illuminates the different reasons why designers and their clients may make specific choices.

Managing brand value is key to an organizations success. Consumers are more loyal to companies where there is perceived shared value. If consumers believe a company is dishonest and treats its workers unfairly they are less likely to continue to purchase the company's products. Protecting the right to operate can be seen as an extension of managing brand value. By getting out in front of regulation, by self-regulating or by obtaining third-party certifications a company will be less likely to have to pay regulatory fines and/or defend themselves against lawsuits which are costly to the brand's reputation and to the bottom line. Organizations are also more likely to look for vendors, employees and partners who share values and it may be easier to develop ongoing relationships in networks of similarly positioned industries (J. Cloud, interview with author, 15 November 2007).

There's nothing wrong with an organization whose primary motivation for adopting more sustainable practices is because it pays. Recycling, reducing materials usage and creating modular systems can save money and can be powerful incentives for change. Being a pioneer and innovating also offers opportunities to tap into the growing market for sustainable goods and services. Finally, healthy, productive organizations need talented, committed and flexible employees. Millennials show a greater interest in working with companies that share their vision than previous generations (Rayapura, 2014) but regardless of their age most people would prefer to work for an organization with values and a mission they believe in.

The behavioural triggers described here are not exhaustive but they highlight how varied motivation can be for individuals and companies alike. For designers looking to develop robust and realistic strategies, evaluating the mission and vision of the organization and assessing the behavioural motivators described above provides greater insight into the decisions made by company employees, upper management and even the consumers who will buy a product or use a service. When MIT's Slone Management Review asked 4,000 managers from 113 countries which internal and external drivers had led to changing business practices in favour of sustainability their answers mirrored many of the same triggers described by Cloud (MIT Sloan Management Review, 2011). The strongest motivator was consumer preference but legislative pressure, resource scarcity and owner demands also played a role in evolving business practices. Regardless of whether a company is motivated primarily by internal or external factors, examining how specific behaviour motivators align with a client's mission and vision makes having conversations about sustainability easier, is almost always better than confronting an organization with their shortcomings head on.

Designers are taught to work within constraints, and this characteristic is one of our greatest attributes. Combined with the use of strategy and iteratively creative processes designers have the ability to produce objects and experiences, which improve people's everyday lives. Reframing constraints can also provide new opportunities for innovation. The real power of design only comes when the designer is understood to be a useful collaborator to businesses, governments and non-profit organizations.

Conclusions

Today the role of the design is complex. It is multifaceted and frankly it lacks a clear playbook but it also offers a greater range of opportunities for success and designers have the chance to be involved in more areas of people's lives than ever before. The following touch points for sustainable design have been adapted from the text *Sustainable Thinking: Ethical Approaches to Design and Design Management* (Sherin, 2013). While they may not be applicable to every project, they are useful markers because they provide an overview of target areas which need to be considered when one is trying to produce a sustainable product or experience.

- **Consumption:** May refer to products or services that reduce the number of objects a person must own overall or can refer to the development of longer lasting products. Some designers suggest we need fewer but better designed objects in our lives and are creating products to fill that niche.
- **Innovation:** Describes the introduction of a new idea, service or product. Innovation may require the development of processes or even in the machinery that is used to make objects and create more sustainable deliverables. In some cases a completely new output or service may be the product of design innovation.
- **Technology:** This may include improvements to systems, manufacturing and production equipment and may require the adoption of new systems or processes and an initial capital investment.
- **Materials:** The sources of raw materials, their method of extraction from the natural environment and their transportation to manufacturing facilities can all be substantial improvements. Additionally, designers should try to use less raw materials and specify those that eliminate or reduce toxicity in a product's lifecycle. Concern for materials should also include the health of people living near extraction or recovery sites.
- **Production:** How an object is manufactured and the various inputs and outputs of production is a key area of focus when improving the environmental performance of a product. This area may require the designer to switch vendors and/or alter their designs so that preferable processes can be used in production. It is important to consider the physical health associated with working in a manufacturing facility.
- **Problem solving:** Often linked to innovation, problem solving examines the ways a designer may approach a problem by redefining what the solution should be or even rethinking the brief. In this area a designer may come up with a completely new product or service or redefine how an existing product is used or manufactured.

- **Reuse/recycling:** One of the biggest problems we face is an overabundance of waste. A key area of focus is the use, reuse and recycling of materials that would otherwise be discarded. Ideally, we should design within a closed loop system thereby transforming waste into useable materials. This target may include making items that are designed to be disassembled, reused, recycled or composted or designing products that are made from recycled or reused material.
- **Efficiency:** One of the most powerful and easy to apply targets of sustainability, efficiency, is often overlooked. It is something that every organization should strive for and an area where at least one improvement is almost always possible. Reducing the amount of energy used in production and/or specifying processes or vendors that use renewable energy is one of the most common ways to achieve greater efficiency.
- **New markets:** Identifying or creating new markets allows designers to create positive links between production and consumption. Identifying new markets is particularly powerful when working in the developing world and trying to find outputs or solutions that can benefit local communities.
- **Storytelling:** Storytelling connects an audience with information. At its core, storytelling provides context and relevance about a product, service or company. It is an undervalued but important touch point for sustainable designers.
- **Fair trade and wages:** Fair trade is a market-based approach that seeks to help producers and workers attain fair wages and equitable working conditions. Fair trade organizations can connect socially conscious designers with producers. Creating opportunities for workers who have previously been exploited to earn fair wages provides benefits for both workers and consumers.
- **Strategy:** Design strategy focuses on successful problem definition and planning rather than traditional visual and object-orientated outputs. Strategists may be part of a larger design team or they may be brought in as consultants to help steer larger projects and help define successful outcomes.
- **Collaboration:** Bringing professionals together from a wide range of disciplines can increase the likelihood that a team will fully understand the problem and will have the expertise to create meaningful and long-lasting solutions. Collaboration also provides opportunities to work on a more diverse set of projects and in different geographic locations serving a broad range of clients and stakeholders.
- **Entrepreneurship:** In addition to working for clients or as part of a larger team, many designers with expertise in sustainability are creating their own companies with the goal of delivering exemplary products and services. Entrepreneurs may start a new business or work to bring a product or service to market using existing distribution channels that haven't been utilized before.

References

Brown, T. (2009). *Change by design*, Harper Business, New York

Casey, V. (2008). The designers accord. Unpublished manuscript

Casey, V. (2016). *In review: 2007–2012. Retrieved* January 13, 2016, from www.designersaccord.org

International Council of Design (2014) First things first manifesto celebrates 50 years, retrieved 12 October 2015 from www.ico-d.org/connect/index/post/1933.php

Merriam-Webster (2015) Empathy, retrieved 12 October 2015 from www.merriam-webster.com/dictionary/empathy

MIT Sloan Management Review (ed.). (2011). *Sustainability: The embracers seize the advantage*, Massachusetts Institute of Technology, Cambridge, MA

Papanek, V. (1985). *Design for the real world: Human ecology and social change*, Academy Chicago Publishers, Chicago, IL

Rayapura, A. (2014). Millennials most sustainability-conscious generation yet, but don't call them 'environmentalists', retrieved 10 December 2015 from www.sustainablebrands.com/news_and_views/stakeholder_trends_insights/aarthi_rayapura/millennials_most_sustainability_conscious

Sherin, A. (2008). *Sustainable: A handbook of materials and applications for graphic designers and their clients*, Rockport Publishers, Gloucester, MA

Sherin, A. (2013). *Sustainable thinking: Ethical approaches to design and design management*, Bloomsbury, London

8

ENGAGING DESIGNERS IN SUSTAINABILITY

Vicky Lofthouse

Abstract

Designers have an immense influence on the modern world but are not currently widely engaged in the sustainability debate. Designers are generally driven by both creativity and innovation, and addressing the sustainability challenge requires both. Every year numerous student designers are engaged with and inspired by the opportunities offered by sustainable design, so on the face of it, engaging designers in sustainable design should be easy.

This chapter recognizes that product designers have great potential to positively influence the environmental and social impact of the products, services and systems that they design. Despite this potential, there is currently little evidence of widespread engagement across the design industry. The different ways that designers can engage in sustainable design across a broad spectrum of activities are presented and discussed. Then, challenges which designers face when it comes to addressing sustainability are reviewed and a number of ways to address these challenges are presented. The chapter concludes by proposing ways in which we can move beyond the status quo and begin to address these challenges in order to more effectively utilize the skills that designers can bring to the sustainability debate.

Keywords: applying sustainable design, product design, case studies, continuous education, practical application

Introduction

In 1971, Victor Papanek accused product designers of creating useless, unnecessary and unsafe products; of wastefully propagating product obsolescence; of creating 'stuff-lust' that promoted materialistic lifestyles (Papanek, 1971). As material consumption continues to grow, epitomized by such marketing tactics as Black Friday and Cyber Monday (Gittleson, 2013), it is unclear as to whether much has really changed in the last 40 years. A more modern voice of the same tone is that of Bruce Nussbaum (2007) who stated in his provocative speech at Parsons School of Design that 'designers suck'. He refers to designers' propensity to design 'crap' and their inability to engage with the sustainability debate, among other things. John Thackara (2007) reflects on this accusation and proposes three possible responses –

to 'argue the toss; cringe with guilt; or, become part of the solution' – he and I favour the third way. As proposed by Nussbaum (2007), we need to start demanding sustainability in design. That said, we should be under no illusion that this is an easy thing to take-up and achieve. Although, in theory, designers have many of the requisite skills to become part of the solution, this is far from simple to orchestrate in practice.

The sliding scale – what do we want from designers?

Designers have an immense influence on the modern world – everything that we interact with, from smart phones, to clothing, domestic products, transportation systems and buildings have been intentionally or unintentionally designed. Added to this, enormous supply chains which can involve 100s of companies across North America, Europe and Asia (Friedman, 2005) in the manufacture of a single product range, mean that the choices designers make can have positive and/or negative impacts which ricochet around the world.

Research has established that given the opportunity, industrial designers have great potential to positively influence the environmental and social impact of the products, services and systems they design (Whiteley, 1993; Sherwin, 2000; Lofthouse, 2001a). In part, this is because of their influence at the early stages of the product development process, where the design brief is more flexible and the most critical decisions with respect to cost, appearance, materials selection, innovation, performance, and perceptions of quality are made (Bakker, 1995; Bhamra *et al.*, 1999). It is also because designers have great influence over values, attitudes and perceived consumer needs which means they are well positioned to help change culturally dominant value systems (Wahl and Baxter, 2008).

While it is widely recognized that designers have a key part to play, there is little discussion as to exactly what that role should be, nor is there generally recognition that there is a spectrum of engagement through which designers can become engaged in sustainability (see Figure 8.1). At the most basic level, those working within product design need to be compliant with environmental legislation such as the Waste Electrical and Electronic Equipment Directive (WEEE) and the Restriction of the Use of Certain Hazardous Substances (RoHS) in Electrical and Electronic Equipment (EEE) Directive (Herat, 2007). This is typically, however, the responsibility of engineers in larger businesses or specialists in an environmental affairs department. To be engaged in sustainable design, designers need to take responsibility for what they agree to design and say 'no' to designing nonsensical products that society really does not need. Though it is often not that straight forward to determine the inherent value of a proposed product or service, single-use, disposable electronic products which are likely to end up in landfill, are a good example of design briefs which should be avoided (or amended).

Following on from this, the design of relevant, valuable and useful products needs to be considerably improved. On a product level this means identifying and applying ecodesign strategies such as energy reduction, material selection, appropriate service life, size and weight reduction and packaging reduction to the product under consideration. This type of product redesign is where the majority of industry practice (where it actually exists) tends to focus. It is also where the majority of ecodesign oriented tools are geared toward (PRé Consultants, 1999; Tischner, 2001; Bhamra and Lofthouse, 2007). Philips' SenseoUp one-cup coffee machine is a good example of this type of approach in practice (see Figure 8.2). A smart interface means that the machine warms up, brews the coffee and shuts down with one touch of a button. As it switches off immediately after the coffee is brewed, a 10 per cent energy saving on previous products is achieved. Its smaller size means that it needs less packaging and causes fewer emissions during transport (Philips Design, 2015). This product also improves on

SCOPE FOR INCREASING YOUR RESPONSIBILITY

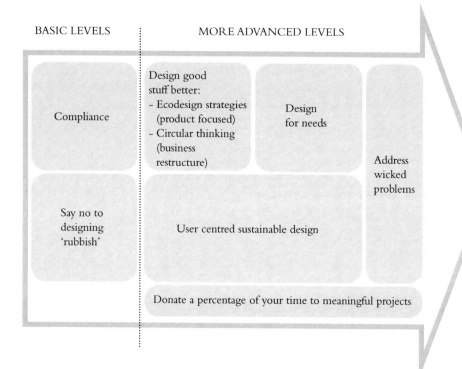

Figure 8.1 The spectrum in which designers can engage with sustainability

Figure 8.2 SenseoUp one-cup coffee machine, Philips Design, 2015

previous generations of coffee machine by utilizing 13 per cent recycled plastics. To achieve this, Philips had to overcome a number of challenges as recycled plastics are only available in dark colours and you can sometimes see spots or flowlines in the plastics, where the material was injected into the mould (ibid.). These restrictions mean that recycled materials can't be used in coloured parts. The baseplate was identified as an appropriate part through which to introduce recycled plastic content into the product. In order to do this part of it was textured to give the recycled plastic a high-quality look and feel. Then a single matte black colour was selected for the complete range instead of many colour variations. Finally, the baseplate was made less visible by focusing attention on the coloured housing above it. This approach enabled the introduction of 90 per cent recycled acrylonitrile butadiene styrene (ABS) plastic from post-consumer electronic waste into the baseplate.

Beyond the incorporation of ecodesign strategies, designers can opt to take a cradle-to-cradle approach (as the design of the SenseoUp demonstrates). This advocates component reuse and material reclamation as a feedstock for new products. These sorts of proposals can be more challenging to get accepted as they often require the restructuring of manufacturing and end of life collection systems, and hence require greater investment from the client. There are also technical challenges to incorporating recycled materials, when previously the component has been designed to use virgin material (Philips Design, 2015). Engagement with this approach is however gaining traction in a number of FTSE 100 companies as a result of the work carried out by the Ellen MacArthur Foundation, whose mission is to accelerate a transition towards a circular economy (as declared on their home page at www.ellenmacarthurfoundation.org).

Braiform, who supply garment hangers, provide an excellent example of this type of business model innovation, moving from a 'throughput model to one that achieves 80 per cent re-use – almost unheard of for such a low-value product' (Ellen MacArthur Foundation, 2015). Their business model works as follows:

> After being contracted by a new partner, Braiform develop a new garment hanger solution, which starts with supplying virgin product into the market. Manufacturers buy these hangers and deploy them before shipping their products. The garments are distributed and during purchase the retailer collects the hangers, sending them back to distribution centres with deliveries. They then return to one of three main re-use centres in Sheffield, and the US, where they are sorted, repackaged and distributed back to garment-producing regions … hangers that cannot be re-used are shredded and used to make new products. As Braiform know that the polymer is pure, they can sell this material to a compounder and it returns to virgin production. Last year, 30 million hangers were made from the company's own waste stream.
>
> *(Ellen MacArthur Foundation, 2015)*

Though at first glance this does not seem to be the typical remit of product designers, there are plenty of innovative opportunities for designers within this type of business model.

We've seen that currently the most popular focus when it comes to sustainable design is on the implementation of ecodesign strategies. During his time at Philips, Chris Sherwin (2004) observed that this meant that ecodesign was carried out entirely by mechanical, electrical or chemical engineers, not by designers:

> [It was not that] Philips designers were not involved in sustainability activities as they were and they still are. It is just that the type of design activities conducted by

> Philips Design, and the types of ecodesign methods and approaches … [used by]
> Philips generally did not match up. The tools and projects simply missed designers.
>   *(Sherwin, 2004, p24)*

In light of this, he reflects that there are 'a number of leading edge companies conducting ecodesign, [where] designers themselves are not generally involved'. Not only is this a missed opportunity, as designers have a unique and important contribution to make (ibid.) but it also indicates a greater mismatch between what we are *telling* industrial designers is ecodesign, and what *actually* is ecodesign (from the perspective of product designers). Sherwin argues that the potential contribution that design can make to sustainable design is quite different from current practices and has the potential to significantly advance sustainability practices. 'Designers are trained to be creative, to challenge precedents and overcome stereotypes. These creative abilities are currently not well utilised within sustainable business' (ibid., p25). This type of 'user-centred sustainable design' is not especially recognized in industry, though is addressed by a number of emerging research fields such as 'Design for Sustainable Behaviour' (Lilley, 2009) and is being incorporated in the development of more sustainable business models (Moreno *et al.*, 2014) There are currently no recognized methodologies for the implementation of this type of sustainable design in an industrial setting.

Designers can also look to move beyond designing commercial products/services and use their skills to address real and more pressing human needs. Needs associated with an ageing and expanding population, environmental crisis, social inequalities and diminishing quality of life – coupled with an awareness of design's potential to contribute positively – have raised wide felt concerns, not least of all by designers themselves, for the implications and responsibilities of product and industrial design's current role (Sparke, 1987; Whiteley, 1993; Cooper, 2005; Walker, 2006; Bhamra and Lofthouse, 2007; Fuad-Luke, 2009; Chapman, 2015). A number of authors believe that designers are well positioned to tackle these types of 'wicked' problems (Buchanan, 1992; Kolko, 2012; Wahl and Baxter, 2008). However these types of problems are not typically given to designers to work on, as they are not commonly challenges that the commercial sector seeks to solve. As such it is often difficult to find an opportunity to get engaged or to engage designers in this type of activity. Berman (2008) proposes that every designer should pledge to spend at least 10 per cent of their professional time on worthwhile projects which repair the world. If each of the estimated 2 million designers in the world were to spend just 10 per cent of their professional time on more sustainable projects, that would be close to 8 million hours a week committed to improving the world in which we live (ibid.). Designers, however, are only part of the solution and need to work with practitioners from a diverse range of disciplines, such as chemistry, biology, geography and politics if they stand any chance of addressing some of the most challenging problems on our planet.

This section has shown that there is a broad spectrum across which designers can engage in sustainable design. Beyond the basic level of activity, engagement of any type can have huge and potentially transformational advantages. In theoretical arguments 'systems innovation' which advocates infrastructure changes, such as a move from traditional agriculture to industry-based food production is advocated over 'product redesign', because of the greater potential for environmental improvement (Brezet, 1997). However, it is important to recognize that any level of engagement brings potential benefits. Widespread adoption of ecodesign strategies, for example, would dramatically reduce the environmental impact of the millions of new products that enter the market every year as well as raising awareness and sensitivity to the broader issues of sustainability.

The theory of engaging designers in sustainability

As mentioned earlier, designers are interested in, and generally driven by, creativity and innovation; addressing the sustainability challenge requires both, and in this way, designers are perfectly situated to engage the challenge. Each year, numerous student designers are inspired by the opportunities offered by sustainable design. At Loughborough University we engage our students by taking a multi-faceted approach. Students are introduced to alternate ways of viewing product development through the introduction of concepts such as eco-efficiency, life cycle thinking and systems thinking. We use Brezet's model of innovation (1997) to demonstrate how moving from Type 1 Innovation (product improvement) to Type 4 Innovation (systems innovation) can achieve higher levels of environmental and social improvement as well as business benefits (Bhamra and Lofthouse, 2007). Students are also introduced to a wide array of approaches such as Design for Happiness (Escobar-Tello, 2015), Design for Behaviour Change (Lilley and Lofthouse, 2009; Lilley, 2009), Social Innovation, Zero Waste and Design for the Circular Economy, in order to encourage them to think about design differently. They are shown a wide range of interesting examples to inspire their creativity and show them how these issues have been addressed by different designers and organizations (Lofthouse, 2001a). They are introduced to a range of quantitative and qualitative tools, such as the Eco Indicator 99 (PRé Consultants, 1999), Design abacus, Ecodesign web (Lofthouse, 2009), Social Issues cards (Lofthouse, 2013) and bespoke tools such as Dirty Carbon, an in-house tool developed specifically to introduce design students to carbon footprinting (Lofthouse *et al.*, 2015). These tools can help them to strategically assess the challenges of a brief, and assess or measure any improvements made. In the second semester they undertake a sustainable design project set by an industrial sponsor, which enables them to apply their research and put the theory into practice. This provides them with a safe environment to 'have a go' at sustainable design and experience the challenges of managing a range of competing requirements (styling, manufacture, environmental stewardship and social justice, for example).

This approach has been seen to produce well-informed graduates with a good understanding of the issues that are relevant to designers as well as providing them with a suite of tools and methods which they can draw on to help them create more responsible products, services and systems. Every year, undergraduate designers from Loughborough University specifically seek out sustainable design related placement and employment opportunities, which is a testament to their interest and engagement in the subject. However, there are currently very few opportunities available (beyond a few specialist SMEs) and even fewer that are advertised via the traditional 'milk-round' employment routes – such as careers fairs, design magazines, blogs and journals – used for recruitment in the UK. Consequently a lot of potential and enthusiasm is not capitalized on.

Current industrial practice

Examples of sustainable design can be found within industry across a wide range of sectors, in a variety of different organizations, and though these examples are important and of great value, they are not evidence of wide spread practice. Success stories are, however, a great way of demonstrating the benefits of good sustainable design practice, and so a cross section of examples are introduced below.

Hiut Denim is a small independent manufacturer and supplier of high quality denim jeans. They are representative of small and macro enterprises set up by individuals who have a deep personal interest in the environment and/or sustainability. They are small and nimble, set their own agenda and typically prioritize sustainability. Hiut's unique selling point is that owners should wait as long as possible before washing their jeans, ideally over six months, in order to get the best out of the fabric. Not only does this improve the quality of the product but also dramatically reduces the water, detergent and energy consumption associated with washing (Hiut Denim, 2015). Additionally, they offer a lifetime guarantee for their products which includes ongoing repair to prolong the life of the product. This type of business model dramatically reduces the carbon and water footprints of denim jeans and makes for an interesting marketing strategy.

At the other end of the spectrum the Nest thermostat (NEST, 2015) was created by Nest Labs, US, in response to an identified gap in the market regarding domestic climate control, which was outdated and underdeveloped (Baynes, 2013). The resulting intelligent thermostat (see Figure 8.3), which drew heavily on the Apple Inc. heritage of the key protagonists involved in its development, helps to reduce energy usage, and consequently consumer bills, by building a deeper understanding of user needs and practices.

Though they could have done more to consider the whole lifecycle of the product, by incorporating a take back element, what they have done, is make energy monitoring desirable and this has the potential to dramatically reduce household energy consumption – currently 29 per cent of overall energy consumption in the UK (Department of Energy and Climate Change, 2014). While sustainability may not have been the key driver for Nest this does not make the achievements any less valuable. The thermostat is an excellent example of how innovative product design and development can be used to drive more sustainable consumption practices.

The Levi's 511 Commuter range of jeans were designed to encourage commuters to cycle 'by making it easier and more comfortable. A strap allows easy transportation of your security lock; nano-coating on the jeans repels rain, crotch support makes them last longer; and reflective strips make you safer' (Sherwin, 2012a). Another great example is that of the award-winning Mu folding plug (Made in Mind, 2015), which dramatically reduces the weight and volume size of the bulky British power plug. This innovative piece of product design leads to great reductions in the carbon footprint of products shipped with this type of plug over the standard design, as it takes up considerably less space in the box.

Figure 8.3 Nest Thermostat, by NEST, 2015

could also help to facilitate ways in which designers can contribute their time to the greater good, outside of/within the framework of day-to-day design and business practice. The successful creation of the Sustainable Apparel Coalition, which brought together competing organizations such as Nike, Puma and Adidas from 60 organizations from across the fashion, textiles and apparel value chain, is proof that this type of approach has great potential. Its vision is for 'an apparel, footwear and home textiles industry that produces no unnecessary environmental harm and has a positive impact on the people and communities associated with its activities' (Sustainable Apparel Coalition, 2015). If they can do it, why can't the product design industry?

Conclusions

The challenges facing our society today, coupled with design's potential to address them, suggest that product and industrial designers should be providing more solutions which contribute positively to the greater needs of society. However, it is clear that this is not a simple or straightforward goal given its apparent conflict with current commercial objectives, and the myriad of complex factors surrounding them. At present, designers and researchers are struggling to resolve these challenges and find an effective way to incorporate them into their role. Although we have some understanding regarding the types of information provision that designers need, more work is needed to support this both in what is provided and how to distribute and potentially share this information. There is also a need for more case studies which celebrate progress and are less militant in what they determine to be good practice. The Red Dott awards already recognize the importance of environmental criteria such as durability and ecological compatibility (associated with materials and manufacturing intensity, energy consumption, disposal and recycling) and social issues such as what a product offers beyond its immediate practical purpose, specifically noting 'emotional attachment' and product longevity as a positive criteria (Red Dott Award: Product, 2015). It is positive to see these criteria making up a third of the overall criteria alongside; degree of innovation, functionality, formal quality, ergonomics, product periphery and self-explanatory quality. Further developments might include recognition of circular thinking or addressing 'real needs' (ibid.).

To move forward in this field there is a real need to equip product designers with the knowledge, skills, interest, support and environment to create socially and environmentally responsible products, services and systems as part of their mainstream work. To do this, continuous education is critical. Currently, designers who have not been trained in sustainability have little opportunity, beyond conference and workshop attendance, to engage in professional development around sustainable design issues. They need to be trained holistically so that they are aware of the many facets and approaches that can be utilized under the banner of sustainable design, while also developing the confidence to utilize and apply them. There is plenty of expertise within our universities to provide this. Combined with better access to high quality, open, transparent case studies this should raise awareness of the benefits and opportunities that sustainable design thinking can bring to product innovation and give designers the confidence to persuade their clients of the benefits of taking a different approach. This would also create opportunities for well-informed graduates and ensure that their enthusiasm is capitalized on.

In an ideal world this additional training would be co-ordinated by a new professional body for design, as this would bring with it a raft of additional benefits. Not least of which would be the creation of a stronger community which would also offer the opportunity to build on the recognized desire to create good design and leverage change with respect to what constitutes good design. This type of community could also oversee a mechanism by which designers employed in the commercial arena could formally contribute a percentage of their time to working on solving 'wicked' problems as part of their professional role.

Notes

1 Stevenson's study (2013) consisted of two studies undertaken in the UK and Ireland. The first was an explorative workshop with 19 participants from academia and design practice. The second consisted of a series of semi-structured in-depth interviews with 31 participants, comprising 22 industrial design consultants; 4 leading academics in the research area and 5 design-related strategic consultants.
2 'When a company, government or other group promotes green-based environmental initiatives or images but actually operates in a way that is damaging to the environment or in an opposite manner to the goal of the announced initiatives. This can also include misleading customers about the environmental benefits of a product through misleading advertising and unsubstantiated claims' (Investopedia, 2015).

References

Bakker, C. (1995) *Environmental Information for Industrial Designers*, Delft University of Technology, Delft
Baynes, A. (2013) Energy: New Business Models, in *Sustainable Innovation 2013: Collaboration, Co-creation and New Business Models*, Centre for Sustainable Design, Surrey, retrieved from http://cfsd.org.uk/events/sustainable-innovation-2013
Berman, D. (2008) *Do Good Design: How Designers can Change the World*, New Riders, Berkeley, CA
Bhamra, T. and Lofthouse, V. (2007) *Design for Sustainability: A Practical Approach*, Gower, Aldershot
Bhamra, T., Evans, S., Simon, M., McAloone, T., Poole, S. and Sweatman, A. (1999) Integrating Environmental Decisions into the Product Development Process: Part 1 The Early Stages, in *EcoDesign '99: First Symposium on Environmentally Conscious Design and Inverse Manufacturing*, IEEE, Tokyo
Brezet, H. (1997) Dynamics in ecodesign practice, *UNEP IE: Industry and Environment*, vol 20, no 1–2 (January–June), pp 21–24
Brezet, H. and van Hemel, C. (1997). *Ecodesign: A Promising Approach to Sustainable Production and Consumption*, UNEP, Paris
Buchanan, R. (1992) Wicked Problems in Design Thinking, *Design Issues*, vol 8, no 2, pp5–21
Chapman, J. (2015) *Emotionally Durable Design: Objects, Experiences and Empathy*, Routledge, Abingdon
Cooper, R. (2005) Ethics and Altruism : What Constitutes Socially Responsible Design? *Design Management Review*, vol 16, no 3, pp10–18
Department of Energy and Climate Change (2014) *Digest of UK Energy Statistics (DUKES)*, Department of Energy and Climate Change, London
Design Council (2010) *Design Industry Research 2010*, Design Council, London
Ellen MacArthur Foundation (2015) Braiform, retrieved from www.ellenmacarthurfoundation.org/case_studies/braiform (accessed 10 December 2015)
Escobar-Tello, M. C. (2015) A New Design Framework to Build Sustainable Societies: Using Happiness as Leverage, *Design Journal*, vol 19, no 1, pp93-115
Friedman, T. L. (2005) Global is Good, *The Guardian*, 21 April, pp17–19
Fuad-Luke, A. (2009) *Design Activism: Beautiful Strangeness for a Sustainable World*, Earthscan, London
Gander, P. (2007) Refill and Reuse to Reduce Costs, *Packaging News*, 1 September, p69
Gittleson, K. (2013) Ten Things You Didn't Know about Black Friday, *BBC News*, retrieved from www.bbc.co.uk/news/business-25110953
Herat, S. (2007) Sustainable Management of Electronic Waste (e-Waste), *CLEAN – Soil, Air, Water*, vol 35, no 4, pp305–310
Herman Miller (2016) Environmental Product Summary – Mirra 2 Chair, retrieved from www.hermanmiller.com/content/dam/hermanmiller/documents/environmental/eps/EPS_MIR2.pdf
Hiut Denim (2015) No Wash Club, retrieved from http://hiutdenim.co.uk/pages/the-no-wash-club
Investopedia (2015) Greenwashing, retrieved from www.investopedia.com/terms/g/greenwashing.asp

Kearins, K. and Klÿn, B. (1999) The Body Shop International plc, in M. Charter and M. J. Polonsky (eds), *Greener Marketing: A Global Perspective on Greening Marketing Practice*, Greenleaf Publishing, Sheffield

Kolko, J. (2012) *Wicked Problems: Problems Worth Solving – A Handbook and A Call to Action*, Austin Centre for Design, Austin, TX

Koninklijke Philips Electronics (2002) Healthy people, sustainable planet, retrieved from www.philips.com/a-w/about/sustainability.html

Lilley, D. (2009) Design for sustainable behaviour: strategies and perceptions, *Design Studies*, vol 30, no 6, pp704–720

Lilley, D. and Lofthouse, V. (2009) Sustainable design education – considering design for behavioural change, *Engineering Education: Journal of the Higher Education Academy Engineering Subject Centre*, vol 4, no 1, pp29–41

Lofthouse, V. (2001a) *Facilitating Ecodesign in an Industrial Design Context: An Exploratory Study*, Cranfield University, Cranfield

Lofthouse, V. (2001b) *Information/Inspiration*, Cranfield University, Cranfield

Lofthouse, V. (2004) Investigation into the Role of Core Industrial Designers in Ecodesign Projects, *Design Studies*, vol 25, no 2, pp215–227

Lofthouse, V. (2006) Ecodesign Tools for Designers: Defining the Requirements, *Journal of Cleaner Production*, vol 14, no 15–16, pp1386–1395

Lofthouse, V. (2009) Ecodesign Tools in Design Education, in *International Conference on Engineering and Product Design Education*, University of Brighton, Brighton, pp384–389

Lofthouse, V. (2013) Social Issues: Making Them Relevant and Appropriate to Undergraduate Student Designers, *Design and Technology Education: an International Journal*, vol 18, no 2, pp8–23

Lofthouse, V. and Bhamra, T. (2000) Benchmarking to Understand Appropriate Communication of Ecodesign – A Collaborative Project, in *Design Research International Symposium on the Dimensions of Industrial Design Research*, Milan, pp397–403

Lofthouse, V., Manley, A. and Shayler, M. (2015) Carbon Footprinting for Design Education, in *Learn X Design: The 3rd International Conference for Design Education Researchers*, Chicago, IL, pp774–789

Made in Mind (2015) The Mu:: Folding Plug, retrieved from www.madeinmind.co.uk/the-mu-folding-plug

Moreno, M., Lofthouse, V. and Lilley, D. (2014) Presenting the Sustainable Consumption Leveraging Model: Adding Value to Business Strategy through User-Centered Design Principles, in *19th DMI: Academic Design Management Conference, Design Management in an Era of Disruption*, Design Management Institute, London, 2–4 September, 2014

NEST (2015) Nest Thermostat, retrieved from https://nest.com/uk/thermostat/meet-nest-thermostat/

Nussbaum, B. (2007) Are Designers the Enemy of Design? *Business Week*, 18 March, retrieved from http://businessweek.com/innovate/NussbaumOnDesign/archives/2007/03/are_designers_the_enemy_of_design--_the_reaction.html.

Papanek, V. (1971) *Design for the Real World : Human Ecology and Social Change*, Pantheon Books, New York.

Philips Design (2015) Senseo Up Coffee Maker, retrieved from www.90yearsofdesign.philips.com/article/6

PRé Consultants (1999) Eco Indicator 99, retrieved from www.pre.nl/eco-indicator99/eco-indicator_99_introduction.htm

Red Dott Award: Product (2015) Red Dott Award: Adjudication Criteria, Retrieved from http://red-dot.de/pd/jury-2015/adjudication-criteria/?lang=en

Sherwin, C. (2000) *Innovative Ecodesign – An Exploratory and Descriptive Study of Industrial Design Practice*, Cranfield University, Cranfield

Sherwin, C. (2004) Design and Sustainability, *The Journal of Sustainable Product Design*, vol 4, no 1–4, pp21–31

Sherwin, C. (2012a) Sustainable Product Design – in Pictures, *The Guardian*, 17 September, retrieved from www.theguardian.com/sustainable-business/gallery/sustainable-product-design-in-pictures

Sherwin, C. (2012b) Embedding Sustainability in All Design, *The Guardian*, 1 October, retrieved from www.theguardian.com/sustainable-business/blog/embedding-sustainability-design-future

Short, T., Lee-Mortimer, A., Luttropp, C. and Johansson, G. (2012) Manufacturing, Sustainability, Eco Design and Risk: Lessons Learned from a Study of Swedish and English Companies, *Journal of Cleaner Production*, vol 37, pp342–352

Simon, M., Evans, S., McAloone, T., Sweatman, A., Bhamra, T. and Poole S. (1998) *Ecodesign Navigator: A Key Resource in the Drive towards Environmentally Efficient Product Design*, Manchester Metropolitan University and Cranfield University, Cranfield

Sparke, P. (1987) *Design in Context*, Bloomsbury, London

Stevenson, N. (2013) A Better World By Design? An Investigation into Industrial Design Consultants Undertaking Responsible Design Within Their Commercial Remits, PhD thesis, Loughborough University, Loughborough

Stevenson, N., Lofthouse, V., Lilley, D. and Cheyne, A. (2011) Complexity and Community: The Relevance of the Design Community for Responsible Design Implementation by Consultant Industrial Designers, in *IDSA International Conference*, New Orleans, LA, 14–17 September

Sustainable Apparel Coalition (2015) Transforming the apparel, footwear, and home textiles industry through: system-wide collaboration, retrieved from http://apparelcoalition.org

Thackara, J. (2007) Foreword, in J. Chapman and N. Gant (eds), *Designers, Visionaries and Other Stories : A Collection of Sustainable Design Essays*, Earthscan, London, ppxvi–xviii

Tischner, U. (2001) Tools for Ecodesign and Sustainable Product Design, in M. Charter and U. Tischner (eds), *Sustainable Solutions: Developing Products and Services for the Future*, Greenleaf Publishing, Sheffield, pp263–281

Wahl, D. C. and Baxter, S. (2008) The Designer's Role in Facilitating Sustainable Solutions, *Design Issues*, vol 24, no 2, pp72–83

Walker, S. (2006) *Sustainable by Design: Explorations in Theory and Practice*, Earthscan, London

Whiteley, N. (1993) *Design For Society*, Reaktion, London

Wilson, G. T., Bridgens, B., Hobson, K., Lee, J., Lilley, D., Scott, J. L. and Suckling, J. (2015) Single Product, Multi-Lifetime Components: Challenges for Product-Service System Development, in *Product Lifetimes and the Environment (PLATE),* Nottingham Trent University, Nottingham, UK, 17–19 June

9

DESIGN FOR SUSTAINABLE BEHAVIOUR

Debra Lilley and Garrath T. Wilson

Abstract

The global impact of designed goods and the role designer's play in accelerating rapid, conspicuous consumption has long been recognized within the profession. As such, considerable effort has been directed towards reducing or mitigating negative environmental impacts caused by mass-manufacture and disposal through so called 'end of pipe' solutions. Less attention, however, has been placed on reducing the impact of use despite tacit acknowledgement among the design community that sustainable designs cannot reach their full potential without targeting user behaviour. Through increased focus on behaviour, and the implementation of suitably informative or persuasive strategies, designers can purposefully alter the way users interact with products to leverage more sustainable use patterns. This chapter provides design practitioners with an introduction to Design for Sustainable Behaviour (DfSB). This is an emergent field of design practice which seeks to understand user behaviour in order to drive the development of products which encourage more sustainable use. Integrating inspirational case study examples drawn from their own and others' practice, the authors chart the origins of DfSB and describe its theories, strategies and design processes. Tools to aid strategy selection are introduced and key ethical considerations reflected on in relation to specific design phases. The authors offer practical advice on designing, installing and evaluating design interventions based on experience and conclude with a discussion of the current limitations and potential future developments in DfSB.

Keywords: sustainable behaviour, user centred design, design strategies

Introduction

In its broadest sense, this chapter is about how we, as design practitioners, can influence or control the behaviour of an individual, and by extension, society, in order to realize a more sustainable world. It is about the design processes, the psychological theories and user-centred design methods that enable us to understand, target, intervene and evaluate our way to a viable and sustainable behaviour change solution while also considering and reflecting upon the ethical issues and debates that surround what some may consider to be a provocative field of design intent and application. Given the complexity of the designer's task and the potentially volatile nature of its output if improperly executed, this chapter has been structured to enable those new to the field to get to grips comfortably with the key themes and arguments, illuminated with examples. This chapter will, in effect, act as a beginner's guide for designer practitioners when undertaking a project that concerns what is termed *Design for Sustainable Behaviour.*

Design for Sustainable Behaviour (DfSB) is an evolving field of design research and practice which sits within the broader context of sustainable design (Wever, 2012; Bhamra and Lilley, 2015). It is concerned with the application of behavioural theory to understand users, and behaviour changing strategies to design products, services and systems that encourage more sustainable use. Since its conception in the mid-2000s (Rodriguez and Boks, 2005; Lilley et al., 2006) a small yet dedicated community of scholars have contributed to the advancement of theories, strategies and design processes for DfSB. However, although there is a lively degree of debate concerning the nuances within DfSB, actively encouraged given the relative immaturity of the field, there is an emerging consensus on what constitutes a DfSB design process. The DfSB design process typically follows a sequence of five phases:

- the forming of an *understanding* of the user's actions in context;
- the informed selection of a behavioural *target*;
- the selection of a single or multiple corresponding behavioural intervention *strategy(ies)*;
- the *production* of appropriate behavioural intervention design solutions; and
- the *evaluating* of the behavioural intervention against the specified target behaviour.

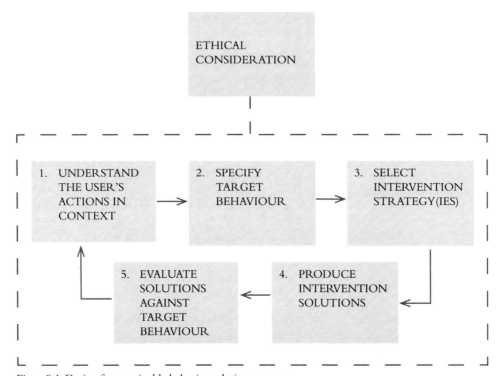

Figure 9.1 Design for sustainable behaviour design process

As depicted in Figure 9.1, though not explicitly a phase in its own right, consideration should be given, throughout the design process, to potential ethical issues which may arise in relation to data collection, the selection of target behaviours and strategies and the resulting behaviour created through the intervention designed (Lilley and Wilson, 2013).

The following sections unpack each of the phases illustrated in Figure 9.1 in more detail to form a comprehensive guide.

Understanding users in context

Deeper understanding of user's intentions and resulting behaviours is crucial as it enables the designer to challenge and affect habit formation (Wilson et al., 2015) – often considered to be at the root of routinized resource consumption. Through increased focus on behaviour, designers can alter the way users interact with products to leverage more sustainable use patterns by shaping individual's perception, learning, and interaction (Tang and Bhamra, 2009). In order to achieve the goal of influencing a change in behaviour towards more sustainable action, it is critical to not only understand the *consequences* of action but, what is also required, is an understanding of the internal and external factors that *influence* user action. On a broader scale, a deeper understanding of the *context* of use allows the facilitating and impeding conditions of infrastructure (such as physical affordances and constraints, as well as social norms, rules and laws) to be interrogated and potentially leveraged.

Models simplify the complexities of behaviours by giving them a tangible and comprehendible form (Darnton, 2008). By integrating and assimilating models from behavioural psychology into DfSB an opportunity is presented to explore and understand the multiple *facets* driving behaviour (Zachrisson Daae, 2014) through a simplified representation of extremely complex, and often quite individualistic, social and psychological structures (Chatterton, 2011). Thus, by disassembling and looking at the component parts of the behavioural construct, those seeking to modify behaviour through design can understand its underlying formation and antecedal structure, while also uncovering multiple points for intervention (Jackson, 2005; Chatterton, 2011). A psychological behavioural model, if we take the broad perspective that the focus is on the individual as the origin or *actor of behaviour*, is also considered to be a *rational decision making process* (rational in terms of being a process with known variables). Therefore, if we know the intentions, habits and facilitating conditions of the user and use context (the internal and external prompts), we can understand and attempt to anticipate what the user's intention to act would be and as a consequence, the resulting behaviours and impacts (Jackson, 2005; Chatterton, 2011). These knowable features are highly attractive to those seeking to influence behaviour towards more sustainable outcomes.

Products can be used in a myriad of different ways for different purposes (Albrechtslund, 2007), depending on the user's goals. A greater understanding of the user's behaviour within the context of use can enable the designer to anticipate multiple-use patterns and resulting actions (Routarinne and Redström, 2007).

By considering and attempting to anticipate the ways in which a technology may be unintentionally appropriated or inappropriately used by intended and unintended users, the designer can be considered to be acting in a reasonably ethical manner (Berdichevsky and Neuenschwander, 1999; Fogg, 2003).

Early research in DfSB sought to identify, appropriate and assimilate models of behaviour from social psychology with varying levels of maturity. Tang and Bhamra (2008), for example, integrated Triandis' Theory of Interpersonal Behaviour (Jackson, 2005) with Anderson's framework for the acquisition of cognitive skill (Anderson, 1982) to explore the formation of habits and the relationship between habitual strength of identified behaviours and DfSB strategies. More recently Hanratty (2015) explored the framing of behaviours in relation to hedonic, gain and normative *goals* through adopting behaviour framing theory (Lindenberg and Steg, 2007).

Ongoing theoretical development has resulted in a collection of models, each with their own literary basis, orientation and emphasis. Although publication dates suggest a linear creation, the development trajectory was not sequential but concurrent, thus limitations arising in one researcher's offering were often not wholly addressed and resolved in another's. As such, consensus on which influencing factors a comprehensive model for DfSB should incorporate has yet to be reached. A full discussion of each model cited in the current literature has, therefore, not been included in this chapter. The authors do, however, suggest that readers refer to referenced works for a more nuanced understanding of these models and their constituent factors.

	Habits	Beliefs	Attitude	Intention	Objective constraints	Subjective constraints	Social norms	Personal norms	Values
Interview		●	●	●		●	●	●	●
Focus group		●	●	●		●	●	●	●
Survey		●	●	●		●	●	●	●
Verbal protocol		●	●	●		●	●	●	●
Conjoint technique			●					●	●
Wants and needs analysis			●					●	●
Card sorting		●							
Group task analysis		●							
Probes		●	●	●		●	●	●	●
Observation					●				
Studying documentation							●		
Video ethnography					●				
Shadowing					●				
User testing					●				
Empathic design					●				
Cultural focussed research							●		
Applied ethnography	●	●	●	●	●	●	●	●	●
Contextual enquiry	●	●	●	●	●	●	●	●	●

Figure 9.2 Matching methods with factors

Source: adapted from Zachrisson Daae (2014)

In order to investigate the driving factors illustrated in such behavioural models in practice, designers typically employ a combination of user-centred design (UCD) methods (see for example Tang, 2010; Elias, 2011). For the designer, Zachrisson Daae's classification of which UCD techniques to apply in order to access which behavioural determinants (depicted in Figure 9.2) provides a valuable overview to inform the selection of suitable methods. Using this matrix it is possible to effectively combine methods to target more than one behavioural determinant, thus maximizing the return on investment in user research.

Having reached an understanding of user behaviour in context, designers must then select, and justify the selection, of the behaviour or behaviours they intend to change as well as a single or multiple corresponding behavioural intervention strategy(ies).

Design for sustainable behaviour strategies

Considerable attention has been given in recent years to expanding and refining the classification and categorization of design for sustainable behaviour design strategies (e.g. Wever et al., 2008; Lilley, 2009; Elias, 2011; Lidman et al., 2011b; Tang and Bhamra, 2011; Lockton and Harrison, 2012; Zachrisson and Boks, 2012). Boks et al.'s survey of the DfSB research community (Boks et al., 2015) however, suggests that Zachrisson and Boks (2012) taxonomy, depicted in Figure 9.3, is most commonly used as their main reference. Regardless of nomenclature, what is consistent across all classifications is the presence of an *axis of influence*, a spectrum or continuum that illustrates control or power in decision-making, with the user or individual at one end and the product or designer diametrically positioned at the other (Lilley, 2007, 2009).

Towards the user agentive end of this scale, are *information* and *feedback* strategies. Feedback is a method by which a product employs an overt visual, tactile or aural indicator in order to inform the user as to their actions. Due to its non-coercive, educational approach, feedback is considered to be a guide to change, enabling control of decision making to reside with the user and their individual interpretation of the feedback offered (Lilley, 2009).

Home energy management systems (HEMS) are a type of intervention that can provide instantaneous feedback on domestic energy consumption back to the user. Typically attached to the main electricity circuit of a home, information is presented via a small, portable electronic device with a numerical display. Common metrics displayed include energy (kWh consumed), environmental (CO_2 produced), or economic impact (£ spent). By providing a performance indicator on the consequences of behaviour, the cognitive connection between action and effect can be strengthened, reflected and acted upon. An effective feedback mechanism should provide information rapidly and be tailored to the user's knowledge and value structures (Van Dam, 2013; Wilson et al., 2015).

In the centre of this proposed axis are *persuading* and *behaviour-steering* strategies (Lilley, 2009; Zachrisson et al., 2011), approaches based on Jelsma and Knot's (2002) definition of scripts but expanded to include Norman's (1988) notion of affordance; concerning the way in which a designer uses the physical or semantic characteristics of a product to prescribe a desired behaviour. By consciously scripting a product through the use of affordances (explicit potential actions), and constraints (explicit potential limitations), a designer can control the user's interaction without forcing action (Jelsma and Knot, 2002).

Most day-to-day products have affordances and scripts built into them as cognitive shortcuts, primarily in order for the user to be able to understand how to use them without having to go through a new, and often quite fatiguing or annoying learning process every time. Based on a socially accumulated visual language, typical examples include the push

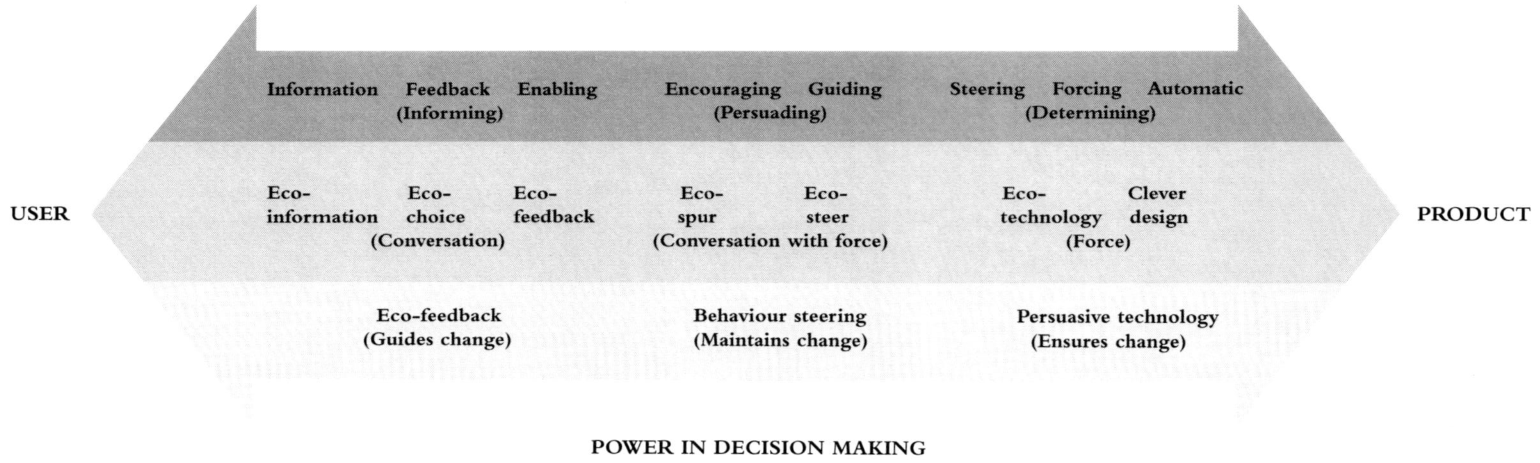

PRODUCT

USER

Information Feedback Enabling Encouraging Guiding Steering Forcing Automatic
(Informing) (Persuading) (Determining)

Eco-information choice (Conversation)

Eco-feedback

Eco-spur (Conversation with force)

Eco-steer

Eco-technology

Clever design (Force)

Eco-feedback (Guides change)

Behaviour steering (Maintains change)

Persuasive technology (Ensures change)

POWER IN DECISION MAKING

Figure 9.3 Axis of influence

Sources: Lilley (2009); Tang and Bhamra (2011); Zachrisson and Boks (2012)

plates and pull bars on a door for opening (depending upon what side of the door you are on), and the handle and spout of a jug or teapot for lifting and pouring (Norman, 1988). An example of a product with intentional scripting to shape behaviour is the Eco Kettle by Brian Hartley which prevents the user from initially filling the heated reservoir, instead filling a secondary reservoir that then requires a conscious pushing of a plunger-like button to measure the quantity of water that the user actually wants to boil.

At the opposite end of the scale from user agentive informing strategies are forcing and determining strategies such as persuasive technology. Persuasive technology, as defined by Lilley (2009), includes Fogg's (2003) theory of captology (a synthesis of computer products and persuasive techniques) however differs by definition through the inclusion of coercive strategies to ensure change, such as intelligent context aware technologies and ubiquitous computing which negate the user's decision making processes (Lilley, 2007, 2009).

Speed bumps that force you to slow down when driving too fast, windows in an office building that open automatically on a hot day to regulate the temperature within, or Nest's smart smoke detector, Protect, that tests itself automatically, are just a few examples of products that use technology to achieve a prescribed consequence, often without the user's explicit agreement or knowledge. If This Then That (IFTTT) technology is one way by which users have started to take control of the automated process and have input, not at the point of action, but at an earlier point in time on their own terms. For example, IFTTT logic can be used to create user codes or 'recipes' such as if my wearable fitness band detects I have awoken, then turn on the socket that controls the space heating (Wilson et al., 2014).

As DfSB research has matured, the division between where strategies fall has been removed to present a fluid spectrum rather than an absolute categorization (Zachrisson et al., 2011). Where a strategy fits within this axis is determined both by the actual and perceived influence of the intervention (Tromp et al., 2011). Devising reliable, defensible and practical methods to inform the selection of which behaviours to target and which corresponding strategy to use, however, has proven more challenging.

Targeting behaviours and strategy selection

If the overall aim of DfSB is to achieve more sustainable actions by users, a key concern when selecting a behavioural target is what constitutes sustainable behaviour? Whereas *environmental behaviour* is considered to result in the least harm to the environment as possible (Steg and Vlek, 2009) and *pro-ecological behaviors* are 'purposeful and effective actions that result in the conservation of natural resources' (Tapia-Fonllem et al., 2013, p712), *sustainable behaviour* presents an expanded scope encompassing both 'actions aimed at protecting both the natural and the human (social) environments' (ibid.). Different behaviours enacted by different users in different contexts, however, result in differing levels of environmental and social impact, both positive and negative. Should, therefore, behaviours be selected on the basis of the severity of their environmental and social impact? And if so, how are such impacts to be measured? And by whom? Whereas arguably key environmental priorities, such CO_2 reduction, remain constant targets (aided by legislative demands), social norms are constantly shifting and what is socially unacceptable behaviour within the public realm today may well become the 'norm' in the future (take for example mobile phone use in public; Lilley, 2007). Is the use of a more forceful intervention warranted if the potential consequences of the target behaviour are considered severely detrimental to society or the environment? Or should free will prevail in all circumstances? These questions are largely rhetorical and, as with many ethical dilemmas, have no definitive answers. It is important, however, to raise them within the designer's mind to ensure the behavioural target is well-chosen and justifiable, and furthermore, that the designer's motivation and intent is reflected upon and scrutinized.

In addition to the somewhat muddied waters of selecting a behavioural target, designers must also carefully consider how to select an appropriate strategy or strategies. Applying a strategy that is too forceful may be met with resistance and rejection (Brey, 2006); conversely, for a more passive strategy such as information provision to be effective the user must be sufficiently motivated to act upon the information and be willing to change (Zachrisson Daae, 2014). Forcing and determining strategies that fall within the remit of ubiquitous technology have a tremendous potential to affect sustainable behaviour. By removing the user from the decision making process an intelligent system could, based on sustainability variables, optimize and automate processes to ensure that the most sustainable action is taken; a fine balancing act between democracy/technocracy and long term sustainable goals. It is important to consider though that removing the user from the decision making process allows 'unsustainable' user actions to be negated, this also separates the user from developing an understanding of the fundamental relationships between cause and effect, potentially leading to further rebound effects and unsustainable consequences. The learning and adapting of one's behaviour in response to feedback is not an option in this more hands-off scenario.

Additionally, the value of the intervention to the user must be considered and weighed against the lack of freedom and choice. For example, an intervention that automated a process and saved the user time and money, such as a smart home thermostat, may be perceived as being more acceptable than an intervention that automatically optimized the office environment, such as automated windows. Hence, the value proposition of the intervention must be considered as well as the boundaries of what the user finds acceptable.

Zachrisson et al.'s (2011) work proposes a set of guidelines that may help the designer in the selection of an *effective* strategy solution, based upon the underlying construct of a psychological behavioural model. Concerned with habits, intentions and constraints, values and norms, and importance/annoyance, the notion is that the designer uses a series of simplified guiding statements and illustrated axis as a tool to help inform and direct the selection of an appropriate strategy. In an early example of the guidelines, under the title of 'Does the user want to behave the intended way?', there is the following guiding statement: 'The less the user wish to perform the intended behaviour, the more control should be given to the product. Pushing the user to do something he/she does not want to do might result in the user stop using the product', under which there are several axes including user in control versus product in control, with the accompanying statement of 'only users who agree with the intended behaviour may be willing to change their behaviour based on information or feedback' (Zachrisson et al., 2011, p366); suggesting that a strategy whereby the user was in control would be an appropriate strategy if the user was willing to change their behaviour. Later iterations of the tool have further streamlined the axes and its usability for designers, resulting in several so-called *Dimensions of Behaviour Change* of how the design strategies should be applied with illustrated examples; including *Meaning* (emotional–reason); *Exposure* (rarely–frequently); *Encouragement* (promote–discourage); *Timing* (before use–after use); *Empathy* (me–others); *Obtrusiveness* (obtrusive–unobtrusive); *Importance* (important–unimportant); and *Direction* (in line–opposing) (Zachrisson Daae, 2014; Zachrisson Daae and Boks, 2014). Though the suitability of the parameters of the chosen axes are open to debate, Zachrisson et al.'s tool provides a valuable aid to strategy selection allowing the designer to give consideration to the appropriateness of a given strategy.

Hanratty's 'Behaviour Intervention Selection Axis' or *BISA* offers an alternative tool for strategy selection based on an understanding of the user's thought processes and associated actions in context (in this case energy consuming behaviours in the home) and their relative level of situationality or reflectiveness (Hanratty, 2015). According to the *BISA* "the more situational behaviour is the more it is driven by context and situation, with perhaps very little mindfulness or cognition from the individual" (ibid, p. 104), the intervention, therefore, should direct the behaviour through employing determining strategies. In a similar vein to Zachrisson et al. (2011), Hanratty also advocates that a requisite level of obtrusiveness (e.g. how much an intervention pushes itself forward into the users sphere of interaction) be applied to support the chosen strategy in order to disrupt and intervene in users routinized thought processes, particularly when dealing with highly situational behaviours (Figure 9.4).

A worked example of the application of the *BISA* can be found in Hanratty (2015) alongside a more detailed explanation of its origin and development. When considering the selection of target behaviours, using either model, it is worth considering if the behaviour itself needs changing at all, or if indeed the *delivered* product functionality is mismatched with the *desired* functionality of the user. For further discussion on this approach to product rather than behavioural adoption, please refer to Wever et al. (2008), Lidman et al. (2011a, 2011b) and Lidman and Renström (2011).

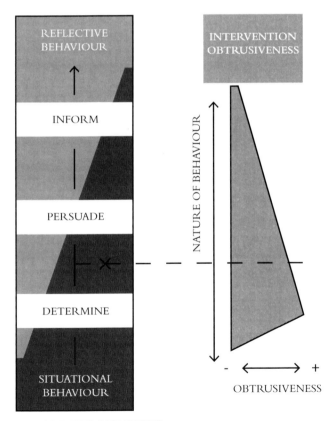

X = TARGETED BEHAVIOUR

Figure 9.4 Required intervention obtrusiveness

Source: Hanratty (2015)

Production of appropriate behavioural intervention design solutions

The development of behaviour changing products has seen considerable growth with a proliferation of designs incorporating behaviour-changing strategies coming to the market in recent years (as described in the numerous examples provided in this chapter). Yet many of these designs have been created independently of the DfSB community and, as a consequence, lack transparency in terms of their process and theoretical underpinning. Those created by DfSB practitioners, such as the shower concept *Enuf* (Hanratty, 2015), have been realized to prototype stage through implementation of a user-centred design process, yet their production has been limited in number and their *real-world* evaluation by users in context limited in length and scope. The value of these studies, however, lies in their exemplification of the application of process and strategy.

The *Enuf* Shower concept (ibid.) was predicated on an understanding of showering practices gleaned from video tours of 11 householders bathroom practices in which family members recounted their routines in context. The analysis of the data identified behavioural drivers such as hygiene, pleasure, waking-up and daydreaming, as well as uncovering relationships between users attitude towards showering (maximizing efficiency) and the duration of the showering activity in relation to the participants age, with younger people tending to shower for longer. Wasteful behaviours such as allowing the water to heat up before stepping under the flow were also observed. With reference to the *BISA* (outlined above), Hanratty determined two key goal frames for the observed showering behaviour; normative goal frames relating to perceived social standards of hygiene was seen to drive the frequency of showering. The duration of the shower, however, was driven by a hedonic goal frame (e.g. comfort, pleasure and privacy) as well as, for those wishing to minimize the amount of time they spent showering to maximize productive time spent on other tasks, the gain goal frame. This analysis led Hanratty to frame showering as deeply situational, an activity performed on a daily basis without conscious deliberation of wasteful behaviours, therefore, the intervention designed needed to 'refocus the participants' reflective attention on the task of cleaning themselves efficiently' (ibid., p. 146) and as such, the level of obtrusiveness required was high. *Enuf* 'is an automatic persuasive shower monitoring device' which uses feedback and behavioural prompts to encourage users to reduce showering times (ibid., p. 148). Through iterative development and pilot testing, *Enuf* was refined to eradicate operational flaws and optimize usability culminating in a 6-week user trial within 6 multi-occupancy households in the UK. To allow a direct comparison of pre and post-installation, baseline data on user behaviour was collected for a 3–4 week period, during which the device remained 'dumb'. The interactive features were then activated. A post-installation evaluation was conducted to assess *Enuf's* effectiveness based on the 3 questions outlined in the Evaluation section below. The trial indicated that the use of *Enuf* did indeed result in reduced showering times.

The experiences of the authors, as well as those of the wider DfSB community, have led to the identification of several practical considerations to account for when designing a behavioural intervention. These are discussed below.

The value of following the entire DfSB process cannot be underestimated. It is acknowledged, however, that although students may have the opportunity (and indeed time) to engage in all phases, practitioners, on the other hand, may have a more defined, bounded role in the product development process in which contribution is limited to one or two particular phases.

Of further benefit is the inclusion of multidisciplinary perspectives in a project team, as the combination of knowledge and skills these subject-areas bring can prove invaluable in the design and implementation of behaviour-changing devices. Within the Low Effort Energy Demand Reduction (LEEDR) project (Wilson et al., 2014), for example, social scientists, engineers and product designers worked collaboratively to develop and test digital design interventions to reduce energy consumption in the private housing sector.

At each stage of the design process, lessons learnt in prior research can be applied to increase the potential for achieving a successful design outcome. When entering the user research phase, for example, consideration should be given to the sample size. Traditionally user-centred studies utilizing qualitative methods tend to favour depth over breadth, resulting in a deep understanding of a specific cohort rather than a statistically significant survey of a larger populous. The value of this rich data should not be undervalued, however, as from the specific, broader conclusions can be extrapolated and tested with a larger, more representative sample; thereby adding to the applicability, validity and reliability of the data. One must also consider who the primary evaluative target user will be, while also taking into account the influence of other occupants. Within the Carbon, Control and Comfort research project (Wilson, 2013), for example, a household within Merthyr Tydfil, Wales was occupied by a mother and daughter who each expressed different levels of acceptability in terms of thermal comfort. Their relative need for warmth resulted in one occupant (the mother) reducing local room temperature via a thermostatic radiator valve while another occupant (the daughter) raised the overall household temperature via the central thermostat in the hall.

Although there may be a temptation to use labour-saving methods, such as existing studies, tools or resources, the use of these in isolation is not recommended. User research can certainly be time-consuming; however, its value in aiding deep comprehension of behaviour in context and building empathy with users is unparalleled. Tools to aid strategy selection and ideation for DfSB can prove useful inspiration for ideation but they are not a substitution for actual user research. Similarly, drawing on user data generated by others, through practical and potentially time-saving, can prove problematic unless the approach is standardized to enable sharing.

There are several design tools that could aid the designer in designing an appropriate solution, including the Fogg Behavior Grid (Fogg and Hreha, 2010); the Design with Intent toolkit (Lockton et al., 2010); the Dimensions of Behaviour Change tool (Zachrisson Daae and Boks, 2014); Lilley and Lofthouse's weighted ethical matrix (2010); and the Design Behaviour website (www.design-behaviour.co.uk). Such tools may be appropriate for facilitating discussion, debate and reflection on the pertinent issues within a design team but it is important to remember that these tools and toolkits are not to be used prescriptively, or as a substitute for understanding the user's behaviour or evaluating an intervention in a real-world context.

Throughout the design development process, the researcher/designer should be cognizant of the fact that they, themselves are an intervention. Without active mindfulness, potential bias may be inflicted through the design choices made, through interaction with users and via the evaluative process. Though objectivity is challenging to maintain when dealing with an artistic endeavour, care should be taken to avoid undue influence. The framing of the initial approach to users, for example, needs to be scrutinized to ensure materials do not lead participants towards a particular behavioural outcome or instigate a premature change in behaviour in response to external prompts. For example, framing the introduction of an intervention intended to reduce energy consumption in explicit terms may trigger other energy-saving behaviours to be enacted. Similarly, the mere presence of the researcher may result in participants consciously or subconsciously altering their behaviour due to their awareness of being observed, a phenomenon known as the *Hawthorne effect* (Roethlisberger and Dickson, 1939). Allowing participants to acclimatize to the device in-situ for a period of time before activating any interactive behaviour-changing features may, however, ameliorate these effects (Hanratty, 2015).

The selection of a strategy or strategies, and the level of persuasion they impose, as discussed previously, should be approached cautiously. The potential for failure in adoption of desired behaviours or possible rebound effects or *game-playing* (escalation of impact as opposed to reduction to *beat* the device) is a distinct reality if the strategy chosen is too forceful or controlling. A weak strategy employed to combat ingrained, habitual behaviours within an obstinate user unwilling to change, however, is unlikely to be effective or sustained. A user's willingness to change can be informed by the *fit* between the behaviour the designer intends to create and previously practiced behaviours (Cialdini, 2001). Yet willingness alone is not sufficient, the circumstances to enable change to happen must also be aligned. Impediments to change are not only structural, such as access to recycling facilities, but also temporal, such as the day of collection. In a study investigating user perceptions towards retrofitting of energy-saving measures within domestic environments, for example, the occupant's stage of life was found to forestall or even prevent home improvements (Mallaband et al., 2013). These life stages, which spanned the birth of a child to the advent of old age, were seen by some as obstructions, yet potentially these and other life changes could signal an opportunity to leverage change by providing the motivation in which to act. Understanding the most *opportune moments* to intervene to ensure successful adoption of new behaviours, therefore, is also a key concern. Within academic research projects the intervention installation period is often determined by project time scales, and may not necessarily constitute the optimum time from the user/behaviour perspective. Though not explicitly explored within DfSB research at present, the integration of theory concerning a user's susceptibility to embrace change, such as the Transtheoretical Model (Prochaska and DiClemente, 2005), may prove beneficial in informing the point of intervention.

The evaluative phase is, in practice, preceded by the installation of the designed device into the context of use. First and foremost, it is necessary to decide upon the length of the testing period as this will determine other practical design features; such as the power supply, participant compensation and data monitoring plan (if consumption data is to be gathered). Having identified the period of testing, the researcher should take steps to ensure the device will function for the full duration of product testing; this may include the choice of power supply (e.g. batteries functional lifespan). They should also try, where possible, to reduce contamination of user evaluation by limiting any discussion or explanation when servicing the device in situ (Hanratty, 2015). While installed, ethical and health and safety issues which may arise; for example, does the intervention draw on the household or workplace energy supply to function? And if so, have participants been duly compensated for any costs they may incur?

All of these issues have the potential to hinder the successful execution of a DfSB intervention; however, with due attention and scrutiny none are insurmountable.

Evaluation

The final stage of the DfSB process is evaluation, yet, surprisingly, this phase has received relatively little attention by scholars. Given the nascent state of Design for Sustainable Behaviour and the lack of longitudinal case studies, especially those that follow through the DfSB design process in its entirety, it is not surprising that there is no one single model or categorization of intervention strategies to which all those practising under this banner subscribe. DfSB is still evolving and many debates are still to be had; that is a good thing. Yet, the lack of a unified framework by which to assess the effectiveness of different strategies in achieving sustained behaviour change has proven to be a hindrance in proving their worth. What is needed to progress the field, and arguably, propel these strategies further into commercial application, is a reliable method of evaluation which demonstrates tangible sustainability improvement. The evaluation of a DfSB intervention can be disaggregated into three core components; an evaluation of the *usability and function* of the designed intervention itself (questions dependent upon the DfSB strategy); an evaluation of the *ecological*, *social* and *economic impact* of the intervention (questions dependent upon the intervention context); and an evaluation of the resulting change in *user behaviour* due to intervention (questions applicable to all DfSB strategies) (Wilson et al., 2013, 2015).

By disaggregating and formalizing the evaluation questions, multiple entry points for analysis can individually or collectively be explored in order to iteratively feed back into the design process as well as for cross-study comparison. This approach gives a more three-dimensional account of the impact of an intervention and avoids the somewhat prevalent and very limited view of only categorizing a behaviour changing interventions success as a percentage reduction in a single sustainability metric (e.g. intervention x reduced energy consumption by y%). Such a limited account not only precludes any evaluation of the actual behaviour change mechanism itself, and by extension how it could be improved through the design process, but also makes the incorrect supposition that a change in behaviour equates directly to a change in, for example, consumption (which we know not to be true due to rebound effects).

Does the design intervention function for the specified context?

Is the usability of the design in line with the user's requirements and expectations, and do the design functions operate as the designer intended? Clearly different DfSB strategies have different criteria against which to assess usability and function and as such questions related to the design of the intervention, for example, how does the accuracy of the feedback information help the user to associate with their actions?, are clearly weighted towards feedback alone and are not applicable to other strategies. The overarching question is still valid: does the design intervention function for the specified context? However, if such specific sub-questions were to be applied to a different strategy then the sub-questions would need to be more appropriate to the intervention strategy and mechanisms employed. Feedback seeks to change behaviour through the provision of information and therefore the sub-questions required are related to this. If one was considering the evaluation of a persuasive or behaviour steering intervention then questions related to cognitive interaction expectations (such as design semiotics) and the use and performance of affordances and constraints (perhaps requiring a physical ergonomics assessment) would be required. Forcing and determining strategies that could entirely negate the user's interaction would perhaps need to be evaluated in terms of installation issues and the requirements of monitoring or maintaining the technology. In short, these sub-questions are dependent upon the strategy.

Is the change in the user's behaviour sustainable?

Through an understanding and measurement of the change in sustainability metrics, the success of a DfSB intervention can be put into perspective against the interventions function and ability to change the user's behaviour. While sustainability is commonly defined in terms of economic, environmental and social pillars (Bhamra and Lofthouse, 2007), each of these pillars are contextual. For example, an intervention may be concerned with reducing the amount of CO_2 (environment) generated from domestic energy consumption, while ensuring that comfort (social) is increased, and that financial burden (economy) is reduced. Interventions with different aims and contexts will require different project specific sustainability impact criteria.

Questions that evaluate the ethical impact of changing the user's behaviour and the ethics of the process itself are not tied to any strategy or context, and are applicable to all design interventions. However, it should be noted that ethical questions asked should not be moralistic, rather they are a proposition of considerations by the designer. They should not be solely reflective, but as a platform from which to integrate other relevant perspectives. Rather than stating that 'the motivations behind the creation of a persuasive technology should never be such that they would be deemed unethical if they led to a more traditional persuasion' (Berdichevsky and Neuenschwander, 1999, p52), it would perhaps be more logical to ask 'was the designer's original motivation for designing a behaviour intervention ethical?' This allows for a wider discussion with the user and other stakeholders without relying on the fragile premise of a universal moral framework. Instead, decisions can be made in reference to the moral frameworks of *relevance*.

Has the user's behaviour changed as a consequence of the design intervention?

The goal of DfSB is to create long-term sustainable behaviour change. Questions have to be asked of a DfSB interventions ability to change the *habitual behaviour* of the user, and therefore, in order to determine if the user's behaviour has changed due to the intervention. It is also necessary to understand the antecedents and the habitual strength of that behaviour targeted for change (i.e. the behavioural baseline).

As outlined previously, by taking a psychological approach, behaviour can be viewed as being a rational decision making process with the individual, or typically termed the user within a design context, being the central actor (Jackson, 2005; Chatterton, 2011). Others, such as Kuijer (2014) and Pettersen (2013) prefer conceptualizing human action in terms of social practice theory, but generally speaking, this is less ontologically aligned with current design practice. Given internal or external stimulus, within this rational process, habits (characterized by frequency of past behaviour and cognitive automaticity) have an overriding priority factor over intention (attitude, social factors and effect), with both intention and habits in turn both ruled by facilitating conditions (external constraining factors, such as situational context) (Bargh, 1994; Jackson, 2005; Verplanken, 2006; Chatterton, 2011). Based on this definition, evaluation questions must focus on changes in context, intentions and cognitive automaticity. For example:

- Did the facilitating conditions constrain or afford opportunities for change?
- Did the users perception of self-concept change?
- Did the user have difficulty in controlling the intended behaviour?

Although behaviour itself is dependent on the specific user and the specific context, the same questions need to be asked as the antecedents of behaviour are present within all action – habitual or not.

To effectively evaluate the impact of a designed intervention, qualitative and quantitative data on existing behaviour within the context of use (a baseline) and behaviour post-intervention is required. Establishing a *baseline* of existing behaviour in context allows any changes or improvements to behaviour derived from the intervention to be measured and quantified in relation to existing influences. This is vital if the efficacy of the intervention is to be demonstrated. Data may be captured through the use of qualitative research techniques, such as observation (Tang and Bhamra, 2012) or, quantitative measurement, such as the length of time a refrigerator door is open, or the number of products correctly disposed of (Elias et al., 2008a, 2008b; Wever et al., 2010). Or ideally, as in Hanratty (2015) – who conducted in-home ethnographic studies as well as capturing energy and water consumption data – a combination of both. In some cases, if considered within the conceptual phase, the device itself can be designed to enable baseline data to be accrued before activating any interactive features, as was the case with the Enuf (ibid.). Although the quantitative techniques lack the in-depth understanding of behaviour afforded through qualitative investigation (behaviour is not measured just by number of repetitions of action), both of these approaches offer different perspectives on how to assess the behaviour of the user and the relative impact of their actions.

Conclusions

This chapter has provided a guide to designing interventions for behaviour change towards sustainable actions for the product design practitioner. It has highlighted the importance of understanding user behaviour in context to appropriately target behaviours to change and provided models and tools to identify behavioural determinants. Two different tools to select behavioural change strategies have been introduced and guiding questions for evaluation of the resulting design outcome provided. The ethical considerations designers should take into account at each stage of the DfSB design process have been elucidated for reflection.

The field of DfSB is growing rapidly; however, there are notable gaps in knowledge which are yet to be addressed. Though strategies differ in their nomenclature, consensus has coalesced around the axis of influence. Furthermore, strategy selection has been strengthened through the development of the Dimensions of Behaviour Change tool and Behavioural Intervention Selection Axis. However, matching the relative severity or significance of the behaviour identified with the strength of an intervention has yet to be firmly established and further guidance is needed. The most obvious omission to the DfSB domain, however, is the lack of real-world application of its strategies and processes to establish their effectiveness in achieving sustained, sustainable behavioural change.

The pressing need to address social and environmental impacts resulting from product use is paramount. We, as design researchers and practitioners, have a unique opportunity to harness the power of design to positively, and ethically, influence user behaviour to create a more sustainable world. Using the tools, strategies and processes outlined in this chapter it is hoped that a new generation of practitioner designers will be inspired to engage in this new and exciting field, and in doing so, further support its evolution.

References

Albrechtslund, A. (2007) Ethics and Technology Design, *Ethics and Information Technology*, vol 9, no 1, pp63–72

Anderson, J. R. (1982) Acquisition of Cognitive Skill, *Psychological Review*, vol 89, pp369–406

Bargh, J. A. (1994) The Four Horsemen of Automaticity: Awareness, Efficiency, Intention, and Control in Social Cognition, in R. S. Wyer, J. and Srull, T. K. (eds), *Handbook of Social Cognition*, 2nd edn, Hillsdale, NJ: Erlbaum, pp1–40

Berdichevsky, D. and Neuenschwander, E. (1999) Toward an Ethics of Persuasive Technology, *Communications of the ACM*, vol 42, no 5, pp51–58

Bhamra, T. A. and Lilley, D. (2015) IJSE Special Issue: Design for Sustainable Behaviour, *International Journal of Sustainable Engineering*, vol 8, no 3, pp146–147

Bhamra, T. A. and Lofthouse, V. A. (2007) *Design for Sustainability A Practical Approach*, Gower Publishing, London

Boks, C., Lilley, D. and Pettersen, I. N. (2015) The Future of Design for Sustainable Behaviour, paper presented at EcoDesign 2015, 2–4 December, Tokyo, Japan

Brey, P. (2006) Ethical Aspects of Behavior Steering Technology, in Verbeek, P. P. and Slob, A. (eds), *User Behavior and Technology Development: Shaping Sustainable Relations Between Consumers and Technologies*, Kluwer, Dordrecht, pp357–364

Chatterton, T. (2011) *An Introduction to Thinking About 'Energy Behaviour': A Multi Model Approach*, Department for Energy and Climate Change, London

Cialdini, R. (2001) *Influence: Science and Practice*, Allyn & Bacon, Boston, MA

Darnton, A. (2008) *GSR Behaviour Change Knowledge Review: An Overview of Behaviour Change Models and their Uses*, Government Social Research Unit, London

Elias, E. W. A. (2011) User-efficient Design: Reducing the Environmental Impact of User Behaviour Through the Design of Products, Doctor of Philosophy thesis, University of Bath, Bath

Elias, E. W. A., Dekoninck, E. A. and Culley, S. J. (2008a) Assessing user behaviour for changes in the design of energy using domestic products, paper presented at 2008 IEEE International Symposium on Electronics and the Environment, 19–21 May, San Francisco, CA

Elias, E. W. A., Dekoninck, E. A. and Culley, S. J. (2008b) Prioritisation Methodology for the User-Centred Design of Energy Using Domestic Products, paper presented at International Design Conference – DESIGN 2008, 19–22 May, Dubrovnik, Croatia

Fogg, B. J. (2003) *Persuasive Technology: Using Computers to Change What We Think and Do (Interactive Technologies)*, Morgan Kaufmann, Burlington, MA

Fogg, B. J. and Hrera, J. (2010) Behavior Wizard: A Method for Matching Target Behaviors with Solutions, in *PERSUASIVE'10 Proceedings of the 5th International Conference on Persuasive Technology*, Copenhagen, Denmark, June 7–10, pp117–131

Hanratty, M. (2015) Design for Sustainable Behaviour: A Conceptual Model and Intervention Selection Model for Changing Behaviour Through Design, Doctor of Philosophy thesis, Loughborough University

Jackson, T. (2005) *Motivating Sustainable Consumption: A Review of Evidence on Consumer Behaviour and Behavioural Change, a Report to the Sustainable Development Research Network*, Centre for Environmental Strategy, University of Surrey, Guildford

Jelsma, J. and Knot, M. (2002) Designing environmentally efficient services: a 'script' approach, *The Journal of Sustainable Product Design*, vol 2, pp119–130

Kuijer, L. (2014). Implications of Social Practice Theory for Sustainable Design, Doctor of Philosophy thesis, TU Delft, Delft

Lidman, K. M. E. and Renström, S. E. (2011) How to Design for Sustainable Behaviour? – A Review of Design Strategies and an Empirical Study of Four Product Concepts, Chalmers University of Technology, Gothenburg

Lidman, K. M. E., Renström, S. E. and Karlsson, I. C. M. (2011a) The Green User: Design for Sustainable Behaviour, in Roozenburg, N. F. M., Chen, L. L. and Stappers, P. J. (eds), *Diversity and Unity, IASDR2011, The 4th World Conference on Design Research*, 31 October to 4 November, Delft, The Netherlands

Lidman, K. M. E., Renström, S. E. and Karlsson, I. C. M. (2011b) I Don't Want to Drown the Frog! A Comparison of Four Design Strategies to Reduce Overdosing of Detergents, paper presented at Conference on Sustainable Innovation 2011, Towards Sustainable Product Design, Farnham, UK

Lilley, D. (2007) Designing for Behavioural Change: Reducing the Social Impacts of Product Use Through Design, Doctor of Philosophy thesis, Loughborough University

Lilley, D. (2009) Design for Sustainable Behaviour: Strategies and Perceptions, *Design Studies*, vol 30, no 6, pp704–720

Lilley, D. and Lofthouse, V. A. (2010) Teaching Ethics For Design For Sustainable Behaviour: A Pilot Study, *Design and Technology Education: An International Journal*, vol 15, no 2

Lilley, D. and Wilson, G. T. (2013) Integrating Ethics into Design for Sustainable Behaviour, *Journal of Design Research*, vol 11, no 3, pp278–299

Lilley, D., Bhamra, T. A. and Lofthouse, V. A. (2006) Towards Sustainable Use: An Exploration of Designing for Behavioural Change, in *DeSForm 2006: European Workshop on Design and Semantics of Form and Movement*, Eindhoven, The Netherlands, pp84–96

Lindenberg, S. and Steg, L. (2007) Normative, Gain and Hedonic Goal Frames Guiding Environmental Behavior, *Journal of Social Issues*, vol. 63, no 1, pp117–137

Lockton, D. and Harrison, D. (2012) Models of the User: Designers' Perspectives on Influencing Sustainable Behaviour, *Journal of Design Research*, vol 10, no 1–2, pp7–27

Lockton, D., Harrison, D. and Stanton, N. (2010) The Design with Intent Method: A Design tool for Influencing User Behaviour, *Applied Ergonomics*, vol 41, no 3, pp382–392

Mallaband, B., Haines, V. and Mitchell, V. (2013) Barriers to domestic retrofit: learning from past home improvement experiences, in Swan, W. and Brown, P. (eds), *Retrofitting the Built Environment*, Wiley-Blackwell, Chichester

Norman, D. (1988) *The Psychology Of Everyday Things*, Basic Books, New York

Pettersen, I. N. (2013) The Role of Design in Supporting the Sustainability of Everyday Life, Doctor of Philosophy thesis, Norwegian University of Science and Technology, Trondheim

Prochaska, J. O. and DiClemente, C. C. (2005) The Transtheoretical Approach, in Norcross, J. C. and Goldfried, M. R. (eds), *Handbook of Psychotherapy Integration*, Oxford University Press, New York, pp147–171

Rodriguez, E. and Boks, C. (2005) How Design of Products Affects User Behaviour and Vice Versa: the Environmental Implications, paper presented at Eco Design 2005: Fourth International Symposium on Environmentally Conscious Design and Inverse Manufacturing, 12–14 December

Roethlisberger, F. J. and Dickson, W. J. (1939) *Management and the Worker: An Account of a Research Program Conducted by the Western Electric Company, Hawthorne Works*, Harvard University Press, Cambridge, MA

Routarinne, S. and Redström, J. (2007) Domestication as Design Intervention. paper presented at Design Inquiries 2007, 27–30 May, Stockholm, Sweden

Steg, L. and Vlek, C. (2009) Encouraging Pro-environmental Behaviour: An Integrative Review and Research Agenda, *Journal of Environmental Psychology*, vol 29, no 3, pp309–317

Tang, T. (2010) Towards Sustainable Use: Design Behaviour Intervention to Reduce Household Environmental Impact, Doctor of Philosophy thesis, Loughborough University

Tang, T. and Bhamra, T. A. (2008) Changing energy consumption behaviour through sustainable product design, in *DS 48: Proceedings DESIGN 2008, 10th International Design Conference*, Dubrovnik, Croatia, 19–22 May

Tang, T. and Bhamra, T. A. (2009) Improving Energy Efficiency of Product Use: An Exploration of Environmental Impacts of Household Cold Appliance Usage Patterns, paper presented at 5th International Conference on Energy Efficiency in Domestic Appliances and Lighting, 18 June 2009, Berlin, Germany

Tang, T. and Bhamra, T. A. (2011) Applying a Design Behaviour Intervention Model to Design for Sustainable Behaviour, paper presented at The Tao of Sustainability: An International Conference on Sustainable Design in a Globalization Context, 27–29 October 2011, Beijing, China

Tang, T. and Bhamra, T. A. (2012) Putting Consumers First in Design for Sustainable Behaviour: A Case Study of Reducing Environmental Impacts of Cold Appliance Use, *International Journal of Sustainable Engineering*, vol 5, no 4, pp288–303

Tapia-Fonllem, C., Corral-Verdugo, V., Fraijo-Sing, B. and Duron-Ramos, M. F. (2013) Assessing Sustainable Behavior and its Correlates: A Measure of Pro-Ecological, Frugal, Altruistic and Equitable Actions, *Sustainability*, vol 5, pp711–723

Tromp, N., Hekkert, P. and Verbeek, P. P. (2011) Design for Socially Responsible Behavior: A Classification of Influence Based on Intended User Experience, *Design Issues*, vol 27, no 3, pp3–19

Van Dam, S. S. (2013) *Smart Energy Management for Households: A Practical Guide for Designers, HEMS Developers, Energy Providers, and the Building Industry*, CreateSpace Independent Publishing Platform, Colorado Springs, CO

Verplanken, B. (2006) Beyond Frequency: Habit as Mental Construct, *British Journal of Social Psychology*, vol 45, pp639–656

Wever, R. (2012) Editorial, *Journal of Design Research*, vol 10, no 1–2, pp1–7

Wever, R., Van Kuijk, J. and Boks, C. (2008) User-Centred Design for Sustainable Behaviour, *International Journal of Sustainable Engineering*, vol 1, no 1, pp9–20

Wever, R., Van Onselen, L., Silvester, S. and Boks, C. (2010) Influence of Packaging Design on Littering and Waste Behaviour, *Packaging Technology and Science*, vol 23, no 5, pp239–252

Wilson, G. T. (2013) Design for Sustainable Behaviour: Feedback Interventions to Reduce Domestic Energy Consumption, Doctor of Philosophy thesis, Loughborough University

Wilson, G. T., Lilley, D. and Bhamra, T. A. (2013) Design Feedback Interventions for Household Energy Consumption Reduction, paper presented at ERSCP-EMSU 2013 Conference, 4–7 June 2013, Sustainable Development and Cleaner Production Center, Boğaziçi University, Istanbul, Turkey

Wilson, G. T., Leder Mackley, K., Mitchell, V., Bhamra, T. A. and Pink, S. (2014) PORTS: An Interdisciplinary and Systemic Approach to Studying Energy Use in the Home, paper presented at UbiComp 2014 Adjunct, 13–17 September, Seattle, WA

Wilson, G. T., Bhamra, T. and Lilley, D. (2015) The Considerations and Limitations of Feedback as a Strategy for Behaviour Change, *International Journal of Sustainable Engineering*, vol 8, no 3, pp186–195

Zachrisson, J. and Boks, C. (2012) Exploring Behavioural Psychology to Support Design for Sustainable Behaviour, *Journal of Design Research*, vol 10, no 1–2, pp50–66

Zachrisson, J., Storrø, G. and Boks, C. (2011) Using a Guide to Select Design Strategies for Behaviour Change: Theory vs. Practice, paper presented at EcoDesign 2011 International Symposium, Kyoto, Japan

Zachrisson Daae, J. (2014) Informing Design for Sustainable Behaviour, Doctor of Philosophy thesis, Norwegian University of Science and Technology, Trondheim

Zachrisson Daae, J. and Boks, C. (2014) Dimensions of Behaviour Change, *Journal of Design Research*, vol 12, no 3, pp145–172

10

MENDING BROKEN PROMISES IN SUSTAINABLE DESIGN

Alex Lobos

Abstract

Sustainable product design is effectively combining solutions that address environmental issues while elevating user experience and achieving success in the marketplace. A closer look at the effectiveness of sustainability strategies in the design process reveals that some of the best efforts in this area do not yield the benefits promised. Examples of these shortcomings include product operation with unnecessary features that push performance beyond environmentally friendly levels, products made out of recyclable materials that still end up in landfills and consumers that do not connect sustainable lifestyles to the products they use. An effective model for consistent benefits in sustainable product design begins with making the right choices for materials, processes and manufacturing so that products have an innately low environmental footprint. Then an understanding of the product lifecycle within a circular economy context ensures that steps such as recyclability and reuse are not ignored as products go through iterative cycles of fabrication, use and repurposing. Lastly, promoting positive user behavior so that products are enjoyable and meaningful enablers of short and long-term sustainable benefits. By having these strategies working together as a multi-layered approach, all stakeholders in a given product's lifecycle will consistently make choices that result in sustainable advantages.

Keywords: sustainability, product design, circular economy, user behavior, systems thinking

Introduction

Sustainability is now established as an essential tool in any designer's tool kit (Robert et al., 2002). Its demand comes from a variety of stakeholders; everyone from businesses to organizations and particularly consumers are all looking for products that reduce environmental impact and promote sustainable lifestyles (Black and Cherrier, 2010; Axsen et al., 2012). Despite skepticism around climate change from some organizations and even from United States Congress (Nuccitelli, 2015), it is widely understood that traditional manufacturing practices need to change dramatically in order to stop exploitation of finite resources. Designers have a key role in defining pathways towards sustainable practices and positive wellbeing while delivering design solutions that perform successfully in the marketplace.

To date, most of the work around sustainable product design has focused on the early stages of the lifecycle. There are plenty of guidelines for sustainable design process, which normally fall into three factors: product specifications around unmet user needs; market considerations around cost, materials, appearance, etc.; and knowledge from designers as they define their final intent (Waage, 2007). These factors define, in large degree, the overall environmental impact of mass-produced objects, which in some products such as laptops, have up 80 per cent of their total energy demand during their fabrication (Williams, 2004). An area frequently looked at for environmental impact is end of life. Recyclability is a key component for measuring how 'green' a product as it reduces landfill waste and provides a method for processing materials for reuse. The reality is, however, that recyclability is not as successful as people commonly assume. Recycling rates in the US, for example, show that about 55 percent of aluminum cans were recycled in 2013 (Environmental Protection Agency, 2015) and electronic waste, which is one of the largest sources of toxic waste, showed a ratio of only 25 percent in 2009 (Environmental Protection Agency, 2011). Recyclability has a large weakness in that its benefits are based on the potential of the recycling act being fully performed and so there is no guarantee that these predicted benefits will occur. This is a big problem when industries increase product complexity in order to accommodate features around disassembly and recyclability, assuming that the metals, plastics and other materials that they use will be disposed of appropriately. If products like these are not recycled they waste materials as well as features planned for end of life.

In order to obtain sustainability strategies that exist in reality and not only in potential, this chapter discusses a set of tools and case studies that promote a more effective product lifespan that integrates sustainability throughout product pre-use, use and post-use. As a starting point is the attention to material and processes that follows ecological, social and economic needs as organized in the Triple Bottom Line (TBL) model (Elkington, 1999; Norman and MacDonald, 2004). The TBL perspective provides products with a more comprehensive view of their sustainable potential that goes beyond environmental benefits. TBL resonates with various manufacturers and it is no longer foreign to designers and engineers. Second is an attention to the entire product lifecycle based on circular economies as an excellent vehicle for rethinking products in a way that guarantees sustainable lifecycles, given that steps in it depend on – and in many cases cannot occur without – the correct completion of the previous step. Third is a strong focus on user behavior towards sustainability, health and wellbeing. Products that promote these types of positive behavior are most times used and maintained in the most effective and sustainable way as they provide satisfaction and benefits to their users both in short and long terms (Chapman, 2009). Users not only benefit from the product performance but also enjoy having an active role in making their products truly sustainable. As overarching goal is the simultaneous implementation of these steps along with other strategies already familiar in sustainable product design. This combination eliminates the assumption that any single sustainability action will happen as it provides as many chances as possible for products to be manufactured, used, and disposed of in the most responsible way.

Broken promises in sustainability

While interest in sustainability grows among manufacturers, suppliers, consumers and other stakeholders it also shows a significant limitation. Its implementation in many cases, particularly during use and end of life, relies heavily on someone making conscious and active decisions. This means that sustainability features in consumer products planned during their development phase are not guaranteed to generate positive results, down the line. Breaking down the term 'sustainability' gives insight to this core limitation. On one hand we have the notion of 'sustaining' as a way of using natural resources without compromising them for future generations (World Commission on Environment and Development, 1987). The need for having the vision of an uninterrupted continuous cycle is the result of shortsighted methods that have provided society with vast amounts of goods and services that result in many of the ecological problems we face today. Whether it is wrong selection of materials, abuse of resources or excessive production, most typical manufacturing processes cannot be maintained forever as they use more resources than what exist or can be replenished. The second part of the term 'sustainability' is its ability to make things right. Ability implies potential and not reality. This means that while there are solutions for issues related to ecological problems, there is no guarantee that these solutions will be implemented. Most manufacturing cycles are so complex that it is very easy to break the cycles that are needed for a successful sustained model to happen. From manufacturers who design their products adequately and with the best materials, to users who know how to dispose of their products correctly to recyclers that process them correctly so that recycled materials make it back to the production cycle, there are just too many variables that can be misunderstood, go wrong, or even worse, just be ignored.

The issue of *potential* versus *reality* can be applied to more specific strategies within sustainability practices. Several key terms around this topic show the same issue: recyclable (as in able to be recycled); compostable (as in able to be composted); or, biodegradable (as in able to be degraded by natural decomposition). While these strategies have the potential to be good solutions, they rely on someone consciously taking the appropriate steps to fulfill them. In the case of a sustainable product, however, achieving environmental benefits can be significantly more challenging than simply pressing a button, or twisting a dial. Biodegradable products are a good example of this failed potential. Disposable tableware made out of starches such as potato and corn has become fairly popular in the marketplace and consumers purchase them because of their ability to decompose in a natural way instead of ending up in landfills. The 'potential' of these products reduces consumer's involvement in their end of life, giving out a false impression that the products will decompose in any setting when in reality they need to sit in special bioactive environments that promote the breakdown of their particles (Gross and Kalra, 2002). It can be argued that plastic ware has the advantage that most consumers know how to recycle it and there is a growing infrastructure that provides recycling bins and collection stations so that this happens. In contrast, consumers don't know what to do with biodegradable tableware and end up throwing it in the trash.

Shifting from potential to reality

As designers began to adopt sustainability practices into their process they were oftentimes puzzled on how to effectively implement them as well as how to communicate their benefits to other stakeholders in the process (Waage, 2007). Designers had good intentions but lacked the technical knowledge to understand the impact of some of their decisions while engineers had a good handle on processes and tradeoffs but showed little understanding of how these choices affect user experience and consumer preference in the marketplace (Lobos and Babbitt, 2013). Luckily, this scenario is becoming uncommon as interdisciplinary collaborations become more prevalent in both academic and professional environments.

From the consumer's perspective, the introduction of sustainable products initially implied tradeoffs such as reduced durability, flawed appearance and higher cost. Even today, consumers continue to struggle with purchase decisions around 'green' products because of factors such as time needed for researching product options, price, lack of information on environmental performance, knowledge needed for understanding eco-benefits and balancing all of these with other general product criteria not related to environmental performance (Young et al., 2010). In the case of automobiles, while most manufacturers offer models with alternative energy technologies such as electric and hybrid technologies, consumers face a price premium and limited availability in comparison to internal combustion equivalent models (Orbach and Fruchter, 2011). Balancing sustainability trade-offs can be difficult, even with products that are apparently simple. Toy manufacturer Lego has spent years trying to find a sustainable alternative to acrylonitrile butadiene styrene (ABS), the plastic it uses to produce its iconic bricks. ABS allows for high tolerances that provide the tight fit and durability that Lego bricks are famous for but it is also harder to recycle than other plastics such as polyethylene. So far the alternatives found for environmentally friendly plastic do not achieve the high tolerances and fit the company needs but a strong push on materials research has prompted Lego to announce its transition to an environmentally sound plastic by 2030, which includes an investment of 1 billion Danish kroner (USD150 million) and the creation of a research center for sustainable materials (Trangbaek, 2015).

MULTI-LAYERED STRATEGIES IN SUSTAINABLE DESIGN

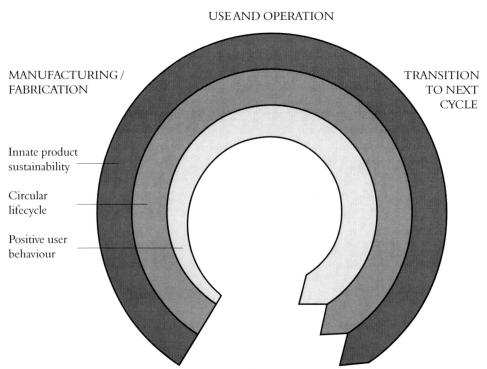

Figure 10.1 A model for effective sustainability in product design is based on three parts laid simultaneously across a product's lifecycle

The best way of moving towards sustainability as a reality that doesn't leave consumers and the planet with unfulfilled promises, begins by understanding how to maximize entire life cycles and turn them into iterative systems. By doing this, you transform sustainable advantage from a variable, into a constant. The model proposed herein for achieving sustainability with certainty combines strategies across the product's lifecycle and involves several actions. These actions are taken by designers and engineers as they design the product, by the product itself during its operation, and perhaps most importantly, by users. The model is composed of three main levels: innate product sustainability as defined by materials and processes during manufacturing; circular lifecycle that guarantees that all steps in a sustainable product lifespan will occur as planned; and, positive user behaviour that leads to achieving short and long term sustainability goals (see Figure 10.1).

Innate product sustainability

This strategy relies mostly on the decisions made during a product's creation, from design to manufacturing which can account for as much as 70 percent of the overall costs for development, manufacturing and use (National Research Council, 1991). It provides insight to the core sustainability of a product by analyzing the materials and processes involved in its creation, which fortunately is an area where most manufacturers are fairly knowledgeable. When sustainability began to be implemented in product design there was a strong focus on lifecycle and maximization of resources. This focus reflects the control that manufacturers have in the front end of the lifecycle as well as corporate responsibilities they have on business practices. In terms of overall benefits for reducing environmental impact, optimizing components in the front end of the lifecycle (such as research, development, fabrication, and transportation) is a very effective way of seeing significant results in a product's environmental footprint. Depending on the product category, the stage of the life cycle that will have the most impact is the manufacturing stage. Most products will have the majority of their resource needs allocated to materials extraction and processing, production (via energy and water) and transportation costs although products with long lifespans such as home appliances actually have most of their environmental impact happening during their use phase. Because of these reasons it is critical to optimize methods for material extraction and selection and fabrication methods with reduced energy and water usage. Making better decisions during this makes also allows for designers and engineers to have full control over how and to what degree these changes happen.

While skeptics see these guidelines for materials selection and processes as limiting for their product development, there are various manufacturers who cleverly turn these limitations into intrinsic features that give their products a competitive edge. Furniture manufacturer Emeco released in 2012 a line of chairs and stools named *Broom* (see Figure 10.2), in collaboration with prominent designer Philippe Starck. These chairs are made from 75 percent recycled propylene and 15 percent wood waste (Emeco, n.d.) which gives them a rugged finish, interesting texture and deep character. These products are as durable as other chairs in their category and go as far as including a recycling symbol No. 5 for polypropylene underneath the seat (see Figure 10.3), meaning that it can be put out on the curb for recycling as is. *Broom* is a good example of sustainability strategies innately embedded in the design of a product.

Figure 10.2 Broom chair

Source: photograph by Alex Lobos

Figure 10.3 Detail of chair's recycling symbol

Source: photograph by Alex Lobos

Circular lifecycle

Traditional industrial systems are linear, meaning there is little consideration on how the end of life of a certain product can lead to the creation of a new one, or on how sustainable their cycle is. It's basically a linear system based on a constant sequence of production and consumption. As issues around depletion of finite resources became obvious more attention was put on how to bend the linear cycle into a circular one, where waste could be used as source for other cycles, mimicking the behavior of natural ecosystems. This approach, known today as circular economy, has been adopted since the 1970s but it has not gained significant attention by consumers and key stakeholders in various industries until recent years (Preston, 2012). The model works on a set of principles that do not necessarily depend on large infrastructures but can be adapted to both small and large-scale environments. The principles include: a systems-based approach with components that are modular, resilient and flexible; use of energy from renewable sources at all parts of the lifecycle; and, elimination of any components that won't have use after the product's useful life, thus becoming waste (Ellen MacArthur Foundation, 2013). A basic example of circular economy can be vegetable gardens, which generate a highly involved participation from the user, generating a continued relationship with the garden, consumption of the produce grown and composting of organic waste that goes back to the soil for new vegetables to grow. This is a radical departure from the consumer-based linear cycle, where people will go to a super market, consume produce, throw away the waste along with the packaging in which the food came, just to make another trip to the store and begin a new cycle all over again, all with minimal interaction with food in its natural state.

While it is relatively easy to imagine how circular economies can be implemented around farming and food, there are ingenious ways of adapting the model to more complex systems such as consumer goods.

An area that requires special attention for improvement of sustainable design practices is that of information communication technologies (ICTs) and electronic waste (e-waste). ICTs include smartphones, tablets, computers and other similar devices, which at their end of life create a wide array of environmental issues due to various factors, all of them complex within themselves. Product complexity puts demands on a large number of materials, many of them from scarce resources that are hard to extract. There are several known issues with the generation of toxic substances either as result of the processing of the materials or as by-products during use and end of life of ICTs (Widmer et al., 2005). The issue is aggravated by the large rate of product replacement, generated, in large proportion, by planned obsolescence (Tang and Bhamra, 2008). In the US the typical lifespan of a mobile phone is just 21 months, which puts enormous demand on fabrication of ICTs but also creates a flow of hazardous e-waste that cannot be handled properly. While short lifespan in ICTs is largely due to consumer preferences and aggressive advertisement, technology advances at an accelerated rate, which can make electronic devices technically obsolete and incompatible, limiting their productivity.

Within ICTs, mobile phones are extremely popular and show continued market growth as a result of their improved performance, portability and convenience. Circular economy can be used for improving ICTs, based on software with extended longevity, better options for reuse, component modularity, cloud-based memory and processing, parts remanufacturing and consumer-based repairs (Benton et al., 2015). When it comes down to designing mobile phones that are environmentally sound, modular architectures are a common approach. The idea is logical and straightforward: most components of the phone such as case, buttons, microphone, speakers etc., remain relatively unchanged from model to model and only a few components become outdated often, such as memory, processors, screens and batteries. The idea of upgrading components instead of replacing an entire device seems to be a natural direction but it is hard to find an example out in the market that executes this principle successfully. While the general concept of a modular phone with interchangeable components is attractive, challenges with technological compatibility, energy output, standardized parts between manufacturers etc. make it a challenging task. A phone concept that is gaining significant traction and shows a promising direction for actual implementation is Google's Project ARA (see Figure 10.4).

The ARA phone, which is similar to other concepts such as PhoneBlocks, is a device with a basic exoskeleton frame and slots that can be populated according to the user's interests and needs, potentially sourced by different manufacturers, making it disruptive enough to revolutionize the mobile phone industry (McCracken, 2014). The business model would require the user to send unwanted modules to the manufacturer to be replaced with new ones, achieving the concept of a circular economy cycle. In theory this model would reduce significantly the amount of e-waste created given that instead of replacing entire products consumers would only replace specific components and keep using the rest of the phone. The concept is raising doubts about its feasibility, business model and even if the modular aspect of the phone would encourage consumers to upgrade components at a higher rate because they feel that they are doing a 'responsible' replacement. Nevertheless, concepts such as Project ARA are interesting examples of how circular economy can be achieved in highly complex product categories.

Another area in hi-tech products that is gaining important momentum is personal fabrication. The rapid growth of 3D printing is empowering people to fabricate their own designs without the need for complex infrastructures. Benefits of this technology include

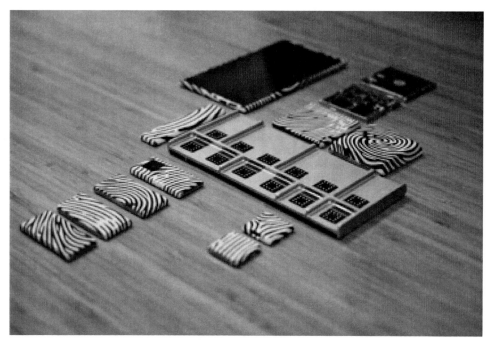

Figure 10.4 Project Ara Spiral 2 prototype

Source: Maurizio Pesce, licensed under CC BY 2.0, available from https://flic.kr/p/qzjYEY

the ability to fabricate goods within a distributed system, innumerable options for mass customization, and a reduced environmental impact as a direct result of simple fabrication methods on site that eliminate transportation, distribution, storage and other factors needed in large scale commercial models (Wittbrodt et al., 2013; Garrett, 2014). With the increase of circular economy systems it is important to watch out for a surplus of artifacts being produced simply because they are easy to print as well as for limited attention to recyclability since users are not required to have plans for end of life as large manufacturers do. Following on the circular economy's principle of using waste as input for future products, solutions for easily recycled unused 3D printed parts is necessary. 3D printers allow consumers to print objects out of materials such as plastic, paper, metal and even food. In terms of plastics, two of the most popular options for 3D printers are polylactic acid (PLA) and ABS. PLA is a good option in terms of environmental impact given that it can be recycled in most facilities. But, as previously discussed, the potential for something to be recycled does not guarantee an environmental benefit.

Dennon Oosterman, Alex Kay and David Joyce, students at the University of British Columbia developed a desktop plastic recycler for common plastics in 3D printing such as PLA and ABS so that they can be reused to print new objects (Streeter, 2015). The ability to recycle materials at home offers significant benefits for achieving closed-loop sustainability in consumer products. The most direct one is savings in terms of materials since users can reuse plastic instead of purchasing new spools. At a larger scale, the notion of recycling and printing products at home eliminates the need for packaging and transportation, which in the case of many product categories are responsible for most of their environmental impact. There is also a utopian advantage to the model where in order to create a new product users have to get rid of something they don't want anymore. In a consumer-driven society that is pushed by consumption beyond actual needs, there is certain magic in obtaining new products without increasing the manufactured landscape and maintaining the same material footprint.

Positive user behavior

Product efficiency provides abundant mechanisms for reducing negative impact in the environment but in order to generate a permanent change in business and society it is critical to look beyond environmental benefits and to enable user sustainable behaviors that transcend what products can contribute by themselves (Spangenberg et al., 2010). As discussed earlier, once consumers start using products, the environmental impact is no longer in control of products themselves. A television set with low energy consumption might offer the promise of being an environmentally friendly choice but if it sits in the home turned on all day long with no one watching it (because the user forgot to turn it off or consciously decided to leave it on as background noise) then the accumulated energy usage will still have a negative impact on the environment. When consumers acquire products that are environmentally friendly but end up being less proactive about having a responsible use assuming that the products won't have negative effects regardless of how they are used, they create what is known as a 'rebound effect' (Hertwich, 2005). Examples of this behavior include people who replace incandescent bulbs with more efficient technologies such as compact fluorescent or LED ones but then leave lights on around the house; or people overusing paper and thinking that putting it in the recycling bin will make everything right. While these behaviors show good intentions, such as selecting light bulbs with better performance or disposing of paper appropriately, they also show how easy it is to take sustainable benefits for granted, resulting in unplanned environmental issues. While some consumers might not feel naturally attracted towards environmentally friendly behaviors, they might be more inclined to minimize the operation of unused devices if they see a higher energy bill due to increased running time. In this way, the balance between sustainable and economic factors in consumer behaviors fluctuates significantly among different groups of consumers (Young et al., 2010). Designers should try to take full advantage of both components when they design products, so that they provide consumer rewards in both sustainable and economic terms. The combination of environmental benefits with other consumer benefits is crucial for the effective and long lasting implementation of sustainable practices.

When consumers purchase products they do it mostly because of needs and wants. While sustainability is important to many people it will not be a core *motivator* for initiating a purchase but rather a *differentiator* when deciding which product to buy, bringing it back to a basic situation of needs and wants. Products that address those basic needs and wants and include sustainability benefits alongside have better chances of success than products that presume to be acquired just because they are greener. Consumers cannot be forced to choose between a product that works well and one that is sustainable; both components need to be merged together and be dependent on each other. A way of achieving this is making sure that products first fulfill common user needs by being useful, enjoyable, durable etc. This creates a connection that results in a more sustainable product with a longer lifespan, offsetting the energy that went into creating it (Lobos, 2014). If users enjoy a product they will be more likely to follow its cues for positive behavior and meaningful activities that are built into it, increasing sustainable benefits further. Products can serve not only to meet needs and wants but also as resources that promote and engage meaningful activities (Desmet and Pohlmeyer, 2013). The idea of promoting positive behavior has been classified in different categories depending on the level of imposition that it has on the user and how direct or indirect its reaction is, ranging in influence from weak to strong and in presence from hidden to apparent (Tromp et al., 2011). Finding the right balance can be challenging as in many cases a stronger persuasion for positive behavior can be perceived as intrusive and undesirable, while a more subtle strategy can be easily ignored. For example, an automobile with a sound system that varies its volume or music selection based on how good (or bad) the driver's habits are might send a clear message to reduce acceleration and frequent braking ... but it will also make for an unhappy driver.

When defining sustainability goals, it is important to focus both on short- and long-term ones that provide larger benefits down the road. For example, household products that use less energy might not yield significant benefits immediately as monetary savings could be measured in fractions of a cent at best. Yet, when added together over longer periods of time and with other products, these benefits can be substantial enough to maintain better user behaviors. This mindset of working towards long-term goals is an excellent way of addressing some of the most challenging sustainability issues that are too big and complex to be solved by individuals. If we want to make a difference in climate change or pollution of a certain eco-system, it will take thousands of people over various decades to obtain a noticeable change.

In contrast to ICTs which have most of their environmental impact during their production phase, other products such as home appliances have up to 90 percent of their total impact happen during their operation. In the case of a washing machine, this is due to their long lifespan and heavy use of energy and water during washing and drying cycles. This product lifecycle provides a different set of needs for implementing the strategies that have been discussed. At a recent collaboration between General Electric and Rochester Institute of

Technology's Industrial Design program, students designed major home appliance concepts that promoted sustainable behavior in order to address the high environmental impact that occurs when products are in use. Graduate students Patricio Corvalán and Aisha Iskanderani teamed up to develop a laundry system named *Acute*, which offers a combination of reduced water and energy use as well offering the user multiple options for making sustainable decisions when using the machines.

Their design is a full-size washing machine with a cylindrical form factor that makes it easier to fit and move around the home. These reduced proportions are possible due to the use of an inverted direct drive to spin the drum, which only needs a dynamic frame to absorb vibration, leaving the unit to perform as free floating; eliminating the need for a boxed shape and a heavy base that keeps the unit in place (see Figure 10.5). One of their key insights during user research identified that while front loading machines use less water and take better care of garments, consumers find top loading machines easier to load and unload. The team's response to the challenge of integrating performance with convenience was solved with a pivoting frame allowing the drum to be swiveled, setting the machine as a top loader for improved accessibility during loading/unloading, and then rotating it forward so that it runs as front loader, using less water (see Figure 10.6). The drum uses a weight sensor to compress the drum to the ideal volume, eliminating unused space that leads to wasted water when running cycles. A closed-loop system allows for water to be filtered and reused throughout a wash cycle, eliminating the need for purging and refilling. This feature also makes the washer extremely portable with no need to be permanently anchored

Figure 10.5 Acute washer concept with floating frame allows for reduced proportions without worrying about excessive vibration

Source: photograph by Patricio Corvalán

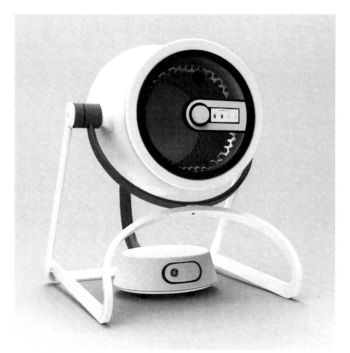

Figure 10.6 Washer can be accessed as a top loader (increasing convenience) and run as a front loader (reducing water consumption)

Source: photograph by Patricio Corvalán

to water inlets and outlets. The washer features a repositionable handle that emphasizes how lightweight and portable the machine is, while also allowing for garments to be hung from the handle to air dry. This feature encourages users to dry clothes without using a dryer, but its actual acceptance would need to be tested if the concept is developed further.[1]

The importance of multi-layered strategies

Achieving true sustainability is no small feat and it cannot be the result of a single effort. This is because most issues around sustainability have scales that transcend individuals, and in many cases, communities. Large issues such as economic development, climate change and limited healthcare are causes of distress to humans and other living beings regardless of political and geographical boundaries.

Even if we scale down some of these issues at levels that are applicable to consumer goods, many challenges still stack up very high and need different types of approaches and solutions. This is why in order to guarantee that sustained practices will occur it is also critical to offer multiple solutions that can work well by themselves, but also work even better together. This multi-layered approach is common in sustainable development, where solutions commonly work as interrelated systems that address different sections on one big problem (Robert, 2000). From short- to long-term solutions, features that reduce impact across the lifecycle, and business plans that promote steady growth it is key for any product to contain as many of these strategies as possible. The biggest challenge for sustainable products is to make sure that consumers make the right choices. If a product offers only one opportunity for its user to behave sustainably the chances of this actually happening are very slim. The more options that products offer their users, the larger the chances of products achieving their sustained potential and fulfilling their promises of reduced environmental impact. Additionally, given the complexity of many products during their lifespan, what might be a good strategy early in the lifecycle might not be the best one as the product approaches its end of life.

The goal for products that follow this approach is to offer a solid base of component parts that provide a guaranteed benefit in terms of sustainable needs. Materials selection and reduced manufacturing and transportation impact are essential considerations for this base. From there, products can start combining short term and immediate benefits that address both everyday needs with sustainable advantages (for example improved portability in a product by using a lighter material). This should also make the product easier to manufacture and to ship, leading to longer terms benefits that can be combined at larger scales and for longer-term solutions (such as disassembly options that eliminate the uncertainty whether a product will be recycled or disposed of properly). This multi-layered approach should not be seen as a complicated system to implement, but rather, as a way of dividing a large challenge into manageable parts that can be addressed effectively and individually, through design.

Conclusions

Sustainable product design has shown a dramatic growth since its beginnings, mostly due to the increased use of strategies that balance perceived notions of 'green design' with features that deliver tangible enhancements across a product's lifecycle. Being able to communicate and to prove positive environmental impact is a key skill in new product development that designers are mastering and sharing with other stakeholders in the process. While using a systems-thinking approach is a widely used for defining solutions while minimizing trade-offs, most solutions still focus only on manufacturing, and end of life stages. Manufacturing decisions that have to do with material selection and low-energy processes are great ways of reducing a product's environmental impact, given that most of them have their largest impact during manufacture. End of life strategies are effective ways of engaging consumers into sustainable practices and also address issues related to waste management and depletion of non-renewable resources. Unfortunately, many efforts for the recycling and reuse of components are not effective because consumers and other stakeholders rarely follow guidelines for recycling. This limitation results in a broken cycle that makes little progress to reduce waste. Additionally, many consumers are not invested enough to change the way that they use products and don't place enough importance on environmental actions such as recycling, reusing and extending product lifetimes.

Emerging models such as circular economy look at breaking down product cycles into closed loops that are easier to control and to follow successfully by industries or communities without need for larger infrastructure common in current economic models. Circular economy enables more participation from consumers and fabricators while making every single component of the cycle essential for its success. The result is a manageable, iterative workflow that minimizes use of new resources and environmental impact while giving consumers a more central role in the process.

Whether products are designed for a small circular economy or for a larger lifecycle, encouraging positive user behavior around sustainability, health and wellbeing, enhances the enjoyment and success of any product. Users who receive immediate benefits and rewards from using their products in a responsible way tend to maintain that behavior, which over time adds to the improvement of communities, society and the planet as a whole. As designers integrate strategies like the ones previously mentioned, they don't need to choose from one or two of them but rather should try to integrate as many of them as they find appropriate. This integration of sustainable features that can be used simultaneously, results in the highest performance possible and also minimizes the likelihood that a product with good sustainable potential will fail to perform in that way and won't be part of a continuously deteriorating cycle. Just as with natural habitats filled with multiple components, each performing predictable roles, small changes in product design and user behavior can cause significant chain reactions that work together to achieve a sustained, perpetual and harmonious macro-system.

Note

1   A video of the *Acute* washer can be watched at: http://youtu.be/T229vm8n_NY.

References

Axsen, J., Tyree-Hageman, J. and Lentz, A. (2012) Lifestyle practices and pro-environmental technology, *Ecological Economics*, vol 82, pp64–74

Benton, D., Coats, E. and Hazell, J. (2015) *A circular economy for smart devices: Opportunities in the US, UK and India*, Green Alliance, London

Black, I. R. and Cherrier, H. (2010) Anti-consumption as part of living a sustainable lifestyle: Daily practices, contextual motivations and subjective values, *Consumer Behavior*, vol 9, pp437–453

Chapman, J. (2009) Design for (emotional) durability, *Design Issues*, vol 25, no 4, pp29–35

Desmet, P. and Pohlmeyer, A. E. (2013) Positive design: An introduction to design for subjective wellbeing, *International Journal of Design*, vol 7, no 3, pp5–19

Elkington, J. (1999) *Cannibals with forks: Triple bottom line of 21st century business*, Capstone, Oxford

Ellen MacArthur Foundation (2013) Towards the Circular Economy, retrieved from www.mvonederland.nl/system/files/media/towards-the-circular-economy.pdf (accessed 24 May 2015)

Emeco (n.d.) Broom stacking chair, retrieved from www.emeco.net/products/emeco-brm-natural-broom-chair-natural-philippe-starck (accessed 12 June 2015)

Environmental Protection Agency (2011) Electronics Waste Management In the United States Through 2009, retrieved from www.epa.gov/epawaste/conserve/materials/ecycling/docs/fullbaselinereport2011.pdf (accessed 10 June 2015)

Environmental Protection Agency (2015) Aluminum Common Wastes and Materials, retrieved from www.epa.gov/osw/conserve/materials/alum.htm (accessed 12 June 2015)

Garrett, B. (2014) 3D printing: New economic paradigms and strategic shifts, *Global Policy*, vol 5, pp70–75

Gross, R. A. and Kalra, B. (2002) Biodegradable polymers for the environment, *Science Magazine*, vol 297, pp803–807

Hertwich, E. (2005) Consumption and the rebound effect: An industrial ecology perspective, *Industrial Ecology*, vol 9, no 1–2, pp85–98

Lobos, A. (2014) Timelessness in sustainable product design, in J. Salamanca et al. (eds), *The Colors of Care: proceedings of the 9th International Conference on Design and Emotion*, Universidad de Los Andes, Bogotá, pp169–176

Lobos, A. and Babbitt, C. (2013) Integrating emotional attachment and sustainability in electronic product design, *Challenges*, vol 4, pp19–33

McCracken, H. (2014) Project Ara: Inside Google's bold gambit to make smartphones modular, *Time Magazine*, February 26, retrieved from http://time.com/10115/google-project-ara-modular-smartphone (accessed 18 April 2015)

National Research Council (1991) *Improving engineering design: Designing for competitive advantage*. National Academy, Washington, DC

Norman, W. and MacDonald, C. (2004) Getting to the bottom of the triple bottom line, *Business Ethics Quarterly*, vol 14, no 2, pp243–262

Nuccitelli, D. (2015) Congress manufactures doubt and denial in climate change hearing, *The Guardian*, 21 May, retrieved from www.theguardian.com/environment/climate-consensus-97-per-cent/2015/may/21/congress-manufactures-doubt-and-denial-in-climate-change-hearing (accessed 30 June 2015)

Orbach, Y. and Fruchter, G. E. (2011) Forecasting sales and product evolution: The case of the hybrid/electric car, *Technological Forecasting and Social Change*, vol 78, pp1210–1226

Otto, R., Ruminy, A. and Mrotzek, H. (2006) Assessment of the environmental impact of household appliances, *Appliance Magazine*, April

Preston, F. (2012) A global redesign? Shaping the circular economy, retrieved from www.chathamhouse. org/sites/files/chathamhouse/public/Research/Energy,%20Environment%20and%20Development/ bp0312_preston.pdf (accessed 3 May 2015)

Robert, K. H. (2000) Tools and concepts for sustainable development, how do they relate to a general framework for sustainable development and to each other, *Cleaner Production*, vol 8, pp243–254

Robert, K. H., Schmidt-Bleek, B., Aloisi de Larderel, J., Basile, G., Jansen, J. L., Kuehr, R. et al. (2002) Strategic sustainable development: selection, design and synergies of applied tools, *Cleaner Production*, vol 10, no 3, pp197–214

Spangenberg, J. H., Fuad-Luke, A. and Blincoe, K. (2010) Design for sustainability (DfS): The interface of sustainable production and consumption, *Cleaner Production*, vol 18, pp1485–1493

Streeter, A. K. (2015) 3-D printing gets a way to instantly recycle plastic waste into new 3-D 'ink'. *Treehugger Magazine*, March 26, retrieved from www.treehugger.com/sustainable-product-design/3-D-printing-plus-way-instantly-recycle-plastic-waste-3-d-ink.html (accessed 28 May 2015)

Tang, T. and Bhamra, T. (2008) 'Understanding consumer behavior to reduce environmental impacts through sustainable product design', in *Unidisciplined!, Design Research Society Conference*, Sheffield Hallman University, pp1–15, retrieved from http://shura.shu.ac.uk/550/

Trangbaek, R. R. (2015) Lego group to invest 1 billion DKK boosting search for sustainable materials. Lego, June 16, retrieved from www.lego.com/en-us/aboutus/news-room/2015/june/sustainable-materials-centre (accessed 24 June 2015)

Tromp, N., Hekkert, P. and Verbeek, P. P. (2011) Design for socially responsible behavior: A classification on influence based on intended user experience, *Design Issues*, vol 27, no 3, pp3–19

Waage, S. A. (2007) Re-considering product design: a practical 'road-map' for integration of sustainability issues, *Cleaner Production*, vol 15, pp638–649

Widmer, R., Oswald-Krapf, H., Sinha-Khetriwal, D., Schnellmann, M. and Bonni, H. (2005) Global perspectives on e-waste, *Environmental Impact Assessment Review*, vol 25, pp436–458

Williams, E. (2004) Energy intensity of computer manufacturing: hybrid analysis combining process and economic input-output methods, *Environmental Science and Technology*, vol 38, no 22, pp6166–6174

Wittbrodt, B. T., Glover, A. G., Laureto, J., Anzalone, G. C., Oppliger, D., Irwin, J. L. and Pearce, J. M. (2013) Life-cycle economic analysis of distributed manufacturing with open-source 3-D printers, *Mechatronics*, vol 23, no 6, pp713–726

World Commission on Environment and Development (1987) *Our Common Future*, Oxford University Press, Oxford

Young, W., Hwang, K., McDonald, S. and Oates, C. J. (2010) Sustainable consumption: green consumer behaviour when purchasing products, *Sustainable Development*, vol 18, no 1, pp20–31

11

SHARING, MATERIALISM, AND DESIGN FOR SUSTAINABILITY

Russell Belk

Abstract

Sharing can reduce resource use, waste, congestion, pollution and senseless accumulation of possessions. We should therefore be happy about the recent hoopla celebrating 'the sharing economy.' With the help of the Internet and digital devices there has been an explosion of successful sharing ventures like Uber, Airbnb and Zipcar. But we must also realize that much of this economy isn't about sharing at all, but rather about selling access through short-term rental rather than ownership. There may still be gains for the environment, but sometimes the goal of the organization is more 'sharewashing' rather than improving the state of the world. That is, sharing provides a pro-social label for what may be exploitative aims. Materialism plays a big role in inhibiting sharing, in encouraging consumer lifestyles with dubious sustainability and in incentivizing business to co-opt and appropriate sharing initiatives in order to profit. The design of products and services also plays a role in encouraging and facilitating sharing. This chapter examines positive and negative takes on sharing and materialism and considers their role in fostering greater sustainability. In spite of counterarguments, the conclusion reached is that sharing may not only promote greater sustainability, it may also inhibit materialism.

Keywords: materialism, sharing, collaborative consumption, design for sustainability

Introduction

Recent technology-enhanced developments in the 'sharing economy' include car-sharing services like Zipcar, ride-sharing services like Uber and home-sharing services like Airbnb. In more intimate contexts parents share resources with children, neighbors share joint labor in community projects and friends share food and drinks with each other. Together, such distributed uses of human and material resources ostensibly make all participants better off and increase the sustainability of both the natural environment and human lives. Motives for such sharing or 'collaborative consumption' vary. Parents share with children out of feelings of love and responsibility. Friends and neighbors share out of reciprocal altruism and as an expression of trust and caring. Strangers may share out of human courtesy or for profit, convenience or environmental concern.

160

Traditionally people share in order to increase their mutual chances of survival (e.g. Stack, 1983). It may therefore seem ironic that it is especially in individualistic affluent economies and classes, where sharing resources is not necessary for survival, that we find the most flourishing new sharing economies. With marketization and privatization, it would instead be expected that resources are fenced off, the commons is dispersed into individual ownership and capital in the forms of land, labor and money are privatized and become individually exploited resources. It would also be expected that growing materialism would lead to less sharing rather than more. Although this hoarding of resources certainly does occur, there are many signs of counter-trends through various forms of resource sharing. In this chapter I attempt to explain these apparent paradoxes and show several ways in which sharing and materialism influence one another in traditional and contemporary economies. I also comment on implications for designing objects and environments that encourage or facilitate sharing.

Sharing

A brief history of sharing

Anthropologists (e.g. Price, 1975) have observed that sharing is the oldest and most universal form of human resource distribution. Rather than regarding objects as *mine* and *yours*, sharing treats them as *ours* – jointly possessed things to which we have joint access (Chen, 2009), even if they are individually owned. Prototypes may be found in mothers caring for infants and household pooling of resources for the care and nourishment of all members rather than just the strongest or most powerful (Belk, 2010). While there are exceptions to this model of resource allocation in some cultures and under some conditions (e.g. Fine, 1980) it has proven robust across many cultures over millennia (e.g. Belk and Llamas, 2012).

Hunter–gatherer societies often had strong norms about sharing with the successful hunter often getting leftovers after others have partaken freely of the bounty (e.g. Bird-David, 2005; Hunt, 2005). Some form of sharing was necessary to enhance the chances of group survival. Sedentary agricultural communities and cities by no means eliminated the practice of sharing and the earlier notion that the commons could serve the entire community persisted widely until the closing of European commons areas with the rise of capitalism (Ostrom, 1990; Polanyi, 1944). Harvests, building construction, irrigation projects and many other tasks requiring a number of people also relied on shared labor within communities. They still do to varying degrees, but capitalism has also resulted in increased privatization of labor, land and capital (Polanyi, 1944; Vikas, Varman and Belk, 2015). Nevertheless, friends and neighbors frequently informally share food, drinks, tools, rides, house-care, childcare and other sundries of daily life, even if the frequency of such sharing, until quite recently, has declined with large scale anonymous cities, multiple worker households, and urban alienation (e.g. Putnam, 2000).

Recently, however, there has been a dramatic upsurge in what has come to be called 'the sharing economy' (Hamari et al., 2016; John, 2012; Sacks, 2011). Botsman and Rogers (2010) detail some of the many products and services that have become part of this sharing economy. For much of the 'sharing economy,' the real model is one of short-term rental of assets like cars and houses rather than sharing in the sense of things being 'ours' rather than 'mine' and 'yours' (Belk, 2014; Bardhi and Eckhardt, 2015). Examples include car-sharing organizations like ZipCar, accommodation sharing services such as Airbnb and ride-sharing services such as Uber and Lyft. Airbnb currently hosts 155 million guests annually or 22 percent more than Hilton Worldwide (PwC, 2015). The 2010 startup, Uber is valued at more than Delta Airlines, United Airlines Continental, and American Airlines (PwC, 2015). PricewaterhouseCoopers estimates that today's sharing economy generates revenues of 15 billion dollars, which will grow to 335 billion dollars by 2025. Notably, despite some progress during 40 years of modern environmentalism and 20 years of work on sustainable development, success has been quite moderate on these fronts. The sharing economy has the potential to create much more progress toward these goals (Brady, 2014; Heinrichs, 2013).

A great deal of the new sharing economy has been facilitated by the Internet and especially by the consumer-engaging possibilities of Web 2.0. Unlike Web 1.0, which provided information that web users could access, Web 2.0 engages them in an interactive fashion such that they both initiate and respond to others online. Attention to these possibilities was dramatically demonstrated by the early success of Napster and the subsequent success of Bit Torrent file-sharing services (Giesler, 2006; Giesler and Pohlman, 2003). Although the film, music and publishing industries fought hard against such peer-to-peer (P2P) file-sharing, it was not until Apple's iTunes store and Amazon's eBooks (Kindle Books) that much inroad was made to stop such sharing practices (Sinnreich, 2013). Still P2P file-sharing continues to flourish and is a major way that many people, especially young people, get access to music and films (Aigrain, 2012). According to a 2009 CBS survey, more than two-thirds of Americans in their late teens and twenties believed that it is sometimes or always fine to download music without paying (CBS, 2009).

But despite free software, Creative Commons licenses and open access source code writing movements (Benkler, 2006; Ghosh, 2005; Hemetsberger, 2012) as well as many arguments on behalf of freely sharing ideas, information and artistic creations (e.g. Hyde, 2010; Lessig, 2001; Sunstein, 2006; Vaidhyanathan, 2001), it appears that attempts to close the Internet commons have been largely successful (Grassmuck, 2012). Digital rights management (DRM) software, and laws with acronyms like TRIPS, WIPO, SOPA, and ACTA have hampered many non-profit attempts to distribute information and digital products freely. To be sure we have successful models of access to information through search engines, blogs, websites, forums, Wikis and other online free access portals. But most of these portals have found a way to monetize their offerings through selling access to user information as well as advertising means to reach them through these same sites. That is, this free access has been achieved at a non-monetary cost in terms of privacy.

Although sharing non-digital products and services has fared somewhat better through neighborhood sharing organizations, tool libraries, events like Really Really Free Markets and FreeCycle (Arsel and Dobsha, 2011), online-facilitated swaps, time banks, home swaps, networked car pools, crowdfunding, and other creative sharing ventures, the nature of most of these efforts keeps them small and local. On the other hand more scalable ventures such as Airbnb, Uber, Bag Borrow or Steal (subscription access to designer handbags) and Zipcar offer services that bring together those offering and those needing products and services by facilitating match-ups or providing inventory and taking a fee for doing so.

As sharing morphs into short-term rental, feelings of altruistic sharing dissipate (Bardhi and Eckhardt, 2012; Belk, 2014; Durgee and O'Connor, 1995; Hellwig, Belk and Morhart, 2016), even though there are still clear benefits to the environment in most cases. Replacing some cars, hotels, parking lots, and banks and sharing rides, human services and tools means not only environmental benefits, but less gridlock and congestion on roads, less wasteful over-consumption, and in some cases, more feeling of community. For example, San Francisco's successful ride-sharing program (allowing access to High Occupancy Vehicle lanes) and Europe's BlaBlaCar ride-sharing service put more people in vehicles, provoke conversations (the 'BlaBla'), and create feelings of commonality.

Design for sharing

An example of the impact of design on sharing is the redesign of the San Francisco School lunch program by IDEO (Butler, 2015; Caula, 2014; Martin, 2013). The school lunches in San Francisco schools were over-budget and under-utilized. Even those eligible for free lunches were no more than 50 percent likely to eat at school and senior high school students and teachers were rarely found in the lunchrooms at all. The IDEO team began by separating grade school, middle school and high school student lunch programs and studied each separately. In grade schools, for example, they found that students were put off by long lunch lines and were intimidated by having to make quick choices in the cafeteria. The students next found a table and ate in silence if they didn't manage to sit with friends. In redesigning the program the design firm completely re-did the lunchroom configuration, making it more like a restaurant. Students had an assigned table with a teacher at it and immediately sat down. The food came to them on mobile trollies and was served family-style. Rather than fixed portions on trays, students ate from round plates, at a round table, and a designated student table monitor helped dish out the food from communal bowls and platters. The food was tied to a curriculum about the environment, food and geography, and a mobile scanner was used to register what was taken and what was left over. Student volunteers also helped in the program and cleanup.

The result was a big spike in eating at school, along with greater satisfaction, less waste and lower costs. By making the elementary school food more like a social event and more similar to shared meals at home, the redesign managed to also inculcate the *feeling* of sharing rather than eating institutional food in a prison-like environment with the former rectangular tables, rectangular trays, and long lines. The previous arrangement was for the convenience of the institution rather than the students and any tie to educational curricula was unthinkable. Although there has been some criticism of the makeover, it mostly centers on how big the improvement was (e.g. Woldow, 2013). Like the round tables and 'Lazy Susan' rotating platforms on tables in some Chinese restaurants, IDEO found a way to redesign the elementary school meal experience in a more social and friendly way, with a communal sharing ethos rather than an individualistic orientation.

This same spirit was evident in the Design for Sharing Conference (November, 2014) held in London. At the conference a number of reports of more and less successful sharing ventures were presented, ranging from micro-libraries, time banking, communal pubs and shared garden spaces to shared sheds, communal shops and crowdfunding. The Internet provided a platform to help organize many of these ventures and a short book analyzing a number of such ventures and lessons learned was produced (Light and Miskelly, 2014).

Design can play a big role in encouraging sharing, not only in terms of products, packaging, locations and services, but also in terms of infrastructure, Internet applications and government support. The social entrepreneurship opportunities are as great, or greater, than the economic entrepreneurship opportunities that have gotten the bulk of attention in treatments of the sharing economy. One of the lessons of San Francisco's lunch redesign is that little things matter. In much of Asia, for example, the beer and sake bottles are quite large and the teacups and sake glasses are quite small. The reason is simple. The bottles are meant for group consumption rather than individual consumption and the small cups and glasses mean that there are ample opportunities to refill the glasses of others at the table. It was once the case in Europe that people sat at a table with common benches and ate off of common long plates called trenchers. Only with the rise of individualism accompanying the rise of capitalism and the Industrial Revolution did individual chairs, plates and silverware become common (Tuan, 1982). Nevertheless, buying rounds and treating others is still a common form of sharing at restaurants, bars and pubs. Reusable containers, recycling bins and eBooks that can be easily given to others all encourage sharing, while disposable objects, fast fashions and digital rights management (DRM) all discourage it.

While many thoughtful design elements can encourage sharing, Schor (2014) urges further study to assess the full impacts of sharing, especially within the commercial sharing economy. She notes that car-sharing services may increase emissions by expanding access to automobiles. Or, that those who rent their possessions to others may use the extra revenue to buy new high-impact products. And with lower cost travel thanks to ride-sharing and home-sharing services like RelayRides and CouchSurfing, people may travel more. She and her research students found that those using Airbnb did in fact take more trips and those using ride-sharing services like Uber used less public transportation, resulting in greater carbon emissions from the car travelers used instead. Schor (2014) also questions whether the use of these sorts of services really result in building social relationships, as is commonly assumed.

The sharing economy may also create new markets as when Bag Borrow or Steal makes designer handbags available to people who could otherwise never afford them. However, while a comprehensive study remains to be done, it seems likely that the net effect of sharing is positive. Much as industry might bemoan file-sharing, car-sharing, tool-sharing and food-sharing services like those found in Germany (Gollnhoffer, Hellwig and Morhart, 2016), they do save resources in manufacturing, transportation and recycling. Furthermore, auto-sharing may make it feasible to try out a hybrid or electric car that would otherwise not be accessible. So strong is the trend toward sharing rides and cars that auto manufacturers like Mercedes, BMW, Audi, Volkswagen, Peugeot and General Motors have started their own car- and ride-sharing services in order to stay in the game. Traditional car rental companies have also gotten involved, as illustrated by Avis's purchase of ZipCar. Bike sharing may also make it possible to get around without owning a car and to not worry about parking. In this case it is municipalities, which have taken the lead in providing such services in order to reduce traffic and pollution in cities. Altogether, sharing services make it possible for us to live less materialistic lifestyles.

Materialism

The role of materialism

Despite the potential for sharing to facilitate less materialistic lifestyles, our ingrained materialism also counters our inclination to share. Materialism has been defined in consumer research as:

> The importance a consumer attaches to worldly possessions. At the highest levels of materialism, such possessions assume a central place in a person's life and are believed to provide the greatest sources of satisfaction and dissatisfaction.
>
> *(Belk, 1984, p291)*

The same source offers a measure of materialism based on three components:

- *nongenerosity;*
- *envy; and*
- *possessiveness.*

All three of these traits may be seen to inhibit sharing our goods with others. Nongenerosity speaks for itself. Envy suggests that we compare and measure ourselves against others, often partly based on our ability to conspicuously consume and to display more and 'better' possessions that make claims about our relative status. And possessiveness is another trait that makes it less likely that we will trust others with our things. Ironically, there is another effect of the possessive element of materialism that could be good for environmental sustainability. If we were more attached to and less possessive of possessions like cars, smartphones, and other digital devices, we should be less willing to trade them in regularly for newer models while the old ones are still quite functional (Monbiot, 1999; Chapman, 2005). In this case other design elements may be invoked in order to increase consumer attachment to possessions (Kleine and Baker, 2004; Schifferstein and Zartkruis-Pelgrim, 2008). Nevertheless, all three components of this measure of materialism suggest that more materialistic individuals and societies should be less willing to share.

An interview with Tim Kasser, who authored *The High Price of Materialism* (2002), summarizes some of his findings:

> the more people care about materialistic goals, the less pro-socially they tend to behave. For example, materialistic goals are associated with being less empathetic and cooperative, and more manipulative and competitive...the more that people care about materialistic goals, the less they care about ecological sustainability and the more their lifestyles tend to have a damaging effect on the planet.
>
> *(True Cost, n.d.)*

These conclusions are backed up by other work as well (e.g. Banerjee and McKeage, 1994). Ironically, the more materialistic people are, the lower the feelings of happiness and well-being they report (Belk, 1985; Burroughs and Rindflesch, 2002; Kasser and Ahuvia, 2002; Richins and Dawson, 1992; Wright and Larson, 1993). It has also been found that spending money on experiences is more satisfying than spending money on possessions (e.g. van Boven, 1995). Besides the shallowness and false promise of materialism, an additional explanation may be found in a study be Caprariello and Reis (2013). Their findings suggest that experiences are more likely than possessions to be shared with others and that this social component of experience brings happiness. On the other hand possessions tend to be consumed in private, depriving the user of both the joy of others and the joy of shared experiences.

No doubt the nature of material possessions and experiences also play a role. Some possessions like interactive games are meant to be enjoyed with others while some experiences (e.g. a safari in Africa; Fournier and Guiry, 1993) can be both highly materialistic and lie far from carbon-neutral sustainable consumption.

Sustainable materialism?

Based on the definition of materialism in the last section, the notion of sustainable materialism should be an oxymoron; the more materialism, the less sustainability. Both the quantity of goods consumed and the heightened value placed on consumption by materialists appear antithetical to sustainability. However, there is another notion of materialism that gives rise to what is being called the sustainable materialism movement. It derives from the postmaterialism hypothesis conceived by Ronald Inglehart (1981, 2008). Inglehart maintains that as we satisfy lower order material needs in a Maslow need hierarchy framework, we move on to higher order, less material needs, such as love and self-actualization and that in so doing become part of a postmaterial society. His approach to measuring materialism involves asking people to select which two of the following values are most important to them:

- Maintaining order in the nation.
- Giving people more say in important political decisions.
- Fighting rising prices.
- Protecting freedom of speech.

Those who choose maintaining order and fighting price rises are labeled materialists and those who choose political empowerment and freedom of speech are labeled post-materialists. Those who choose a different combination are placed in a middle category. Based on this scale he is able to show a growth of post-materialism in Europe over the post-Second World War years as well as a low correlation between post-materialism and national wealth.

Inglehart's measures are more macro and abstract than the consumer research focus on the desire for and meanings of possessions. They have been criticized on a number of grounds including these. Nevertheless findings using Inglehart's measures have been used to suggest that there is a new materialism afoot – one that can embrace a desire to have a more sustainable world. This has led to several papers (e.g. Salonen and Ahlberg, 2013; Schlosberg, 2011) as well as one recent conference (Sydney Environment Institute, 2013) devoted to the topic of pursuing sustainability through postmaterialism. Nevertheless, we've heard the predictions of the death or decline of materialism before (e.g. Elgin and Mitchell, 1977; Schor, 1998) as well as the reports of many optimistic expectations that such trends are just over the horizon and will be realized soon (e.g. Elgin, 1977, 1981; Gould, 1988; Gregg, 1936; Kaza, 2005; Nearing, 1954; Schumacher, 1973; Shi, 2001; Wann, 2007). While the new imperatives of the most recent global financial crisis as well as global warming may add urgency to achieving these optimistic forecasts, any significant and sustained movement away from materialism is hard to find. If anything, as the economically developing world grows, the trend is in the opposite direction (e.g. Davis, 2000; Dermé, Sharma and Sethi, 2014; Lu, 2008; Mathur, 2014; Osburg, 2013; Pandey, 2014). Former have-nots of the world are eager to catch up with the haves in terms of housing, travel, automobile ownership, and, more generally, material lifestyle. Simplicity is a difficult premise for them to buy into.

Supply side materialism

Materialism is not just a demand side phenomenon involving consumption. By supply side materialism I don't simply mean that marketing, promotion and advertising help to fuel consumer materialism. Rather, it is an inherent characteristic of business and entrepreneurship in capitalist economies to try to design ways to capitalize on, co-opt or appropriate new sharing or simplifying opportunities arising among consumers in order to make a profit. Such corporate materialism is one factor that distinguishes small scale consumer-initiated non-profit sharing such as that occurs among family, friends and community from the pseudo-sharing, for-profit, collaborative consumption and short-term rental that occurs when businesses intervene between people in what is otherwise P2P sharing (Belk, 2014; Bardhi and Eckhardt, 2015). Belk (2010) notes the fuzzy boundaries in borderline cases of sharing as it shades into commodity exchange or gift giving. Scaraboto (2015) also details some of the hybrid economies that emerge at these borders. Businesses nominally embracing the sharing economy is also a practice that has been termed *sharewashing* – an effort to dress-up profit-seeking businesses in the nobler garb of sharing (Light and Miskelly, 2014).

This practice has become a target for recent criticisms of the sharing economy and has promoted suggestions for using a more apt descriptor such as pseudo-sharing, collaborative consumption, the gig economy, or short-term rental (Roberts, 2015). We can separate the criticisms of the sharing economy into several categories. One involves the argument that new practices such as Airbnb, Uber and Lyft compete unfairly against hotels, motels, taxis and car rental companies. Critics suggest that the unfairness arises because many of those who offer rooms and rides through these services do not pay taxes on their earnings, buy insurance, undergo safety and hygiene inspections or abide by municipal laws such as those vetting drivers and licensing taxis (e.g. Baker, 2014; Leonard, 2014b). A second sort of criticism is that while small scale informal sharing is born out of altruism or friendship and builds a sense of community, most of the mediated formal sharing platforms are motivated by profits, often at the expense of low-paid drivers or other participants (e.g. Leonard, 2014a; Morozov, 2014). A sense of injustice and irony is palpable in these critics' comments:

> The supposed environmental benefits of the sharing economy are likewise laughable: while we are asked to share our cars with neighbours – it's cheaper and greener! – the rich [read: sharing economy CEOs] keep enjoying their yachts, limos and private jets.
>
> *(Morozov, 2014)*

Furthermore, while sharing was initially a matter of survival, it is now seen as something that only those who can afford to hire an Uber private car, reserve an expensive parking space or rent a luxury home can indulge in (Cagle, n.d.). These same privileged users then press municipal governments for non-regulation of these new ventures in the interests of creating 'a more level playing field' (Leonard, 2013). Far from the social justice perspective of sharing for a more equitable and equal world, sharing ventures, in this view, are seen to have just the opposite effect. A related concern is that the gig economy not only undercuts taxi drivers, restaurant workers and hotel employees and puts them out of work, but also forces them and others into the low-paid, uninsured, no pension plan no health insurance work needed to make ventures like Uber and Lyft work. All in all, the indictment of the gig economy is that it has appropriated the term sharing while remaining true to none of the premises of what is truly sharing by some more sober reckoning (Marszalek, 2014). Here the materialism of corporate greed is seen to quickly trump community caring.

Conclusion

In many cities of central California like Fresno, easy to grow fig trees produce more figs than their owners can possibly consume. Some put notices on Craigslist or Kijiji announcing that they are free for the taking. When others with fig trees in their yards are asked, they most commonly grant ready permission to help yourself. This is a type of sharing where the owners get to feel good, the gleaners are grateful and the community benefits in the feelings of trust and solidarity generated. A similar sort of win-win situation was found in the early days of Napster when Sean Parker found a way for owners of digital music and movies to freely exchange recordings with each other. And neighborhood shared gardens, toy libraries, tool libraries and other communal sharing opportunities serve a similar desire for less waste, more use and more shared feelings of neighborliness.

It is a big jump from these small-scale non-profit ventures to 6-year-old Uber, which, as I write this, has been valued at $50 billion. Yet Uber owns no cars, does no advertising and merely offers an application that brings drivers and riders together to reach a specified destination at a competitively bid price that is paid online when the booking is made. This scaling up of old fashioned hitchhiking has found a way to take the danger out of getting a ride and the wait and precariousness our of hailing a taxi cab, at a price that is often below that which would be paid in a cab. Thanks to the reputation economy of rating drivers, passengers, hosts and guests, many collaborative consumption ventures create a form of trust and certainty (e.g. Masum and Tovey, 2011; Solove, 2007). As with the Industrial Revolution and the Computer Revolution, the Sharing Revolution disrupts the economy and employment. But neither of the previous two revolutions caused an economic collapse and both created new types of jobs to replace the old ones they obsolesced. The same is likely to be true of collaborative consumption.

The car-sharing and ride-sharing sectors of collaborative consumption are often given the greatest attention because they have the greatest opportunity to positively affect the environment through reducing automobile ownership, parking acreage, air pollution and traffic congestion. But home-sharing services like Airbnb and CouchSurfing also reduce the amount of water use, land use and energy use compared to hotels (Dechert, 2014). As we have seen, there are issues to be worked out in terms of fairness, regulation, externalities, taxation and other aspects of the Sharing Revolution. But a movement of this magnitude signals another unique affordance of the Internet and Web 2.0. We have not yet seen the end of growth in resulting collaborative consumption opportunities and adoption of existing sharing opportunities, Because there are battles being waged between the old economy and the new economy, it is too early to say just how much impact these changes will have. Witness the up and down battle between the music industry and P2P file-sharing. Much of the battle has already been won. Imagine going back to print encyclopedias and printed library catalog cards instead of online information searches using Google.

We may also see with this Internet transformation a decline in the materialism that still holds back a full embrace or access over product ownership. As we learn to share more and own less, we may realize that materialistic acquisitiveness imposes a great burden of ownership. To the extent that we can be as happy with ready access to things rather than personally archiving, maintaining and safeguarding them, sharing may truly offer a substantial step toward sustainability.

References

Aigrain, P. (2012) *Sharing: Culture and the Economy in the Internet Age*. Amsterdam: Amsterdam University Press

Arsel, Z. and Dobscha, S. (2011) Hybrid Pro-social Exchange Systems: The Case of Freecycle, *Advances in Consumer Research*, vol 39, no 1, pp. 66–67

Baker, D. (2014) The Downside of the Sharing Economy, *Counterpunch*, May 28, www.counterpunch.org/2014/05/28/the-downside-of-the-sharing-economy/, last accessed July 31, 2015

Banerjee, B. and McKeage, K. (1994) How Green Is My Value: Exploring the Relationship between Environmentalism and Materialism, in *Advances in Consumer Research*, vol 21, pp. 147–152

Bardhi, F. and Eckhardt, G. (2012) Access Based Consumption: The Case of Car-Sharing, *Journal of Consumer Research*, vol 39, no 4, pp. 881–898

Bardhi, F. and Eckhardt, G. (2015) The Sharing Economy Isn't About Sharing at All, *Harvard Business Review*, January 28, https://hbr.org/2015/01/the-sharing-economy-isnt-about-sharing-at-all

Belk, R. (1984) Three Scales to Measure Constructs Related to Materialism: Reliability, Validity, and Relationships to Measures of Happiness, in *Advances in Consumer Research*, vol 7, pp. 291–297

Belk, R. (1985) Materialism: Trait Aspects of Living in the Material World, *Journal of Consumer Research*, vol 12, no 4, pp. 265–280

Belk, R. (2010) Sharing, *Journal of Consumer Research*, vol 36, no 6, pp. 715–734

Belk, R. (2014) Sharing versus Pseudo-sharing in Web 2.0, *The Anthropologist*, vol 18 no 1, pp. 7–23

Belk, R. and Llamas, R. (2012) The Nature and Effects of Sharing in Consumer Behavior, in Mick, D., Pettigrew, S., Pechmann, S. and Ozanne, C. (eds), *Transformative Consumer Research for Personal and Collective Well-Being*, New York: Routledge, pp. 625–646

Benkler, Y. (2006) *The Wealth of Networks: How Social Production Transforms Markets and Freedom*, New Haven, CT: Yale University Press, US

Bird-David, N. (2005) The Property of Sharing: Western Analytical Notions, Nayaka Contexts, in Widlok, T. and Tadesse, W. (eds), *Property and Equality, vol 1, Ritualisation, Sharing, Egalitarianism*, New York: Berghahn, pp. 201–215

Botsman, R. and Rogers, R. (2010) *What's Mine is Yours: The Rise of Collaborative Consumption*. New York: Harper Collins

Brady, D. (2014) The Environmental Case for the Sharing Economy, *Bloomberg Businessweek*, September 24, www.bloomberg.com/bw/articles/2014-09-24/the-environmental-case-for-the-sharing-economy, last accessed July 31, 2015

Burroughs, J. and Rindfleisch, A. (2002) Materialism and Well being: A Conflicting Values Perspective, *Journal of Consumer Research*, vol 29 no 4, pp. 348–370

Butler, K. (2015) Happy Meals: Can San Francisco Reinvent the School Cafeteria? *The Atlantic*, March, online edition, www.theatlantic.com/magazine/archive/2015/03/happy-meals/384981/, last accessed July 29, 2015

Cagle, S. (n.d.) The Case Against Sharing: On Access, Scarcity, and Trust, *The NIB*, https://thenib.com/the-case-against-sharing-9ea5ba3d216d, last accessed July 31, 2015

Caprariello, P, and Reis, H. (2013) To Do, to Have, or to Share? Valuing Experiences over Material Possessions Depends on the Involvement of Others, *Journal of Personality and Social Psychology*, vol 104, no 2, pp. 199–215

Caula, R. (2014) School Lunches, Design Boom, May 1, www.designboom.com/art/a-cafeteria-designed-for-me-ideo-05-01-2014, last accessed July 29, 2015

CBS (2009) Poll: Young Say File-sharing OK. *CBS News*, February 11, www.cbsnews.com/stories/2003/09/18/opinion/polls/main573990.shtml, last accessed July 28, 2015

Chapman, J. (2005) *Emotionally Durable Design: Objects, Experiences and Empathy*, London: Routledge

Chen, Y. (2009) Possession and Access: Consumer Desires and Value Perceptions Regarding Contemporary Art Collection and Exhibit Visits, *Journal of Consumer Research*, vol 35 no 4, pp. 925–940.

Davis, D. (ed.) (2000), *The Consumer Revolution in Urban China*, Berkeley, CA: University of California Press

Dechert, S. (2014) Homesharing With AIRBNB: Greener Than Your Usual Hotel, *Clean Technica*, August 11, http://cleantechnica.com/2014/08/11/homesharing-airbnb-greener-usual-hotel/, last accessed July 31, 2015

Dermé, S., Sharma, M. and Sethi, N. (2014) Structural Changes Rather than the Influence of Media: People's Encounter with Economic Liberalization in India, in Mathur, N. (ed.), *Consumer Culture, Modernity and Identity*, New Delhi: Sage, pp. 145–147

Durgee, J. and O'Connor, G. (1995) An Exploration into Renting as Consumption Behavior, *Psychology and Marketing*, vol 12, no 2, pp. 89–104

Elgin, D. (1977) Voluntary Simplicity, *Co-Evolution Quarterly*, Summer, pp. 5–18.

Elgin, D. (1981) *Voluntary Simplicity: Toward a Way of Life that Is Outwardly Simple, Inwardly Rich*, New York: William Morrow and Company, US

Elgin, D. and Mitchell, A. (1977) Voluntary Simplicity: Lifestyle of the Future? *The Futurist*, vol 11, pp. 200–209

Fine, S. (1980) Toward a Theory of Segmentation by Objectives in Social Marketing, *Journal of Consumer Research*, vol 7 no 3, pp. 1–13

Fournier, S. and Guiry, M. (1993) An Emerald Green Jaguar, a House on Nantucket, and an African Safari: Wish Lists and Consumption Dreams in Materialist Society, *Advances in Consumer Research*, vol 20, 352–358

Ghosh, R. (ed.) (2005) *CODE: Collaborative Ownership and the Digital Economy*, Boston, MA: MIT Press

Giesler, M. (2006) Consumer Gift Systems, *Journal of Consumer Research*, vol 33 no 2, 2006, pp. 283–290

Giesler, M. and Pohlman, M. (2003) The Anthropology of File-sharing: Consuming Napster as a Gift, *Advances in Consumer Research*, vol 30, pp. 273–279

Gollnhoffer, J., Hellwig, K. and Morhart, F. (2016) Fair is Good but What is Fair? Negotiations of Distributive Justice in an Emerging Non-monetary Sharing Model, *Journal of the Association for Consumer Research*, vol 1 no 2, special issue on ownership and sharing

Gould, P. (1988) *Early Green Politics: Back to Nature, Back to the Land, and Socialism in Britain, 1880–1900*, Basingstoke: Palgrave Macmillan

Grassmuck, V. (2012) The Sharing Turn: Why We are Generally Nice and Have a Good Chance to Cooperate Our Way Out of the Mess We Have Gotten Ourselves Into, in Sützl, W. Stalder, F. Maier, R. and Hug, T. (eds), *Cultures and Ethics of Sharing*, Innsbruck: Innsbruck University Press, pp. 17–34

Gregg, R. (1936) *The Value of Voluntary Simplicity*, Wallingford, PA: Pendle Hill

Hamari, J., Sjöklint, M. and Ukkonen, A. (2016) The Sharing Economy: Why People Participate in Collaborative Consumption, *Journal of the Association for Information Science and Technology*, vol 69, no 9, pp. 2047–2059

Heinrichs, H. (2013) Sharing Economy: A Potential New Pathway to Sustainability, *Gaia*, vol 22, no 4, pp. 228–231

Hellwig, K., Belk, R. and Morhart, F. (2016) Shared Moments of Sociality: Embedded Sharing within Peer-to-peer Hospitality Platforms, in Hall, S. and Ince, A. (eds), *Sharing, Gifting and Reciprocity: Everyday Moral Economies and Politics of Crisis*, London: Routledge

Hemetsberger, A. (2012) 'Let the Source Be with You!' – Practices of Sharing in Free and Open-Source Communities, in Sützl, W. Stalder, F. Maier, R. and Hug, T. (eds), *Cultures and Ethics of Sharing*, Innsbruck: Innsbruck University Press, pp. 117–128

Hunt, R. (2005) One-Way Economic Transfers, in Carrier, J (ed.), *A Handbook of Economic Anthropology*, Cheltenham: Elgar, pp. 290–301

Hyde, L. (2010) *Common as Air: Revolution, Art, and Ownership*, New York: Farrar, Straus and Giroux

Inglehart, R. (1981) Post-materialism in an Environment of Insecurity, *American Political Science Review*. vol 75 no 4, pp. 880–900

Inglehart, R. (2008) Changing Values among Western Publics from 1970 to 2006, *West European Politics*, vol 31 Nos 1-2, pp. 130–146

John, N. (2012) Sharing and Web 2.0: The Emergence of a Keyword, *New Media and Society*, vol 15 no 2, pp. 167–182

Kasser, T. (2002) *The High Price of Materialism*, Boston, MA: MIT Press

Kasser, T. and Ahuvia, A (2002) Materialistic Values and Well-being in Business Students, *European Journal of Social Psychology*, vol 32, pp. 137–146

Kaza, S. (2005) *Hooked! Buddhist Writings on Greed, Desire, and the Urge to Consume*, San Francisco, CA: Shambhala

Kleine, S. and Baker, S. (2004) An Integrative Review of Material Possession Attachment, *Academy of Marketing Science Review*, vol 1, pp. 1–39

Leonard, A. (2013) Millenials Will Not be Regulated, *Salon*, September 20, www.salon.com/2013/09/20/millennials_will_not_be_regulated/, last accessed July 31, 2015

Leonard, A. (2014a) 'Sharing Economy Shams': Deception at the Core of the Internet's Hottest Businesses, *Salon*, March 14, www.salon.com/2014/03/14/sharing_economy_shams_deception_at_the_core_of_the_internets_hottest_businesses/, last accessed July 31, 2015

Leonard, A. (2014b) You're Not Fooling Us, Uber! 8 Reasons Why the 'Sharing Economy' is all about Corporate Greed, *Salon*, February 17, www.salon.com/2014/02/17/youre_not_fooling_us_uber_8_reasons_why_the_sharing_economy_is_all_about_corporate_greed/, last accessed July 31, 2015

Lessig, L. (2001) *The Future of Ideas: The Fate of the Commons in a Connected World*, New York: Random House

Light, A. and Miskelly, C. (2014) *Design for Sharing*, Sustainable Society Network, Northumbria University, UK

Lu, P. X. (2008) *Elite China: Luxury Consumer Behavior in China*, Singapore: John Wiley and Sons

Martin, C. (2013) Improving School Lunch by Design, *New York Times*, October 16, online edition, http://opinionator.blogs.nytimes.com/2013/10/16/rethinking-school-lunch/?_r=0, last accessed July 29, 2015

Masum, M. and Tovey, M. (2011) *The Reputation Society: How Online Opinions are Reshaping the Offline World*, The MIT Press, Cambridge, MA

Marszalek, B. (2014) The Sharing Economy = Brand Yourself, *Counterpunch*, May 26, www.counterpunch.org/2014/05/26/the-sharing-economy-brand-yourself, last accessed July 31, 2015.

Mathur, N. (2014) Modernity, Consumer Culture and Construction of Urban Youth Identity in India: A Disembedding Perspective, in Mathur, N. (ed.), *Consumer Culture, Modernity and Identity*, New Delhi: Sage, pp. 89–12

Monbiot, G. (1999) We're Not Materialistic Enough, *The Guardian*, May 29, online version, www.monbiot.com/1999/05/29/were-not-materialistic-enough/, last accessed July 29, 2015.

Morozov, E. (2014) Don't Believe the Hype, the 'Sharing Economy' Masks a Failing Economy, September 28, *The Guardian*, online edition, www.theguardian.com/commentisfree/2014/sep/28/sharing-economy-internet-hype-benefits-overstated-evgeny-morozov, last accessed July 31, 2015

Nearing, S. (1954) *Man's Search for the Good Life*, Harborside, ME: The Social Science Institute

Osburg, J. (2013) *Anxious Wealth: Money and Morality Among China's New Rich*, Stanford, CA: Stanford University Press

Ostrom, E. (1990) *Governing the Commons: The Evolution of Institutions for Collective Action*, Cambridge: Cambridge University Press

Pandey, S. (2014) Consumer Agency of Urban Women in India, in Mathur, N. (ed.), *Consumer Culture, Modernity and Identity*, New Delhi: Sage, pp. 71–88

Polanyi, K. (1944) *The Great Transformation*, New York: Beacon

Price, J. (1975) Sharing: The Integration of Intimate Economics, *Anthropologica*, vol 17 no 1, pp. 3–27

Putnam, R. (2000) *Bowling Alone: The Collapse and Revival of American Community*, New York: Simon & Schuster

PwC (2015) The Sharing Economy, Consumer Intelligence Series, PricewaterhouseCoopers, http://download.pwc.com/ie/pubs/2015-pwc-cis-sharing-economy.pdf, last accessed July 27, 2015

Richins, M. and Dawson, S. (1992) A Consumer Values Orientation for Materialism and its Measurement: Scale Development and Validation, *Journal of Consumer Research*, vol 19, no 4, pp. 303–316

Roberts, J. (2015) As 'Sharing Economy' Fades, these 2 Phrases are Likely to Replace it, *Forbes*, July 29, http://fortune.com/2015/07/29/sharing-economy-chart/, last accessed July 31, 2015.

Sacks, D. (2011) The Sharing Economy, *Fast Company*, April 18, online edition, www.fastcompany.com/1747551/sharing-economy, last accessed July 31, 2015

Salonen, A. and Ahlberg, M. (2013) Towards Sustainable Society: From Materialism to Post-materialism, *International Journal of Sustainable Society*, vol 5 no 4, pp. 374–393

Scaraboto, D. (2015) Selling, Sharing, and Everything in between: The Hybrid Economies of Collaborative Networks, *Journal of Consumer Research*, vol 42 no 1, pp. 152–176

Schifferstein, H. and Zartkruis-Pelgrim, E. (2008) Consumer-Product Attachment: Measurement and Design Implications, *International Journal of Design*, vol 2 no 3, pp. 1–13

Schlosberg, D. (2011) From Sustainability to a New Materialism, Sustainability Forum, www.policyinnovations.org/ideas/briefings/data/000212, last accessed July 29, 2015.

Schor, J. (1998) *The Overspent American: Upscaling, Downshifting, and the New Consumer*, Harper Perennial, US

Schor, J. (2014) Debating the Sharing Economy, Great Transition Initiative, www.greattransition.org/publication/debating-the-sharing-economy, October, last accessed July 29, 2015

Schumacher, E. (1973) *Small is Beautiful: Economics as if People Mattered*, New York: Harper and Row

Shi, D. (2001) *The Simple Life: Plain Living and High Thinking in American Culture*, Athens, GA: University of Georgia Press, US

Sinnreich, A. (2013) *The Piracy Crusade: How the Music Industry's War on Sharing Destroys Markets and Erodes Civil Liberties*, Amherst, MA: University of Massachusetts Press.

Solove, D. J. (2007) *"I've Got Nothing To Hide" and Other Misunderstandings of Privacy*, George Washington University Law School, US, retrieved from http://tehlug.org/files/solove.pdf

Stack, C. (1983) *All Our Kin: Strategies for Survival in a Black Community*, New York: Basic Books

Sunstein, C. (2006) *Infotopia: How Many Minds Produce Knnowledge*, Oxford: Oxford University Press

Sydney Environmental Institute (2013) Sustainable Materialism: An Environmentalism of Everyday Life, November 29, http://sydney.edu.au/environment-institute/events/what-is-sustainable-materialism-an-environmentalism-of-everyday-life/, last accessed July 29, 2015

True Cost (n.d.) A Conversation with Tim Kasser, http://truecostmovie.com/tim-kasser-interview/, last accessed July 29, 2015

Tuan, Y.-F. (1983) *Segmented Worlds and Self: Group Life and Individual Consciousness*, Minneapolis, MN: University of Minnesota Press

Vaidhyanathan S. (2001) *Copyrights and Copywrongs: The Rise of Intellectual Property and How it Threatens Creativity*, New York: New York University Press

Van Boven, L. (1995) Experientialism, Materialism, and the Pursuit of Happiness, *Review of General Psychology*, vol 9 no 2, pp. 132–142

Vikas, R., Varman, R. and Belk, R. (2015) Status, Caste, and Markets in a Changing Indian Village, *Journal of Consumer Research*, 42 (October).

Wann, D. (2007) *Simple Prosperity: Finding Real Wealth in a Sustainable Lifestyle*, New York: St. Martin's Griffin

Woldow, D. (2013) Is IDEO's Vision Harming San Francisco's School Lunch Program, November 12, www.beyondchron.org/is-ideos-vision-harming-san-franciscos-school-lunch-program/, last accessed July 29, 2015

Wright, N. and Larson, V. (1993) Materialism and Life Satisfaction: A Meta-Analysis, *Advances in Consumer Research*, vol 6, pp. 158–175

12

A JOURNEY OF
TWO DESIGNERS

Yorick Benjamin

Abstract

Sustainable design (SD) appeals to our need to do good, but twists our design mind into thoughts of uncertainty and delivers a thread of anxiety. To help the designer to decide on these complex relationships, many theories, tools and methods have been proposed over the years that attempt to steer designers and help them realize products and services that have less impact on the biosphere. There are many academic and theoretical models, from the quantitative to the qualitative. They cross one idea with another and often merge and collide into a confused and over complex whole. This chapter explores the journey of two designers (myself, and Jonathan Stedman) with the shared aim of designing and developing a sustainable product for everyday use. The aim is simple, but as everyone knows who has explored these issues the journey is complex. There are many unknowns and hidden layers that trip-up the designer and give challenge to their design decisions and judgements. Every physical element of the product and the system that surrounds its realization, and the services that underpin it, have an impact that needs to be understood and weighted; what is good, what is bad and how do we define either? On this product development journey we draw upon ideas from a variety of models in an eclectic fashion while wholeheartedly taking a pragmatic approach to realizing a real product for everyday use. The product developed is a bus shelter for public transport. The development from a design idea to public use is presented as a narrative to explore one way of working towards a sustainable product. It is a practice based design case study in which we find some good design solutions, and some problems. Intentionally, this chapter does not significantly draw upon other references or publications as it is based on a modest but real sustainable design journey. It is the journey itself that provides the case study, and the final outcome (shelters and systems) the impact.

Keywords: material resilience, life cycle assessment (LCA), cyclic, low carbon, practice based

Defining borders

In broad terms, SD approaches and tools are conceived to reduce the negative impact of human made products and services. They achieve this to a varying degree and in one way or another. How we measure the success of these methods is always important, yet often overlooked, as without measurement we do not know if we have done the right thing. Out of the assessment options open to us, carbon reduction is the headline grabber – the designer's 'gold' currency.

There are numerous terms and methods that connect with the notion of SD. For example: green design; eco design; product, service, system (PPS); cradle to cradle (C2C); design for the circular economy; environmentally conscious design; sustainable product development; and, design for social innovation. Then a subset of layers, or enablers if you like: reuse; renewable; recycle; longevity; low carbon; multifunctional; upcycle; and, life cycle assessment (LCA). Although individually positioned and contextualized, these approaches cross one side of a divide to another and in reality each method often crosses the territorial boarder of another. This is by no means an exhaustive list and not an attempt to justify or evaluate these approaches. They are referenced to underline the fact that there are many procedures that engage at different levels with the common aim of contributing to 'sustainable development'. However, as in the case of defining what we mean by 'sustainable development' our sustainable design methods tend to remain generic in nature and need a lot of tailoring when practically applied. In other circumstances they are so targeted at a specialism that they are not useful to the nomadic and open role of designers who frequently cross disciplines and sectors. In keeping with the confused state of methods and their defined boundaries we also seem to reinvent what has gone before. For example, some current terms are cyclic in their own right, such as cleaner production, industrial ecology and waste prevention studies. For example, van Weenen (1990) considered the pre-extraction of raw materials, energy and material flows (think *biosphere* and *technosphere*) and associated toxicology many years ago … ideas that reappear in both the circular economy and cradle to cradle models.

It is not surprising that we have created such monumental environmental problems for ourselves; we need to think carefully about how we can alleviate the ongoing damage to the biosphere. Since humanity discovered the abundance of carbon based energy we have aggressively accelerated the throughput of materials and energy with great ingenuity to meet our product-service needs (Osborne, 2014). Coupled with population growth, this is a heady mix of pressure and requires fresh new approaches, such was the case of *Natural Capital* where we attempted to balance economic and ecological needs within the resources available to us (Hawken, 2010).

Today, while we wait for majority to recognize and value our natural capital it follows that in general mass-produced products and services have damaging energy and material impacts to the biosphere. They also carry within them worrying toxins and carcinogens and may be a result of inhuman or poor working conditions. If it is a truism, 'that as a norm most products and services have a negative impact on the biosphere', it follows that one of the first SD strategies a designer should ask themselves is whether a product is needed at all? This brings us back to the fundamental question of what is good, what is bad and who decides?

Need

Perception of product need is a personal and highly subjective viewpoint and is dependent upon context. Many readers will know that the relationships between design, consumption and need were addressed and championed several decades ago in a number of seminal texts, most notably, *Design for the Real World* (Papanek, 1971). In thinking about meeting need we aim to optimize our valuable resources taken from the biosphere for worthwhile applications, and place the human condition at the heart of the design process. If we wisely invest the resources we have on things we truly need it reframes the negative impacts of a given product or service as a more understandable compromise. Some areas that may be considered essential to meet human needs are: transportation to move ourselves; resources such as food; education because the more we learn the more we should care, positively innovate and improve; textiles for climate and physical protection; healthcare to keep us stronger longer; communication methods to spread knowledge and understanding; housing to protect and nurture; agriculture to feed and sustain; and, energy to optimize the productivity of our services, systems and products. There may be other areas to consider and add, but the common thread is that these are useful and realistic product-services realms that are needed by practically all societies.

Nevertheless, how we interpret the detailed delivery of these realms and what models we use to invest and implement our precious resources to meet these needs is often questionable and driven by unsympathetic and destructive values. Sustainable design can contribute and make a positive change to all these areas. There are scores of design opportunities that can service the needs of billions of people. Let's try to realize them through more diligent forms of design.

Opportunity

In 2008 Transport for London (TfL) announced an intriguing competition to design an iconic new bus shelter for the city. The opportunity to establish a product that could share a place with Sir Giles Gilbert Scott's famous K6 Red Telephone box was a product designer's dream. There were 53 entries including many well-known design companies and large urban infrastructure manufacturers. The high product delivery numbers were tempting. The design was to replace 11,000 (mainly) metal *Insignia* shelters with an investment in excess of £44,000,000.

Deciding on need

Fully appreciating that a bus shelter is not life changing or critical to human survival, the brief did seem to meet a real 'need', nevertheless. The shelter is an important element in a much bigger logistical transport system that contributes to low carbon living and makes bus travel more pleasurable and comfortable. The system has potential to reduce the number of cars on the road and thus lead to related improvements in health, wellbeing, air quality and mobility around the city. The London's network of shelters service millions of travellers weekly and are a key part of London's street furniture, and visual landscape, providing safe access and drop off points for bus users. Furthermore, it not difficult to recognize the social, economic and environmental benefits if a sustainable design solution could be realized and presented to the public as an integral part of their everyday lives. With all this in mind, we entered the competition.

Stage 1

The first stage of the competition was to submit a fairly comprehensive document to a technical specification committee comprising 45 members, who would evaluate all the entries over several days. They were looking for proposals that had the potential to be iconic but also demonstrated a real understanding of the project's technical demands and requirements. In addition to overall aesthetics and usability criteria, the committee paid close attention to areas such as structural engineering; DDA compliance; supply chain resilience; effective delivery and installation regimes; maintenance; and, very basic but indicative cost.

The TfL bus shelter brief did not mention sustainable design at all in the specification. Nevertheless, we submitted an outline proposal for a product we named the D4S Shelter (with D4S standing for 'design for sustainability') and were somewhat surprised when the design was shortlisted as one of nine proposals to be selected for further development. Another unexpected result was that the submitted proposal scored highest for technical rigour and understanding of the brief. We had assumed that a shelter made predominately from wood was unlikely to progress in the competition due to technical concerns over the material; virtually all urban shelters are made of steel, aluminium or stainless steel. Furthermore, the supply chain for metal (ferrous and non-ferrous) is both sophisticated and mature, and therefore the cost is reasonably predictable for the high volume production of extruded and rolled components. In contrast, the durable woods required for this project (we were planning to use oak) are much harder to guarantee supplies for and estimating the cost is therefore less reliable. To put this into perspective, the procurement of wood at this project scale would be over 5,000 cubic metres. Unlike many other commodities, hardwoods such as oak do not have a robust price index due to unknowns such as specific species, harvesting routines and processing stages. In the UK there is a standing supply of oak of 69.4 million cubic metres (Forestry Commission, 2014) on a growing cycle of 100–150 years. This means that supply is variable over time and this extended cycle impacts on predicting price. Therefore, it is very difficult to make direct cost comparisons with alternative materials such as steel and this makes large-scale procurement more problematic.

Procurement

A meaningful SD approach with client involvement often challenges their current management systems, introduces new unaudited materials, interferes with sub-contractor arrangements, champions materials and systems with minimal test and structural engineering data and asks the client to spend on unproven markets. This missing proof and evidence causes great difficulty for common procurement practice and moving to contract. It raises an early and often insurmountable constraint for designers working towards more sustainably designed products and services. If a designer specifies an environmentally benign material such as oak because they are convinced it has positive technical and environmental attributes over a more established traditional material such as steel, it does not mean the material will be accepted by the client. It is likely that its market penetration is very limited (because it is not proven in that specific setting), which means it will be unavailable for the production of mass produced products. Very few clients will take the risk of supply chain failures as that can have a catastrophic impact on their business. Frustratingly, when specifying material substitution in any meaningful volume as a SD strategy, it is likely to fail due to a lack of supply chain resilience, convincing backup data and market and supplier endorsement. The default procurement position, therefore, is business as usual, where complex industrial materials are favoured that may well be toxic, energy intensive, non-recyclable or only partially so, and highly resistant to decay.

It follows that procurement departments in the public sector need product endorsements and greater confidence in the product supply chain. To achieve this, these chains must be resilient and guaranteed. There is accountability to consider and paperwork to sign off. These departments are typically conservative and risk averse. So even though most regional, national and international government procurement policies support sustainable development as a key priority, there are systemic internal barriers to procuring more sustainably designed products. With this point in mind, a design competition is a good route to generating interest in new sustainable designs. However, to be clear, putting a sustainable design competition winner into production and risking capital is quite another step.

Common language

The lack of follow-through on public procurement for SD is disappointing, and does much to bar smaller companies entering the market with novel SD products. Although only a qualitative observation, surely there are many opportunities lost for both the designer and the procurer? For example, bus shelters (and street furniture in general) are a highly visible and a rare opportunity for public authorities to demonstrate to the public their commitment to the green agenda – even to those traveling past in cars! It is perfectly understandable why public procurement departments feel insecure or are unable to back the unknown. However, they are in a good position to make a difference if obstacles are overcome, or removed. In addition, they have many great opportunities across the proposed areas of need to support SD: transportation; education; textiles; healthcare; communication; housing; and, energy.

Another key procurement obstacle is the lack of numeric technical data that is fundamental to the procurement process for low impact and sustainable materials. In a competing market where mature products have a track record, the SD concept often stands forlorn and naked apart from some excited yet unproven claims. Therefore we need to use the tools at our disposal that speak to procurers in a language they understand to gain support and a contract for SD products and services. This is where life cycle assessment (LCA) becomes a valuable tool and was very powerful in the TfL project. If you are making claims about your SD product you need to justify them; LCA provides quantified data, which is a language that both procurement departments and clients understand and value. Most importantly, LCA helps proposals to become economically-meaningful, as clients know there is a value in carbon savings in real cash terms and through PR and marketing differentiation. Once short-listed in the TfL competition, and to support the D4S shelter proposal, we approached Pré in The Netherlands. They are a well-respected company in the sector, and developers of the world's leading LCA software, SimaPro.

Material switching

Pré were very generous with their support and expertise and produced an LCA of the reference product – the current and existing Insignia shelter used by TfL. This would be compared with the new D4S Shelter we had designed in response to the brief. However, for Pré to carry out a meaningful LCA, they need all the data (material types, processes, transportation, volume, sizes, etc.) related to the components of the D4S so they could make a full and detailed comparison. This proved tricky, as for example, at this point we could not specify the main timber elements as we were still working on the best choice for the project.

Up to this time we had been certain that the D4S would be manufactured in oak. However, we were concerned that we lacked the experience and supply chain to support the use of this material. The use of oak requires a craftsperson's knowledge that we did not possess, but more fundamental was that movement (twisting, expanding, contracting etc.) in the material can range from 2 to 3 per cent, which is a considerable amount. We felt this was an issue as it would cause assembly and maintenance difficulties when it came to replacing components. For example, if after 5 years a shelter was installed and one of its posts was severely damaged by a lorry hitting it, would a supplied replacement component fit? All the evidence we collected showed that follow-on maintenance and repair required skilled workers and may lead to servicing problems.

One of our project specification aims was to remove all tooling by designing a SD product that was created in 3D CAD and went into production from the digital file without specialist knowledge of wood (the knowledge focus being CAD and digital manufacturing). This approach would enable agile and bespoke developments for special sites and interest groups. We needed a wood that was easily machined into components, had minimal movement, and as such, could be replaced using the same CAD files some years later – attributes you can guarantee when using steel or aluminium. At this point we made a key decision and switched the wood specification from oak to 'sweet chestnut'. The advantages were that sweet chestnut mainly grows in short usable lengths and because of this limitation, if it is not a fence post, it is commonly manufactured into an engineered wood as glue laminated timber (often referred to as *glulam*). It is not the purpose of this text to go into great detail about sweet chestnut. Nevertheless, the key benefits are that glulam sweet chestnut is a lot less prone to movement, and that there is ample woodland supply under cultivation near London in the south east of the UK. Furthermore, as in the case of oak it does not need treatment, is reasonably hard wearing and should mellow to a pleasant grey over time.

Supportive data (SimaPro)

Having carried out as much research as we could on sweet chestnut, Pré completed the LCA (quickscan). The following information is taken from a personal communication making a comparison of the Benjamin Stedman bus shelter and the Insignia bus shelter, in which the following methodology was used:

> A comparison will be made between the reference shelter (Insignia) and D4S shelter using the Eco-indicator 99 method (H/A perspective), expressed in Points (Pt). 1000 Pt equal the total environmental impact of an average European citizen. The CO_2 emissions were calculated using the IPCC 2007 GWP 100a method, expressed in CO_2 equivalents. CO_2 uptake is taken into account in both these methods. To calculate the LCA SimaPro 7.1 software was used and the data was taken from the Ecoinvent 2.0 database. The functional unit used in this screening was: 1 occupied bus shelter location during 30 years.
>
> *(PRé Consultants, personal communication, 2008)*

From the SD perspective, the results were very positive. The SD strategies that had been used to conceptually design the D4S shelter showed that great environmental wins were possible:

Overall the Insignia shelter scored 559 Pts, the D4S Shelter scored 53 Pts, meaning the new design was less than 10% of the environmental impact of the Insignia shelter. Translated into percentages, if the Insignia shelter scores 100% the D4S Shelter scores –2%. The Insignia shelter causes an equivalent of 8.7 metric tons of CO2 to be emitted through its manufacture and installation, whilst the D4S shelter was carbon negative, with a net uptake of 166kg of CO2.

(PRé Consultants, personal communication, 2008)

Taking the above figures into account the overall benefits are substantial:

- Designing with wood instead of steel, and applying SD logic to other components such as the concrete foundation, removed $11,000 \times 8.7$ metric tons of CO_2 = 95,700 tons of CO_2.
- Sequestering $11,000 \times 166kg$ of CO_2 within the D4S design gave a carbon credit of 1,860 tons CO_2.

Adding the above figure together the D4S shelter made from wood had the potential to remove 97,560 tons of CO_2 when compared to the steel Insignia shelter. The low carbon figure represented a big win for using wood.

These results were exciting, not least because the Insignia is actually an excellent design and serves London's traveling public very well. It is economically designed but robust, simple and understated. It takes on the role of public servant very effectively and in our view as a steel shelter it is well executed. However, it is a baseline model, meaning that there are numerous more complex and more resource intensive shelters on the market, which would score even more negatively than the Insignia.

Beyond carbon

The LCA had thrown up very helpful data to convince TfL that significant CO_2 savings could be realized. However, there were also other useful benefits from the human health, ecosystem and resource depletion results. Within the LCA the biosphere and technosphere material cycles were also assessed. Combined with climate change impacts are other factors such as associated toxicology (Method: Eco-indicator 99 (H) V2.05 / Europe EI 99 H/A / weighting), the study includes: carcinogens; respiratory organics; respiratory inorganics; climate change; radiation; ozone layer; ecotoxicity; acid/eutrophication; land use; minerals; and, fossil fuels.

In Figure 12.1, the impact differences between the two designs on the three main parameters can be clearly seen. The Insignia shelter scores 559 Pts, whereas the D4S Shelter scores 53 Pts. If we examine the human health data in Figure 12.2 (below) the differences between the two designs are obvious. At a time when we focus on carbon statistics these figures are worth remembering as designers tend to put these factors to one side when thinking about SD and focus on other more tangible issues such as embodied energy, recycling, multifunctionality, patina and such like.

The benefits on human health of realizing many more products that are demonstrably benign is difficult to quantify due to the huge scale of the issue. However, we only have to look in the ocean or at our bread and cereal bars (Ecologist, 2013) to know that we are pushing the limits of biodiversity and our environs that support human health.

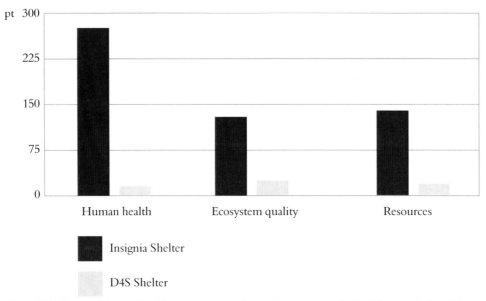

Figure 12.1 Overview human health, ecosystem quality and resources analysis of the two shelter designs

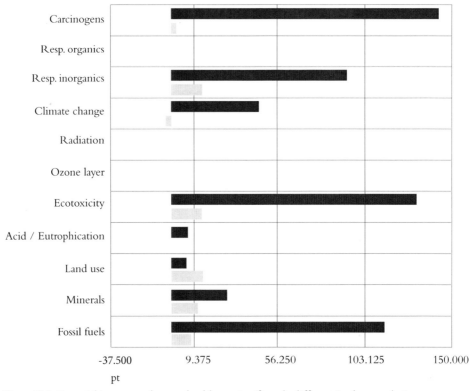

Figure 12.2 Potential impacts to human health are significantly different in the two designs

Figure 12.3 D4S Shelter for TfL incorporating SD strategies of product longevity reuse, colocation, future proofing and back-to-grid solar and renewable resources

D4S Shelter overview

The D4S shelter shown in Figure 12.3 had been designed with attention to aesthetics, appropriateness and economics. The design met all the requirements of the TfL brief. The shelter demonstrated best practice in sustainable product design and embodied many innovative yet practical cost effective solutions. The design was intentionally understated to fit within the streetscape for an anticipated period of 30 years, or more. It was to be made of high quality engineered materials: sweet chestnut, stainless steel, glass and prompt lime mortar. The aim was for it to age gracefully and avoid becoming a stylistic relic of 2010. Natural materials and future proof ICT facilities were combined in a well-considered design with the aim of encouraging public affection.

The shelter offered people generous seating, increased lighting, digital information, good visibility and a secure environment. Furthermore, the natural wood was maintenance free. The design was modular and would fit both flat and sloping sites based around half bay modules that facilitated many variations. ICT could be fitted into the seating bay at any time next to the totem post (the tallest post shown in Figure 12.1), which also doubled as a flagpole.

Sustainable design strategies

The D4S design was proactively based on principles of SD. The sweet chestnut as the main material choice was one contributing factor to the overall scheme, which included the following:

* *Renewable resources with socio economic advantages*: The main material, FSC certificated sweet chestnut, was to come from 18,000 hectares of coppice woods in West Sussex, sustainably harvested for more than 200 years. CO_2 is absorbed in the growth of the wood and stored (see previous LCA data). All glulam components were also to be made in West Sussex so resources, labour and transportation of products were relatively local to London.

- *Reuse*: The shelter was designed to fit to the existing Insignia foundation. The D4S foundations were to be fitted to the cut off Insignia posts. Steel reinforcement would be attached; over this a precast mould is placed and set horizontal. The entire foundation assembly is then fixed in situ in just 20 minutes using fast curing lime 'Prompt', as used by the Romans. With no invasive foundation work it was conceivable that shelter installation would be reduced to one day from the normal two days required. This aim would contribute significant environment and cost savings while reducing inconvenience to motorists and pedestrians. The reuse proposal for foundations would lead to saving energy in production and transportation for the supply of approximately 16,500 tons of concrete. The D4S was also designed to use the same glass as the Insignia. It was estimated that this would result in approximately 60,000 glass panes from the existing installed 'Insignia' model being reused. Their glass would be reclaimed, refurbished and fitted to the D4S. New glass would only be used if needed.

- *Renewable energy*: The roof of the D4S was designed with embedded solar panels to provide back-to-grid renewable energy. This energy gain was not included in the LCA calculation but was a further SD proposal to offset the manufacture of the D4S and its operational power requirements. The solar panels on 11,000 shelters came to approximately 30,000m^2 and payback for energy used in D4S manufacture was estimated at 10 years.

- *Colocation*: An additional saving in material and environmental terms was the colocation of the timetable information case (see ICT, future proofing) and the flagpole as a part of the shelter design. These were both integrated into the shelter design as a 'totem' and to reduce street clutter, meaning there would be no need to dig 11,000 holes, fill them with concrete and supply flagpoles.

- *Future proofing*: The D4S Shelter was designed with an area that served three purposes: it was a seat bay, or could be used for advertising posters (within the technical specification) or become a robust ICT housing for touchscreen information and timetabling. Removing the seat and glass, then slotting in 40mm thick tongue and groove glulam planks to create a box with a void achieved this. As decisions were made on ICT modules they could be added *ad hoc* to the box simply by removing the appropriate planks. All power and auxiliaries were housed in the box, which could also be installed double width to become a much larger information area. A small innovation that supported future proofing, and the overall resilience and serviceability of the D4S, was the inclusion of a secure 13-amp plug socket. This was for workers doing service and repair work. For example, if the external advertising client (Clear Channel) needed to change the size of an advertising unit, this task could be performed on site using the power socket, with minimal street disruption. Like most wooden structures, the shelter glulam components are very adaptable. Within limits, parts can be remade and upgraded, adapted on site and changed any time after the original installation. These unanticipated changes are very difficult on metal shelters, which are difficult to retrofit upgrades to in a neat and integrated fashion, and not generally future proof. The inclusion of the socket would help workers carryout many of these tasks without the need to bring a separate generator to site.

- *Product longevity*: From an aesthetic perspective the D4S was conceived to be an understated design and fit in with the street scape for many years to come. With the exception of the solar panel, CCTV, infrared detectors and ICT totem and electrics, all other components were specified to have a minimal 30-year service life. The main wooden structure enabled new components to be easily upgraded at a later date and could be easily repaired by local woodworkers without specialist tools. The aim was to create a shelter that would have double the product life span of the Insignia.

- *Optimization*: Throughout the product design and associated services we made a conscious effort to 'optimize' the use of all materials. For example, the integrated totem (flag, timetable and ICT) reduces the amount of materials and time needed to install the units and lessens those impacts on the streetscape.

Disappointment, but nevertheless

At this time (2009) and for all sorts of unknowns, which have never become clear TfL cancelled the competition. The finalists that included ARUP, Conran Design and Priestman Goode were extremely disappointed (being polite here) but the competition coincided with a change in the Mayor of London. London's transport is a key part of its political landscape and at £44,000,000 investment a highly visible asset; there were a lot of interested parties. Along with the other competitors we were disappointed, but nevertheless, there were some positives. We had determined that LCA input was very important for procurement, and this had meant that we had designed the D4S in far greater detail than the competition demanded. We established a supply chain model, a complete bill of materials (BOM), 3D CAD at component level and with all sub-assembles detailed. The design was fully specified to go into prototyping iterations, and so we were already at an advanced stage. Although this sudden and unforeseen change in direction cost us a lot of additional work it was very informative and educational; we felt that we had managed to design a shelter that would serve the public well, while being an implicit advert for sustainable design. Moreover, even though the competition had been cancelled, we knew that the design had been well received. Although it was the only entry that was designed with sustainability to the fore, this approach had supported its progression throughout the competition. In this way, the whole process had given us confidence to look further into engineered wood as the *new metal*, and support this with a range of SD strategies. The design had proven to be competitive on cost and materials. To date, however, we had not produced any tangible, real world evidence for procurement departments to work with.

The next generation: insightful procurement

In 2011, the enlightened procurement department of Cornwall Council put out a tender for the 'Design of Sustainable Bus Shelters'! Given its geographic position, environment and its wealth of natural resources, Cornwall is striving to become recognized as a green peninsula and as the developer of a smart innovation and knowledge-based economy. Given the previous comment on the procurement process it was admirable that this council was prepared to take a risk and back their sustainable development transport policies. The project was demanding and the procurement department was fully behind their brief with the following specification:

- Bus shelters should seek to be zero carbon in sourcing, manufacture and operation. The prototype design will provide at least a zero carbon design, endeavouring to provide carbon capture in sourcing and fabrication/manufacture but excluding erection/installation.
- They should have a very low carbon demand in operation.

- Design information should demonstrate the sustainability of each shelter in manufacture, construction, use and decommissioning. This should be achieved through considering the following issues associated with materials: sourcing, transportation, production methods, energy use in sourcing, production and operation, and reuse/recycling/disposal to landfill upon decommissioning (Morgan, 2013).

This is the sort of brief sustainable design practitioners want to see from their public bodies. It seemed that all the work we carried out for TfL would have some future after all and we tendered for the contract. The results were as follows. There were 15 expressions of interest in the original contract from a variety of organizations. 14 of these sent representatives to the supplier information event and 10 responded to the request for quotation. We were the successful tenderer and scored 21/25 for quality and 4.5/5 on the 'design for zero carbon' aspect (ibid., p1).

Material selection

Having won the contract, the next step was to design a new shelter range for Cornwall and this change in locale led us to re-evaluate the appropriateness of sweet chestnut. After all, Cornwall council acted as if they actually wanted to have their SD commissioned shelter put into production, so it had better be right! Sweet chestnut is a fine material and there are many socio economic and environmental reasons to support it. Many British woodlands are in decay and by specifying sweet chestnut we help encourage woodland management and support biodiversity. Even so, we had concerns regarding production supplies and cost, and given that there is a seismic shift on liabilities when a design is no longer a concept and is put into production, it is essential that the supply chain is robust. We do not know if our assessment was just, but we were concerned enough to be wary of committing fully to sweet chestnut and we looked for alternative woods. We had been tracking the development of modified and engineered woods for some years and we revisited Accoya. After due diligence we specified Accoya for the new shelters. Accoya wood results from a patented process in which softwood is modified by acetylation. The benefits are remarkable, and some key features follow:

- Rot proof (warranted for outside use for 50 years, 25 years if submerged in water)
- Class A, the best level of durability, like teak (EN 350-1 and EN 335-1)
- Indigestible to microorganisms and insects
- Treatment happens throughout the material so there are no weak spots
- Tremendous dimensional stability in which the wood movement and expansion is less than 1%
- Excellent machinability allowing 3D CAD direct to product manufacturability
- All wood used for Accoya is produced from well managed sustainable sources including FSC, PEFC and other regionally certified woods
- The acetylation improves the insulation properties of the original softwood
- Reusable and recyclable, or safe to incinerate for bio-energy
- Accoya has been awarded numerous awards including Cradle to Cradle Certification Gold (C2C-Centre, undated).

This wood was the *new metal* that we had been looking for, possessing the structural and dimensional stability of steel (but without the rust problem) and with the look, warmth, texture and machinability of wood. We just had to convince the council of the change.

Making the case

We covered a great deal of data in assessing the suitability of Accoya and made numerous comparisons. We gained a lot of information which is either confidential or beyond the scope of this text. It is a material that is undergoing numerous tests for durability; coating treatments and structural properties. However, for the purposes of this SD journey there were two key areas of concern that the client had:

1 The transportation distance involved for the wood to be used
2 That it was not locally or nationally available.

The predominant tree species for Accoya is radiata pine, shipped from New Zealand. It could not be a worse scenario! However, like much of what we think is sustainable and unsustainable, when we look in depth we find another story, it's all part of deciding on 'how to do the right thing'?

Transportation review

The transportation calculations were particularly revealing. It would be natural to assume that the shipping of radiata pine all the way to Europe from New Zealand would be very negative when compared to using sweet chestnut but to make sense of the comparison we need to consider a broader range of parameters, such as the carbon footprint of sweet chestnut and Accoya. Although the pine is coming from the other side of the world, its growth yields (from certified forests) and far superior carbon sequestration can be used to offset the additional transportation requirement. In land use and carbon sequestration Accoya is more than four times as effective as Sweet Chestnut as it provides greater timber growth per hectare. This means that it is a more efficient use of land committed to renewable resource production. This reflects the wood used and not full carbon captured by the tree. Additional carbon will have been sequestered in the timber waste, in the tree litter and in the remaining trunk and root system. The real value of Carbon sequestration cannot be assessed until the end-of-product life and the consequences of CO_2 release. This is common to both materials. It should also be noted that transportation by sea verses truck is over eleven times more efficient in reducing CO_2 impact (Purse and Muss, 2009). After further research and discussion the agreement was reached that Accoya would be used for the shelters due to its robust supply chain, material properties and environmental credentials.

Mini, Midi and Maxi sustainable design shelters

After three prototypes, ten pre-production shelters were installed in Cornwall. Through this process, a modular system was realized that has three marketed models: the Mini, Midi and Maxi. The council then tendered the range to manufactures and the winning company was awarded a £1,500,000 four-year framework contract. We continue to advise and develop the range within the contract; as of early 2016 there are seventy shelters installed in Cornwall.[1] It is a great shame we could not source suitable timber locally to the quality required, but it was not to be (the UK imports 80% of the wood in consumes). However, out of eleven companies involved in the manufacture of the shelters nine are based in Cornwall. The project has had a direct input to local jobs and in a small part made these companies more resilient during a difficult economic recession.

Figure 12.4 Shelters install in 15 minutes minimizing disruption and environmental impact

The latest designs include many SD features, some new and some adopted from the work with TfL. All materials used in the shelters are of high quality. The engineered wood structure and roof (10mm toughened glass, stainless steel, mechanical fixings) all have a projected 50-year service life, or more. We believe the Accoya timber sequestered CO_2 results in a very low carbon footprint compared to that of the metal shelters. The integrated timber flagpole and timetable facilities further offset the use of other metal components. The shelters are built offsite on a digitally manufactured concrete foundation slab (85% waste pulverized fuel ash and 15% cement) in a production plant to ensure quality control and improve working conditions. This approach enables the delivery of shelters to be very efficient. All shelters only require a shallow 20cm hole to be dug to crane in the shelter on its concrete base. The shelters take just 15 minutes to install as shown in Figure 12.4, glazers then fit the glass in approximately 2 hours. This method means that the two days normally taken to install a shelter has been massively reduced and common problems of hitting gas, electrical, water and fibre optic supplies is avoided (traditional shelters have a 50cm cube of concrete under each post and these utility services are very problematic).

Sustainable design features

Figure 12.5 provides an overview of the Maxi shelter; the numbers should be cross referenced with the number column in Table 12.1. This table explores some of the SD interventions that the design has explored, providing a qualitative indicative list for discussion purposes. Figures 12.6 and 12.7 show two of the shelter designs that capture the SD features listed in Table 12.1, demonstrating how these features work in the fully installed final products, on site.

Figure 12.5 Maxi shelter for approximately 16 users

Table 12.1 Sustainable design features of the Maxi shelter

Number	SD feature	SD tag
1	Designed and mainly manufactured in Cornwall supports local jobs based upon a knowledge based economy.	SOCIOECONOMIC–ENVIRONMENTAL
1	Design based on 90 × 90mm sections. Large posts are designed as 90 × 290mm so that they can be cut down to three 90 × 90mm posts allowing minimal waste for saw cuts and planning rather than making individual 90mm posts, which is more resource intensive.	SUSTAINABLE PRODUCTION; OPTIMIZATION; ENERGY EFFICIENCY; LOW-IMPACT MATERIALS
1	Over engineered structure and digital manufacturing enables bespoke custom shelters to be manufactured on a one off basis.	EMOTIONAL DURABILITY; PERSONALIZATION; LOCALIZATION; LONGEVITY
1	Other than cleaning and repairing vandal caused damage shelters are not expected to need any servicing. Damage, wear and tear are expected to be minimal due to the high build quality and the heavy-duty materials specified.	LONGEVITY; ENERGY EFFICIENCY; LOW-IMPACT MATERIALS
1	Timber construction means that local woodworkers can repair quickly if needed.	SOCIOECONOMIC–ENVIRONMENTAL; PERSONALIZATION; LOCALIZATION
1	All timber components mellow to a silver grey in 2–5 years helping to disguise marks and graffiti. Natural finish and self-healing patina.	LONGEVITY; ENERGY EFFICIENCY; LOW-IMPACT MATERIALS; EMOTIONAL DURABILITY
1	Remove graffiti using just water (power jet), sand paper or woodworkers plane; no chemicals.	LONGEVITY; ENERGY EFFICIENCY; LOW-IMPACT MATERIALS
1	Integrated totem (flag pole and timetable).	LONGEVITY; ENERGY EFFICIENCY; LOW-IMPACT MATERIALS; COLOCATION; FUTURE PROOFING

Continued...

Table 12.1 continued…

Number	SD feature	SD tag
1	Accoya engineered wood, manufacturers material warranty 50 years. Less than 1% material movement allows retrofitting over 50 years. Durability Class A (like teak).	LONGEVITY; RENEWABLE RESOURCE; CASCADE; REUSE; CARBON SEQUESTER; SUSTAINABLE PRODUCTION; ENERGY EFFICIENCY; LOW-IMPACT MATERIALS
1	Fully modular structure. Digitally manufactured design to meet different site needs (e.g. solar roof or unusual bespoke sites via CAD with no tooling).	PERSONALIZATION; ENERGY EFFICIENCY; AGILE JUST IN TIME PRODUCTION; FUTURE PROOFING; SUSTAINABLE PRODUCTION
3	Square shaped foundation slab enables shelters to rotated 90 degrees and be sited 'back to wind' to give users best protection. All sites have a survey to assess prevailing wind and weathering.	EMOTIONAL DURABILITY; LONGEVITY; OPTIMIZATION; ENERGY EFFICIENCY
3	Hiab delivery and 15 minute installation system means that shelters can be relocated as needed. Enables fast delivery cycle saving energy and re-siting of shelters any time anywhere.	REUSE; OPTIMIZATION; LONGEVITY; FUTURE PROOFING; ENERGY EFFICIENCY; HEALTH AND SAFTY; WORKING CONDITIONS; LOW CARBON MATERIALS/SERVICE
3	Concrete raft made with 85% Cornwall-sourced waste aggregate (PFA). Can be made back to aggregate as infill at end of life.	RECYCLE; REUSE; OPTIMIZATION; LONGEVITY; LOCALIZATION
4	Pavers made with 85% waste aggregate from local sources. Optional, to utilise local material such as brick, slate or granite. Standard shelters have 2 × 2m concrete raft.	RECYCLE; REUSE; OPTIMIZATION; LONGEVITY
5	Triccoya roof, manufacturers material warranty 60 years with water replant and anti-graffiti coating.	LONGEVITY; RENEWABLE RESOURCE; CARBON SEQUESTER; SUSTAINABLE PRODUCTION; ENERGY EFFICIENCY; LOW-IMPACT MATERIALS
6	Support for local shelter themes through the use of 'Patterns' (e.g. routed lettering and patterns can be applied to give a shelter a local theme).	EMOTIONAL DURABILITY; PERSONALIZATION; LOCALIZATION
6	Generous low conductive timber seating as standard increased comfort compared to metal or plastic seats.	EMOTIONAL DURABILITY; CASCADE
2, 7	10mm toughened glass (recyclable). High specification has result in only 3 broken panes over 3 years. High visibility throughout as requested in national user surveys.	LONGEVITY; ENERGY EFFICIENCY; OPTIMIZATION
8	Low energy LED lighting with 18-year service life. One of the most energy efficient proven products on the market.	ENERGY EFFICIENCY; LOW CARBON; LONGEVITY; SIMPLE MAINTENANCE
9	A4 stainless steel components throughout. 100% recyclable.	REUSE; OPTIMIZATION; LONGEVITY; FUTURE PROOFING; CYCLIC FINITE RESOURCES (C2C)

Figure 12.6 Mini cantilever design: a compact design for low footfall sites and for narrow pavements

Figure 12.7 Midi, the square base design allows installation in 90° increments for weather protection

Conclusions

A key conclusion that can be taken from this modest sustainable design journey is that there is a huge difference between SD theory and practice. Having a theory is useful, but at some point, your design must be implemented in volume and be in use if it is to make the difference you so passionately strive to make; otherwise the work of the designer offers little to the greater cause of sustainable development.

While acknowledging a clear difference between *developed* and *developing* countries, there are many projects presented as Sustainable Design that are not produced in any meaningful volume, or indeed, really needed. This is especially true of the 'upcycling' of numerous materials such as electrical wire into jewellery, card into furniture and tins into lamps. All noble efforts that suspend waste but do not make any real difference to the problems we face. Undoubtedly, these projects are fun to do and perhaps they have become so visible because of this very reason – they are *doable*. However, they are generally simple projects to implement and do not confront the contractual, financial, market, technical and compliance barriers that impede the mass production of sustainably designed products and services, in the vast majority of cases.

To make a difference, we need mass produced products that are genuinely useful to humanity and a good investment of our time, energy, materials and services. Not incremental tweaks or modest energy gains, but sustainable design that always considers holistic systems and the small details within. To realize this fundamental change we must enter into complex new ways of creating and sustaining our material world. These requirements have been known for years and we are still a long way from achieving the integrated holistic approach that will help conserve our diminishing resources. Although engaged designers can explore these integrations in their work and highlight the opportunities, many of the mechanisms needed to go to market are beyond the control of the designer. Brave clients and well-placed ambassadors are essential to progress sustainable design – especially those who have the role of buying (procuring) and selling products and services at scale.

However, our experience over numerous projects has been that getting a client to accept a disruptive sustainable design solution is a challenge. A painful conclusion is that although a design team may produce the most appealing, appropriate and rigorous design, if it is not proven it poses a risk and is thus a very hard sell. Therefore, the likelihood of a procurement department awarding a contract is remote. This affects the opportunities to develop sustainable products and services in high volume for real world applications. Public procurement can directly support and empower sustainable design solutions but needs to take more responsibility and greater risks. Business as usual is not proactive enough. From a national level and through to UN and EU (International Governmental Organizations) strategic sustainable development policies are in place and well intentioned, but these rarely seem to translate into bold procurement on the ground.

To unlock this public procurement sector, designers need a language that procurement specialists and clients can respond to, and that is an LCA set against a commonly understood reference product. This can be an expensive option prior to an order but it does provide compelling numeric data (which reduces risk), and helps give buyers confidence when dealing with the unknown aspects of a project.

The TfL project provided a theoretical understanding of what we wanted to design and how. Four years later, it led to the production of a shelter range that explored these ideas, in a practical and applied way. We conclude that this only came about because of benign and bold sustainable design procurement. Sustainable product designers need more of the same. Indeed, the shelter project does not make a significant contribution to reducing CO_2

or in mitigating human health impacts as the scale is too small. However, it is a start, and the knowledge gained can be scaled. The research underpinning our design is now being applied in a number of larger projects that have the potential to drawn down thousands of tonnes of timber from appropriate sources. These projects may help shift the reliance on finite resources to renewables in sectors that had not previously considered the use of timber. We have concluded that timber can act as a sustainable, renewable and economically viable alternative to aluminium and steel. Furthermore, it is very scalable for the manufacture of products as no tooling is required; 3D CAD files can be passed straight through to mass production. In addition, with the right variant, the designer does not need extensive traditional timber knowledge to be successful.

If the public sector can organize public procurement so that small agile sustainable design companies and supply chains can secure contracts that meet in areas of need (such as transportation, education, textiles, healthcare, housing, agriculture, energy etc.) we may well realize tremendous benefits for society, the general economy and the environment. Our modest project has put £1,500,000 into the local economy and supported local employment, and nine of the eleven companies involved in the shelter's supply chain are based in Cornwall. We would hope that the seventy shelters installed provide better service to the traveling public, and given their longevity, generate an excellent return on investment to the local authority.

In summary, we propose that designers should try to design products in volume that meet a need, think in holistic systems, optimize small details, give confidence to buyers through initial LCA quick scans and target public sector procurement. If the means was there, imagine what could be achieved by a large group of engaged sustainable designers supported by more benign public procurement.

Note

1   The full range can be viewed online at: www.naturalshelter.com

References

C2C-Centre (undated) The gateway for Cradle to Cradle knowledge, expertise and professionals. Retrieved from www.c2c-centre.com/product/building-supply-materials/accoya®-wood-radiata-pine-alder (accessed 31 July 2015).

Ecologist (2013) Harmful weedkiller in your bread and cereal bars. Retrieved from www.theecologist.org/News/news_analysis/2217533/harmful_weedkiller_in_your_bread_and_cereal_bars.html (accessed 3 August 2015).

Hawken, P. (2010) *Natural Capitalism: The Next Industrial Revolution*. Earthscan, London.

Morgan, D. (2013) GPP in practice: Designing green, low carbon bus shelters. Green Public Procurement (GPP), issue 28, Case Study 61. European Commission – Directorate General Environment. Retrieved from http://ec.europa.eu/environment/gpp/pdf/news_alert (accessed 31 July 2015).

Osborne, R. (2014) *Iron, Steam and Money: The Making of the Industrial Revolution*. Random House, London.

Papanek, V. (1971) *Design for the Real World: Human Ecology and Social Change*. Pantheon Books, New York.

Purse, L. and Muss, H. (2009) Greenhouse gas emissions assessment for Accoya Wood – Public Version, Camco. Retrieved from www.accoya.com/wp-content/uploads/2013/09/Greenhouse-Gas-Emissions-Assessment-for-Accoya-Wood-CAMCO-11Dec2009.pdf (accessed 31 July 2015).

Van Weenen, J.C. (1990) *Waste Prevention: Theory and Practice*. Technische Universiteit, Delft, The Netherlands.

PART III

Materials and processes

Far more than form-giving skins, materials mediate between the physical and psychological worlds, cultivating meaning, expectation and prejudice. This materials experience is powerful, and serves to govern the perceived value, physical and emotional durability and ecological impact of products. Despite this, materials are still grossly undervalued in terms of their potential to contribute to the meaningfulness of human experience. Resources – as we like to call matter for which we have a commercial use – are being transformed at a speed far beyond the natural self-renewing rate of the biosphere; in the past six decades we have consumed, poisoned, destroyed or incinerated the majority of them.

This third part comprises five chapters, each engaging themes of resources, materials and processes, and their social, ecological and political contexts. The contributors writing in this part draw together previously disconnected scholarship in haptic perception, sustainable materials, additive manufacturing, materials innovation, environmental politics and user experience. In doing so, they reveal the rich and sophisticated domain of resources and materials and the central role they play in shaping sustainable products and experiences. Their chapters may be summarized as follows:

13 Conflict minerals and the politics of stuff – *Colin Fitzpatrick*
    Conflict minerals are an increasingly critical issue in discourses surrounding the social and political impacts of product design. This chapter outlines creative responses to support the design and production of electronic products that use tin, tungsten, tantalum and gold (3TG).

14 Materially yours – *Elvin Karana, Elisa Giaccardi and Valentina Rognoli*
    This chapter illuminates the way in which materials behave differently with the passing of time. Depending on the product design strategy adopted, users experience this change either as graceful ageing, or unwanted decay, greatly influencing the nature and longevity of materials experience.

15 Mediating matters – *Nick Gant*
    Materials are central to the physical and experiential dimensions of sustainability. This chapter reveals how materials mediate complex social, political and cultural values; exploring new methods to elevate the value of waste materials, and the rich histories they carry.

16   Print to repair: 3D printing and product repair – *Miles Park*
      This chapter shows how replacement parts can be printed in a range of materials,
      when and where they are required. Despite the practical and economic benefits that
      3D printing can bring, few brands offer 3D printed replacement parts, or print to
      repair services.
17   Unmaking waste – *Robert Crocker*
      While governments and businesses need to play their part in creating a 'circular
      economy' – where resources are more highly valued and waste is minimized – to
      'unmake waste' on this scale requires designers to both understand how and why
      unnecessary waste is created in the first place.

As users we are fickle when it comes to materials. We tweet the term 'plasticy' to criticize a low-quality toaster, yet do so using the polymer-cased smartphone we value so dearly. Materials are unstable. They age, wear, scratch, dint and burnish. They develop patina, adding memory, history and value to the object experience, and deepening the resonance it has with the user. Yet, the story of materials runs far deeper than what the eye, and hand, can perceive. We see a slick plastic and metal chassis and assume that inside is a battery, a speaker of some sort and extensive complex circuitry that we will most likely never see, but can assume is there. Actually peer beneath these glossy, scratch free skins of polymers and alloys, and an inner material world is revealed of far greater technical complexity. Beneath the product surface, the theatre of materials is performed at an atomic level, with unfathomable depths of ecological and social consequence.

Electrical and electronic equipment (EEE) contains both ecologically and socially destructive cocktails of minerals, precious metals and noxious compounds, including: tin, tungsten, tantalum and gold (3TG), arsenic, cadmium, copper, lead, manganese and zinc. A child's remote-control tank, for example, contains a thumbnail-sized microchip, containing over 65 per cent of the elements in the periodic table. Many of the elements commonly used in everyday household products have no known replacement (e.g. rhenium, rhodium, lanthanum, europium, dysprosium, thulium, ytterbium, yttrium, strontium and thallium), yet we use them in a carefree and disposable way. This is a nonsensical way to use these precious, finite materials. In terms of technological capability, a scarcity of just a handful of these elements could send us back in time by decades. These tiny wafers of semiconducting material used to make complex integrated circuits, are found at the heart (or should I say, *mind*) of most electronic products made today – from toasters and smartphones, to microwave ovens and wind turbines.

Shift our gaze toward one of these products, the smart phone, and the situation continues to increase in mind-boggling impossibility. Place the average smart phone on a set of weighing scales and it will come out close enough to 200g, give or take a few grams depending on the brand and model. It's no surprise then, that people inadvertently associate such lightness with an equivalent descent in ecological and social impacts. Yet, if we look at the *true weight* of the smart phone in terms of its total energy and resource footprints, involving all the processes involved in bringing this complex yet magical product into being, it weighs something in the region of 500kg … that's half a tonne. To put this into some kind of context, the average horse ways half a tonne! Therefore, every time you lift this product to your ear to take a call, or hold it flat in the palm of your hands to read a text, think about the horse, and the incredible wait that sits at your fingertips. Indeed, for sustainable product design to be effective, we need to look beyond the 200g smartphone, and see the entire 500kg whole product context in which the phone sits.

Through this approach, we can begin to navigate the complexity and identify optimum points for intervention within the system.

Let's not forget, materials don't come out the ground in packets or test tubes, ready for use. Raw materials must be extracted and processed, and consume great quantities of natural resources in the process. With the exception of surface-based renewables, practically all materials, basically, start out as a giant hole in the ground. They must be mined from several thousand tons of earth and rock, shipped many hundreds of kilometres to be crushed, scorched, processed and refined into usable forms. Only then, can they be shipped to other manufacturing sites around the world to be joined with other materials, and manufactured into component parts like clips, switches, LEDs or even microchips.

Today's products – electronic or otherwise – are riddled with an astonishing array of resource narratives. For example, mining of tin, tungsten and gold is linked with war and conflict in central Africa. Surprising then, to learn that there is more gold in a tonne of discarded phones than a tonne of rock extracted from a gold mine; due to their design and manufacture, the rock-bound gold is currently more economically viable to extract than its phone-bound counterpart. It is often either shipped to less regulated parts of the world for incineration, or stockpiled and left to decay over centuries along with countless other precious minerals and resources, inseparably fused together through a slapdash approach to manufacturing and production. In an age of steadily rising resource prices, and dwindling levels of natural reserves, process and resource inefficiencies like this make absolutely no sense.

13

CONFLICT MINERALS AND THE POLITICS OF STUFF

Colin Fitzpatrick

Abstract

Conflict minerals have become an important issue in the discourse surrounding the social and political impact of high-tech consumption with the Democratic Republic of Congo (DRC) being the primary focus for NGOs and legislators concerned with this issue. This chapter gives a brief insight into the nature of the conflict in the DRC and draws on a literature review to demonstrate that the complexity of the conflict goes beyond the simple narratives that circulate. It proceeds to outline the main uses of tin, tungsten, tantalum and gold (3TG) in electronics and briefly discusses some of the different direct responses open to product designers which include sourcing materials from outside the DRC, designing 3TG out of products entirely and engaging with the conflict free sourcing initiative that has emerged. It speculates as to how each of these strategies might impact upon the people affected by the conflict. It concludes by questioning the extent to which designers and consumers should be exclusively burdened with the responsibility for resolving these issues. The chapter, ultimately, proposes that efforts should be made to channel the awareness-raising opportunities that the use of these materials present into developing a new narrative for a wider set of solutions for conflict resolution, peacebuilding and sustainable development.

Keywords: conflict minerals, Democratic Republic of Congo, Dodd-Frank, 3TG

Introduction

Over the past decades, with the increasing proliferation of electronic products, there has also been a growing interest in, and awareness of, their life cycle impacts from consumers, producers and regulators alike. Concern for the environmental and social impacts of electronic products is now widespread which is reflected in an array of laws covering topics such as material selection through the Restriction of Hazardous Substances Directive (RoHS), Registration, Evaluation, Authorization and Restriction of Chemicals (REACH), energy use through the Energy related Products Directive (ErP) and waste through the Waste Electrical and Electronic Equipment Directive (WEEE). Industry initiatives to demonstrate they are taking these issues seriously are pervasive, eco-labels validating specific levels of environmental performance are widespread and NGOs routinely advocate for improved conditions at both ends of the supply chain, from resource extraction and production, through to the end of life when products become waste. This is not to say that we are even close to achieving sustainability in modern consumption patterns but it is at least on the agenda. Most recent to join the array of concerns about the sustainability of products has been conflict minerals.

Resources have often played a role in conflict and drugs, oil and diamonds have all been connected with fuelling conflict related activities (Le Billion, 2003). More specifically related to electronics has been the use of minerals from provinces in the east of the Democratic Republic of the Congo and their role in the funding of warlords involved in hostilities. These materials are to be found in almost every electronic product imaginable, performing functions fundamental to their operation. The next section will include a detailed discussion how they are integral to the workings of modern electronics.

In order to consider how a designer can engage with this issue it is necessary to provide a brief background to events in the DRC to even partly demonstrate the complexity of this situation. What should be clear from the outset is that there will be no straight answers. Due to this complexity there is no clear cause and effect that can be mapped between the decisions of the designers and the welfare of the people of the eastern DRC. What we can do is try to develop our understanding of the situation in a little more detail and use this to guide us in our choices, knowing that we will never be certain of the impact of that choice. We should stay mindful of the situation, stay abreast of developments in DRC, hope that the situation improves and our choices simplify. Until then we need to move beyond the simple cause and effect narratives that circulate, so that we may begin to wrestle with the real complexity of the issues.

The Democratic Republic of the Congo ranks second from bottom in the UN Human Development Index, just one away from the position as the least developed nation on earth. Following a deeply troubled formation under colonial rule DRC gained independence in 1960 with its early years plagued by political and social instability. Independence did not improve its fortunes and by the outbreak of the First Congo War (1996–1997), triggered by a mass exodus during the Rwandan genocide and including Rwandan, Ugandan and Angolan government involvement, it was effectively a failing state with a non-functioning economy, widespread ethnic tensions, corruption and a complete lack of government control in many regions (CIA, 2015). The Second Congo War, also referred to as the Great War of Africa (1998–2003), started for largely the same reasons and resulted in approximately 4 million deaths (Coghlan, 2006). This war is known for its many massacres and atrocious acts of brutality with sexual violence being a prominent instrument of conflict (Gettleman, 2012). In spite of a formal end to the war in 2003, the hostilities in the east never fully abated and rebel groups backed by Rwanda and Uganda continued their campaigns of violence and human rights abuses. In 2013, a joint offensive between the DRC army and the UN defeated the M23 group which had taken control of a number of cities in the area but the situation in the region is still regarded as being highly unstable (BBC, 2015).

The first official attention to the connection between mining and conflict in the DRC came from a UN panel of experts report in 2002 which found that even as the intensity of the Second Congo War diminished criminal groups linked to the armies of Rwanda, Uganda, Zimbabwe and government of the Democratic Republic of the Congo will not disband voluntarily and have built up a self-financing war economy based on mineral exploitation (United Nations, 2002). This artisanal mining is often undertaken by children and in very unsafe and unhealthy conditions (Hahn et al., 2013).

It is the role of the revenues from mines controlled by certain rebel groups that has brought the world's focus to conflict minerals. In the years following this report, attempts to highlight the issue by a number of international NGOs were largely unsuccessful. It wasn't until the connection between these minerals and the high tech products used by consumers in developed countries was highlighted that the issue really began to gather momentum (Lezhnev and Prendergast, 2009; Prendergast, 2009). The issue became framed as the consumption of high-tech electronics in the global north being the primary cause of violence in the DRC, with sexual abuse of women and girls the main consequence. While this provided a compelling narrative to get the attention of consumers in developed countries it has also received considerable criticism for over-simplifying the situation and ignoring other causes and victims of the conflict (Autesserre, 2012; Open Letter, 2014; Siggins, 2014).

What exactly are conflict minerals and what are they used for?

In the US, where section 1502 of the Dodd-Frank Act was the first piece of national legislation to address the issue, 'conflict minerals' are defined as columbite-tantalite, also known as coltan (from which tantalum is derived); cassiterite (tin); gold; wolframite (tungsten); or their derivatives; or any other mineral or its derivatives determined by the Secretary of State to be financing conflict in the Democratic Republic of the Congo or an adjoining country.

At the time of writing, the EU is also currently considering legislative measures and the current text which is being negotiated between the commission and the parliament expresses a wish to curtail opportunities for armed groups and security forces to trade in tin, tantalum and tungsten, their ores, and gold from conflict-affected and high-risk areas where conflict-affected and high-risk areas are defined as meaning: 'areas in a state of armed conflict, fragile post-conflict as well as areas witnessing weak or non-existent governance and security, such as failed states, and widespread and systematic violations of international law, including human rights abuses' (European Parliament, 2015). The proposed EU text also provides a mechanism to update the list of relevant materials.

Collectively these materials are commonly referred to as 3TG (tin, tungsten, tantalum and gold) and, in spite of the common perception that they are only used in high-tech consumer products such as mobile phones and laptops, they have widespread uses across a broad range of industries which are discussed below.

Tin (Sn)

Tin has been used by humans since pre-historic times, most notably through alloying it with copper to create bronze. Major applications today include food packaging, construction and transportation. Its dominant use in electronics is in solder for electrical and mechanical connection between components and the printed circuit board. For a significant subset (smart phones, laptops, desktops, tablets, displays, servers) of major consumer electronics products it has been shown to constitute 2 per cent of global use (Fitzpatrick et al., 2015). The global recycling rate of tin is estimated to be greater than 50 per cent (UNEP, 2011).

Tungsten (W)

Tungsten is an extremely hard material with the lowest coefficient of thermal expansion of any metal and has the highest melting point of all the elements. Its major applications include it being used as part of cutting or wear-resistant parts and applications requiring high density.

In electronics it has uses in chip manufacture and also in vibration motors commonly used in mobile phones. Its use in consumer electronic products is estimated at 0.1 per cent of global production (Fitzpatrick et al., 2015) and its recycling rate is estimated to be between 10 and 25 per cent (UNEP, 2011).

Tantalum (Ta)

Tantalum is a relatively scarce metal that is best known for its corrosion resistance. It is frequently used as a minor component in alloys and due to its inertness has many applications in lab equipment and also notably in medical implants and bone repair. It has two main uses in electronics; capacitors and integrated circuits. Tantalum capacitors are regarded as the very best in-class by electronic engineers. Largely because, among other benefits, they have no known wear-out mechanisms and have the best volumetric efficiency available which is very important when space is at a premium as it often is in portable equipment. Its other use is in semiconductors is as a barrier layer to prevent copper spoiling the microelectronics when it is used as bond wire or for component interconnection. The global share of tantalum in consumer electronics is estimated to be 15 per cent (Fitzpatrick et al., 2015) and its recycling rate is estimated to be less than 1 per cent (UNEP, 2011).

Gold (Au)

Throughout history gold has been one of the most revered and valued of materials. It is aesthetically attractive, highly corrosion resistant, extremely malleable and a good conductor. Its major use is in jewellery and as a currency reserve. Its uses in electronics are as bond wire between integrated circuits and their packages and as plating for connectors. Consumer electronics is estimated to consumer 3 per cent of global production (Fitzpatrick et al., 2015) and its recycling rate is estimated to be greater than 50 per cent (UNEP, 2011).

Dodd-Frank and its impact

As mentioned in the previous section, the first significant legislative response to have emerged in response to public concerns about conflict minerals has been the Dodd-Frank Act (2010) from the United States which required companies listed in a US-based stock exchange to make a publically available declaration to the Securities and Exchange Commission (SEC) that they have made sufficient efforts to determine if their products contain 3TG emanating from the DRC or neighbouring countries. The EU looks set to follow suit but at the time of writing it is unclear if it will be a mandatory requirement which will apply on the product level, as the parliament wants, or if it will be a voluntary requirement at a material level, as proposed by the commission. However, it looks likely that there will be some degree of harmonization in the compliance requirements which should not lead to a duplication of efforts, and in turn, some progress is likely to be made.

Given that there can be up to 9 tiers of suppliers between the original equipment manufacturer (OEM) which places products on the market and the mines from which the minerals are extracted, compliance with Dodd-Frank was completely uncharted territory for producers (Young, 2012). To help them to navigate it, the Conflict Free Smelter Programme (CFSP) emerged as a joint initiative of the Electronics Industry Citizenship Coalition (EICC) and the Global e-Sustainability Initiative (GeSI) (both are collaborations among a range of electronics industry actors in the sustainability space). The smelting stage was identified as the key stage to focus on due to it being a 'pinch point' (i.e. the place in the supply chain with the fewest number of actors and therefore the easiest to target). The CFSP uses an independent third party audit to identify smelters and refiners that have systems in place to assure sourcing of only conflict free materials. The audit standards have been developed according to the global standard 'OECD Due Diligence Guidance for Responsible Supply Chains of Minerals from Conflict-Affected and High-Risk Areas'. The CFSP also provides funding to support smelters to participate in this programme. Observing the foundation of this programme and the provision of funding clearly demonstrates the disproportionate dominance of the electronics industry considering the wide range of other sectors which also use these materials.

Originally developed by the International Tin Research Institute (ITRI), this system essentially relies on a mine risk assessment and a 'bag and tag' mechanism to create a chain of custody and due diligence system that validates that the minerals arriving at the smelter have come from a mine that has 'green' status. It uses two types of bar-coded tags, each with unique reference numbers and clearly visible areas of allocation: a *mine tag* and a *processor tag*. These are each added to the bags of minerals at extraction and processing. The tagging is accompanied by data collection which provides a record of the process. However, there are reports that smuggling is rampant (Global Witness, 2013).

At the time of writing, there are 46 tantalum, 72 gold, 17 tungsten and 44 tin smelters/ refiners certified as being CFSP compliant and at this stage it is reported that 70 per cent of tin, tungsten and tantalum mines in Eastern Congo have conflict free status with only 35 per cent of gold mines having this certification.

However, criticism of Dodd-Frank has been widespread for the impact of its unintended consequences (Kinniburgh, 2014; Wolfe, 2015; Seay, 2012). For complex reasons, likely connected with Dodd-Frank but also for domestic political motivations, the Congolese president Joseph Kabila imposed an embargo on minerals from the key provinces of North and South Kivu which lasted from September 2010 until March 2011 (Geenen, 2012). This had the effect of causing widespread unemployment due to the reduction in extraction but perversely actually reinforced insecurity and militarization in the region as mining could now only take place in a clandestine fashion involving increased levels of bribery. However bad we might imagine life to be for an artisanal miner, when the only livelihood option for many people was removed it led to widespread school drop-outs as people could no longer afford fees, malnourishment spread and even rudimentary healthcare was unaffordable. The decreased economic activity also impacted other sectors of the local economy as the logistics channels which had transported the minerals were also used for food and other commodities and so trade was reduced. Soon after this ban was lifted a *de facto* embargo of Congolese minerals soon took its place when large international smelters refused to accept the material as not all of it could yet be guaranteed to be conflict free. The overall effect was again disastrous for the region in the short term (Aronson, 2011) but it is reported that wages in conflict free mines are now higher than before and that conditions for former 3T miners have slowly improved with alternative opportunities (Bafilemba et al., 2014). On the downside, many of these former 3T miners now work in militarized gold mines which have been much more difficult to take on due to the potential for smuggling that exists for gold due to its high value. The adverse effects experienced by the subjects of concern during this period, the miners and their families, demonstrated that stopping to source materials from the conflict affected areas would not automatically release the workers from slavery into better lives.

What options do product designers have?

While this is only a very brief synopsis of the situation in eastern DRC it is enough to realize how complex the decision making processes around the use of tin, tantalum, tungsten and gold are for designers who want to develop products which are ethically acceptable to them and their consumers. So, what options exist and what outcomes are likely from these decisions?

If you would like to guarantee that products are 100 per cent conflict free then this can probably only be achieved by adopting a strategy of sourcing all materials from outside the DRC entirely, and happily project yourself as 'conflict free' and not contributing to the hated warlords. Taking everything into consideration it would be a relatively easy option for large multinationals, with valuable brands at stake, to adopt this approach. However, the flip side of this boycott option is that there are many regions in the DRC that are completely uninvolved in the conflict which will be adversely affected by this decision. Even in the mines affected by conflict this approach would simply eliminate one of the only economic opportunities available to local people.

Alternatively it would be possible to eliminate or significantly reduce the use of these materials in electronic products. For example, per product gold use is already in significant decline for economic reasons with innovations such as copper bond wire (as opposed to gold) in integrated circuit packages. Eliminating the option to interchange memory and processor will also reduce gold use (but will also eliminate the possibility for the user to upgrade) as will reducing the number of external ports. Not having a vibrate function would take out the tungsten in one move and tin could be reduced by using conductive epoxies instead of solder (this is technically possible but not mainstream). Eliminating tantalum is probably the most difficult and would depend on the available space in the product as alternative equivalent capacitors will be larger. There are also alternatives to tantalum in semiconductor barrier layers when copper is used in the device. Yet, while it might be technically possible to design out conflict minerals, like in the previous scenario, it is hard to see how this would actually improve the lot of the people affected by the conflict.

Another option for designers and manufacturers is to get behind the Conflict Free Smelter Programme, as described earlier, and only source components which are certified as such. In spite of some of the criticisms about its potential weaknesses, this programme does help to support economic activity in one of the poorest regions in the world. Imagining for a moment that 100 per cent of the mines in DRC eventually became certified as conflict free, the big question that needs to be posed is whether this would have the effect of shutting down the warlords or would they simply move on to other illicit sources of income to fund their operations? As it is argued that the minerals themselves are not the driver of the conflict but only one of a range of other causes including land conflict, poverty, corruption, local political and social antagonisms and hostile relationships between state officials including security forces and the general public then it could be argued that it is unlikely to have any overall benefit on the population.

One noteworthy and design-led response to these issues has been that of Fairphone, which started as an awareness raising exercise about conflict minerals in 2010 and evolved into a social enterprise in its own right in 2013 to use commercial strategies to reach its social goals. It released its first product, the Fairphone, in 2013 and was preparing to release the Fairphone 2 at the time of writing. The Fairphone concept has evolved from its original position of focusing on conflict minerals to a position where it has high aspirations for environmental and sustainability hotspots throughout the lifecycle of their mobile phones. What is very refreshing about their approach is that they openly admit that they don't have all the answers, that creating a truly 'fair' product is a step-by-step journey, and that many social and environmental issues across the lifecycle are simply impossible to achieve right now (Fairphone, 2015). They are open and transparent about achievements, the areas where they have not yet made progress and have the goal of stimulating discussions such as this one about fairness, what it means and how it can be achieved. They also direct a portion of their revenue to projects on the ground in the DRC.

Other examples from the electronics sector of deep engagement with the issue can be witnessed at Intel, Dell, HP, Apple and Philips among others who continue to commit to sourcing of materials within DRC that can support a sustainable local economy and have been to the forefront of the. By contrast, engagement by the automotive sector seems to have come only recently and has a much more compliance oriented approach to the topic with little commitment to in-country solutions evident. But, to what extent should designers and consumers be burdened with the responsibility for resolving conflicts such as the situation that exists in the eastern DRC? While it is certainly true that eco design can be employed to achieve quantifiable improvements in the environmental performance of products in specific impact categories, no such certainty exists for the social implications of design decisions. In any case, even if they were known to be effective, the share of conflict minerals which are used in consumer electronics would be much too small to have such a transformational effect.

The placing of such responsibility on designers and consumers to change the world through consumption as is happening with the issue of conflict minerals could actually be distracting attention away from other more reliable sources of conflict resolution and sustainable development.

Conclusions

> One person, not littering, will not singlehandedly solve the litter problem, but on the other hand, the litter problem will never be solved if one continues to litter
>
> – *David Parnas*[1]

So it seems that any single action taken by product designers cannot credibly be claimed to improve the problems of the DRC and its people. However, there are no quick fixes for most major problems in the world and single actions can rarely solve them. Does this mean that nothing should be done? Of course not. Such binary arguments are often used to oppose projects or initiatives related to climate change for example, that 'such and such' individual action is too small to make a difference so it is pointless to proceed with it. However, the climate change situation differs in that there is an established and evolving narrative available that allows small actions to be explained as part of a bigger picture that will involve transformational change of the energy landscape. At present, the discourse surrounding conflict minerals is missing this wider narrative and needs to create one that moves beyond the simple framing that is currently available to the general public. Of course, cutting off a revenue stream to the warlords is necessary, but stopping there is simply not enough. The CFSP should be seen as only the start and now it needs to be worked out what else needs to happen.

Companies who produce high-tech products are well placed to advocate for a wider solution for the DRC. Instead of thinking in terms of their consumers they should think about citizens and how these citizens in developed countries can play a constructive role as advocates for others caught in such extremely difficult situations in faraway places. Delivering solutions to situations such as those in the DRC lie beyond the capacity and mandate of private corporations, and the teams of individuals who work within them. It would be much more effective for NGOs and producers of equipment alike to work to activate citizens to this end than to pretend that straightforward interventions and solutions are what are required. Efforts to use the guilt of first world consumers and their consumption of high-tech gadgets to effect change in developing countries should focus on finding and implementing on-the-ground efforts in sustainable economic, social and environmental development. It should look at what role they can play to canvass their governments to provide leadership within the international community to find a peaceful resolution to the conflict and a sustainable pathway for the DRC.

Note

1 This comment from renowned software engineering David Parnas was made when discussing his opposition to the missile defense project 'Star Wars' in the 1980s.

References

Aronson D. (2011) How Congress Devastated Congo, *New York Times*, 7 August, retrieved from www.nytimes.com/2011/08/08/opinion/how-congress-devastated-congo.html?_r=0 (accessed 25 November 2015)

Autesserre, S. (2012) Dangerous Tales: Dominant Narratives on the DRC and their Unintended Consequences, *African Affairs*, 111(443), pp202–222

Bafilemba F., Mueller T. and Lezhnev S. (2014) The Impact of Dodd-Frank and Conflict Minerals Reforms on Eastern Congo's Conflict, June, Retrieved from www.enoughproject.org/reports/impact-dodd-frank-and-conflict-minerals-reforms-eastern-congo%E2%80%99s-war (accessed 25 November 2015)

BBC (2015) Democratic Republic of Congo Profile –Timeline, *BBC News*, 4 August, retrieved from www.bbc.com/news/world-africa-13286306 (accessed 25 November 2015)

CIA (2015) The World Fact Book, retrieved from www.cia.gov/library/publications/the-world-factbook/geos/cg.html (accessed 25 November 2015)

Coghlan, B. (2006) Mortality in the Democratic Republic of Congo: A nationwide survey, *Lancet*, 367, pp44–51

European Parliament (2015) Union System for Self-certification of Importers of Certain Minerals and Metals Originating in Conflict Affected and High Risk Areas, 20 May, retrieved from www.europarl.europa.eu/sides/getDoc.do?pubRef=-//EP//TEXT+TA+P8-TA-2015-0204+0+DOC+XML+V0//EN (accessed 25 November 2015)

Fitzpatrick, C., Olivetti, E., Roth, R. and Kirchain, R. (2015) Conflict Minerals in the Compute Sector: Estimating the Global Use of Sn, Ta, W, and Au in Selected ICT Products, *Environmental Science and Technology*, 49 (2) pp974–981

Geenen, S. (2012) A Dangerous Bet: The Challenges of Formalizing Artisanal Mining in the Democratic Republic of Congo, *Resources Policy*, 37(3), pp322–330

Gettleman, J. (2012) The World's Worst War, *New York Times*, 15 December, retrieved from www.nytimes.com/2012/12/16/sunday-review/congos-never-ending-war.html (accessed 25 November 2015)

Global Witness (2013) Putting Principles into Practice, retrieved from www.globalwitness.org/sites/default/files/library/Putting%20principles%20into%20practice.pdf (accessed 25 November 2015)

Hahn H. P., Hayes, K. and Kacapor, A. (2013) Breaking the Chain; Ending the Supply of Child-Mined Minerals, October, retrieved from www.pactworld.org/sites/default/files/PACT%20Child%20Labor%20Report%20English%202013.pdf (accessed 25 November 2015)

Kinniburgh, C. (2014) Beyond Conflict Minerals: the Congo's Resource Curse Lives On, *Dissent Magazine*, Spring, retrieved from www.dissentmagazine.org/article/beyond-conflict-minerals-the-congos-resource-curse-lives-on (accessed 25 November 2015)

Le Billion, P. (2013) Getting it Done: Instruments of Enforcement, in I. Bannon and P. Collier (eds), *Natural Resources and Violent Conflict*, World Bank, Washington, DC, pp215–286

Lezhnev, S. and Prendergast J. (2009) *From Mine to Mobile*, Enough Project, Washington, DC, retrieved from www.enoughproject.org/files/minetomobile.pdf (accessed 25 November 2015)

Open Letter (2014) Open Letter, retrieved from https://ethuin.files.wordpress.com/2014/09/09092014-open-letter-final-and-list.pdf (accessed 25 November 2015)

Prendergast, J. (2009) Can You Hear Congo Now?, retrieved from www.enoughproject.org/files/Can%20Your%20Hear%20Congo%20Now.pdf (accessed 25 November 2015)

Seay, L. E. (2012) *What's Wrong with Dodd-Frank 1502? Conflict Minerals, Civilian Livelihoods, and the Unintended Consequences of Western Advocacy*, Working Paper 284, May, Center for Global Development, Washington, DC, retrieved from www.cgdev.org/files/1425843_file_Seay_Dodd_Frank_FINAL.pdf (accessed 25 November 2015)

Siggins, L. (2014) Amnesty Expert Criticises 'Misleading' International Campaigns, *The Irish Times*, 2 July, retrieved from www.irishtimes.com/news/social-affairs/amnesty-expert-criticises-misleading-international-campaigns-1.1853059 (accessed 25 November 2015)

UNEP (2011) *Recycling Rate of Metals: A Status Report*, UNEP, Nairobi, retrieved from www.unep.org/resourcepanel/Portals/24102/PDFs/Metals_Recycling_Rates_110412-1.pdf (accessed 25 November 2015)

United Nations (2002) Final Report of the Panel of Experts on the Illegal Exploitation of Natural Resources and Other Forms of Wealth of the Democratic Republic of Congo, 16 October, available online at www.pcr.uu.se/digitalAssets/96/96819_congo_20021031.pdf (accessed 25 November 2015)

Wolfe, L. (2015) How Dodd-Frank Is Failing Congo, *Foreign Policy*, 2 February, retrieved from http://foreignpolicy.com/2015/02/02/how-dodd-frank-is-failing-congo-mining-conflict-minerals (accessed 25 November 2015)

Young, S. (2012) *Conflict-Free Minerals Supply-Chain to Electronics*, Electronics Goes Green 2012+, Berlin

14
MATERIALLY YOURS

Elvin Karana, Elisa Giaccardi and Valentina Rognoli

Abstract

Materials embedded in products behave differently with the passing of time. This can be witnessed either as graceful ageing, or as material degradation. Some materials can appear to be 'alive': they can sense and respond, and change state; they can show different 'faces' depending on applications and circumstances; they can remain personal and appropriate over time. Materials can reflect fashions in a particular era, or they can exhibit timelessness, for example. Such experiential qualities of materials inevitably affect the way we use, and the time span we possess, everyday products. In this chapter, we propose three strategies, which focus on the potential experiences we have with and through the materials of products that last; these are: (1) embrace imperfection; (2) do it yourself; and (3) multi-situated materials. With the term 'materially yours', we highlight the idea of *resilience thinking*, in which *the most responsive to change* will survive. We capitalize on this thinking in all three strategies, by offering a sense of ambiguity, curiosity, flexibility and openness in material thinking in design. We further explain these new strategies with a number of illustrative cases throughout the chapter.

Keywords: materials experience, imperfection, multi-situated materials, DIY materials

Introduction

The title *Materially Yours* pays homage to *Eternally Yours*, a project created by Ed van Hinte, Henk Muls, Arnoud Oddin and Lisbeth Bonekamp in 1995. The aim was to generate and disseminate knowledge about the interlinked processes of design, production and use of durable products and services, which through their qualities provoke longer-lasting, 'eternal' use. The project – now considered seminal – explored the life of products by tapping into the psychological aspects of product consumption, and exploring the hidden complexities behind our relationships with a range of objects. The project developed three key approaches to extend product life; these are: shape and surface (design); sign and scripts (non-material aspect); and, sales and services (marketing). Almost 100 researchers, designers and policy makers formed the Eternally Yours network. The project resulted in two books: *Eternally*

Yours: Visions on Product Endurance (van Hinte, 1997) and *Eternally Yours: Time in Design* (van Hinte, 2004). The first book focuses mainly on sustainability and defines how design should work to create a more resource-efficient and equitable world. Its main message is that we should design products towards which people can develop attachment and that they will keep for longer. The second book maps out the ways in which products can be designed and planned as such that their value can be sustained to keep them in 'use' for longer. It tells the story of Vivian, which is used as a name of any product, to illustrate the ideal future product designed for lifespan extension by sustaining their value for long time. The name Vivian, which means 'living', was chosen to avoid the abuse of words like products or objects. Vivian's story is richly illustrated with examples to convey the main theme of the book.

In the Eternally Yours project, it is emphasized that products must have the *material ability* as well as the *material opportunity* to age in a graceful way (van Hinte, 1997). Jonathan Chapman elaborates on this issue, stating that:

> Designing products with the capability to deliver complex enduring narrative experiences is not simply a matter of specifying materials that age well; although, this is a part of it. Instead, provocative design concepts must emerge that challenge our social desire for a scratch-free and box-fresh world, illustrating how the onset of ageing could concentrate rather than dilute the experience of an object.
>
> *(Chapman, 2014, p141)*

Along similar lines, with 'Materially Yours' we examine and suggest ways to turn down the noise of production and consumption (van Hinte, 1997) and give more attention to the experiences we have *with* and *through* the materials of products. Before moving forward, let us first explain what we mean by the term 'materials experience'.

Materials experience

While our experiences with a product may originate from – or be moderated by – a wide variety of sources, one of the prominent sources is the physical reality of a product: the wood of the table, the plastic of the kitchen utensil, the leather of the handbag (Karana et al., 2015a, p17). Materials embedded in such products behave differently in respect to the passing of time, which can be witnessed either as graceful ageing, or as material degradation. Materials can also reflect fashions in a particular era, or they can exhibit timelessness, for example (Chapman, 2005; Candy et al., 2008; Ramakers, 2002; Saito, 2007). Materials are experienced in different ways, in different interactions between people and materials, or in different settings, and these qualities can change over time. The properties of a material, the product in which a material is embodied, one's previous experiences and expectations, and social and cultural values inevitably affect how we experience and thus act upon materials (Karana, 2009). Taken together, these aspects may construct a different materials experience for different individuals.

No matter what the resulting experience for different individuals is, all materials are experienced at four experiential levels (Giaccardi and Karana, 2015); these are *sensorial*, *interpretive*, *affective* and *performative*, and they affect each other in a non-sequential manner. Our first encounter with materials occurs at a *sensorial level*, through touch, vision, smell, sound and taste. The sensorial component of experience is omnipresent and inevitable. We like the smooth surface of a metal laptop, and we dislike a sticky rubber handle. The *interpretive level* concerns how we interpret and judge materials, that is, the situated meanings we ascribe to them after the initial sensorial encounter. Meanings we attribute to materials are usually personality characteristics and associations (such as feminine, modern, traditional, toy-like, elegant, etc.), and are not factually part of a material's properties or embodiment (i.e., a material is not literally feminine or masculine). The *affective level* concerns emotions, which arise often unconsciously, and the affective dispositions that are triggered by our inner thoughts, beliefs and attitudes. We can be fascinated or disappointed by the qualities of a material embodied in a specific product. For instance, the easily scratched surface of an electronic product might disappoint us, or the extreme lightness of a chair might surprise us. The *performative level* refers to the active role of materials in shaping our ways of doing and practices. The performances we establish around products are significantly influenced by the experiential qualities of materials at all four levels.

In an earlier study, we asked what crossovers we could identify between material experiences and sustainability concerns (Karana et al., 2015a). There is a growing interest among scholars particularly for the aesthetics of sustainability. This has been named by others as the 'aesthetics of environmentally sensitive products' (Walker, 1995), 'total beauty' (Datschefski, 2001), 'green aesthetics' (Saito, 2007), 'sustainable aesthetic' (Branzi, 2008) and 'sustainable beauty' (Hosey, 2012). These aspects are highlighted to be taken into account in designing for sustainability and dealing with the potential impediments on that path (Dobers and Strannegård, 2005). It is emphasized as a powerful means to influence and determine behaviour, attitudes and actions in a society (Saito, 2007; Manzini, 1994; Vezzoli, 2007; Orr, 2002) and to impart a sense of new lifestyle, real socio-cultural values and the whole philosophy of sustainability (Zafarmand *et al.*, 2003).

These earlier works of scholars mainly focus on expressing the 'sustainability' of a product through the aesthetic (sensorial) qualities of the design; materials' role in this endeavour is inevitable. In previous studies, we elaborated on our sensorial experiences with materials in relation to sustainability. For example, when we think a material expresses 'naturalness' (interpretive level), which in many daily contexts affects people's product preferences and possession. Krista et al. (2016) elaborate on the effect of 'naturalness' perception on the preference of textiles in garments.

Our account in this chapter is neither about 'material aesthetics' of sustainable products, nor the 'functional/physical durability of materials'; such issues are taken for granted and have been covered in the materials science, design and engineering literature to a great extent. Instead, we suggest that experiences a material can mediate at all four experiential levels can contribute to longer lasting products. This is because when materials are open to change and interpretation, they adapt, evolve and mature over time. These products, in other words, become 'materially yours'.

Strategies for materially yours

We propose three strategies, which suggest ways of using materials at different experiential levels to assist in the design of longer lasting products; these are:

1 embrace imperfection;
2 do it yourself (DIY) materials; and
3 multi-situated materials.

With these strategies for 'materially yours', we also aim to highlight aspects of *resilience thinking* (Walker and Salt, 2006; Zolli, 2013; Chapman, 2005, 2014) which suggests that the most responsive to change will survive. Chapman explains:

Change, and the impermanence of all things has forever troubled us humans – that whispered taunt, just beneath the level of awareness, that reminds us of our own mortality, and that of all things on earth. As streams of matter and energy flow continuously in and out of each other, we realize that the one constant in all of this is change itself. The more we attempt to overcome this fact, the less in tune with natural processes our thinking becomes, and the more alien our resulting practices become. In evolutionary biology, it is not the strongest species that survive, nor the most intelligent, but the most responsive to change. In resilience thinking, this innate capacity to absorb disturbance, and accept change (rather than defensively resist and block it), is key to success.

(Chapman, 2014, p140)

We apply and develop this thinking in all three strategies, by offering a sense of ambiguity, curiosity, flexibility and openness in material thinking, and indeed, the design of materials.

Embrace imperfection

Technological development has led, and been driven by, a trend towards perfection. The predominance of automation processes and quality controls have led to the almost total elimination of errors and imperfections in the made world. Thus, what we have witnessed is the dominance of an aesthetic model tied to perfection in every sphere of human life: the body, the style of life, products and their materials (Rognoli and Karana, 2014). On the contrary, according to the Japanese notion of *Wabi Sabi*, in which the asymmetrical, the unfinished, the broken, the shattered and the reassembled, are all important aspects for our sensorial enjoyment of the world around us. This is a world that is continually changing its 'perfect' state. *Wabi* identifies the rustic simplicity, the freshness or the silence. It can also refer to quirks or defects generated in the process of construction, which add uniqueness and elegance to the object. *Sabi* is beauty or serenity that accompanies aging, when the life of the object and its impermanence are highlighted by the patina and the wear, or any visible repairs (Koren, 2002; Sartwell, 2006; Juniper, 2003).

Giving value to imperfection (Ostuzzi et al., 2011) and particularly, giving value to imperfect material qualities (as suggested by *Wabi Sabi*) leads to a reconsideration of the relationship that we have with everyday products. For example, imperfect material qualities can be endearing (sensorial level), can be perceived as natural and mundane (interpretive level), can help to create a bond between an object and the user (affective level). These objects, whose materials express a new aesthetic, offer new ways and forms of interaction (performative level), which are richer, more enduring and sometimes 'fuzzy' (Chapman, 2005) based on more unpredictable and uncertain forms of interaction (as opposed to clear, unambiguous forms of interaction).

Materials derived from natural (and relatively unprocessed, or *raw*) resources, such as wood and stone, have the potential to generate unique aesthetics inherent to their physical character. These anomalies inherent to materials can be kept and mobilized in design. This has been successfully adopted as a strategy by a number of designers. Nao Tamura's recent design, the 'Rings' stool, beautifully illustrates this approach, for example. The designer states that the size of the rings is never the same and year-by-year the stool records its history slowly, like a tree. In other words, the each Rings stool has different aesthetic qualities (i.e. sensorial level), and they accumulate their users' history in unique ways. This inevitably affects the meanings we attribute to the stool over time (i.e. interpretive level) and how we build an emotional bond (i.e. affective level).

If the materials are recycled, there is also a high possibility to create unique aesthetic qualities because often they have non-homogeneous structure with various colours or inclusions like we experience in the 'Parupu' chair for children by Claesson Koivisto Rune for Sodra. The chair is made from a composite material, based solely on recycled paper pulp and a biodegradable plastic, developed by Innventia (Sweden). Similarly, if the materials originate from food waste, re-used materials or discarded objects, they offer unique textual and visual experiences. Coffee cups designed with waste coffee grounds by Lou Io show how the irregularities due to waste coffee grounds are kept and valorized in design (Figure 14.1). In both Parupu chair and the Io's coffee cups, we see that each product has unique colour shades and textures (i.e. sensorial level). In both we can recognize the raw material (which is paper in Parupu chair and coffee grounds in the Io's cups), which might elicit surprise (i.e. affective level), or evoke the meaning 'environmental friendly and natural', (i.e. interpretive level) which may make us appreciate the product and keep it longer (i.e. affective level).

Designing with anomalies and defects inherent to the material or created through manufacturing processes has long been emphasized in the design domain. Italian architect and designer, Gaetano Pesce, was one of the first to stress the importance of imperfection and deformity with regard to its expressive and symbolic potential. His design style usually celebrates the beauty of chance and the uniqueness of the imperfections caused by a manufacturing process, and material, where each piece is unique and original. In this way, bubbles, defects and dimensional changes are all embraced as part of the production process. One of his classics reflecting this thinking is 543 Broadway Chair, designed in 1993 (Figure 14.2). Each seat and back is different; as when the resin is poured into the moulds, the workers add the colour of their own preference, by hand.

In every industrial process there occur anomalies by accident, and these are ordinarily avoided or rejected. When this is deliberately sought, and the parameters are deliberately set for the purpose of creating such design *defects*, designers may create unique, idiosyncratic objects as a result of a traditional industrial process. The Happy Misfit Armchair, designed by Rutger de Regt from Handmade Industrials, for example, was developed through a flexible moulding system using a balloon and polystyrene pearls (Figure 14.3). Applying restrictions to the mass enabled the designer to sculpt and form each Happy Misfit individually as a unique handmade object, with unique aesthetic qualities, yet through an industrial machine.

Figure 14.1 Coffee cups designed with waste coffee grounds by Lou Io

The above examples show how the qualities inherent to materials are kept and valorized to elicit unique aesthetic experiences. Placing Hassenzahl's *hedonic needs* (2010) in the context of materials experience, we suggest that unique and imperfect qualities of materials trigger experiences of *popularity* – as a feeling of being liked and appreciated, with influence on other people, through possession of unique personal belongings. For example, knowing that a stool you possess, though industrially produced, is one of a kind, you will tell its story to your friends with pride, it will be your personal belonging … it will be materially yours. Through the lens of aesthetics, the materials in the above examples, due to their inherently imperfect natures, will stay appropriate over time as they will envelope and normalize scratches, colour changes, wears and tears more easily than their shiny and perfectly smooth peers, which instead will not accumulate the traces of time and use in an aesthetically pleasant manner, and will most probably be thrown away even though they still work/function perfectly.

No matter what its shape or material, it is inevitable that any surface, in time, will gradually lose its initial qualities. In fact the chemical/physical properties of the material, as well as the environmental stress and its use, always leads the surface of a material through an inexorable

Figure 14.2 543 Broadway Chair designed by Gaetano Pesce

Figure 14.3 The Happy Misfit Armchair, designed by Rutger de Regt from Handmade Industrials

decline. Therefore, a material's aging is dependent on the nature of the material itself and the operating conditions at hand. From an experiential point of view, some materials 'degrade' while others 'mature', by losing, maintaining or improving certain inherent qualities. The positive term of *maturity* is usually used for natural materials such as stone, paper, wood and leather, which over the years can acquire scents, colours and textures. These characteristics far from diminishing their quality, instead acquire an aura of antiquity and preciousness. As van Hinte states (1997), many natural materials were once alive; they have already naturally aged and are therefore in possession of an innate ability to deal with time. We do seem to share consistent responses concerning which materials 'age well' or not (Saito, 2007):

> Concrete becomes more ugly every passing year, looking greasy if smooth, squalid if rough; glass-fibre decays more disagreeably than stonework … Much corrosion – rust on iron, tarnish on silver, white crust on lead and tin – is normally odious; only to copper and bronze does a time- introduced oxidized surface add the luster of a noble patina.
>
> *(Lowenthal cited by Saito, 2007)*

The term *patina* is used today in a broad sense, denoting all processes connected with the aging of surfaces of artefacts with the passage of time (such as tarnish on a copper surface occurring by oxidation, or a sheen on wooden furniture). This patina often accompanies the maturation of certain materials, especially natural materials, making them also aesthetically appealing (Candy et al., 2008; Robbins et al., 2015a). In Manzini's words (1986), contemporary 'ephemeral, transient and instantaneous' materials, represented so well by synthetic polymers, degrade without dignity. For this reason, such materials reach a level of unacceptable degradation because they are not able to respond, above all, to the aesthetic requirements (Fisher, 2004). At that point in time they are usually discarded. The quality of material surfaces thus acquires also a cultural dimension (yet unexplored) on aging; an ability (or not) to stand the test of time by recording transitory signs with (or without) losing value to people (Manzini, 1986, 1990). Papanek (1995) stated that the environmentally and socially orientated design of the twenty-first century has to include 'graceful aging' as the first fundamental principle, since materials that have aged well hold great appeal. Chapman (2014, p141) also emphasizes that 'patina is a necessary design consideration to assist the extension of product lifespans in graceful and socially acceptable ways'. The Paris-based designer Lee West illustrates this approach in his recent design, Brass Watering Can (Figure 14.4). This product develops a patina over time as the metal oxidizes if the user decides not to polish it often. West explains how 'the collection aims to have longevity from an aesthetic and qualitative point of view. Hopefully people will want to use these objects regularly and enjoy watching them age.'[1]

Another example is *Underskog* designed by Kristine Bjaadal, which illustrates how the wear and tear of materials tells stories about how products have been used (Figure 14.5). The designer argues that we appreciate the aging of wood, stone and leather, yet textiles, we throw away as soon as the first thread breaks. Her work poses the question: could it be possible to make a fabric that grows more beautiful with wear and tear? When *Underskog*'s top layer, which is made of velvet, is being worn, the hidden floral pattern is slowly revealed. The parts that wear and reveal the pattern underneath mediate how people act upon the chair and how it has been used. Bearing in mind how the material of a product will change over time, designers can create products which will evolve and mature with the user. Such products that witness the passing of time with their users will evoke the experience of *relatedness* such as one would have when in regular contact with others who care, and with whom we are familiar, in this case with 'a product' through its matured, lifelong materials.

Designing with and for imperfection mainly capitalizes on the material at the first three experiential levels (sensorial, interpretative and affective), yet this does not explicitly mobilize the performative qualities of materials. Robbins et al. (2015b), on the other hand, suggest a design approach that communicates 'traces of use' via the performative qualities of materials used on particular technological products. They aim to help people understand how these products are used on a daily basis and the role that they come to play in our lives. We foresee that such products may elicit the experience of *autonomy,* where one may experience having control and being the cause of one's own actions. Seeing how your actions are mediated upon the material surface (in other words seeing how your own personal traces are conceived over time) it is argued that one will have a deeper and enduring relationship with the product. We elaborate on the power of 'self-producing' toward longer lasting products in the following strategy.

Figure 14.4 Brass Watering Can which develops patina over time, designed by Lee West

Figure 14.5 Underskog designed by Kristine Bjaadal

Do it yourself materials

The DIY approach and the revaluation of a crafts and self-production approach in product design is also supported by the democratization of technological practices (Tanenbaum et al., 2013) in terms of commonly used production labs, low cost and accessible fabrication tools and open and shared knowledge about production processes. These dynamics around DIY practices have led to the emergence of many new materials for product design. Recently, we have introduced such materials created and/or shaped by DIY practices as 'DIY materials' which are: 'created through individual or collective self-production experiences, often by techniques and processes of the designer's own invention, as a result of a process of tinkering with materials' (Rognoli et al., 2015, p693). They can be new materials with creative use of other substances as material ingredients, or they can be modified or further developed versions of existing materials.

In DIY materials, design capability is influenced and shaped through 'learning by doing'. As Lee (2015, p21) argues, the designer becomes an alchemist willing to self-produce materials following the magic conversion of one substance into another. 'Material perfection was sought through the action of a preparation (Philosopher's Stone for metals; Elixir of Life for humans), while spiritual ennoblement resulted from some form of inner revelation or other enlightenment (Gnosis, for example, in Hellenistic and western practices)'. In DIY material design practices, the designer becomes a craftsperson, able to build and to modify the tools for his/her purpose (Rognoli et al., 2015) to create new material proposals (Karana et al., 2015b). A result of the DIY material design process is new aesthetic expression grounded on imperfect aesthetic qualities that show the existence of an alchemist's (i.e. designer's) manual labour and craftsmanship, and hence traces of humanity, in search of perfection.

Such self-produced materials elicit a sense of ambiguity, curiosity and surprise among those who come into contact with the results. For example, finding out that a given material comes from recycled coffee grounds or is made from recycled plastics collected from oceans. In this way, Marlène Huissoud shows the potential of insects as an innovative future material ingredient. The designer has experimented largely with *propolis*, a biodegradable resin that honey bees collect from trees and use as a sealant for their hive (Figure 14.6).

Another example is Xylinum Cones by Jannis Huelsen with Stefan Schwabe for Science Gallery/Dublin, who use living organisms to grow geometrical objects. The project uses bacteria cellulose characterized by high purity, strength, mouldability and increased water-holding ability (Figure 14.7). After a growth period of three weeks, the cellulose cones are dried and added to a sculptural assembly. The main motivation of the Xylinum Cones is on the one hand to prove the reproducibility of organically grown objects, but on the other, to find a balanced level of geometric precision and organic diversity.

When considered through the lens of materials experience, the first strategy (embrace imperfection) and the second (DIY materials) converge on a common understanding of valuing traces of humanity and nature. On the other hand, in DIY materials, there are two additional layers which strengthen the relationships we have with products. The first is the act of 'making', so being proud of your act of doing and creating; the second is to reveal the unique, yet unknown, new material qualities, so being proud of the new aesthetics you could achieve. These ambiguous new materials are open to interpretation. We argue they create new opportunities for building new relationships between people and the products they are embodied within.

Figure 14.6 Propolis made of insects by Marlène Huissoud

Figure 14.7 Xylinum Cones by Jannis Huelsen with Stefan Schwabe for Science Gallery/Dublin

Multi-situated materials

Materials of a given product are decided upon both functional and experiential requirements, which are often determined in relation to an envisioned *situational whole* (Karana, 2009). In other words, with a pre-defined scenario, the material of a product is imagined to be used in a particular manner, or as a facilitator in a particular context of use, or both. However, pre-defined scenarios do not accommodate for the huge variety of situations people encounter in the day-to-day use of products (Brandes et al., 2009), nor do they account for ongoing change. These situations are far from being static and homogeneous (Jencks and Silver, 2013; Giaccardi and Fischer, 2008). Not only is there great variety in the everyday lives, needs and motivations of people, these needs and motivations are also continuously changing with the changing capabilities and routines that we develop by accommodating products in our lives.

Creating products that can be assimilated in practice does not empower people to cope with changing needs and situations of use that are, in reality, often in flux. A study on everyday home practices (Giaccardi et al., 2016) has revealed that products have the ability to support a variety of different practices according to their movements, temporalities and relationships with other objects – in other words, their performative qualities. However, product design has the tendency to ignore heterogeneity, preferring instead to focus on individual aspects of the larger and more integrated whole. Despite one of the central tenets of user-centred design being 'know your user', design research often prioritizes needs over people, so that people are defined in relation to anticipated use, and the design is then adapted to the supposed 'specific needs' of a given scenario of use.

Empowering people to resourcefully address the variety in situations of use and ongoing change requires new forms of openness in the materiality and functionality of designed objects. It requires designs that can adapt and remain appropriate for the wide variety of situations they may end up in (Kuijer and Giaccardi, 2015). Think of how a walking cane is used 'in practice' also to reach things, push a button or *call* the neighbour upstairs (Forchhammer, 2006). Another example of this is a recently designed yoga set by Joseph Guerra and Sina Sonrab, who expresses the idea of designing yoga products that wouldn't

Figure 14.8 Yoga set by Joseph Guerra and Sina Sonrab

Giaccardi, E. and Fischer, G. (2008) Creativity and Evolution: A Metadesign Perspective, *Digital Creativity*, vol. 19, no. 1, pp19–32.

Giaccardi, E. and Karana, E. (2015) Foundations of Materials Experience: An Approach for HCI, in *Proceedings of the 33rd SIGCHI Conference on Human Factors in Computing Systems*, ACM, New York, pp. 2447–2456.

Giaccardi, E., Speed, C., Cila, N. and Caldwell, M. (2016). When Objects Become Co-ethnographers: Potentials of a Thing-Centered Approach in Design and Anthropology, in R. C. Smith et al. (eds), *Design Anthropology Futures*, London: Bloomsbury.

Hassenzahl, M. (2010) *Experience Design: Technology for all the Right Reasons*, Morgan & Claypool, San Rafael, CA.Hosey, L. (2012) *The Shape of Green: Aesthetics, Ecology, and Design*, Island Press, Washington, DC.

Jencks, C. and Silver, N. (2013) *Adhocism: The Case for Improvisation*, Cambridge, MA: MIT Press.

Juniper, A. (2003) *Wabi Sabi: The Japanese Art of Impermanence*, Tuttle Publishing, Chicago, IL.

Karana, E. (2009) Meanings of Materials, doctoral dissertation, Delft University of Technology, Delft, The Netherlands.

Karana, E., Pedgley O. and Rognoli V. (eds) (2014) *Materials Experience: Fundamentals of Materials and Design*, Butterworth-Heinemann, Oxford.

Karana, E., Pedgley, O. and Rognoli, V. (2015a) On Materials Experience, *Design Issues*, vol. 31, no. 3, pp16–27.

Karana, E., Barati, B., Rognoli, V. and Zeeuw van der Laan, A. (2015b) Material Driven Design (MDD): A Method to Design for Material Experiences, *International Journal of Design*, vol. 9, no. 2, pp35–54.

Koren, L. (2008) *Wabi-Sabi: For Artists, Designers, Poets and Philosophers*, Imperfect Publishing, Point Reyes, CA.

Krista, O., Karana, E. and Soto-Faraco, S. (2016) Perception of Naturalness in Textiles, *Journal of Materials and Design*, vol. 90, pp. 1192–1199.

Kuijer, L. and Giaccardi, E. (2015) Considering Artifacts as Co-performers, paper presented at Animals, Automated Devices and Ecosystems: A Symposium on the Agencies of Dynamic Non-humans in Theories of Practice, Barcelona, 9–10 October.

Lee, J. (2015) *Material Alchemy. Redefining Materiality within the 21st Century*, Bis Publisher, Amsterdam.

Manzini, E. (1986) *The Material of Invention: Materials and Design*, Arcadia Edizioni, Milan.

Manzini, E. (1990) *Artifacts: Towards a New Ecology of the Artificial Environment*, Domus Academy, Milan.

Manzini, E. (1994) Design, Environment and Social Quality: From 'Existenzminimum' to 'Quality Maximum', *Design Issues*, vol. 10, no. 1, pp37–43.

Orr, D. (2002) *The Nature of Design: Ecology, Culture, and Human Intention*, Oxford University Press, Oxford.

Ostuzzi, F., Salvia G., Rognoli V. and Levi, M. (2011) The Value of Imperfection in Industrial Product, in *Proceedings of Designing Pleasurable Products and Interactions*, DPPI11, Milan, pp361–369.

Papanek, V. (1995) *The Green Imperative: Ecology and Ethics in Design and Architecture*, Thames & Hudson, London.

Ramakers, R. (2002) *Less+More, Droog Design in Context*, 010 Publishers, Rotterdam:

Robbins H., Giaccardi E. and Karana E. (2015a) De-commodifying the Device: A Materialist Design Approach for Communication With and Through Connected Objects, presented at The Future of Making: Where Industrial and Personal Fabrication Meet workshop, Critical Alternatives 2015, Aarhus, Denmark.

Robbins, H., Giaccardi, E., Karana, E. and D'Olivo, P. (2015b) Understanding and Designing with (and for) Material Traces, *Studies in Material Thinking*, vol. 13, no. 1, retrieved from https://www.materialthinking.org/sites/default/files/papers/0143_SMT_Vol13_P03_FA.pdf

Rognoli, V. and Karana, E. (2014) Towards a New Materials Aesthetic Based on Imperfection and Graceful Ageing, in E. Karana, O. Pedgley and V. Rognoli (eds), *Materials Experience: Fundamentals of Materials and Design*, Butterworth-Heinemann, pp145–154.

Rognoli, V., Bianchini, M., Maffei S. and Karana, E. (2015) DIY Materials, *Materials and Design*, vol. 86, pp. 692–702.

Saito, Y. (2007) *Everyday Aesthetics*, Oxford University Press, Oxford.

Sartwell, C. (2006) *Six Names of Beauty*, Routledge, Abingdon.

Tanenbaum, J. G., Williams, A. M., Desjardins, A. and Tanenbaum, K. (2013) Democratizing Technology: Pleasure, Utility and Expressiveness in DIY and Maker Practice, in Proceedings of CHI 2013, 27 April–2 May, Paris, France, pp2603–2612, retrived from https://pdfs.semanticscholar.org/1553/79ab94e87ee9cf7648eb53dfc8749887eee7.pdf

Van Hinte, E. (ed.). (1997) *Eternally Yours: Visions on Product Endurance*, 010 Publishers, Rotterdam, The Netherlands.

Van Hinte, E. (ed.). (2004) *Eternally Yours: Time in Design. Product Value Sustenance*, 010 Publishers, Rotterdam.

Vezzoli, C. (2007) *System Design for Sustainability. Theory, Methods and Tools for a Sustainable 'satisfactionsystem' Design*, Maggioli Editore, Milan.

Walker, S. (1995). The Environment, Product Aesthetics and Surface. *Design Issues*, vol. 11, no. 3, pp. 15–27.

Walker, B. and Salt, D. (2006) *Resilience Thinking: Sustaining Ecosystems and People in a Changing World*, Island Press, Washington, DC.

Zafarmand, S. J., Sugiyama, K. and Watanabe, M. (2003) Aesthetic and Sustainability: The Aesthetic Attributes Promoting Product Sustainability, *The Journal of Sustainable Product Design*, vol. 3, no. 3–4, pp.173–186.

Zolli, A. (2013) *Resilience: Why Things Bounce Back*, Simon & Schuster, New York.

15

MEDIATING MATTERS

Nick Gant

Abstract

This chapter explores material communication and the use of recycled and waste materials as a means to engineer communicative and therefore *valuable* products. It explores methods for elevating the value of waste materials through unearthing and highlighting the narratives and histories that are embodied within them. Through this chapter, I explore how the process of designing with recycled materials may exploit these *material memories* to bring value to products. The term *mediating matters* also refers to the capacity for materials to mediate stories, and develop new languages pertaining to the branding of more sustainable consumption. This text considers how materials can convey ideas and issues of sustainability through a material vocabulary that helps to broker engagement between consumers and matters in the world. As consumer habits continue to evolve in today's *post-awareness-raising* scenario, products also need to evolve to be both reflective of this change and in catalysing further transition in consumer consciousness and behaviour. Materials mediate complex meanings and values (social, personal, political for example) that often go beyond their performance or function. As well as being central to the physical issues of sustainability, materials have agency in the communication of these issues and play a role as actors within the narrative of sustainability – materials have a *voice* in this social and cultural dialogue. This chapter will explore how methods for more nuanced material articulation can be applied in the creation of highly valued and more sustainable, consumer products. The corollary being that the sustainability of the material is in-turn part of the product's value and is often also central to the way the product expresses this value. Finally I will argue for greater significance being placed on *material literacy* and the material language of recycling when designing eloquent, sustainable products.

Keywords: re-meaning, re-valuation, embodied stories, product poetics, virtuous circularity

Matter-reality

In many respects, sustainability could be considered a matter of matter. Much of the *stuff* we consume is material, and the materiality of things is fundamental to both the impact and culture of consumerism. When, as designers, our ideas, visions and concepts become reality, inevitably matter will be consumed in the process of their realization. Before we create products we also create *material products* – vsuch as medium-density fibreboard (MDF) or polycarbonate sheet – which as well as giving form and function, also provide the underpinning visual, textural and physical language of objects. As we manufacture and consume products we consume matter and transform it into different states. During this process, the mining, processing, movement and consumption of solid, liquid and gas in turn creates new states of matter in the form of waste, pollution and emissions. In the UK, data for 2012 (DEFRA, 2015) suggests that the combined consumption of materials through UK extraction and imports equates to 590 million metric tonnes. Design therefore has a direct impact on the earth due to the specified use of materials (Thorpe, 2007). Consequentially, designers have both a duty and responsibility to be conversant in both the impact and potential of materials in the design of the products they propose. Designers also need to be aware of new advances in materials that help minimize impact. Indeed, the design of materials is an often under-represented but key driver of product design as a creative discipline, and frequently leads to the development of evermore-sustainable products. Equally, designing more sustainable systems and processes can also have a direct impact on natural resource consumption, and in the generation of waste. In the UK, waste materials going to landfill has decreased from 25 million tonnes in 2010, to 20 million tonnes in 2012 (<20%) and effective waste management also results in a reduction of problematic carbon emissions that is calculated as saving 4,258,233 tonnes of carbon emissions in the UK alone. So matter does matter.

More sustainable products

As a starting point, this may seem like a contradiction in terms – the consumption of ever expanding choices of products is still (and is likely to remain for the foreseeable future) the reality until less consumptive models prevail. Whilst this is still the case, materials continue to play a part in championing the delivery and consumption of *more* sustainable products.

The notion of a *sustainable product* may be seen as oxymoronic, as more of anything suggests sharp contradiction. However, it is unhelpful to characterize sustainability as an absolute. Rather, sustainability is a goal, which requires incremental transition towards it and a diversity of variations on how it is achieved (Fletcher, 2007). There is no time to try and resolve whether the state of sustainability is or is not by definition an absolute, and equally, there will be those who suggest not to consume at all is the only model for achieving true sustainability. However, in an age of consumerism we might also need to consider a scenario where *more* product designers choose to design *more* products and services that are *more* sustainable than their predecessors. If sustainability is achievable as a symbiosis between people, profit and the planet, then materials have a central role to play in the transition to sustainability through their prevalence within the physical things we sell and buy.

Meaning matters

We buy products for reasons beyond pure function and choices are often made through issues of the heart, not just the head. Designers are expected to create products transferring certain meanings and it is materials that in part carry this (Karana, 2010). In this way, the product narrative, language, semantics and semiotics have become a ubiquitous part of product design (Steffen, 2009). It is suggested that materials are separated into two clear categories; first the technical aspects, for performance and function and second for user-interaction, in terms of communication and personality (van Kesteren et al., 2007). Materials do not simply provide material function alone but should deliver meaningful experiences beyond mere utility (Karana *et al.*, 2015).

Many products offer little in terms of material language. Their conformity and repetition of the same vernacular to the point of indecipherable difference, results in clones competing with one another in the marketplace. Often, their material form and language is monotonous and even disingenuous, as fake polymer representations of undefined semi-metallic forms become inert as a meaningful vocabulary through a lack of authenticity and meaning. In contrast, materials can perform a role as the facilitator of meanings and values in society. As designers we have the opportunity to articulate these through the materials we use. Materials have 'character' derived from how they are form and age and how people feel about them (Ashby and Johnson, 2002) and their character can play a lead role in the stories of product design.

So, what are the new brand stories or meaningful products, and how will they respond to the contemporary context? Sustainability is an increasing part of consumer consciousness and brands are, essentially, about promises. How can more sustainable products articulate, communicate and mediate brand meanings in a more effective, visceral way? Can recycled materials utilize their meaning in the creation of consumer value and their adoption or acceptance of more sustainable values? Brands need to create tangible, meaningful connections with their customers and increasingly the expression of a material is the underpinning of design (Houseley, 2009).

The *value* of materials is often not so much the consequence of its role as the provider of function or performance but is a result of interactions with the user and the context in which user, product and material are situated. Indeed, this can be in relation to the cultural or contextual *spaces* in which the materials can gain identity (Shove et al., 2007). Equally it is suggested that materials may not in and of themselves contain *meaning*, but meanings can be formed through interactions and associations in context (Chapman, 2014). Consumers are continually searching for meanings and narratives that interrelate and help narrate their lives; bringing value to their experiences as owners and users of material things. In a sustainable and ethical context we are already utilizing the language of materials to mediate more advanced forms of communication with consumers that reflect more nuanced, sustainable values.

Our relationship to certain personal, value-based consumer beliefs can develop and offer deep and sustained consumer relationships, such as those some consumers have with, say, organic foods (Noel, 2009). These experiences can trigger more motivated, *feel good* factors, which further enrich consumer experience. These kinds of *attitude objects* can be a person, advertisement, issue or object with which one has an attitude towards. It might be, then, that materials could also be seen as *attitude objects*. Indeed, marketers often aim to exploit or expose attitudes, which consist of consumers' cognitive, affective and cognitive responses in terms of how they think, feel and act. The corollary of this is that we may think of the waste matter being generated as a result of these three factors, in total reverse. On this flipside, when we engage with what would otherwise be waste materials, we are actually engaging with the *matters of behaviour.*

Virtuous-circular economy

The linear process of digging holes in the ground, extracting matter, manipulating that matter and processing it into new states of matter, manufacturing the matter into new things only for those things to be hastily dispensed of and returned to the ground or burned is a fundamentally flawed concept – lets agree on that! So we endeavour now to model, define and deliver a more circular economy, which recycles matter through a more sustainable and efficient set of interlinked processes. The potential material saving of a circular economy is estimated at over 1 trillion dollars a year (Ellen MacArthur Foundation, 2015, p10). This enables new possibilities to prevent waste, but also it affords new opportunities to create value, or represent values. This can be achieved through the meaning that is constructed in the physical returning of our materials within such a system, but additionally, in the value that is bestowed upon these materials when they are reformed into new products.

In a similar way to how we grant importance when encountering antiques that contain the essence of former lives, uses and experiences, recycled materials also develop and gather importance as their lives are extended. This, in turn, affords the materials a sustained cognitive interaction with us and this connection is sustained as it changes and grows, over time. The continued and cyclical process of recycling is itself a form of *meaning-making*. As such, it is a powerful method for gathering, exploiting and reforming material meanings in the made world. This is a humanizing process of correlating the experience and regeneration that is constructed through the material interactions with our world; the processes we undertake as humans and contexts in which we coexist. To differing degrees, when we engage with *recycled materials*, we are aware of their provenance, aware of a journey they may have been on, and we can form a sense of a history. Therefore, as users, we contrive a notion of a narrative that accompanies that object. Recycled materials are embodied with the accompanying sense of both human and material experience through the processing of their various former lives – they embody ghosts of their former lives, if you will.

Many of our social interactions revolve around sharing our life histories and experiences with one another. As we move through our lives, we collect experiences which help form our character, and, whilst we ourselves are physical things (matter), it is our life experiences that are also essential to how we interact with other people and give meaning to our lives. We therefore value both the process of gaining experience, and the recounting of these physical and experiential journeys, to ourselves and to others. Similarly the life of a material, object or product can add meaning to it and it is through use that we give life and meaning to material things.

Whether it is a conscious or determined act, or not, to design using recycled materials is, in part, to recite and recount the experience that material has undergone. The values attached to this process of recycling can actually be exploited when encouraging the act of recycling in consumers, if offered as both a physical reward and as a meaningful incentive. There is a circle-of-virtue that is constructed when a consumer recycles a material if they can configure a sense of that material being returned to them. Whether through a product that they use made from the recycled material or that they encounter a notion of the material being reused somewhere else and especially if the actual material they have recycled is deployed, then the consumer experience is what we might refer to as a 'virtuous-circular-interaction'. In opposition to this, when we waste things there is no circularity in the interaction, as we need not encounter the material or object again. Equally in this scenario, the opportunity to build or recycle the meaning is also lost. Now that recycling is considered a normal part of many social contexts, we can no longer *flush-and-forget* when dispensing of our materials – we have a duty to see their lives extend, but equally, we can anticipate and relish their return.

By designing with this in mind, we are also authoring authenticity. This is because the physical embodiment of the act of recycling is manifest in the material and therefore new, more ethical interpretations of the material now apply. This kind of authentic engagement with material, even in fairly crude form, can offer a greater sense of meaning and value than those with a faux polymer masquerading as metal, for example. Recycled materials have significant cultural value and meaning within the post-awareness-raising consumer context. We therefore need to more fully understand how to deploy these as powerful tools of resource efficiency and behaviour changing product semantics.

Mediating materials

Aside from the important role recycling has within the tangible, physical context of consuming matter, the issues themselves can be embodied and expressed through more abstract notions of a material language. In this way, materials can be deployed as vehicles for *product-propaganda, product-protest, object activism* and *meaning making* (Gant and Dean, 2012). When communicating through objects, Julia Lohman describes how the meaning is created through the materiality of the object. The material becomes words; the design becomes syntax. The piece speaks without the detour of language (Williams, 2012). Material discourses influence repertoires of positional storytelling, in and through which objects acquire (and lose) aspects of symbolic meaning (Shove et al., 2007). Yet, materials themselves are also active agents in the communication of issues and the establishment of meaning. Materials have agency in the presentation, articulation and discussion of issues as actors within the broader narrative of sustainability. It can also be said that the language of recycling is the language of the systems and processes that enable it, which correlate in some products that overtly present this – communicating the capacity to be recycled and that they are of recycled origins (Manzini, 1997). We actually construct meaning and value through the materials we choose and the complexity to which we understand and deploy their origin, history and process as part of the object narrative we compose.

Making meaning

The transformative nature of designing and making products with recycled materials is turning waste into wonder. This is a cherished *rags-to-riches* story of recycling transformed by the maker as a kind of Fairy Godmother in the process of creating beauty, from modest means. The composing of material narratives as ingredients in a story is to craft experience and material dialect. To a greater or lesser degree, the act of making forms meaning. Something made in a factory by low paid workers, in a sterile environment offers one type of meaning, and where as to be made from materials, 'fished' from the oceans is another meaning. The interaction in material, making and form can help imply or amplify a material's social, cultural or political history and this includes championing ethical or sustainable origins or aspirations. The composition and interrelationship of material and making processes form a kind of performance process that is often used as activism, propaganda and protest. Overt making methods are deployed to deliberately reject the hidden, 'dark arts' of manufacture in favour of humanizing and championing the role of making and manufacture as a key context in the creation of meaningful things. Materials are characterized and placed centre stage; 'acts of making' form a prologue, setting the scene that shapes a plot that is realized through the material manifestations of the product. This is not so much the social acts of making in a connecting community sense (Gauntlett, 2011), but rather, this process seeks to anthropomorphize through the conscious attribution of human and ethical qualities (Sennett, 2008).

Materials manufacture and in particularly recycled material manufacture, often mediate process through the visual language and attributes of the material. And the language of the *event* that transforms the material from a former state (virgin) into its new state (recycled) is often a significant and prominent strategy in the designed application of recycled matter. For example, composite material boards (such as chipboard or recycled plastics) often tell a story of their origins as wood- or polymer-based products. Designers often deploy these materials as a means to portray greater levels of sustainability or to articulate those values through designed products and spaces. The frequency of how these materials are used leads to consumers learning the meanings of the materials (see Hekkert and Karana, 2014). The chipped-up parts of a mobile phone, drinks bottle or car tyre, reformed within a new surface vocalizes a sense of history and of former lives. Thus, recycled materials can narrate the states of being, which through the transformative event of being recycled can change (Steffan, 2009). For makers, the process of recycling and the nuanced ways in which this process is undertaken can form part of an articulate language and sophisticated narration that becomes embodied in the final object. This connection is mediated through the material, as the object's form can often be of little consequence when compared to the communicative power of the material as a vehicle for meaning. The transformative, iterative or expressive act of recycling a material is in itself meaningful in relation to a range of historical, technical, conceptual and cultural contexts. The *conspicuous transformation* of recycled matter forms new 'raw' material (Skov Holt and Holt Skov, 2008) when the tell-tail signatures and ghosts of identifiable waste, reincarnate through novel, pressed polymers. The *remoulding of the rejected* enables new compositions that, like remixing music, can blend new variants or material sub-cultures of mashed-up, cultural connotation and dialect. The dull equality of mass-production can be infiltrated by *happy accidents* (Ingledew, 2011) and the idiosyncrasy of the 'one-off' is merged with moulded regularity as materials and meanings are re-embodied and recomposed en masse.

Poetic products

Products and materials that relate back to the causal factors or origins of the problem can forge poetic links, which resonate with consumers whilst clearly highlighting the need for the intervention within the issue. This is not only potentially a closed loop recycling system but also a more poetic idea that presents a cognitive closing of the loop, conceptually. The recycling of plastic waste to make plastic refuse sacks is, of course, not such a compelling product story, but when designers and makers utilize and deploy an enhanced level of technical material understanding, with a distinct eye for irony, the result can be a revelation in object communication.

One of my graduate students, British designer and materials researcher Adam Fairweather has been investigating the engineering of waste coffee grounds as a material resource for some time, initially at our labs and workshops here in Brighton. Through rigorous experimentation he has unearthed properties in the development of coffee-based polymers and composites, which not only enable qualities that other 'traditional', oil derived polymers do not have, but also make it compatible with some mainstream manufacturing processes and applications. What's important here, however, is that he has applied this back within the industry that creates the material as a by-product. Compostability and a resistance to ultraviolet degradation are not often attributes that a composite material can boast, in addition to more *natural* attributes such as biodegradability, or low toxicity, for example. Equally, its ability to be moulded into various forms for use in extreme environments also demonstrates the range of performance attributes afforded through harnessing the untapped potential of overlooked waste materials. Coffee cups and coffee machines all using materials created from the waste coffee grounds evoke a warm sense of well-being when you engage with their natural beauty. Indeed, the materials help to also highlight the problem of consumption and the ethical responsibilities consumers have (and some brands also consider) when consuming this ubiquitous, everyday product. The material is sourced through considerate means; offering benefits to communities from the countries where the material is sourced, whilst also being considerate of the material life span and possibilities for issues including circulation, end of life and, low emission degradability.

Another one of our student's work that exemplifies this is that of Anna Bullus's 'Gumdrop Bin', which is a chewing gum bin made from recycled chewing gum. This highly acclaimed proposition is an elegant product pun, which both visually and materially relates to the blowing of a bubble-gum-bubble. Again, it utilizes conventional mass-manufacturing techniques to enable a closed loop system. The 'gumdrop bin' harvests waste chewing gum, which in turn, forms its own supply chain for the creation of more bins and a material language that is authentic, charming and importantly, memorable. All this, whilst serving to responsibly solve an environmental problem (waste chewing gum, and associated impacts of street clean-up) that costs local authorities considerable public money to deal with. Through in-depth material design, a poetic narrative is played-out between users and the product, through a descriptive, physical manifestation of the issue. So eloquently and composed is this material story and the effectiveness of both the symbolism and technical function is difficult to ignore, or misunderstand.

By recycling the material both physically and symbolically, distinctive material stories are scripted and deployed within products that articulate new values and forms of design that resonate powerfully with users.

Provenance and place

As users we are inconsistent when evaluating the provenance of the materials we engage with throughout our daily lives. We do not necessarily consider the origin of the polymers in our sweatshirt, yet we might overtly consider the origins of the wool in our cardigan. The value systems we consider as consumers and users can have both positive and negative consequences when we seek to demand products of a certain provenance, and geographic location or community. It may or may not be *sustainable* to import and export products of a particular material heritage around the world, but nonetheless materials that relate directly to a place can have significance, meaning and value that have proven to sustain demand in many retail sectors. In part, this will be due to the special, unique or idiosyncratic qualities of the product, but also of the mythology, culture and stories that are associated with a particular place. These sensibilities can often form aspirational desires, which heighten the value of materials and products and can even elevate them to luxury status.

Another way to consider provenance and place is to consider *locality*. Locality has not always been synonymous with product design, as a predominately decentralized, global enterprise. However, in a reflective context design considers options to enhance both the creative content of products and in relating them to more meaningful considerations for the future. Indeed, it might be argued that product design has *made it* when a designer can front the world's largest and most profitable company developing products of ubiquity globally. However, within the complexity of the consumer context and values, this could simultaneously be seen as both pinnacle and hiatus. When the notion of *design* equates to mass-manufacture in zero-tolerant, cloned forms, which spawn countless indecipherable replicas of equal hollow homogeny, then there will certainly be sectors of design and designers, brands and consumers, that will

Figure 15.1 Coffee cups and coffee machine made from waste coffee, by Adam Fairweather

Figure 15.2 Gumdrop Bin made from waste chewing gum, by Anna Bullus

seek to redefine the value of these monopolizing establishments. This may be to get us to 'think differently' (ironically the former strapline of one such global brand) or to offer new considerations and values, which may be more sustainable.

In the globalized context of product design, *local* as a concept may have been prejudiced against as a result of perceptions of things that are *narrow* in focus, lacking aspiration or limited in diversity. Some designers and makers are continually reconsidering the local as a means to write new material meanings and construct and promote alternative value systems that can more effectively meet contemporary consumer contexts and concerns; a shift that even extends to global brands.

We might liken consideration of the local to that of *food miles*, in which producers and consumers are concerned with the miles that produce has travelled and consequential environmental impact of our daily intake of food. To buy local is often to potentially recalibrate our consumer choices to offer greater benefit to communities, locally, whilst simultaneously lessening the environmental impact of our consumption. In addition, local initiatives also aim to get a product that is perhaps fresher, less standardized and more characteristic of a given place or season for example. This combination of multiple meaningful benefits can tap into different value systems that align with a range of principles, processes and narratives with which we may want to relate to as discerning consumers and designers. Rightly or wrongly, product designers and brands see this as an opportunity – either way, these opportunities exist to create more sustainable attributes or outcomes as a result, and are therefore worthy of pursuit.

The 'Farmer's Market' range of training shoes by New Balance (2012) unapologetically shout about *locality* and use local waste materials as part of the material language and narrative composition of their product (see Figure 15.3). The brand uses this language to carry a message of localism and pride-in-provenance. It seeks to directly deploy the identity of farmers markets where traditionally local producers come together to sell local produce direct to the local community.

My own research and that of my colleague, Tanya Dean, seeks to define and systematize the methods by which materials can be composed or deployed by designers and makers as a means to generate meaningful material narratives. Indeed it is an interrelationship between the product, the process, the user and the material, which forms the basis upon which to compose such scenarios for the development of value. This process is catalysed when using waste materials and their embedded histories and experiences. This programme of design research is entitled 'Sole-Searching' and uses the creation of shoes made from waste materials as part of the methodology and as a vehicle for the research. One example of a method from 'Sole-Searching' is presented through the 'Flip-Flopsam and Jetsam' shoes (2011). In this instance the 'provenance and place' method is deployed and tested by engaging local people in the process of collecting waste plastics from their local beach. By using this material to form a memento of the event (forming a pair of flip-flops on a converted heat press, using collected waste plastic) the significance of the event is locked into the materiality of the object. The hypothesis was that the *feel-good factor* generated through participation in this act of local activism, becomes embodied when the rubbish is transformed into a unique product. This experience is further amplified by the addition of a map of the local area that forms the grip of the sole, courtesy of the etched heat plate on which the thermoplastics are melded together. The product also stands as a means to promote the act of communal clean-ups (in this case promoted by the UK Marine Conservation Society) whilst highlighting the issue that is the cause of the waste material – what we might consider to be a 'product-protest or propaganda' (Gant and Dean, 2013).

Figure 15.3 New Balance 'Farmer's Market' trainers (2012)

Source: photograph by Nick Gant

Figure 15.4 Flip-Flopsam and Jetsam (2011): flip-flops made from plastic beach waste embossed with a map relating to the source of material, by Nick Gant and Tanya Dean

Local no longer needs to be perceived as a negative connotation and at odds with the concerns of global organizations – in fact it can be a rich source of creative sustenance and context for meaning making. Also the consideration and perception of *place* can be international when we relate it to our own environment and that of shared systems like the air, the landscape and the seas and oceans. Kieran Jones and Studio Swine's Sea Chair (2013) and Gyrecraft (2015), G-Star Jeans (2014) and Ed Carpenter's shoe for Adidas (2015) all recycle the potential resource of plastic waste from the sea, whilst at the same time authoring material mediations which generate awareness of what have become the material legends of the oceanic gyres. With 'Flip-Flopsam and Jetsam' (2011), Gant and Dean's concern was not only to clear beaches of this problematic material but perhaps more pertinent was to test if we could drive a local sense of significance and pride into the material and make meaning through making for those who collected it. Additionally could the material then elevate the value of the object as a consequence of the process? The act of harvesting and processes in situ, amongst a *caring* community embodies the material with greater significance and elevates the material value through experience and interaction that is co-related to locality and even a time and a place.

'Ghost fishing' nets are fishing nets that are disposed of at sea by the fishing industry and continue to catch fish despite no humans benefiting from the catch. Dr Nick Hill from the London Zoological society and Interface Carpets project pays fishermen in the Philippines to fish for these problematic waste nets. The provenance of material is projected through the material towards customers in foreign places. The substance itself becomes embodied in a literal, material way to that place and its wildlife and people and customers are invested in a part of this narrative. This process drives a conscious demand for the nets as a *mediating material embodied with meaning* and in-turn creates more sustainable economies that provide solutions to ecological issues.

Material literacy

When trying to describe the potential there is to script meaningful material stories, the terms 'recycling and up-cycling' don't capture the rich diversity and sophistication of the material language available, which is being explored and deployed by designers and makers. Our verbal and textual repertoire lacks the nuance of the dialogues being formed within material products and such deficits can serve to stifle the culture of recycling as design tool for projecting meaning. This is a challenge, both for consumer culture, and for product design education. If we take plastics as an example, *plastic* is a term that is ripe for reinvention (Gant, 2005). There are, of course, protective commercial benefits of differentiating and branding types of plastic (Lycra and Perspex, for example) as a means to diversify a negative generic identity (Shove et al., 2007). However, this must go further and we need to be able to distinguish between complex polymers and champion the role of more sustainably progressive materials by a revolution of language and well-communicated, authentic, material, brand promises. All made things are to some degree artificial and it is the technical interference that may have been what defined the *depth of the artificial* and their relational *distance* from being natural (Manzini, 1986). However, a move to more complex eco-polymers and a more diverse appreciation of the variations of recycling requires a shift in thinking and in practice. Designers and consumers need to develop a more refined language and understanding about the evolving complexity that polymer developments offer us within contexts of sustainability if we are to perpetuate and demand their use. Over simplified beliefs that *plastics* are limited in their value due in part to their inexorable link with *cheap products* (and times), the context of future visions for sustainability again opens up new spaces for the reconsideration of the role of this complex material. For example, we might need to rethink the value and rescript the story of injection moulded clogs as efficient, waste minimizing, lightweight and packaging-free propositions. What might have once been seen as a product forever diminished by historic perceptions of cheapness, requires objective evaluation in the context of their potential carbon-savings, when you compare them to that of some natural traditions (Berners-Lee, 2010). By creating new clogs from old clogs we can further enhance and articulate the value of this product and even offer an alternative sandal to that stereotypically considered the tree hugger's apparel of choice! Of course, we also need to be much more careful with this versatile material commodity, and like all materials, plastics should be used wisely and literately, and not be abused mindlessly and illiterately.

Raising awareness of material abuses through the use of oceanic waste in a product provocation adds new cultural value to the consideration of plastics in our lives and in our environment but also evolves our material dialogues. Such material design can remind us that we should take care to reuse and recycle this potentially harmful, yet highly versatile and efficient material. When our recycled material is returned to us in new forms (like when our bottle of fizzy drink becomes the team colours for our favourite soccer stars), it reminds us of the collective value and responsibility we have in managing our materials.

Greater (sustainable) material literacy – and more literate (sustainable) materials – is where the designer, as the author, can command material language and invite greater participation through championing more expressive, dynamic, meaningful material experiences (products). There is enormous scope create a diverse outputs through the creative application of waste and in changing the perception of waste (Bramston and Maycroft, 2014). However to innovate and change something, we first need to understand it. Only then can it be mastered and we can become more conversant, languid and articulate with it, which will increase the value of our propositions.

Conclusions

Being a *sustainable* product designer and maker may often require us to a material raconteur, orator or storyteller (Gant and Dean, 2013). There are of course the dangers of fake and faux and designers have sometimes 'sold out' the story of material value through inauthenticity. Fake versions of carbon fibre's unique characteristic slate grey-weave are deployed as a means to trick us into thinking that our football boots, car dashboards or even aftershave bottles could be constructed by a Formula 1 car technician or NASA engineer. We must also be attuned to this insincere approach to material language, and the manipulation of material meaning. As consumers, we switch *on* and *off* our material language translators. As designers, when it comes to deciphering material semantics, we simply have not developed the material literacy required to effectively converse or interpret what they mean. By learning through making we can evolve a tacit understanding of the intricacies of materiality as designers. Through this process, we can also learn how to construct critical cultures of material meaning, which can enrich consumer and brand experiences. A lack of material literacy in product design can serve to limit products to nothing more than mere material typecasts, or stereotypes. Design that is based on a deeper material knowledge can extend the dialogue between objects, critical issues in society and the environment, mediated by and articulated through materials. Without a better rapport with our materials, we distance ourselves from the objects we use, this lessens the potential for repair, maintenance or upgrading (Walker, 2006). We also miss the opportunity to fashion and construct new meanings and value – values that are relevant to, and demanded by, our contemporary consumer contexts. Walker suggests a typology and series of aesthetic identifiers for *unsustainable products*, which may be as important as literacy in *sustainable materials*. In either instance, our disconnection with materiality serves to limit our understanding of the reality of matter itself.

As well as being central to the physical issues of sustainability, materials have agency in the communication of these issues and can ironically mediate the messages of a more sustainable society to an unsustainable consumer culture. If deployed well, materials can provide a powerful and articulate *voice* in the societal and cultural conversation. They can facilitate and sustain engagement with issues and catalyse behavioural change through their capacity to communicate. This kind of *object-activist* approach is a definable method deployed in mainstream manufacturing as well as by a diversity of product designers and makers, who are using products as a means to carry strategic messages of sustainability and ethics to consumers mediated by materials.

References

Ashby, M and Johnson, K. (2002) *Materials and Design*, Elsevier, Oxford.

Berners-Lee, M. (2010) *How Bad are Bananas?* Profile Books, London.

Bramston, D. and Mycroft, N. (2014) Designing with Waste, in E. Karana, O. Pedgley and V. Rognoli (eds), *Materials Experience*, Elsevier, Oxford, pp123–134.

Chapman, J. (2014) Meaningful stuff, in E. Karana, O. Pedgley and V. Rognoli (eds), *Materials Experience*, Elsevier, Oxford, pp135–143.

DEFRA (2015) *Digest of Waste and Resource Statistics – 2015 Edition*, DEFRA, London, retrieved from www.gov.uk/government/uploads/system/uploads/attachment_data/file/422618/Digest_of_waste_England_-_finalv2.pdf

Ellen MacArthur Foundation (2015) *Towards a Circular Economy: Business Rationale for an Accelerated Transition*, Ellen MacArthur Foundation, Cowes, retrieved from www.ellenmacarthurfoundation.org/business/reports/ce2014

Fletcher, K. (2007) Clothes That Connect, in J. Chapman and N. Gant (ed.), *Designers Visionaries and Other Stories*, Earthscan, London, pp118–130.

Gant, N. (2005). Plastics Design: The Unlikely Pioneer of Product Relationships, in *Proceedings of the 1st International Conference on the Art of Plastics Design*, Paper No. 6, Rapra Technology, Shrewsbury.

Gant, N and Dean, T. (2012) Meaning Making, paper presented at Making Futures Conference, Plymouth.

Gant, N and Dean, T. (2013) Sole-Searching: Mediating Material Narratives for Meaningful Products, paper presented at Research Through Design Conference, Northumbria University.

Gauntlett, D. (2011) *Making Is Connecting*, Polity, Cambridge.

Hekkert, P. and Karana, E. (2014) Designing Material Experience, in E. Karana, O. Pedgley and V. Rognoli (eds), *Materials Experience*, Elsevier, Oxford, pp3–11.

Houseley, L. (2009) *The Independent Design Guide*, Thames & Hudson, London.

Ingledew, J. (2011) *A–Z of Visual Ideas*, Lawrence King, London.

Karana, E. (2010) How Do Materials Obtain Their Meanings? *Journal of the Faculty of Architecture Middle East Technical University*, vol 27, no 2, pp 271–285.

Karana, E., Barati, B., Valentina, R. and van der Laan, A. Z. (2015) Material Driven Design (MDD): A Method to Design for Material Experiences, *International Journal of Design*, vol 9, pp35–54.

Manzini, E. (1986) *The Materials of Invention*, Arcadia Edizioni, Cagliari, Italy.

Manzini, E. (1997) The Aesthetics of Recycling is Not in the Product, in N. Drabbe (ed.), *Refuse–Reuse. Making the Most of What We Have*, Exhibition Catalogue of the First European Arango International Design Exhibition, Cultural Connections, Utrecht.

Noel, H. (2009). *Consumer Behaviour*, AVA Academic, New York.

Skov Holt, S. and Holt Skov, M. (2008) *Manufactured: The Conspicuous Transformation of Everyday Objects*, Chronicle Books, San Fracisco, CA.

Sennett, R. (2008) *The Craftsman*, Penguin, London.

Steffen, D. (2009) Meaning Narration in Product Design. In *Proceedings from the International Conference on Designing Pleasurable Products and Interfaces*, 13–16 October 2009, University of Technology, Compiegne, France, retrieved from www.academia.edu/212571/Meaning_and_Narration_in_Product_Design

Thorpe, A. (2007) *The Designers Atlas of Sustainability*, Island Press, Washington, DC.

van Kesteren, I. E. H., Stappers, P. J and Bruijn, J. C. M. (2007) Materials in Products Selection: Tools for Including User-Interaction in Materials Selection, *International Journal of Design*, vol 1, pp41–55.

Walker, S. (2006) *Sustainable By Design*, Earthscan, London.

16

PRINT TO REPAIR

3D printing and product repair

Miles Park

Abstract

3D printing offers new opportunities and particular advantages for creating replacement parts. This technology is particularly suitable for producing complex forms that can be created in a range of materials on demand and at a location where they are required. A 3D printed part co-exists as a digital design that can be changed or customized as required without the need to create moulds or custom tooling. In mainstream consumer product sectors there remains few if any examples of major brands offering 3D printed parts, or print to repair services. But in specialist fields, such as medical, aerospace and the maker movement community, 3D printed replacement parts are becoming increasingly common. Additional to the many practical and economic benefits that 3D printing can bring to producing replacement parts, the technology also promises environmental benefits. As an additive technology that builds parts, layer-by-layer, material use and waste can be minimized when compared with many other manufacturing processes. Further dematerialization is possible as a consequence of producing spare parts on demand. This reduces the need to warehouse or stock certain parts. By locating 3D printers where spare parts are needed significant energy savings could be achieved, as parts do not need to be shipped over long distances. 3D printing affords the efficient and economical reproduction of parts when they are scarce or no longer available. This can extend the lifespan of products that would otherwise become obsolete.

Keywords: 3D printing, product repair, replacement parts

Introduction

3D printing is now being applied to applications well beyond its original use as a rapid prototyping tool in product development. One particular use that is starting to emerge is the 3D printing of spare or replacement parts. It offers an entirely new means to provide parts for repairing products when spare parts are scarce or unavailable.

While current examples of this activity remain isolated to specialist industry sectors and individual applications, there exists a huge potential to prolong the lifespans of many products through 3D print to repair. 3D printing can provide efficient and effective access to replacement parts. In addition to environmental benefits of prolonging product lifespans, 3D printing offers the potential to reduce environmental impacts. Parts can be printed on demand; thereby reducing the material intensity and cost invested in stockpiled parts. Parts can also be printed at locations where they are required, thereby reducing energy use associated with transport and distribution over long distances. This chapter explores the advantages, opportunities and constrains of 3D printing replacement parts for product repair.

Digital disruption

Digital disruption is rolling through a succession of industry sectors with an increasing impact upon our everyday experiences and activities. The way we consume goods and services continues to be reshaped by digital technologies. The catalyst for this disruption was first delivered by the Internet revolution. It has enabled an almost frictionless acceleration in the global trade of goods and services by rebuilding a new infrastructure around digital economies. As a consequence, the first wave of digital disruption changed the way we listen to music, watch movies, shop and access and share information. The next wave of digital disruption will be on a physical level and will change the way many products are designed, made and function. Along with the emergence of the Internet of things, autonomous vehicles, advanced materials and robotics, 3D printing is indicative of further disruptive changes that are starting to occur (Manyika et al., 2013):

'While we are still adjusting to and making sense of the first wave of digital disruption led by the digitization of information, disruption is now moving into the physical and product level' (Hagel et al., 2014, p17).

There exists much excitement, speculation and hype about the transformative possibilities that 3D printing will bring to how products are designed, manufactured, distributed and sold. Technology forecasting firm Gartner track emerging technologies, on their Gartner hype cycle (2015). They claim that mainstream consumer adoption of 3D printing is between five to ten years away, but for business and medical applications the biggest impact is currently under way: 'As with most disruptive technologies it is likely that we will overestimate potential 3D printing in the short while underestimating it in the long term' (Kietzmann et al., 2015, p214).

3D printing is an additive manufacturing technology where parts are built incrementally, layer by layer. It enables a new way of conceptualizing manufacturing as parts are grown, unlike the 'heat, beat and treat' of subtractive manufacturing processes from the past (Benyus, 1997). A part co-exists as a digital file that can be easily updated and shared. This file instructs a 3D printer to build a physical object of almost unlimited complexity without the need for custom tooling or moulds, machining or the assembly of multiple components.

Conspicuous production

3D printing fits within an evolving ecosystem of increasingly affordable enabling digital technologies and accessible online platforms. These include 3D printers, 3D scanners, laser cutters, CNC routers and a host of programmable devices (such as Arduino, Raspberry Pi and other microcontrollers). They are enabling individual makers and entrepreneurs to remix, customize and create new products and services. Aided by online trading platforms (such as Etsy, eBay) and specialist 3D printing services (such as GrabCAD, 3D Hubs, Thingiverse, Shapeways and Sculpteo), individuals can now connect to a vast distributed network to share and market 3D print files and products. With lower cost barriers and increasing accessibility, makers are now afforded incredible powers of production and distribution to create and share in a globalized economy (Anderson, 2012). This represents a new form of democratized production by enabling a sidestepping of traditional barriers to manufacturing and distribution (Manyika et al., 2013). As Sammartino (2014, p7), put it, 'The power base of industrial companies is breaking up with. It's flipping from the few to the many.' As the next wave of change unfolds, novel ways are possible for the design, production and distribution of 3D printed replacement parts. It will create equal opportunities for large manufacturing brands and individual makers. This trend will be beneficial for products that were destined to become obsolete due to the scarcity of replacement parts. In this context, 3D printing is a highly disruptive technology (Kietzmann et al., 2015).

Product obsolescence

Products become obsolete due to multiple reasons that can be generalized as being either 'absolute' or 'relative' (Cooper, 2010). Absolute obsolescence is determined when the durability of a product is expended and is no longer able to function as originally intended. This may be due to misadventure, poor design or low quality of materials and manufacture. It may be due to the failure of one critical component that is irreplaceable. On the other hand, relative obsolescence occurs due to a range of indirect psychological, economic or technological reasons. Relative obsolescence is when a replacement decision is discretionary (ibid.). This form of obsolescence can be simply due to changing fashion or changing perceived needs. Equally, it may occur due to diminished performance or appearance when compared with newer, more technologically advanced products. Relative obsolescence also has an economic dimension. If it is determined that the running and maintenance cost for a product are excessive it makes good economic sense to replace it. Likewise, it may be unviable to attempt a product repair due to issues such as cost, or scarcity of spare parts.

Product repair

An affordance for repair and the availability of spare parts are contributing features for a product's resilience against obsolescence. Increasingly, many consumer products are becoming difficult to repair. There are many reasons for this, including difficulty in disassembly and non-serviceable internal components. Moreover, many consumer products are difficult to repair simply due to the non-availability or cost of spare parts (Stahel, 2010; Twigg-Flesner, 2010). This is not an uncommon situation. There is an absence of any legal requirement for manufacturers or supplies to make parts or repair facilities available (Twigg-Flesner, 2010). Televisions are a notable example to illustrate this common scenario. They have, since the 1970s, become gradually more reliable and energy efficient. As a consequence, the number of TV repair businesses has declined. In more recent times, televisions have become digital flat screen devices that are subject to frequent model updates driven by the marketing of technological novelty. Often when a television does require a repair it is likely to be replaced (if covered by warranty) or deemed un-repairable due to the non-availability of parts.

For individuals who wish to take a DIY approach to repair, there exist an increasing number of online resources. There are countless videos and demonstrations produced by individuals and businesses on how to fix and repair an extraordinary diversity of products. iFixit (2015) are a prime example of an online business that promotes a DIY approach to product repair – fixing anything from a can opener to an iPad. Additional to their videos and step-by-step teardown guides for fixing a wide range of consumer products, they provide a parts and tool store. Around the world community based and social enterprises are also playing an increasing role in promoting product repair. The Restart Project (2015) is a UK based social enterprise, and Repair Café (2015), a Dutch non-profit organization, encourages repair by holding regular workshops to empower people to repair electronic products in order to reduce e-waste.

Rise of the replicators

3D printing has over the last 20 years progressively become firmly integrated into many product design, development and prototyping settings. However, in more recent times it has been applied to purposes beyond the product design and development stage to the extent that it is starting to displace some manufacturing activity. In other words, it is not limited to producing product models and prototypes, but producing viable end use products. The technology is also being applied to fields as diverse as surgical implants, food production and jewellery, as well as finding a role within schools, homes and remote locations such as at sea and in space.

As an additive manufacturing process, 3D forms are printed by adding and solidifying small layers of material at a time. Printers build physical artefacts from a variety of materials using a digital file in STL format. A STL file renders the surfaces in a computer-aided design (CAD) file as a mesh of triangles. 3D printer slicing software converts this into machine code to print a physical part. Recent improvements in the technology now mean that high performance parts can be produced in a range of plastic, metal and ceramic materials. While personal desktop machines are limited in this capacity, the range and performance of materials continues to improve (Torabi et al., 2014). Fused deposition modelling (FDM) is the most common technology used by such printers. A plastic filament, often acrylonitrile butadiene styrene (ABS) or polylactic acid (PLA), is extruded like spaghetti through a heated nozzle that follows a precise tool path to create an object in layered increments.

Self-replicating machines

Originating in 2005, the open source Reprap 3D printer project marked the origins of low-cost 3D printing. The project was supported by a community of maker enthusiasts who were encouraged to share both knowledge, and print files. The machine was conceived to print (self-replicate) many of its own components (Reprap, 2014). In 2008 the RepRap 1.0 'Darwin' successfully reprinted over half its 3D printed parts. Reprinting a replacement part could readily renew a worn or broken component. A key benefit of this process is that parts can be upgraded as a means to improve the performance of the printer, thus contributing to the evolution of the Reprap project. This intrinsic ability to reproduce and self-replicate remains a central feature of 3D printing. By using the properties of the digital data (i.e., a stream of ones and zeros that can be replicated) that are programmed to control a mechanism for constructing new parts, 3D printing is analogous to biological reproduction.

The role of makers

Central to the ongoing development of personal low cost 3D printers has been the contribution of many individual enthusiasts and small start-up enterprises. Collectively they represent the *maker movement*. The maker movement consists of a distributed community

Figure 16.1 The Ultimaker Original is offered as a DIY kit that can be upgraded

of craftspeople, tinkerers, hackers, hobbyists, designers, inventors and start-up enterprises (Hagel et al., 2014). The ethos of the maker movement is to hack, repair and repurpose products. This is summed-up by a light-hearted manifesto titled *The Maker's Bill of Rights: To Accessible, Extensive, and Repairable Hardware*, which states:

'If you can't open it, you don't own it' (Jalopy, 2005, p154).

Along with the original RepRap, many machines utilize open source software or hardware. This approach enables developers and users to mix and match various components to build, modify and upgrade their machines. A good example of this approach is the Dutch Ultimaker original 3D printer. It uses an open-source Arduino logic board and is available fully assembled or as a self-assembly kit. Since its launch in 2011, numerous upgrades have been developed by the Ultimaker team, many individual users also design and share upgraded 3D printed parts.

Digital ecosystems

Alongside the rapid development of 3D printing is a growing digital ecosystem of individual users, technology developers, small and large businesses. A key feature of this is the growing online marketplace for products and services that enable individuals and businesses to share and sell 3D printed products and resources. Shapeways, based in New York, Sculpteo, based in France, and Materialise, based in Belgium are all examples that offer makers a chance to share and sell their 3D print designs. There are numerous other vibrant online communities that offer support and tips, products and services. A notable example of a specialist online community is 3D Hubs. It enables individual owners of a 3D printer to register their location and the capabilities of their machine to offer a local pay for print service.

3D printing replacement parts

3D printing offers new opportunities and advantages for creating replacement parts. Since parts are built in incremental layers from information derived from a digital file, no expensive moulds or custom tooling is required. This makes the technology particularly suitable for small or batch production runs. Customized and low volume designs can be produced on demand. Replacement parts can be printed when they are required and reduce the need to physically stock spare parts for some future anticipated demand, which may or may not transpire. The production cost per individual part can often be lower as no tooling expenditure needs to be amortized across the production run. Coincidently, when tooling is required for short run or pre-production injection moulded plastic parts, 3D printing can be used to produce a low cost 'bridge' tool. A bridge tool is a printed soft tooling process that enables moulded parts to be made available before a full production hard steel tool is cut.

3D printing can create parts of great complexity. Internal voids and lattice structures, undercuts and complex internal geometry are possible. Such forms would not be possible within a single injection moulded, cast or machined part (Crane et al., 2014). This benefit results in further cost savings as multiple components and the assembly of subcomponents can be simplified into one part:

'Paradoxically, the ability to produce individual components with more complex geometries allows designers to produce entire sub-assemblies using fewer subcomponents, reducing complexity at the system level' (ibid., p5).

3D printed parts coexist as digital design files that can be changed or customized at any stage of a production cycle. Each design exists in a software environment as a constant 'beta' – offering continuous opportunities to evolve and change the design of a given part. This gives rise to the opportunity to improve the design of a replacement part and to address reasons for its initial failure. Replacement parts can be further customized for individual customer requirements, or model variants.

Table 16.1 General advantages for 3D printing replacement parts

Advantages	Description
Tooling	No custom tooling is required for moulds, jigs or formers to create parts of varying complexity. This can contribute to lower part costs. When tooling may be required for low-volume injection-moulded parts 3D printing can also be used to create bridge tooling.
Part complexity	3D printing is ideal for complex forms. This offers an advantage compared to other manufacturing processes where complex parts must often be fabricated out of multiple subcomponents.
Design freedom	Designing parts for 3D printing is much simpler compared to injection moulding or die-casting processes. The designer does not need to consider the design constraints of these processes.
Parts revision and customization	A part design exists as a digital file. As software, it can be modified, improved and changed as required with few cost penalties. As there is no tooling and minimal set-up costs, only the digital design file requires revision to create a new part.

Examples of print to repair

Examples of 3D printing replacement parts are mostly found at either end of an organizational hierarchy. In specialist industry sectors, notably aerospace, defence and medicine the application of 3D printing for replacement parts is expanding and finding new applications as the technology develops. At the other end, it is the many individuals and independent entrepreneurs who are designing, creating and sharing 3D designs and 3D printed parts for product repair. This polarization is reflective of the 3-D printing technologies on offer. On one side, high-cost sophisticated machines are capable are producing parts in a range of high-performance materials to fine tolerances, while the other side is represented by the increasing availability of low-cost desktop machines.

Specialist applications

In specialist applications, such as aircraft replacement parts and surgical implants, 3D printed replacement parts are establishing a role and proving to be advantageous over traditional methods. With a replacement parts inventory of about 3.5 million items, Airbus (2014) and other aircraft firms have embarked upon a program of printing replacement parts (Economist, 2013). The advantages are apparent when you consider the amount of spare parts that need to be stored, identified and dispatched for any given aircraft type over its operational lifespan. For an Airbus A300 and A310 series aircraft this means provisioning spare parts until 2050. This locks up a huge amount of resources, storage space and capital (Airbus, 2014).

For medical applications the advantages of 3D printing replacement parts differ. 3D printing can offer individual customized surgical implants and prosthetics for each patient without the need to create moulds and special set-ups. Parts can be produced quicker and at a much lower cost than traditional methods. Furthermore, 3D printers can be located where parts are required and not where production takes place. This advantage becomes clear when parts are required in remote locations and when normal distribution channels are unavailable. An extreme example is the use of a 3D printer on the International Space Station (NASA, 2014). For similar reasons, various Navy vessels house 3D printing facilities on-board.

Individual maker applications

At the other end of a production hierarchy there are the many individuals and independent entrepreneurs. They are harnessing the enabling technologies of CAD, 3D printers and online resources to create and share an increasing portfolio of replacement parts. These parts range from specialist interest needs to more general household items. The sharing and availability of designs for 3D printer parts are available on websites such as Thingiverse, which is owned by MakerBot – a popular brand of 3D printer. It hosts 3D print files contributed by many individuals and are available for download. Among the numerous 3D print designs on offer are various replacement parts. Another online service, Shapeways, offers the additional service of providing actual 3D printed parts for purchase in a range of materials and colour choices. Individuals contribute their 3D print designs to be hosted on the site and receive a percentage for each sale.

A simple replacement latch, which holds down the lid of a Panasonic bread maker offers a good example of how this service works. The redesigned latch is available for sale through Shapeways and is claimed to be superior to the original part due to its construction from a stronger material (stainless steel). The designer created the part, as the original part is

Figure 16.2   Redesigned bread maker latch printed in laser-sintered stainless steel

Source: photograph by Susan Parker

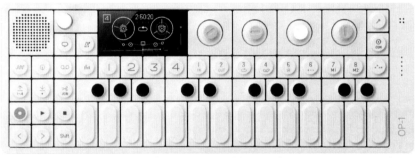

Figure 16.3 3D print files for replacement and customisable knob for the OP-1 music synthesizer

Source: Teenage Engineering (files can be downloaded from the company's website: www.
teenageengineering.com/press/op-1)

unavailable from Panasonic. The designer, a trained engineer and competent CAD user
describes this process:

> Whilst I measured the old part for general size and features, my own implementation
> is a from-scratch design. It is also not desirable to make a direct copy since stainless-
> steel printing tolerances and feature parameters have to be taken into account. The
> overall shape is similar, as it has to perform the same job and fit as a replacement.
>
> *S. Parker, personal communication, 19 January 2015*

Consumer product sector applications

In the consumer product sector there are surprisingly few examples of manufacturing brands
offering 3D print to repair services – either by direct supply of 3D printed replacement parts,
or, by providing downloadable 3D print digital files through a 3D printing bureau. One firm

that has taken the lead is a small Swedish firm called Teenage Engineering who make a music synthesizer – the OP-1. They offer their customers the ability to download 3D print files or purchase 3D printed replacement knobs and accessories through their online 3D print service, Shapeways (2012).

Environmental benefits

Additional to the many practical and economic benefits that 3D printing can bring to replacement parts, the technology also promises environmental benefits. As an additive technology, material use and waste can be minimized when compared with many other manufacturing processes. A further environmental benefit is possible as a consequence of producing spare parts on demand. This reduces the need to warehouse or stock certain parts. By locating 3D printers where spare parts are needed, significant energy savings can be achieved, as parts do not need to be shipped over long distances. 3D printing affords the efficient and economical reproduction of parts when they are scarce or no longer available. This can extend the lifespan of products that would otherwise become obsolete, and consequently discarded.

Dematerialization

3D printing is an additive manufacturing process. It minimizes material use when compared to subtractive manufacturing processes such as machining and punching that produce swarf and offcuts. However, it is not entirely free of waste. When a 3D printer commences printing material is laid down to create a bed on to which the part is build. Furthermore, printed parts often require support structures during the print build process. Upon completion both the bed and the support structure material are removed from the part then discarded. Machines also need periodic maintenance – including flushing, priming or purging – that contributes additionally to waste. Despite these minimal inefficiencies, far greater potential for dematerialization is that 3D printed spare parts can be printed on demand when they are required. This just-in-time approach reduces the need to hold an inventory of stockpiled parts, often at multiple locations, in anticipation of eventual use.

Energy saving

A flow on benefit from a dematerialization of stockpiled parts is that information can be shipped and not physical parts. As 3D printed part coexist as digital information. This can be sent electronically to a printer located close to where parts are required. In addition to the speed at which digital information can travel, sending data and not physical parts (bytes and not bits) has a clear advantage in terms of transport energy savings and reducing demand on transport infrastructure.

Prolonging product lifespans

3D printing replacement parts offer an opportunity to extend the lifespans of many manufactured products. Already we are seeing examples of this in the specialist industry sectors where 3D printer parts can extend the service life of aircraft, cars and other niche product sectors. 3D print replacement parts offer an ideal solution when spare parts become scarce or no longer available. Overtime, a product can become orphaned when a supplier or

Table 16.2 Environmental advantages for 3D printing replacement parts

Advantages	Description
Dematerialization	3D printing is an additive manufacturing process that minimizes material use when compared to subtractive manufacturing processes. A greater potential for dematerialization is that 3D printed spare parts can be printed on demand when they are required reducing the need to hold on inventory of stockpiled parts.
Energy saving	As 3D printed part coexist as digital information, this can be sent to a printer located close to where parts are required reducing transport and energy use.
Prolonging product lifespans	3D printing replacement parts offer an opportunity to extend the lifespans of many manufactured products. 3D print replacement parts offer an ideal solution when spare parts are scarce or no longer available.
Redistributing production	Low-cost 3D printing creates new opportunities for individual makers by placing the tools of production and distribution in the hands of the consumer.

the parent company no longer exists. For example, American entertainer Jay Leno has built a reputation for 3D printing spare parts for his extensive vintage car collection (Koten, 2013). Meanwhile obsolescence continues to be significant every day challenge in the consumer products sectors. What is notable at this early stage of 3D printing replacement parts is that it is the initiative of many individuals who are providing designs for 3D printed replacement parts, and not of large manufacturers or spare part suppliers. While individuals take the lead in providing parts for various consumer electronic and household items, the major manufacturing brands remain notably absent from this activity.

Small is beautiful: Redistributing production

3D printing and associated digital technologies enable a redistribution of where things are made and who designs and makes them. Low cost 3D printing creates new opportunities for individual makers to become producers in a distributed but highly connected digital landscape. In this scenario, localized micro-factories represent a new form of democratized production. They challenge the incumbent and, often, unsustainable model of highly centralized manufacturing that is reliant upon extensive and far-reaching supply chains and distribution channels.

Constraints

Despite the numerous benefits discussed above, there are a number of obstacles that are constraining the wider adoption of 3D printing and 3D printed replacement parts. These constraints concern existing design and business practices, limitations of current technology and legal issues around ownership and liability.

Business as usual

In many consumer product sectors product lines are refreshed frequently. In highly competitive markets that are focused upon sales volume and turnover – such as consumer electronics and kitchen appliances – product lines are updated annually. Updates may consist of no more than a facelift to the external appearance of a product, or it may be more substantial, providing as an incremental rise in performance. This frequency of change creates a challenge to repair many of these products. The cost of stocking and supplying spare parts for frequently revised product lines can be prohibitive. As a consequence, spare parts are often unavailable, especially for superseded models. Service centres, when they do exist, are often outsourced, creating a further logistical distance from the production of spare parts. For products covered by warranty, a frequent remedy is to replace the product, as spare parts are unavailable. There is often little economic or business incentive to provide replacement parts, and no legal requirement for a manufacturer or retailers to make parts available (Twigg-Flesner, 2010).

Technical constraints

Notwithstanding the rapid and recent development of 3D printing, there remain disadvantages with the current technology for 3D printing spare parts. This is especially true for low-cost desktop printers. They are still in an adolescent stage of development (France, 2014); few have the performance and reliability that we often expect from other equipment. Printers are often temperamental and require constant surveillance when printing. Personal desktop machines can create dimensionally acceptable and robust components, but parts will often fail to print as planned, requiring modifications to the design or the machine settings.

High-end professional 3D printers have fewer limitations, but to become more competitive with existing manufacturing technologies they need to become much more cost competitive. They also need to offer a broader range of printable materials with better performance characteristics (Crane et al., 2014). In addition, the speed of producing a 3D printed part is poor when compared to many other manufacturing techniques, such as injection moulding plastics.

While specialist technical knowledge is required for designing 3D printed parts, it is less than what is required for some other manufacturing technologies. Product designers need to become familiar with the both capabilities and limitations of the process. Creating a new part from scratch, or reverse engineering an existing part, requires CAD knowledge and product design skills. While 3D scanning promises to simplify this process, the technology is still in its infancy. Raw scans inevitably require cleaning-up and adjusting in 3D Design software before printing is possible. Unlike the ubiquitous 2D inkjet or laser paper printer, 3D printers are inherently more complicated to operate than simply executing a simple keyboard command 'ctrl + p'.

Intellectual property rights

A distinctive feature of 3D printing is the ease at which designs can be copied and shared. This raises a concern about intellectual property rights (IPR). In simple terms, the concern is about the uncertainty about who owns what, to print, share or sell? But how a 3D printed part is protected remains unclear since digital property rights remain a poorly defined field (ACIP, 2014).

A 3D printed part exists as two separate elements: a physical part (the object) and the digital file. Copyright exists automatically with a digital file (by virtue of authorship), but it is uncertain how it applies to a 3D printed functional part (Weinberg, 2015). However, a part may be protected as a registered design and in certain circumstances, if the part is independent from other components and has new functional advantage, a patent may be sought to protect it.

Clarity regarding IPR protection is missing in this rapidly evolving technology sectors. Disruptive technologies, such as 3D printing, highlight these inadequacies. In Australia, the Advisory Council on Intellectual Property (ACIP) is currently reviewing registered design law. In the course of their review they found:

> In particular, technology is transforming the nature of design and making 'virtual' or software designs more important, but design protection is tied to whole, physical products. Further, 3D printing and scanning technologies enable online circulation of designs but such activities are not captured by design law and, in at least some cases, copyright may be of no assistance.
>
> *(ACIP, 2014, p2)*

The law and how it applies on these matters varies from country to country. This adds further complexity to how IPR may be applied in the common situation of a file being hosted on a web server in one country but used for printing in another. Web-based file sharing platforms and 3D printing bureaus have similar concerns. The US-based 3D printing service, Shapeways, request that creators of 3D designs do not infringe other people's IP rights. They focus upon copyright and have a take-down procedure for designs that may infringe IP (Shapeways, 2015). File sharing platform, Thingiverse, is described as a thriving design community for discovering, making, and sharing 3D printable things (Thingiverse, 2015) and encourages the use of Creative Commons licensing arrangements.

As 3D printed replacement parts move into mainstream consumer markets many of these current obstacles are likely to be resolved. The advantages for both producers and the consumers will eventually outweigh the current uncertainties of disruptive change presented by 3D printing.

Product liability

Under consumer law products and parts must be safe and meet customer guarantees. In this regard 3D printed replacement parts may be difficult to regulate for manufacturing brands, especially if parts are printed without any quality control. For example, a downloaded replacement part design file printed by an individual on a low cost desktop printer would produce in a variety of results. Replacement parts that require a critical fit with other components, or perform a critical function need to be of a consistent quality. In such cases, in order to maintain quality, 3D printed parts supply may best be restricted and supplied by a manufacturing brand or authorized 3D print bureau.

Taking print to repair to market

How might this work in practice? Most manufacturing brands now provide user guides and product manuals as a downloadable PDF documents. Some go further by providing downloadable service and technical repair information. By doing so, they can significantly reduce costs by eliminating the need to print and distribute documentation, while providing consumers the convenience of locating and accessing up-to-date information. Likewise, 3D printed replacement parts could be provided as downloadable files. In addition to the numerous advantages discussed above, it would offer manufacturing brands a means to generate insight, better understand their customers and learn how their products are performing in use, by collecting data on part enquiries and file downloads.

3D printed replacement parts could be distributed to customers in a number of additional ways. For a manufacturer or brand wishing to maintain tight control of the availability of 3D printed parts, it could offer a print on demand service managed through its existing spare parts distribution channels.

Another method that offers a potentially greater advantage for producers and consumers is to partner with a 3D printing bureau service. By doing so, a manufacturer can outsource what is often considered a costly and peripheral activity. Instead, the stocking and supplying of replacement parts could be managed by a service that specializes in 3D printing and shipping parts. We're likely to see more examples of this type of activity in the future as major manufacturing brands and retailers start to explore partnerships with 3D print bureaus (Harris, 2014). Alternatively, a manufacturer may adopt an open source approach by making available freely downloadable STL print files for anyone with access to a 3D printer to reproduce replacement parts.

Conclusion

While 3D printing may herald a profusion of new and unnecessary products, it could equally transform how products are designed, manufactured, distributed and sold. 3D printing replacement parts demonstrates an evolutionary step towards this transformation. It offers the opportunity to extend product lifespans by providing re-printable replacement parts when existing part inventories are exhausted, or no longer exist. The technology enables the repositioning of production both in terms of location (printing parts in places where they are required), and structure (by placing the tools of production and distribution in the hands of the consumer).

3D printing will continue to rapidly improve and will become increasingly prolific in mainstream consumer markets. The technology will become more affordable for individual ownership and will be easier to use. Technical and regulatory obstacles will eventually be resolved that will contribute to the acceptance by manufacturing brands to provide 3D print information and parts, and consumer confidence to obtain 3D printed replacement parts. Manufacturing brands could partner with online 3D print services, and as a result, new business opportunities will emerge capitalizing on this transformative technology. When a product fails and replacement parts are unavailable or scarce, 3D printing can offer a means for quick and efficient repair to prolong its lifespan.

References

ACIP (2014) *Review of the Design System.* Options Paper. Advisory Council on Intellectual Property, December. Retrieved from www.acip.gov.au/pdfs/Options-Paper-for-the-Review-of-the-designs-System.pdf (accessed 5 February 2015).

Airbus (2014) How 3D Printing Is Delivering Airplane Parts On Demand. Retrieved from www.forbes.com/sites/airbus/2014/07/15/how-adding-a-new-dimension-to-airplanes-is-delivering-parts-on-demand (accessed 21 July 2015).

Anderson, C. (2012) *Makers: The New Industrial Revolution.* Crown Business, Danvers, MA.

Benyus, J. (1997). *Biomimicry.* Quill, William Morrow, New York.

Cooper, T. (2010) The Significance of Product Longevity. In T. Cooper (ed.), *Longer Lasting Products: Alternatives to the Throwaway Society.* Gower, Farnham, pp3–36.

Crane, J., Crestani, R. and Cotteleer, M. (2014) *3D Opportunity for End-Use Products Additive: Manufacturing Builds a Better Future.* Deloitte University Press, New York.

Economist (2013) 3D Printing Scales Up. Retrieved from www.economist.com/news/technology-quarterly/21584447-digital-manufacturing-there-lot-hype-around-3d-printing-it-fast (accessed 7 September 2013).

France, A. (2014) 3D Evolution. Make: Annual. *Guide to 3D Printing*, vol 42, November.

Gartner (2014) Gartner Says Consumer 3D Printing Is More Than Five Years Away, 30–34. Retrieved from www.gartner.com/newsroom/id/2825417 (accessed 22 July 2015).

Hagel, J., Seely Brown, J. and Kulasooriya, D. (2014) *A Movement in the Making*. Deloitte University Press, New York.

Harris, E. (2014) Hasbro to Collaborate With 3D Printing Company to Sell Artwork. Retrieved from www.nytimes.com/2014/07/21/business/hasbro-selling-my-little-pony-fan-art.html (accessed 21 July 2015).

iFixit (2015) About iFixit. Retrieved from www.ifixit.com/Info (accessed 21 July 2015).

Jalopy, M. (2005) *A Maker's Bill of Rights to Accessible, Extensible, and Repairable Hardware*. Make: Technology in your time, vol 4, November. O'Reilly Media, Sebastopol.

Kietzmann, J., Pitt, L. and Berthon P. (2015) Disruptions, Decisions, and Destinations: Enter the Age of 3D Printing and Additive Manufacturing. *Business Horizons*, vol 58, no 2, 209–215.

Koten, J. (2013) Who Says Jay Leno Isn't Cutting Edge? *The Wall Street Journal*, 10 June. Retrieved from www.wsj.com/articles/SB10001424127887324866904578517090180869864 (accessed 10 June 2013).

Manyika, J., Chui, J., Bughin, M., Dobbs, R., Bisson, P. and Marrs, A. (2013) *Disruptive Technologies: Advances That Will Transform Life, Business, and the Global Economy*. McKinsey Global Institute, New York.

NASA (2014) Open for Business: 3D Printer Creates First Object in Space on International Space Station. Retrieved from www.nasa.gov/content/open-for-business-3D-printer-creates-first-object-in-space-on-international-space-station/index.htm (accessed 8 February 2015).

Repair Café (2015) About the Repair Café. Retrieved from http://repaircafe.org/about-repair-cafe (accessed 21 July 2015).

Reprap (2014) Welcome to Reprap. Retrieved from http://reprap.org/wiki/RepRap (accessed 12 December 2014).

Restart (2015) About Restart. Retrieved from http://therestartproject.org/about (accessed 21 July 2015).

Sammartino, S. (2014) *The Great Fragmentation: And Why the Future of Business is Small*. Wiley, Milton.

Shapeways (2012) Teenage Engineering Make CAD Files Available to 3D Print Replacement Parts. Retrieved from www.shapeways.com/blog/archives/1647-teenage-engineering-make-cad-files-available-to-3d-print-replacement-parts.html (accessed 21 July 2015).

Shapeways (2015) Shapeways Content Policy and Notice Takedown Procedure. Retrieved from www.shapeways.com/legal/content_policy (accessed 9 February 2015).

Stahel, W. (2010) Durability, Function and Performance. In T. Cooper (ed.), *Longer Lasting Products: Alternatives to the Throwaway Society*. Gower, Farnham, pp157–178.

Thingiverse (2015) About MakerBot Thingiverse. Retrieved from www.thingiverse.com/about (accessed 10 February 2015).

Torabi, P., Petros, M. and Khoshnevis, B. (2014) Selective Inhibition Sintering: The Process for Consumer Metal Additive Manufacturing. *3D Printing and Additive Manufacturing*, vol 1, no 3, 152–155.

Twigg-Flesner, C. (2010) The Law on Guarantees and Repair Work. In T. Cooper (ed.), *Longer Lasting Products: Alternatives to the Throwaway Society*. Gower, Farnham, pp195–214.

Weinberg, M. (2015) Wrongs and Rights: Make. *Annual Guide to 3D Printing*, vol 42, 14.

17

UNMAKING WASTE

Robert Crocker

Abstract

Modern consumerism is based upon the individual's ongoing quest for an idealised good life, a better life promised through the enjoyment of the 'best' and 'latest' in consumer goods. This mental perfectionism requires the frequent upgrading of objects and environments and the abandonment of what seems old, imperfect or well used. Waste is thus continuously produced, and in ever larger volumes, to make way for the new. Waste-making on a global scale is supported by standard economics, government policy and business practice, which routinely externalise the environmental costs of this wasting of resources. Since the production of consumer goods now involves such limited responsibility for the waste that is generated, and the waste of over half the world's population is not formally managed or disposed of, much of this waste becomes pollution. This chapter argues that while governments and businesses need to play their part in creating a 'circular economy' where resources are more highly valued and waste is minimised, to 'unmake waste' on this scale requires designers to both understand how and why unnecessary waste is created in the first place. The purpose of 'unmaking waste' is thus to create products that are more durable, can be used for longer periods and can be remade, or turned into other products at the end of their lives. This reconfiguration of design and manufacturing will give material form to the circular economy, one where there is limited waste, and where every product can be safely reused or remade into another, and where all waste is understood as a 'misallocated' resource.

Keywords: consumerism, waste, waste-making, obsolescence, sustainable design

Introduction

Modern consumerism is a waste-making culture, in which objects, spaces and buildings are prematurely 'aged' and devalued, and then turned into waste, in order to make room for the new. Driven by the urgency of the bottom line, and in most nations unencumbered by legislation that might require a more careful use of resources, designers must continuously style novel products and gadgets to gain market share for their clients or employers, often without much thought as to where these might end up. Consumers of these products, according to standard economics, must buy more, more quickly, and use what they buy for ever-shorter periods of time. As a result, they increasingly dispose of what they own or use sooner, often before the object concerned is broken or unusable. From an economic perspective, this can be seen as the creation of rising productivity and efficiencies created by technological change: as the price of goods fall in response, there is a corresponding take up of more goods by more people, and a consequent pressure on their 'free' time, that is time that is not allocated to activities that involve using these goods (Bianchi, 2008).

The result of this is a 'hyper-consumption', or accelerated consumerism; an expanded and extended form of post-war mass-consumption, which is now enabled in particular by the greater efficiency and speed of networked systems of information, communication and transportation (Lipovetsky, 2011). We can now find something and buy it in the store or online within a few seconds, whether this is an investment, a piece of software, an mobile phone, a new sofa or an apartment (Tomlinson, 2007; Rosa, 2003). It might take a few days for anything we buy online to reach us, but time and place no longer have the same limiting roles they once did: instant transactions, affordable, short-lived products, and a large array of choices in every domain, all add their weight to this hyper-consumption, shifting cultural norms towards a greater materialism and an equally obsessive quest for saving more time (Ryan, 2014; Schor, 2005; Rosa, 2003).

Partly through technological change, time and place have decreased in importance as barriers to consumption since the 1980s, and also as barriers to production. For example, products like smartphones contain complex parts from all over the world, assembled in separate facilities and then put together in a factory ready for shipping (Xing, 2014; Princen, 2002b). Most large companies like Apple or Samsung can no longer easily tell where the different materials in their products come from (Kreuger, 2008; Rotter et al., 2014). Supply chains have become longer and more complex, and this is true in most domains, from cars to shoes and textiles, with many large companies remaining ignorant about, or indifferent to, where their products are made, by whom, and at what social or environmental cost (Nimbalker et al., 2015).

The prices of many everyday items have fallen relative to incomes, and this has further stimulated demand, leading to an intensification of mass-consumption in the West, a pattern now evident in most developing nations too (Schor, 2005). New large middle classes in Asia have become the most rapidly expanding market for many branded goods, with the demand for cars, phones and many luxuries visible everywhere in China, India and southeast Asia (Jaffrelot and van der Veer, 2008; Zhang, 2010). Consumer debt enabled by the credit card, another innovation dependent on computerisation, has also extended the capacity of each consumer to spend, further adding to global demand (Bernthal et al., 2005; Pettit and Sivanatham, 2011).

The cultural aspects of this hyper-consumption are often bundled together in the term, 'consumerism', which is often defined as the individual's pursuit of the good life through various accelerated material or virtual means. A 'way of life and state of mind' closely entangled with the individual's sense of identity and social worth, consumerism, for those who can afford it, involves a pursuit of the 'best' and 'latest' from an expanding array of possible market choices (Smart, 2010, pp8–10; Crocker, 2013a). This primarily takes hold through comparison, with what others have, or what might be 'out there' in the media, and how this might enhance the individual's life in some way. Comparison and social competition also play an important role in increasing the intensity and spread of consumerism (Dwyer, 2009a; Nelissen et al., 2011).

Hyper-consumption is often driven by the individual's quest for the more useful, which is sold to the consumer as a 'solution' to a 'problem', a problem that in many cases perhaps was not noticed until such a promise was first made (Strasser, 1998; Slater, 2007). For example, in various experiments with making coffee making, I have tried perhaps 10 machines over the last twenty years (see Morris, 2010). Like many consumers I make the mistake of thinking that I can make a 'café-style' coffee at home on the cheap, and find a 'remedy' for my desire to do so. Instead, over time I accumulate interesting stovetop models, usually 'justified' to myself, at least, by my knowledge of design, and also a handful of cheaper electric machines, most of which do not live up to their claims (Gregson et al., 2007). I still frequent my local coffee shops, and certainly making the occasional coffee at home has not reduced my many visits to cafés near where I work (Morris, 2010; Manzini, 2002).

In contrast to the attitudes of our grandparents' generation, where coffee was often made by grinding fresh beans by hand and then pouring boiling water on them in a jug or coffeepot, we now search for 'the perfect cup', and expect a higher standard in what we buy. Large sums are now spent on fully automated or instant capsule machines, many of them short-lived, and creating new sources of hard-to-recycle waste (Brommer et al., 2011). My own experience is fairly typical: after months of fitful use, the least useful of my coffee machines is slowly pushed down a mental ladder of less useful objects into the deeper recesses of our kitchen cupboards. The more practical ones stay at the front, while the others, after remaining as clutter for some years, are given away to charity or friends (Gregson et al., 2007; Makovicky, 2007).

Apart from the burdens of choice, of being offered so many goods in each domain (Schwartz, 2010) one of the central problems of hyper-consumption, of buying 'more' just because we now can, is managing the 'old', the less valued that accumulates everywhere (Gregson et al., 2007). In the home as at work, cheaper, more abundant supplies of goods in every domain demand attention, and once bought, push out the not so useful, the 'old' or redundant (Scheibehenne, Greifeneder and Todd, 2010). The kitchen is an especially 'restless' zone for this movement of things between the categories of 'new' and 'old'. Like making coffee, preparing food is an art that can always be improved or accelerated, and so many buy what they don't use, or at least what they don't use for long. The old must make way for the new, even if it is still functioning. The kitchen itself is also subject to the same pattern, with dissatisfaction with function, space and style often driving more frequent renovations (Parrott et al., 2008; Shove and Hand, 2005). This is made more likely by increasing mobility, with many now changing homes more frequently, pushed to do so by work or family reasons, or, again, just because we now can (Jensen, 2009; Bianchi, 2008).

At work, at home and in the public sphere, it is now assumed that the new must bump out the old, and more frequently. More and more goods, and more choices, have led to a corresponding emphasis on higher standards in what is possessed, which has changed the home itself, dramatically expanding its size and its typical contents, and creating a series of reality TV shows on home 'make-overs' and renovation (Allon, 2008). Old homes are knocked down and replaced by new ones, with the average size of Australian homes now approximately double what they were in the 1950s (Clune et al., 2012). To perform something 'better', and possess the 'best', seems not only to require more 'stuff', and correspondingly more time and effort, but more space, more bedrooms, more bathrooms and more storage (Hamilton, 2002; Parrott et al., 2008). The inseparable partner of this increase in demand is a parallel increase in waste; for the new continuously grows in variety and volume and, meanwhile, the old must be dislodged and replaced. In this way consumerism becomes a kind of mental perfectionism and materialism, which shapes how objects and space are valued, and at every scale (Campbell, 2004; Kasser, 2002).

What is already 'there' can soon seem not quite good enough in comparison to the better or 'best' seen elsewhere. And this soon bumps out the 'not quite good enough' and makes it seem ready for replacement, even if it is still functioning. The idea of possessing the latest and at least the 'better' also becomes entangled in the individual's sense of self (Campbell, 2004). While possessing quality second-hand goods is quite acceptable, since their value has been revived in their rediscovery and repossession, the drivers for discard and renovation are still embedded in consumerism and its haunting perfectionism – from working fridges replaced in the new kitchen because they are the wrong colour, to old but perhaps beautiful houses demolished to make way for brand new, but much larger ones. These and many similar acts of restless waste-making have become normalised; often justified by some imagined standard of 'better' or 'best'. The environmental costs of this increasing material mobility and more rapid replacement are never addressed, and rarely even noticed, the waste that is created being distanced from view (Clapp, 2002; Dauvergne, 2008).

Planning to create waste in global consumerism

From the consumer's perspective, what is used now has to be 'better', and more perfect, if not the best, and this requires more frequent updating or replacement, and often more clutter, both within the home and outside it (Makovicky, 2007). The desire for, and capacity to purchase the new, continuously creates waste, which can be best defined as what is no longer valued, at least relative to the 'better' and 'newer' (Dinnin, 2009). In much of the developing world, where the collection, separation and managed disposal of waste does not occur, the end result of this accelerated process of waste-making is increasing pollution, for waste in the wrong place rapidly becomes environmentally damaging. Indeed, it is estimated that only 48 per cent of the world's population has access to even elementary waste management services, a similar proportion to those with functioning sanitation (ISWA, 2014b, p5).

Collectively human beings now produce an estimated 4 billion tonnes of solid waste each year, and this is growing (ISWA, 2014b, p5). Without expert management and recovery efforts, this waste gets dumped 'somewhere else', and in a mixed-up state, often in the universal plastic bag, which makes any reuse difficult. In most of Asia, South America and Africa, everywhere that the blight of poverty thrives, waste pickers remove what is of value from this mixed-up waste, with the rest taken to vast open dumpsites, which are again picked over (Loschiavo dos Santos, 2014). Since the businesses that reuse or recover resources from wastes concentrate on those wastes whose resale value is assured, most other waste ends up as pollution in these nations; an invasive problem for all those without the capacity (or money) to escape its influence. Recent estimates suggest that over 64 million people now live in or near the world's largest 50 dumps, with many of these dumpsites affecting local rivers and lakes, and the health of those who live on, or adjacent to them. This figure does not include the next 500 or so still very large dumps, which suggests a very large number of people, the size of a modern nation, is now directly affected by the presence of, and pollution deriving from, all wastes (ISWA, 2014b, p76).

Since there is no 'away', when it comes to waste, much of the developing world's wastes, and quite a bit of the developed world's wastes, especially plastic bags and bottles, end up in waterways and oceans (Moore and Phillips, 2012; Liboiron, 2013a). This too has become 'pollution', and no longer 'waste'. It is estimated that around 8 million tonnes of this 'unmanaged' plastic waste enters the oceans each year (Hardesty and Wilcox, 2015). Indeed, the oceans now contain more plastic by weight than plankton, and more and more ocean wildlife are being poisoned or crippled by this plastic, including of course the plasticizers that are released with these (Liboiron, 2013b; Meikle, 1997). The figures speak for themselves. According to the International Solid Waste Association (ISWA), in 2012 288 million tonnes of plastics were produced, but only 15 million tonnes of this was recycled (ISWA, 2014b; and see ISWA, 2014a). Since only 15 million tonnes is being recycled and the oceans are receiving around 8 million tonnes per year, this suggests that a deluge of over 100 million tonnes will be wasted each year, much of this 'escaping' our waste management and recycling systems. As O'Brien notes, it is 'pure fantasy' to pretend, given the scale of this problem, that 'waste' can be solved technically; it just will not 'go away', at least without rethinking the whole system of production and consumption as it presently stands (O'Brien, 2008, p5).

So much documented damage, including Climate Change, now derives from global consumerism's primary requirement to make room for the new, and evermore frequently (Dinnin, 2009). So making space for the new, or making waste, is now a normal, in-the-background strategy, in most industrial production, with engineers, designers and marketers all working towards this end, to bring forward the 'natural end' of their products more quickly, in order to ensure a more frequent purchase of the 'latest' (Slade, 2006). Following this logic, waste has to be rendered more quickly invisible to the producer as well as to the consumer (see Nagel, 2013). So in food production, waste is made at the farm, in the warehouse and in the store, all to ensure that the consumer is presented with a more perfect–looking abundance of products to choose from. In a world where far too many go hungry, this type of wasting is particularly abhorrent, with many supermarkets now locking up and burying their wasted, but still edible, products, rather than giving them away (Stuart, 2009).

Making waste today is carefully designed, planned for, and managed, largely for the benefit of its producers. Four interdependent waste–making strategies are typically used by manufacturers, often in combination, to encourage and accelerate waste-making in consumption, so as to sell more products, and more often, within what is increasingly being understood as a 'linear' economy – a one way street to wasting. The first is visual or *relative obsolescence*, where the appearance and design of a product is altered frequently to ensure that what is bought soon appears 'old', or goes 'out of date' quickly. The second is *functional obsolescence*, where short-lived components are included in a product to ensure these will compromise its functioning. The third is systemic or *technological obsolescence*, where the product is rendered redundant, left behind and made useless by incremental technological change (Park, 2010; Slade, 2006). The fourth, which is still much neglected, is marketing or *promotional waste-making*, where the product is sold and priced in a way that ensures premature, planned discard (Crocker, 2012).

Most designers are all familiar with the first form of waste making, stylistic or *relative* obsolescence. It is relative because it is comparative. All cars, for example, must periodically change style, to ensure that sooner, rather than later, their owners will want to upgrade to the new (Park, 2010; Guiltnan, 2009). Similarly, *functional* obsolescence is often built in to products, so that even quite durable ones will break down and require expensive repairs, thus encouraging upgrading. From power tools and watches to mobile phones and hot-water systems, these 'ready to fail' inclusions, sometimes a specially designed component such as a battery that cannot be replaced, make for more frequent resales (Slade, 2006; Guiltnan, 2009). In *systemic* or technological obsolescence upgrading is forced upon consumers by larger systemic changes, such as the change from analogue to digital broadcasting. Suddenly everyone has to dispose of their TV, with these TVs unable to be sold anywhere analogue transmission has ceased (Slade, 2006; Park, 2010).

The final form of deliberate wasting, *promotional waste-making*, is often not included in discussions of obsolescence, but it has become increasingly significant. So, for example, large telecommunication providers 'give' a new phone to customers signing a new contract. In this way consumers are encouraged to dispose of their existing (and still useable) phone, and to take another 'better' one at the start of each contract. This requirement to dispose of the 'old' and take up the new is reinforced by the phone's guarantee being attached to the length of each contract (Crocker, 2012; Mooallem, 2008). This is not to claim that old phones are thrown away: in fact, only around 10 per cent are disposed of for official 'recycling', with the rest stockpiled in bottom drawers, or passed on to friends and families. This is an indication that consumers, driven to 'give up' their phones by marketers, do not necessarily want to throw away what they still value and can use (Crocker, 2012).

These four strategies are often used in combination to encourage faster waste-making in different domains. Each provides the consumer with more convincing reasons to discard what they have, to see what is already owned as 'less perfect', even if it is still working. So keeping the old phone beyond the guarantee is no longer in the consumer's interests: there is a time cost associated with 'bothering' to keep it (Bianchi, 2008). Using redundant technology, such as a tape-recorder, becomes difficult and then impossible, and repairing most common items is often more expensive than the price of new ones. IKEA furniture, for instance, contains proprietary fixing systems, and so if these break (or more typically, the chipboard into which they are screwed breaks) it is common to find the item itself thrown away. Toasters are another obvious example, at least outside Japan, Korea and Taiwan, where much greater strides have been made in reviving a culture of repair (see Kim et al., 2013). These are in most nations now cheaper to buy than to repair. So the consumer sees few easy choices but to upgrade, becoming 'locked in' to a treadmill marked by frequent, and often unnecessary, purchases and upgrades (Park, 2010; Evans and Cooper, 2010; Cooper, 2004).

The environmental load of this accelerated waste-making is worth considering here. If, for example, an average mobile phone is now engineered through marketing, financial contracts, technical construction and design to only last one to two years, then the volume of mobile phones produced will increase proportionately to the rising number now 'required' by this larger market (Ongondo et al., 2011; Lundgren, 2012). On the other hand, if consumers were encouraged to keep their phone for four or five years, and these were made to last for four years, as most of the early ones were, and the marketers encouraged consumers to keep their phones, production would be more than two times less per user than it is now (Crocker, 2012). Further, if these products were made to be disassembled, to be internally upgradeable, it is quite possible that the average lifespan of the mobile phone could increase to four or five years. To put this into perspective, this is a difference between needing to use an average of perhaps 20 phones over the course of a user's lifetime, as opposed to an average of 40 or more phones needed by the average user over the course of their life now.

Existing commercial waste-making strategies like this take advantage of the fact that they are now free of all regulatory interference, and that government economists unwittingly encourage this trashing of the planet by insisting on 'growth' at almost any cost. The box of the new 'free' mobile phone or $100 printer, for example, will have all the 'ticks' indicating compliance with the 'best' environmental and quality standards and regulations, but these are made worthless by the fact that the consumer is simultaneously being encouraged to discard them, often while they are still working, within a year or so of purchase. Apart from in a few nations like Japan, South Korea and Germany, there are very few serious 'take back' laws in place, and so what the consumer must throw away becomes, literally, someone else's problem (Crocker, 2016). While all the large telecom providers seem proud of their environmental standards, as are Apple and their rivals, and indulge in some hyperbolic claims to promote their green credentials, the reality is rather more grim: excess production and energy use leads directly to excess consumption, which leads directly to waste, pollution and, ultimately, Climate Change (Crocker, 2013b).

Waste making as devaluation and avoidance of shame

One of the central problems here is how waste and pollution are perceived and understood (Graeber, 2012; Alexander and Reno, 2012; O'Brien, 2008). Times have changed since Douglas wrote her famous book on *Purity and Danger* (1966) and even since Thompson wrote his *Rubbish Theory* (1979). For the content, volume and pervasive nature of modern waste has been transformed, as has our ability to measure and record it. For example, it is now possible to photograph plankton glowing with ingested microplastics (Liboiron, 2013a, 2013b), and to measure heavy metal pollution in large areas, and also in fish in the Arctic, and of course the presence of dangerous gasses in the upper atmosphere (Dauvergne, 2008; Liboiron, 2013b). The 'Anthropocene' age is, to a great extent, the product of this waste-making on a vast scale, and the continuing extracting, processing and wasting of natural landscapes and resources. Integrating what is understood through science with the insights of anthropology, sociology and philosophy has therefore become urgent, and the humanities too must play a leading role, alongside the social and environmental sciences, in this task of exposure (Solli *et al.*, 2011).

This is because measurement in itself can become a way of masking what waste is from ordinary people, and thus legitimising it as the normal but invisible by-product of generally beneficial economic activity. So for example CO_2 emissions are constantly monitored in the belief that a reduction in these will indicate less environmental degradation and thus a slowing of Climate Change (IPCC, 2014). But most people, including most in business, cannot grasp the significance of the rising proportions of greenhouse gasses in the atmosphere. But they can understand the dangers of a hotter sun, of more damaging storms and floods, and more pollution and waste. They can also often quickly grasp the need to end all planned and deliberate waste making and pollution, and to reshape our economic systems to 'price out' this damaging excess, and of revaluing the resources in materials now thrown away (IPCC, 2014; Yuan et al., 2006; Webster, 2015). For this reason businesses and politicians, from China to Europe, have been quick to grasp the significance of the idea of a more circular and resource-efficient economy.

Making waste, as this suggests, in its present form requires a linear economy and a consumer culture that encourages a continuous process of devaluation to make room for the new, and thus more consumption. This also begins in the mind, and not just in the mine or factory. It is certainly reinforced by the way waste can be made so easily disposed of, soon becoming invisible to human eyes and ears, distanced from the maker of waste, and from any consequences this waste might produce in some 'distant' environment (Clapp, 2002; Thompson, 1979). This devaluation often begins in a state of comparison with the new, or at least 'newer', and for this reason, consumerism is of increasing interest to environmentalists and government agencies, with the UN and the IPCC placing increasing emphasis on 'sustainable consumption' and various strategies for increasing 'circularity' in production (IPCC, 2014).

Price plays an important role in most mental calculations of relative value. A cheaper price attached to a useful product like a printer conditions the mind to devalue the product more quickly, both at the till and in use, and in most places this makes discard and replacement practically easier. Many 'cheap' products therefore fall into a more rapid cycle of waste making, from cheap tools and kitchenware, to mugs, glasses and t-shirts, and indeed much of what is to be found in discount stores everywhere (Shell, 2009). This tendency to seize upon, use and then discard the cheap is also true among producers, much of it driven by the urgency of the bottom line. The effect of this is 'linearity', of rapidly made cheap goods, rapidly consumed and used, and then as rapidly discarded (Schor, 2005; and see Rosa, 2003).

How things are valued, and how waste is first conceived in the mind, as Douglas reminds us, is an ancient affair, and pre-exists the systems that are now in place to encourage waste making (Douglas, 1966; and see Strasser, 1999). Indeed, people have always tended to identify with what they possess (Belk, 1988; Csikszentmihalyi, 1993). But what the consumer accepts and possesses, or rejects as their own, is entangled in a more mobile, modern sense of identity and social value (Ahuvia, 2005; Campbell, 2004). So while possessing a new Mercedes might bestow some sense of personal achievement and social value upon its owner, possessing what falls out of date such as an old and battered Mercedes, or worse, not possessing any car at all, might be taken as indicators of a lower social standing, and experienced as shame (Binkley, 2009; Scheff, 2003). Much the same story can be seen in manufacturers, where name and image, headquarters, plant, product and brand are all used as touchstones of identity and social standing (Crocker, 2013b).

Advertising and marketing tend to suggest that the consumer's lifestyle, body or environment is insufficient in some way *without* the new product being promoted. This continuously brings to attention the perceived value of the consumer's appearance and possessions: it is difficult now in many circumstances to avoid seeing what is owned, comparatively – that is *extrinsically* – through the eyes of others (Dwyer, 2009a, 2009b; Binkley, 2011). Not having sufficiently acceptable or up-to-date possessions creates or reinforces a sense of *lack* and shame: there is social pressure placed on the consumer, through the media and by example, to feel inferior to someone who possesses a more desirable product. Through such frequent opportunities for comparison the older, and cheaper, declines in relative value more quickly, while owning or enjoying the latest and the 'best' become more important goals to attain.

The threat of scarcity is a significant thread running through both the psychology and economics of modern consumerism (Mullainathan and Shafir, 2013). Children are particularly vulnerable to this sense of lack and the shame it generates, since their sense of self is under development and their place in the world still insecure (Hill, 2011; Schor, 2004). The sense of lack and personal shame created by the *absence* of a particular product and the qualities it allegedly bestows on the user is experienced particularly acutely, and is continuously reinforced by peers and reflected back in the media. So it is not uncommon to find stories that focus on the antics of teenagers bullying or harassing each other because one is seen to lack certain cool things (or looks), or for some becoming depressed and anxious because they believe that, in some way, they are not 'good enough' (Binkley, 2009; Scheff, 2003; Mullainathan and Shafir, 2013).

An important reminder of this darker side of consumerism is the novel and later film, *American Psycho* (Ellis, 1991), a 1980s parable about the destructive power of social competition, materialism and perfectionism in consumerism. In this dark tale the psychopathic anti-hero becomes jealous of, and then kills, a series of victims because they have some personal item that looks better than the equivalent he possesses, in one case a 'beautiful' business card. The killer must 'win' the game of social competition, and destroy his own sense of lack and shame, by killing his 'rivals'. Ellis's horror story holds up a sharp mirror to the perfectionism in everyday consumerism and the social competition it legitimises; without the 'perfect' and 'best', Ellis's consumer-killer is unsatisfied, and shamed (Muratovski, 2013; Malkmes, 2011; Binkley, 2009).

Searching for the 'better' and 'best' requires a restless search, since it is ultimately unattainable, with each 'best' soon eclipsed by the next, a more subtle implication of the storyline in *American Psycho*. This can also be seen at work in branding, since each valued brand must 'evolve' from one product to its next iteration, for example, from the iPhone 4 to the iPhone 5. Like a renovated house, the new version of the same-brand product is necessarily 'even better' than the earlier one. But how long can this last? It appears that more than two thirds of new mobile phones typically replace older ones still in use. While much of this is triggered by the contractual arrangements involved in this 'promotional waste-making', the brand's mobility from one product to the next is also an important trigger for 'upgrade' (Kim and Paulos, 2011; Crocker, 2012).

Reshaping the waste-making linear economy

Waste-making in consumerism can be seen as a legacy of existing systems of production and distribution, a 'sunk-cost effect' of linear industrialised systems, where products are rapidly manufactured, distributed, used and disposed of, before being replaced by the 'next best thing'. 'Sunk costs' are irrecoverable prior investments, and a 'sunk-cost effect' or 'legacy effect' is the sense of commitment resulting from such prior investments (Kelly, 2004; Cunha and Caldieraro, 2009). Sunk-costs in this way tend to reproduce a status quo, in both material and social terms, and this status quo cannot easily be undermined (Janssen et al., 2003). This is because sunk costs normalise existing systems and related expectations, and generate their own social acceptance and support, however environmentally destructive these might be (Crocker, 2016, chapter 4).

Sunk-cost effects soon manifest in public discourse as 'sunk-cost fallacies' (Gunia et al., 2009; Janssen et al., 2003), especially in those who most directly benefit from 'the way things are'. These are self-justifying and ideological explanations for an ongoing commitment to 'how we do things here'. Social or environmental problems associated with a successful and profitable industry are typically 'externalised' exploiting such fallacies (Princen, 2002a, 2002b). Sunk-cost fallacies tend to explain away damaging effects and emphasise the benefits of the system in question. They can thus lead governments or companies to deny the causal relationship between a product and its environmental damage. For example, asbestos manufacturers continued to deny any responsibility for the negative impacts of their products on health until forced to admit this in the courts (Tweedale and Warren, 1998). Changing a large and profitable system because of a supposedly 'external' cause is costly, and thus to be avoided, so it seems (see Zerubavel, 2006).

Designers need to be aware of the likely existence of the 'sunk-cost effect' and its impact on slowing or opposing sustainable change, especially since it is the elite that is most likely to cling to such sunk-cost fallacies (Janssen et al., 2003). For this reason most sustainable design often takes the form of incremental change towards a distant goal. For example, in an ideal world many engaged in sustainable product design would like to see consumers use a bicycle, walk or take a tram, rather than a car to commute to work, but most are aware that the car, and its associated practices and infrastructure cannot be abandoned overnight: everyday life in many cities requires access to a car (Soron, 2009; Sanne, 2002).

For this reason, designers must carefully consider the *ends* to which a product is required, the service it is fulfilling, and the social and material contexts in which a related unsustainable activity presently takes place (Ayres, 1999). This 'systems view' of the car has many parallels to 'capabilities theory'. We look to human needs not in terms of what already might exist, which might be scarred with injustice, exclusion, or environmental degradation, or some other evil, but instead look to the functional purpose responding to the original human need, which might have become embedded (and distorted) in the present system, in this case, the 'service' of transportation that the car serves (Ayres, 1999; Soron, 2009; Robeyns, 2005).

A problematic product, such as a car, might be replaced by a new more collaborative system, a 'product-service system', in which the need the existing service meets is now provided through more collective forms of consumption that more efficiently delivers the required service, where and when it is required. Xerox's famed photocopier product service system is a pioneer here, but there are more and more innovative examples (Vezzoli, 2013). For instance, while most Australian cities were remodelled post-war to become more 'car-friendly' (Lundin, 2008), as were many in Europe, the rising costs of car ownership have helped encourage more city dwellers to walk, cycle, use public transport and sometimes also use services like 'Go Get', a localized, car rental service that operates rather like a club. Each Go-Get car can be parked in locations across each city, and then booked online and used by individuals with an access code. Such shared services save these occasional drivers a lot of money, and considerable time (Cohen and Keitzmann, 2014). They also dramatically reduce the environmental impact of individual car ownership and use. Without possessing a car we find we do not need to drive 'down to the shops' for a bottle of milk, but can walk or cycle instead. In short, we take more 'incidental exercise' which adds greatly to our well-being.

Much also can be learnt by considering the *context* of the problem that appears to need a solution, and the existing product's relations within this context. Can such an object be placed within a different system of provision, so that the object can be reconfigured towards more sustainable outcomes (Manzini et al., 2008; Manzini, 2015)? For example, the supply of mobile phones could well be turned into another type of product service system, and the product itself improved and made internally upgradable, within a modified version of current waste-generating marketing systems. Products do not have to be toxic, unrecyclable, unrepairable, lacking durability and thus short-lived, and individually owned. In fact, there are clear benefits to be gained by the consumer if we can increase the quality and durability of such products (Evans and Cooper, 2010). The system that sells the service to the consumer does not need to become a barrier to sustainability. The individually owned mobile phone could be leased on a three year basis, with each phone 'owned' by the leasing company, which then takes responsibility for its functioning, and for all aspects of this service, including remanufacturing at the end of its life. Apple, for example, could develop such a system if sufficient regulatory encouragement was apparent (Vezzoli, 2013; Manzini, 2015).

Another important consideration here is the supporting role of *social technologies* in enabling such sustainable changes. For instance, it is becoming more common for consumers to sell or swap unwanted goods with others online, using a variety of exchange platforms. These increase efficiency by reducing the distance between buyer and seller, but also serve to localise the relationship. So it is now common for some stores to sell local vegetables and fruit using online social systems that link local producers to the storekeeper, rather than to the cumbersome logistical system of large-scale supermarkets. These 'heavier' systems require much higher profit margins, since bulk volumes must be stored and distributed as required, often across vast distances. More localised and more circular systems, enabled by social ITC platforms, where the store-keeper can sell 'the small, the imperfect and the unpackaged' from local growers, can cut out more than half the waste that supermarkets and their centralized systems currently require (Stuart, 2009).

There are also many technical and material interventions that can be achieved to reduce the environmental load of many products (Park, 2010). Many of these again involve undoing the established techniques that lock in early discard or prevent repair and reuse. For example, most toasters now will only last two or three years, simply because one or two parts are notoriously short-lived, unable to cope with the misuse most users regularly subject such appliances to. In Japan, with stricter legislation in place, this is no longer possible: repair is obligatory and every toaster sold is expected to be repairable (Chong et al., 2009). Certainly, as this shows, these failing parts could be replaced and redesigned. Packaging can also benefit from a dramatic reduction in many spheres. The aim of this is to design out waste wherever possible, to ensure that this waste is reusable, and to transform the experience of consumption so that the consumer does not feel obliged to repeatedly upgrade, and to prematurely discard.

Finally, in terms of *appearance*, much more could be done to fit the product to the consumer's needs, rather than to entice the consumer to adopt an 'exciting' but poorly designed product. Products that are loved, reliable and long-lived, if designed well, will not be abandoned so easily (Chapman, 2005). Products where lifecycle information about them is not concealed but made plain, both through the design and the labelling, can also provide convincing arguments for longer-term use. For example, in France lawmakers are now considering a labelling scheme where estimated 'length of life in use' will be mandated, and then linked to product stewardship laws that require 'return to maker' after disposal. These twin legal requirements could well encourage manufacturers to adopt longer-term strategies, and consumers to have more confidence in their products, and not resort so rapidly to upgrade (Khaleeli, 2015).

Conclusions

A critically important thread, binding together these various approaches to reducing waste and overconsumption is the goal of circularity, of creating a circular economy. Such a circular economy enables the generation and sometimes doubling of economic activity through turning waste into productive resources, reducing lengthy chains of provision and distribution, and reducing distances and time between producer and consumer (Webster, 2015). So the gardener's green waste might be collected and passed on through the waste collectors to the soil company, which then turns it into compost and sells it back to the gardener. Without the soil company this waste would go to landfill, and be rendered valueless, creating methane and other possible environmental problems. Similarly, the builder can now reuse much of his demolished building, crushing the concrete from a demolished building and reusing it in the floor of his next building (e.g. see www.zerowaste.sa.gov.au). In other recent examples, tyres have been recycled for fuel for making steel, and other waste products, for building material and for energy (Sahajwalla, 2015).

For what drives the circular economy and makes it so attractive as a way out of our present waste-making system is its reduction in distance between producer and consumer, as well as its multiplication of opportunities to produce services – and economic activities – within a 'closed' cycle or loop of production, use, discard and reuse (Webster, 2015). It is assumed in this model that materials are scarce and need to be reused, and that new technologies of communication can be used to re-localise production and consumption in activities that generate little or no waste, minimise emissions and negate the present need for toxics in production (ibid.). Waste (and pollution) is to be 'designed out' of the loop, and consumers are encouraged to co-create, where possible, solutions to their own problems using social technologies. We do not have to create waste to find the 'good life': potentially, at least, the good life is already here, within our towns and communities.

While there are many different approaches taken by individuals and groups towards the goal of the circular economy, most emphasise three interrelated principles: first, developing clearly defined goals that embody a closed-loop, no-waste system in a particular material and cultural context; second, developing new or better social communication tools to link 'end-users' and other stakeholders to producers within a system, to help 'co-create' this closed-loop system, in this way ensuring that all can benefit from it without many of the problems of inequity that have developed in our present linear system; and finally, to shift focus from some glossy perfection in consumption as 'possession' towards a deeper form of consumer satisfaction based upon experience and relationship. These three principles, visible in 'Living Labs', 'Transition' towns, and other movements towards sustainable consumption, should be incorporated into the sustainable designer's toolkit. 'Unmaking Waste' in this way could become a strategy for design transition, towards a more circular, 'zero waste' economy.

References

Ahuvia, A. C. (2005) 'Beyond the Extended Self: Loved Objects and Consumers' Identity Narratives', *Journal of Consumer Research*, vol 32, pp171–184

Alexander, C. and Reno, J. (2012) 'Introduction' in Alexander, C. and Reno, J. (eds), *Economies of Recycling: The Global Transformation of Materials, Values and Social Relations*, Zed Books, London, pp1–33

Allon, F. (2008) *Renovation Nation: Our Obsession with Home*, University of New South Wales Press, Sydney

Ayres, R. U. (1999) 'Products as Service Carriers: Should we kill the messenger or send it back?' in *United Nations University: Zero Emissions Forum*, United Nations University, Tokyo, retrieved from http://archive.unu.edu/zef/publications_e/ZEF_EN_1999_01_D.pdf (accessed 1 May 2015).

Belk, R. W. (1988) 'Possessions and the Extended Self', *Journal of Consumer Research*, vol 15, no 2, pp139–168

Bernthal, M. J., Crockett, D. and Rose, R. (2005) 'Credit Cards as Lifestyle Facilitators', *Journal of Consumer Research*, vol 32, No 1, pp130–145

Bianchi, M. (2008) 'Time and Preferences in Cultural Consumption' in Hutter, M. and Throsby, D. (eds) *Value and Valuation in Art and Culture*, Cambridge University Press, Cambridge, pp236–260

Binkley, S. (2009) 'The Civilizing Brand: Shifting Shame Thresholds and the Dissemination of Consumer Lifestyles', *European Journal of Cultural Studies*, vol 12, pp21–39

Binkley, S. (2011) 'Psychological Life as Enterprise: Social Practice and the Government of Neo-liberal Interiority', *History of the Human Sciences*, vol 24, no 3, pp83–102

Brommer, E., Stratmann, B. and Quack, D. (2011) 'Environmental Impacts of Different Methods of Coffee Preparation', *International Journal of Consumer Studies*, vol 35, no 1, pp212–220

Campbell, C. (2004) 'I Shop therefore I Know I Am: The Metaphysical Basis of Modern Consumerism' in Ekstrom, B. and Brembeck, H. (eds) *Elusive Consumption*, Berg, Oxford, pp27–44

Chapman, J. (2005) *Emotionally Durable Design: Objects, Experiences and Empathy*, Earthscan, London

Chong, J., Mason, L., Pillora, S. and Giurco, D. (2009) *Briefing Paper: Product Stewardship Schemes in Asia: China, South Korea, Japan and Taiwan*, Institute of Sustainable Futures, University of Technology Sydney, July, retrieved from www.environment.gov.au/.../product-stewardship-asia.doc (accessed 1 May 2014)

Clapp, J. (2002) 'The Distancing of Waste: Overconsumption in a Global Economy' in Princen, T., Maniates, M. and Conca, K. (eds) *Confronting Consumption*, MIT Press, Cambridge, MA, pp155–175

Clune, S., Morrissey, J. and Moore, T. (2012) 'Size Matters: House Size and Thermal Efficiency as Policy Strategies to Reduce Net Emissions of New Developments', *Energy Policy*, vol 48, pp657–667

Cohen, B. and Keitzmann, J. (2014) 'Ride On! Mobility Business Models for the Sharing Economy', *Organization and Environment*, vol 27, no 3, pp279–296

Cooper, T. (2004) 'Inadequate Life? Evidence of Consumer Attitudes to Product Obsolescence', *Journal of Consumer Policy*, vol 27, pp421–449

Crocker, R. (2012) 'Getting to Zero Waste in the New Mobile Communications Paradigm: A Social and Cultural Perspective', in Lehmann, S. and Crocker, R. (eds) *Designing for Zero Waste: Consumption, Technologies and the Built Environment*, Routledge, London, pp115–130

Crocker, R. (2013a) 'From Access to Excess: Consumerism, "Compulsory Consumption" and Behaviour Change' in Crocker, R. and Lehmann, S. (eds) *Motivating Change: Sustainable Design and Behaviour in the Built Environment*, Routledge, London, pp 11–32

Crocker, R. (2013b) 'Ethicalization and Greenwashing: Business, Sustainability and Design', *Design for Business: AGIDEAS Research*. 2, pp162–175

Crocker, R. (2016) *Somebody Else's Problem: Consumerism, Sustainability and Design*, Greenleaf, Sheffield.

Csikszentmihalyi, M. (1993) 'Why We Need Things' in Lubar, S. and Kingery, W. D. (eds) *History from Things: Essays on Material Culture*, Smithsonian Institute, Washington, DC, pp20–29

Cunha, M. and Caldieraro, F. (2009) 'Sunk-Cost Effects on Purely Behavorial Investments', *Cognitive Science*, vol 33, pp105–113

Dauvergne, P. (2008) *The Shadows of Consumption: Consequences for the Global Environment*, MIT Press, Cambridge, MA

Dinnin, A. (2009) 'The Appeal of Our New Stuff: How Newness Creates Value', *Advances in Consumer Research*, vol 36, pp261–265

Douglas, M. (1966) *Purity and Danger*, Routledge & Kegan Paul, London

Dwyer, R. (2009a) 'Making a Habit of It: Positional Consumption, Conventional Action and the Standard of Living', *Journal of Consumer Culture*, vol 9, no 3, pp328–347

Dwyer, R. (2009b) 'The McMansionization of America? Income Stratification and the Standard of Living in Housing, 1960–2000', *Research in Social Stratification and Mobility*, vol 27, pp285–300

Ellis, B. E. (1991) *American Psycho*, Vintage, New York

Evans, S. and Cooper, T. (2010) 'Consumer Influences on Product Lifespans' in Cooper, T. (ed.) *Longer Lasting Products: Alternatives to the Throwaway Society*, Gower, Farnham, UK pp319–350

Graeber, D. (2012) 'Afterword: The Apocalypse of Objects: Degradation, Redemption and Transcendence in the World of Consumer Goods' in Alexander, C. and Reno, J. (eds) *Economies of Recycling: The Global Transformation of Materials, Values and Social Relations*, Zed Books, London, pp277–290

Gregson, N., Metcalfe, A. and Crewe, L. (2007) 'Moving Things Along: The Conduits and Practices of Divestment in Consumption', *Transactions of the Institute of British Geographers*, New Series, vol 32, pp187–200

Guiltnan, J. (2009) 'Creative Destruction and Destructive Creations: Environmental Ethics and Planned Obsolescence', *Journal of Business Ethics*, vol 89, pp19–28

Gunia, B. C., Sivanatham, N. and Galinsky, A. D. (2009) 'Vicarious Entrapment: Your Sunk Costs, My Escalation of Commitment', *Journal of Experimental Social Psychology*, vol 45, no 6, pp1238–1244

Hamilton, C. (2002) *Overconsumption in Australia*, report by the Australia Institute, retrieved from www.tai.org.au/documents/dp_fulltext/DP49.pdf (accessed 20 March 2011)

Hardesty, B. D. and Wilcox, C. (2015) 'Eight Million Tonnes of Plastic Are Going into the Oceans Each Year', *The Conversation*, 13 February, retrieved from http://theconversation.com/eight-million-tonnes-of-plastic-are-going-into-the-ocean-each-year-37521 (accessed 1 March 2015)

Hill, J. A. (2011) 'Endangered Childhoods: How Consumerism is Impacting Child and Youth Identity', *Media, Culture and Society*, vol 33, pp347–362

IPCC (2014) *Climate Change 2014: Synthesis Report*, Contribution of Working Groups I, II and III to the Fifth Assessment Report of the Intergovernmental Panel on Climate Change. IPCC, Geneva, Switzerland

ISWA (2014a) *Waste Atlas: The World's 50 Biggest Dumpsites: 2014 Report*, Leeds University and ISWA, retrieved from www.atlas.d-waste.com/Documents/Waste-Atlas-report–2014-webEdition.pdf (accessed 1 May 2015)

ISWA (2014b) *Globalization and Waste Management: Final Report*, ISWA, retrieved from www.iswa.org/fileadmin/galleries/Task_Forces/TFGWM_Report_GWM_LR.pdf (accessed 1 May 2015)

Jaffrelot, C. and van der Veer, C. (eds) (2008) *Patterns of Middle Class Consumption in India and China*, Sage, London

Janssen, M. A., Kohler, T. A. and Scheffer, M. (2003) 'Sunk-Cost Effects and Vulnerability to Collapse in Ancient Societies', *Current Anthropology*, vol 44, no 5, pp722–728

Jensen, O. B. (2009) 'Flows of Meaning, Cultures of Movements – Urban Mobility as Meaningful Everyday Life Practice', *Mobilities*, vol 4, no 1, pp139–158

Kasser, T. (2002) *The High Price of Materialism*, MIT Press, Cambridge, MA

Kelly, T. (2004) 'Sunk Costs, Rationality and Acting for the Sake of the Past', *Nous*, vol 38, no 1, pp60–85

Khaleeli, H. (2015) End of the Line for Stuff that's Built to Die? *Guardian*, 5 March, retrieved from www.theguardian.com/technology/shortcuts/2015/mar/03/has-planned-obsolesence-had-its-day-design (accessed 1 May 2015)

Kim, S. and Paulos, E. (2011) 'Practices in the Creative Reuse of e-Waste', *CHI 2011*, session: Sustainability 2, Vancouver, Canada, retrieved from www.cs.cmu.edu/~sk1/papers/ewaste_chi_camera_ready.pdf (accessed 1 May 2014)

Kim, Y. J., Kang, D. H., Kim, M. G. and Qureshi, T. I. (2013) 'Analytical Study on the RoHS of Plastic from Waste Electrical and Electronic Appliances', *International Journal of Environmental Research*, vol 7, no 4, pp903–908

Kreuger, D. A. (2008) 'The Ethics of Global Supply Chains in China – Convergences of East and West', *Journal of Business Ethics*, vol 79, pp113–120

Liboiron, M. (2013a) 'Modern Waste as Strategy', *Lo Squaderno: Explorations in Space and Society*, vol 29, no 9–12, retrieved from www.losquaderno.professionaldreamers.net/?cat=162 (accessed 1 May 2015)

Liboiron, M. (2013b) 'Plasticizers: A Twenty-first Century Miasma', in Gabrys, J., Hawkins, G. and Michael, M. (eds) *Accumulation: The Material Politics of Plastics*, Routledge, London, pp22–44

Lipovetsky, G. (2011) 'The Hyperconsumption Society' in Ekstom, K.M. and Glans, K. (eds) *Beyond the Consumption Bubble*, Routledge, London, pp25–36

Loschiavo dos Santos, M. C. (2014) 'Lessons from Plastic and Cardboard Cities: Waste, Design and the View from the Edge' in Loschiavo dos Santos, M.C., Walker, S. Lopes, S., and Goncalves Dias, F. (eds) *Design, Waste and Dignity*, Editora Olhares, São Paulo, pp41–54

Lundgren, K. (2012) *The Global Impact of E-Waste: Addressing the Challenge*, ILO, Geneva

Lundin, P. (2008) 'Mediators of Modernity: Planning Experts and the Making of the "Car-Friendly" European City', in Hard, M. and Misa, T. J. (eds) *Urban Machinery: Inside Modern European Cities*, MIT Press, Cambridge, MA, pp257–279

Makovicky, N. (2007) 'Closet and Clutter: Clutter as Cosmology', *Home Cultures*, vol 4, no 3, pp287–309

Malkmes, J. (2011) *American Consumer Culture and its Society: From F. Scott Fitzgerald's 1920s Modernism to Bret Easton Ellis' 1980s Blank Fiction*, Diplomica Verlag, Hamburg

Manzini, E. (2002) 'Context-Based Wellbeing and the Concept of Regenerative Solution: A Conceptual Framework for Scenario Building and Sustainable Solutions Development', *Journal of Sustainable Product Design*, vol 2, pp141–148

Manzini, E. (2015) *Design, When Everybody Designs: An Introduction to Design for Social Innovation (Design Thinking, Design Theory)*, MIT Press, Cambridge, MA

Manzini, E., Walker, S. and Wylant, W. (eds) (2008) *Enabling Solutions for Sustainable Living: A Workshop*, University of Calgary Press, Calgary

Meikle, J. (1997) 'Material Doubts: the Consequences of Plastics', *Environmental History*, vol 2, no 3, pp278–300

Mooallem, J. (2008) 'The Afterlife of Cell Phones', *New York Times Magazine*, 13 January, retrieved from query.nytimes.com/gst/fullpage.html?res=980DE1DD1F3CF930A25752C0A96E9C8B63, accessed 20 February 2011

Moore, C. J. and Phillips, C. (2012) *Plastic Ocean: How a Sea Captain's Chance Discovery Launched a Determined Quest to Save the Oceans*, Avery, New York

Morris, J. (2010) 'Making Italian Espresso, Making Espresso Italian', *Food and History*, vol 8, no 2, pp155–183

Mullainathan, S. and Shafir, E. (2013) *Scarcity: The True Cost of Not Having Enough*, Penguin, London

Muratovski, G. (2013) 'Advertising, Public Relations and Social Marketing: Shaping Behaviour Towards Sustainable Consumption' in Crocker, R. and Lehmann, S. (eds) *Motivating Change: Sustainable Design and Behaviour in the Built Environment*, London, Routledge

Nagel, R. (2013) *Picking Up: On the Streets behind the Trucks with the Sanitation Workers of New York City*, Farrar, Strauss and Giroux, New York

Nelissen, R. M. A., van de Ven, N. and Stapel, D. (2011) 'Status Concerns and Financial Debts in Adolescents', *Social Influence*, vol 6, no 1, pp39–56

O'Brien, M. (2008) *A Crisis of Waste? Understanding the Rubbish Society*, Routledge, London

Ongondo, F. O., Williams, I. D. and Cherrett, T. J. (2011) 'How Are WEEE Doing? A Global Review of the Management of Electrical and Electronic Wastes', *Waste Management*, vol 31, pp714–730

Park, M. (2010) 'Defying obsolescence' in Cooper, T. (ed.) *Longer Lasting Products: Alternatives to the Throwaway Society*, Gower, Farnham, pp77–106

Parrott, K. R., Beamish, J. O., Emmel, J. M. and Lee, S.-J. (2008) 'Kitchen Remodeling: Exploring the Dream Kitchen Projects', *Housing and Society*, vol 35, no 2, pp25–42

Pettit, N. C. and Sivanatham, N. (2011) 'The Plastic Trap', *Social Psychological and Personality Science*, vol 2, no 2, pp146–153

Princen, T. (2002a) 'Consumption and its Externalities: Where Economy Meets Ecology' in Princen, T., Maniates, M. and Conca, K. (eds) *Confronting Consumption*, MIT Press, Cambridge, MA, pp23–41

Princen, T. (2002b) 'Distancing: Consumption and the Severing of Feedback' in Princen, T., Maniates, M. and Conca, K. (eds) *Confronting Consumption*, MIT Press, Cambridge, MA, pp103–131.

Robeyns, I. (2005) 'The Capability Approach: A Theoretical Survey', *Journal of Human Development*, vol 6, no 1, pp93–117

Rosa, H. (2003) 'Social Acceleration: Ethical and Political Consequences of a De-synchronized High Speed Society', *Constellations*, vol 10, no 1, pp3–33

Rotter, J. P., Airike, P., and Mark-Herbert, C. (2014) 'Exploring Political Corporate Social Responsibility in Global Supply Chains', *Journal of Business Ethics*, vol 125, no 4, pp581–599

Ryan, M. (2014) 'Apartment Therapy, Everyday Modernism, and Aspirational Disposability', *Television and New Media*, vol 15, no 1, pp68–80

Sahajwalla, V. (2015) 'Green Manufacturing: Recycling End-of-Life Polymers in Steel Making: An Example of Successful Translation of Research into Industry' in Thornton, K., Crocker, R. and Thornton, C. (eds) *Unmaking Waste: Transforming Production and Consumption in Time and Place: Proceedings*, retrieved from http://unmakingwaste2015.org/wp-content/uploads/2015/09/UMW_Cover_Foreword_Table-of-Contents-.pdf (accessed 1 October 2015)

Sanne, C. (2002) 'Willing Consumers – or Locked-In? Policies for a Sustainable Consumption', *Ecological Economics*, vol 42, pp273–287

Scheff, T. J. (2003) 'Shame in Self and Society', *Symbolic Interaction*, vol 26, no 2, pp239–262

Scheibehenne, B., Greifeneder, R. and Todd, P. M. (2010) 'Can There Ever Be Too Many Options? A Meta-Analytic Review of Choice Overload', *Journal of Consumer Research*, vol 37, pp409–425

Schor, J. S. (2004) *Born to Buy: The Commercialized Child and the New Consumer Culture*, Scribner, New York

Schor, J. S. (2005) 'Prices and Quantities: Unsustainable Consumption and the Global Economy', *Ecological Economics*, vol 55, no 3, pp309–320

Schwartz, D. T. (2010) *Consuming Choices: Ethics in a Global Consumer Age*, Rowman and Littlefield, New York

Shell, E. R. (2009) *Cheap: The High Cost of Discount Culture*, Penguin Books, New York

Shove, E. and Hand, M. (2005) 'The Restless Kitchen: Possession, Performance and Renewal', in E. Shove (ed.) *Kitchens and Bathrooms: Changing Technologies, Practices and Social Organisation – Implications for Sustainability*, University of Manchester Press, Manchester

Slade, G. (2006) *Made to Break: Technology and Obsolescence in America*, Harvard University Press, Cambridge, MA

Slater, P. (2007) 'The Gadgeteer: Sex, Self and Consumerism in Stuff Magazine', *Language and Ecology*, vol 2, no 1, pp1–8

Smart, B. (2010) *Consumer Society: Critical Issues and Environmental Consequences*, Sage, London

Solli, B., Burström, M., Domanska, E., Edgeworth, M., González-Ruibal, A., Holtorf, C., Lucas, G., Oestigaard, T., Smith, L. and Whitmore, C. (2011) 'Some Reflections on Heritage and Archaeology in the Anthropocene', *Norwegian Archaeological Review*, vol 44, no 1, pp40–88

Soron, D. (2009) 'Driven to Drive: Cars and the Problem of "Compulsory Consumption"' in Conley, J. and McLaren, A. T. (eds) *Car Troubles: Critical Studies of Automobility and Auto-Mobility*, Ashgate, Farnham, pp181–197

Strasser, S. (1998) '"The Convenience is Out of this World!": The Garbage Disposer and American Consumer Culture' in Strasser, S., McGovern, C. and Judt, M. (eds) *Getting and Spending: European and American Consumer Societies in the Twentieth Century*, Cambridge University Press, Cambridge, pp263–280

Strasser, S. (1999) *Waste and Want: A Social History of Trash*, Henry Holt, New York

Stuart, T. (2009) *Waste: Uncovering the Global Food Scandal*, W. W. Norton, New York

Thompson, M. (1979) *Rubbish Theory: The Creation and Destruction of Value*, Oxford University Press, Oxford

Tomlinson, J. (2007) *The Culture of Speed: The Coming of Immediacy*, Sage, London

Tweedale, G. and Warren, R. (1998) 'A Case in Point: Morality and Paternalism in the Asbestos Industry: A Functional Explanation', *Business Ethics*, vol 7, pp87–96

Vezzoli, C. (2013) 'System Design for Sustainability: The Challenge of Behaviour Change' in Crocker, R. and Lehmann, S. (eds) *Motivating Change: Sustainable Design and Behaviour in the Built Environment*, Routledge, London, pp276–290

Webster, K. (2015) *The Circular Economy: A Wealth of Flows*, Ellen MacArthur Foundation, Cowes, retrieved from www.ellenmacarthurfoundation.org/publications/the-circular-economy-a-wealth-of-flows (accessed 1 July 2015)

Xing, Y. (2014) 'China's High Tech Exports: The Myth and the Reality', *Asian Economic Papers*, vol 13, no 1, pp109–123

Yuan, Z., Bi, J. and Moriguichi, Y. (2006) 'The Circular Economy: A New Development Strategy in China', *Journal of Industrial Ecology* vol 10, no 1–2, pp4–8

Zerubavel, E. (2006) *The Elephant in the Room: Silence and Denial in Everyday Life*, Oxford University Press, Oxford

Zhang, L. (2010) *In Search of Paradise: Middle-Class Living in a Chinese Metropolis*, Cornell University Press, Ithaca, NJ

PART IV

User experience

Products shape experience, and designers influence the character of these experiences in powerful ways – we are creators of experiences, not simply of objects. Through designing products with a focus on both the quality and longevity of user experience, we enhance our ability to influence their perceived value, social performance and ecological impacts. In considering both the tangible and intangible dimensions of user experience, we activate, shape and steer user experiences to foster more resilient partnerships between people and their material worlds; designing for sustainable behaviours, new routes to resource efficiency and greater product value.

This fourth part examines the meaningful proxies, triggers and metaphors embedded within product experiences as far ranging as toothpicks and televisions to brogues, bathroom suites and construction materials, to expose alternative understandings of the immaterial culture underpinning our stuff, and the manifold dialogues we are continually engaged in with the plethora of designed objects and environments that touch our lives. Each of the six chapters engages the part's core theme of user experience and longevity. The contributors writing in this section draw together previously disconnected scholarship in user experience, transition design, developmental psychology, interaction design and design activism. Their chapters may be summarised as follows:

18 Emotional sustainability – *Deana McDonagh*
   This chapter discusses how specific stages of life impact the meaning we attach to products. Individuals are dynamic with existing, changing and emerging needs. The product design challenge, therefore, is to satisfy these changing functional and emotional needs of users.

19 Pleasant experiences and sustainable design – *Juan Carlos Ortíz Nicolás*
   User experience aims to understand how people make sense of products, services or interfaces. This chapter outlines four aspects of 'pleasant experience', and provides creative direction for producing such experience in the design of sustainable products.

20 Surprising longevity – *Silvia Grimaldi*
   This chapter shows how surprise, when designed into the product experience, can contribute to the longevity of a product, creating a timeline of *before* and *after* the surprising event, structuring the experience as a story in our mind.

21 Design for sustainable use using principles of behaviour change – *Casper Boks and Johannes Zachrisson Daae*
    Following a complete design process – from problem finding, user research and analysis, to ideation, conceptualization and user testing – this chapter illustrates the power of Design for Sustainable Behaviour (DfSB) as an interdisciplinary approach, now and in the future.
22 Hacking the probe-head: manipulations for social sustainability – *Otto von Busch*
    Through the use of devices, design sorts and consolidates human behaviors to propel the status quo. This chapter shows how hacking transforms systems of exclusion into more inclusive systems that propel user experience, sustainability and social justice.
23 Transitions in sociotechnical conditions that afford usership: sustainable who? – *Cameron Tonkinwise*
    Lifestyles structured around 'usership' – rather than 'ownership' – are less materials intense, yet they may also be less autonomous. This chapter highlights recent shifts to information technologies and design, and their influential roles in shaping 'sharing economies'.

So, what does user experience have to do with sustainability? Indeed, it may appear that generating meaningful synthesis between such apparently disconnected ideas is like trying to nail ice cubes together. As users, we mine the glossy surface of material culture in search of experience and meaning, the nature and character of which, influenced by each user's personal register of previous material encounters and experiences. In this way, we are each entwined within several distinct systems of objects, simultaneously, each occupying different depths of material experience. These objects may well sit side-by-side on our shelves, but are divided by fathoms, in an experiential sense. This constantly shifting assemblage of trainers, teapots and toasters are deployed to reflect our equally dynamic and unstable identities. In this respect, material consumption may be understood as an aspirational process, in which the material you possess is the destiny you chase. Like a shadow that follows you around, this *stuff* defines you, whether you like it or not. However, as our identities evolve and change, so too must the products we deploy to both mirror and project these unstable, shifting identities.

Sustainable product experience can be loosely directed by designers but never fully controlled. Indeed, some product experiences simply can't be designed, or planned by design – the coffee cup becomes a paperweight at some breezy outdoor café, or the dining chair becomes a stepladder when the light bulb pops. However, product designers are authors of experience, casting objects as mediators of mystery, fiction, wonder and awe – not just as dull and servile boxes that perform 'tasks' seamlessly. Take denim jeans for example. You have a close relationship with your jeans. Your jeans are like a second skin, worn and moulded and torn by your everyday experiences. Purchased like blank canvases, jeans are worked on, sculpted and personified over time. Jeans are like familiar old friends providing animated narrative to life – a repository of memories – mapping events as and when they occur.

Products are mediators of experience and meaning; the sustainability, longevity and efficiency of the product use phase are largely determined at the design stage. Sustainable product designers, therefore, must understand their role as authors of experience, in addition to a wider set of physical parameters and conditions.

In terms of product use, the point of sale is just the beginning of the product story. A pair of handmade leather brogues for example, will improve with age by softening and developing patina through use. Much of this is due to the use of materials, in this case, leather. Yet, despite its excellent ageing qualities, leather places a heavy burden on the environment. The leather equivalent produces 15kg CO_2 – over twice as much. The average synthetic shoe produces about 8kg CO_2, through materials processing, manufacturing, transportation and packaging. In addition to the high carbon intensity of cattle farming, the process of 'growing' leather creates a great deal of methane, or CH_4 as it is scientifically known. As a greenhouse gas and main contributor to climate change, CH_4 is 25 times more potent per kilo than CO_2. Herein lies the dichotomy – higher material impacts versus shortened product lifespans. Synthetic materials are at times more sustainable than natural ones, as they can be kept within material flows on a cradle-to-cradle (C2C) methodology. Leather can be used in a way, which extends product life, and in so doing, reduces levels of consumption and waste. While on the other hand, leather has a heavy ecological burden.

In today's throwaway society, where products are desired, purchased, briefly used and promptly land filled to make way for more, consumption and waste are rapidly spiralling out of control with truly devastating ecological and social consequences. In many cases, products are discarded long before their time simply because the complexity and range of experience they deliver is pathetically narrow, and thus short-lived. The 'throwaway society' is, sadly, nothing new and has been in the public lexicon since about 1955. In fact, it was as early as 1932 when American economist Bernard London first introduced the term, 'planned obsolescence' (made popular by Vance Packard in his monograph *The Waste Makers* of 1963) as a means to stimulate spending among the very few that had money at that time. This proposed shift toward an increasingly disposable material world was initially proposed as a solution to dark economic crisis experienced during the Great Depression in the US (1929–1939).

At the time, the ecological impacts of this drive toward planned product failure could not have been anticipated or understood in the 1930s. Today, however, we are all too aware of the devastating social and ecological pressure these short-term industrial practices create. That's not to say that longer is always better. For example, unless retrofit is an option, you really should recycle that vintage refrigerator from the 1950s, and upgrade to a modern, energy-efficient one. However, we are currently experiencing a seismic shift in thinking, from the creation of short-lived product experiences, to that of longer-lasting material experiences and services. Collectively, this transition shapes future design paradigms for sustainable materials, products, services and experiences, which expand the frontiers of product design in the twenty-first century.

say, but what they actually mean (Rapaille, 2006). Interpreting actions, feelings and aspirations are what make design research, design thinking and the design process so engaging.

The most successful products, services and environments offer the user a positive experience. Chapman refers to them as 'the experiential fabric of daily life' (Chapman, 2005, p19). Apple products, for example, satisfy the needs of a socially – and to some extent, prestigious – connected lifestyle. Adidas sporting products satisfy the aspirational need for a healthier life, even if tennis shoes may never actually see a tennis court, they have satisfied this need, to some extent. Visit your nearest supermarket or shopping mall and you will observe examples of aspirational clothing being worn, such as sports apparel that may never actually be used for any sport-related activity. With the rise in popularity of television cooking programmes, there does not seem to be an increase in cooking within the home. By being part of the cooking process (e.g. observing), aspirational needs are satisfied: 'People feel before they think. The implication for business? Value gets assigned emotionally, not rationally' (Hill, 2010, p14).

Chapman (2005) discussed research from a UK supermarket chain (Sainsbury's) that found their customers who purchased organic produce developed a sense of well-being. The act of acquiring 'organic' satisfied a need in itself. An extension of the organic movement is 'buying local' (e.g. local breweries, cheese makers), and can be seen in restaurants presenting this as 'farm to table' offerings.

Design is about creating an experience that resonates with the user, ideally over a long period of time. It is worth noting at this point that the customer (person who purchases the product) may be different than the user (person who uses the product). This is noteworthy as a product may function perfectly well and be accepted for retail, but if it does not resonate with the user, then it may be underused, misused or worse still, returned and/or disposed of. An example of such disconnects are unwanted Christmas gifts.

Why do we (as receivers) thank the givers, only to store such unwanted gifts before we finally dispose of them, and without becoming overwhelmed by guilt or shame, which is an interesting concept in itself? The time period of 18–24 months seems to be the unspoken standard for storage prior to disposal. Products that have a chance of extending their shelf life need to enhance the product–user (emotional) relationship. User needs are dynamic. Needs are ever changing and designers need to be aware of current needs, emerging needs and to a degree foresee the unforeseeable needs (McDonagh, 2015). Indeed, emotional connections are essential for a sustained user experience to take place: 'Being on-emotion is more important than being on-message' (Hill, 2010, p47).

In order for designers to better understand users (the purchasers and consumers of their products) it is critical that they consider the wide ranging functional and emotional needs of people. These range from the tangible (e.g. anthropometric data of users, price points, materials) and less tangible (e.g. user's aspirations, cultural needs, impact of colour used). Designers' toolkits have expanded and developed to include user research (McDonagh, 2015) in the last 20 years. Without sensitivity to users, the design outcome tends to be more of an exercise in styling rather than generating positive, and potentially transformative, user experiences. As new technologies are developed, the way in which the person engages and interacts with that technology, can present unexplored challenges and new opportunities. For example, with the increase in wearable technology (e.g. FitBits, Nike+) we need to consider what else a person would be wearing (e.g. clothes, watch, jewellery) in order to fully appreciate the user context, and the way in which these new products sit alongside existing material goods. For example, accessing wearable technology may be more challenging in winter than in summer due to layering of clothing, while the intensity of light in the summer months may make the interface difficult to read.

Why do designers need to think about ageing and disability?

Buying into a brand may not be appropriate for some users; they may require a less overt statement. For many, assistive technology devices still carry a stigma (e.g. walking stick, leg braces), but with designers applying increased sensitivity to the user, it is hoped that such products no longer carry any stigma. An example of such a product that has transformed from assistive technology to a fashion item, are spectacles.

Loe (2011, p5) notes that 'By 2020, for the first time in history, Americans over sixty-five will outnumber those under fifteen', and 'The fastest growing age group in America is composed of those eighty-five years and over.' Why should designers care about the ageing population? Because the profile of users is changing. The population is changing. People are living longer and expecting a higher quality of life than the generation before them. Having a disability is no longer perceived as a barrier to having a good quality of life. In addition, we have injured war veterans returning that are young and having to renegotiate the material landscape. We need to rethink ageing and disability (Loe, 2011; McDonagh et al., 2010). Assistive technologies that need to satisfy the functional and supra-functional needs of these two populations offer designers both an incredible challenge, as well as developing numerous new business models and design opportunities. Rethinking ageing and disability is the next frontier, and provides unprecedented opportunities for innovation and transformation through design.

In healthcare, assistive and supportive technologies are more popular than ever before. Devices that are placed under the skin already exist within the mainstream (e.g. pacemakers, pain-killing devices), but in the coming decades, we will be relying on the development of technically sophisticated devices to support healthcare (e.g. sensors, monitors and screening devices) as never before. Being socially connected is proving a significant contributor to healthy ageing (Loe, 2011). The way we share and/or communicate our geographic location, our social interactions, monetary transactions may supersede all the objects we currently carry with us everywhere we go (e.g. identification, mobile telephone, camera, paper currency, credit cards).

The role that product designers play within the consumerisation of technology is paramount. In this way, design offers the bridge between the technologies, engineers and scientists and that of the *lived experience* of user. Mediating the technology in an empathic way for the user is not merely a matter of size, colour and choice of material. Technology alone is not selling products, it is the meaning such products offer users that prove successful in the marketplace.

Material landscape

The material culture we create within our homes is often a reflection of the external world and culture in which we live, while also representing our private world (Miller, 2001). Entering a person's home environment for the first time is significant, as it provides the observer with an impression of the host that goes beyond the public persona they have so carefully constructed. Objects, paintings, furniture, what we store in our refrigerators, are all 'real' indicators of our human values. This will begin to explain why it is so stressful when someone 'new' visits your home environment. In some cultures you may never be invited to a person's home and this is acceptable, while in other cultures the home is more socially accessible.

> The 20th century witnessed a steady societal migration away from deep communal values toward a fast-food culture of nomadic individualism and excessive materialism

… today empathy is consumed not so much from each other, but through fleeting embraces with designed objects.

(Chapman, 2005, p18)

The home environment is typically both a private space (e.g. place to sleep, eat and relax) and a semi-private space (e.g. friends and family gatherings). It is also one of the most revealing ways in which we communicate our life's journey, tangibly, through objects (e.g. trophies, family photographs), less tangibly through 'feeling' (e.g. lighting, colour scheme). Holistically the home represents a series of life choices, experiences and aspirations that have accumulated, iteratively, over time. Furthermore, it is not always what is present in the home, but sometimes what is not present (e.g. lack of family photographs or loved ones). It is your life story.

A house encompasses an array of different materials, from furniture and fixtures to ornaments and décor, collectively creating a dwelling experience that is greater than the sum of the parts. For these are more than mere 'things', they are a collection of appropriated materials, invested with meaning and memory, a material testament of who we are, where we have been, and perhaps even where we are heading. They are what transforms our house into a home… They bind our past with our present and our possible futures, thereby framing and reflecting our sense of self.

(Hecht, 2001, p123)

Consider what happens when a person breaks the law within the US, for example. Depending on the severity of the crime, they may end up imprisoned. The process of taking someone away from their personal possessions, putting them in a facility without a unique identity is part of the punishment, and dehumanisation of the convicted individual. Now let us consider how we support elders who may fall and need medical attention, or they can no longer look after themselves, or their home environment is not adequate. We take them away from all their personal possessions and put them into a facility without their own unique identity. Having your familiar worldly possessions taken away can be traumatic when they represent the individual and the life they lived.

Have you ever considered why we tend to stage our home environments before anyone visits us? We tend to remove the anti-dandruff shampoo away from sight, remove all clutter and empty the cat litter tray! We remove stigmatised products and further contribute to the pretence of effortless living (no clutter, clean living spaces). At the end of the day, we are inviting friends over to share our living spaces but even at our most relaxed we can be sensitive to how our personal living spaces are perceived by others.

Life's stages

If 'apparel oft proclaims the man' (Shakespeare, *Hamlet*, act 1, scene 3, lines 55–81), the products we surround ourselves with, and the environments we spend our time in, will significantly *proclaim* our daily experiences. We pass through various life stages from being a child through to an ageing citizen, with various levels of dependency on others and our environments along the way. Making sense of the world, the people in it and the objects that we surround ourselves with can be empowering or disempowering depending on our context. The aim of this chapter is to encourage new product developers to ensure more balanced design outcomes for the user. User interaction and engagement with the products they surround themselves with needs to offer a longer-lasting and more meaningful relationship, over time. The design shift, therefore, is from increased numbers of meaningless objects, to fewer numbers of meaningful possessions.

What has become of paramount importance for many teenagers is their appearance, and the appearance of the peer-group they associate with. Their clothing, footwear, hair style, jewellery and so forth, represents one of their initial platforms by which they communicate and express themselves. They become a walking shrine to the music they listen to, the celebrities they follow and the sociocultural groups they feel affiliated with. In some way, they become an extension of their private space (their bedroom) and take their value system out into the public domain.

> As we change and grow throughout our lives, our psychological development is punctuated not only by meaningful emotional relationships with people, but also by close affective ties with a number of significant physical environments, beginning in childhood.
>
> *(Cooper Marcus, 2006, p4)*

For a university student living away from home for the first time, the degree to which their coffee cups coordinate with the kitchen cupboards will probably be of little concern to them. Once a person purchases their first home then such concerns become elevated, because their personal environment now begins to represent them more closely. Before this point, most purchasing choices were made by others (e.g. parents, landlords); now they are solely responsible for their living environment and therefore take greater care over the image it portrays. Their material landscape will now reflect their success, achievements, ability to organise and so on. It is almost as if allowing others to witness our dirty pots and unwashed laundry would result in one becoming a social outcast. This would help to explain why entertaining in one's home can be so stressful. How we authentically use our homes, and how we like to present our homes, may be significantly different.

Wolfe and Snyder (2003, p126) have identified 'four seasons of life' in terms of consumption. Considering stages of life in terms of the relationship individuals have with their material landscape is important (see Table 18.1).

Table 18.1 Four seasons of life

Stage	Season	Overview
Childhood	Spring	A time of learning about oneself, others and gathering a relatively small cluster of personal possessions. Learning through playing is demonstrated. Children tend to be consumers of products rather than customers.
Early adulthood	Summer	Focuses on developing an identity distinctive from childhood. This is often the stage where individuals become more sensitive to their material possessions as a means to express themselves. The individual at this stage is engaged in primary material acquisition as both consumer and customer. They are becoming somebody.
Middle adulthood	Fall	Signifies a slowing down of acquisition and an emphasis on possessions offering deeper meaning. Inner self-development, with work-life balance becomes a priority for the individual.
Later adulthood	Winter	Is the final stage and there tends to be an emphasis on reduction of possessions, also known as 'downsizing'. Making sense of the life lived and coming to terms with mortality.

Source: based on Wolfe and Snyder (2003, p126)

Though there is personal variance between the four stages, generally speaking, over a typical life span, we carry fewer possessions towards later adulthood as compared with early adulthood, and their value and meaning can deepen.

Figure 18.1 represents the main stages of user product purchasing and consumption patterns, if we assume a long and healthy life span. Even before we are born (0–9 months), there tends to be a significant amount of preparation and purchasing on our behalf (pre-acquisition stage). In effect, we own a range of products and services without even being part of the purchasing decision, we literally consume.

The next stage involves the baby becoming its own person (acquisition). They begin to express their preferences when choosing what they wear, how they arrange their bedrooms and so on. From being born, they begin to become more aware of their command of space, material objects and their parents attention. This is a relatively long stage where the individuals, typically, go through school, first job, marriage, children and such like, where material comforts become one of the main focuses for working so hard.

According to Wolfe and Snyder (2003), the de-acquisition stage can begin around 55 years of age. Often around the time their children have *flown the nest* (left home) and there is a realisation that *less* may indeed be *more*. At this stage, to focus shifts dramatically, to become more on meaningfulness of one's life and the legacy you leave behind rather than ephemeral and rapidly updating sequences of material ownership.

The post-acquisition stage represents the stage in one's life where you require more support than ever in adulthood to maintain a healthy lifestyle. There is a similarity to young children that need help with dressing, preparation and cooking of meals, and medical issues may dominate daily living.

The latter stage is one of focusing on the life that has been lived, and this is why this is referred to as the reflection stage. This is the stage of life where the least number of objects are required. A handful of photographs, selection of jewellery and books may represent the life once lived.

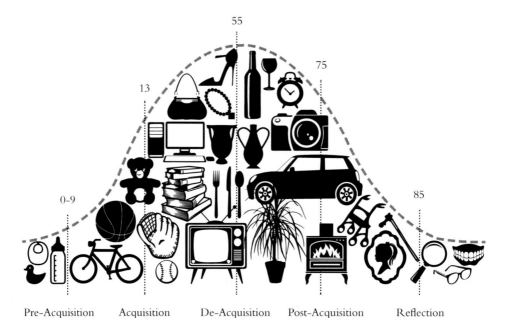

Pre-Acquisition   Acquisition   De-Acquisition   Post-Acquisition   Reflection

Figure 18.1 The four key life stages and their relation to material consumption

Recognizing the role that designers play in introducing products, new technologies and new ways of performing tasks to users with varying abilities, provides an opportunity to enhance quality of life for all. Taken to the extreme, this could literally enable people to live independently (in their own homes, surrounded by their own meaningful possessions) for as long as possible. We cannot afford to overlook and diminish the impact potential failed user-product relationships have on the individual. Living independently, on one's own terms, becomes challenged by thoughtless food packaging, home appliances, difficult to fasten clothing and so on.

Emotional sustainability

Emotion drives reason more than reason drives emotion.
– Hill, 2010, p15

Emotional sustainability requires products to satisfy existing, emerging and foreseeable needs (both functional and emotional). The functional needs tend to be more tangible, while the emotional needs can be more visceral and elusive. Supra-functionality refers to emotional, cultural, aspirational and social needs. These may not be measurable, but that does not render them any less critical for the user; Calne (1999, p215) notes that 'The essential difference between emotion and reason is that emotion leads to actions while reason leads to conclusions.'

Only measuring what is measureable can remove the essence from user experience that would make the difference. The individual may not even consciously be aware they have such needs but an empathic designer within a new product development team needs to ensure a product, service or environment supports the user beyond immediate use, and object utility.

If the products one is surrounded with privately (e.g. at home), semi-publicly (e.g. work environment) and publicly (e.g. public transport, access to building) are not empowering, enabling or ensuring independent living, they are probably diminishing quality of life, level of independent living and ultimately disadvantaging the individual.

Unwanted birthday and/or Christmas gifts tend to strike a chord with individuals from different age groups, cultures and backgrounds. A gift is typically given with love and friendship, yet at the same time, if it does not match or fulfil our emotional needs, it can come to symbolise disconnects between how one views themselves, and how your friends and family view you. This is not about economic value (e.g. how much the gift costs) but rather, how the gift does not fit into our material landscape.

Trying to live with a product purchase that fails to meet our needs can strip us of our dignity; it can interrupt our daily tasks, extend the amount of time completing tasks and diminish future purchasing choices. A product that fails to deliver what we need from it can sometimes feel like a failed (product) relationship; often you even grieve a little before you finally dispose of it. For many rational thinkers this may seem extreme, but you are sharing your life, your intimate personal space with these objects. In this way, products are critical props in our life stories.

Enhancing functionality

One performance indicator of a person developing their independence is being able to dress themselves. As we age, possibly develop disabilities (e.g. reduced hand grip and dexterity, reduced sensitivity in our finger trips) we begin to experience new challenges with clothing that diminishes independence. Difficulty with opening and closing zips, fastening buttons, tying shoe laces, applying make-up and, what has to be one of the most challenging activities of all, pulling up the zip on the back of a dress. Yet with more thoughtful design, we can continue to wear the clothes we enjoy throughout our full life span, regardless of diminished abilities. By enhancing functionality, for all age groups, brands can develop and accompany individuals throughout their lives and design products that more effectively meet their changing needs.

Twenty years ago, Velcro was a relatively stigmatised material as it was associated with assistive technology, such as products for the elderly. Walk down any high street today, however, and you will notice Velcro has gone mainstream. It is used in high priced, prestigious fashion apparel, performance sports shoes and quality luggage. This would indicate that all age groups benefit from ease of use and efficiency, but also that 'stigma' associated with materials and processes can, indeed, be overcome. In the process, the additional choice for all leads to more stylish and appropriate foot wear for all age groups with diverse abilities.

Buttons can also be a significant barrier to purchase and use for all ages. Rarely are they large enough for the average hand, and they are not shaped to offer the user significant purchase in order to locate the button through the fabric. What happens over time is that ageing users begin to avoid purchasing clothes with such tricky elements. This is extremely disappointing on many levels. Clothing companies are missing out on a key target group, ageing users have their purchasing choices significantly diminished and brands lose their appeal. By rethinking fasteners for clothing, brands can become reinvigorated.

Gradual journey into disability

As our abilities begin to change over our life span, one needs to be aware of how our personal material landscape impacts our daily life … The author realised recently that she had personally been avoiding buttons for several years due to limited grip and dexterity in her hands. This feels like a gradual journey into disability, and ageing. The following image (Figure 18.2) illustrates an alternative to buttons that is both stylish and does not scream 'this person has diminished abilities'. Being able to dress yourself in the clothes that have meaning for the individual is a critical element in feeling, and being, independent.

Two main areas of products that are in need of exploration and development are food packaging and medical/health related products. For many of us, we have experienced the frustration of attempting to open food packaging that has been less than an enjoyable experience. Cereal (such as granola) being flung around the kitchen while you attempt to wrestle with the airtight bag. Food that is stored in either the freezer or refrigerator requires another level of skill, as the product can now be both cold and slippery. Having to purchase additional devices to assist the user in opening basic food packaging is not acceptable, on any level. Poor user experience, poor functionality and – this has to be said – poor design.

We are living in an ageing world, where increased use of medication is becoming the new norm for many. What is surprising is how difficult medication packaging can be for the vast majority of people, young and old. With attention to detail, this type of thoughtfulness and user-centred design results in increased sales. The following example illustrates (Figure 18.3) how a manufacturer has packaged medication for pain that actually seems to acknowledge that when you reach for such a product you may not be feeling your best. The medicine relieves the pain of arthritis and recognises the difficulty many users experience trying to open such containers. The lid was designed specifically for users with arthritis; by wrapping a thin layer of silicone around the lid in a relatively stylish manner, the product is not screaming 'disability' but rather inviting all members of a family, young and old, the opportunity to access the medication. Additionally attention was paid to the bottle itself to ensure the user could more effectively grip the oval, than in the case of the more classic 'round' form. The Arthritis Foundation awarded this design an 'Ease of Use' Commendation.

Thoughtful and sensitively designed outcomes can open up the market for the manufacturer, and contribute to the vast population living independently for longer. Abandoning the conventional wisdom of the dominant group (also referred to as COWDUNG) (Waddington, 1977) we as designers need to reimagine how we can make the most mundane moments in the day, truly satisfying, and meaningful, for all.

Figure 18.2 Alternative to buttons, metal bar and hoop as clothes fastener (top, fastened; bottom, unfastened)

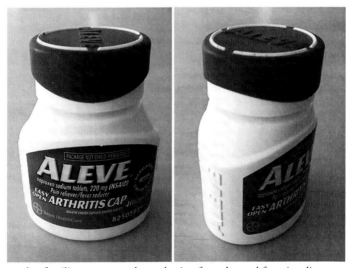

Figure 18.3 Example of a silicon wrap on the packaging for enhanced functionality

Conclusion

As our consumer base is growing older and living longer, products need to offer meaning over a longer time period, and to a wider array of user types. More people than ever will be within the age group 55–75 years of age, who may be 'empty nesters' or recently retired, seeking new and deeper meaning to life. Products that fail to offer meaning beyond their functional use will become waste very quickly – they will be abandoned, underused and/or misused, and/or not purchased at all. The concept of what is considered 'functional' needs to expand to encompass less tangible needs, to ensure the product development process is inclusive and effective for all. Design outcomes that offer a balanced approach, of both functional and emotional needs for the consumer, tend to be more intuitive to use, offer value beyond the functional and provide a meaningful addition to a person's material landscape.

Emotional sustainability goes beyond tangible design considerations such as the choice of material, the manufacturing process, and so on. It is a mind-set that provides the user with multiple layers of meaning within a product. Enabling the product to be customised, updated and/or refreshed thus reflecting the users current stage in life, not only the stage when they originally purchased the product. Designers have a unique opportunity to respond to user needs and deliver meaning through products, services and environments. Striking an effective balance between functionality and supra-functionality is key to achieving emotionally sustainable design.

Moving forward, designers need to consider the following:

- Users purchase meaning not just function
- Broad range of abilities should be able to engage with products
- The material landscape impacts the individual significantly
- The life stages of the user matter enormously
- Encourage longer and deeper user-product relationships
- Enhance functionality for all

We need to ensure the products, services and environments we create, meet existing user needs (as we are now), emerging needs (as we will be in the near future) and the unforeseeable needs (as we may become due to an accident or ageing). Designers have the unique opportunity to empower the user and bring more meaning to the products we engage with every day. Let those daily tasks become opportunities for joy and empowerment.

References

Calne, D. B. (1999) *Within Reason: Rationality and Human Behavior*, New York: Pantheon.

Chapman, J. (2005) *Emotionally Durable Design: Objects, Experiences and Empathy*, London: Earthscan.

Cooper Marcus, C. (2006) *House As a Mirror of Self: Exploring the Deeper Meaning of Home*, Lake Worth, FL: Nicholas-Hays.

Hecht, A. (2001) Home Sweet Home: Tangible Memories of an Uprooted Childhood, in D. Miller (ed.), *Home Possessions: Material Culture Behind Closed Doors*, Oxford: Berg, pp123–145.

Hill, D. (2010) *Emotionomics: Leveraging Emotions for Business Success*, 2nd edn, Philadelphia, PA: Kogan Press.

Loe, M. (2011) *Aging our Way: Independent Elders, Independent Lives*, New York: Oxford University Press.

McDonagh, D. (2015) Design Students Foreseeing the Unforeseeable: Practice Based Empathic Research Methods, *International Journal of Education Through Art*, 11(3): pp421-431.

McDonagh, D., Thomas, J., Sears, S. and Peña-Mora, F. (2010) Empathic Design Research Strategy: People With Disabilities Designing for All, in A. Silva and R. Simoes (eds), *Handbook of Research*

Trends in Product Design and Development: Technological and Organizational Perspectives, Hershey, PA: IGI Global, pp58–79.

Miller, D. (ed.) (2001) *Home Possessions: Material Culture Behind Closed Doors*, Oxford: Berg.

Rapaille, C. (2006) *The Culture Code: An Ingenious Way To Understand Why People Around The World Live And Buy As They Do*, New York: Broadway.

Verganti, R. (2009) *Design-Driven Innovation: Changing the Rules of Competition by Radically Innovating What Things Mean*, Boston, MA: Harvard Business Press.

Waddington, C. H. (1977) *Tools for Though,* St Albans: Paladin.

Wolfe, D. and Snyder, R. E. (2003) *Ageless Marketing: Strategies for Reaching the Hearts & Minds of the New Customer Majority*, Chicago, IL: Dearborn.

19

PLEASANT EXPERIENCES AND SUSTAINABLE DESIGN

Juan Carlos Ortíz Nicolás

Abstract

User experience aims to understand how people make sense of products, services or interfaces. A relevant issue in user experience is to investigate the goodness and pleasantness of experiences in human–product interaction. This chapter outlines four aspects of pleasant experience that are relevant to human–product interaction and are infrequently considered in the design of sustainable products: *hedonic adaptation*, *positive emotions*, *pragmatic and significant experiences*, and *the role of context in the user experience*. The chapter describes in detail these four aspects and suggests ideas that designers may consider to enhance pleasant experiences in the design and use of sustainable products.

Keywords: pleasant experiences, user experience, sustainable design, experience design

Introduction

In the current context, humans use thousands of products during their lifetime. For example, cars, computers, ticket machines, blenders, furniture and so forth. The reasons to use them are many (e.g. to explore, to communicate or to learn). From the many products that people are in touch with every day, they remember, maintain and collect just a few. The reasons to keep them may be related to the appearance of the product, others may be clever solutions for a particular task or are mementos of a person or event; in other words, we maintain products that are meaningful to the self (Csikszentmihaly and Rochberg-Halton, 1981).

In the field of user experience an object that is meaningful to the self has been linked to an object that helps a person grow and flourish (Ortíz Nicolas, Aurisicchio and Desmet, 2013a). For example, a musical instrument that allows a person to become the musician they want to be. In a similar line, scholars have suggested that products should elicit experiences that have a positive effect on people (Hassenzahl, 2010). Recent research has shown that people prefer to be in touch with products that enhance an overall pleasant experience (Desmet, 2012; Diller, Shedroff and Rhea, 2005). A general definition of this term is a positive evaluation of the Human–Product Interaction. Professional designers are also interested in learning methods to design pleasant experiences (Porter, Chhibber and Porter, 2008; Ortíz Nicolas,

Aurisicchio and Desmet, 2013c). Nevertheless, it seems that at present, designers rely predominantly on approaches based on their intuition and personal knowledge of positive emotions and pleasant experiences (Porter, Chhibber and Porter, 2008; Chhibber Porter, Porter and Healey, 2004; Ortíz Nicolás, Aurisicchio and Desmet, 2013c). Industry can also benefit from pleasant experiences. A study of consumers' complaints by Den Ouden and colleagues (2006) revealed that businesses commonly deal with customer complaints based on an instrumental approach (i.e. ensuring that products effectively meet the technical specifications). More so, their study identified a rise in non-technical complaints (e.g. expectations, and desires of the customer). Several of these complaints resulted in goods being returned within a just a few days of purchase. The authors conclude that the traditional way of looking at product quality and reliability is no longer suitable for handling those type of complaints. A way to handle them is to better understand consumers' experiences in all the phases of their interaction with the artefact, as it will help capture the various complex motivations and reasons for dissatisfaction.

User experience is relevant to sustainable product design because it can influence the acceptance or rejection of designed products based on sustainable methods. A factor that defines the valence of an experience as pleasant or unpleasant is emotions. Research in the field of emotions has indicated that they are actionable (Frijda, 1986). Therefore, a person can reject a product that elicits disgust or approach one that elicits inspiration, for example. It is important for designers to reflect on the desired actions that users may have with the products that they design. Therefore, a planned strategy to make people notice sustainable products is to consider what positive emotions the product should elicit to stimulate feelings of approachability.

Another reason to consider pleasant experiences in the design of sustainable products is that they help designers consider how users see and understand products. For example, users may become more interested in cooking tasty dishes for relatives, and to achieve their goal they will use a set of products (pans, spoons, stoves, etc.). It is common that such products are a means to complete tasks or activities that are relevant for the user. Activities and tasks, therefore, can be considered in the design of products based on interaction characteristics (e.g. how products should be designed to enhance a fluent cooking experience). User experience insight is relevant to sustainable product design because it considers the nature of highly involved experiences within human–product interaction. If the experiences are pleasant the user may accept (keep) the product, if they are negative the user may reject (discard) it. Clearly, the social and ecological implications of this behavioural cycle are significant.

The aim of this chapter is to expose how user experience can more effectively align with sustainable design to help create products that respect the desires and motives of humans. To achieve the latter the focus is placed on pleasant experiences. The chapter outlines four key aspects that have been identified in the study of pleasant experiences in human–product interaction, yet are rarely considered in the actual design of sustainable products.

This chapter is divided into four main sections. The first presents an explanation of user experience and pleasant experiences with products. The second section describes in detail the four aspects related to pleasant experiences and suggests ideas that designers may consider to enhance them in the design of sustainable products. The third section discusses the findings generated through research into these areas. Finally, the fourth section draws conclusions and proposes future directions.

A brief introduction to user experience

User experience is part of *human experience* and its interests are on technology (McCarthy and Wright, 2004; Mahlke and Thuring, 2007), interactive products (Hassenzahl, 2010; Forlizzi and Battarbee, 2004), products (Desmet and Hekkert, 2007; Gentner, Bouchard and Favart, 2013) in synthesis within artefacts (Ortíz Nicolas and Aurisicchio, 2011). In this way, user experience can be understood as the overall impression and evaluation that results from a complex and vivid phenomenon that occurs when a person interacts with an artefact in a particular context. In principle, it is subjective and therefore is influenced by the personal characterises of the user. Furthermore, user experience emerges from the intertwined works of perception, action, motivation, emotion and cognition in dialogue with the world (i.e. place, time, people and objects; Hassenzahl, 2010).

Research into user experience attempts to understand how users make sense of products in a particular context and time. For example, McCarthy and Wright (2004) have presented four threads of experience: *sensual*, *emotional*, *compositional* and *spatio-temporal*. The *sensual* thread is concerned with the sensorial engagement with a given situation. The *emotional* thread is concerned with the judgments of value that users ascribe to products based on their particular needs and desires. The *compositional* thread is concerned with relationships between the parts, and the whole, of an experience (e.g. the characteristic of a mobile phone and the relations between these, the user and the setting). The *spatio-temporal* thread distinguishes between public and private space, and recognizes comfort zones and boundaries between the self and others, or between temporal notions of present and future. At least four elements impact the experience with artefacts: the user, the interaction, the artefact, and the context (Ortíz Nicolás and Aurisicchio, 2011; Gentner, Bouchard and Favart, 2013). Users bring their knowledge, senses, values, emotions and needs to the experience. The resulting interaction is the basic relationship that binds the user and the artefact. The artefact is an object made by a human being(s) that performs technical and non-technical functions. The context is the scenario where the interaction occurs (Ortíz Nicolas and Aurisicchio, 2011).

Pleasant experiences with products

Pleasure has been linked to physical (e.g. enjoying food), ideological (e.g. reading a novel), social (e.g. being with friends) and psychological (e.g. solving a puzzle) aspects in product design (Jordan, 2000). The work of Jordan has had significant impact in user experience research. He was one of the first scholars to acknowledge the role of pleasure in human–product interactions and to suggest how pleasure can be considered in design practice. One of the limitations of his work, however, is that it maintains a general concept of pleasure (Desmet, 2012).

In the field of user experience it is relevant to understand what makes a good experience. Hassenzahl (2010) argues that the experience-oriented approach can be useful to understand what makes an experience positive, pleasurable and good, as well as to try to deliver pleasant experiences through product design (Hassenzahl and Tractinsky, 2006). For example, Blythe and Hassenzahl (2003, p95) explain that pleasant experiences are often related to objects and activities that are absorbing and personally meaningful – they contribute to the self-definition of users. More so, these experiences are long-lived (i.e. users tend to stick to objects and activities that allow them to enhance themselves). The focus on pleasant experiences has also theoretical support from other fields of research such as psychology. For example, Hektner and colleagues (2007) explain that the various theories that have flourished throughout the history of psychology suggest that individuals generally look for pleasure, and avoid pain. It can be expected, then, that users look for pleasant experiences with products. In addition, the focus on pleasant experiences implies a tendency towards a user's pursuit of well-being. In this line, scholars have suggested that a strong reason for understanding users' experiences with products is to improve their lives (Forlizzi and Battarbee, 2004; McCarthy and Wright, 2004; Law et al., 2008)

A pleasant experience with a product is a phenomenon that is influenced by many factors. The intensity of the experience and the involved emotions indicate that there are different levels of pleasure in human–product interactions; for example, a calm and relaxing experience versus an exciting one (Ortíz Nicolas, Aurisicchio and Desmet, 2014). A pleasant experience is influenced by the activities undertaken with products, the richness of the interaction, the product attributes (aesthetic, symbolic and instrumental functions), the needs fulfilled and the positive emotions triggered (Ortíz Nicolás, 2014). There is also some evidence to indicate that the most pleasant experiences with products are those that involve activities that are personally meaningful (Blythe and Hassenzahl, 2003; Ortíz Nicolás, 2014) and rely upon the user (active agency), not the product, as in the case of the experience that a person lives when playing the piano (Ortíz Nicolás, Aurisicchio and Desmet, 2013a) This supports the argument that design needs a shift in emphasis from products, to users (Jordan, 2003; Chapman, 2005; Hassenzahl, 2010; Ortiz Nicolás and Aurisicchio, 2011; Desmet, 2012).

How experience affects relationships with products

In this section I present how pleasant experiences can be used to influence sustainable design solutions. Alternatives to the design of pleasant experiences are also introduced in human–product interaction.

Hedonic adaptation

One of the core findings of subjective well-being research is that people adapt to material advances, requiring continued increases to achieve the same level of satisfaction (Brickman, Coates and Janoff-Bulman, 1978; Frederick and Loewenstein, 1999; van Boven and Gilovich, 2003). This phenomenon is called *hedonic adaptation* (Frederick and Loewenstein, 1999). For example, Chancellor and Lyubomirsky (2011) explain that a person enjoys a newly remodelled bathroom for a season, but over time it becomes less noticeable and brings fewer positive feelings. The bathroom that used to be new has now become ordinary and completely faded into the background of one's conscious experience.

Hedonic adaptation is a challenge for sustainable product design because the current alternatives to deal with it are based on refinements to an endless cycle of design, production and consumption. New solutions have to increase the level of satisfaction that the user has in comparison to the previous version of the product. In this context, a new, shiny and powerful product is launched into the market to replace the old one. This action accelerates the disposal of products because the consumer has a new alternative to upgrade his/her hedonic standards. Hedonic adaptation explains in some degree the phenomenon that Chapman (2005) identifies: the majority of products are still *working* when disposed. The current economic system – which to some degree, relies upon consumption – takes advantage of hedonic adaptation, by creating newer versions that are better in some way but accomplish the same need as their predecessors. This model is effective for economic reasons but ineffective for sustainability because it will never fulfil the consumer's hedonic needs, as they are permanently increasing. Chancellor and Lyubomirsky (2011) suggest that hedonic adaptation encourages overspending and indebtedness in the US, although we may suggest that the same occurs in many countries.

It is important that designers become more familiar with the phenomena of hedonic adaptation because they can suggest alternatives to diminish its effects, which ordinarily include the early disposal of products. There are products that deliver pleasurable experience to the user and the level of pleasure is maintained for a long period of time (e.g. a Rubik's cube). This product has been on the market since its invention in 1974 with good acceptance, and, the design has been hardly changed during this time. We suggest that this product has been designed in a way that diminishes hedonic adaptation. Based on the typology suggested by Jordan (2000), the Rubik's cube (Figure 19.1) delivers psychological pleasure (i.e. solving a puzzle). Analysing the product further by considering its appearance, interaction and involved activity the findings are: the appearance of the product does not change (i.e. the Rubik's cube is a cube before, during and after its use). The interaction is also constant, as users have to rotate the different faces of the cube during its use. The activity is constant, people have to solve the puzzle. The challenge, however, is different and it has to be solved by the user. The user is responsible to deal with the situation (i.e. active agency). Based on its properties of randomness, users work to solve new puzzles each time, therefore the pleasure to solve it is in some degree, always new.

There are other products that have been on the market for a long period of time and the design has not been modified (e.g. Lego bricks). This product also involves active agency, in which the user is responsible for creating something with the blocks. It also offers potentially limitless possibilities of creation. Designers then can consider how the products they create may deal with hedonic adaptation and formulate designs accordingly. For example, they can create a product that allows different configurations. From time-to-time the user will have the option to reorganise and customise it. Designers can also create products that allow different ways to interact with it (e.g. an MP3 that users can squeeze, press or punch to active its main functions). Designers can also develop products that are delivered in parts. This idea is better explained with the following analogy already suggested by Chancellor and Lyubomirsky (2011): a way to extend savouring a chocolate bar could be as simple as dividing it into squares and eating one piece per day instead of devouring it all in a single sitting. Research supports the idea that breaks are beneficial for positive experiences, such as enjoying a television programme, but detrimental for negative experiences, such as enduring a dental drill (Nelson et al., 2009; Chancellor and Lyubomirsky, 2011).

Figure 19.1 The Rubik's cube

Focusing on positive emotions

There is a shift in product design from a tool-oriented, to an experience-oriented, approach (Jordan, 2003; Hassenzahl, 2010). This shift has suggested that user experience should focus on the pleasant side of experience (Hassenzahl, 2010; Ortíz Nicolás and Aurisicchio, 2011). One way to accomplish this goal is to focus on positive emotions. Emotions are a promising aspect because they are at the heart of experience (Hassenzahl, 2010) and they colour it (McCarthy and Wright, 2004). In other words, emotions are a key factor that defines the experience as pleasant, or unpleasant. Therefore, an alternative to understand and design pleasant experiences is to focus on positive emotions.

In a study investigating pleasure and design, Porter et al. (2008) identified that designers tend to rely upon 'quick and dirty' research methods, with little awareness of techniques and data specifically related to user pleasure. In addition, these scholars also identified that designers expressed great interest in a 'resource' that would give them access to information about the emotional needs of specific user groups (ibid.). More recent studies have shown that, beyond their own tacit understanding, designers have little knowledge about positive emotions (Desmet, 2012) and that when they are trying to evoke emotions through their designs, they rely on self-referential approaches (i.e. experimentation or solid concept definition) (Ortíz Nicolás, Aurisicchio and Desmet, 2013c). Experimentation refers to trial and error processes aimed at identifying the triggers of a positive emotion, while solid concept definition to the early proposal of a concept waiting for it to 'connect' with the user and elicit positive emotions in him or her (ibid.). These findings confirm the interest of designers in emotions and the need to approach their study systematically.

Emotional design aims to intentionally elicit emotions in users through appropriately designed solutions. To fulfil this aim, a three-step process was identified based on previous research (Desmet and Dijkhuis, 2003; Demir, Desmet and Hekkert, 2010; Yoon, Desmet and van der Helm, 2011):

1 *Select a positive emotion:* Based on the characteristics of the project, one or several target emotions are selected to be evoked by the design solution.
2 *Understand the emotion:* Based on theoretical and empirical approaches, the selected emotion or emotions, are studied to understand their eliciting conditions.
3 *Create design solutions:* Based on the knowledge gathered in the previous step, designers create solutions that aim at eliciting the selected emotion or emotions.

Differently from previous research where emotions were investigated during the design project (step 2 of the design process – 'Understand the emotion'), we have studied and understood selected emotions in advance. The studied emotions were: *anticipation, confidence, inspiration* and *sympathy.* We carried out research to study the multi-componential characteristics of the positive emotions based on appraisal structures and thought-action tendencies (Ortíz Nicolas, 2014). Appraisal structures characterise internal or external aspects of an individual experiencing an emotion (Scherer, 2005). An example of an appraisal structure is motivation – the situation is consistent (or inconsistent) with what the person wants. Thought-action tendencies characterise behavioural and cognitive aspects of the individual experiencing an emotion (Fredrickson, 1998). For example, when experiencing fear it can be easily observed if people have an urge to flee (Frijda, 1986) With the data gathered, a plausible description of each emotion was obtained and later used to create a tool that explains in detail the experience of the emotions, and also the triggers of each of them (see Figure 19.2).

An interesting issue that was identified based on the emotions' thought-action tendencies was that participants to our study reported that they would maintain a product if it made them feel confidence. This is relevant to sustainable design because designers can aim to elicit confidence with a particular product as a strategy to stimulate people to keep the product instead of throwing it away, or repair it when it breaks. In relation to products that elicit inspiration it was identified that when the emotion is elicited in people they want to get their hands on the product that triggers the emotion. This is also relevant to sustainable design because it can be used as a strategy to draw attention towards sustainable products.

DESIGNING INSPIRATION

Inspiration is experienced when a person unexpectedly identifies with an idea, insight or object that shows them possibilities to grow and flourish.

APPRAISAL STRUCTURE	THOUGHT-ACTION TENDENCIES
When experiencing Inspiration: - The situation is consistent with what people want. - Under the reported situation it was unexpected to experience inspiration. - It is triggered by circumstances. - It increases self-esteem. - People have the power to control the situation, however, the outcome is unpredictable. - Mental effort is involved. - There is coping potential involved e.g. by using skill and knowledge to handle the situation.	When experiencing Inspiration people: - Identify with the situation/product. - Pay attention to the situation/ product. - They get their hands on the product. - They reflect on the situation/product. - They create as a result of feeling inspired - They open up about possibilities.

CONNECTION	FLOURISH	POSSIBILITIES	GRACE
- Create unexpected solutions that connect with the user. The connection can be regarding enjoyable activities such as reading, cooking, or cycling. - Explore solutions that 'connect' with the user in different levels, e.g. ideological, spiritual, or professional.	- Seek solutions that help people grow and flourish. - Seek solutions that trigger people's imagination. - Seek solutions that improve people's current situation. - Consider how to involve a future positive expectancy.	- Challenge users by presenting them new possibilities, e.g. a lamp that uses a new and sustainable source of energy. - Stimulate people to reflect about an interesting topic, e.g. people can reflect on a product when it is manufactured with a new process. - Stimulate opportunities for self-expression and creation. - Create solutions that are flexible in its outcome, e.g. Lego bricks are a source of several possibilities.	- Design solutions that allow people create beauty. - Seek smart solutions, that are ingenious and original. - Seek solutions that allow users to focus on their source of inspiration, e.g. by creating transparent interactions. - Create beautiful products in terms of appearance and interaction.

Figure 19.2 A tool that aims to communicate how people experience inspiration

A tool that we developed based on the gain data of the studied emotions is called the 'design ingredients tool'. It provides a rich and multi-component description of an emotion (see Figure 19.2). It can be seen that the tool includes:

1 appraisal themes;
2 appraisal structures;
3 thought-action tendencies; and
4 design ingredients (i.e. ideas that designers could consider and use to evoke an emotion).

Detailed information on the study of the emotions, as well as the tools developed for each emotion, can be found in Ortíz Nicolás (2014). The outlined process and tools were evaluated by product designers in a workshop, the details of which can be found in (Ortíz Nicolas, Aurisicchio and Desmet, 2013b). Designers reported that the process helped them frame the design task from an emotional perspective, and create solutions accordingly. For example, confidence can be triggered by the good performance of the product or by the act of overcoming a challenge with the help of a product. These triggers point out strong differences in relation to the designed products. For example, eliciting confidence based on a product that works well focuses on the product, while eliciting confidence based on challenges focuses on the user. The design process emerging from this research proposes a systematic approach that represents an alternative to the self-referential approaches that designers commonly rely upon. Product designers also positively evaluated these tools; explaining that the tools provided a structured view of emotions, which helped focus on the design process and support decision making. Designers also indicated that a benefit is related to the detailed knowledge of an emotion that the tools provide. The multi-componential research of emotions is an alternative to generate reliable data. The gained knowledge can later be used to design emotional products that enhance a pleasant experience.

The role of the context to define design challenges

User experience is holistic in principle (McCarthy and Wright, 2004; Hassenzahl, 2010; Ortíz Nicolás and Aurisicchio, 2011). A key factor that impacts on the experience is the context. By studying user experience in a particular setting, new services or products can be suggested to improve the experience. Identifying unfulfilled needs in a particular situation could be a great start to create sustainable solutions. In this line, I align with Chapman (2005, p10) who mentions that in times in which product development and innovation have predominantly focused on technology and away from users it is important to understand how to provide experiences that impact on users' lives.

User experience takes place in a context. When users interact with an artefact they are not only influenced by the product, but also by the context in which the interaction takes place. In the field of user experience Forlizzi (2007) indicates that context is understood as a complex, dynamic set of factors including the social, historical and cultural. Based on a literature review six sub-elements of context have been identified in the field of user experience: physical, systemic, social, cultural, situational and temporal (Ortíz Nicolás and Aurisicchio, 2011). Taking into account the role of context in the design of sustainable products, it is important to create solutions that are fit for that context. Bloch (1995), for instance, identified that societal and cultural aspects influence the physical form of a product, which is an unquestioned determinant of its market success.

It is well known that design aims at fulfilling users' needs, and this is a fundamental value that product designers develop during their training. Outside of the discipline of design, however, this view is often challenged. Jean Baudrillard (1969) mentions that there is an inexhaustible mine of imaginary solutions to stereotyped needs. It is difficult to deny the latter when many designers aim to design a new chair (i.e. a product that fulfils a stereotyped need). The solution itself may be new and designers may succeed to create a personal style or mark. It is valid that designers explore their interests, however, from a sustainability point of view it could be questioned if there is a real need to create a new chair when there are already great solutions on the market. Studying the context in which the user experience occurs has the potential to identify needs that are not fulfilled, or are not stereotyped. This can be a great key to engaging with sustainable product design.

Let us assume that a group of designers have to redesign a hospital bed. This bed is used in a particular physical space with particular characteristics (i.e. physical context). The bed is also part of a system of products (e.g. a heart scanners, oxygen machines, trolleys). The room in which the bed is located is used by different people (e.g. patients, nurses, and medical doctors) and for different purposes (e.g. to recover, to check, or to attend). This is what we called the social context. The cultural context is related to the conventions that a group of people share (e.g. values, languages, norms). In the case of the design of a new bed, the cultural context could be considered in the use of icons and language. The situational context is related to the set of circumstances in which a person is during the experience. In this line, there are beds that are used to recover and others that are used in surgery. By taking into account the different sub-elements of the context and analysing them it is possible to identify current problems that could be avoided in the new solution. For example, in relation to the systemic context, the bed can be designed to avoid any hassle related to the connection with other devices. In relation to the social context, it can consider the role that nurses have in the treatment of the patient by observing how they work, the reports that they created and so forth. It may be that nurses, who work in different shifts, use the bed as communication channel, leaving notes for nurses on the next shift. By acknowledging the role of the context in the user experience the solution can be designed to fit in the context, and be more closely related to the needs of patients, medical doctors and nurses. In other words, by including the role of the context in the design solution, the user experience can be significantly enhanced.

In the previous example we focused on a particular product, but we could also have focussed on a particular space (e.g. intensive therapy or the room to treat third degree burns). The study of the context is relevant for sustainable product design because it can help to develop user-oriented products. This is in comparison to products that are designed to meet (supposed) market needs as a way to maintain economic growth.

Significant experiences

It is well known that people assign meaning to products, or objects. Moreover, many designers aim to create products that have a positive impact on people's lives. In a previous study I explored how people experience great products. Eighteen respondents participated to the study. No explanation of *great* was given because I aimed to understand how users valued products. The only condition was that the respondents had to select a product from his/her point of view was *great*. I also prepared an in-depth interview to study the experience that the product enhances in the user (Ortíz Nicolás, 2014). The data was analysed and two types of experiences with great products were identified: *pragmatic* and *significant* (Ortíz Nicolás, Aurisicchio and Desmet, 2013a).

Eight experiences were classed as *pragmatic*. Participants explained that the greatness of their products is linked to how well the products perform their instrumental functions (i.e. what the product is meant to do). They also reported that the products were easy to use and that they did not need special skills to use them. Other product attributes, such as appearance or novelty, were seen as extras but not the core of the experience. The large majority of the participants (7) whose experiences were classed as pragmatic indicated that they were not emotionally attached to the product that they chose.

Ten experiences were classed as *significant*. Participants explained that the greatness of the products is related to how suitable the products are for them (i.e. how well they adapt to the users). They explained that with the help of their products they can express themselves, for example, by creating new music or pictures, and do enjoyable activities. They also reported that in order to use the products they refined or developed some skills (e.g. playing the piano, or mixing music). This indicates that users have an active role in human–product interaction, and that participants to this research seem to be aware of it. In addition most of the participants (6) reported that they were emotionally attached to the products because they were either mementos of happy times (e.g. a gift) or of enjoyable activities (e.g. playing music with an instrument). In addition, the large majority of the participants (9) reported that the products reflected something about themselves (e.g. their personal interests and creativity).

The term *significant*, as used to characterise this experience, refers to a constructive view of human experience involving five key aspects (namely: active agency, order, self, social-symbolic relatedness and lifespan) and was taken from constructive psychology (Mahoney, 2004). This view emphasizes the importance of meaningful actions by a developing self in complex and unfolding relationships (ibid.). In the following paragraphs I explain in detail the five aspects that Mahoney identified as part of significant experiences. After each explanation an example extracted from the data (the selected product was a Polaroid camera; Figure 19.3) is presented. By following this approach I aim to suggest the relevant aspects to consider when aiming at enhancing significant experiences in human–product interactions.

Figure 19.3 A Polaroid camera that enhances a significant experience

First, human experiencing involves continuous *active agency*, meaning that the user is responsible to direct the situation:

> I only use it for very special occasions. It is not something like my phone that I would carry all the time. It is something that I use because I have been thinking about. I have to plan in advance, it is not that I have it in my pocket and use it, then that is even more special because the film itself is very expensive so I can't use it whenever. That's what makes it very precious. I have to think when to use it, and treasure it.

Second, *order* reflects the contention that much human activity is devoted to meaning-making processes. This is a more complex aspect, however, designers can approach this aspect by undertaking problems that are significant for people (e.g. sustainability, poverty, or joy):

> I think the product does [reflect something about her] because not many people would bother getting a Polaroid camera and it needs a lot of research and patience, it is an investment of time. For example, a decent digital camera costs maybe £300 today and to be honest, I would rather spend £10 on my Polaroid and £190 on the film and have all those photos in my hands. The fact of being able to take a photo, have it straight away, pass it around, keep it and maybe give to someone as a present is amazing. It means a lot to me.

Third, the organization of personal activity is fundamentally *self-referent*. This is why user experience is relevant to understand how people live/understand a particular phenomenon:

> [A great product is] something that is suitable for you and that you use very often and do not get bored of. It also needs to be something you are comfortable with … it is really funny because it also contributes to my identity, I think.

Fourth, individuals cannot be understood apart from their organic embeddedness in *social and symbolic* systems. Any design solution should be contextually related in order to create significant experiences:

> I love to take pictures of people when they do not know that I am taking a picture of them. I also surprise people and take a picture of them. I did it once when I took a picture of a friend after I just told her happy birthday, she was surprised.

Finally, all of this active, meaningful and socially embedded self-organization reflects an ongoing developmental flow of the experience (i.e. *lifespan*). In other words the experience is dynamic, and in order to create a significant experience the design solution has to envision how it is going to develop over time:

> I still consider it as great as on the first day. Even though, I saw other cameras that had better features but their prices were over £100 and I was like 'aaaaaah, what if I had seen this one before', but now I really like mine: it does everything I want it to do, and I have some memories, so it is an even greater product.

The considerations involved in designing pragmatic and significant experiences are different. In the former, the designer can focus on creating a product that excels at its instrumental function and interaction. In the latter, the designer has to consider that there are many factors involved (i.e. active agency, order, self, social-symbolic relatedness and lifespan). A way to solve active agency, for example, is by creating solutions that stimulate users to have the control over the product. The five factors involved in significant experiences can be used as a guide to design them.

Discussion

In this chapter I have shown how pleasant experiences can contribute to the design of sustainable products. Pleasant experiences offer alternatives to overcome problems that product-centred approaches, such as product lifecycle, have. One problem may be that a product that is perfectly defined based on product lifecycle analysis can be rejected if it frustrates the user.

Pleasant experiences are valuable to sustainable design solutions because they can influence the acceptance of designed products based on sustainable methods. For instance, designing for particular positive emotions have different effects on the human–product interaction. Eliciting confidence through product design may stimulate people to keep the product with them until it stops working, or breaks. Eliciting inspiration may be used as a strategy to draw attention towards the product, because it will excite users and they may approach it. Understanding pleasant experiences offer alternatives to deal with phenomenon such as hedonic adaptation. The current alternatives to deal with it are based on an endless and ecologically destructive cycle of design, production and consumption. New solutions have to increase the level of satisfaction that the person has in comparison to the previous version of the product. Designers can suggest alternatives to diminish the effects of hedonic adaptation (e.g. early disposal of products).

Finally, pleasant experiences are context related. Understanding the context in which the solution is going to coexist can be beneficial to creating better solutions (e.g. those that are fit for the context). Another benefit is that designers can identify needs that are not fulfilled, and are not stereotyped. This can be a great start to achieving sustainable product design.

The four examples that I have used to clarify the role of pleasant experiences in sustainable product design may be relevant for particular situations (e.g. pragmatic experiences for medical devices). On the other hand, products that aim to enhance a significant experience may be those that can help people flourish (e.g. musical instruments). It can also be that a company decides to diminish the launch of new products into the market. Thus, the solutions can consider how to diminish hedonic adaptation as a strategy to maintain people's satisfaction for a long period of time. Designers, therefore, have to carefully consider which strategy is suitable for the particular challenge that they are dealing with, at any given time.

During recent years, product design processes have been challenged because they focus on the instrumental function of the product (Jordan, 2003, pxii). This approach, focusing on human physical and cognitive capabilities, has delivered artefacts that have helped users perform tasks with an emphasis on instrumental function. Rafaeli and Vilnai-Yavetz (2004) have noted that if not satisfied, the instrumental functions of an artefact tend to elicit negative emotions (e.g. frustration). However, if adequately implemented, they do not necessarily promote positive emotions either (e.g. fun). Therefore, the design of products has to consider other relevant issues. For instance, it has been identified that human hopes, fears, dreams, feelings and self-image are important in the design of products (Jordan, 2000;

Chapman, 2005). In other words, functionality, sustainability, usability and pleasure are different attributes of a product, and they have to be aligned to create a pleasant experience (Hassenzahl, 2010). In addition, the design process needs to be modified. A typical way to start the design process consists of writing a brief that states the functions that the product has to perform (e.g. instrumental and aesthetic) (see Crilly, Maier and Clarkson, 2008). A limitation of this approach is that *thinking of* different functions and designing them as separate elements neglects an important aspect such as the experience delivered by the product. Indeed, it has been suggested that consumers are more interested in the overall experience provided by an artefact than in the specific functions that it performs (Chapman, 2005, p19). Thus, an approach that considers the experience of users is needed in design. This chapter suggests four such approaches to consider and design the overall pleasant experience.

Experience design, however, is a complex task, as designers have to develop skills to include the experience during their design process. For example, it has been suggested that designing an experience is a question of balance. Changing the weight of one feature will have an effect on all of the others (Costello and Edmonds, 2007). Therefore, designers have to develop skills to create balanced solutions in relation to the aimed experience. Similarly, the potential solution has to consider how to balance the role of pleasant experiences with current sustainable design methods (e.g. biomimicry, cradle to cradle, product lifecycle analysis) to create integral products. For example, lifecycle analysis could be considered a tool to measure the environmental consequences of a product. Biomimicry, on the other hand, inspires design. These two approaches deal with sustainable design from a different perspective. Interestingly, in both cases considering the design of pleasant experiences can complement the overall solution. To integrate pleasant experiences and sustainable design, multidisciplinary teams may be required. People with different perspectives can help create more balanced and integral solutions. It has to be acknowledged that user experience aims to create products that are human centred, not market oriented. This means that solutions have to be created based on the needs of the user instead of the needs of the market. This is particularly relevant for hedonic adaptation, which has thus far been primarily used to stimulate the pace of consumption. A new product is exciting at first but people adapt and get used to it quickly. Therefore, a new product is launched into the market which promotes fresh excitement and fast consumption. Hedonic adaptation explains, to some degree, why people continue to purchase and possess, yet never reaching a point when their life is sufficiently pleasurable and satisfying. The consequence is run away materialism, in which more and more money is spent and less and less happiness is derived from it (Chancellor and Lyubomirsky, 2011). It has to be acknowledged, however, that any approach that challenges consumption may not be so readily accepted by industry.

There is evidence to show that experiences are better at making people happy in comparison to material possessions (van Boven, 2005). An example of an experience is a holiday trip with friends and family. Experiences are better at making people happy because they are more open to positive reinterpretations, are a more meaningful part of one's identity and contribute more to successful social relationships (van Boven, 2005). In addition, experiences are difficult to compare (e.g. is it possible to compare my holidays in relation to my friends?). Comparison, however, is possible with products. Take for example cars, each year a new model hits the market and the user can compare all their features and qualities. The issue that I want to point out is that products are an element of our experiences and only some can influence people's happiness. In our holiday trip we may want to record pictures with our friends that later will remind us the nice time that we have together. To record a picture we need a material possession (i.e. a camera). This does not mean that the camera automatically adds to my happiness. Research in user experience has identified that products enhance particular experiences (e.g. autonomy, relatedness and so forth; Hassenzahl, Diefenbach and Göritz, 2010), and that only some experiences enhance product attachment (i.e. significant experiences; Ortíz Nicolás, Aurisicchio and Desmet, 2013a). We therefore can speculate that particular products help a person flourish and grow and only these add in some degree to his/her happiness. The latter case shows the importance of considering human hopes, dreams and motivations in the design of sustainable products (Jordan, 2003; Chapman, 2005; Hassenzahl, 2010).

Conclusions

Pleasant experiences and sustainable design deal with relevant issues for humankind. Throughout this chapter I have identified potential benefits that support the inclusion of pleasant experiences in the design of sustainable products. For instance, products that enhance significant experiences stimulate product attachment. This is relevant to sustainability because this phenomenon can avoid the early disposal of products. In addition, in this chapter I have characterised pleasant experiences and have suggested some strategies to design products that will elicit them. By providing designers with detailed knowledge about pleasant experiences I believe to have contributed to making the challenge of designing them more feasible.

To fully embrace sustainable product design there is a need to employ multidisciplinary approaches. In this line user experience is an important contributor. I would like to conclude this chapter by suggesting that the development of new products should not only rely on economic reasons but also on the potential benefits for society and the living environment. User experience is a powerful and effective means to create such products.

References

Baudrillard, J. (1969) *El sistema de los objetos*, Siglo XXI, Mexico City

Bloch, P. H. (1995) 'Seeking the Ideal Form: Product Design and Consumer Response', *Journal of Marketing*, vol. 59, no. 3, pp16–29

Blythe, M. A. and Hassenzahl, M. (2003) 'The Semantics of Fun: Differentiating Enjoyable Experiences', in Blythe, M. A., Overbeeke, K., Monk, A. F., and Wright, P. C. (eds.), *Funology from Usability to Enjoyment*, Kluwer Academic Publishers, London, pp91–100.

Brickman, P., Coates, D. and Janoff-Bulman, R. (1978) 'Lottery Winners and Accident Victims: Is Happiness Relative?' *Journal of Personality and Social Psychology*, vol. 36, no. 8, pp917–927

Chancellor, J. and Lyubomirsky, S. (2011) 'Happiness and Thrift: When (Spending) Less is (Hedonically) More', *Journal of Consumer Psychology*, vol. 21, no. 2, pp131–138

Chapman, J. (2005) *Emotionally Durable Design. Objects, Experiences, and Empathy*, Earthscan, London

Chhibber, S., Porter, C. S., Porter, J. M. and Healey, L. (2004) 'Designing Pleasure; Designers' Needs', in *Proceedings of the Fourth International Conference on Design and Emotion*, Ankara

Costello, B. and Edmonds, E. (2007). 'A Study in Play, Pleasure and Interaction Design', in *Proceedings of the 2007 Conference on Designing Pleasurable Products and Interfaces*, August, Helsinki, pp76–91

Crilly, N., Maier A. and Clarkson P. J. (2008) 'Representing Artefacts as Media: Modelling the Relationship between Designer Intent and Consumer Experience', *International Journal of Design*, vol. 2, no. 3, pp15–27

Csikszentmihalyi, M. and Rochberg-Halton, E. (1981) '*The Meaning of Things: Domestic Symbols and the Self*,' Cambridge University Press, MA

Demir, E., Desmet, P. M. A. and Hekkert, P. (2009) 'Appraisal Patterns of Emotions in Human–Product Interaction' *International Journal of Design*, vol. 3, no. 2, pp41–51

Den Ouden, E., Yuan, L., Sonnemans, P. J. and Brombacher, A. C. (2006) 'Quality and Reliability Problems from a Consumer's Perspective: An Increasing Problem Overlooked by Businesses?', *Quality and Reliability Engineering International*, vol. 22, no. 7, pp821–838

Desmet, P. M. A. (2012) 'Faces of Product Pleasure: 25 Positive Emotions in Human–Product Interactions' *International Journal of Design*, vol. 6, no. 2, pp1–29

Desmet, P. M. A. and Dijkhuis, E. (2003) 'A Wheelchair Can be Fun', in *Proceedings of the 2003 International Conference on Designing Pleasurable Products and Interfaces-DPPI '03*, New York, pp22–27

Desmet, P. M. A. and Hekkert, P. (2007) 'Framework of Product Experience', *International Journal of Design* Vol 1, no. 1, pp 57–66.

Diller, S., Shedroff, N. and Rhea, D. (2005) *Making Meaning: How Successful Businesses Deliver Meaningful Customer Experiences*, New Riders, San Francisco, CA

Forlizzi, J. (2007) 'The Product Ecology: Understanding Social Product Use and Supporting Design Culture' *International Journal of Design*, vol. 2, no. 1, pp11–20

Forlizzi, J. and Battarbee, K. (2004) 'Understanding Experience in Interactive Systems', *Designing interactive system*, pp261–269

Frederick, S. and Loewenstein, G. (1999) 'Hedonic Adaptation', In Kahneman, D., Diener, E. and Schwarz, N. (eds), *Well-being: The Foundations of Hedonic Psychology*, Russell, New York, pp302–329

Fredrickson, B. L. (1998) 'What Good Are Positive Emotions?' *Review of General Psychology* vol. 2, no. 3, pp300–319

Frijda, N. H. (1986) *The Emotions*, Cambridge University Press, Cambridge, MA

Gentner, A., Bouchard, C. and Favart, C. (2013) 'Investigating User Experience as a Composition of Components and Influencing Factors', in *Proceedings of Int. Association of Societies of Design Research Conference*, Tokyo, pp319–330

Hassenzahl, M. (2010) 'Experience Design: Technology for All the Right Reasons', *Synthesis Lectures on Human-Centered Informatics*, vol. 3, no. 1, pp1–95

Hassenzahl, M. and Tractinsky, N. (2006) 'User Experience-A Research Agenda' *Behaviour and Information Technology*, vol. 25, no. 2, pp91–97

Hassenzahl, M., Diefenbach, S. and Göritz, A. (2010) 'Needs, Affect, and Interactive Products-Facets of User Experience'. *Interacting with Computers*, vol. 22, no. 5, pp353–362

Hektner, J. M., Schmidt, J. A. and Csikszentmihalyi, M. (2007) *Experience Sampling Method: Measuring the Quality of Everyday Life*, Sage Publications, London

Jordan, P. W. (2000) *Designing Pleasurable Products*, Taylor & Francis, London

Jordan, P. W. (2003) 'Foreword', in Blythe, M. A. et al (eds), *Funology: From Usability to Enjoyment*, Kluwer Academic Publishers, Dordrecht, ppxi–xiii

Law, E. L. C., Roto, V., Hassenzahl, M., Vermeeren, A. P. O. S. and Kort, J. (2009) 'Understanding, Scoping and Defining User Experience: A Survey Approach', in *Proceedings of the 27th International Conference on Human Factors in Computing Systems*, ACM, pp719–728

Mahlke, S. and Thuring, M. (2007) 'Studying Antecedents of Emotional Experiences in Interactive Contexts', in *Proceedings of the SIGCHI Conference on Human Factors in Computing Systems,* San Jose, CA, US, April 30–May 3, pp915–918

Mahoney, M. J. (2004) 'What is Constructivism and Why is it Growing?' *Contemporary Psychology*, vol. 49, pp360–363

McCarthy, J. and Wright, P. (2004) *Technology as Experience*, MIT Press, Chicago, MA

Nelson, L. D., Meyvis, T. and Galak, J. (2009) 'Enhancing the Television Viewing Experience Through Commercial Interruptions' *Journal of Consumer Research*, vol. 36, no. 2, pp160–172

Ortíz Nicolás, J. C. (2014) Understanding and Designing Pleasant Experiences with Products, PhD dissertation, Imperial College London, London

Ortíz Nicolás, J. C. and Aurisicchio, M. (2011) 'A Scenario of User Experience', in *Proceedings of the 18th International Conference on Engineering Design (ICED11)*, vol. 7, Copenhagen pp. 182–193

Ortíz Nicolás J. C., Aurisicchio M. and Desmet P. M. A. (2013a) 'How Users Experience Great Products', in *Proceedings of the 5th International Congress of International Association of Societies of Design Research*, Tokyo, pp5546–5557

Ortíz Nicolás, J. C., Aurisicchio, M. and Desmet, P. (2013b) 'Designing for Anticipation, Confidence, and Inspiration', in *Proceedings of the 6th International Conference on Designing Pleasurable Products and Interfaces*, Newcastle upon Tyne, pp31–40

Ortíz Nicolás J. C., Aurisicchio M. and Desmet P. M. A. (2013c) 'Differentiating Positive Emotions Elicited by Products; An Exploration of Perceived Differences between 25 Positive Emotions by Users and Designers', in *Proceedings of the International Conference on Engineering Design*, Seoul, pp1–10

Ortíz Nicolás, J. C., Aurisicchio, M. and Desmet, P. M. (2014). 'Pleasantness and Arousal in Twenty-Five Positive Emotions Elicited by Durable Products', in *Proceedings of the Colors of Care: The 9th International Conference on Design and Emotion*, Ediciones Uniandes, Bogotá, pp221–227

Porter C. S., Chhibber S. and Porter, J. M. (2008) 'What Makes You Tick – An Investigation of the Pleasure Needs of Different Population Segments', in Desmet, P. M. A., Erp V. J. and Karlsson, M. (eds), *Design and Emotion Moves* , Cambridge Scholars Publishing, Cambridge, pp 324–361

Rafaeli, A. and Vilnai-Yavetz, I. (2004) 'Instrumentality, Aesthetics and Symbolism of Physical Artifacts as Triggers of Emotion' *Theoretical Issues in Ergonomics Science*, vol. 5, no. 1, pp91–112

Scherer, K. R. (2005) 'What are Emotions? And How Can They Be Measured?' *Social Science Information*, vol. 44, no. 4, pp695–729

Van Boven, L. (2005) 'Experientialism, Materialism, and the Pursuit of Happiness', *Review of General Psychology*, vol. 9, no. 2, pp132–142

Van Boven, L. and Gilovich, T. (2003) 'To Do or to Have? That is the Question' *Journal of personality and social psychology*, vol. 85, no. 6, pp1193–1202

Yoon, J., Desmet, P. M. A. and van der Helm, A. (2011) 'Design for Interest: Exploratory Study on a Distinct Positive Emotion in Human–Product Interaction', *International Journal of Design*, vol. 6, no. 2, pp. 67–80

20

SURPRISING
LONGEVITY

Silvia Grimaldi

Abstract

In everyday language a *surprise* is a sudden or unexpected event; psychologically though, the emotions of surprise is the reaction to the sudden or unexpected event. Surprise is one of the six primary emotions and it heightens attention to prepare us to react. If the surprise happens to be a positive one, then that positive emotion will also be heightened by the surprise and the surprise will make the event more memorable. The way we interpret the world is tied to narrative; we not only remember and recall events as stories, but we interpret them as stories as they are happening. In a similar way, product experiences have a narrative element because the series of events that make up the experience happen in time, and narrative helps us to make sense of time. Adding a surprise to a product experience creates a timeline of *before* and *after* the surprising event, and this can help to structure the experience as a story in our mind. In addition this story is emotionally charged because of the surprise, so it will stay with us longer, and the object itself will evoke that emotion and that narrative, and it will be an object we become more attached to and are less likely to prematurely dispose of. Analysis of design examples help to show how this works from a user perspective, and a design technique to incorporate meaningful surprises into the product experience is described. The chapter concludes by showing how surprise, when designed into the product experience, can contribute to the longevity of a product.

Keywords: surprise, product experience, emotional design, narrative, experience design

Introduction

Recently, people have been looking at their passports more closely, and being surprised by what they find. In particular Norwegians, Canadians and Finns have been debating online which passport is the most interesting. When looked at under black light (ultraviolet or infrared, invisible to the eye) the Canadian passport illuminates with additional images to complete the printed scenes. The Finnish passport when used as a flipbook shows an animation of a walking moose. The Norwegian passport has been the subject of a competitions held by the National Police Directorate of Norway for its redesign. The winning sketches by Neue

Design Studio feature landscapes that come alive with scenes of the northern lights when black light shines upon the pages.

Why is this surprising? Hardly anyone would look at their passports as examples of interesting design, as it is mostly a dry and somewhat bureaucratic document. However, a lot of technology and research goes into producing passports, making them harder to counterfeit. Gorgeous, romantic images of the northern lights are not what you expect to see in a passport. But it does make sense, from a cultural point of view, as the northern lights are a famous feature of the natural landscape of the country, and from a technical point of view, as black light is often used to add a layer of security to passports. Perhaps more importantly, though, is the poetic meaning; one reason why this is so striking, is that the northern lights glow when the passport is in the dark of a black light echoing the way they glow in the dark

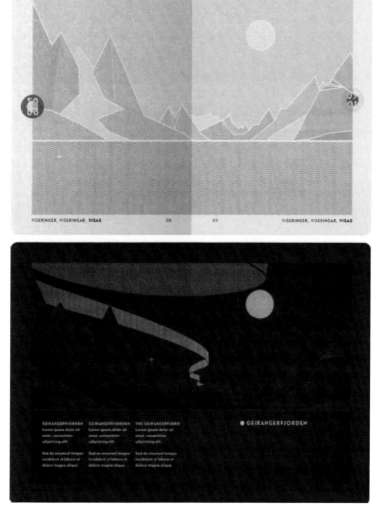

Figure 20.1 Passport design sketches from the competition held by the National Police Directorate of Norway, designed by Neue Design Studio. Design sketches will not be identical to the final issued passports

sky. In a similar way one of the pages of the Canadian passport illuminates with fireworks in the sky of the printed scene. A black light logo would have done the job, but it wouldn't have been as surprising or as memorable. The relevance of the design adds to the surprise and sustains the sense of wonder through time.

What is surprise?

Everyone has been surprised before. In common language, surprise is a sudden or unexpected event. This event will be different than what we thought was likely to occur, or what we assumed would occur. A surprise changes the story of what we had assumed would happen and replaces it with another one with a different, unexpected ending.

If surprise is something that is unexpected it is inevitably dependant on people's expectations, which themselves are based on our experience of the world. By having seen and used a lot of mugs I can expect a mug to look like a cylinder with a loop on one side. I know it can contain a liquid, and the loop/handle can be used to grip the mug with. I know I can expect it to be hot because I have used it to contain hot liquids before. I know it is usually made of ceramic, and I know its approximate weight. I know my experience of the object will probably include filling it with a hot liquid, gripping the handle, and drinking from it, putting it back down on the table, etc. Even for an object as simple as a mug, or perhaps because it is such a simple object, this list of expectations could go on and on. These expectations and affordances allow us to approach an object that we have never seen before (a particular mug) and be able to know what its function is, how to use it, whether caution is necessary when approaching the object, etc.

Clues or signs, being based on past experiences, are necessarily dependant on the cultural context of the user. Some signs can be considered more universal (though none can be considered completely universal) like the signs that tell the user what material the object is made of. Nevertheless most signs are culturally specific, especially when we analyse their interpretation, for example what the material represents (e.g. white ceramic – sanitation). It is therefore virtually impossible to think of a universal surprise. If surprise is based on breaking, or disrupting people's expectations, it is necessary to have an audience whose expectations are more or less the same in order to surprise them all. However, the feeling of surprise is universal, and all humans feel this emotion regardless of their cultural predisposition.

The psychology of surprise: can a sudden emotion create longevity of experience?

Psychologists define surprise as part of the set of six basic human emotions, based on the standard set of emotions first compiled by P. Ekman (2014). These are surprise, joy, sadness, disgust, fear and anger (ibid.). These six emotions are defined as 'basic', 'universal' or 'primary', because they are the ones that we learn earlier in life and the ones that are also common to most mammals; and from these all other emotions are made to derive (Desmet, 2004).

The first scientist to catalogue human emotions was Darwin, who places surprise in a scale that goes from attention to surprise to astonishment and amazement, and talks about these emotions as closely related to the category whose scale goes from fear to horror. Both of these categories of emotions are a 'response to a sudden stimulus'. In the second scale, the fear to horror one, the stimulus is obviously a negative one that might threaten your existence; in the first scale, which includes surprise, the stimulus is unknown, and the reactions described by Darwin are all geared towards heightening the person's attention (e.g. eyes wide open) and preparing the body for a reaction (e.g. tense muscles). Because the stimulus of surprise is unknown, the body prepares itself to be able to best deal with what is coming. In this way, surprised people are more receptive to noticing things and have an enhanced perception of what is around them (Darwin, 1998).

Antonio Damasio is a neurologist who pioneered the study of emotion and human consciousness by studying patients with brain damage. He has shown that emotions are necessary to run a regular life and have particular implications for decision-making. Individuals who have brain damage in areas of the brain related to emotions seem unable to make 'rational decisions' and will make 'personal and social decisions [that] are irrational, more often disadvantageous to their selves and to others than not' (Damasio, 2000, p40). Technically speaking, emotions are chemical and neural responses to stimuli from the outside or from memory, and they have a regulatory function within the body, which has a number of implications for the physical state of the person and for the person's state of mind. By changing the mental state of a person, they make the person experience what is around them in a different way and make a mental association between the particular stimulus (object or event that caused the emotion) and the emotion felt (ibid.). The emotional state that was associated with the stimulus will be remembered whenever the person is thinking of that particular stimulus or whenever this is encountered again.

This is particularly important for emotions that are often sudden, like surprise. As surprise is the reaction to a sudden or unexpected stimulus, it puts the surprised person in a state of mind in which other senses and other emotions are heightened. If these other emotions associated with the event are positive ones, like joy, happiness or pleasure, this positive state will be amplified, and then remembered when coming into contact again with the surprising object.

This association can be seen very prominently in infants, through what Daniel Stern calls RIGs ('repetitions of an interaction that has been generalized') (Stern, 2000). For example, the way adults play with babies is a delicate balance between familiar and unfamiliar elements. On the one hand, the baby is more interested in familiar modes of interaction because they remind the baby of the previous times that interaction has taken place and evokes the previous situation. In such instances, babies can be found playing with a toy in the same way their mother plays with them (ibid.). But by observing babies in their interactions, it is clear that if the game remains exactly the same, the baby loses interest in the game and gets distracted. Another typical RIG interaction is the peek-a-boo game, based on a combination of repetition and surprise. The first times the baby plays the peek-a-boo game it creates a little anxiety, since the mother's face disappears. But when it reappears, the relief and joy at seeing it again make the game fun. Therefore the mother repeats the game to produce the same emotional response in the baby. But the baby soon gets bored of the game and his reactions start diminishing; the mother will instinctively start varying the game, she'll use a different object to cover her face, or change her tone of voice, or the timing with which she uncovers her face to keep the baby interested.

The game soon turns into a RIG, evoking the feeling of joy again even when the game is played with other people, and even when the baby knows that the mother is still there. Initially, the baby finds interest in the game because of the pleasant surprise of finding that mum is still there, but after a few repetitions what drives the baby's interest is knowing that the mother is still there, being in on the joke in a way, and the situation evoking the initial pleasant emotion again. By evoking the surprise, the other feelings associated with it are also evoked, such as the joy of seeing the mother again.

Surprising stories

These concepts are applied in most narrative mediums, from public speaking to the way a narrative is set-up in books, films and music. Haydn's *Surprise Symphony* (Symphony No. 94 in G major) was revolutionary for the time because in the middle of a very quiet *Andante* second movement, which is based on the variation on a universally well-known popular tune of the time, all of a sudden there is an outburst in a *Fortissimo* tune, which gives the symphony its nickname of *Surprise Symphony*. There are several anecdotes about why Haydn did this, ranging from being angry with people who fell asleep during his performances to trying to outdo colleagues in the music world. Either way it is interesting to notice how the whole second movement is set up: it is extremely quiet and calm at the beginning, following a familiar and traditional first movement. And all of a sudden, with no warning, following a short pause, an extremely loud chord is played. It then goes back to being really quiet and mellow. The loud chord is repeated again several times throughout the whole movement; the small pause is followed sometimes by the loud chord, and sometimes by a mellower one in tone with the rest of the movement (Schwarm, n.d.).

The balance between the familiar and the surprising can be achieved on many different levels; to set up something familiar we can repeat it until it becomes familiar, or we can use something that already is well known. The surprise can then be achieved by playing with the user's/viewer's expectations derived from the repetition or from the context. These different types of surprises are used quite a lot in film, both when setting up suspense, and when using archetypal or stereotypical characters in unconventional ways. It is necessary in film to set up a familiar context in order to draw people in and make them relate to the characters. The film has to have familiar elements in order for the viewer to relate to it, but at the same time it has to have some surprising elements in order for the viewer to stay interested.

Surprise can be used in films to amplify different sorts of feelings; it is used to amplify fear in horror movies, to create suspense in mystery films or to make the jokes funnier in comedies. One of the most memorable surprises in film is the scene from *Jaws* (1975), when the shark is first seen coming out of the water. The situation is calm and the main character is speaking. Knowing it is a horror film about sharks one would expect to see a shark. But knowing horror films one expects the usual build-up of music and situation. Then the shark shoots out of the water. The shark is seen out of the water several times throughout the three movies, but the way surprise is used in that moment makes this particular scene the most memorable one of the whole trilogy. When we watch the film again, the same feeling is evoked again, though we are fully expecting the shark to pop out.

What we expect of films is derived from our experience of events in real life as well as our experience of stories and films. When viewing a narrative fiction film the viewer's main activity is that of forming hypotheses about the way the story will unfold; these hypotheses are either validated or disproved as the story develops as expected or with surprising turns of plot (Bordwell, 1985). We can make hypotheses about the plot because we have expectations about how events unfold based on our own lives, the typical forms of stories, expectations about particular genres and particular characters, props, locations, etc. These expectations are called 'schemata' (ibid.). Bordwell describes four types of schemata, two of which are of particular interest to product designers: *prototype schemata* and *template schemata*.

Prototype schemata are used by the viewer to recognize what characters, props and locales contribute to the story. So, if you see a hooded character with a gun in a dark alleyway you expect something violent is going to happen. This is similar to the way we interpret semiotic signs about objects, such as affordances or object types. *Template schemata* are used by the viewer to understand the chronological plot of a story from a narrative structure that may not be linear. They allow viewers to slot the information into place and reconstruct the film's plot. Template schemata allow us, for example, to understand a cause and effect sequence, no matter what order it is presented in. Interestingly, plots are easier to remember when told in ways that are closest to these template schemata (or typical story structures). Most people will also retell a narrative in a way that is closer to a template schemata, though the initial story may not have followed such a linear structure (Bordwell, 1985).

Surprising things

An interaction with an object contains a sequence of events that happen over time; designers can design or direct these events to create a particular experience with the object, and template and prototype schemata can be a valuable way of looking at these sequences of events (Grimaldi, 2015). Designers can use the properties of template schemata to create patterns of surprise and predictability within a product experience, for example designing 'dramaturgical structures' into the story of the interaction (Löwgren, 2009). Template schemata also aid in understanding cause and effect patterns. Thus, keeping these in mind while designing might also help to create objects to which users might assign certain behavioural patterns (or even a *will*) if the object appears to cause a particular effect. In addition, designers might apply template schemata to make sequences of events better conform to particular story structures, and therefore be more memorable. Prototype schemata might also help designers establish what you may or may not expect from an object, and this may lead to objects that are surprising when designers play with these expectations (Grimaldi, 2015).

There need to be familiar elements in surprising objects in order to make us expect something from them, and a level of trust needs to be established. When you trust an object you know the object because it is part of a familiar class of objects that you have contact with all the time. This is trust at first sight, derived from your knowledge of the category of objects rather than the specific object itself. This is more prominent with objects that have turned into archetypes, which everyone within the given culture already knows how to use. In a sense, it is harder to use surprise in digital objects for example, because we don't trust them, and we don't have such preformed expectations about the way they should work.

Surprising objects demand more attention from the user, simply because when an unexpected event occurs 'ongoing activities and information processing are interrupted and attention is focused on the unexpected event' (Ludden et al., 2004, p3). This can be achieved in a playful way and the surprise will be a pleasant one. In terms of product design, the designer can make use of a surprise reaction because it captures attention to the product, leading to increased product recall and recognition, and to increased word-of-mouth (Derbaix and Vanhamme, 2003; Vanhamme and Lindgreen, 2001). This is because the object is remembered is through a 'story of the experience' and this story is usually one that the user will tell to others. Creating a story around an object turns that object into a memento or *souvenir* of the experience, and in that sense, it becomes a special object to be cherished and kept rather than abused and discarded.

The benefits of creating emotional attachment to objects are clear. People treat objects that they are attached to with much more care, they service and repair them rather than throwing them out, and in general they will use them for a much longer period of time (Chapman, 2015; Govers and Mugge, 2004). Furthermore, when people have special bonds with a particular object, that object will be more enjoyable to use, and the user will be willing to cope with minor problems in its operation or appearance (Norman, 2003). 'There is something Orwellian about the distribution of emotions in our world: All objects can get some emotional attachment, but some objects get far more than others.' (Damasio, 2000, p58). There are many reasons why people become emotionally attached to objects; sometimes these have to do with the object itself, and could be based on things like the look of the object or on its comfort. More often than not though the emotional attachment has to do with a past experience with the object, either in the way that the object was acquired, for example a family heirloom or a memento, or in the fact that it was present at an important time, and reminds the user of an event, for example the piece of clothing worn on a first date (Csikszentmihalyi and Halton, 1981). In many cases, the object is special because it is associated with a particular person or event; in other words, the object is special because of the story behind it. The emotion is therefore not always present in the object, but it is present through the way the object reminds the user of the way they felt in a certain moment or situation. This act of remembrance is dependent on, and inseparable from, the story itself. The story is necessary to facilitate the memory of the object, which then triggers the same emotion.

The concept of *narrativity* is relevant here (Abbott, n.d.; Herman et al., 2005). If we look at an interaction with an object in narrative terms, we are looking at a sequence of events presenting more or less opportunities for being told as an interesting, engaging and memorable story. A surprising object possesses more narrativity – more potential to be retold as a story. This is because a surprising event in a product interaction sets up a story, an interaction with a surprising object will be more prone to be interpreted and retold as a story, it will have more potential for narrative interpretations, or narrativity (for more on narrativity and design, see Grimaldi, 2013, 2015).

Events and experiences in our lives are often interpreted in the moment and remembered and recounted as stories (Bruner, 1991; Dewey, 2005; Forlizzi, 1997; Hassenzahl, 2010; Löwgren, 2009; Abbott, 2008; Bal, 2002; Young and Saver, 2001). In fact, people who have brain damage in the narrative parts of the brain (known as *dysnarrativia*) have problems remembering events, as memory appears to function on a narrative level, and in severe cases even forming a sense of self, because this is so tied to our personal narratives (Bruner, 1991; Sacks, 1998; Young and Saver, 2001). When thinking of a product experience as it unfolds over time, a surprising object will necessarily set up a narrative, for the simple fact that there is a point in time, the surprise, that divides the whole experience into a *before* and an *after*, and this creates a timeline and a narrative of sorts. The surprising event structures the experience of the object into a more traditional narrative (McKee, 1999) and the closer to conventional narratives a story is the easier it is to remember and retell (Bordwell, 1985; for a more thorough review of narratives in design see Grimaldi et al., 2013).

By breaking your expectations, a surprising object also makes you aware of the fact that you do have expectations about objects, and of what these expectations are. The *before* is therefore related to your expectations, and the *after* is the discovery. It is as if the object, or the designer, were telling you something about yourself. In this way the object is not used but discovered, and through the process of engagement, allows you to discover something about yourself as well. The narrative is therefore transformed from a story about the object doing something, to a story about yourself, about the way the object made you feel and about the way you think. The comparison between the way a person felt before and the way that person felt after the surprise creates a story, and in this story the user is the protagonist. The concepts of 'user as protagonist' and 'designer as author' are widely explored by Anthony Dunne in *Hertzian Tales*, in relation to electronic objects (Dunne, 2008). It is possible, though, to extend the concept to all objects that provide a narrative experience to the user. The designer is therefore not only designing the object itself, but also the product experience of which the user is the protagonist (Dunne and Raby, 2001; Dunne, 2008).

The result of focusing on surprise to design objects might be that the object actively encourages the user to interpret it as having a will, or agency, and somehow directing the story of the interaction, fostering more emotional attachment to the object and increasing the narrativity of the object, the gusto that someone might have in retelling the story of their interaction, increasing word of mouth and recall (Grimaldi, 2015).

Surprising designs

In order to review examples of surprising design, these are divided into types of surprise based on what the surprising element is, and how and when in the product experience the surprise is encountered. The three categories are:

- Seeing is believing?
- Using is believing
- What is happening?

These categories are not meant to be an absolute metre to set objects apart, as most of the objects described will fit into more than one category, to differing degrees. They are nevertheless useful to provide a good frame of reference to discuss and compare surprising objects and to set some parameters for design work.

Seeing is believing? is based on first impressions and a purely visual surprise. It is the most instant and probably harder to sustain type of surprise, based on visual impact and visual incongruities. *Using is believing* is still an instant type of surprise, but it is based on the incongruity between what an object looks like and how it functions or feels. *What is happening?* includes objects which do not behave as expected or change their behaviour over time, or whose behaviour is unexplainable. In this way it is the one creating surprises that are most prolonged in time, since the behaviour only manifests itself on certain occasions, and it takes many repetitions of the behaviour to start trying to understand it logically.

Seeing is believing? Surprise based on visual impact

This category is the most immediate, and it contains all of those objects that are surprising at first sight. Many different types of surprising elements fit into this category; the surprise can be about the perceived material and the way in which this is used ('how does that stand up?') or about the viewer's cultural expectations ('is it a chair or a hammock?'). In any case, they are based on previously acquired knowledge.

Design objects in this category work on the principles of displacement and recognition; they take elements from a certain context, particularly elements that signify a certain context, and then apply them to a different context with surprising results. The contradictions work at first sight at inducing emotions, but the way that emotion is sustained is through reflection. At first sight one might be induced to think, 'yes, it is nice, it is fun, but why?' but upon reflection the reason is discovered, and it starts to make sense. Because you came to that conclusion yourself, somehow you understood what the designer was trying to tell you, you feel engaged in a virtual dialogue with the designer – or with the object itself. In a way you feel like you were let in on a joke.

Marcel Wanders's *Knotted Chair* plays with the contrasts between the visual elements of the product, and what these elements signify to the viewer/user. These visual signs come from different contexts; the overall shape references a traditional chair. Therefore the function of

Figure 20.2 Knotted Chair by Marcel Wanders

the object is clear and the viewer will know how to use it and that it is meant to be used. On the other hand the material and the way the structure is achieved through knots has diverse references, from hammocks to fishing and rock climbing, which reinforce the impossible look of the object. The reference to hammocks, in particular, makes one aware of the fact that the 'rope' should not be holding itself up but should be attached to something, in suspension. This feeling that rope should not be able to hold itself up and should definitely not be able to hold a person's weight is reinforced by the fact that the material is not yet known in this sort of application, and there are no other examples that one can refer to understand how it works (Manzini and Cau, 1989).

Hector Serrano's *Waterproof Lamp* for Metalarte plays in a similar way with displacement. It uses the archetypal table lamp shape, but places it in a swimming pool, therefore not only taking the object out of context, but including an element of danger, since a regular lamp would be very dangerous in a swimming pool. The shape of the lamp also references the shape of a lifebuoy, creating an additional layer of contrast between the image of danger created by the electricity in the water and the image of safety associated with the lifebuoy.

The *Spineless Lamps* by Frederik Roijé work on a different plane; they reference the shape of a generic table lamp, but they appear to be partially melted and to have lost their shape. They would appear damaged if you didn't encounter them on the shelf of a shop or in a museum, and if you didn't see them close to the others. On closer inspection, one sees that they are actually porcelain, which is a material that is not usually used for this type of lamp, but rather associated with fancy dinner plates and serving bowls – it is seen as a delicate and precious material. The shape of the lamp on the other hand is one typical of a utilitarian cheap lamp made with inexpensive materials. This contrast adds an additional layer of surprise and an additional layer of meaning to the piece.

The risk in this category is to create a novelty object; an object that is mildly surprising for a second and is quickly discarded and forgotten. It is important therefore that the object functions on many different levels, and that the viewer will not necessarily 'get it' all immediately. Ideally, it will be something that the viewer will reflect on and maybe

Figure 20.3 Waterproof Lamp by Hector Serrano

Figure 20.4 Spineless Lamps by Frederik Roijé

understand later in time. Even if the understanding is not put into words, it creates a sort of fascination in the viewer because the comparison, though surreal, will be strangely familiar.

Using is believing: surprise through interaction

In a similar way to the previous category, the surprise is instant and could be considered a one off. The difference is that this category requires the user to not only look at the object, but also interact with it physically and there is a different approach to how the expectations to be broken are set up. While the previous category relies heavily on previously acquired knowledge, in this category it is possible to set up in the object itself certain expectations deriving from the way it looks. As a consequence, the surprising elements, which in this category can include the difference between how a material looks and how it feels or the difference between the affordances of the object and how the object is actually to be used, are a comparison between sight and other senses, or sight and function.

David Rockwell's *Grand Central Chair* is used in a waiting area in Grand Central Station in New York. This chair uses the language of traditional wingback armchairs and luxury travel in both its shape and its colours. It effectively looks like a cartoon caricature of an old-fashioned waiting room chair. But when the chair is used there are several surprises. First the chair is slightly over-scaled, which is not noticeable at first sight. When sitting in it, this scale difference gives a feeling of protection and of having turned into a child. The second one is that the material used, while it looks like it might be a soft material, is similar to stone in texture and temperature. The material is also used in a way that conceals its tactile properties, since it is shaped into a very soft form. The shape-based surprise plays on the expectations that people gain from the armchair sign.

The surprise in Hella Jongerius's *Soft Urn* is completely based on the material used; the form of the vase is very traditional and recognisable, and it would not be noticed at first sight in a group of vases. But when the object is used it is obvious that the material is not ceramic but rubber, and that the whole vase is soft. This is particularly effective when we think of the associations that a vase-form has, with a precious object that needs to be placed on a pedestal for fear of knocking it over and having it shatter. Rubber achieves the opposite effect, being a common and inexpensive material that can easily be mass-produced, and definitely impossible to shatter.

Paul Hessels's *Socket Light* plays with our expectations in a similar way, glowing like a nightlight when something is plugged into it. The electrical socket is probably one of the

Figure 20.5 Grand Central Chair by David Rockwell

Figure 20.6 Soft Urn by Hella Jongerius

most mundane and utilitarian objects imaginable. Nobody expects it to do anything besides receiving electrical plugs. The fact that it light up adds a small surprise and makes the user notice the socket, which they wouldn't usually notice, while still staying within the vocabulary of electricity and things that are found plugged into sockets, such as nightlights. In this case the surprise is also in recognizing that it is really not that surprising; it makes complete sense that a socket, which provides electricity, should also glow with that same electricity. In realising this we also realize that the accepted way in which sockets are designed, the standard for these, is not a necessity but a choice. Sockets could have been designed in any number of other ways, and a lot of these ways make perfect sense or add something to the use of this object. The surprise provides us with the opportunity to not overlook this object but to reflect on why such a small and obvious change should be so surprising.

This process of setting up expectations is similar to the repetition of interactions, and the way this process is broken by the surprise is similar to what is done in narrative media to hold people's interest through breaking prototype schemata. By making an object look like something familiar, a sort of rhythm is established based on the viewer's knowledge of the signs given. The surprising element is what breaks this rhythm and makes the user pay attention to the object. As in other narrative forms, it is not essential that the object completely conceal the presence of a surprising element, as long as that element remains somewhat unknown, or hidden. The surprising element in this category happens and has the most impact only once, on the first use. But again it is the presence of additional meaning that makes the emotion persist through time. By thinking about the object later on, one discovers more surprising elements that are not necessarily as immediate.

What is happening? Behavioural surprise

This category is the most diverse of the three; the unifying feature within the category is the fact that the surprise is not instant but it is discovered gradually through repeated interactions with the object. Within this category it is possible to make full use of the narrative structure of repetition and surprise, since the objects behave in different ways at different times. In this way the surprise has the possibility of being sustained over time, since the user will make hypotheses about what triggers the object's incomprehensible behaviour, and will expect it to react according to the hypothesis formed. The user will then have to wait for the situation s/he suspects triggers the reaction to happen again, and when the object does not react, a new theory will be formed.

In our everyday life one common source of this type of surprise are other people or pets. They act in ways we think we can predict, but they do not always follow the same rules we would like to apply to them. Even when we think we can predict the behaviour because we *know* the person or pet very well, the predictions can never be accurate.

Dunne and Raby's work with electromagnetic waves has produced some objects which could fit into this category, but the way in which they fit needs to be explained. All of the objects in the collection have a set behaviour based on their response to electromagnetic waves. They are meant to make the user aware of the presence of this *hertzian space* and interact with this space in a physical way. The objects were tested by finding volunteers that would 'adopt' these objects, live with them and then describe their reactions to the objects.

It is interesting to notice that the people who were using these objects in their home did not fully understand what triggered their behaviour. Of course, they knew they were responding to electromagnetic waves, but being that these are normally hidden from our view, it was often hard for them to picture what exactly was causing the object's behaviour. This sense of unpredictability is what many of the users found most interesting; they spent hours trying to figure out why the object was behaving in a certain way, moving the object about the house to find a place it 'enjoyed' and generally caring for the object and checking

Figure 20.7 Nipple Chair by Dunne and Raby

on it often to see how it was doing. The *Nipple Chair* had this effect on Neil, its user. Its form is very archetypal, but with two footrests and two 'nipples' on the backrest. When the chair is placed near electromagnetic waves, the nipples start moving. What intrigued Neil about the chair were those situations in which he did not understand what made it move. In particular, he describes coming home from work, and as he approaches the chair, it starts to move. 'When you come home at night, it speeds up and you think "Oh, it's pleased to see me."' (Dunne and Raby, 2001, §5). This can be explained through static electricity, since he had carpeted floors and the build-up of static electricity is picked up by the chair. But since Neil did not understand what was triggering it, he anthropomorphized the response, by assigning human-like motives to the chair's behaviour.

Throughout his interview, Neil refers back to how his lack of understanding and control over the chair's behaviour is what fascinated him the most. If there were a programmable interface, the chair would lose its meaning. He also spoke of how it is this lack of control that made him interact with the object in a way that is more similar to communicating with a human. Also, in his opinion, a combination between the lack of control and the attention to aesthetics is what distinguishes the chair from a gadget, and therefore gives the chair a much higher possibility of being kept and cherished for a longer period of time than any gadget.

Jim Rokos's *Gauge* vase sets up a time-based surprise by tilting. The vase is at an angle, slightly precarious in its balance, and as the water evaporates the angle of the vase gets steeper. This increases the sense of precariousness but also reminds you to water the plant by making you realize why the vase is more tilted.

The first two categories are both based on instant types of surprises, and when successful they have a lot of initial impact on the user, but they are not necessarily objects whose surprise is repeatable over time. However if the surprise is able to create a story with the user, and an emotional attachment, this will sustain the interest of the user for longer. The third category unfolds over time and it creates the possibility that these objects will be treated in a way that is similar to living things makes them also very prone to emotional attachment. However, the risk is that the object itself won't be as interesting at first sight.

Figure 20.8 Gauge by Jim Rokos

Designing for surprise: the Ta-Da Series

The *Ta-Da Series* is a series of three objects, consisting of a lamp, a stool and a set of coffee tables, designed through a technique of opposites and gut reactions to deliberately create a surprising user experience. (This will be described briefly here; for a full description please see Grimaldi, 2006, 2008). Using this technique allows designers to find, out of the infinite number of surprises that could be incorporated into the product experience, one that is relevant, has some meaning and stimulates thought and reflection in the user. It also allows the designer to set up a coherent narrative for the product experience, starting from an initial situation in which the object may have some incongruous elements, different from the user's expectations and beliefs, to then having an event unfold through the surprise. This could be through sight, touch, or through prolonged use, and then the closure comes from understanding or resolving the initial incongruities.

It is therefore important to think of how the original scene is set up. How will the user first approach the object? Can any suspense build-up based on the way this first approach is designed? How will the unexpected or surprising element be discovered? How is the suspense resolved? Does this sequence achieve the desired effect, or the desired closure to the story? The first step is to assess which objects will be used and what their main characteristics are; which of these might be essential to an object (without that it wouldn't be the same object) and which instead could be changed. For example what characteristics make a lamp a lamp? An essential one is that it makes light; if it doesn't make light it wouldn't be a lamp. The second step is to find the opposite of one non-essential but still associated characteristic and turn it into a design concept. For example, fragility is usually associated with lamps, but it is not essential to its 'lampness'. The third step is to incorporate gut reactions as a way to reinforce the message and have it persist over time. For example, a fragile lamp sitting on the edge of the table creates a gut reaction to want to move it to a safer place. In the case of the *On-Edge Lamp* (below) the lamp sits on the edge of the table when it is on, and this reinforces the contrast between what we expect of the lamp (fragility) and what we are surprised by (the change of material to rubber).

The *On-Edge Lamp* sets out the scene by visually referencing art deco glass lamps, but sitting on the edge of a table. The user might see this and instinctively try to move the lamp to a safer spot on the table. When moving the lamp the user will be surprised to discover that it is made of rubber, and also that it only turns on when it is perching precariously on the edge of the table, when it is fully on the table surface the lamp turns itself off. The resolution to the story is the understanding of the designer's intention, as well as an understanding of their own preconceptions and gut reactions, and this will make the user smile. Though the object is initially puzzling, the user will then be surprised (emotionally charged event) and will then find closure in the positive realization of the designer's intention. The precariousness of the lamp's positioning adds suspense to the story, the surprise is the punch line and the discovery that the lamp doesn't break provides closure and a happy ending. When used again, the sense of suspense becomes playful, though the gut reaction will continue to affect us when we see the lamp out of the corner of our eye. We will be reminded of the emotions felt at first interaction and the happy ending will make us smile again.

Conclusions

Surprise is a powerful emotion and it makes us more receptive to what is going on around us. It can also heighten any positive or negative impact that our experience has, because it adds the emotional charge of surprise. When thinking about designing products in terms of

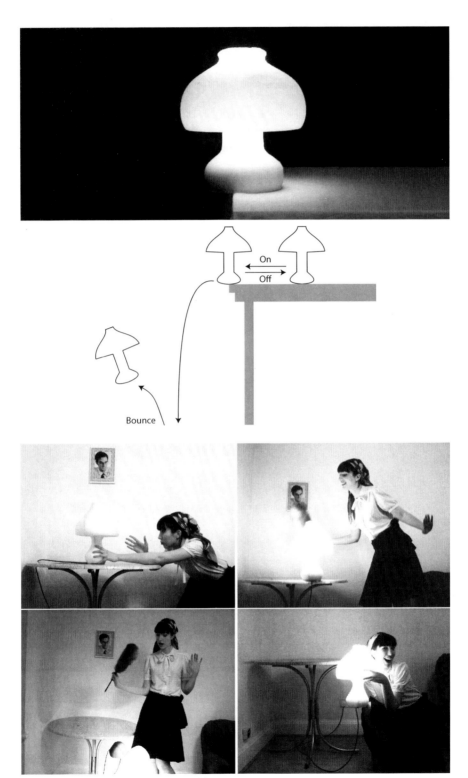

Figure 20.9 On-Edge Lamp by Silvia Grimaldi

how people will interact with them, and how this experience of interacting with the object unfolds over time, incorporating surprising elements within a product experience helps to focus the user's attention and to make the experience more memorable. In addition, the surprising element helps to make the positive or negative emotions in the product experience more emotionally charged.

The way we interpret, remember and retell these product experiences is tied with narrative, as narratives are used to make sense of time, and time-based events. When we look at the way interactions with objects unfold over time, it makes sense to describe these product experiences in narrative terms. Adding a surprise to a product experience also facilitates this narrative interpretation, as it creates a timeline of before the surprise and after the surprise, and the user can compare their own feelings and ideas in the two stages.

Surprise is used extensively in narrative media to capture the audience's attention and to progress the narrative through techniques such as suspense. Understanding how this works, through prototype and template schemata for example, can help designers to look at when in the product experience it is most appropriate to introduce surprising elements in order to aim for the most impact. In addition, because a surprising story is necessarily emotionally charged it will stay with us longer, and seeing the product again will remind the user of the emotions felt.

Looking at the product experience through a narrative lens, the designer can envision what the user's process of discovery will be. The designer can then 'direct' the user's experience of the product through designing-in events that will happen at particular moments in time, for example details that may only be noticed once the object is seen closer up, or once the object is touched, or when the object is used over a longer period of time. If these events make sense to the meaning of the product experience narrative, this will also add a level of reflection for the user which may happen after encountering the object. The designer can't possibly control how every user will approach and interpret the designed object, but by understanding emotions and narrative, the designer can build in clues that are likely to trigger particular reactions at particular points in the experience. By understanding surprise in more detail the designer can include relevant and meaningful surprising elements that may shape the story of the interaction for the user.

In this way though, surprise is a sudden emotion and we can only be truly surprised about an event once. After that, the object that surprised us will become part of a narrative in our mind about the first product experience. Though the surprise is not sustained over time, the attachment to the object created by the surprising product experience and the narrative around this can be sustained over time. Whenever the user sees or uses the surprising object again they will be reminded of the initial interaction and the emotions created in that interaction will be evoked. This makes the object more likely to be one that is kept, maintained, cherished and repaired when broken, rather than discarded before its time.

References

Abbott, H. P. (n.d.) Narrativity, in Hühn, P., et al. (eds), *The Living Handbook of Narratology*, Hamburg University Press, Hamburg, retrieved from www.lhn.uni-hamburg.de/article/narrativity

Abbott, P. (2008) *The Cambridge Introduction to Narrative*, Cambridge University Press, Cambridge, UK.

Bal, M. (2002) *Travelling Concepts in the Humanities: A Rough Guide*, University of Toronto Press, Canada.

Bordwell, D. (1985) *Narration in the Fiction Film*, University of Wisconsin Press, Madison, WI.

Bruner, J. (1991) The narrative construction of reality, *Critical Inquiry* vol 18, no 1, pp1–21.

Chapman, J. (2015). *Emotionally Durable Design: Objects, Experiences and Empathy*, Routledge, Abingdon.

Csikszentmihalyi, M., Halton, E. (1981) *The Meaning of Things: Domestic Symbols and the Self*, Cambridge University Press, Cambridge.

Damasio, A. (2000) *The Feeling of What Happens: Body, Emotion and the Making of Consciousness*, new edition, Vintage, London.

Darwin, C. (1998) *The Expression of the Emotions in Man and Animals*, Oxford University Press, Oxford.

Derbaix, C., Vanhamme, J. (2003) Inducing word-of-mouth by eliciting surprise – a pilot investigation *Journal of Economic Psychology*, vol 24, Issue 1, pp99–116.

Desmet, P. M. A. (2004) From disgust to desire: How products elicit emotions, in McDonagh, D., Hekkert, P., Erp, J. van, Gyi, D. (eds), *Design and Emotion*, CRC Press, Abingdon, pp8–12.

Dewey, J. (2005) *Art as Experience*, Perigee Books, New York.

Dunne, A. (2008) *Hertzian Tales: Electronic Products, Aesthetic Experience, and Critical Design*, MIT Press, Cambridge, MA.

Dunne, A., Raby, F. (2001) *Design Noir: The Secret Life of Electronic Objects*, August/Birkhäuser, New York.

Ekman, P. (2014) Expression and the nature of emotion, in Scherer, K. R., Ekman, P. (eds), *Approaches to Emotion*, Psychology Press, Brighton, pp319–344.

Forlizzi, J. (1997). Designing for experience: An approach to human-centered design, Master of Design in Interaction Design, Department of Design, College of Fine Arts, Carnegie Mellon University.

Govers, P. C., Mugge, R. (2004) 'I love my jeep, because it's tough like me': The effect of product-personality congruence on product attachment, in *Proceedings of the Fourth International Conference on Design and Emotion*, Ankara, Turkey.

Grimaldi, S. (2006) The Ta-Da Series: presentation of a technique and its use in generating a series of surprising designs, Presented at the 5th International Design and Emotion Conference, Chelmers University of Technology, Gothenburg, Sweden.

Grimaldi, S. (2008) The Ta-Da Series – a technique for generating surprising designs based on opposites and gut reactions, in Desmet, P. M. A., Karlsson, J. van E. (eds.), *Design and Emotion Moves*, Cambridge Scholars Publishing, Newcastle-upon-Tyne, pp165–190.

Grimaldi, S. (2013) Story of use: Analysis of film narratives to inform the design of object interactions, in Brandt, E., Ehn, P., Johansson, T. D., Hellström Reimer, M., Markussen, T., Vallgårda, A. (eds.), *Nordes 2013: Experiments in Design Research*, The Royal Danish Academy of Fine Arts, Schools Architecture, Design and Conservation, Copenhagen, pp374–377.

Grimaldi, S. (2015) Narrativity of object interaction experiences: A framework for designing products as narrative experiences, in Benz, P. (ed.), *Experience Design: Concepts and Case Studies*, Bloomsbury Academic, London, pp57–68.

Grimaldi, S., Fokkinga, S., Ocnarescu, I. (2013) Narratives in design: A study of the types, applications and functions of narratives in design practice, in *Proceedings of the 6th International Conference on Designing Pleasurable Products and Interfaces, DPPI '13*, ACM, New York, pp201–210.

Hassenzahl, M. (2010) *Experience Design: Technology for All the Right Reasons*, Morgan & Claypool Publishers, San Francisco, CA.

Herman, D., Jahn, M., Ryan, M.-L. (eds) (2005) *Routledge Encyclopedia of Narrative Theory*, Routledge, Abingdon.

Löwgren, J. (2009) Toward an articulation of interaction aesthetics, *New Review of Hypermedia and Multimedia* vol 15, no 2, pp129–146.

Ludden, G. D., Schifferstein, H. N., Hekkert, P. (2004) Surprises elicited by products incorporating visual-tactual incongruities, in *Fourth International Conference on Design and Emotion*, Ankara, Turkey, retrieved from www.studiolab.nl/manila/gems/ludden/paperDE.pdf (accessed 1 December 2015).

McKee, R. (1999) *Story: Substance, Structure, Style and the Principles of Screenwriting*, Methuen Publishing, London.

Manzini, E., Cau, P. (1989) *The Material of Invention*, MIT Press, Cambridge, MA.

Norman, D. A. (2003) *Emotional Design: Why We Love (or Hate) Everyday Things*, 1st ed. Basic Books, New York.

Sacks, O. W. (1998) *The Man Who Mistook His Wife for a Hat and Other Clinical Tales*, Simon & Schuster, New York.

Schwarm, B. (n.d.) Surprise Symphony: work by Haydn, *Encyclopedia Britannica*, retrieved from www.britannica.com/topic/Surprise-Symphony (accessed 15 September 2015).

Stern, D. N. (2000) *The Interpersonal World of the Infant: A View from Psychoanalysis and Developmental Psychology*, Basic Books, New York.

Vanhamme, J., Lindgreen, A. (2001) Gotcha! Findings from an exploratory investigation on the dangers of using deceptive practices in the mail-order business, *Psychology and Marketing* vol 18, no 7, pp785–810.

Young, K., Saver, J. L. (2001) The neurology of narrative, *SubStance* vol 30, no 1–2, pp72–84.

21

DESIGN FOR SUSTAINABLE USE USING PRINCIPLES OF BEHAVIOUR CHANGE

Casper Boks and Johannes Zachrisson Daae

Abstract

This chapter briefly sketches and visualizes how Design for Sustainable Behaviour (DfSB) has developed into an interdisciplinary research field within the past 10 years. Research within this field has resulted in an ever growing database of case studies that investigate an increasing number of behaviours and practice. These case studies differ considerably in terms of case study setup, user centred methods applied, target problems addressed, design methodology used, proposed solutions and tests whether the solutions have led to (sustainable) behaviour change. Few, if any cases follow a complete design process, including problem finding, user research, analysis, ideation, conceptualization and testing. In this chapter, one major (on spatial heating using woodstoves) and two smaller (on dishwashing and sustainable sleeping) projects illustrate how using Principles of Behaviour Change – an approach developed at the Norwegian University of Science and Technology (NTNU) – can inform such a complete process. Though the case studies may inspire how to do a design project aimed at developing interventions to create sustainable behaviour, existing insights by no means provide a final answer how to approach these and similar research questions. The chapter concludes with some insights into how the field could develop further.

Keywords: Design for Sustainable Behaviour, design for sustainability, case studies, use phase, environmental improvement

Introduction: an increasing focus on the use phase

The first formal decade of ecodesign research, which spans approximately 1995 to 2005, saw relatively little attention to the use phase of products, and thus for the human and social aspects of sustainable product design. Common ecodesign strategies focused mainly on various Design for X (DfX) approaches, such as design for disassembly, recycling and remanufacturing, and on various material applications. Strategies related to usage had of course been considered from the early days of ecodesign, but most of these strategies were likewise based on indirect material and end-of-life considerations (Boks and McAloone, 2009); life time extension, for example, appealed to postponing the end-of-life stage, and avoiding the need for further material use.

Reduction of energy use focused on using technologies requiring less energy consumption, and thus increasing energy efficiency that way.

It was not uncommon to state that researchers and designers used a lifecycle perspective, but in reality, they contributed with 'end-of-lifecycle' solutions; focusing on the means to consumption (the product) instead of the practices involved in consumption itself (use). Research into sustainable consumption has traditionally had relatively little connection to sustainable design at the product level – in terms of research community; these topics traditionally attracted interest from scholars with distinctly different backgrounds and academic perspectives to product designers. Academic research in the sustainable product design domain has often been carried out in the design engineering tradition, usually with limited intent to make truly interdisciplinary connections, such as building or extending scientific theory in, from, with or for, other scientific domains including the social sciences, natural sciences or management sciences, for example. A lot has changed in the past decade, however. Nowadays, many scholars see the potential that design research offers to transdisciplinary perspectives into the development of sustainable solutions.

The rapidly emerging field of Design for Sustainable Behaviour (DfSB), which serves as an example of a transdisciplinary enquiry, investigates, at various levels, how to influence the sustainability impact of consumers' activities, by studying their behaviours and practices, developed over time and in space. As a result, we have seen an academic network develop, which organizes international workshops and other forms of scholarly cooperation, several dedicated special issues of acknowledged scientific journals, as well as doctoral dissertations devoted to this theme. Figure 21.1 visualizes the (arguably) most significant academic events related to the development of DfSB as a field of academic interest. It should be noted that the figure represents a very Northern European perspective, which the authors choose to justify by the fact that the bulk of DfSB literature originates from a limited number of northern European universities. Adjacent fields, such as sustainable human–computer interaction (HCI), critical design and persuasive technology focus on similar research questions but do not affiliate themselves with DfSB.

Case studies

DfSB literature provides a rapidly growing database of case studies investigating an increasing number of behaviours. Daae and Boks (2015a) provide a large overview of 27 case studies that have focused on attempts to design products that reduce the environmental impact of using them. These case studies were primarily taken from DfSB literature and are categorized according to the type of product that was focused on, the targeted behaviour change, the way the case studies were set up, the design challenge found, the proposed solutions, the methods used for testing and the results achieved. Such an overview serves the purpose of providing an illustration of the diversity and magnitude of the existing studies. An analysis of the overview suggests that case studies are polarized in their approach, and either explore the target problem or test the effectiveness of potential solutions. Very few studies report an entire process, from the identification and investigation of the behaviour to the evaluation of possible ways of improving it. Even fewer calculate or predict the potential effectiveness of the proposed solutions.

Partially in response to this observed lack of case studies, a project was carried out at the Norwegian University of Science and Technology to apply an entire DfSB process, including all aspects that other studies so far only partially covered, including prototype building and testing of environmental effects of changed behaviour; the latter being one of

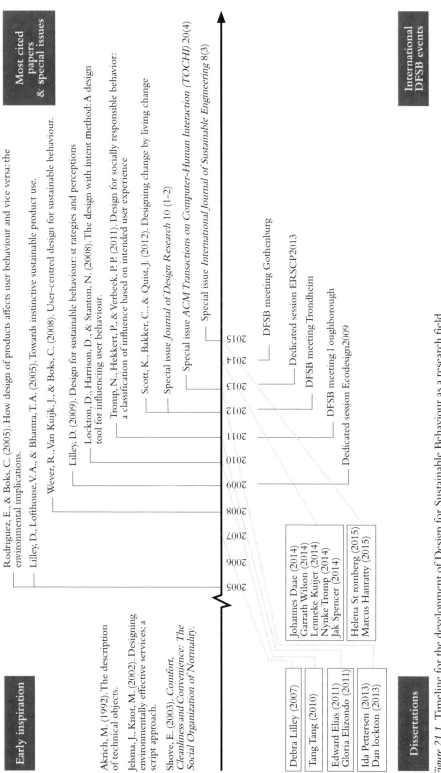

Figure 21.1 Timeline for the development of Design for Sustainable Behaviour as a research field

Source: Boks et al. (2015)

the most important omissions in most DFSB studies in literature (Wilson, 2013). The goal of the study was to investigate whether an alternative design of a woodstove, informed by principles of design for behaviour change, could allow for a type of user interaction that is more in line with recommended behaviour, and whether this would result in reduced emissions. At the time of the commencement of the study, there were very few available methods, providing direct support for design projects aiming at achieving such behaviour change.

The research approach for this project was inspired by the application of a user-centred design for sustainable behaviour process, which has been proposed as a tool referred to as Principles of Behaviour Change (Zachrisson et al., 2011; Boks and Daae, 2013b). The tool, which is based on insights from behavioural psychology, aims at helping designers make informed decisions about which design principles to apply when aiming to achieve a desired behaviour change for a target group. It suggests the consideration of a variety of user centred research methods, depending on which aspects of the user may be of particular interest given the behaviour to be studied.

The core purpose of the Principles of Behaviour Change is to identify the most promising types of design principles that may positively influence user behaviour. It makes use of a landscape that allows the sorting of design principles based on two parameters: the degree of control that a product allows the user to have over his or her behaviour, and the degree of subtlety or obtrusiveness that is designed into the solution (see Figure 21.2). Previous research (Zachrisson and Boks, 2011, 2012) revealed these two dimensions to be important ways to distinguish between design principles, but a substantial amount of additional dimensions may assist distinguishing between and selecting design principles (Daae and Boks, 2014).

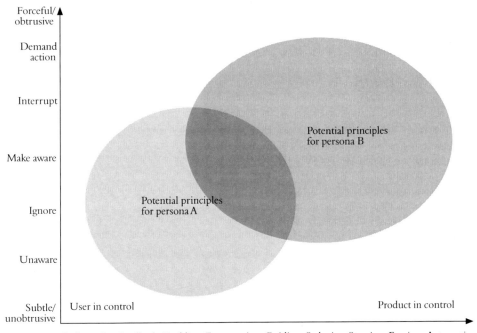

Figure 21.2 Control–obtrusiveness landscape

The idea behind this is that some design principles likely will work better for certain users in certain situations, than for others. In order to appropriately select feasible design principles for different groups of users with similar characteristics, a variety of user research methods can be used (an extensive overview of tools and their suggested application is provided by Daae and Boks, 2015b). The application of the Principles for Behaviour Change is further illustrated by the wood stove study in the next section, and by two smaller case studies in the section thereafter.

Design of a DfSB solution for ineffective burning of wood in woodstoves

For countries like Norway, fine particle, carbon and dioxin emissions resulting from burning firewood in woodstoves represent a significant environmental impact, because most households use woodstoves as a heating source. The majority of environmental impacts during the entire lifecycle of a woodstove occur during the use phase, in particular during start-up and the end phase of the burning process (Ozil et al., 2011). Emissions depend not only on the type and condition of woodstove and firewood, but also on user interaction with the stove (Haakonsen and Kvingedal, 2001; Karlsvik and Oravainen, 2009). Air supply for most modern stoves still requires manual operation by the end-user and can normally be regulated by two separate handles; one handle for ignition air through the bottom grate and a second handle to regulate the air supply to the primary combustion zone for setting the desired burn rate. The main combustion air controls the overall combustion intensity as given by the instantaneous burn rate at any time in the primary combustion zone. All modern stoves also apply what is called a secondary burnout zone where additional preheated air provides oxygen for gaseous hydrocarbons and particle burnout in the plume slightly above the main combustion zone. Active regulation of the ignition air is mainly required only when lighting the stove, where it should be fully open during a certain period, normally between 5 and 15 minutes, to support sufficient air until self-sustained combustion has been established, after which it is normally closed. For the remaining burnout and charcoal phase the effect can be set by adjusting the handle for the main combustion air. Many wood stove manufacturers also recommend lighting the stove with the door partly open. Lately recommendations for lighting woodstoves is to light the fire from the top, although this is not yet commonly applied.

A 2011 informal survey by consumer interest website www.DinSide.no, found that among 1,765 readers of a web-article about how to use a woodstove, only 10 per cent answered that they followed this recommendation. Based on this knowledge on how stoves and their users behave, there appears to be potential for reducing emissions by designing woodstoves that are likely to improve the way people interact with them. Therefore, at NTNU a project was initiated to investigate this potential by improving the design of the stove's user interface. The initiative was a collaboration between NTNU, SINTEF (Scandinavia's largest independent research organization), and Norwegian woodstove producer Jøtul, who contributed both with technical advice, participation in workshops and the development of prototypes for the final testing.

In the user research phase of the wood stove project, applied ethnography was used, where an approximation of real life product use was analysed to better understand why users behave the way they do, both consciously and subconsciously, based on interviews and analysis of video-recorded observations. Seventeen participants, all of whom used a woodstove on a regular basis, were recruited in the area around Oslo, where they lived in apartments, houses and semidetached houses. All participants were visited at home, video recordings were made of the participants firing up the woodstove, and semi-structured interviews addressed why and how they had done this the way they did, as well as other firewood energy and sustainability relate issues. Throughout each interview (which took on average one hour) participants were asked to maintain the fire in the woodstove, allowing for observation of adjustment of the air valves and reloading of wood, in cases where this was done. As expected from the choice of method, the user research resulted in an extensive and rich base of information. A summary was made of each interview and formed the basis of the creation of four *personas* (Miaskiewicz and Kozar, 2011); Personas descriptions that were created for this study were:

- *Persona 1*: a user who sees burning firewood as a hobby, is very knowledgeable but still eager to learn.
- *Persona 2*: a user who believes they know everything but does many things wrong.
- *Persona 3*: a user, who enjoys burning firewood but finds it difficult and is insecure, is interested in learning but does not care too much.
- *Persona 4*: a user who does not care and just wants everything to be as easy as possible.

In addition to the development of the personas, an overview was made of various recorded elements of behaviour that differ from the recommendations for optimal burning. These included burning wood that is too moist, using paper and cardboard to start the fire, kindling the fire from the bottom of the wood instead of from the top, not giving flames sufficient air when firing up, reducing the air too much while burning, closing the secondary air while leaving the primary air open and leaving the door ajar too long.

The goal for the design phase was to design a woodstove that would potentially make all four personas use it more in line with recommended behaviours, and as a result, it would be accepted by all the personas. To support this process the personas and the types of sub-optimal behaviour were used as input to idea generation, analysis and evaluation, and finally, concept development. To generate ideas, a workshop was arranged at Jøtul in May 2012 with seven participants from their product development, marketing and the technical departments. At the start of the workshop, the results from the user research and the personas were presented. The participants were then asked to brainstorm ideas for how to make people use a woodstove more in line with recommended behaviour, particularly targeting the list of sub-optimal behaviours. To keep the challenges simple the personas were given limited emphasis during the idea generation, although they were brought up from time to time to spur the generation of additional ideas. By analysing the results from the design workshop and excluding overlapping ideas, a number of distinct ideas were identified. These ideas were positioned in the control–obtrusiveness landscape, according to how much control and attention they demanded from the user (see Figure 21.3).

As suggested in the Principles of Behaviour Change guide, the next step was to identify those areas of the landscape that will potentially result in a desired behaviour change, which are acceptable or not acceptable for the different personas (Figure 21.4).

Combining results from the previous steps allowed for identification of the most suitable ideas, which were evaluated in collaboration with the design and technical experts at Jøtul on the basis of their feasibility and how easily they could be included in a product prototype. As a result, it was determined that the prototype should include a combination of some of the ideas, which also directly respond to some of the most obvious shortcomings of the vast majority of the woodstoves on the Norwegian market, where almost all the woodstoves

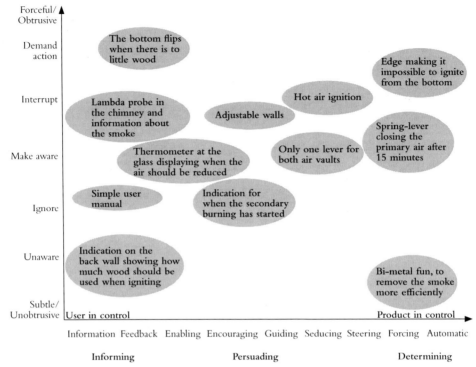

Figure 21.3 Ideas for design interventions plotted into the control–obtrusiveness landscape

have separate leavers for primary and secondary air with no obvious information about the difference between the two. The consequence is that many users do not understand the difference and how they should be adjusted according to each other. As a result, they often do it wrong.

It was concluded that the prototype should have one lever, to make it impossible for the user to close the secondary air but leave the primary air open. When the lever is pulled all the way out, both air valves are completely open; when it is pushed in a bit, the primary air closes but the secondary air is kept open. The further it is pushed beyond this point, the more the secondary air closes, until it is pushed all the way in and the secondary air is completely closed. Also, almost none of the woodstoves on the Norwegian market provides users with information where the air adjustment leavers should be positioned during different stages of the burning process. To help the user understand the different positions of the lever, icons were provided at the position where:

1 both primary and secondary air are completely open (to be used during ignition);
2 primary air is closed but secondary air completely open (to be used for rapid burning); and
3 when primary air is closed and secondary air almost but not completely closed (to be used for slowest possible burning).

To our knowledge, no existing woodstove helps the users understand when the most appropriate time is to make adjustments to the air in this way. The prototype was also equipped with a thermometer on the window at the front of the woodstove, indicating

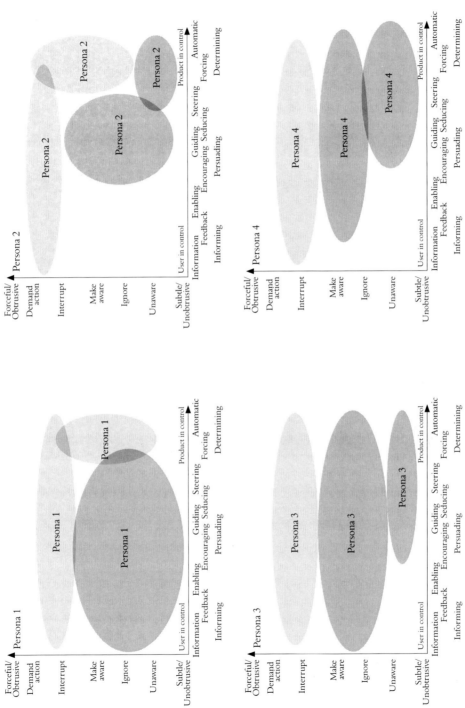

Figure 21.4 Finding out how different personas would react to various control–obtrusiveness combinations

when the air should be adjusted. Lastly, the prototype was accompanied by an easy to read, illustrated user manual.

Details of the testing phase are provided in Daae *et al.* (2016). In short, 20 participants, all woodstove users on a regular basis, would come to the lab, answer a few questions about their woodstove experience and burning habits, and light a fire in one of the woodstoves – not knowing that there were two, and not knowing the intention of their participation in the test. No explanations were given of how to operate the woodstove, but before lighting the fire the participants were asked to explain what they believed the purpose was of the different parts of the woodstove. During the burning process, the test leader paid attention to what the participant did, but without commenting on it. After the test, the participants of the prototype were asked specifically about whether they had noticed (and used) the steps on the air vault lever, and what they thought of it. All participants were provided with the same choice of lighters, matches and quantity of wood. Measurements were made every minute of the emissions of CO_2, CO, O_2 and NO_x. In addition, the weight of the remaining wood and temperature development in the smoke was recorded, and the total fine particle (PM) emissions were measured.

None of the participants that used the prototype consulted the user manual and the few who noticed the thermometer, thought it was part of the measuring instruments and not something they should pay attention to. However, half of the participants using the prototype noticed the icons and letters before or during the beginning of the burning process, and they all used it actively, both by adjusting the air according to the icons and by naming the letters when talking about what they were doing. Among the participants who did not notice the icons, four out of five were very enthusiastic about them when they were asked about them after the test. They also said they believed they would have interacted differently with the woodstove, if they had noticed them before the test. Only one participant was uncertain about their meaning and thought it would not have affected her if she had noticed them at the beginning of the test.

The way the participants used the woodstoves was analysed to evaluate to what extent their behaviour was in line with the recommendation. Particular attention was given to whether the participants had lit the fire from the top, closed the primary air when it burned properly or adjusted the secondary air and achieved a successful secondary burning.

These criteria, together with other observations and the general evaluation of what the participants had done, provided the basis for rating their behaviour. Based on this evaluation, it was apparent that the five participants who noticed the icons either behaved identical to, or quite in line with, the recommendations. They also closed the primary air, adjusted the secondary air and achieved good secondary burning. Though the sample size was small (the stoves needed to become cold again after every test, allowing for one test per day), the evaluation of all the test results suggested that the prototype resulted in better burning processes than the conventional woodstove. For example, after each test, the ash was removed from the woodstoves, but no other cleaning was done. Before the testing, both woodstoves were almost unused and consequentially had completely clean glass at the sides and on the door. During the testing, the glass surfaces on the conventional woodstove gradually got increasingly opaque, whereas the glass on the prototype stayed clean.

The results indicated that it is worthwhile to explore further how the design of ovens may be improved and do further testing without the variation in the way the participants lit the fire. The primary function of the combined lever was to simplify the air adjustment and avoid the situation where the wrong air valve is closed. Possibly the thermometer could have simplified this even further, but as none of the participants noticed this, the test was unable to evaluate this aspect. However, further simplification of the adjustment of the air valves, and possibly other aspects of the interaction with the woodstove, are undoubtedly possible and potentially valuable.

The fact that only half of the participants who used the prototype noticed the icons, none noticed the thermometer and none consulted the simplified user manual, is in line with the known challenges connected to affecting a habitual behaviour (Klöckner and Matthies, 2004; Verplanken and Wood, 2006), which is likely to be the case for regular woodstove users. In the context of the woodstove, this presents a challenge, as our ethnographic research suggests that a design that would be obtrusive enough to break user habits is unlikely to be accepted by users. Thus, the way the behaviour changing aspects of a new woodstove are presented would benefit from additional research. The lack of attention given to the user manual may also be a consequence of the lack of attention that is generally paid to user manuals, across a broader spectrum of household products. The thermometer was interpreted as one of the many measuring tools attached to the woodstove, and thus may have had more effect if applied in a non-laboratory setting.

The use of Principles of Behaviour Change to evaluate the likelihood of the ideas resulting in the desired behaviour change and being accepted by users, contains a number of potential challenges. First of all, the positioning of the ideas in the landscape is difficult, particularly because the position may depend strongly on how the principle is applied, not only on the type of principle. The results of the analysis only indicate that particular types of principles have the potential to result in the desired behaviour or are likely to be accepted by the user. There may also be several other aspects of the design of a product that also affect the success of the design (Daae and Boks, 2014). Nevertheless, the tool does provide some new insight and can provide additional understanding of how the product affects the user, in addition to the exclusion of directly unsuitable ideas from the ideation process.

Master's-level research projects

The woodstove case study described above was carried out in the context of PhD research at the Department of Product Design at NTNU. Several dozen smaller, though still extensive studies have been carried out as well, mostly as semester-long projects in the context of a Sustainable Design course (Boks and Daae, 2013a, 2013b). Most of these research-based student projects have followed the Principles for Behaviour Change approach, discussed in this chapter. In the subsequent sections, two of these projects are briefly presented, to illustrate how the approach may inspire research processes, factors to investigate and the use of user centred methods to apply in a design for sustainable behaviour process. Though each project was based on following the same Principles of Behaviour Change approach, they all adapted this method to their own needs, sometimes with innovative approaches and ways to visualize the process and findings.

Design of a DfSB solution for ineffective hand washing of household dishes

In a project aimed at manual dishwashing behaviour, students used structured observation and structured interviews to develop new insights on behavioural patterns, equipment use, kitchen layout, what users washed up manually, water temperatures and overall cleanliness. They found that bad (unsustainable) behaviours included using too much detergent, running the tap for unnecessary periods of time, using excessively hot water and over-cleaning. It was also found that many users believed they were acting in an eco-friendly way, but in practice were not. Several key factors were found to affect these behaviours, including: habits; outdated beliefs of what was correct dishwashing behaviour; an urge to speed up the process; the amount and type of dishes that needed to be cleaned; lack of vacant space in the dishwasher; equipment available; boredom with the chore itself; and, lack of knowledge about when dishes are sufficiently clean according to general standards and the standards of household members in particular.

A matrix was produced, linking bad (unsustainable) behaviour and cause, which proved very insightful for getting an idea of the solution finding space. It was, for example, common that users only considered water use when thinking in terms of environmental impact, and disregarded the environmental consequences of excessive detergent use.

In this project the Master's-level students adapted Lockton's distinction of users (Lockton et al., 2012), and categorized 'shortcut' (ease is important, adverse to change, lazy, will not investigate, read, notice or put any effort into making a change), 'in between' (distant concern for environmental issues but not at the cost of speed and effectiveness) and 'thoughtful' users (concerned, eager to learn, but still require convenient solutions that give evidence of sustainability before adoption is considered). Using the control-freedom landscape, the group decided to focus on the 'in between user'. It was found that these users are unlikely to want to be controlled by the product, but probably not offended if the product steered the user towards the desired behaviour, as long as it was not too obtrusive. Results from the observations suggested that most users were not reluctant to change their behaviour towards more sustainable patterns as long as it would not inconvenience them, but would jump at a solution to make dishwashing more efficient in terms of time and labour. Therefore the key principles that a solution could incorporate were encouraging, guiding, seducing or possibly mild steering, depending on how much the solutions would need to appeal to those that are most unlikely to change their behaviour. Feedback should be limited to positive reinforcement of good behaviour to keep delivered information mostly unobtrusive. The design dilemmas derived centred around: how to design a product that appears hygienic given that dishwashing is a 'dirty' activity, and how to create something new and exciting with the capability of changing habitual behaviour without it being too obtrusive or determining.

After several iterations with ideation and concept development, this inspired a concept that based on a roller, dispensing just enough detergent to get the job done, in an unobtrusive, hygienic and user friendly way. Combining sloping surfaces, the students created a product that clearly communicates use and direction to potential users. The area around the ball gathers the dirt and keeps the surrounding area clean. The rounded overall shape appears hygienic, with no nooks and crannies where dirt can accumulate. The product is still adjustable in terms of placement so the user retains full control in this regard.

USING TOO MUCH DETERGENT

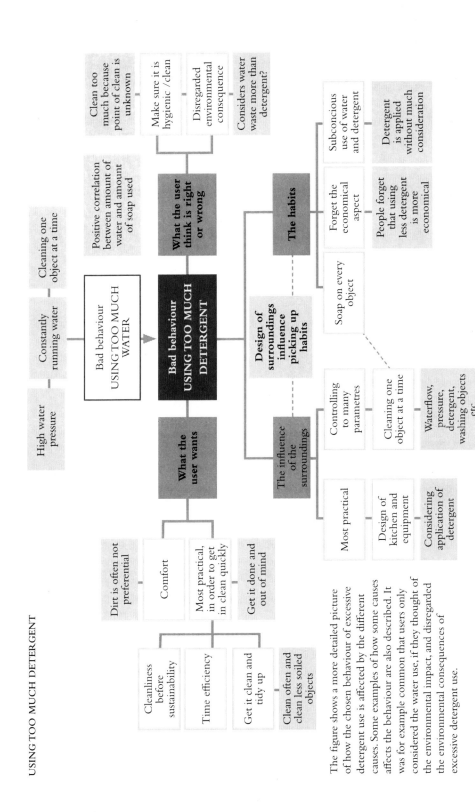

Figure 21.5 Reasons for using too much detergent

RESEARCH PROCESS

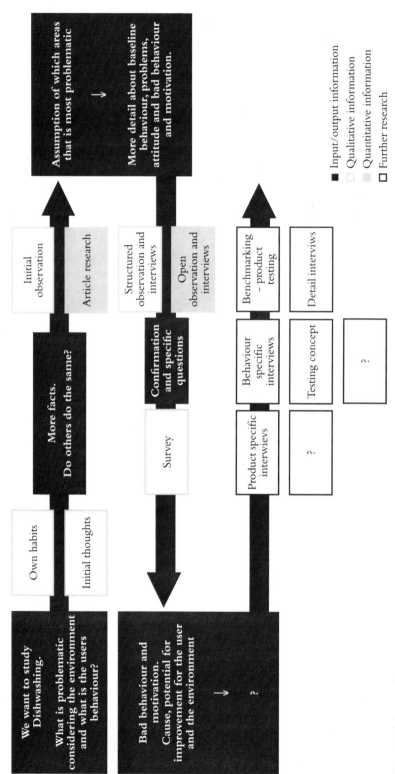

Figure 21.6 Research process

Figure 21.7 The *Roll design solution developed in response to case study data and insight

Design of a DfSB solution for ineffective use of heaters while sleeping

It is widely understood that people spend nearly one-third of their lives sleeping. However, less understood are the heating requirements for sleeping environments, especially in a northern country with long harsh winters such as Norway. In this project, a team of Master's-level students chose to study sleeping habits related to spatial heating during sleeping in student dwellings. This project was undertaken to explore the opportunities for design interventions that could reach those who use more energy for heating than necessary in single-room student accommodations. The students conducted fieldwork to gain understanding of the mindset of various student/consumer groups, seeking to understand what these people do and value when they sleep, and what they would consider to be acceptable for their respective comfort levels. The objective was to develop the groundwork for the design of an effective and appealing product. The students started off by mind mapping all aspects related to sleep, and were particularly active in finding relevant scientific literature on topics such as measurements of temperatures in sleeping rooms, duration of sleep, the effect of humidity on quality of sleep and overheating due to fear of getting too cold. In addition to an online survey for mapping sleep habits the students developed a cultural probe diary that respondents could use to share experiences with hardware use, in the context of their room layouts (such as beds, mattresses, bedlinen) and the heating system (under floor heating, panel heaters, radiators, heat pumps etc.).

It was found that approximately a quarter of the survey participants choose to turn on/up their heating when they felt too cold. Furthermore, 60 per cent of the respondents chose to open the window when their room was too warm. Some of them may also reduce the room heating temperature at the same time, however, this was a relatively small percentage of respondents. Through the survey, it became evident that people generally use more heat than is necessary. This was shown to occur on a daily basis for general use prior to sleep (such as studying, reading, eating, etc.) and users did not adjust their heating in accordance to their sleep preferences. The probes further revealed habits such as turning on the heater fully upon entering the room or just before sleeping, sleeping in little or no clothing and drinking certain beverages that affect body temperature.

It was also found that bed position in relation to the thermostat or the window affected behaviour, as does the type of bed. Another finding was that the context of sleeping makes many people extremely sensitive to what is considered disrupting, stressful or frustrating actions that may be required for establishing a desired behavioural pattern; they value their sleep so much that they are not willing to make any sacrifices in terms of perceived desired heat and comfort levels, such as leaving control over heat levels to an automatic thermostat. Further interesting findings were related to convictions and beliefs: people keep the heat on all night because they are scared of getting cold, they leave (often simultaneously) the windows or door open because they think airing out brings health benefits and they believe that the health effects of sleep outweigh any environmental consequence of unsustainable behaviour. As a result, bedrooms often end up being too warm or hot during the night.

Related to this, people fail to take steps to regulate bed and body temperatures prior to and during sleep. The easy solution is to warm up the entire room. Focusing on the bed temperature instead of room temperature could reduce overall heat usage. By focusing on these two behaviours, the ambition was to reduce the impact of the above observations. Based on these insights, the students identified three main behavioural patterns, and developed three *personas* accordingly.

- *Persona 1*: is aware of his/her energy usage, and keeps track of it in some way or another. Is generally environmentally responsible (such as using extra blankets when cold, turning off electronic devices before sleep).
- *Persona 2*: prefers to be warm and get fresh air at the same time, leaving the window open with the heat turned on. Routinely charges smart phone and laptop at night. Is open to changes if they do not compromise convenience too much.
- *Persona 3*: may or may not behave routinely environmentally friendly when engaged in other activities, but will not compromise or bulge when it comes to sleeping habits. Sticks to sleeping routines and will not give away control to for example automatic thermostats.

A number of design dilemmas were consequently identified. First of all, the sleep temperature preference is highly variable. While one individual prefers warm sleeping temperatures, there are others who prefer cooler sleeping environments. In other words, what is comfortable for one person may be unbearable for another. Moreover, many student dwellings are multi-functional and accommodate not just sleeping, but also eating, relaxing and studying. These different activities also typically require variable temperature settings. This makes designing an intervention challenging when the aim is to cater for a significant user group. In addition to individual characteristics and body behaviour, people also possess varying aptitudes when it comes to electronic products and devices. Early on in the research, the students considered technology-based solutions, but this also created a dilemma: if a design solution was to be technology-based, different technology competencies of users must be taken into account. In the end, the product must exhibit intuitive functionality to all potential users, so that even the laziest of users were not put off. Another consideration was that the target group (students) is highly mobile. For example, many students change dwellings quite frequently for various reasons, posing challenges on a design solution particularly if the device is to have intelligent memory (remembering user habits).

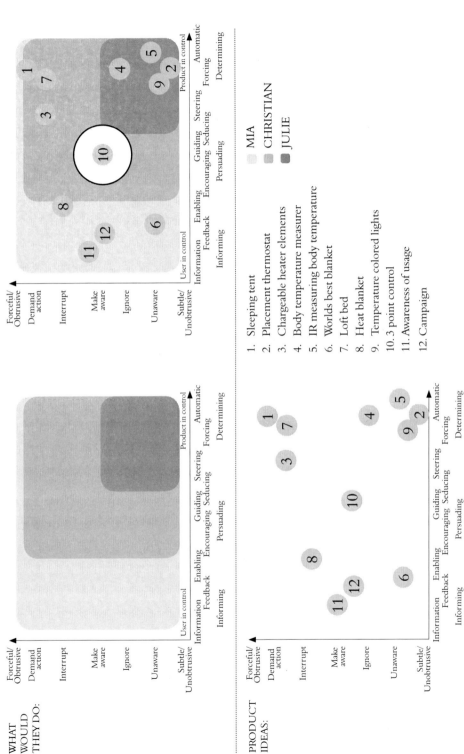

WHAT WOULD THEY DO:

PRODUCT IDEAS:

1. Sleeping tent
2. Placement thermostat
3. Chargeable heater elements
4. Body temperature measurer
5. IR measuring body temperature
6. Worlds best blanket
7. Loft bed
8. Heat blanket
9. Temperature colored lights
10. 3 point control
11. Awareness of usage
12. Campaign

MIA
CHRISTIAN
JULIE

Figure 21.8 Mapping 'forceful/subtle' and 'user in control/product in control' scenarios

Through a design ideation phase, the students selected twelve ideas that could contribute to solving the core design challenges that were identified. These included sensors measuring body temperature controlling the heater, creating lighting that provide a correct or incorrect sense of actual room temperature, creating a microclimate around the bed and various other architectural solutions. The students realized that the key to the solution was to increase the ease with which bedroom temperatures can be appropriately adjusted, and that awareness and motivation are the key aspects to triggering environmental gains with respect to sleep – at least for persona one and two, who are willing to delegate some level of control to technology. Using the Principles of Behaviour Change landscape to arrange the solutions according to what users may prefer or be sensitive to, it was decided to focus on a three-point control device consisting of a heater adapter, control panel and a cell-phone application; essentially connecting the heater to the alarm function on the smart phone, allowing the heater to understand when the user goes to bed and plans to wake up, enabling it to adjust heat to a desired, sustainable and healthy level. This was also motivated by the fact that existing solutions to adjust the heat, traditional programmable panel heaters, are designed for people that actively should make an effort to reduce their energy consumption. They are static, in the sense that they (after programming) lower the temperature at the exact same time each day, regardless of when you go to sleep, and at what time you get up. This functionality automatically excludes the majority of users. The solution was partially inspired by one of the cards of the Design with Intent toolkit (Lockton, 2013), the one that suggests to make the desired behaviour the default behaviour.

Conclusions

This chapter has provided insights into how a user-centred design process may lead to suggestions for reducing environmental impacts during use phase interaction between users and products. The user-centred design process described in this chapter is informed by behavioural psychology, and makes use of the toolkit of methods that designers have available. This toolkit exists of widely used methods such interviews, observation and ethnography, as well as methods developed specifically for changing behaviour, such as Principles for Behaviour Change and Design with Intent.

In the main case presented, which focused on the redesign of a woodstove, the process covered everything from problem identification, anthropological research and several iterations of ideation and redesigning, to blind testing by comparing emissions from a conventional and a prototype woodstove. Two smaller cases were also discussed to show variations on this approach, developed as far as the design conceptualization phase.

This, however, by no means implies that research has provided a final answer as to how approach these and similar research questions. Design for Sustainable Behaviour is young field, which has still much to gain from more extensive cross fertilization with fields such as practice theory, persuasive technology and behavioural psychology. Therefore, a key challenge for future research will be to test whether effects of (re)design interventions are truly sustainable in the long term, as we (sometimes) assume (too easily) they will be. Neither does the current state of the art provide a meaningful roadmap to implement such approaches within industry and the public sector. In the future, DfSB must expand its focus, to include the role of other actors relevant to design and use and the development of interventions involving multiple actors (Pettersen, 2013). Another approach could be to take DfSB approaches and apply them on firms, or on other societal stakeholders. Looking upon them as actors, in the same vein as we look at individual consumers as actors, we can think of ways of informing or forcing them, or most interestingly, seducing them to integrate sustainability into their activities.

Acknowledgements

This chapter is partly based on recent publications in the *International Journal of Sustainable Engineering* (Daae and Boks, 2015a) and the *Journal of Design Research* (Daae et al., 2016), as well as a conference paper by Boks et al. (2015). The authors also acknowledge the students that have indirectly contributed to this article through their assignments for the sustainable design course at NTNU's Department of Product Design.

References

Boks, C., Daae, J. (2013a) 'Towards an Increased User Focus in Life Cycle Engineering: Re-engineering Manufacturing for Sustainability'. *Proceedings of the 20th CIRP International Conference on Life Cycle Engineering*, Singapore, 17–19 April.

Boks, C., Daae, J. (2013b) 'From Teaching Sustainable Product Design to Teaching Sustainable Behaviour Design'. *Proceedings of Cumulus 2013, The 2nd International Conference for Design Education Researchers*, Oslo, 14–17 May.

Boks, C., McAloone, T. C. (2009) 'Transitions in Sustainable Product Design Research'. *International Journal of Product Development*, vol 9, no 4, pp429–449.

Boks, C., Lilley, D., Pettersen, I. (2015) 'The Future of Design for Sustainable Behaviour, Revisited'. *Proceedings of Ecodesign2015*, December, Tokyo, Japan

Daae, J., Boks, C. (2014) 'Dimensions of Behaviour Change'. *Journal of Design Research*, vol 12, no 3, pp145–172.

Daae, J., Boks, C. (2015a) 'Opportunities and Challenges for Addressing Variations in the Use Phase with LCA and Design for Sustainable Behaviour', *International Journal of Sustainable Engineering*, vol 8, no .3, pp148–162.

Daae, J., Boks, C. (2015b) 'A Classification of User Research Methods for Design for Sustainable Behaviour'. *Journal of Cleaner Production*, vol 106, pp680–689.

Daae, J., Goile, F., Seljeskog, M., Boks, C. (2016) 'Burning for Sustainable Behaviour', *Journal of Design Research*, vol 14, no 1, pp42–65.

Haakonsen, G., Kvingedal, E. (2001) *Utslipp til luft fra vedfyring i Norge Utslippsfaktorer, ildstedsbestand og fyringsvaner*. Statistics Norway, Norway.

Karlsvik, E., Oravainen, H., (2009) *Guidebook – Effective and Environmentally Friendly Firing of Firewood*. Intelligent Energy Europe, Luxembourg.

Klöckner, C., Matthies, E., (2004) 'How Habits Interfere with Norm-Directed Behaviour: A Normative Decision-Making Model for Travel Mode Choice'. *Journal of Environmental Psychology* vol 24, no 3, pp319–327.

Lilley, D., Wilson, G. T. (2013) 'Integrating Ethics into Design for Sustainable Behaviour'. *Journal of Design Research*, vol 11, no 3, pp278–299.

Lockton, D. (2013) 'Design with Intent: A Design Pattern Toolkit for Environmental and Social Behaviour Change'. Doctoral dissertation, Brunel University School of Engineering and Design.

Lockton, D., Harrison, D., Stanton, N. A. (2012) 'Models of the User: Designers' Perspectives on Influencing Sustainable Behaviour'. *Journal of Design Research* vol 14, no. 10(1–2), pp7–27.

Miaskiewicz, T., Kozar, K. A. (2011) 'Personas and User-Centered Design: How Can Personas Benefit Product Design Processes?' *Design Studies* vol 32, pp417–430.

Ozil, F., Tschamber, V., Haas, F., Trouvé, G. (2011) 'The "Zero-CO" Domestic Fireplace: A Catalytic Solution to Reduce Pollutants'. *Management of Environmental Quality: An International Journal* vol 22, pp429–439.

Pettersen, I. N. (2013) 'Changing Practices: The Role of Design in Supporting the Sustainability of Everyday Life'. Doctoral dissertation, Norwegian University of Science and Technology.

Verplanken, B., Wood, W. (2006) 'Interventions to Break and Create Consumer Habits'. *Journal of Public Policy and Marketing* vol 25, pp90–103.

Wilson, G. T. (2013) 'Design for Sustainable Behaviour: Feedback Interventions to Reduce Domestic Energy Consumption' Doctoral dissertation, Loughborough University.

Zachrisson, J., Boks, C. (2011) 'Obtrusiveness and Design for Sustainable Behaviour', *Proceedings of Consumer 2011*, 18–20 July, Bonn.

Zachrisson, J., Boks, C. (2012) 'Exploring Behavioural Psychology to Support Design for Sustainable Behaviour Research'. *Journal of Design Research* vol 14, no 10(1–2), pp50–66.

Zachrisson, J., Storrø, G., Boks, C. (2011) 'Using a Guide to Select Design Strategies for Behaviour Change: Theory vs. Practice'. *Proceedings of EcoDesign 2011, Design for Innovative Value Towards a Sustainable Society*, Kyoto, Japan, 30 November–2 December, pp362–367.

22

HACKING THE PROBE-HEAD

Manipulations for social sustainability

Otto von Busch

Abstract

Design designates; it guides and leads us towards specific types of behaviors. Designers serve to defend and propel the interests of the client, who wants to lead their customers or users into a relationship of dependence and addiction. Through the clever use of devices, apparatuses and affordances, design sorts and consolidates human behaviors to propel the status quo. However, there can be many forms of resistances, and one form is hacking – the manipulation of the mechanisms which guide and exclude, such as locks. In this way, the craft of manipulation is the central feat of hacking. It is the material intervention of trespassing into systems in order to change and tune them towards becoming counter-systems. This text examines how hacking can be used to manipulate systems of exclusion into more inclusive systems; affecting the designed guidance devices in order to propel both sustainability and social justice.

Keywords: hacking, sustainability, activism, probe-head, social justice

Designations: coercive affordances

To most of us, the everyday environment that we call home is shaped by human intentions, ideas of function and aesthetics. Even our nature today bears marks of human engagements, and some propose we now live in a geological age which carries a mark of human actions on a planetary scale (often referred to as the *Anthropocene*). As humans, on both an individual as well as a collective scale, we are born into design. We wrap our bodies into design and use design to get by in our designed everyday. We live in designed environments, and even our exit from this life happens within a designed space of objects, techniques and rituals. At every occasion, design structures and devises our course of life as we are framed, coupled and networked by traditions, intentions and practices.

Design *designates*, and I would like to draw attention to how it does so. Design *directs* our attention and perception to notice what is regarded as important, such as language, signs, abstract concepts, symbols and machines, which makes us see things we could not see with our own senses (just think of microscopes, X-ray cameras or space probes). Design *assigns* itself to be of use, enhancing and modifying human behavior (just think of everyday tools, functional clothes or ergonomic furniture). Design also *delegates*, it takes over some of my own labor, decisions and troubles (just think of washing machines, pocket calculators and suggested playlists), while also creating dependencies on others, such as specialist repairs or abstract systems of service or updates.

The more user-friendly design is, the better it designates our behavior. It also leaves us ignorant to how we are being directed. A user-friendly design manipulates us; it coerces us into a designed path of action. The better and more efficient it is, the less we notice our obedience to it. We are so consumed with our own empowerment, we fail to see how our new powers came at a price: our compliance to be guided and coerced. This is especially problematic when shifting towards more sustainable solutions for living. Not only are many of our unsustainable environments very user-friendly (our addiction to cars, or recent coffee-to-go lifestyle), we often fail to see how intricately bound to them we are (such as our rising need for electricity in order to be 'social' with each other).

Other designations are more blatant. They can be explicit obstructions, such as speed bumps, or mechanisms of exclusion, such as gates at the metro which make sure I have paid for my ticket. They can be seemingly innocent, such as can-openers for right-handed people, which are impossible to use with the left hand. Other designation mechanisms can be more abstract forms of exploitation, such as offshore sweatshops or economic systems of segregation and extortion. Human culture revels in design and this can be both a benefit and a hazard. Yet, when we speak of design, we most often focus on the benefits.

Mechanisms of designation

Any randomly chosen issue of a popular design magazine will be full of designation machines; endless images of *devices* and *apparatuses*, each and every one with its own designated *affordances*. As objects designate our behaviors, they are often amalgamations of these mechanisms. Some types of designs are *devices*. As highlighted by design researcher Martin Avila "a device (Latin *divisa*, *divisus*; division) divides, that is, organizes, arranges, frames our environment and defines limits and possibilities of relation" (Avila, 2012, p31). The device fragments the world, sharpens action towards certain uses but also delimits other fields of action. Other designs are *apparatuses* (Latin: *apparare*; to prepare). As emphasized by cultural theorist Vilem Flusser, the apparatus is tool that "lies in wait … it sharpens its teeth in readiness" (Flusser, 2000, p21), ready to spring into action. Such tools can be simultaneously a mechanical object, such as Flusser's example of the camera, as well as its abstract reflection, the regime of visuality manifested through photographic representation, which in turn resonates well with Giorgio Agamben's notion of the apparatus as a mechanic of power (Agamben, 2009). All forms of design also have designated *affordances*, symbolic or material properties that guide the user's actions with them, their intended purpose of use (Norman, 1988). The concept of affordances may also serve us well as we trace how everyday design coerces, sorts and consolidates our behaviors.

If we focus on how design designates, as in the previous examples, it can be useful to think of these mechanisms as "abstract machines," to use a term by philosophers Gilles Deleuze and Felix Guattari (2005). According to Deleuze and Guattari, two of the primary abstract machines are those of *sorting* and *cementing*. As we move through life we are guided through psychological, social, material and environmental settings, already put there before we were born, and these guiding operations are further reproduced by our own actions: we make others repeat what we want them to do. We take part in "sorting operations" and "consolidation operations" through our everyday actions. These designed systems organize, stratify and code the world.

Sorting is the compartmentalizing of people through micro-categorizations through classifications, distinctions, symbols and rankings, using all kinds of means (clothes, dialects, forms, passports, and grades for example). Using the vocabulary of Cassirer we could call these distinctions "symbolic forms" as man is a "symbolic animal" (Cassirer, 1944). The other force is the *cementing*, the concrete materialization of symbolic categorizations. This implies the sorting process materializes into physical structures of society, congealed into inalterable forms, which strictly limits the potential for the emergence of new and different determinations: the mortar which reproduces social and material processes has fixed the result of the sorting. Following the thinking of Deleuze and Guattari, the form and shape of society is ordered and affixed by these two structure-generating principles, the concrete forces embodying the same abstract machines or engineering diagrams.

Yet, the sorting does not happen with any pre-ordained course or inherent meaning. There may be strategies or overarching ideologies effecting the construction of the everyday environment. However, sorting always happens at the local level, sometimes in what seems like a haphazard way, yet governed by behavioral repertoires supported by several guidance devices. The sorting can be an evolutionary event, such as natural selection of a germ-line from a population, or a social event, such as a court of law, distinguishing between the innocent, or the guilty. Whereas natural selection is replicated and consolidated through reproduction, the decision from a court of law in turn is firmly coupled with the prison, which consolidates the verdict into freedom or imprisonment. This kind of sorting takes place in many fields; among other things it can for example be *coded*, such as compatible or incompatible languages, or *genetic*, such as which populations can intermix and reproduce, or *medical*, sorting between healthy and sick, whom to medicate and whom to not, or *national*, sorting between passport-holding citizens, and undocumented aliens. Within the everyday realm of design, it also sorts us into right-handed or left-handed, who can access a space through the stairs and who cannot, what size of feet fits into women's shoes or not, who has the strength to twist open a can or not, what file-format can be copied, and so on.

Concerning sustainable design, the sorting may happen on the level of how regulations deem what is considered a "healthy" life. An example can be levels of hygiene, which in itself is also pushed by lifestyle markers and consumption patterns. For example, what smells an individual may suggest (how often must we shower and wash clothes, use of perfume etc.), which in turn affects other sustainable behaviors, such as cycling to work. I may choose not to bike, or push for more sustainable laundry habits, if I feel socially excluded by tacit norms at my glamorous workplace.

To bring attention to where sorting and consolidation takes place, Deleuze and Guattari suggest a function they call *probe-heads*, or "*tetes chercheuses*, guidance devices" (Deleuze and Guattari, 2005, p190). This is the sharp-edge of sorting and guidance operations, or what we could call the "front-end," bearing in mind it is an intrusion and, sometimes violent, conflict zone. The probe-head is a switch that sorts, in or out, right or left, free or captive, just before the following compartmentalization and consolidation mechanism kicks in. The probe-head is what philosopher Manuel DeLanda translates as "searching device," a shortsighted sorting device that "explores a space of possible forms" (DeLanda, 1997, p139). He defines the sorting "strictly as the result of the coupling between a population of replicators ... and a sorting device (of any kind)" (DeLanda, 1999). The probe-head, as an abstract device (not a metaphor), is enacted through natural, material or social forces, laws, or design. It is the very edge of the sorting device; it orders and pushes matter, populations, or ideas into the cementing process and the formal operations of society, replicating and materializing designs, orders and commands through social obligations, like abstract categories, such as citizenship, or qualities, such as degrees or diplomas, etc. Probe-heads also manifest in material functions that include or exclude us, unlocks or locks the doors and exits, borders or exams. DeLanda gives the example from biology, of species and populations, geology, of rocks and sediments, and of various social contracts and conditions, such as laws and religious codes, guiding weddings, offspring, and trade agreements (DeLanda, 1997).

Especially DeLanda's last examples of probe-heads interact smoothly with the realm of design: the tacit social contracts such as custom, tradition and informal praxis. The social ways of being and our value systems are most often hidden to us, we are shaped by them and have trouble noting how we are formed by them, and socially addicted to them. Everyday behavior is intrinsically guided by minimal social rewards and punishments. They are part of the consolidation processes which makes sure that life stays somewhat predictable; they preserve the status quo for good and bad. Through continuous feedback-loops, recognition and affirmations, or judgments and penalties, such behaviors anchor us into our everyday, while simultaneously make sure we don't resist or "rock the boat," even when we are faced with wrongdoings. Indeed, as peace researcher David Cortright notices, most of us fail to speak out even to blatant oppression:

> We fear the loss of job security or position; we worry how family, friends, and employers will view us. We are so entangled in the comforts of society that we find it difficult to take risks, even for causes we hold dear.
>
> *(Cortright, 2009, p33)*

Designated systems and countersystems

According to the acclaimed critical designers Anthony Dunne and Fiona Raby, most everyday designs reinforce the "status quo" (Dunne and Raby, 2001), rather than questions the conditions of consumer society. On a similar note, design theorist Tony Fry has convincingly put forward the claim that most design not only sustains the existing order, but is also a form of "defuturing," which severely constrains our options to make our societies more sustainable (Fry, 1999). Even acclaimed design perspectives (such as participatory design and co-design) risks reproducing tacit forms of coercion, or turning the change agent into a *collaborateur*, colluding with current exploitative regimes of consumerism and politics of domination (Cooke and Khotari, 2001). The very system of consumerism compels us to collaborate with unsustainable conditions and lifestyles, which severely limits the avenues to radically address the roots to the unsustainable paradigm of consumerism. Sociologist Gideon Sjoberg has made a call to examine alternative social arrangements that explicitly challenge the systems supporting the status quo; a move towards perspectives that offer a "countersystem" approach (Sjoberg et al., 2003).

Sjoberg calls for a countersystem approach, highlighting how systematic wrongs needs to be confronted by opposing systems, not just small "fixes." This, however, necessarily produces various levels of conflict. Over the last few decades there has been a calling to expose disagreement, dissensus and "agonism." Agonism shows how there is asymmetry of power, and "wrongs" are being committed within the existing system, thus exposing tensions and contradictions. Agonism highlights how the system is not based on tacit consensus – that all parts are agreeing or everything runs smooth – instead it highlights how the system is a "thing," an assembly of designed and conflicting parts, a product of imbalanced compromises (Björgvinsson, Ehn and Hillgren, 2012). As underlined by interaction designer Pelle Ehn, the thing is both an object and a parliament of different opinions coming together to address the *political* – the conflict of forces, wills, populations, affects, trajectories and ethics, into a process of "thinging" (Ehn, 2008). As proposed by design theorist Carl DiSalvo, design agonism is a central concept in his "adversarial design," which in turn is a strategy of critical design which exposes inconsistencies and disagreements, and becomes a type of political design, based on agonism, and contestation (DiSalvo, 2012, p2).

Intervening in systems

A systemic approach to design unveils how parts interact, and are networked into larger wholes, into social ecologies. Yet, a systemic perspective of design also raises a specific question: where is design to intervene in a system?

Environmental thinker Donella Meadows text, "Leverage Points: Places to Intervene in a System," is a much cited resource on identifying how to push systems towards more sustainable goals. In order to affect change in systems, Meadows stresses, one needs to find and intervene at specific leverage points, where a small local shift can produce big changes that ripple throughout the whole system: "leverage points are points of power" (Meadows, 1999, p1). As Meadows famously argues, intervening at the level of parameters (such as standards and taxes) has a low factor of impact, whereas the more abstract levels (affecting incentives, values, and goals) produces deeper and more systemic change. Following Meadows' advice may however confuse designers used to intervening at the tangible level of the world, through the redesign of products, objects, or tools.

On yet another level, a designer may ask how the tangible interventions of design may even touch such abstract phenomena as poverty or oppression, which are also most often parameters in unsustainable environmental conditions. Using Meadow's framework, a designer will need to mobilize a wide participation to change the social conditions that reproduces our current unsustainable culture waste-making. One way to address Meadow's call for action would be to follow Paulo Freire's *Pedagogy of the Oppressed* (1970), where the subjugated or marginalized must be active participants in their own emancipation, "so that through transforming action they can create a new situation, one which makes possible the pursuit of a fuller humanity" (ibid., p32). Freire urges that this process is facilitated by a problem-solving education, which talks back to the current social condition, and "strives for the *emergence* of consciousness and *critical intervention* in reality" (ibid., p81). So, what can designers really do on this social level?

One such critical intervention into reality, which has been popular within artistic endeavors such as "social practice," is the reference to acupuncture. Artistic director Darren O'Donnel has called such artistic interventions on an interhuman level "social acupuncture" (2008). They are strategic social acts in civil society, which aims to redistribute the energies throughout the social whole. According to O'Donnel, whereas Western medicine is focused on underlying reasons for disease such as bacteria, and aims at treating them momentarily, Eastern medicine sees the whole body in a continuous feedback process. Microbes are always there, but they just matter when your immune system is compromised. Similarly, O'Donnel sees holistic problems in the *social body* of today which affects its social immune system:

> The lack of free public space for unstructured discourse can be seen both as symptomatic of a democratic deficiency and as contributing to the situation, in what amounts to a feedback loop, each contributing to deterioration of the other.
>
> *(O'Donnel, 2008, p48)*

Thus, interventions into the body as well as the social system require a holistic approach, with no aspect isolated or analyzed without taking the whole system into account. Releasing healing energies through the body could apply also socially, O'Donnel continues:

> Theoretically, then, the same thing should apply to the social body: small interventions at key junctures should affect larger organs, in turn contributing to feedback loops that can amplify and affect the distribution of energy resources.
>
> *(O'Donnel, 2008, p49)*

As O'Donnel highlights, social acupuncture aims at healing and redistributing social energies, thus changing the processes of everyday life. Acupuncture does not work by putting the needles at any random place. Instead the interventions much touch specific conduits of social life, questioning the status quo, bringing awareness to the world and pushing for change of social practices; they must modulate and manipulate the social world.

The craft of manipulation: hacking

In much political theory, manipulation is done by those in power as a Machiavellian game of powermongering. Example of this may include the false directions of propaganda, the deception and deceit that reinforces obedience, and leaders who steer elections in their favor with spin and cunning. Manipulation is also the craft of deceptive mythical gods, such as Lucifer "the deceiver" and not least Plato's *Demiurge,* who the Gnostics made into the knowledgeable craftsman who misleads man to take the world of appearances for reality (Meyer, 2003, p5). In this way, the craftsman was *cunning*; that is, "artfully deceitful", "crafty" and with "fraudulent dexterity" (Herzog, 2006, p71).

Political theorist William Riker coined the term *Heresthetics*, after the Greek word for choosing and electing, for a specific form of political cunning, or a "political art" (Riker, 1986, pix). Riker differs heresthetics from of other forms of political manipulation, such as rhetoric and persuasion, as it changes political outcomes *without* changing peoples' underlying preferences. Instead, Riker posits that manipulation is a form of politics which interferes with the decision-making process, setting it up in a partisan manner, of managing the act of choosing (for example by changing the order in which decisions are made). It is a maneuvering of political forces and positions, or as he puts it, "this is what heresthetics is about: structuring the world so you can win" (ibid., pix). Using game theory and examples of how politicians have manipulated rational choices in their favor, Riker expose how decisions can be tilted. Applying *Deleuzoguattarian* terminology, I would like to argue that Riker points to how the probe-head in decisions can be influenced, by the very specific "craft" of guiding the processes of politics.

It is important to notice here that craft, also political craft, is an intervention, often a physical one, manipulating a system on both an abstract and concrete level. As Riker posits, it is a tinkering with material and procedural operations rather than a matter of persuasion or awareness of minds.

As craft theorist Glenn Adamson shows in *The Invention of Craft* (2013), craft is a physical manipulation that overrides barriers between tools, systems and labor organization. In Adamson's example, Alfred C. Hobbs picking of the Bramah patent lock at the world exhibition in 1851 exposed how the fraudulent dexterity of a craftsman can outsmart the systemic ingenuity of the engineers, and how manual action can challenge the predictability of devices. Adamson objects to the modern perspective that industrialism marginalized craft, a view especially asserted by nineteenth-century craft revivalists such as John Ruskin and William Morris, to instead highlight how the skilled hand has a tendency to continuously reinvent its place in the world (Adamson, 2013, p45). As Adamson states, industrialization did somewhat push artisans onto the factory floors, but they also claimed a central position of manually building the mechanisms of mass-production through their specialization and division of labor.

These transformations did not, as is often claimed, de-skill workers. Rather, the modern invention of craft literally put artisans "in their place." In fact, it was precisely their workers' valuable skills that motivated capitalists to invent techniques of controlling them. As "craft technique was isolated as a subject of concern in its own right through division and explication, the person executing the technique was – in a countervailing move – made to seem inconsequential or generic" (Adamson, 2013, pxix). Thus, the potential of artisan skills were robbed of agency, displaced within cultural heritage institutions or dismissed as irrelevant, while in reality, they were at the center-stage of industrial innovation and modernity itself. It was the artisan's power of manual intervention and manipulation that needed to be supervised and controlled: both a necessity and problem of industry.

Craft is itself a powerful form of control, but precisely because of that potency, a telescoping system of larger forces seeks to control it. "Craft's fate in modern times has been to manipulate and be manipulated in turn" (ibid., pxx).

As I would like to argue, it is the fraudulent potency of craft, exactly that it can manipulate matter and systems, which adds to its tacit forcefulness in the world, and intimately connects craft practices to the contemporary phenomenon of hacking. Indeed, it is no accident hacking emerges out of the lock-picking community, inheritors to Hobbs's feat of outsmarting the Bramah lock, a manual skill similar to the technical manipulation, or "phreaking," of telephone systems (Levy, 1994; Thomas, 2002).

Whereas many theorists have highlighted how hacking can be seen as a form of do-it-yourself (DIY) activity, or even forms of critical civic interventions (Ratto and Bolger, 2014), I would like to define hacking not as any form of making, but the specific manipulation of sorting and guidance-mechanisms, or the operational interventions at the level of the probe-head. Rather than being simply a productive craft, or a disseminated mode of production, hacking can manipulate probe-heads. There are thus "better" objects to hack, instances which need more *strategic* intervention, and therefore unlocking more potential, short-circuiting more of the sorting and consolidation operations. Thus it is no accident that the concept of hacking has an undertone of illegality, as it challenges established systems of control, exclusion and sorting. Yet, this illegality should not be confused with crude sabotage. Hacking is a form of material cunning, a fraudulent dexterity; it not only opposes, it also proposes.

Even if the demarcation between hacking and cracking is highly porous, it could still be of interest to try to distinguish between the two. Whereas programming guru Eric Raymond simply makes the distinction: "hackers build things, crackers break them" (Raymond, 2001), it is important to stress how hacking is the conscious 'trickery and manipulation of a system' (Cramer, 2003), which by its very nature is a form of interference and trespassing. The *Jargon File* (the lexicon for hacker slang) also exhibits traits of opposition rather than mere construction under the entry of "hacker": "A person who enjoys exploring the details of programmable systems and how to stretch their capabilities, as opposed to most users, who prefer to learn the minimum necessary" (Jargon File, n.d.).

As financial activist Brett Scott argues, "hackers challenge the binary by seeking *access*, either by literally 'cracking' boundaries – breaking in – or by redefining the lines between those with permission and those without. We might call this *appropriation*" (Scott, 2015). However, as anthropologist Christopher Kelty (2008) points out, hacking, or the practice of "geeks," by manipulating systems, trespassing and opening for new practices, the worldview of the geeks is infused into the world, and by being "out of control," thus clashes with power. New practices intrude on closely guarded territories, upset modes of authority, and overturn previous divisions of power. Geeks are thus "involved in the creation of new things that change the meaning of our constituted political categories" (ibid., p94). Every hack contains elements of a crack, breaking into new territories in order to produce local change.

If hacking has a productive element, I think it would resonate well with feminist Barbara Deming's metaphor of the "two hands," which both *oppose* and *propose* (Deming, 1971). Deming's form of resistance aims to control and reform the relationship between activist and opponent, or more precisely, to take active part in reforming the *guiding principles* between opponents:

> The more the real issues are dramatized, and the struggle raised above the personal, the more control those in nonviolent rebellion begin to gain over the adversary. For they are able at one and the same time to disrupt everything for him, making it impossible for him to operate within the system as usual, and to temper his response to this ... They have as it were two hands upon him—the one calming him, making him ask questions, as the other makes him move.
>
> *(Deming, 1971, p207)*

As the hack confronts the probe-head, the opposing lock, door, policeman, court, or code, it aims to influence the guidance device through a double action: one hands interferes or stops, while the other points to the alternative. And not only that: whereas one hand stops or calms the opponent, the other constructs the alternative, making sure *means and ends coincide* in the same gesture, and at the same time. An act of opposition does not point towards an abstract goal, which will materialize in a distant future, but instead the moving hand produces and embodies the new, even in the smallest form.

From a more activist stance, let's take the example of the sit-ins of the American Civil Rights movement in the 1960s. By the very act of trespassing, of sitting at a segregated luncheon, the activist not only transgresses a symbolic border, but also acts constructively as the counter itself gets desegregated, if only for the moment the protester sits there. The segregating probe-head, the local directive as well as its physical manifestation, its device, is temporarily hacked. The one hand displaces injustice, breaks through a mechanism of exclusion, while the other enacts justice, promoting the act of trespassing and desegregation. The chair reserved "for whites" was temporarily occupied and thus desegregated when a person of color sat on it. Means and end coincided in one act, segregation was opposed, the seat was desegregated, even only for the time of the sit-in. Also, in order to oppose the sit-ins, the opponents had to stop the constructive act of desegregation, thus blatantly enacting their racist stance and revealing the direct violence of segregation and the probe-head itself. The manipulation and displacement of the probe-head enacted justice locally, but also exposed the cruelty of the sorting devices and turned public opinion towards the cause of the civil rights movement.

Hacking for sustainability

So what can hacking as a practice for sustainable design be? On a basic level, it can be any small modification that makes a gadget consume less energy, or a tinkering that prolongs the lifespan of a product. A well-known example may be the Toyota Prius hack, where car owners found a way to make the hybrid car run longer on its batteries, recircuiting the electronics of the car and installing an extra button to activate the new eco-mode of the car (Gordon, 2006). It may also be an intervention, such as repair or maintenance, which makes the user invest attention and time and thus prolong the products emotional durability (Chapman, 2005), which in turn often also adds to the product's patina (Fletcher, 2015). However, as I mentioned earlier, such wide interpretations of hacking may miss the confrontational qualities of hacking, that it is a craft that trespasses and manipulates systems, not merely adds to the existing world. Perhaps it may even be possible to say that the definitive quality of hacking, compared to any DIY-activity, is exactly that it trespasses, it challenges control and thus continuously borders on the illegal.

Illegal sustainable practices may be easier to find than one may first assume. For example, in some parts of the US, it is highly contested, or even deemed illegal to live off-grid, even if the homesteader is totally self-sufficient. Health and sanitation regulations, such as having an approved water supply or being connected to the electricity grid, clash with personal ideals of what is considered a healthy living environment, both on an individual and more collective level (Hren, 2011). In some instances, collecting rainwater may, for example, be counted as theft of property from downstream water-rights owners. Yet, as author and "earthonaut" Stephen Hren emphasizes so eloquently, we cannot know what conditions can be sustainable until we test, and all too often we face laws and regulations that challenge such experiments even before we set out to test. Popular initiatives in sustainable living, which may seem harmless to most (such as urban gardening) may clash not only with laws concerning plants or livestock within city limits, but also property values and the aesthetic ideals of a neighborhood. A small sustainable initiative may thus clash with regulations written to secure peace and consensus within a community.

In many cases, a hack highlights a conflict not only between individual and governmental regulations, but also between personal and collective values, and this is another contributing factor to the conflicts concerning hacking. In his approach to open sources programming, Eric Raymond starts with an aphorism, how "every good work of software starts by scratching a developer's personal itch" (Raymond cited in Moody, 2002, p150). As Raymond mentions, the itch, an immediate personal problem or obstacle in one's way, may be one of the individual impulses on why to put in the efforts to hack, trespass or improve something in the first place. But it may also distort the basic ethical model of hacking; in whose name does a hacker trespass, and what are the communal benefits of an individual's urge to scratch an itch? As hinted by political philosopher Michael Sandel, we may know civic virtues, because "when politics goes well, we can know a good in common that we cannot know alone" (Sandel, 1998, p183).

Following Hren's discussions on how sustainable living may clash not only with modern conveniences, but also with regulations and laws, I would like to propose two basic modes of hacking. I will discuss their implications on social sustainability and how I would suggest a push towards sustainable manipulations for civic purposes. The first mode is the *clandestine* type of hacking, perhaps a style that most connote to the term "hacking"; a secretive act, which aims to dodge the probe-head unnoticed, such as an act of lock-picking or phone "phreaking." The second mode is an *explicit* type of hacking, where the act aims to draw attention to itself, creating momentum and public debate, and thus aims to affect the public operations of the probe-head.

Clandestine and explicit forms of hacking

In the realm of sustainable design, one example of clandestine sustainable actions may be that of "guerrilla gardening," where gardeners do not have the legal rights to utilize, often a private or public property that is not being cared for, or an abandoned site. As author and gardener Richard Reynolds puts it, guerrilla gardening is "the illicit cultivation of someone else's land" (Reynolds, 2008, p5). However, even if the act of gardening itself may be clandestine and done under cover, the results may be very obvious, and these results may be the strength of the action in the first place. The clandestine operations of the gardeners, often involving trespassing, point to the accessibility of abandoned places, and may thus produce leverage for political decisions concerning the underutilized green areas of the neighborhood. However, as with other forms of community engaged urban beautification, it may also lead to unintended forms of gentrification and displacement.

Cultivating capabilities or crafts may also affect the probe-head. The ability to forge a passport for refugees may enable migrant mobility on an international scale. This ability may be invaluable in order to transport someone over a crucial national border, yet the skill may prove less valuable for social movements or for getting a job once inside the new country. The manipulation of documents thus only locally and temporarily affects the probe-head of a national border. Yet the act of forging also affirms the border by reproducing its power, and the forging skill is indeed a perfect reproduction of the probe-head itself: the better I become at forging the passport will, if discovered, trigger processes to further sharpen the probe-head with more safe passports. Thus the clandestine hack tends to amplify the mutual and ongoing arms-race mechanisms between hacker and probe-head.

Another form of social hacking addressing the probe-head of national borders may be the US sanctuary movement, which was especially active in the 1980s, hiding refugees and asylum seekers. The assassination of Archbishop Oscar Romero while serving communion caught the world's attention to the civil wars in Latin America and the refugees fleeing the violent conflicts (Wuthnow and Evans, 2002). Following this, a lot of small Christian communities in North America offered to give sanctuary to the refugees, even against the governmental decrees against doing so. Even if most of their practice was clandestine, hiding refugees and avoiding government crackdown, they also tried to challenge the ruling regime of fear, such as the fear of being caught. Instead, part of their tactic was emphasizing how citizens themselves can overrule one oppressive form of (state) government with their own form of governing; that a community itself decides to give refugees asylum and a residency permit for the very same community. Their emphasis was on how community itself is the basic form of *governing*, not the abstract government, governing by decrees from far off in the capital. Instead, the community itself claimed absolute sovereignty to decide whom to grant sanctuary (Lippert, 2005):

> The Sanctuary Movement argued that they were not committing acts of civil disobedience, but civil initiative, upholding laws their government disregarded. The Sanctuary Movement attorneys argued that the workers were not 'smuggling,' because their immigrants were refugees who had legitimate asylum claims.
>
> *(Smith-Christopher, 2008, p449)*

Thus the community's decision to grant asylum to a refugee was a higher moral ruling than that of the abstract entity called *law* or *state government*. The action of granting sanctuary thus displaces one form of abstract government with our own, more concrete form of direct governing; displacing state-appointed probe-heads to make sure means and ends coincide in action. What was first a clandestine hack became an explicit event, and even if the actions resulted in prison sentences for some of the activists involved, the public opinion pushed for reform of US refugee policies.

As apparent in the example above, explicit manipulations, which were what became of the clandestine sanctuary actions in the trials, tend to look more like acts of civil initiative or disobedience; a highly practical and material practice pushing against political boundaries. Like the Prius-hack, the aim is to make the trespassing or manipulation of the probe-head public and thus accessible to all. The point is to make it obvious and radical enough to affect the policies and laws guiding the probe-head in the first place. Some actions, such as the sit-ins discussed earlier, explicitly challenge immoral or unsustainable laws. Others become powerful symbolic events, such as the craft protests in the 1980s at Greenham Common Women's Peace Camp (Hopkins and Harford, 1984) or some of today's "craftivist" actions (Greer, 2014).

An example of explicit manipulations that have a direct impact on the probe-head can be the actions by the Swedish organization GIL (Gothenburg's Cooperative for Independent Living). GIL is an organization supporting the rights of assistance and accessibility, especially for people with disabilities. The organization has for many years merged activism and media stunts with their lobbying and service to the community. An event that made many headlines was the production of a "CP-doll" in 2012; a toy doll with cerebral palsy. "CP" is also a Swedish insult roughly equivalent to "retard." The text on the packaging stated: "The retard doll GIL. Treat her like a real retard!" The text continues: "She doesn't swear, have sex, drink or poop. So much better than a normal retard." The doll provoked a lot of discussion in media on the treatment of people with disabilities and the societal as well as social accessibility to people with variable or atypical abilities. The doll specifically addresses the often well-meaning but subjectively invalidating treatment of people with disabilities. Anders Westgerd, spokesperson of GIL, said in an interview:

> We came up with the concept for GIL because the members of our cooperative, myself included, were sick and tired of people treating us with prejudiced niceness, as if we were kids or had an inferior intellect. We wanted to do something that provoked people to think about how they treat us. I am sick and tired of people talking over my head, saying stuff like, 'should he really be drinking when he's in a wheelchair?
>
> *(Westgerd in Larsson, 2012)*

The last remark in the statement above also became the point of departure for the next campaign of GIL, the production of a specific beer for "retards," the "CP-beer" (*CP-öl*), a CPA, "a completely normal CP beer." The beer sticker states:

> CPA is a beer that is especially suited for you with disabilities. It is designed to reach parts of the brain that does not otherwise activate. Not activated in you, the imbiber, but rather the people whose prejudice makes such a simple thing as going to the pub with friends harder. We CAN order ourselves. We MAY drink beer. We may even get drunk.
>
> *(Author's translation from Swedish)*

"There's a moral panic about disabled people wanting to drink alcohol. Why shouldn't we be able to get drunk just like anyone else?" Westgerd states after the release. "Many people don't think about how hard it is to have to go in through the backdoor or be carried down stairs. When something like that happens you feel diminished at once," and he continues: "The beer will become like an accessibility certificate" (Westgerd in Genborg, 2013).

It is this last feature that is special about the CP-beer, and made it radically different from the previous media stunts of GIL. In order for an establishment to sell the beer, it had to be wheel-chair friendly and follow the accessibility regulations set by GIL and its members. Thus the beer not only became a tool to raise discussion and awareness, but also materially it became a probe for changing the environment and layout of bars, so they could sell the beer. The beer thus tackled two probe-heads: both the prejudices of people, and the material properties of gaining spatial access from a wheel chair. The bar, a device that makes a division between the abled-bodied and disabled, allowing access to the first while excluding the second, has been manipulated – its lock has been picked. With the beer, means and ends coincide in action to promote the cause of inclusion, accessibility and social sustainability.

Conclusions

While hacking may have many similarities to DIY activities, many which are initiatives towards sustainability, forms of home-steading, renegotiations of agency and divisions of labor and liability, I find it important to stress how hacking engages with conflict. In every hack there is a little crack, and, as Leonard Cohen sings, it's through the crack the light gets in.

Very few struggles for justice have affected political institutions successfully without confrontation. But, likewise, few struggles have brought about social betterment without the constructive part of actively building the alternative. The strength in Deming's "two hands" approach is that it reminds us how two movements can be combined, and means and ends made to coincide.

The world of design is full of probe-heads, and substantial monetary and political interests have rigged them to preserve power to the few. This has produced societal dependencies on unsustainable regimes of production and distribution in everything from food, clothes, housing, care, energy and transport, as well as within the cultural fields, such as education. The democratic struggle to change such regimes and affect the probe-heads is both a matter of environmental design, but simultaneously, an urgency to enact social justice. As with the Sanctuary Movement, justice is a matter of civil initiative; we, the people, need to uphold the laws and moral obligations our governments and especially the market disregard. Hacking is a call to mobilize our skills and efforts towards such goals, not only on an abstract level, but by concrete interventions into the systems we need to change.

But as Brett Scott argues, we need to be aware the means and methods may easily be hijacked in the interest of preserving the status quo. We need to stay sharp, keep raising the bar. As Scott posits, the "hacker" is today not necessarily a subversive character, but has also been bought by an innovation-obsessed venture capitalist culture. To Scott, in today's entrepreneurial culture, hacking has become gentrified:

> Gentrification is the process by which nebulous threats are pacified and alchemised into money. ... The process is repetitive. Desirable, unthreatening elements of the source culture are isolated, formalised and emphasised, while the unsettling elements are scrubbed away ... We are currently witnessing the gentrification of hacker culture. The countercultural trickster has been pressed into the service of the preppy tech entrepreneur class.
>
> *(Scott, 2015)*

Yet, in its manipulation of the probe-head, a hack mobilizes a mix of entities, devices, laws, people and practices. These are not easily controlled, not even by the forces of gentrification, but may continue be tools for trespassing. As Adamson argues, the craftsman has always the potential of manipulating the engineered system of control and exclusion. One cunning hand is for trespassing and opposition, while the other is for redirection and propositions.

The DIY magazine *Make* may have played an essential part in the gentrification of hacking, having tamed and coerced the practice into compliance with the current status quo. Yet, if we are to take ownership of our living environment and make it more sustainable, we may still use the *Make* motto and apply it to more of the political sorting mechanisms that structure our democracy: "if you can't open it, you don't own it" (Jalopy, 2005).

References

Adamson, G. (2013) *The Invention of Craft*, Bloomsbury, London

Agamben, G. (2009) *What is an Apparatus? And Other Essays*, Stanford University Press, Stanford, CA

Avila, M. (2012) Devices: On Hospitality, Hostility and Design, Dissertation, University of Gothenburg

Björgvinsson, E, Ehn P. and Hillgren, P.-A. (2012) Design Things and Design Thinking: Contemporary Participatory Design Challenges, *Design Issues*, Summer, vol 28, no 3, pp101–111

Cassirer, E. (1944) *An Essay on Man: An Introduction to a Philosophy of Human Culture*, Yale University Press, New Haven, CT

Chapman, J. (2005) *Emotionally Durable Design: Objects, Experiences and Empathy*, Routledge, Abingdon

Cooke, B. and Khotari, U. (eds) (2001) *Participation: The New Tyranny?*, Zed Books, London

Cortright, D. (2009) *Gandhi and Beyond: Nonviolence for a New Political Age*, Paradigm, Boulder, CO

Cramer, F. (2003) Social Hacking, retrieved from http://artwarez.org/projects/nagBOOK/texte/florian_eng.html (accessed September 15, 2015)

DeLanda, M. (1997) *A Thousand Years of Nonlinear History*, Zone Books, New York

DeLanda, M. (1999) An Interview with Manuel DeLanda, *Switch Interviews*, retrieved from http://switch.sjsu.edu/web/v5n1/deLanda (accessed September 15, 2015)

Deleuze, G. and Guattari, F. (2005) *A Thousand Plateaus: Capitalism and Schizophrenia*, University of Minnesota Press, Minneapolis, MN

Deming, B. (1971) *Revolution and Equilibrium*, Grossman, New York

DiSalvo, C. (2012) *Adversarial Design*, MIT Press, Cambridge, MA

Dunne, A. and Raby, F. (2001) *Design Noir: The Secret Life of Electronic Objects*, Birkhäuser, Basel

Ehn, P. (2008) Participation in Design Things, *Proceedings of Participatory Design Conference* (PDC), October 1–4, Bloomington, IN, pp92–101

Fletcher, K. (2015) Local Wisdom: An International Fashion Research Project Exploring the 'Craft of Use', retrieved from www.localwisdom.info (accessed September 15, 2015)

Flusser, V. (2000) *Towards a Philosophy of Photography*, Reaktion, London

Freire, P. (1970) *Pedagogy of the Oppressed*, Seabury Press, New York

Fry, T. (1999) *A New Design Philosophy: An Introduction to Defuturing*, UNSW Press, Sydney

Genborg, L. (2013) A Completely Normal CP Beer, *Göteborg Daily*, April 17, retrieved from www.goteborgdaily.se/news/a-completely-normal-cp-beer (accessed September 15, 2015)

Gordon, J. (2006) Hack Your Hybrid – Activate EV Stealth Mode, Get Rid of the BEEP, and More!, *Treehugger*, January 31, retrieved from www.treehugger.com/cars/hack-your-hybridaactivate-ev-stealth-mode-get-rid-of-the-beep-and-more.html (accessed September 15, 2015)

Greer, B. (2014) *Craftivism: The Art of Craft and Activism*, Arsenal Pulp Press, Vancouver

Herzog, D. (2006) *Cunning*, Princeton University Press, Princeton, NJ

Hopkins, S. and Harford, B. (1984) *Greenham Common: Women at the Wire*, Women's Press, London

Hren, S. (2011) *Tales From the Sustainable Underground: A Wild Journey with People Who Care More About the Planet Than the Law*, New Society Publishers, Gabriola Island

Jalopy, M. (2005) Owner's Manifesto, retrieved from http://archive.makezine.com/04/ownyourown (accessed September 15, 2015)

Jargon File (n.d.) Hacker, retrieved from www.catb.org/jargon/html/H/hacker.html (accessed September 15, 2015)

Kelty, C. (2008) *Two Bits: The Cultural Significance of Free Software*, Duke University Press, Durham, NC

Larsson, M. (2012) Some Serious Thought Was Put Into This Retarded Doll, *Vice*, August 24, retrieved from www.vice.com/en_uk/read/some-serious-thought-was-put-into-this-retarded-doll-0000326-v19n8 (accessed September 15, 2015)

Levy, S. (1994) *Hackers: Heroes of the Computer Revolution*, Penguin, New York

Lippert, R. (2005) *Sanctuary, Sovereignty, Sacrifice: Canadian Sanctuary Incidents, Power, and Law*, University of British Columbia, Vancouver

Meadows, D. (1999) *Leverage Points: Places to Intervene in a System*, The Sustainability Institute, Hartland, retrieved from www.donellameadows.org/wp-content/userfiles/Leverage_Points.pdf (accessed September 15, 2015)

Meyer, M. (2003) Gnosticism, Gnostics and the *Gnostic Bible*, in W. Barnstone and M. Meyer (eds), *The Gnostic Bible: Gnostic Texts of Mystical Wisdom from the Ancient and Medieval Worlds*, New Seeds, Boston, MA, pp1–20

Moody, G. (2002) *Rebel Code: The Inside Story of Linux and the Open Source Revolution*, Basic Books, New York

Norman, D. (1988) *The Psychology of Everyday Things*, Basic Books, New York

O'Donnel, D. (2008) *Social Acupuncture*, Coach House Books, Toronto

Ratto, M. and Bolger, M. (2014) *DIY Citizenship: Critical Making and Social Media*, MIT Press, Cambridge, MA

Raymond, E. (2001) How to Become a Hacker, retrieved from www.catb.org/esr/faqs/hacker-howto.html (accessed September 15, 2015)

Reynolds, R. (2008) *On Guerrilla Gardening: A Handbook for Gardening without Boundaries*, Bloomsbury, London

Riker, W. (1986) *The Art of Political Manipulation*, Yale University Press, New Haven, CT

Sandel, M. (1998) *Liberalism and the Limits of Justice*, Cambridge University Press, Cambridge

Scott, B. (2015) The Hacker Hacked, retrieved from http://aeon.co/magazine/technology/how-yuppies-hacked-the-original-hacker-ethos (accessed September 15, 2015)

Sjoberg, G., Elizabeth G. and Cain, L. (2003) Countersystem Analysis and the Construction of Alternative Futures, *Sociological Theory*, vol 21, no 3, pp210–235

Smith-Christopher, D. (ed.) (2008) *Battleground Religion*, Greenwood Press, Westport, CT

Thomas, D. (2002) *Hacker Culture*, University of Minnesota Press, Minneapolis, MN

Wuthnow, R. and Evans, J. (2002) *The Quiet Hand of God: Faith-Based Activism and the Public Role of Mainline Protestantism*, University of California Press, Berkeley, CA

23

TRANSITIONS IN SOCIOTECHNICAL CONDITIONS THAT AFFORD USERSHIP

Sustainable who?

Cameron Tonkinwise

Abstract

While sustainable design strives for quantifiable change, it has a history of ending up advocating for radical socioeconomic change. For instance, life cycle assessment (LCA) research pushed sustainable design researchers to promote systems of shared product use as a way of radically reducing the materials intensity of society. Initial efforts toward these 'product service systems' in the mid-2000s proved premature. This chapter describes more recent changes to information technologies and their use within consumer societies that appear to be more compatible with 'sharing economies'. Pathways for transitioning toward more sustainable ways of resourcing everyday life appear to be opening up. However, these opportunities are not without their own dangers: lifestyles structured around 'usership' rather than ownership may be less materials intense, but also less autonomous. Designers have considerable power in determining which way 'sharing economies' turn.

Keywords: dematerialization, product service systems, sharing economy, transition design

Quantitative unsustainability

Design aims to create things that will improve the quality of human lives. This often involves selecting materials that have been manufactured to perform better in more predictable ways for longer (e.g. plastics, non-ferrous metals, low-e glass, etc.) – as compared to the more or less readily available materials produced by natural ecosystems (e.g. timber, wool, mud-brick, etc.). Concentrating materials through industrial processes to deliver higher performance invariably results in substances that are no longer tolerable to natural ecosystems. These pollutants can then damage beyond repair the very natural ecosystems upon which we depend for other aspects of our quality of life (e.g. air quality, water quality, soil quality, etc.). Much sustainable design is therefore an attempt to negotiate this trade-off between performance and toxicity in our built environments.

Our societies are, however, unsustainable for a whole other reason. This concerns less the quality of the materials with which we furnish everyday life – something that is, at least technically, fixable – and more the quantity (Schmidt-Bleek, 1993). In large part because design is constantly trying to improve the quality of every aspect of our lives, we (in the global consumer class) have too much stuff. Each of those innumerable things requires vastly larger amounts of materials and energy to make (precisely because their materials have been synthesized to higher levels of quality) and run (Schmidt-Bleek, 2001). And each of these things is in actual use far less than it could be, as it is rapidly replaced by other 'better' things and so displaced to landfills where its components and materials are difficult to recover. The rate at which we are dispersing resources – both for use as materials and to convert into energy – out of negentropic natural systems with our linear economies of extraction → manufacture → retail → household → waste stream is now even more unsustainable than its toxic side-effects.

Sustainable design must also therefore reduce societal materials intensity. More sustainable societies would be ones that service everyday living with fewer things. Lowering materials intensity is also about slowing rates of material flows. A sustainable society with fewer things is also a society with longer lasting things, and/or things that get used more while they last. As Schmidt-Bleek noted with his formula 'Materials Intensity per Unit Service (MIPS)', societal sustainability can be enhanced by minimizing the left-hand side – lightweighting – or it can be enhanced by maximizing the right-hand side – increasing service intensity to improve materials productivity. In sum, sustainable design should entail trying to get more use out of things: this could be through longer use, more uses or more users.

More use(r/s)

With this last proposition, we arrive at ideas of 'shared use', 'decoupling use and ownership' and 'usership'. The jargon conceals a seemingly straightforward argument (Gardner, 1999):

- a device can be designed to be somewhat less toxic and/or more energy efficient;
- but that percentage improvement in eco-performance can quickly be undermined once an increased percentage of those devices is sold;
- most of those devices sit idle most of the time in people's households because they are devices that are only needed occasionally;
- it is therefore feasible that one device could be used by many households if it was possible to create a system that coordinated when and where a device was needed;
- fewer devices, used more productively, would deliver enduring factor gains in eco-performance that are not possible with incremental percentage improvements in the eco performance of individually sold and used products.

I am paraphrasing here the work of sustainable design researchers throughout the late 1990s (Cooper and Evans, 2000; Stahel, 1986) and early 2000s, primarily in Europe, Scandinavia and the UK. It is important to see the way in which these arguments developed out of technical assessments of sustainability performance, such as life cycle analysis (LCA), but then arrived at – or, almost backed into – questioning notions of 'property' in radically sociopolitical ways.

These were not, by the way, arguments for (ecological) socialism (as in the work of Andre Gorz and Murray Bookchin). The research from a decade ago that built the case for less materials intense societies was also less focused on the peer-to-peer versions of 'sharing economies' that are more dominant today, and that I will focus on later in this chapter. Rather, the focus was on 'product-service systems' that were more business-to-consumer in nature. Consider the widely cited typology that was the basis of the large *SusProNet* research project (Tukker, 2004):

- **Product-oriented PSSs**: use life extension services added to products owned in conventional ways by households (e.g. help desks, warranties, maintenance/repair/ upgrade).
- **Use-oriented PSSs**: pooled products available on a pay-per-use basis (e.g. laundromats, printing services centres, tool libraries) or temporarily loaning products (e.g. car hire, car share, ride share).
- **Result-oriented PSSs**: true services in which the customer not only does not need to own the product, but does not even use the product as it is instead part of the service provider's equipment (e.g. energy services companies under performance contracts for delivering set levels of lighting and heating, flooring services combining carpet leasing, cleaning, repair and refurnishing; Oliva and Quinn, 2003).

Whilst the second category, Use-oriented PSSs, includes peer-to-peer sharing (me lending you my lawn mower), the focus in the early 2000s was on businesses selling access to, or leasing, fleets of equipment. These are situations of decoupled use and ownership but they are far from communism; they were instead explicitly designed as commercial business innovations. This was part of the argument at the time, an argument that has a demand-side and a supply-side.

Sustainable design can deliver 'cleaner production', but significant ecologically damaging impacts, if not the majority, occur post-production, in the use of a product and its disposal. Sustainable consumption tries to persuade product owners to be more careful about what they do with their goods, but with only ever limited success. One of the constraints in this regard is the fact that households, as homes, offer respite from the market and work. Sustainable consumption has a tendency to want households to be more business-like about their goods. To be concerned about the asset value and operating costs of all your household equipment and maximizing their resource productivity by auditing energy and waste is not an especially attractive way of practicing everyday life. Sustainable design researchers advocating for product service systems (PSSs) recognized that it was more feasible to outsource the practice of enhancing the sustainability of product use and disposal to businesses, than it was trying to convert households over to the business of sustainable asset management. 'Home services' could aim to resource households in more sustainable ways, as specified through performance contracting, freeing householders to simply live in those serviced environments (Quist, 2007; Halme, 2012). Hence, the research advocated for business-to-consumer versions of use-oriented PSSs, rather than peer-to-peer systems.

On the supply side, one of the major obstacles to 'strongly sustainable business models' is that current systems are centred on volumes of retail sales. Not only was after-sales outside of core business, but enhancing utilization intensities directly countered the profitability of selling more and more products. The underlying policy directive of Dematerialising Productive Service Systems research, especially in Europe in the early 2000s, was therefore to convince manufacturers to shift into service provision. The aim was to find ways in which businesses could generate value from resource productivity, aligning the objectives of profitability with ecological sustainability, at least in regard to material intensity (van Halen *et al.*, 2005). PSSs hoped to complement waste minimization directives like Extended Producer Responsibility by shifting economies from sales to leasing in order to facilitate the logistics of product take-back. Talk of these 'closed loop' systems has today been replaced by the alliance between advocates of the Circular Economy and of the Sharing Economy. The added advantage of servicization from a European perspective was that it should have allowed European manufacturers to shift out of a 'race-for-the-bottom' competition with East Asian manufacturers into higher margin, longer-term relations with local customers.

This research was then, from the perspective of both consumers and producers, promoting the idea that businesses maintain ownership of their products and instead sell the use of, or even just the outcomes from professional use of, those goods – what has been called 'Functional Sales' (Stahel, 2010) or the 'Access Economy' (Rifkin, 2000). This is perhaps a less radical proposition than all goods being rendered shareable between households, but it is still a fundamental shift in the economies around which late consumer capitalist societies are organized. While less participatory than currently hyped versions of the 'Sharing Economy', it still entails a radical re-categorization of things in general. In the scenarios of PSSs researchers, nearly all the household equipment with which we live would not actually be owned by us. Consider for instance that such performance contracts would mean having service providers regularly entering homes to tweak or even replace (their) equipment.

The important point for my purposes here is to underline the arc of this research. Research centred on the technicalities and economics of sustainability ends up changing the nature of 'being at home.' It might have been too challenging to convince households to become more sustainable citizens in relation to their possessions, but is getting households to outsource their material sustainability to businesses less revolutionary?

I would like to explore this shift in sustainability research at a more abstract level before returning to the issue of post-ownership economies.

Unintentional change

The discourse of sustainable design tends to oscillate between the utopian and bureaucratic, between revolution and reformism.

On the one hand, it is almost impossible to stay focused on the technical issues of making *x* or *y* more sustainable; that comparative ('more sustainable') demands you nominate what it is that you are aiming to be more sustainable than, which then leads to question, 'what are you sustaining?' (Fry, 2009). On the other hand, any scheme for radically different ways of living must be able to explain its sustainability in terms of the mundane matters of energy sourcing, waste disposal etc., and of course, just how on earth we get from this unsustainable here to that sustainable there (Tonkinwise, 2012).

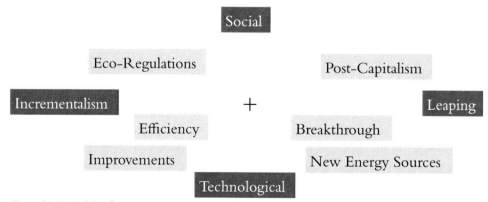

Figure 23.1 Models of transition to more sustainable futures

This is why Ulrich Beck's approach to sustainability is, to my mind, one of the most insightful. Beck reframes sustainability in terms of 'risk' – something that productively converges the technical and the social (Beck, 1995a, 1995b). The decision as to whether a community sources its energy from nearby fracked natural gas or not will involve consideration of the technical assessment of the ecological impacts of that option. But the decision in the end should not be determined by those technicalities, as if there is some determinable threshold to necessarily acceptable risk. What kinds of dangers people are prepared to live with will always vary depending on those people's values. There will always remain the unavoidably political question for the community: 'do we want to live with those risks (even at those levels) at all?'

The question that Beck promotes as the essence of sustainability – 'how do we want to live?' – has the appearance of being quite quotidian. But it contains a subversive potential (much like Herman Melville's Bartleby the Scrivener, whose 'I would prefer not to' was taken up during Occupy Wall Street). For in the background of the community evaluating fracking, for instance, is the issue of whether or not they may 'have to' live with those risks given their economic situation and their current levels of energy consumption. 'How do we want to live?' opens up the possibility of that community choosing a more restrained, effortful and/ or local lifestyle to avoid living with the risks associated with a fossil fuel extraction industry. In that case, the community would appear to be deciding against what is thought necessary, opting for something quite revolutionary – to live in a completely different way.

The obverse of the question, 'what are you seeking to sustain?' is, 'what are you prepared to change, or, what would you like to change?' In the context of this second question, it is often depressing how non-radical some sustainable utopias actually are. For example, scenarios sketching out resourcing systems that have broken completely with globalized capitalism will often still envision people living for the most part in heterosexual nuclear families in single-family dwellings with jobs and modes of transport. Peter van Wyck once complained that the issues of ecological risk should be treated as opportunities for profound transformation, not just in how we are, but also more fundamentally, what we are, or who (van Wyck, 2005, p112). This is perhaps still the problem with the question, 'How do we want to live?' – it presumes a mostly unchanged 'we' choosing (hopefully not just like a consumer shopping) a different mode of living. What if that future way of living changes, or involves changes to 'us' fundamentally? If we live in entirely new way, we will become different kinds of people. Who we were when we decided to live in a new way could be unrecognizable to who we subsequently become after the change. For instance, if we decided, for the sake of sustainability, to give up private property, we would not in the future be simply the same people minus all our possessions. If we were, we would be very unhappy. Instead, we might change into people who experience satisfaction from being without things, or who feel that there is something delightful about always engaging with our peers whenever we need this or that thing.

These kinds of 'systems-level' changes to how, and so who we are, are in fact not things available to us to make (consumerist) decisions about. By necessity, the high or base level of change we are now talking about is something that must happen 'to us' rather than 'by us' – we are subject to it, not the subject driving it. Or to be less philosophical, these kinds of changes are systems effects. They are over-determined by multiple factors in which many things change simultaneously and comparatively quickly, what ecosystems theorists call 'transitions'. Interestingly, these kinds of changes, though radically transformative of everything, can be the result of seemingly smaller progressions which converge in unexpected ways. In other words, revolution can come from bureaucratic gestures, if we can learn to pay attention to the indirect effects of those gestures on more fundamental qualities.

Becoming digital

Let me give two quite different kinds of example before moving finally onto the topic of usership in the sharing economy.

At the turn of the millennium, a major and increasing source of energy consumption was screen-based technologies – televisions, but more so computers. The cathode ray tube (CRT) screens were not only significant energy loads (up to 200% that of the computer processors they made communicable), but they were also major heat loads for office buildings, requiring their own wattage again in cooling equipment. Further, the technology – beaming electrons at photosensitive materials – had material depleting consequences that led to a high rate of turnover of computers and a consequent mass of electronic equipment waste (e-waste).

At some point, liquid crystal display (LCD) screen technologies were developed to cost levels that made them outcompete CRTs, rendering them largely obsolete. Despite the waste initially generated by the rapid replacement of CRTs with LCDs, we saw significant reductions in energy consumption within developed nations with large information economies, primarily in their offices, not least because cooling requirements dropped by an order of magnitude. Though disruptive within its market, these screens were the result of wider incremental improvement in technology, one that was developed without reference to issues of ecological sustainability. Nevertheless, with the diffusion of these screens, our societies made a major shift in the direction of less impacting futures.

Except. The cheapness, thinness and durability of these screens afforded a massive diversification of screen-based technologies. Offices could fit many more computer-based personnel in offices because of the reduced profile and heat load of computers. Each of those employees could now have a work and/or private laptop, and then a smart phone, and then a tablet. In addition, portable access to the internet afforded by smart mobile phones exponentially increased demand for internet resources and services, especially audiovisual material. Reductions in computer screen related energy consumption in offices has been more than offset by increased energy consumption by all the screen-less computers in server farms around the world delivering content to all those portable screens.

There are many other implications, some of which I will return to in relation to possessions and sharing. For now, register that the arrival of LCDs, out of a very non-sustainability-vision-driven technical process, created a bifurcation point that allowed the (information and communication technology dominated) world to undertake a significant transition. More sustainable societies have not been the outcome; though one set of ecologically impacting systems (CRTs) have effectively gone extinct as a result.

My second example also concerns communication and information technologies, but rather than the technical side, such as screens, it relates to the social side, how we perform through our screens. It is common to point out the speed with which computational devices both developed (i.e. Moore's Law) and diffused (i.e. the ever faster market penetration rates for computers, mobile phones and then smart phones). It is important to remember that a rapidity of supply-side production cycles is only possible if there is an equally rapid social change on the demand-side. It is not that the former simply imposed itself, necessitating the latter; rather, there had to be have been significant social learning occurring that afforded, if not drove, what technologies were developed. However, a consequence of all that speed of development tends to be historical amnesia, even if we are talking about things that should just be in our short-term memory.

For instance, in the post-Facebook era it is often forgotten that the first decade of 'the internet' was structured in large part around anonymous collaborative interactions. Beyond the merely functional communications of email and organizational websites, and quite apart from attempts to establish retail e-commerce, which stalled with the bursting of the first dot.com bubble, there were large amounts of time and resources invested by internet users in spaces of play, like the MUDs and MOOs, that evolved into Second Life and online gaming. The emergence of these domains and practices enabled very significant but mostly unintentional cultural learning in relation to 'being online'. There were three aspects to what was learned, over and above any technical literacy.

The first concerns 'identity'. As was noted at the time by Sherry Turkle (1995) and Fernando Flores (1998), anonymity allowed 'users' to develop and perform multiple identities online. Certainly, these were initially only in addition to being a conventional person 'in real life'. However, it is now apparent that the very notion of identity was being transformed into something that was not inherited or fixed, but continually and iteratively created. When, for commercial reasons (trackability), social networking platforms insisted on 'true identity', this did not limit the practice of people constructing their identities through constant online display.

The second concerns 'sociality'. Virtual worlds, because they were virtual, were relatively low risk environments in which to experiment with encounters with strangers, or at least with people with whom you might only have a very thin connection ('communities of interest'). It is frequently noted that 'the internet' allows more people to connect outside of their geographic communities than ever before in the history of humanity. But 'can' does not automatically mean 'is.' The difference between the two in this case is social learning, something that required extensive experimentation over time in online encounters. The process has not been smooth – flaming, cyber-bullying, phishing and self-reinforcing bubbles of xenophobia – but the success of social networking platforms does suggest that people have developed ways of negotiating with other people who are less than friends, but more than strangers. It is not that people have learned to trust each other online, or that technical developments now safeguard interactions; rather, our sense of sociality has modified.

The third concerns 'digital ontology'. Digital files do not have discernible physical presence. In addition, files are perfectly replicable and so distributable. Recent developments in 'cloud-based' data storage and retrieval indicate that an increasing number of people have been normalized to the insubstantial nature of the digital. Again, I would argue that participation in the collaborative construction of various kinds of online worlds was part of this social learning. Importantly, at this point, the success of music and video streaming services suggest that people have not only learned to consider digital collections reliable even if distributed, but are prepared to do away with their own (physical) collections altogether. This raises interesting challenges to our established notions of ownership, in a material sense.

All three of these emergent cultural phenomena overlap: identity being a social projection of your use of virtual things for more-than-just-strangers, for instance. And all three overlap with the screen developments mentioned previously: identity can be ongoing, displayed because of the multiple screens through which we access our various 'things' and activities; and what we are, have and do is cloud-based and merely deployed through various interfaces, which are readily replaceable. Just as with screen developments, there is nothing inherently good here. Cosmopolitan aspects to digital sociality can still be quickly undermined by the narcissism of online identity production and display, for example.

In this section, I have sketched out this overly schematic social history of digital screen practices to demonstrate that significant structural changes can occur along with seemingly incremental technical changes. I am arguing that these profound social changes need now to be placed alongside the ambitions for societal 'dematerialization' through 'servicization'. I argued previously that technical, if not bureaucratic sustainable design research, ended up, in relation to PSSs investigations, advocating for the seemingly radical proposition of doing away with ownership. When those arguments were made in the early 2000s, usership did seem as far-fetched as capitalism morphing unproblematically into communism. Such arguments were, at best, only feasible when imagined as complex business-to-business innovations.

Yet, the situation is now quite different. Not by design, but by the ways in which we (in networked economies) coevolved with screen-based technologies. There is consequently enormous sustainable materials intensity reduction potential in our current situation – but it is also clear that there are equally significant social consequences. To engage effectively with this, we are first going to have to decide how we want to live, and who we are.

Sharing economies

It should be noted that the first (mostly European) wave of effort aimed at developing usership-based sustainable service systems failed, both in practice – the research-led innovations failed to be economically sustainable – and in theory – analysis suggested that even if such innovations had been taken up by the market, the reduction in materials intensity would not have significantly enhanced societal sustainability (Tukker, 2004).

The second wave of usership-based systems that are now highly visible, even if still statistically marginal – AirBnB, Uber and then all the other 'startups' attempting to be the AirBnB or Uber of things other than accommodation and private mobility – has been market-led. They appear to have (for now) economic sustainability. This is most likely because the sociotechnical conditions, such as the digital sociality I have tried to describe, must be different enough to now afford such initiatives.

An important factor to add to all the changes sketched out above is locational media. It has taken a while for hand-held devices to become small enough (with respect to computational speed and scale of memory – a 64GB phone for instance), and for the supporting infrastructure to become large enough (with respect to pervasive granularity – think of the accuracy of digital map services), to enable widespread real-time locational services. It is precisely this that has proved to be the tipping point for sharing economies. AirBnB, Uber and similarly designed digital platforms can deliver a level of service convenience that makes, other factors being equal in a networked society, sharing privately owned goods like a spare room or car, competitive. I can simply press a button on a phone to find almost immediate mobility or accommodation. Precisely because these systems make use of distributed resources rather than locationally fixed resources (such as a hire-car yard, or a hotel), getting the mobile interactions right was not just necessary in terms of lowering the transaction costs involved, but was the key to accessing the value they mobilize.

As was recognized by one of the first major advocates of sharing as a strategy for developing more sustainable economies – Walter Stahel – these systems are effectively a form of fuel switching. To use a service rather than (individually own) a product means using human power rather than fossil fuels (embodied in the manufactured materials of that product). This in itself can be a source of the sustainability of service systems; though the agriculture that feeds humans is not currently sustainable, it should be able to be much more sustainable, especially in terms of carbon emissions, than fossil fuels.

But this point foregrounds that what sharing economies access are not just products, dispersed in under-utilized ways amongst private households, but people, who must also be to some extent cast as under-utilized – from weekend AirBnB hosts to between-jobs Uber drivers. Where are these extra-labour hours coming from?

One argument is that, ironically, they are coming from, or being necessitated by, precisely the sustainable materials intensity reductions that digital technology has finally enabled. Productivity gains from computerization have been famously missing. But as was mentioned earlier, real digital convergence does appear to now be happening. One smart device is replaces several others – still and video cameras, Walkmans, phones, navigation devices and libraries. Physical collections of movies, music and books are evaporating along with the systems that play them. There is no need to invent sharing systems for what has been digitized (if each individual can afford to buy their own virtual copy). To 'digital natives' supposedly, a smart phone and laptop is their sole source of work ('creative class'), entertainment ('cable cutters'), mobility ('car cutters') and shopping. Conservative pundits recently argued that the middle class should stop complaining about income inequality because all they now need is one device and a few subscriptions to have access to exponentially more than their wealthier (in real terms) parents ever did.

This way of speaking is caricaturish, but there is reason to believe that something of this phenomenon is having an economic effect. The recent Global Recession appears to have been triggered by a combination of real estate speculation, financial engineering and petroleum price increases due to peak conventional oil. But the failure of developed economies to recover (apart from the bailed out top end) does seem to be related to people needing to buy less stuff. Mobile digital technologies have demonstrated that making do in austere times with less can be a kind of liberation, especially for those moving to larger urban environments – places that do not need the incoming younger generation to build new suburban houses and then fill them with individually owned things from big box stores.

The result however is a flat economy. Those not in design and tech firms, or funding design and tech firms, struggle to find jobs with growing wages. They then must not only be recipients of sharing economy services but also, if not only, the providers of those services. This can be spun positively: Freelancers using their 'slash slash' status (as in 'waiter/actor/ childcarer') to also be creative, activists and/or carers. Or it can manifest negatively: the Gig Economy Precariat struggling to survive as the last elements of the welfare state are removed. Which way sharing economies unfold is matter of both design and politics; it will depend on the extent to which these systems can promote solidarity between those who make use of platforms like AirBnB and Uber, and those who labour to ensure their value and convenience.

For my purposes in this chapter, I want to just underline the wider point, that the consequence of systems of usership, whatever their ecological sustainability, play out in the space of employment, or social sustainability. We seem to be witnessing at the moment another one of those technical-bureaucratic-incremental, yet nevertheless over determinedly radical shifts. In this case, sharing economies 'disrupt' what it means to have a job, something that throughout the twentieth century was made central to our identity. It seems that in addition to challenging notions of property, meaning things we own, usership also challenges the very nature of own-ness – our 'proper identity'. Van Wyck's challenge, to let sustainability afford radical change to who we are, and not just how, does appear to be taken up by what is happening around sharing economies.

Conclusions

This chapter has been arguing at a conceptual level, which tends to render things in overly stark terms. Often when promoting usership and sharing economies, there is the claim that all product categories should be subject to such dematerialising product service systems. I do not think that anyone has ever explicitly argued this. There has always been the sense that being a person in a sustainable society would involve a mix of ownership and usership for different kinds of people at different life stages, and in different sociocultural contexts. Research into systems of usership often comes up with novel versions of these mixes, such as when the *SusHouse* project advocated for underpants to be disposable (the real opposite of sharing), or when Ursula Tischner and Martin Charter (2001) recommended decoupling the refrigerators casing (to be built into dwellings and so shared by subsequent occupants) from compressor (which was owned to taken from property to property by tenants).

Translated to the question of work and identity, this would mean having a mix of 'kinds of identities', not just multiple forms of the one identity. In other words, sustainability is not just a matter of how we want to live, but who we want to be.

References

Beck, U. (1995a) *Ecological Politics in an Age of Risk* Polity, Cambridge

Beck, U. (1995b) *Ecological Enlightenment: Essays on the Politics of the Risk Society* Humanities Press, Atlantic Highlands, NJ

Cooper, T. and Evans, S. (2000), *Products to Services*, Sheffield Hallam University Center for Sustainable Consumption, Sheffield

Flores, F. (1998) Information Technology and the Institution of Identity: Reflections since Understanding Computers and Cognition, *Information Technology and People*, vol 11, no 4, pp351–372

Fry, T. (2009) *Design Futuring: Sustainability, Ethics and New Practice*, Bloomsbury, London

Gardner, G. (1999) Our Shared Future: More Sharing-of Property, Products, and Time May be just the Antidote Our Disconnected Communities Need, *World Watch*, no 12, pp10–20

Halme, M. (2012) *Sustainable Consumer Services: Business Solutions for Household Markets*, Routledge, Abingdon

Oliva, R. and Quinn, J. (2003) *Interface's Evergreen Service Agreement* Harvard Business Review Case Study, Boston, MA

Quist, J. (2007) *Backcasting for a Sustainable Future: the Impact after 10 Years*, Eburon Uitgeverij, Delft

Rifkin, J. (2000) *The Age of Access: The New Culture of Hypercapitalism, where All of Life is a Paid-for Experience* J. P. Tarcher/Putnam, Los Angeles, CA

Schmidt-Bleek, F. (1993) *The Fossil Makers*, Birkhäuser, Berlin (translation downloadable at http://factor10-institute.org/publications.html)

Schmidt-Bleek, F. (2001) MIPS and Ecological Rucksacks in Designing the Future, in *Environmentally Conscious Design and Inverse Manufacturing: Proceedings EcoDesign 2001*, IEEE, Piscataway, NJ, pp1–8

Stahel, W. (1986) Product Life as a Variable: The Notion of Utilization, *Science and Public Policy* vol 13, no 4, pp185–193

Stahel, W. (2010) *The Performance Economy*, Palgrave Macmillan, New York

Tischner, U. and Charter, M. (2001) 'Sustainable Product Design' in Charter, M. and Tischner, U. (eds), *Sustainable Solutions: Developing Products and Services for the Future*, Greenleaf Publishing, Sheffield, pp118–139

Tonkinwise, C. (2012) Weeding the City of Unsustainable Cooling, or, Many Designs rather than Massive Design, in Tilder, L. and Blotstein, L. (eds), *Design Ecologies: Essays on the Nature of Design*, Princeton University Press, Princeton, NJ

Tukker, A. (2004) Eight Types of Product–Service System: Eight Ways to Sustainability? Experiences from SusProNet, *Business Strategy and the Environment* vol 13, no 4, pp246–260

Turkle, S. (1995) *Life on the Screen*, Simon & Schuster, New York

Van Halen, C., Vezzoli, C. and Wimmer, R. (2005) *Methodology for Product Service System Innovation: How to Develop Clean, Clever and Competitive Strategies in Companies*, Uitgeverij Van Gorcum, Assen, The Netherlands

Van Wyck, P. (2005) *Signs of Danger: Waste, Trauma, and Nuclear Threat*, University of Minnesota Press, Minneapolis, MN

PART V

Systems and services

Conventionally, industrial activity involves a linear production-consumption system with inbuilt environmental destruction at either end; sustainable product design activity over the past 45-years has made these wasteful and inefficient ends of the scale, marginally less wasteful and inefficient. However, we need to move away from this linearity in our design thinking, to reconnect with design on a more circular and systemic level, if we are to achieve the degrees of transformation our current situation demands.

This first part comprises six chapters; drawing together previously disconnected scholarship in design innovation, design for the circular economy, service design and social innovation. In doing so, they reimagine the role of products in more closed-loop, service-oriented contexts. Their chapters may be summarized as follows:

24 Product service systems and the future of design – *Tracy Bhamra and Ricardo J. Hernandez*
    This chapter shows how providing access to performance and experience – rather than just more materials and products – enables more systematized, resource efficient and socially purposeful forms of product design, and product use.

25 A consumer's perspective on the circular economy – *Ruth Mugge*
    A circular economy is regenerative by design, ensuring biological and technical resources remain in flow, through several product iterations. This chapter introduces strategies for greater emotional durability in products, and ensuring a *second life* through refurbishment.

26 Designing circular possessions – *Weston Baxter and Peter Childs*
    In a circular context, consumer interactions with possessions are being altered and redefined. This chapter explores the changing idea of possession: what it is, how an object becomes one and why it is important for the circular economy.

27 Which way to turn? Product longevity and business dilemmas in the circular economy
    – *Tim Cooper*
    A circular economy offers the potential for resources to be used more sustainably. This chapter considers the significance of product longevity for enhanced environmental sustainability, consumer loyalty and industry growth, and the implications for product design.

28 How about dinner? Concepts and methods in designing for sustainable lifestyles –
    Annelise de Jong and Ramia Mazé
    Issues of ecological sustainability – such as water, energy and waste – are at stake in
    sustainable product design. However, as this chapter shows, so too is attention and
    sensitivity to how products and services impact, or alter, socio-cultural practices,
    rituals and routines.
29 The Sustainable Energy for All Design Scenario – *Carlo Vezzoli and Elisa Bacchetti*
    Sustainable development is not possible without sustainable energy for all; distributed
    renewable energy systems are central to this goal. This chapter presents the *Sustainable
    Energy for All Design Scenario*, which relocating design in a new social, economic and
    technical system.

Compared to the entire life cycle of materials – from mining, processing, refinement, shipping and fabrication – final products are a fairly fleeting moment. Sadly, few designers even consider the use phase of a product, never mind end-of-life. We need to build end-of-life consideration into the whole system of a product; reframing end-of-life as a moment in a longer trajectory of materials and energies, which flow *through* products, rather than *end up* in them. We can design for end-of-life to ensure that when the moment does arrive, systems are in place to deal with take back, disassembly and material recovery, to keep resources in continuous flow.

In temporal terms, products do not exist in isolation; they are the result of decades of iterative design decisions, each one believed to be an improvement on the former. Through this continually unfolding process, typologies of products adapt and evolve in line with the values and aspirations of the people developing them, at that time. Over years and decades of such refinement, products become increasingly specific and peculiar, relying on highly specific resources flows, manufacturing processes and technical infrastructure, to support their formation. As a result of this excessive specificity, any disturbance to these highly specialized conditions spells disaster. Analogous situations can be seen in ecology, whereby a particular species, or organism, evolves to thrive in highly specialized conditions. Provided the conditions remain the same, the specialist thrives. However, this specialism also makes them highly vulnerable to threat and extinction, should the delicate balance of those highly specialized conditions change in any way – which they invariably do.

The shift to a more resource efficient, service economy requires an equivalent shift in the way we design and manufacture products themselves. For example, when products are leased they get much heavier use, by multiple users, across their lifetime. In this context, repair and the availability of spare parts, is built-in to the design and planning of product lifetimes, because the economic model depends on it. In addition, products designed to be repairable tend to be easier to disassemble at end of life, as they are designed to quickly take apart and their internal components are readily accessible. In this way, the service economy is a great catalyst for designing longer-lasting, repairable and sustainable products. The act of repair itself has led to the emergence of partisan communities, united by a shared frustration with the status quo – seas of fixable products habitually tossed aside, and tribes of dormant makers cordoned off from the process of creation by a failing economic system. These emerging communities of object-activists seize back control over the destiny of their material possessions. In so doing, they cut waste, reduce rates of consumption and increase product value and longevity.

A circular economy is regenerative by design; keeping products, components and materials at their highest utility and value by separating technical and biological cycles. In the circular economy you are a *user* of materials, not a *consumer*. This changed role must be communicated effectively at all levels of design culture, from design education in schools, colleges and universities, through to the everyday working practices and values of design businesses, cultural institutions and policy makers. The interlinked processes of design, manufacture, use and disposal need to be redesigned, to align with the core principles of a circular economy. Only by doing this will we generate commercially viable means to increase rates of reuse and recycling to address material security issues. Many designers are becoming increasingly aware of this, though culture shifts take time – some say they are multi-generational.

If you were to start with a blank sheet of paper and design a product service system from the ground up, the results would bear little or no resemblance to the material goods with which we are so familiar, today. In a more resource efficient system, products would: use fewer materials; be designed for ease of upgrade, repair and disassembly; and, would be shared by communities, not owned by individuals. Product service systems provide access to function, performance and experience, rather than just more materials and products. Through these interventions, the walls separating manufacturer from user crumble, to reveal a more reflexive space in which users become co-creators of material experiences – making the transition from ownership to usership.

24

PRODUCT SERVICE SYSTEMS AND THE FUTURE OF DESIGN

Tracy Bhamra and Ricardo J. Hernandez

Abstract

Product service systems (PSS) can be viewed as one approach towards more sustainable production and consumption. This chapter outlines the reasons why PSS could be a useful approach to sustainability in the future. In particular it highlights the three main types of PSS, product oriented, use oriented and results oriented, which can be considered by designers wanting to make the shift away from purely product focussed approaches. By understanding the benefits of each type of PSS a designer will be able to choose the best option to help develop an integrated system of products and services which can provide benefits for both the customer and the environment.

Keywords: circular economy, consumption, manufacture, sustainable product service systems

Introduction

It is clear that wherever we are in the world we are now living in a service economy. In 2013, services contributed to 73.5 per cent of GDP of the European Union as a whole with some countries such as United Kingdom, France, Belgium and Denmark seeing more than three quarters of their GDP coming from them (Eurostat, 2015). Even in low-income countries such as India, services constitute over 50 per cent of GDP (Cali *et al.*, 2008).

To date, the move from selling products to providing services has not particularly been driven by environmental issues but instead by business concerns such as increasing competitiveness, reducing costs, serving a market's need for speed, convenience, flexibility or specialist skills, improving corporate identity, or responding to a discrete business opportunity (Rocchi, 1997; White et al., 1999). Goedkoop et al. (1999) identified several drivers for moving towards product service systems, which included the threat of legislation, responding to client's wishes, and the company considering themselves environmentally and socially responsible.

Traditional linear models of production and consumption usually referred to as *cradle-to-grave* have proved not to be the best option, especially from an environmental point of view (Kok et al., 2013). The extraction, transformation, consumption and disposal of valuable resources in a linear way has resulted in overexploitation and extinction of non-renewable resources, pollution, social problems and has exceeded the capacity of the planet to sustain our activities. Facing this panorama of problems, new types of economies have emerged aiming to change the paradigm from linear models to circular ones (Ellen MacArthur Foundation, 2012).

In these emerging models functions replace products, and concepts such as reuse, remanufacturing, closed materials cycles, dematerialization, visualization and collaboration are central to the desired change (Botsman and Rogers, 2011; Esslinger, 2011). Sustainable product service systems (PSS) are an approach that has shown potential to operate effectively under this new circular logic. This is partly because sustainable PSS are built with similar concepts to the ones that are central to circular economies and also because it is acknowledged that the changes needed to achieve sustainable standards of living have to be at the level of systems beyond just isolated products and services (UNEP, 2009). According to the Ellen MacArthur Foundation (2012) the development of circular economies should be supported by four building blocks circular economy design, new business models, reverse cycles and enablers and favourable system conditions. All of these are closely related to the conditions also needed to develop sustainable PSS.

For consumers, the shift towards PSS could result in lower costs and fewer problems associated with the buying, use, maintenance and eventual replacement of products (UNEP-DTIE, 2001). The quality of the service, and the degree of consumer satisfaction, may improve with PSS because the service provider has the incentive to use and maintain equipment properly, increasing both efficiency and effectiveness (ibid.). It might also result in greater diversity of choices in the market, in terms of maintenance and repair services, payment schemes and different schemes of product use that suit the customer best in terms of ownership responsibilities (Mont, 1999).

There are however considerable barriers to overcome when a company considers offering PSS. Offering services requires a deeper understanding of the client's business and production processes and a greater degree of trust is required when the service provider takes over in-house activities (White et al., 1999). There is, by and large, a poor understanding of costs associated with PSS – and services in general – both on the supply and demand side, making it difficult to determine how to charge for knowledge and information (ibid.). In general, there is a lack of information available to the consumer to influence their purchasing decision, such as lifetime costs of ownership (UNEP-DTIE, 2001; Zaring et al., 2001). For some types of services, customer psychology can be an important barrier, since offering services can mean moving towards a situation of non-ownership, especially since current economic and social infrastructures have developed to reinforce individualistic lifestyles and routine activities based on unsustainable modes of private consumption (UNEP-DTIE, 2001; White et al., 1999). Finally, a lack of senior management support within the company for offering PSS can be a challenge which arises as a result of either a lack of understanding of PSS and their benefits, or the resistance to change (Zaring et al., 2001).

Making the transition to product service systems

According to Cook et al. (2006) there has been an urgency to respond to increasing pressure from competitors, and the determination to create more value to better address customer needs. This has motivated, in certain industrial sectors, the development of new services and combinations of products and services to complement existing products or in some cases substitute them. These emerging combinations of products and services have been defined in different ways as PSS (ibid.; Goedkoop et al., 1999; Mont, 2002b). Despite the different definitions that can be found in the literature there is a common classification generally accepted that presents PSS as a combination of products and services that can go from 'pure' products at one extreme to 'pure' services at the other (Tukker and Tischner, 2004). This classification implies that the transformation from traditional products to PSS can be made at different levels. It is possible to find systems where products still play a key role and services are developed to complement and improve the offer, such as in the case of warranties, but also other systems where services are central and products play a more marginal role.

This transition from products, to systems of products and services acting together, can be understood also as part of a major transformation from traditional approaches of making, selling and buying physical products to emergent models focused on services and the provision of functions rather than things. In these functional economies – or, *performance economies*, as Walter Stahel (2010) describes – the satisfaction of needs and the concept of development is detached from the materiality of products and instead supported by the provision of functions where businesses and people change their roles from producers to providers and from consumers to users (Manzini and Vezzoli, 2003; Mont, 2002b; Vezzoli et al., 2014). In the end, all business solutions comprise a combination of products and services and even 'pure' services are supported by products. However, in the context of a PSS, the leading role of products has become displaced by the role services play in the system, and this has caught the attention of academics and researchers.

Motivations and challenges to move towards product service systems

From a business perspective, adding value to the business and improving customer satisfaction have been major drivers in the transition from models centred on products to PSS (Beuren et al., 2013). These drivers are associated with the opportunities PSS represent in terms of increased resource efficiency, savings related to reductions in the use of materials and energy, expansion of markets due to flexible offers and loyal relationships between businesses, their customers and other stakeholders. Despite the importance of these economic motivations, the shift from products to PSS has also been associated with better environmental and social ways to satisfy customers' demands than traditional product-oriented solutions (Manzini and Vezzoli, 2003; Mont, 2002b; UNEP, 2009; Vezzoli et al., 2014). This potential of PSS to create and deliver value to customers, while causing less environmental and social harm than traditional offers based solely on physical products, is strongly associated with strategies like dematerialization and virtualization (Beuren et al., 2013).

The use of these strategies, along with the implementation of the PSS concept in industry has taken place in both the business-to-business (B2B) and business-to-consumers (B2C) markets. In both cases, the characteristics of PSS are very similar and the main definitions and classifications apply. The PSS oriented to B2B markets are usually called Industrial PSS (IPSS), while PSS oriented to B2C markets are named simply as PSS. One key difference between the two orientations is that whereas many IPSS have been developed, they mainly focus on achieving industrial efficiencies. In contrast, PSS seem to pay more attention to the environmental and social benefits they can provide.

Despite the opportunities and benefits a shift from products to PSS might bring, this transformation represents significant challenges for any business initiating the process. These challenges are associated for example with the increase in responsibility over the products and services throughout multiple life cycles, the change of roles between producers and consumers, the participation of diverse actors in the development of the systems and the new knowledge and skills required to deliver these PSS. Of course, most of these challenges are linked to the design of the systems themselves. Design of PSS is complex, as the reflexive links between the product and the service need to be taken into account to ensure the product supports the value of the service and also to ensure that the abstract value of the service if expressed in the design of the product (Creusen, 2011). In relation to the participation of different actors in the design of the systems, the creation of alliances and collaborations in the development of sustainable PSS become critical (De Bruijn and Tukker, 2002), as the dynamics involved are too complex to be effectively tackled from within a single disciplinary or sectorial paradigm.

Despite the PSS concept being relatively new, it has been almost thirty years since the first definitions appeared and probably fifty since the first cases in industry were identified. However the number of PSS in the market place is still very low. This narrow adoption of the concept by industry, particularly in the case of sustainable PSS, can be explained by different factors, including: partial understanding of the PSS concept (Cook et al., 2006; Hernandez-Pardo, 2012), limited knowledge regarding sustainable business models (Hernandez-Pardo, 2012), lack of evidence of successful cases that can be transferable to different business scenarios (Cook et al., 2006; Mont, 2002a), and the absence of market incentives and appropriate regulations.

Product service systems and sustainability

Not all product service systems can be considered to be sustainable. However, it is possible with PSS to look at options for radically reducing resource use or even breaking the link to consumption. In the longer term, this could be more sustainable than other offers currently in the market.

Types of product service systems

Three basic types of PSS are recognized according to the combination and importance of each tangible and intangible component in the offer (Cook et al., 2006; Mont, 2002b; Tukker and Tischner, 2004). The first, *product-oriented PSS* arises where there is a product complemented by services which enable that product to be maintained, replaced or updated. In this case, the physical product usually remains the property of the customer (Cook et al., 2006). An example of these are additional warranties which might accompany electrical products. These type of PSS have the benefit of potentially extending the life of the product though adopting a number of strategies such as reuse, repair, reconditioning or upgrading.

The second is *use-oriented PSS*, where the tangible product is the property of the producer and the customer pays for the use of the product and the services of the system. Generally this is for a specific period of time or number of service units. This category includes leasing, sharing, and pooling systems (Cook et al., 2006). Car Sharing schemes are an example of these type of services. The sustainability benefits of these types of services come from the high intensity of use of the products, meaning that less products are needed overall.

Finally, there is *result-oriented PSS*, where the producer owns the product and there is a specific result that the user pays for. In these PSS the producer can choose the most efficient products and services to deliver the predefined result. One example of this type of PSS is paying for clean clothes rather than buying a washing machine or paying to use one (Roy, 2000). If this type of results oriented service considers sustainability at the design stage then significant reductions in material and energy consumption per unit of service can result. In

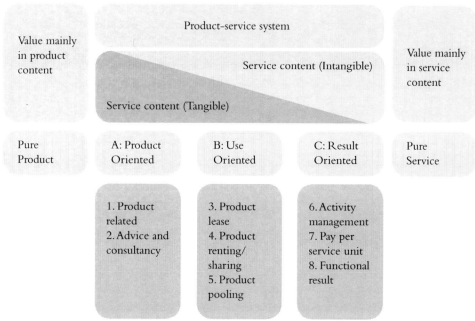

Figure 24.1 Main categories and subcategories of product service systems

Source: Tukker and Tischner (2004)

these scenarios, the best economic interest of the service provider is to guarantee the best possible service to the customer while using the minimum amount of resources.

It is recognized that any PSS requires organizational changes in order to be successfully developed and delivered (Maxwell and van der Vorst, 2003; Roy, 2000; Tukker and Tischner, 2004). The initial organizational situation, and the type of PSS that will be developed, define the level of change needed. Tukker (2004) divides the three basic types of PSS in eight subcategories as shown below.

It is clear that result-oriented PSS, which includes activity management, pay per service unit, and functional results, are those with the most potential to achieve benefits in environmental, social and economic dimensions (Mont, 2002b; Tukker and Tischner, 2006) as there is more freedom and space to optimize the system and satisfy customer needs.

Sustainable product service systems and the implications for designers

The design of sustainable PSS has many implications for designers. Many of these implications are related, for example, to the fact that a PSS is not sustainable by default; it has to be consciously designed to create value from an environmental, social and economic perspective. Other implications are associated with some of the characteristics that differentiate a sustainable PSS from other models, such as a focus on customization and the variety of actors involved in the provision of the system; characteristics that in the end are the ones that produce the benefits by which this type of system is recognized. Below, the most relevant of these implications to be considered in the design of sustainable PSS are discussed.

Sustainability

The view that PSS are more sustainable models of production and consumption is linked to the concept of result-oriented systems (Roy, 2000; Tukker, 2004). It is especially in these types of systems that businesses have the right incentives to provide their customers with a function that will satisfy their needs in a process that can generate environmental, economic and social benefits. This makes result oriented PSS the more promising, from a sustainability point of view.

In practice, the potential of result-oriented PSS to be sustainable, relies heavily on the freedom that providers of the systems have, to produce the results that are agreed with their customers (Tukker and Tischner, 2006). This freedom is partly due to the fact that the focus in these systems is on the *results* and not on the products or services creating those results, and because the ownership of the products and services used to produce the results is retained by the providers of the systems. These conditions represent an important opportunity for providers to achieve significant gains in resource productivity as they can be motivated to deliver the results agreed using less materials, optimizing the system to reduce maintenance and repairs, using products with longer life cycles and that are suitable to be recycled, remanufactured and reused, consuming less energy and using better and more efficient technologies (Dewberry et al., 2013; Tukker, 2004). The gains in resource productivity that these decisions can generate are directly associated with the potential of PSS to be sustainable. For the designer of the system, these decisions represent a set of interesting challenges that have to be addressed to take full advantage of the opportunity.

Products to be used as part of a sustainable PSS should be designed taking into consideration issues such as the source of materials, labour used to source the materials, long life cycles, upgradeability, end-of-life scenarios, types and amounts of energy needed to produce the products and also to operate them, and consumables needed during the usage stage, for example. These considerations imply that sustainable PSS demand that the products are designed that are friendly to the environment and responsible to society (Mont, 2002a; UNEP, 2009). Existing 'eco-design' guidelines can be a valuable tool for designers to partially address these requirements, at least in relation to the environmental performance of products.

However, products do not act in isolation, and services also have to be designed to deliver performance that creates value from a sustainability point-of-view. For example, these could be services that use only efficient and clean sources of energy, that are easily accessible to different types of user and that promote positive social values like respect and transparency. Unlike the design of sustainable products, there is considerably less guidance for designers when they are designing sustainable services. One of the biggest challenges designers face when designing sustainable PSS is to assure that products, services, infrastructure and people work together to create value (Manzini and Vezzoli, 2003) without producing unwanted rebound effects. One way to avoid these negative effects is to design, as part of the PSS, products and services that encourage and reinforce sustainable behaviours in all the actors involved in the production and use of the systems (Meijkamp, 1998).

Variety of actors involved

According to Morelli (2002), PSS are produced by the interactions of different actors. In those interactions each one of them brings to the system their social, cultural and technological background, knowledge and experience, enriching the process and also making it more complex. For Baines et al. (2007, p7) this interaction in the case of sustainable PSS is not just desirable, it is a necessity 'outside the focal organization, several stakeholders may need to be involved in the process, as competitive and sustainable PSS solutions can rarely be provided by a single company'.

From a designer's point-of-view this multiple set of actors interacting in the production and delivery of the PSS means different interests and motivations driving their participation in the provision of the system (Vezzoli et al., 2014). Designers are then facing not only the challenges associated with the design of sustainable products and services, but also those associated with the articulation of these actors' demands (Manzini and Vezzoli, 2003). In practice it can mean bringing together different manufacturers of products with several service providers under particular regulations and market conditions. In this context, designers can act as articulators usually in charge of producing and exchanging artefacts in the form of sketches, maps, diagrams and prototypes, between the actors involved in the process. The purpose of this use and exchange of artefacts is that everyone involved in the provision of the system shares a common knowledge about the system, finds their space to participate in the process and fulfils their responsibilities and roles within the system. This expansion of the design field from the production of physical products in the traditional view of design, to more holistic roles articulating actors, functions and concepts (Borja de Mozota, 2003) has been important for the emergence of highly innovative and complex system, such as sustainable PSS.

Providers extended involvement and responsibility

One of the biggest transformations sustainable PSS demands from producers is the shift from the traditional relationship of the seller and buyer to new ones in the form of the provider and user. This shift represents a mind-set change from product-oriented models to function-oriented systems (Baines et al., 2007). It is a transformation implying a closer relationship between the providers of the systems and their customers, as the involvement and responsibility of the providers go beyond the production of physical elements (Mont, 2002b). The role of these providers in a sustainable PSS involves, in addition to the production of physical elements, their participation in the delivery of different types of services. This may be on a long term basis such as with maintenance, renting and leasing, and may also take action with the physical elements of the systems such as with recycling, remanufacturing and reuse after the use has finished (Tukker, 2004). This larger involvement and responsibility of the providers has to be supported by products that are designed to last longer, to be easily repaired and to use materials that can be recovered and reintegrated into systems. These conditions are meant for designers to also expand the requirements they traditionally use in a design process where products are usually expected to perform in single life cycles only. This expansion of the set of requirements designers should take into account also affects the design of services themselves.

User orientation and multiple users

According to Baines et al. (2007, p7) PSS should be designed to respond better to individual cases than traditional offers. They state, 'A PSS must be designed, made and delivered on a case-by-case basis and viewed from a client's perspective.' This characteristic of PSS of being user-oriented is related to one important aspect that should be taken into account in the design of a sustainable PSS: the variety of types of users a PSS can have, and the importance of customization and flexible designs to respond to that variety. Designers should be aware when designing the physical elements and the services of the systems, in contrast to traditional offers based just on products or even just on services, it is very common for a PSS to have to cover the requirements of a larger range of users. It means that products and services that are part of a sustainable PSS have to be designed in a way that makes them flexible and highly customisable to respond to many different needs coming from a wide variety of potential users.

An additional aspect to consider in relation to users when designing a sustainable PSS is that because of the user-orientation of the system, and the necessity to cover a large range of user needs, it is very common to involve the users in the design process. According to Baines et al.:

> The relationship between the customer and the company plays a key role in the design of an effective PSS. Early involvement with the customer is essential to achieve a solution that responds to customers wants and needs ... users should be treated as innovators, emphasizing a shift to what they term as value co-creation process, whereby professional customers and end-users play an organized and important role in designing.
>
> *(Baines et al., 2007, p7)*

This participation of users in the design process adds further complexity to an already complex process if it is considered that the design of the systems usually involves different kinds of actors from the production perspective (Morelli, 2002) – as mentioned earlier, designers have to assume a very holistic role of articulation that goes beyond traditional approaches of design.

Service design

Services are fundamental elements in a PSS (Goedkoop et al., 1999; Mont, 2002b; Tukker and Tischner, 2004). These services, working together or being supported by products and particular infrastructures, are responsible for much of the value the systems create. Furthermore, the sustainable performance of a PSS is associated with gains in resource productive that relies mainly on the use of services instead of physical products (Dewberry et al., 2013; Tukker, 2004). The importance services play as part of a sustainable PSS is undeniable, and it is because of this importance that the design of those services should be more carefully considered.

While the first approaches in service design adopted and adapted some of the methodologies and tools used in product design, particular characteristics of services demand the use of new and specific approaches and tools. However, one of the biggest challenges designers face when designing services, as part of sustainable PSS, is the lack of methodologies and tools to support the process of developing those services. According to Morelli (2002, p6) 'while products are easily represented through technical drawings, there are not many metaphors and graphical tools available to represent the immaterial component in services and the relationship between material and immaterial elements of a product/service system'. From this statement, it is possible to affirm this challenge goes beyond the design of the services; it relates also to the representation of the relationships between products, services, infrastructure and actors in the whole system – as Morelli explains it, relationships and interactions between 'material and immaterial elements'. Finally, an additional implication in relation to the design of services as part of sustainable PSS regards the training of designers. This is because service design is a relatively new field of study and therefore designers should be aware of the necessity to develop new methodologies and tools but also the necessity to gain additional competencies.

Conclusions

Considering all the challenges outlined in this chapter, it is clear that there is a low adoption of sustainable PSS in the market (Vezzoli et al., 2014). This is partially due to the fact that linear models of production and consumption are not favourable for operations based on systems that rely on collaborative connections between different actors, reverse cycles, virtualization, and dematerialized offers. It might be the case that the systemic essence of sustainable PSS requires a more suitable context of operation; a context that is better aligned with the characteristics of circular economies than to the ones embedded in conventional linear models.

This can be illustrated by one of the most commonly mentioned examples of sustainable PSS in the literature. In the 1980s, Xerox Corporation introduced the idea of integrated document management systems that changed its traditional mode of operation, from producing and selling photocopying machines to providing a photocopy and printing system. This shift in the mode of operation brought the necessity to redesign their products to make them more suitable for reuse, remanufacturing and recycling. It also required the introduction of new actors and the establishment of new collaborations to guarantee the success of the operation. Despite the fact that Xerox was offering the system, in order to assure the collection of machines and their re-introduction to the production system at different stages (reuse, repair, remanufacturing or recycling), Xerox had to engage in new collaborations with third parties to operate the collection, cleaning, disassembling and distribution of the machines and their components to the right production plants and final disposal sites. Without these connections the reverse cycles would not have worked, the final functions of the system could not have been provided and the environmental benefits associated with this sustainable PSS would not exist. Xerox created the system and the network of actors and responsibilities to provide the promised results, but the reality is that not many companies are in the position to develop these systems and do not currently possess the required infrastructure to develop a sustainable PSS. If the conditions at a macro level are not favourable it will be very unlikely that the wider adoption of the PSS concept will be achieved. Circular economies might be the right context at macro level to trigger the development of this type of sustainable system.

Finally, this change of paradigm, from linear production and consumption models to circular economies, not only relates to the necessity of collaborative connections, it is also associated with the products and services that will operate better in these emerging contexts. It is regarding those products and services that the alignment between circular economies and the development of sustainable PSS becomes stronger. In general terms, the products and services required to operate and create value in a sustainable PSS are based on almost the same characteristics products and services will require in order to operate effectively in circular economies – the overlaps are notable and significant. These characteristics include, in the case of products, to be suitable to be reused, repaired, remanufactured and recycled, and to avoid the use of toxic materials or components that cannot be used in cycles. In addition they could include using energy efficiently and from renewable sources, avoiding the use of non-renewable resources, and designing in a flexible way to allow upgrading, multiple uses and diverse scenarios of use. In this sense the future of sustainable product and service design is strongly linked to the future of this change of paradigm, from linear to circular economies. The products that we currently call sustainable or environmentally friendly might have to evolve in line with this shift and as part of new types of models and systems like sustainable PSS.

References

Baines, T. S., Lightfoot, H. W., Evans, S., Neely, A., Greenough, R., Peppard, J., Roy, R., et al. (2007). State-of-the-Art in Product-Service Systems. *Proceedings of the Institution of Mechanical Engineers, Part B: Journal of Engineering Manufacture*, *221*(10), 1543–1552.

Beuren, F. H., Gomes Ferreira, M. G. and Cauchick Miguel, P. A. (2013). Product-Service Systems: A Literature Review on Integrated Products and Services. *Journal of Cleaner Production*, *47*, 222–231.

Borja de Mozota, B. (2003) *Design Management*, Skyhorse Publishing, New York.

Botsman, R. and Rogers, R. (2011). *What's Mine is Yours: How Collaborative Consumption is Changing the Way We Live*. HarperCollins Publishers, London.

Cali, M., Ellis, K. and Willem te Velde, D. (2008) *The Contribution of Services to Development: The Role of Regulation and Trade Liberalisation*. Overseas Development Institute, London.

Cook, M. B., Bhamra, T. A. and Lemon, M. (2006). The Transfer and Application of Product Service Systems: From Academia to UK Manufacturing Firms. *Journal of Cleaner Production*, *14*(17), 1455–1465.

Creusen, M. E. H. (2011). Research Opportunities Related to Consumer Response to Product Design. *Journal of Product Innovation Management*, *28*, 405–408.

De Bruijn, T. and Tukker, A. (2002). *Partnership and Leadership: Building Alliances for a Sustainable Future*. Springer, New York.

Dewberry, E., Cook, M., Angus, A., Gottberg, A. and Longhurst, P. (2013). Critical Reflections on Designing Product Service Systems. *Design Journal*, *16*, 408–430.

Ellen MacArthur Foundation (2012). *Towards the Circular Economy: Economic and Business Rationale for an Accelerated Transition*. Ellen MacArthur Foundation, Cowes.

Esslinger, H. (2011). Sustainable Design: Beyond the Innovation-Driven Business Model. *Journal of Product Innovation Management*, *28*, 401–404.

Eurostat (2015). National Accounts and GDP. Retrieved from http://ec.europa.eu/eurostat/statistics-explained/index.php/National_accounts_and_GDP#Main_GDP_aggregates.

Goedkoop, M., Van Halen, C., Te Riele, H. and Rommens, P. (1999). *Products Service Systems, Ecological and Economic Basics,* Dutch Ministries of Environment and Economic Affairs, The Hague.

Hernandez-Pardo, R. J. (2012). *Designing Sustainable Product Service Systems : A Business Framework for SME Implementation*. Loughborough University, Loughborough.

Kok, L., Wurpel, G. and Ten Wolde, A. (2013). *Unleashing the Power of the Circular Economy*. IMSA Amsterdam, Amsterdam.

Manzini, E. and Vezzoli, C. (2003). A Strategic Design Approach to Develop Sustainable Product Service Systems: Examples Taken from the 'Environmentally Friendly Innovation' Italian Prize. *Journal of Cleaner Production*, *11*(8), 851–857.

Maxwell, D. and van der Vorst, R. (2003). Developing Sustainable Products and Services. *Journal of Cleaner Production*, *11*(8), 883–895.

Meijkamp, R. (1998) 'Changing consumer behaviour through eco-efficient services: an empirical study of car sharing in the Netherlands', *Journal of Business Strategy and the Environment*, 7(4), 234–244.

Mont, O. (1999). *Product-Service Systems, Shifting Corporate Focus from Selling Products to Selling Product-services: A New Approach to Sustainable Development*. Report no. 288, December. AFR, Sweden.

Mont, O. (2002a). Drivers and Barriers for Shifting towards More Service-Oriented Businesses: Analysis of the PSS Field and Contributions from Sweden. *Journal of Sustainable Product Design*, *2*, 89–103.

Mont, O. (2002b). Clarifying the Concept of Product–Service System. *Journal of Cleaner Production*, *10*(3), 237–245.

Morelli, N. (2002). Designing Product/Service Systems: A Methodological Exploration. *Design Issues*, *18*(3), 3–17.

Rocchi, S. (1997). Towards a New Product-Services Mix: Corporations in the Perspective of Sustainability. MSc thesis, IIIEE, Lund University, Lund, Sweden.

Roy, R. (2000). Sustainable Product-Service Systems. *Futures*, *32*, 289–299.

Stahel, W. (2010) *The Performance Economy*. Palgrave Macmillan, Basingstoke.

Tukker, A. (2004). Eight Types of Product–Service System: Eight Ways to Sustainability? Experiences from SusProNet. *Business Strategy and the Environment, 13*(4), 246–260.

Tukker, A. and Tischner, U. (2004). *New Business for Old Europe: Product-Service Development, Competitiveness and Sustainability*. Greenleaf Publishing, Sheffield.

Tukker, A. and Tischner, U. (2006). Product-Services as a Research Field: Past, Present and Future. Reflections from a Decade of Research. *Journal of Cleaner Production, 14*(17), 1552–1556.

UNEP (2009). *Design for Sustainability D4S: A Step by Step Approach*. UNEP, Nairobi.

UNEP-DTIE (2001). *The Role of Product Service Systems in a Sustainable Society*. UNEP-DTIE Paris, France.

Vezzoli, C., Kohtala, C. and Srinivasan, R. (2014). *Product-Service System Design for Sustainability*. Greenleaf Publishing, Sheffield.

White, A.L., Stoughton, M. and L. Feng (1999). *Servicizing: the Quiet Transition to Extended Producer Responsibility*. Tellus Institute, Boston, MA.

Zaring, O., Bartolomeo, M., Eder, P., Hopkinson, P., Groenewegen, P., James, P., de Jong, P., Nijhuis, L., Scholl, G., Slob, A. and Örninge, M. (2001). *Creating Eco-efficient Producer Services*. Gothenburg Research Institute, Gothenburg, Sweden.

25

A CONSUMER'S PERSPECTIVE ON THE CIRCULAR ECONOMY

Ruth Mugge

Abstract

A circular economy in which material flows are restored through closed-loop processes can diminish the negative effect of consuming durables on the environment. Although recycling has received a lot of attention over the past few decades, this is actually not the preferred loop in a circular economy because it implies that much value is lost. This chapter takes a consumer's perspective on two of the more inner circles of the circular economy: prolonging the product's *first life*, and giving the product a *second life* through refurbishment. To prolong the first life, it is necessary that consumers can maintain and repair a product without much cost and effort. However, merely considering such technical durability is insufficient because many products are replaced while still functioning properly. Designers should strive to design products that are also emotionally durable by stimulating the attachment the owner experiences with his/her product. Product personalization, gracefully aging materials and storytelling are presented as effective design strategies to stimulate product attachment. Nevertheless, it seems impossible to stimulate product attachment for all types of products. Accordingly, designers need to consider the other inner circles of the circular economy as well. A promising strategy is to give products an effective second life via refurbishment. At present, consumers perceive refurbished products as having lower quality. For refurbishment to work, consumers need to accept refurbished products as substitutes for new products. Several opportunities are discussed to enhance the perceived benefits of refurbished products and reduce the perceived risks through product design.

Keywords: consumer behaviour, product attachment, refurbishment, remanufacturing, circular economy

Introduction

Consumer durables generally follow a linear 'Take, Make, Dispose' route, in which products are produced, consumed and discarded, ending up as landfill or in incinerators. In Europe, 2.7 billion tonnes of waste were produced in 2010 of which only 40 per cent was reused/

374

recycled (Ellen MacArthur Foundation, 2013). It is clear that this is undesirable from a sustainability perspective because it implies that scarce resources are going to waste. At present, a circular economy is recognized as an important approach to diminish the negative effect of consuming durables on the environment. A circular economy is 'an industrial system that is restorative or regenerative by intention and design' (ibid.). It counters the linear 'Take, Make, Dispose' route in that the circular economy aims to restore material flows through closed-loop processes. By closing the loop, valuable resources are reused and less waste is created. Today, many companies and designers interested in closing the loop for consumer durables approach the circular economy from the well-known viewpoint of recycling materials (see most outer circle of the technical materials loops in Figure 25.1). However, recycling requires the complete dismantling of a product by bringing it back to its constituent raw materials. It is generally impossible to recycle a complex electronic product 100 per cent, and therefore, much value is lost through the process. In this respect, the Ellen MacArthur Foundation (ibid.) propose that recycling is actually not the preferred loop in the circular economy, and more attention should be paid to the inner circles (see Figure 25.1). The tighter the circle, the less a product has to be changed and the more value is preserved. As a consequence, the saving potentials in terms of waste, material and energy are much greater for the inner circles than for recycling.

In this chapter, I explore two of these inner circles. First of all, the most inner circle implies that the product is intended to stay longer with the first user. This requires that products are technically durable so that consumers can easily maintain them, but also that products are emotionally durable. Specifically, I present product attachment as a strategy to prolong the product's first life. Even though encouraging such emotional durability is important, it is discussed later in this chapter that it remains questionable whether product attachment can serve as a successful strategy for many categories of product. Accordingly, it is worthwhile to explore other inner circles of the circular economy – specifically, the inner circle of refurbishment. Refurbishment is the process of collecting a used product, assessing its condition and replacing and/or upgrading parts in order to resell the product to other consumers (Pigosso et al., 2010).

An important difference of these two inner circles in comparison to the outer circle of recycling is that the consumer/user plays a much more prominent role. Consumers are often unaware that a product includes recycled materials, due to which this is unlikely to affect their perceptions of the product. On the contrary, the success of the inner circles of the circular economy strongly depends on consumers' behaviour and perceptions towards the products involved. Only if consumers' perceptions towards their own product remain positive over an extended period of time, will they be encouraged to keep the product. Correspondingly, consumers need to perceive ample benefits in refurbished products and not too many risks in order to see these as alternatives for new products. By taking a consumer's perspective on the circular economy, this chapter aims to provide insights that can help designers who want to design products for a circular economy and thereby contribute to a more sustainable society.

Prolonging the product's first life

Most products are disposed of because consumers have replaced them with new ones. Encouraging consumers to keep their products for a longer period of time thus implies that their replacement decision is postponed. Consumers replace products for many different reasons. To successfully address the most inner circle of the circular economy, designers

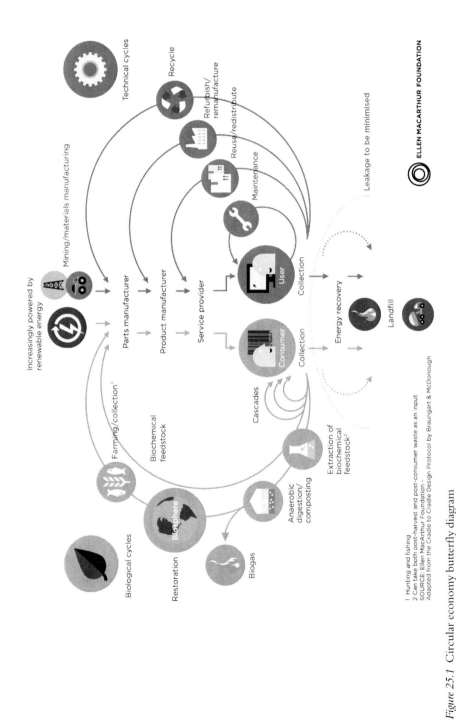

Figure 25.1 Circular economy butterfly diagram

Source: Ellen MacArthur Foundation (2013)

need to tackle these replacement reasons within the product design process itself. First of all, consumers often replace products because they are malfunctioning. Designers can tackle this replacement reason by designing products that are technically durable and that will properly function for an extended period of time. Providing easy maintenance, repairability, durability, and long-life guarantee can thus serve as potential product life extension strategies (Mugge et al., 2005; van Hemel and Brezet, 1997; van Nes, 2003). At present, many products are designed without taking repair into consideration. As a result, consumers usually consider repairing products an expensive and complex endeavour. By changing the design of the product in such a way that repairing it will be easy, affordable and even desirable, consumers will be more inclined to do so. An example of a company employing this strategy is Fairphone (www.fairphone.com). Fairphone has recently launched the new modular smartphone Fairphone 2 (see Figure 25.2). This smartphone is designed to empower consumers by enabling them to repair the smartphone themselves. Specifically, components that are identified as susceptible to defects (e.g., battery, camera, screen) can be easily removed and replaced with new components by using only a simple screwdriver. By selling the new components, Fairphone can generate sales from the maintenance of products, rather than simply the selling and reselling of products.

Nevertheless, it is unlikely that merely focusing on products' technical durability will be sufficient for postponing consumers' replacement decisions. In fact, many products are replaced even though they were still functioning properly (van Nes, 2003). Consumers have many other reasons than purely functional ones to buy new products and replace their old ones. For example, technological improvements may trigger completely new perceived needs, service benefits or operational features in products. After being exposed to these new products, consumers' perception of what is preferred in a certain product may change. For example, during the last decade consumers' anticipated features in smartphones (e.g., larger screens, better cameras, faster internet) have changed considerably, thereby triggering a recurrent need for new and incrementally improved smartphones. Although a modular design can partly serve as a solution by being able to upgrade certain components, it is not always possible to incorporate advanced, new technologies in older devices. Finally, fashion trends may also shift consumers' desires by causing people to feel their product is outdated.

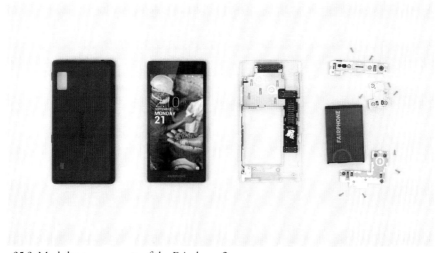

Figure 25.2 Modular components of the Fairphone 2

As a consequence, the desire for a new model that follows the latest fashion style can trigger a replacement need.

Despite the attraction of new products, there are also plenty of examples in which consumers have little desire to replace a product, even though it may perform unsatisfactorily, show signs of wear and tear or does not follow the latest fashion trends. We say that these products are 'emotionally durable' (Chapman, 2005, 2009) and people experience attachments to these objects (Mugge et al., 2005, 2008). If a person experiences attachment to his/her own product, this product obtains an additional source of attraction, and thus they are more inclined to keep this product, and postpone replacement. Stimulating product attachment may thus be another way to tackle the most inner circle of the circular economy. The next section will discuss product attachment in more detail and will present design strategies that designers can use to design emotionally durable products.

The value of product attachment for prolonging a product's first life

Product attachment is defined as 'the strength of the emotional bond a consumer experiences with a specific product' (Mugge et al., 2008, p. 426). Being attached to a product suggests that a consumer experiences a strong relationship with the product and that this product triggers his/her emotions. In general, people experience stronger and more positive emotions to the products to which they feel attached (Schultz et al., 1989) and these products may be among their favourite or most special possessions.

Attachments to products tend to develop as a result of the *special meaning* that the product conveys (Csikszentmihalyi and Rochberg-Halton, 1981). A special meaning can develop if a product provides the owner with something exceptional, over and above its utilitarian meaning. Due to this special meaning, the product becomes extraordinary and the owner will put effort into preserving this special meaning. Consequently, experiencing attachment to a product can prolong the first product life. An example is a family heirloom that was inherited from one's grandfather, and therefore, has gained a deep symbolic meaning besides it pure utilitarian one.

Based on the literature on people's most treasured, special or favourite possessions (Ball and Tasaki, 1992; Kleine et al., 1995; Schifferstein and Zwartkruis-Pelgrim, 2008; Schultz et al., 1989; Wallendorf and Arnould, 1988), Mugge et al. (2008) have proposed the following four determinants of product attachment:

1　*Pleasure*: the product provides the owner with pleasure.
2　*Self-expression*: the product expresses the owner's identity.
3　*Group affiliation*: the product expresses the owner's belonging to a group.
4　*Memories*: the product reminds the owner of the past.

I will discuss each determinant in detail below and illustrate the determinant using a product to which I personally feel attached.

Pleasure

Prior research has concluded that people can become attached to products because these products evoke pleasure (Mugge et al., 2010; Page, 2014; Schifferstein and Zwartkruis-Pelgrim, 2008). An example is the television screen (Figure 25.3). Besides the joy of being able to watch great movies and television shows, this screen provides me with a superior picture quality and a beautiful widescreen. Due to its superior utility in comparison to most other television screens, this particular television screen provides me with pleasure, which is the source for my emotional bond with the product. As is described in the literature, if products provide the owner with superior utility (e.g., additional features, higher quality) or superior appearance, these products may evoke pleasure that is not necessarily evoked by other similar products (Jordan, 1998). Consequently, the product can gain a special meaning and a feeling of attachment may grow.

Figure 25.3 My television screen

Figure 25.4 My Tube Light

Self-expression

People may also experience attachment to products that help them to differentiate from others and express their own identity and personality (Ball and Tasaki, 1992; Govers and Mugge, 2004; Kleine et al., 1995; Schultz et al., 1989; Wallendorf and Arnould, 1988). This determinant of product attachment can be illustrated by the emotional bond I have with my lamp. I own a Tube Light that was designed by Eileen Grey in 1927 (see Figure 25.4). The lamp has a modern, minimalist and practical design. Given that I consider myself to be a modern, pragmatic and down-to-earth female, these qualities in the product design fit well with the way I see myself. As a consequence, I believe that the lamp is expressive of my identity and thus the lamp has obtained a special meaning to me.

Group affiliation

The third determinant of product attachment is group affiliation. Group affiliation suggests that a product expresses a person's desirable connections to a group. If a product expresses such group affiliation, it can gain an additional symbolic meaning, which can trigger the development of an emotional bond with the product (Kleine et al., 1995; Schultz et al., 1989). People can simultaneously belong to many different groups, such as their family, friends or social groups. An example of a product to which I feel attached because it makes me feel part of a group is the Alvar Aalto vase (aka Savoy vase; see Figure 25.5), which was designed in 1936 for the brand Iittala. The vase is a well-known and iconic piece of design that has remained popular for many decades. Furthermore, I bought it when I was a visiting design researcher at the School of Arts, Design and Architecture of Aalto University. Due to these specific associations, the Aalto vase serves as a symbol that I am part of the design community, and I experience attachment to it.

Figure 25.5 My Aalto vase

Figure 25.6 My bear sculpture

Memories

Finally, people can become attached to products because they serve as reminders of the past (Kleine et al., 1995; Mugge et al., 2010; Page, 2014; Schifferstein and Zwartkruis-Pelgrim, 2008). Due to the (physical) association between the object and a special person, place or event in the past, these products can acquire a strong, symbolic meaning. My bear sculpture (see Figure 25.6) serves as a good example of determinant memories. When I visited the Canadian Rocky Mountains about ten years ago, I was eager to see a bear in the wild. Unfortunately, I was not so lucky to see one at first. During these first days, I came across some very nice bear sculptures in the souvenir shops, but I said to myself that it would be weird to purchase a bear souvenir without having seen an actual bear. After one week, I finally came face to face with a black bear who was just walking by the side of the road. It was an amazing experience to see how such a huge animal can move so quickly and gracefully! After seeing the bear, I decided to buy my bear sculpture. Now, merely looking at it still reminds me of one of my most fascinating experiences with nature. In other words, the product has acquired a narrative and due to this unique personal history the product has gained a special meaning for me (Chapman, 2009).

Replaceable versus irreplaceable products

The four product examples I have used to illustrate the determinants of product attachment demonstrate that there is a hierarchy in the experience of attachment (see Figure 25.7; Mugge et al., 2008). First of all, a person can be attached to a product for relatively general product features, related to the product's functionality or appearance. Even though the owner believes these features to be special there are, in fact, many more products within the category that have similar or superior features. As a result, replacing these products will be straightforward and it is unlikely to result in the loss of the special meaning. For example, it would not be difficult for me to find another television screen that can give me the same amount of (or even more) pleasure. Correspondingly, it would be possible to find another lamp with aesthetic qualities that express my identity. It is highly questionable whether this type of attachment will actually discourage people to replace their products because it evokes only minimal attraction to the owned product. As long as the special meaning can be easily taken over by other products, it is probable that the experience of product attachment will only be short-lived. Then, other products in the market that can provide the same meaning,

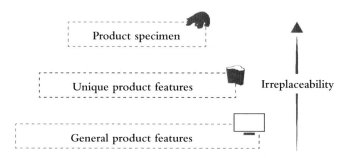

Figure 25.7 Hierarchy of product attachment

but also have new features and/or follow the latest fashion, will persuade people to replace their product prematurely. For designers interested in prolonging the product's first life, this type of attachment may thus be less effective.

Rather than being attached to an object for its general features, attachment can also take place due to unique product features. In other words, the owner is attached to a specific product variant (Mugge et al., 2008), which suggests that a specific type of product has a special meaning to the owner. My Aalto vase is an example of this type of attachment, because any other Aalto vase could equally symbolize that I am part of the design community. As the attachment is focused towards one specific object, this may provide better opportunities for prolonging the product's first life than being attached to the product for its general features. Nevertheless, it remains possible to replace the product without losing its special meaning.

Lastly, a person may experience attachment to a specific product specimen. Then, another object cannot take over the product's special meaning, even though it is physically identical. For example, the context in which the object was obtained or used can be inimitable, making the product irreplaceable. 'An irreplaceable possession is one that a consumer resists replacing, even with an exact replica because the consumer feels that the replica cannot sustain the same meaning as the original' (Grayson and Shulman, 2000, p. 17). In other words, the special meaning that is triggering the experience of attachment is deeply anchored in the object to the point where the product and its meaning have become inseparable. For example, as it was this specific bear sculpture that I bought in Canada directly after seeing the bear in the wild, the sculpture has *absorbed* this very unique and memorable context, making it irreplaceable.

Product attachment will provide the best opportunities for prolonging the product's first life if people feel that the product is irreplaceable. Then, people have a clear incentive to keep their current product because replacing it would mean that the special meaning that is deeply anchored in the object would be lost. Several design strategies have been proposed in order to create products that are inextricably connected to their special meaning.

Strategies to design irreplaceable products

Product personalization is the first design strategy that has received attention in the literature (Grant et al., 2013; Mugge et al., 2009). Product personalization implies that a consumer is involved in the design process of his/her own product, and serves to some extent as a designer (Blom, 2000). During the personalization process, the product is adapted to better fit a consumer's preferences and needs regarding the functionality and aesthetics of the product, and thereby it can gain the symbolic meaning of self-expression. Because only this specific product resulted from the consumer's participation in the design process, the product's special meaning is likely to have a factual connection to the object. Mugge et al. (2009) demonstrated that if people personalize the appearance of their bicycle, they deem this product to be more self-expressive and unique, and therefore experience a stronger emotional bond with it. Even though their findings suggested that the more consumers are involved in the personalization process, the stronger the emotional bond will become, there is a downside to giving consumers ample design freedom. For example, people may feel the risk of spoiling a product because they are not sufficiently skilled. Consequently, designers need to steer the personalization process by giving consumers the feeling that they are truly creating their own unique product, while supporting them in this task to prevent possible spoiling.

An example of the personalization design strategy is the Pop Light, designed by Rina Bernabei and Kelly Freeman (see Figure 25.8). The Pop Light comes as a DIY paper light shade. The lamp triggers the owner to become the co-designer by simply popping out holes from the pre-perforated panels. With hundreds of design possibilities, the Pop Light enables people to creatively make their very own and unique pendant light, while reducing the possibilities to spoil the product during the design process.

Another design strategy that may encourage consumers to develop long-lasting emotional bonds to their products is by embodying these in *gracefully aging materials* (Mugge et al., 2008; Rognoli and Karana, 2013). The gracefully aging materials strategy implies that the product is manufactured using materials that will wear gracefully in time, and acquire patina. In most situations, consumers consider signs of wear and tear – such as scratches and dents – negatively. However, there are some exceptions. Just think of a leather jacket that in time acquires a personal touch, and fits better. In this respect, new materials could be designed that have the ability to change in an aesthetically pleasing manner. Due to these changes, the shared history between the owner and the object is symbolized within the product, due to which the product can become irreplaceable. Designers need to closely consider how to apply these materials in order to elicit positive associations over time.

Storytelling is a third design strategy that may lead to the experience of attachment. Storytelling suggests that the product serves as a narrative for the past experiences of the

Figure 25.8 Personalization strategy: Pop Light by Bernabeifreeman

owner. It is related to the gracefully aging materials strategy in that they both demonstrate the shared history between owner and product. However, whereas the strategy to embody a product using gracefully aging materials generally represents the use period as a whole, storytelling suggests that the product tells a more specific and predetermined narrative through design. An example is Growing, a lamp designed by Marc Benito Padró (see Figure 25.9). The front of this lamp is covered in black paint, due to which it initially only shines light to the back. After purchase, the owner is encouraged to use the lamp to measure his/ her children's height, annually. By carving the height of the child in the black paint, an illuminated line appears. By doing this each year, the lamp will serve as a reminder of past times. Consequently, these product changes will have a deep and special meaning for the owner, and the product and meaning will be inextricably connected, which will make the lamp irreplaceable.

Figure 25.9 Growing, designed by Marc Benito Padró (2014)

Source: cargocollective.com/marcbpadro

Limits to the value of product attachment

It is clear that it will be difficult for designers to stimulate the most inner circle of the circular economy through product attachment. In many situations, the experience of an emotional bond with a product will not be sufficient as the special meaning can be readily taken over by other products, and is thus likely to be short-lived. In order for product attachment to contribute to prolonging the product's first life, and the circular economy, the special meaning should be deeply anchored in the product, due to which the product and its meaning become inseparable, and the product irreplaceable. Then, replacing the product would imply that the person loses the special meaning and thus a genuine and long-lasting attraction to the owned product is achieved.

Even though product personalization, gracefully aging materials and storytelling are presented as potential design strategies that can help designers to strive for such long-lived product attachment, these design strategies may also have their limitations. For example, when personalizing products, the owner needs to spend a lot of physical and mental effort in the product in order to design the product in such a way that it will become self-expressive. People may be willing to do so for product categories that are important for them and thus for their identity. Some examples are furniture, cars, bicycles and laptops. Nevertheless, it remains questionable whether many people would be willing to personalize other product categories, such as their washing machine, iron and lawn mower. Accordingly, the design strategy of product personalization may only be applicable to certain product categories. Similar concerns can be raised for the strategies gracefully aging materials and storytelling. For example, gracefully aging materials implies that frequent physical interaction takes place between the owner and the product. Only through such engagement will the material begin to show interesting signs of aging. However, people own many products that are only used incidentally, such as certain tools and kitchen utensils. Although product attachment can be a useful strategy for certain product categories, it may be less likely to succeed for others.

Taking into account the notion that many people also derive pleasure from the mere act of purchasing new objects, it will be very challenging to encourage people to stop purchasing new products by keeping the products they own for a longer period of time. Designers who want to contribute to a circular economy thus need to consider the different circles in a circular economy that a product can go through in order to reach the full potential of circular products. The next section will discuss refurbishment as another means to close material loops.

Giving products an effective second life via refurbishment

After the first owner has disposed of a product, this product may return to the original equipment manufacturer (OEM) or another third-party, where it is restored to a functional and satisfactory state. This process is called refurbishment. After this refurbishment process, the product is sold to new consumers (Rathore et al., 2011). Contrary to recycling, the original product's functionality is preserved and products are offered a second life with only limited new resources needed. Different types of refurbishment exist:

1. The refurbished product can be merely functionally restored to a good functioning state by verifying proper operation, (data) cleaning and if needed replacing broken parts.
2. The product can be aesthetically restored by replacing parts that show wear and tear.
3. The product can be functionally upgraded, resulting in a technically superior product.
4. The product can be aesthetically upgraded, resulting in a different appearance than the original.

At present, refurbishment is commonly implemented in computers and smartphones and mostly focuses on restoring the functions and aesthetics of the product for resale. Besides electronics, refurbishment can be implemented in many other product categories (e.g., furniture, home appliances, baby equipment). Considering changing market and environmental conditions (e.g., raw material prices, environmental awareness), refurbishment is gaining interest among original equipment manufacturers (OEMs) producing various consumer products. This raises the question how designers should design products for refurbishment. While design research has begun to investigate refurbishment, until now it has solely focused on the development of tools to assist designers in improving products' assembly/disassembly (Hatcher et al., 2011; Tchertchian et al., 2013; Zwolinski and Brissaud, 2008). This will make it easier to refurbish the product after its first life has ended. However, the value of product design for refurbishment must go far beyond the streamlining of assembly/disassembly capabilities. In order to more fully contribute to a circular economy through refurbishment, designers need to design the refurbished product in such a way that it will trigger positive consumer responses. Only if consumers are willing to accept refurbished products as substitutes for new products, can refurbishment contribute to a sustainable society.

Consumers' evaluation of refurbished products

The few prior consumer studies that investigated refurbishment suggested that there is a market for refurbished products, but consumers' willingness to pay (WTP) and quality perceptions are lower for refurbished products than for new ones (Essoussi and Linton, 2010; Harms and Linton, 2016; Hazen et al., 2012; Michaud and Llerena, 2011; Wang and Hazen, 2016). At present, people lack awareness of the existence of refurbished products, and as a result, refurbished products are often not taken into consideration. Yet, even when consumers are aware of refurbished products, they have a misconception of what refurbishment entails (van Weelden et al., 2016). Generally, people do not know what to expect from refurbished products and tend to interpret them as similar to second-hand, which reduces their perceived value. This perception is unhelpfully reinforced by the marketing of current refurbishment companies who generally market refurbished products as cheaper alternatives of expensive new products, and thus only focus on the financial benefit. Although refurbishment is similar to second-hand in the sense that both have been previously used by other people and offer a financial benefit over new products, categorizing refurbished products as second-hand does not do justice to the value of refurbished products. As a result, consumers judge the trade-off between the perceived risks and benefits of refurbished products more negatively than is actually appropriate.

Van Weelden et al. (2016) propose an approach towards increasing consumer acceptance of refurbished products. According to this approach, the starting point is to build a strong product basis. To reach the full potential of refurbishment, designers could search for ways on how to increase the benefits that are offered by refurbished products, while reducing the perceived risks through product design. In the following section, I present several preliminary design strategies to influence consumer acceptance of refurbished products.

Design strategies to increase consumers' acceptance of refurbished products

Besides the clear financial benefit, refurbished products can provide additional benefits to consumers if designed well. First of all, it would be possible to highlight the environmental benefit of refurbished products. Thus far, people are often unaware of the environmental benefits that refurbished products offer. Providing consumers with information about the environmental benefits of refurbishment has been shown to positively influence consumers' evaluation of refurbished products (Harms and Linton, 2016; Michaud and Llerena, 2011). In addition to providing consumers with information through marketing activities or eco-certification, a potential design strategy would be to make this environmental benefit more clear in the design of refurbished products. For example, refurbished products could have an aesthetic upgrade that symbolizes the environmental benefit. If the environmental benefit is clearly communicated in the product, the owner can use this to express their environmental consciousness. It may also be possible to use packaging design as a cue for the environmental benefits. Consumers use the visual appearance as a cue for their perception of a packaging's sustainability (Magnier and Schoormans, 2015). It is also possible that applying eco-packaging for refurbished products may also help to communicate the environmental benefit of the refurbishment process.

Another approach would be to turn the negative connotation of the first use into a positive one. Although people tend to have negative associations with second-hand products, this is not necessarily true for all situations. When considering antiques, for example, people tend to consider the prior usage of a product in a far more positive way. The heritage that the product embodies then serves as an additional advantage that a new product could never offer. If designers are able to integrate the prior usage as a positive attribute in the refurbished product, this could give the product a unique and additional benefit over a new one. For example, a refurbished baby stroller could communicate a personal story of the positive experiences of the first owner and the interactions with his/her baby and the stroller. By reading these stories, the memories that the first owner has shared with the product are transferred to the new owner, thereby adding a deeper layer of meaning to the product. Obviously, this is only one solution in which memories can be shared and much more design opportunities exist.

It would also be worthwhile to strive for a reduction of the perceived risks associated with refurbished products. Prior research has demonstrated that information provision can reduce the risks associated with refurbishment (Michaud and Llerena, 2011; Wang et al., 2013). Consumers may value information about product age, possible damages, how the product was used and use intensity (van Weelden et al., 2016). Designers could integrate information about the use history in the product design to convince new consumers about the potential of refurbishment. For example, when purchasing a second-hand car it is custom to know and assess the amount of kilometres the car has covered or access a record of its service history. Probably, it would be possible to integrate similar approaches into the design of different product categories.

To further reduce the perceived risk of refurbished products, designers could consider the role of product appearance. Past research has demonstrated that consumers use the appearance of a product to draw inferences about experience attributes, such as its performance quality and ease of use (Creusen and Schoormans, 2005; Mugge, 2011; Mugge and Schoormans, 2012a, 2012b). It may thus be worthwhile to resurface refurbished products in order to remove signs of wear and tear that may negatively affect consumers' evaluation. Designers should already address this in the design process by uncovering which parts are most likely to show signs of wear and tear, and how to design for an easy resurfacing of these parts.

Conclusion

One of the major challenges for today's society is to keep the present welfare level attainable for future generations, which implies that the harmful effects of acquiring this welfare level on the environment need to be minimized. By encouraging closed-loop processes, in which products keep their value longer, the harmful effects of consumption on the environment can be diminished. However, the success of such a circular economy strongly depends on consumers' behaviour and perceptions. Consumers do not currently appear to take responsibility for prolonging products' lifetimes themselves and are sometimes even unaware of the environmental problems caused by their consumption behaviour (Cox et al., 2013). In this chapter, I propose that designers can play a critical role in realizing the potential of a circular economy by influencing consumers' behaviour and perceptions through product design. Several design strategies are presented that address two inner circles of the circular economy by encouraging consumers to either prolong the lifetime of their own products or to accept refurbished products as viable substitutes for new products, thereby giving products an effective second life. Although, as the literature shows, these strategies seem promising, more empirical research is needed to understand the scope of their potential effects and limitations. Only if designers have a comprehensive understanding of consumers' needs and wants can they design circular products that will contribute to a more sustainable society.

References

Ball, A. D. and Tasaki, L. H. (1992) 'The role and measurement of attachment in consumer behavior', *Journal of Consumer Psychology*, vol 1, no 2, pp155–172

Benito Padro, M. (2014) *Emotionally durable lighting: An exploration of emotionally durable design for the lighting domain*, Delft University of Technology, Delft

Blom, J. O. (2000) 'Personalization – A taxonomy', in *CHI 2000 Conference on Human Factors and Computing Systems*, New York, pp313–314

Chapman, J. (2005) *Emotionally durable design: Objects, experiences, and empathy*, Earthscan, London

Chapman, J. (2009) 'Design for (emotional) durability', *Design Issues*, vol 25, no 4, pp29–35

Cox, J., Griffith, S., Giorgi, S. and King, G. (2013) 'Consumer understanding of product lifetimes', *Resources, Conservation and Recycling*, vol 79, pp21–29

Creusen, M. E. H. and Schoormans, J. P. L. (2005) 'The different roles of product appearance in consumer choice', *Journal of Product Innovation Management*, vol 22, no 1, pp63–81

Csikszentmihalyi, M. and Rochberg-Halton, E. (1981) *The meaning of things: Domestic symbols and the self*, Cambridge University Press, Cambridge

Ellen MacArthur Foundation (2013) *Towards the circular economy: Economic and business rationale for an accelerated transition*, vol 1, Ellen MacArthur Foundation, Cowes

Essoussi, L. H. and Linton, J. D. (2010) 'New or recycled products: how much are consumers willing to pay?', *Journal of Consumer Marketing*, vol 27, no 5, pp458–468

Govers, P. C. M. and Mugge, R. (2004) "I love my Jeep, because it's tough like me': The effect of product-personality congruence on product attachment', in Kurtgözü, A. (ed), *Proceedings of the Fourth International Conference on Design and Emotion*, Ankara, Turkey

Grant, K. E., Straker, K., Muller, C. and Wrigley, C. (2013) 'The search for individualism: Self-expression through product personalisation', *International Journal of Designed Objects*, vol 6, no 1, pp17–29

Grayson, K. and Shulman, D. (2000) 'Indexicality and the verification function of irreplaceable possessions: a semiotic analysis', *Journal of Consumer Research*, vol 27, no June, pp17–30

Harms, R. and Linton, J. D. (2016) 'Willingness to pay for eco-certified refurbished products: The effects of environmental attitudes and knowledge', *Journal of Industrial Ecology*, vol 20, no 4, pp893–904

Hatcher, G. D., Ijomah, W. L. and Windmill, J. F. C. (2011) 'Design for remanufacture: a literature review and future research needs', *Journal of Cleaner Production*, vol 19, no 17, pp2004–2014

Hazen, B. T., Overstreet, R. E., Jones-Farmer, L. A. and Field, H. S. (2012) 'The role of ambiguity tolerance in consumer perception of remanufactured products', *International Journal of Production Economics*, vol 135, no 2, pp781–790

Jordan, P. W. (1998) 'Human factors for pleasure in product use', *Applied Ergonomics*, vol 29, no 1, pp25–33

Kleine, S. S., Kleine, R. E. and Allen, C. T. (1995) 'How is a possession "me" or "not me"? Characterizing types and an antecedent of material possession attachment', *Journal of Consumer Research*, vol 22, pp327–343

Magnier, L. and Schoormans, J. (2015) 'Consumer reactions to sustainable packaging: The interplay of visual appearance, verbal claim and environmental concern', *Journal of Environmental Psychology*, vol 44, no December, pp53–62

Michaud, C. and Llerena, D. (2011) 'Green consumer behaviour: an experimental analysis of willingness to pay for remanufactured products', *Business Strategy and the Environment*, vol 20, no 6, pp408–420

Mugge, R. (2011) 'The effect of a business-like personality on the perceived performance quality of products', *International Journal of Design*, vol 5, no 3, pp67–76

Mugge, R. and Schoormans, J. P. L. (2012a) 'Newer is better! The influence of a novel appearance on the perceived performance quality of products', *Journal of Engineering Design*, vol 23, no 6, pp469–484

Mugge, R. and Schoormans, J. P. L. (2012b) 'Product design and apparent usability: The influence of novelty in product appearance', *Applied Ergonomics*, vol 43, no 6, pp1081–1088

Mugge, R., Schoormans, J. P. L. and Schifferstein, H. N. J. (2005) 'Design strategies to postpone consumers' product replacement: The value of a strong person–product relationship', *The Design Journal*, vol 8, no 2, pp38–48

Mugge, R., Schoormans, J. P. L. and Schifferstein, H. N. J. (2008) 'Product attachment: Design strategies to stimulate the emotional bonding to products', in Hekkert, P. and Schifferstein, H. N. J. (eds), *Product Experience*, Elsevier, London, pp425–440

Mugge, R., Schoormans, J. P. L. and Schifferstein, H. N. J. (2009) 'Emotional bonding with personalized products', *Journal of Engineering Design*, vol 20, no 5, pp467–476

Mugge, R., Schifferstein, H. N. J. and Schoormans, J. P. L. (2010) 'Product attachment and satisfaction: Understanding consumers' post-purchase behavior', *Journal of Consumer Marketing*, vol 27, no 3, pp271–282

Page, T. (2014) 'Product attachment and replacement: implications for sustainable design', *International Journal of Sustainable Design*, vol 2, no 3, pp265–282

Pigosso, D. C., Zanette, E. T., Ometto, A. R. and Rozenfeld, H. (2010) 'Ecodesign methods focused on remanufacturing', *Journal of Cleaner Production*, vol 18, no 1, pp21–31

Rathore, P., Kota, S. and Chakrabarti, A. (2011) 'Sustainability through remanufacturing in India: a case study on mobile handsets', *Journal of Cleaner Production*, vol 19, no 15, pp1709–1722

Rognoli, V. and Karana, E. (2013) 'Toward a new materials aesthetic based on imperfection and graceful aging', in Karana, E., Pedgley, O. and Rognoli, V. (eds), *Materials Experience: fundamentals of materials and design*, Elsevier, Amsterdam, pp145–154

Schifferstein, H. N. J. and Zwartkruis-Pelgrim, E. P. H. (2008) 'Consumer-product attachment: Measurement and design implications', *International Journal of Design*, vol 2, no 3, pp1–14

Schultz, S. E., Kleine, R. E. and Kernan, J. B. (1989) '"These are a few of my favorite things": Toward an explication of attachment as a consumer behavior construct', in Scrull, T. (ed.), *Advances in Consumer Research*, Association for Consumer Research, Provo, UT, pp359–366

Tchertchian, N., Millet, D. and Pialot, O. (2013) 'Modifying module boundaries to design remanufacturable products: the modular grouping explorer tool', *Journal of Engineering Design*, vol 24, no 8, pp546–574

Van Hemel, C. G. and Brezet, J. C. H. (1997) *Ecodesign; A promising approach to sustainable production and consumption*, United Nations Environmental Programme, Paris

Van Nes, N. (2003) *Replacement of durables: Influencing product life time through product design*, Erasmus University, Rotterdam

Van Weelden, E., Mugge, R. and Bakker, C. (2016) 'Paving the way towards circular consumption: Exploring consumer acceptance of refurbished mobile phones in the Dutch market', *Journal of Cleaner Production*, vol 113, pp743–754

Wallendorf, M. and Arnould, E. J. (1988) '"My favorite things": A cross-cultural inquiry into object attachment, possessiveness, and social linkage', *Journal of Consumer Research*, vol 14, no March, pp531–547

Wang, Y. and Hazen, B. T. (2016) 'Consumer product knowledge and intention to purchase remanufactured products', *International Journal of Production Economics*, vol 181, part B, pp460–469

Wang, Y., Wiegerinck, V., Krikke, H. and Zhang, H. (2013) 'Understanding the purchase intention towards remanufactured product in closed-loop supply chains: An empirical study in China', *International Journal of Physical Distribution and Logistics Management*, vol 43, no 10, pp866–888

Zwolinski, P. and Brissaud, D. (2008) 'Remanufacturing strategies to support product design and redesign', *Journal of Engineering Design*, vol 19, no 4, pp321–335

26

DESIGNING CIRCULAR POSSESSIONS

Weston Baxter and Peter Childs

Abstract

The notion of possession is one of the most fundamental concepts that guide everyday behaviour. Paradoxically, it is often poorly understood. This is particularly true in a circular context where consumer interactions with possessions are being altered and in some cases redefined. Thus, an understanding of possession serves as a useful, if not necessary, prerequisite to designing circular products, services and systems. This chapter explores the idea of possession: what it is, how an object becomes one and why it is important for the circular economy. Possession is understood through a human-centred lens that considers the consumer's state of mind towards and relationship with an object. A state of possessiveness can be attained for material or immaterial objects and for objects that may or may not legally belong to the person. The discussion is presented within a design framework that discusses the motives and routes that lead to the state of possession. This framework is substantiated by looking at affordance principles and paths associated with possession. Each section includes a theoretical discussion as well as practical examples and insights that can be incorporated into the product design process itself. This chapter aids in understanding interactions relevant to the circular economy such as the maintenance and care that comes with object attachment and adoption of access-based consumption models. Understanding and designing for these desired interactions should be the first priority of designers followed by an establishment of laws, regulations and policies to support them.

Keywords: possession, psychological ownership, object attachment, emotional attachment, circular economy

Introduction

With a transition to a circular economy, consumers are encouraged to change their interactions with objects. A product longevity approach would have consumers keep and maintain their objects longer. New business models push for access, rather than ownership. Access schemes and growing second-hand markets present consumers with objects with 'contamination' from previous use. Usage and disposition decisions are now of great interest to researchers and increasingly involves discussion of legislation and other behavioural interventions. Under these situations, the traditional view of consumer possessions are being studied, altered, and, in some cases redefined.

The concepts of possession, ownership and personal property are among the most fundamental to who we are and how we engage with the world around us. Without understanding possession, for example, it would be difficult to understand the purpose of selling, gifting, and stealing objects (Snare, 1972). Indeed, possessive behaviours are engrained in our evolutionary and cultural background. Hundreds of millions of years ago animals began exhibiting possessive behaviours when scarcity compelled competition (Aunger and Curtis, 2015). Adam Smith, the 'Father of Modern Economics' has said that one of the sacred laws of justice is to guard a person's property and possessions (Smith, 1790). Consistent with these ideas, our research has shown that individuals often talk about possessions first in the context of what they mean to the owner and second with regard to how laws and regulations support those behaviours.

The legal-centric approach to possessions is useful if you are designing rules of a system. However, in a circular system, much is still changing and rules are still being determined. Rather than first focusing on the legal fabric that supports the system, our focus is on properly framing the mental state that is called possessing or owning an object. Individuals may, for example, feel a sense of ownership for things they don't legally own (Pierce, Rubenfeld and Morgan, 1991; Van Dyne and Pierce, 2004) or conversely, they may never take possession of things that are legally theirs (McCracken, 1986). By focusing on the mental state, we can transition to a system based on the needs of the consumers first and then make appropriate legal and business infrastructure to support these needs. This approach, for many, will reframe the concept of possessions, and the role products play in the experiential lives of users. Discussions about possessions and relationships to objects have been explored extensively in the literature. What seems to be missing is a coherent, human-centred narrative about possessions aimed to aid in the design of circular products and systems.

In this chapter, we examine the processes associated with possessing an object. To achieve this, we build on psychological ownership theory – the notion that individuals enter a mental state in which they feel an object is 'theirs' (Pierce, Kostova and Dirks, 2001). Thus, the terms possession and ownership are used interchangeably to refer to those things mentally perceived as belonging to a person. As we hope will be illuminated throughout the chapter, behaviours associated with possession such as maintaining, engaging with, and properly disposing of objects, help determine the desired outcomes within the circular economy and should prove useful for designers. The theory of psychological ownership presents fundamental motives for wanting to own and routes to achieving the mental state of ownership. We expand this model and place it within a design framework. The model and subsequent insights and commentary have been substantiated through several qualitative studies.

This approach to understanding consumer possessions is useful for design in at least two ways. First, it addresses why and how individuals seek to own objects. As the name suggests, this ownership is a psychological representation of the individual's relationship to the object and subsequently is bound by interactions rather than legalese. Using this nuanced approach to understanding interactions leading to psychological ownership helps explain the consumer concerns that have curbed access-based consumption models. In these models, companies retain ownership and provide access to consumers but consumers may still be able to, and want to, develop feelings of ownership to it. In other words, this approach helps explain what it is consumers want from the concept of ownership and then allows the 'system' to support that. Evidence for the usefulness of this approach is seen in California's Native Americans who are often referenced for their notion of ownership that differed from that of the modern western culture. For the Native Americans, an area would become theirs if they frequently used and tended to it through which they created a system of usufruct rights at both an individual and communal level (Anderson, 2005). Similarly, designing circular possessions will benefit from first understanding how and why individuals make objects theirs and then supporting (or appropriately accommodating for) this through systemic mechanisms such as laws, regulations and policies.

The second way in which this approach is useful in design deals with product longevity. Product longevity is a function of both the technical and emotional durability of an object (Chapman, 2005). The emotional durability (or durability of emotional attachment) of an object is methodically explained through psychological ownership theory. That is to say that if object attachment is defined as a perceived psychological closeness to an object (Baumeister and Wangenheim, 2014), then psychological ownership represents an extreme form of this closeness – one in which the object may become part of an extended self (Belk, 1988). Shu and Peck (2011) directly link psychological ownership to attachment and show how it contributes to loss aversion. Other studies support this link to loss aversion (Baer and Brown, 2012; Kahneman and Knetsch, 1991) and highlight additional consequences of attachment such as higher evaluation (Franke, Schreier and Kaiser, 2010; Reb and Connolly, 2007) and feelings of stewardship (Hernandez, 2012). In a wider perspective, we see psychological ownership theory useful in providing a coherent model for attachment (Baxter, Aurisicchio and Childs, 2015a), the elements of which are stressed in a number of design-oriented attachment studies (Mugge, Schifferstein and Schoormans, 2006, 2010; Mugge, Schoormans and Schifferstein, 2009; Desmet and Hekkert, 2007; Norton, Mochon and Ariely, 2011). Beyond perhaps other approaches, this approach discusses the paths and processes of attachment and detachment (referred to in this chapter at times as possession and dispossession) such that design can deal with both. For some, this direct link between psychological ownership and attachment will be new in part because attachment is often associated with strong, positive affect. In reality, attachment and affect are independent measures that can have countervailing effects on the evaluation of an object (Shu and Peck, 2011). Building on this work, we view psychological ownership the same as attachment and also use this term throughout the document.

It is easy, but inaccurate, to think of possession as a stage-gate process beginning at the point of purchase and ending at disposition. Possession, as defined as a mental state, is much more fluid. Feelings of possession can emerge through exposure to simple stimuli frequently encountered before or without purchasing an object such as touching or seeing objects (Peck and Shu, 2009). Similarly, it is not difficult to identify things in our legal ambit of possessions of which we have never truly taken possession (e.g. some gifts). In this regard, any feelings of ownership may lead, lag, or never include legal ownership. Disposition, as a physical act, also could be preceded or followed by an emotional dispossession of the object. Any object that is still in a person's legal ownership but has been emotionally dispossessed is only waiting temporarily before it is properly disposed. A previous study (Baxter, Aurisicchio and Childs, 2015b) found that the reason consumers discard and keep objects is consistent with the psychological ownership framework, below. Thus, any design interventions around acquiring and disposing of possessions should focus on the physical act *and* the mental state of the consumer. By focusing on the mental state of possessing objects, consumer behaviour is viewed as a fluid process that more accurately represents behaviours of interest in design.

The next section of this chapter presents a framework for designing objects that produce psychological ownership. Subsequent sections explore the process of possessing, and dispossessing objects. This work is the culmination of several studies focused on uncovering the interplay between possessions and consumers under various circular contexts. Our intent is that by understanding these processes, designers are better equipped to produce human-centred designs within the circular economy.

A framework for psychological ownership

Psychological ownership is the mental state in which individuals feel that an object is theirs. Within this chapter, we refer to this state as having 'possession' of an object. The theory of psychological ownership describes the motives (the why) and routes (the how) leading to this mental state (Pierce, Kostova and Dirks, 2003). It follows that ownership is a result of user interactions and experiences. In the perspective of existing experience design frameworks the motives and routes can be thought of as be-goals and do-goals, respectively (Pucillo and Cascini, 2014; Hassenzahl, 2010). Previous work by the authors has mapped and expanded this connection to create the framework in Figure 26.1 (Baxter, Aurisicchio and Childs, 2015a). A major part of this expansion included the identification of affordance principles intended to help guide design. The final column of the framework, actions or motor-goals, represents the actions that result in the routes being achieved. The actions that lead to feelings of possession, particularly those contributing significantly, can be thought of as 'possession rituals' as described by McCracken (1986). Actions are specific to each product and are not discussed in this chapter.

This framework is bidirectional. Specific behaviours (i.e. actions performed through routes) are driven by the motives in the framework. It is also possible, however, to entice actions through design that fulfil motives and bring about feelings of ownership without the drives of the motives. An example of actions leading to feelings of ownership occurs when consumers help create an object; a process referred to as the 'IKEA effect' (Norton, Mochon and Ariely, 2011). Neither the routes nor the affordance principles are mutually exclusive and will often work together for greater impact.

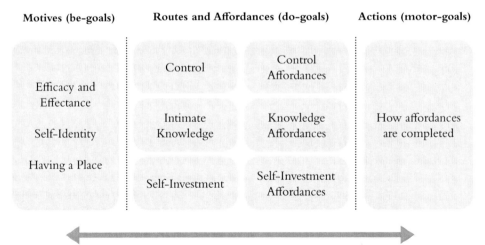

Figure 26.1 Framework for psychological ownership-based attachment to possessions

Source: Baxter et al. (2015a)

The remainder of this section discusses the motives, routes and affordance principles found within the framework. Though we present this with regard to targeted physical objects, this is a holistic framework in which any object, physical or non-physical in nature, can be applied. For example, developing attachment (or psychological ownership) of a brand could be included in the framework. A number of non-physical targets may be of interest to the readers of this chapter. For example, developing psychological ownership over energy usage or the earth's resources could lead to more responsible behaviours. There is no reason why these too cannot be addressed through the psychological ownership framework. In these cases, designers should look to the framework to determine how users fulfil (or could fulfil) the routes to ownership.

Motives

Psychological ownership is driven by three motives: efficacy and effectance, self-identity, and having a place to dwell (Pierce, Kostova and Dirks, 2001, 2003). Efficacy and effectance is the desire to feel competent through the ability to impact one's surroundings. Self-identity is the desire to create, continue, and/or transform one's public and/or private identity. Having a place to dwell is the desire to gain and preserve physical, emotional, and mental security through familiar surroundings.

Routes

There are three routes to achieving psychological ownership: control, intimate knowledge, and self-investment (Pierce, Kostova and Dirks, 2001, 2003). Control is the ability to use or transform an object when and how desired. Intimate knowledge comes as users acquire information about the object. Self-investment is the expenditure of time, money, physical effort, and/or psychological energy into an object. Importantly, a prerequisite to these routes is that the object attracts or engages the user to the point a route can be pursued.

Affordances

Design intended to achieve a mental state within a user is difficult because it cannot be forced or guaranteed. It can, however, be designed for through affordances (Pucillo and Cascini, 2014). Affordances are the possible interaction with and use of an object based on the properties of the object and the capabilities of the user (Norman, 2013). Each route can be thought of as a desired interaction that can be achieved through affordances between the user and the object or environment. Thus, a previous study identified affordance principles to help better understand and design for each of the routes (Baxter, Aurisicchio and Childs, 2015a). Affordances at this level are still broad and allow room for tailoring specific design features to the problem at hand. These principles are not thought to be exhaustive but rather act as a guide to help designers think about ways to evaluate and create objects or the environments in which objects are used. The affordances are presented in Table 26.1 with short descriptions but are described in more detail in previously published work (ibid.).

In total, 16 affordance principles were identified through and categorised according to the route (control, intimate knowledge, and self-investment) that they afford (see Table 26.1). All affordance categories were considered as widely as possible to reflect diverse interactions. Control affordances describe spatial and temporal control as well as the user's ability to change the object. Intimate knowledge affordances reflect ways to allow an object to communicate

Table 26.1 Affordance principles aiding in the creation of psychological ownership

Affordance principle	Description
Control	
Spatial	Physically manipulate the object
Configuration	Arrange the object settings
Temporal	Use of the object when desired
Rate	Use as much of the object as desired
Transformation	Change the object as a result of interaction
Intimate knowledge	
Ageing	Capture stories in object changes as it ages with the user
Disclosure	Convey origins and former experiences
Periodic signalling	Communicate on an event-dependent basis
Enabling	Mediate meaningful experiences
Simplification	Eliminate distractions
Proximity	Communicate through closeness
Self-investment	
Creation	Bring something or part of something into existence
Repair and maintenance	Service the object
Repository	Collect and store valuables within the object
Emblems	Signal information about identity
Preference recall	Remember previously established preferences

Source: Baxter et al. (2015a)

more accurately with the user. This communication occurs through object features as well as contextual factors. Self-investment affordances represent the range of user effort spent on interacting with an object. The remaining sections describe how this framework relates to taking possession, having possession and dispossessing of objects.

Taking possession

Taking possession of something occurs through interactions in a time-dependent process. While feelings of possession or psychological ownership can occur with a first interaction with an object such as touching or seeing the object (Peck and Shu, 2009), more meaningful possession will typically develop over multiple interactions. These interactions reflect the framework presented in the previous section. The routes have a type of directionality between the user and target objects of ownership. Control and self-investment are typically things done by the user to the object, whereas intimate knowledge is the result of the user interpreting information communicated by or about the object. Understanding these directions helps inform how various interactions with consumers (e.g. co-creation, mass customization, designed affordances, associated service offerings, marketing and promotion) impact attachment or ownership.

Through numerous interviews, we have sought to extract general paths to developing attachment or psychological ownership. We did this through inquiring about the user's relationship to and interactions with the object through time (Baxter, Aurisicchio and Childs, 2015b). We found that paths are primarily determined in three ways. First, significant increases in attachment occur when users engage in focused interactions with an object such as configuring, repairing or researching an object. Second, gradual increases in attachment result over time due to improved ability to control the object, routine effort required in interacting with the object and knowledge received through use. Finally, used objects may create feelings that they are foreign, contaminated and belonging to someone else. We have depicted four common paths in Figure 26.2. Path B represents a typical path of attachment for an object – large initial attachment and continued increase as the user learns to better control and cares for the object over time. Path A results from heightened attachment activities (e.g. mass customization) making a steeper slope in the initial attachment. Path C occurs when the object is standardized so as to limit progression through focused interactions. Finally, Path D occurs when users engage with objects used by other people and feel the object is not theirs until they 'cleanse' it from traces of the previous owner. The obvious line not discussed here is the one in which the user develops no psychological ownership for the object.

An example of these paths is seen with car use. Path A might represent an owner's attachment to a car that has been customized and thus showing increased up-front effort. Path B would be a car as normally purchased. The focused interaction in this path being primarily the search for the car and money (i.e. self-investment) spent. Path C might be a company car that a person did not choose or purchase but does get to know through frequent use over time. Finally, Path D might be a car acquired second-hand or temporarily accessed with reminders, usually unwelcome, of the previous user.

The negative interaction shown in line D is common and perhaps will be increasingly so in the context of a circular economy. It represents one form of contaminated interaction. In a previous study we defined contaminated interaction as 'the process through which the quality, meaning, or value of an object changes due to interaction with someone or something'

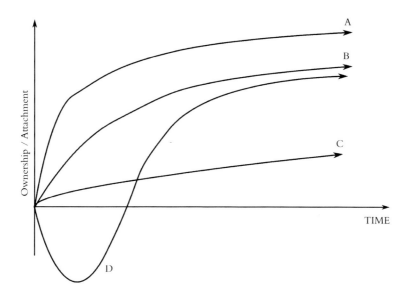

Figure 26.2 Four common paths for developing attachment or psychological ownership

Source: Baxter et al. (2015b)

(Baxter, Aurisicchio and Childs, 2016). In this same study, we found that contamination arose in three ways: hygienic contamination, utility contamination, and territorial contamination. Hygienic contamination occurs when an object threatens a person's health or feeling of hygienic cleanliness. Utility contamination occurs when an object's functional attributes are damaged. Territorial contamination results when objects seem to be 'marked' by another person. A single indicator of previous use (e.g. a bad smell) can change perceptions linked to multiple drivers (e.g. hygiene and territory).

There are at least two ways this discussion contributes to product design. First, there is a process to helping people develop possessions and it can be understood through the framework we have presented. This process results in any number of paths created by specific interactions with objects but we have listed some common paths in Figure 26.2. Importantly, the initial point of time occurs with the first interaction, not the point of purchase. Thus, activities such as searching and special ordering can become important within this framework. If the object is sold, it can help to increase the attachment before sale and influence the amount a consumer is willing to pay. If the object is not sold, this can be used to induce other behaviours that accompany psychological ownership that will be discussed further in the next section.

The process of overcoming contamination is an important path to be considered in circular systems. One interviewee in our research recounted her experience of buying a faux fur coat at a second-hand store. Initially excited about the purchase, she took the coat home and tried it on again. She soon became dismayed when she examined it closely because it smelled of the previous owner. Washing and airing the coat out did not work so she put the coat in a bag with coffee beans and sealed it for several days. When she took it out, her coat no longer smelled of the previous owner thanks to her great effort and she now enjoys a coffee-scented coat that she feels is very much hers (see how this mirrors line D of Figure 26.2). Not many users are willing to put the same type of week-long effort that this person did. We do not suppose that all used objects will be contaminated and disrupt the flow of materials. However, materials within a circular economy, by definition, will have had a former life and be reused. Designers should consider how their objects might be perceived as they become used and take steps to address this accordingly.

Second, this discussion contributes to the design of access-based consumption models. Users participating in these schemes are often limited in terms of how or when they can use an object and the transient use does not allow them to readily develop a self-identity or place to dwell. Thus, all three motives for ownership are threatened. This provides more insight into the phrase, 'people want a hole, not a drill' variously attributed to multiple sources (Botsman and Rogers, 2010; Norman, 2013). Some people certainly do want to achieve 'the end' and do not care about 'the means' but this is not always the case, and when it is, 'the end' that consumers desire may be poorly understood. Accordingly, it might be more correct to say that people want efficacy and effectance, self-identity and a place to dwell, not (legal) ownership. The process of achieving these goals within access models is complicated by contaminated interaction shown in line D. In many access schemes, the time of usage is short enough that users only feel the contamination and never emerge to have a positive experience. However, design can aid in helping users overcome contamination and, when desired, fulfil the motives of the psychological ownership framework.

Possession

Once an object has become a possession it is treated differently. This is because possessions are objects with a significant relationship with users. At a basic level, a possession reflects the fulfilment of the framework motives – efficacy and effectance, self-identity, and having a place to dwell. Coupled with this is a sense of stewardship over the object (Davis, Schoorman and Donaldson, 1997; Hernandez, 2012). It follows that this stewardship often directly reflects maintaining each of the motives. An object that heavily influences efficacy and effectance, such as a tool, might be regularly cared for to maintain performance. An object reflecting an outward-facing identity, such as a car or clothing, might be carefully maintained to reflect the desired identity. Finally, the desire to have a place to dwell leads people to clean and organize an environment as they want and keep familiar objects with them. When there is no feeling of ownership or possession objects are often abused through use rather than cared for.

It is worthwhile to look at examples of interactions with possessions to better understand the behaviours that come with it. The native tribes of Vanuatu are an indigenous people who, similar to the Native Americans discussed in the introduction, view property ownership different from the colonial version of land ownership. These tribes do however have significant possessions in the form of swine. As Miles (1997) reports, pigs in Vanuatu have significant importance and for a long time, pig ownership and pig killing has conveyed status, wealth and informal power. Over time, these customs have changed with more influence from the outside world. Still, pigs hold great importance in the country and as recently as 1991, pigs have been traded in exchange for a commuted jail sentence. These pigs are groomed, cared for, named, beautified (e.g. through manipulation of teeth), traded, and wept over (ibid.). These behaviours are a reflection of the routes described in the framework (i.e. control, intimate knowledge, self-investment) and the outcomes often desired for consumers possessing an object in a circular economy (e.g. stewardship, care or maintenance).

Another interesting example of interacting with a possession comes from one of the original papers on psychological ownership. Pierce and colleagues (Pierce, Kostova and Dirks, 2003), recounted the behaviours of truck drivers in a local mine. Originally, drivers showed no feeling of ownership over a truck until the company changed its policy to assign each driver to a specific truck. The company retained legal ownership but the truck was used each day by the same driver. Slowly, behaviours toward the trucks began to change. The company found that drivers started to take possession of the trucks and refer to them as 'my' truck, clean the interior and attend to mechanical maintenance. One driver even named his truck and had his name painted on the door of the car using his own money. Simple policy changes such as this one could see significant behaviour change toward objects, at a range of scales.

Developing feelings of possession requires effort (as seen in the previous section). This effort can be a deterrent for many users and could result in poor brand perception and more abuse to objects during use. Design can help reduce the effort required to develop feelings of possession by guiding users through the routes of the framework. In the case of sharing, design needs to retain this effort across multiple uses. Many cars, for example, have two sets of keys. When one person enters the car, the key is recognised and all the settings – mirrors, seat position, radio station, etc. – conform to that user. Through design, the effort of taking possession of the car is not lost after each use but is remembered and called-upon in future situations.

We do not suppose that feeling possession for something will always lead to environmentally friendly behaviours. For example, electricity is an invisible object not often thought about as a possession. However, homeowners who have installed solar panels seem to view their 'solar electricity' differently. This energy is often uniquely theirs because they went through specific effort to create it (i.e. self-investment) and they get feedback about its use (i.e. intimate knowledge). In turn, some consumers view this as an opportunity to 'spend' their energy by purchasing something they otherwise would not have bought such as an electric dryer. Any potential gain from the solar panels are then minimised or eliminated through the acquisition of more creating a rebound effect.

Dispossessing

Dispossession is the process individuals go through to relinquish an object as 'theirs'. Similar to the discussion on taking possession of objects, dispossession is unique from disposition in that disposition is the actual act of removing the object from your environment while dispossession is the process of mentally relinquishing the object. We focus on dispossession because it differentiates between the moments when an object has become mentally *and* physically removed from ones material world. An object that has been dispossessed might as well be counted as waste since the act of disposing is merely a formality of physically doing what has already been done mentally. Similarly, an object may be disposed of physically but it is spoken of as if it is still a possession. In these cases it is also common for people to 'keep the objects alive' through photos, stories and other memories that leave the person grasping for what physically once was but mentally may still remain (e.g. a childhood toy).

Paths to dispossession rely on the same interaction between users, motives and routes as did the paths to possessing. As was the case before, there are as many paths to dispossession as there are products and ways to interact with them. Through our qualitative studies we have identified trends in the interactions as they relate to dispossession. These paths are presented in Figure 26.3. Line H represents the nostalgia many users have for objects. Sometimes, nostalgia moves people to keep an object despite other issues such as broken components or outdated technology. The line is dotted to represent feelings of ownership that were sometimes directed to former possessions that are no longer physically in the person's control. In these cases, the feeling of possession was maintained through images, stories and other means and it was common for people to talk about the object as if it was just in the other room. If the object was kept alive by something physical, such as a photograph, great care was transferred to the physical object. Line G occurs when an object becomes distanced from a user. With distance, the 'intimate knowledge' of the object decreases and the subsequent psychological ownership weakens. Line F follows a similar curve as line G but differs in that it is an active interaction. The active interactions here mean that a user is still engaged with the object but is beginning to find the object boring or has become otherwise disenchanted by it. Users described this type of dispossession with a number of objects including video games, furniture and even spaces (e.g. rooms in a house). An effort to avoid this disenchantment or boredom may be one of the reasons why people often rearrange furniture in a room in their home. By rearranging furniture, an act of hedonic adaptation, the room becomes fresh and explorable and can contribute to the efficacy and effectance motive (e.g. you are competent through manipulating your surroundings) and the intimate knowledge motive because you have more you can learn about the room setup. Finally the sharp dispossession found in line E reflects the situation where a motive is suddenly no longer met. This can be the result of changes in the object itself (e.g. it is broken), new products on the market that fulfil the motives better (e.g. upgrading to the newest technology), or changes to the person (e.g. transitioning to a new identity).

These paths to dispossession help guide thinking around design within a circular economy. Most obvious is the way this can be used to approach designing for the emotional durability

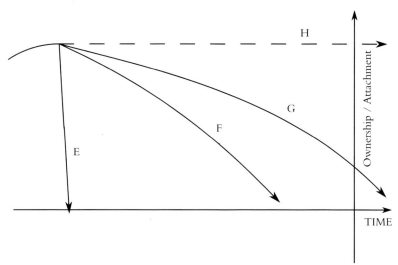

Figure 26.3 Common paths for detachment and absolving psychological ownership

of an object (Chapman, 2005). Any hope to extend product longevity requires that we understand how well the object can continue to fulfil the psychological ownership motives. Important factors to consider include: replacements available on the market, changes in identity and how well the object itself ages. Emotional durability also deals with the boredom or disenchantment expressed toward certain objects (line F). An important design question in itself regards how to make 'timeless' pieces that do not leave the user bored. We would expect timeless objects to continue to rise in feelings of ownership though not all stimuli achieve this. Some types of art deemed 'bad' by scholars and critics, for example, are shown to decrease in liking scores the more a person is exposed to them (Meskin et al., 2013). Other strategies to create objects with which consumers remain engaged, such as modular or personalized designs, should be employed when possible.

There seems to be an inherent usefulness in changing the vocabulary from emotional durability or attachment to ownership. In defining the term 'emotional durability', Chapman (2005) refers to a full spectrum of human emotion, both positive and negative, as playing a part in extending the life of products. Yet, the term seems to carry with it strong connotations that the user needs to have some sort of positive emotion associated with or directed towards the object. The same is true of attachment. This is not the case. Users may feel any number of emotions toward an object – happiness, sadness, frustration, excitement, etc. – and still keep and use the object. This was most readily seen with one of our interviewees who owned an electric tool given to him by family. The tool was expensive and was more than ten years old. Over the years, numerous new product releases had taken place but he continued to use the machine because it continued to work well and would be expensive to replace. The interview became particularly interesting when the respondent told us that he hated the machine. He hated it not because of how well it did the job, but because of the emotion associated with using it. He had a major fall-out with the person who gifted the machine a number of years earlier and each time he used the machine it reminded him of the pain of that experience. Was it 'emotionally' durable? Sure. He regularly maintained it, had fixed it multiple times, and transported it through several moves. Did he want to get rid of it? Absolutely. By talking about objects as possessions or psychologically owned, we avoid the connotations dealing with emotions in terms of their positive or negative bias.

Unsurprisingly, some motives are more 'durable' than others. Through our interviews we tracked the reasons for dispossessing (and eventually disposing) of an object. The efficacy and effectance motive is relatively weak because products in this category are often subjected to advances in technology and natural degradation that occurs through use that limits its life. Self-identity is a stronger motive because it is mainly susceptible to major changes in identity that can often be predicted such as transitioning into teenage years, moving to a new house, moving out of a parent's house, going from college to a career, single to married and so on. The strongest motive was having a place to dwell. These consumer 'places' are often rooted in emotions and help the person feel safe or secure through familiar objects. This place can be developed and cultivated as specific memories and experiences are associated with objects that create feelings of nostalgia. Consumers often keep objects fulfilling their 'place to dwell' for a long time even when it incurs a significant cost.

Conclusions

In this chapter we have argued that designing in the circular economy requires an understanding and at times a redefinition of possessions. Unfortunately, designed products and services often change the notion of possessions without considering the consumer. Through a human-centred approach, we present a narrative around what it means to possess something and how and why it is done. We have intentionally avoided legal notions of possessions in this process and have relied on a possession as a mental state. The result has been a discussion of the processes and behaviours associated with possessions including design conclusions contained in each section. Our aim is to help designers understand consumer interactions with circular possessions and then develop policies, regulations and laws to support these interactions.

Designing circular possessions is about understanding scarcity and abundance. Consumers fight for scarce things and freely exchange the abundant. Consumers have a scarce amount time, money, space and energy to invest in objects and they are forced to make trade-offs in how they fulfil the motives. For example, many respondents reported that they would keep an object but the cost of repair had become too high. In other situations, respondents reported that the purchase of one new item for a room in their home conflicted with another piece (e.g. mismatched furniture) and they had to discard one to create the 'place' they desired. Scarcity is also found in personal objects with sentiment attached or objects such as property which, by its nature is scare. Abundant objects (mass produced products, electricity, water, etc.) freely move in and out of a person's possession. A person is happy to exchange out the hardware for their smartphone because the hardware is abundant but the internal contents (address book, photo library, etc.) is a scarce prized possession that will not be given up easily. Designers should differentiate the abundant and scarce aspects of their offerings to more effectively align consumer behaviours.

We have presented a theoretical contribution in this chapter. In our research, this has proven useful in helping explain many of the problems and opportunities within a circular economy and inspiring several research questions. The theory has also proven useful in informing design directions for the development of circular possessions. At the end of each section, we highlighted insights designers can use to understand how the ideas are applicable to their work. These insights are founded on understanding possessions and are applicable to product designers, policymakers and businesses. In this way, designers, policymakers and businesses need to work together to understand and design circular possessions.

References

Anderson, K. (2005) *Tending the Wild: Native American Knowledge and the Management of California's Natural Resources*. Berkeley, CA: University of California Press.

Aunger, R. and Curtis, V. (2015) *Gaining Control: How Human Behavior Evolved*. Oxford: Oxford University Press.

Baer, M. and Brown, G. (2012) Blind in one eye: How psychological ownership of ideas affects the types of suggestions people adopt. *Organizational Behavior and Human Decision Processes* 118(1): 60–71.

Baumeister, C. and Wangenheim, F. V. (2014) *Access vs. Ownership: Understanding Consumers' Consumption Mode Preference*. Retrieved from http://papers.ssrn.com/abstract=2463076 (accessed 4 September 2014).

Baxter, W. L., Aurisicchio, M. and Childs, P. R. N. (2015a) A psychological ownership approach to designing object attachment. *Journal of Engineering Design* 26(4–6): 140–156.

Baxter, W. L., Aurisicchio, M. and Childs, P. R. N. (2015b) Using psychological ownership to guide strategies for slower consumption. In T. Cooper, N. Braithwaite, M. Moreno and G. Salvia (eds), *Product Lifetimes and the Environment (PLATE) Conference Proceedings, Nottingham, 17–19 June*, Nottingham: CADBE, Nottingham Trent University, pp1–8.

Baxter, W. L., Aurisicchio, M. and Childs, P. R. N. (2016) Materials, use and contaminated interaction. *Materials and Design* 90: 1218–1227.

Belk, R. W. (1988) Possessions and the extended self. *The Journal of Consumer Research* 15(2): 139–168.

Botsman, R. and Rogers, R. (2010) What's mine is yours. Retrieved from www.tantor.com/SellSheets/1920_MineIsYours.pdf (accessed 21 May 2014).

Chapman, J. (2005) *Emotionally Durable Design: Objects, Experiences and Empathy*. London: Earthscan.

Davis, J. H., Schoorman, F. D. and Donaldson, L. (1997) Toward a stewardship theory of management. *Academy of Management Review* 22(1): 20–47.

Desmet, P. M. and Hekkert, P. (2007) Framework of product experience. *International Journal of Design* 1(1): 57–66.

Franke, N., Schreier, M. and Kaiser, U. (2010) The 'I designed it myself' effect in mass customization. *Management Science* 56(1): 125–140.

Hassenzahl, M. (2010) Experience design: technology for all the right reasons. In J. M. Carroll (ed.), *Synthesis Lectures on Human-Centered Informatics*. San Rafael, CA: Morgan & Claypool Publishers, pp1–95.

Hernandez, M. (2012) Toward an understanding of the psychology of stewardship. *Academy of Management Review* 37(2): 172–193.

Kahneman, D. and Knetsch, J. L. (1991) The endowment effect, loss aversion, and status quo bias. *Journal of Economic Perspectives* 5(1): 193–206.

McCracken, G. (1986) Culture and consumption: A theoretical account of the structure and movement of the cultural meaning of consumer goods. *Journal of Consumer Research* 13(1): 71–84.

Meskin, A., Phelan, M., Moore, M. and Kieran, M. (2013) Mere exposure to bad art. *The British Journal of Aesthetics* 53(2): 139–164.

Miles, W. F. (1997) Pigs, politics and social change in Vanuatu. *Society and Animals* 5(2): 155–167.

Mugge, R., Schifferstein, H. N. and Schoormans, J. P. (2006) A longitudinal study on product attachment and its determinants. In K. M. Ekstrom and H. Brembeck (eds), *European Advances in Consumer Research*. Gothenburg, Sweden: Association for Consumer Research, pp. 641–647.

Mugge, R., Schifferstein, H. N. J. and Schoormans, J. P. L. (2010) Product attachment and satisfaction: understanding consumers' post-purchase behavior. *Journal of Consumer Marketing* 27(3): 271–282.

Mugge, R., Schoormans, J. P. L. and Schifferstein, H. N. J. (2009) Emotional bonding with personalised products. *Journal of Engineering Design* 20(5): 467–476.

Norman, D. A. (2013) *The Design of Everyday Things: Revised and Expanded Edition*. New York: Basic Books.

Norton, M., Mochon, D. and Ariely, D. (2011) The 'IKEA effect': When labor leads to love. Harvard Business School Marketing Unit Working Paper 11-091. Retrieved from http://papers.ssrn.com/sol3/papers.cfm?abstract_id=1777100 (accessed 14 March 2014).

Peck, J. and Shu, S. B. (2009) The effect of mere touch on perceived ownership. *Journal of Consumer Research* 36(3): 434–447.

Pierce, J. L., Kostova, T. and Dirks, K. T. (2001) Toward a theory of psychological ownership in organizations. *Academy of Management Review* 26(2): 298–310.

Pierce, J. L., Kostova, T. and Dirks, K. T. (2003) The state of psychological ownership: Integrating and extending a century of research. *Review of General Psychology* 7(1): 84.

Pierce, J. L., Rubenfeld, S. A. and Morgan, S. (1991) Employee Ownership: A Conceptual Model of Process and Effects. *Academy of Management Review* 16(1): 121–144.

Pucillo, F. and Cascini, G. (2014) A framework for user experience, needs and affordances. *Design Studies* 35(2): 160–179.

Reb, J. and Connolly, T. (2007) Possession, feelings of ownership, and the endowment effect. *Judgment and Decision Making* 2(2): 107–114.

Shu, S. B. and Peck, J. (2011) Psychological ownership and affective reaction: Emotional attachment process variables and the endowment effect. *Journal of Consumer Psychology* 21(4): 439–452.

Smith, A. (1790) *The Theory of Moral Sentiments*, 6th edn. London: A. Millar.

Snare, F. (1972) The concept of property. *American Philosophical Quarterly* 9(2): 200–206.

Van Dyne, L. and Pierce, J. L. (2004) Psychological ownership and feelings of possession: three field studies predicting employee attitudes and organizational citizenship behavior. *Journal of Organizational Behavior* 25(4): 439–459.

27

WHICH WAY TO TURN?

Product longevity and business dilemmas in the circular economy

Tim Cooper

Abstract

A circular economy offers the potential for resources to be used more sustainably. While the concept is primarily associated with recycling, there are added benefits to be gained from slowing cycles of resource use through longer product lifetimes. Noting a growth of political and academic interest in the topic, this chapter considers the significance of product longevity for environmental sustainability, consumers and industry, and the implications for design. Findings from recent research on consumers' expectations of product lifetimes are summarized and their maintenance and disposal behaviour explored. The feasibility of product lifetime labelling is assessed, together with other policy options for encouraging increased product longevity. Industry has historically been blamed for planned obsolescence and criticism of companies operating with traditional 'linear' business models continues. Alternative business models that could enable companies to increase their products' lifetimes while remaining competitive are identified. Finally, the potential role of designers in this emerging debate is considered.

Keywords: circular economy, product lifetimes, obsolescence, consumer behaviour, business models

Product longevity in a circular economy

The concept of a circular economy, which in recent years has increasingly attracted the attention of governments, industry and civil society, represents a long-overdue recognition that the throughput of materials in industrial economies is unsustainable. Locked into the traditional, linear economy mind-set, politicians and industrialists were, until recently, reluctant to engage in the debate, aware that it challenges many fundamental norms of economic policy, how businesses generate revenue and people's relationship with possessions. This, however, appears on the verge of change. When the *EU Action Plan for the Circular Economy* was launched in December 2015, European Commission Vice President Frans Timmermans noted its implications: 'The circular economy is about reducing waste and protecting the environment, but it is also about a profound transformation of the way our entire economy works' (European Commission, 2015a). Earlier in the year, leading industrialist Frans van Houten, Chief Executive of Philips Electronics, wrote positively about it: 'The circular economy has the potential to help us make better decisions about resource use, design out waste, provide added value for business, and proceed along a secure route to society-wide prosperity and environmental sustainability' (Ellen MacArthur Foundation, 2015, p5).

Like sustainable development, the circular economy is a concept open to different interpretation. The term is primarily associated with recycling, or 'closing resource loops'. In addition, it is commonly – though not consistently – assumed to embrace longer product life-spans as a means of slowing the throughput of materials. The Ellen MacArthur Foundation (2014, p16) has advocated 'the power of circling longer', which it describes as 'maximising the number of consecutive cycles (be it repair, reuse or full remanufacturing) *and/or the time in each cycle*' (my emphasis); it does so on the grounds that 'each prolonged cycle avoids the material, energy and labour of creating a new product or component' (ibid.). Thus the *Action Plan for the Circular Economy* not only increases targets for recycling but also anticipated measures to increase product lifetimes, and even reopened the debate on planned obsolescence (European Commission, 2015b).

The reasons are worth exploring. Recycling is generally regarded as environmentally beneficial because it addresses threats relating to resource security and energy consumption (and thus carbon emissions) by reducing virgin material inputs for a given level of production. In the widely recognized waste management hierarchy it is considered preferable to the disposal of products in landfill or 'energy recovery' through incineration. Nonetheless recycling has environmental impacts and technical limitations that are well known to designers, engineers, environmental scientists and social scientists (Cooper, 1994; King et al., 2006; Allwood, 2014; Moreno et al., 2014).

The potential environmental gains from a circular economy based on recycling alone are limited. For example, the frequency with which discarded goods are replaced and unwanted items recycled is critically important because, in addition to materials degrading, energy is used in each cycle. Furthermore, a strategy limited to increased recycling leaves open the possibility that the stock of consumer goods will increase in an expanding economy, necessitating additional use of virgin material. This suggests a tension between economic growth and the vision of a circular economy: 'if demand for goods is growing and is the sum of replacement and new demand, the supply of recycled material can never match demand until new demand ceases' (Allwood et al., 2011, p366). Beyond current economic and logistical obstacles (which might, in principle, be overcome), there are also technical constraints such as degradation of materials during recycling processes. Allwood (2014, p474) concludes: 'Recycling is already well developed when it is commercially attractive, is impossible for some materials, and for most recycling systems it is only possible to maintain material quality by mixing recycled material with virgin material.'

The case for increased recycling is accepted by most industrialists, in principle, and their primary concern is that any government intervention should provide for fair competition (e.g. CECED, 2015). One somewhat cynical observer suggested that companies welcome recycling as it provides them with 'an environmental excuse for instant obsolescence' (Fairlie, 1992, p280). Increasing product lifetimes through greater durability, repair and reuse represents a far greater challenge, not least because it could threaten economic growth. The Ellen MacArthur Foundation (2015) has sought to allay such fears in a report which claimed that the circular economy would add 7 per cent growth to the global economy by 2030, yet this raises questions about how growth fits with 'one planet living' (Schoon et al.,

2013). Research by UNEP (2011) demonstrated that the 'material footprints' of countries remain very strongly coupled with economic growth: as countries become more affluent they generally consume more biomass, construction materials, fossil fuels and metal ores.

In a traditional linear economy characterized by a 'take, make and dispose' mindset, economic growth is fuelled by consumerism. Unless consumers become convinced of a need to change their purchasing and disposal practices, transformation to a circular economy is unlikely (Jackson, 2009; Evans and Cooper, 2010; Cox, J. et al., 2013). While industry is criticized for producing goods designed for unduly short life-spans, it is equally true that households discard many appliances, furniture, clothing and other items that are still functional (e.g. Curran, 2010; ERM, 2011; WRAP, 2012). A shift to a circular economy that goes beyond increased recycling thus requires changes in consumption patterns as well as in design and production.

This chapter outlines recent knowledge about product lifetimes within the context of the circular economy and its potential for application in industrialized nations. It starts by considering, in turn, the significance of product longevity for environmental sustainability, consumers and industry. It then draws upon evidence of consumers' expectations of product lifetimes and their behaviour at the three key stages of acquisition, use and disposal. The response of industry to the re-emerging product lifetimes agenda is outlined next, tracing its origins with reference to planned obsolescence and reviewing recent insights into business models that enable companies to increase product lifetimes while remaining competitive. Finally, some implications for designers are considered.

The significance of product longevity

Contemporary consumption in industrial economies involves a fast throughput of goods (Cooper, 2005) and yet the widening gap between rich and poor is leaving many people dissatisfied (Wilkinson and Pickett, 2009), fuelling envy and aspirations for greater affluence. According to Schoon et al. (2013, p5), 'our current models of economic growth are working neither for the poorest or the planet.'

Consumption in such economies is widely regarded as unsustainable, threatening raw material security, causing excessive pollution and waste, and contributing to climate change. The quantity of materials extracted from natural resources and consumed worldwide has doubled over just thirty years, reaching 72 billion metric tonnes (Gt) in 2010, and is projected to reach 100 Gt by 2030 (OECD, 2015). By 2050 the world economy is expected to quadruple and global population is set to rise from 7 billion to 9.2 billion, leading the Organisation for Economic Co-operation and Development (OECD) (ibid., p10) to conclude that 'confronting the scale of these challenges requires more ambitious policies to increase the resource productivity at all stages of the material life cycle.'

Increased recycling might mitigate negative environmental impacts to some extent, but an ever-growing throughput of goods and materials caused by frequent product replacement cycles is clearly unsustainable on a finite planet. Bocken et al. (2016, p309) conclude that a circular economy requires 'slowing resource loops', the prolonged use and reuse of goods over time, as well as 'closing resource loops', the reuse of materials though recycling. Previously Cooper (2005, p54) has advocated 'slower consumption', described as 'slowing the rate at which products are consumed (literally, 'used up') by increasing their intrinsic durability and providing careful maintenance.'

Even if products are recycled the frequency of product replacement cycles is significant because of the implied energy consumption, as well as the residual waste. Energy is used throughout the process of replacement: in the transportation of end-of-life products, disassembly (or shredding) and transformation into recyclate (i.e. secondary raw material), and the production and distribution of new products. Carbon emissions are thus 'embodied' in products: an estimated 270kg CO_2 equivalent in the case of washing machines and 2.9 tonnes in that of cars (Skelton and Allwood, 2013). This explains why product lifetime optimization has become an important element in the climate change debate (Scott et al., 2009).

The significance of product lifetimes to environmental sustainability has begun to attract unprecedented levels of interest from international agencies, governments, public authorities and academics (Babbitt et al., 2009; Brook Lyndhurst, 2011; ERM, 2011; Gutierrez et al., 2011; Cox, J. et al., 2013; Wang et al., 2013; Bakker et al., 2014a; Bakker et al., 2014b; Cooper et al., 2015; Echegaray, 2015; Wieser and Troeger, 2015; Coats and Benton, 2016; Hennies and Stamminger, 2016; Prakash et al., 2016; Rivera and Lallmahomed, 2016). While firm, comprehensive data remains elusive, not least due to methodological issues in measuring product life-spans (Oguchi et al., 2010), recent research suggests that life-spans in certain categories of products are in decline (Wang et al., 2013; Bakker et al., 2014b; Prakash et al., 2016). Latterly, there has been a strategic shift from waste management to waste reduction; in the European Union (EU), the Waste Framework Directive (2008/98/EC) requires all member states to publish a waste prevention programme and in the UK this resulted in an unprecedented government commitment to 'making it easier for people and businesses to find out how to reduce their waste, to use products for longer, repair broken items and enable reuse of items by others' (HM Government 2013, p13). In his Foreword, the environment minister declared: 'Products should be designed to use fewer resources from the start and with longer lifetimes, repair and reuse in mind' (ibid., p3).

The EU's Ecodesign Directive (2009/125/EC), previously applied to energy efficiency, is now being used to address product lifetimes. Its 'implementing measures' can require products placed on the market in member states to meet certain criteria that include 'extension of lifetime' expressed through 'minimum guaranteed lifetime, minimum time for availability of spare parts, modularity, upgradeability, reparability.' More generally, governments in many countries are encouraging product longevity by supporting schemes aimed at the reuse of products discarded in a functional condition, notably appliances and furniture. In 2016, Spain became the first European country to set a mandatory national reuse target: its waste management plan for 2016–2022 requires at least 2 per cent of furniture, textiles and electrical items to be redirected from landfill and recycling to repair and resale (McDowall, 2016).

In addition to the environmental implications, product lifetimes are significant to consumers. Knowing the whole life cycle costs of purchasing and using a product, including its anticipated life-span and typical maintenance costs, would enable consumers to make better decisions.

Market research studies typically show that price is accorded the highest priority in consumers' purchasing decisions – predictably, as most have limited budgets – followed by product quality. Unfortunately, the different components of 'quality' (aesthetics, range of features, efficiency in use and other attributes, as well as durability) are often not disaggregated and consequently the relative importance of durability to consumers is not always easy to gauge.

Premium quality products are generally expected to be more durable than other models and therefore, in most cases, environmentally beneficial (Cooper, 2010; ERM, 2011). In the absence of information from manufacturers on their anticipated lifetimes, however, consumers remain uncertain as to whether they are of higher build quality and likely to last longer than other models. In the case of electrical and electronic goods, for example, 'the increasing complexity of products and the trend to differentiate models by additional features has made near-term prospects for an enhanced price-reliability association unlikely' (Boyle and Lathrop, 2008, p212). This reinforces evidence from previous research about the uncertain relationship between price and quality (e.g. Rao, 2005).

There are, of course, consumers who are not especially concerned about product lifetimes, affluent enough to be untroubled by the cost of frequent replacement and largely disinterested in the environmental implications of waste. This explains the large proportion of functional products discarded before they have reached the end of their intended life. Such products may have either failed to solicit an 'emotionally durable' sense of value and attachment (Chapman, 2005; Mugge et al., 2005) or were not designed in such a way as to be upgraded, upcycled or adapted in response to technological and aesthetic trends (van Nes and Cramer, 2005; Han et al., 2015).

Product lifetimes are also significant for industry, notably in connection with replacement cycles and brand reputation. The frequency of replacement is an important determinant of sales volumes, especially in industrial nations, where most households already own the more essential consumer durables (Bayus, 1988; Guiltinan, 2009). The apparent decline in certain product lifetimes has been attributed to pressure on manufacturers to maintain sales that leads them to introduce stylistic changes to make older products appear 'out of date' and to reduce product prices by making minor, incremental reductions in quality (Stahel, 2010). In addition, companies carefully manage the product life cycle (i.e. the period between when a product is conceived and its removal from the market) in order to maximize profit; they do so through marketing and pricing strategies and decisions to withdraw support for repair and servicing (e.g. availability of parts).

Product lifetimes also contribute to brand reputation. An ability to demonstrate product lifetimes above the industry norm is important to companies operating at the premium end of the market, as they need to maintain their reputation and to justify higher prices (Mackenzie et al., 2010). Miele, for example, states on its website that its products are tested for 20 years usage, while watch manufacturer Patek Philippe's advertisement proclaims: 'You never actually own a Patek Philippe; you merely look after it for the next generation.'

Expectations and acquisition: do users want products to last longer?

A societal shift toward increased product longevity will require greater understanding of people's experiences with their possessions: their attitudes to product lifetimes and expectations of them, their sense of attachment to possessions and how carefully they maintain them, and their decisions to dispose of them. Survey evidence and qualitative studies have increased understanding in recent years (e.g. Brook Lyndhurst, 2011; Gutierrez et al., 2011; Wang et al., 2013; Bakker et al., 2014a; Echegaray, 2015; Prakash et al., 2016; Wieser and Troeger, 2015; Hennies and Stamminger, 2016) but the research base is still relatively narrow.

The most substantive overview of attitudes to product lifetimes in Britain concluded that consumers are used to constant and rapid updating of products and are not especially concerned about the environmental consequences of the 'throwaway society' (Brook Lyndhurst, 2011; Cox, J. et al., 2013). Expectations of product lifetimes were 2 years or less for most clothing items, under 5 years for most consumer electronics and small appliances, and between 5 and 10 years for beds, sofas, carpets, curtains, televisions, washing machines and cookers; they only exceeded 10 years for kitchen units, wardrobes and boilers. As participants were asked when they would replace products rather than when they expected products to fail beyond repair, the figures do not take account of reuse. The data was obtained from a series of discussion groups and due to the small sample ($n = 115$ consumers) cannot be generalized to the UK population, but it provides a general indication of current expectations. The researchers concluded that, while directly comparable historic data is lacking, consumer expectations appeared lower than in the past.

Subsequent UK research on product lifetimes looked in more detail at electrical goods and clothing. A quantitative survey on electrical and electronic equipment (EEE), with a much larger sample ($n = 1,104$), concluded that 'product lifetimes are not a front-of-mind consideration for most consumers when buying products, but are still held to be important' (Knight et al., 2013, p39). Older consumers and people in lower income groups appeared to attach relatively more importance to product lifetimes. Expectations for several products were investigated. Consumers expected vacuum cleaners to last for 5 years, washing machines 6 years and fridges 8 years, on average, and in each case a clear majority (at least 70%) indicated that they were 'very' or 'quite' satisfied with how long such products last. As people with the highest expectations of longevity had the highest level of satisfaction (and vice versa), it appears that they adapt their expectations on the basis of experience (ibid.). The earlier study (Brook Lyndhurst, 2011; Cox et al., 2013) concluded that the expected lifetime of so-called 'workhorse products' (items valued principally for their service utility) was associated with a desire to avoid the expense and inconvenience of repair or replacement; many consumers did not envisage replacing such products before the end of their functional life and wanted them to last as long as possible. Less importance was attached to the lifetime of 'up to date products' (consumer electronics such as televisions and laptops), which consumers expected to upgrade periodically to the latest technology.

Surveys have also been undertaken on consumers' clothing behaviour (WRAP, 2012) and, specifically, their expectations for clothing lifetimes (Langley et al., 2013). Both provided evidence of consumer interest in increased product lifetimes. Among purchasing criteria, 'made to last and look good for longer' was deemed more important than 'fashionable': 61 per cent of respondents sought the former, compared to only 46 per cent for the latter. Moreover, many consumers appeared willing to change their behaviour. Asked about their ability and willingness to buy longer lasting garments, 38 per cent chose the option 'I could do more to buy items that are made to last and would like to do so' (WRAP, 2012, p20). Lifetimes varied by type of clothing: jackets, ties, coats and outdoor wear were typically expected to be 'actively used' for over five years, in contrast with less than three years for underwear, leggings, socks, tights and stockings (Langley et al., 2013).

Among a range of policies that could encourage greater product longevity (Cooper, 2010), one that has attracted particular attention is improved product lifetime information. A European Commission (2013) survey of over 25,000 consumers revealed that 38 per cent did not feel informed about the life-span of products and 92 per cent wanted product life-spans to be indicated. A UK survey similarly revealed that 'consumers do not feel knowledgeable about how long fridges, washing machines and vacuums last' (Knight et al., 2013, p4). Currently there is a general lack of transparency about product lifetimes from manufacturers and retailers, a rare exception being light bulbs, for which stating the 'average rated life' is a legal requirement. Variations in the length of guarantees for certain products may signal different anticipated lifetimes but consumers often have to resort to intrinsic cues given by a product's physical characteristics (e.g. thickness or perceived strength of material), extrinsic cues (e.g. price, packaging, brand or store image and country of origin), anecdotal information from the media or friends, or personal experience (Schiffman and Kanuk, 2001; Cooper and Christer, 2010).

The feasibility of promoting a more widespread use of lifetime labelling has been questioned. Lifetimes are reasonably predictable when primarily determined by design and production quality, as in the case of refrigeration equipment and solid wood furniture. For many types of product, however, there is potential for considerable variation, as lifetimes may be influenced by the intensity with which the products are used, the level and quality of care and maintenance, and climatic variables that can accelerate degradation (e.g. sunlight, temperature and dampness). Products used with different degrees of frequency, such as cars, washing machines and toasters, would need labels based on metrics such as mileage or cycles of use rather than time, or a grading scheme (as with energy labels). Labelling products that demand regular maintenance is especially problematic because lifetimes may depend on how this is undertaken; for example, whether care label procedures are followed when laundering clothes (Cooper et al., 2013) and vacuum cleaner bags, filters and brush heads are regularly checked (Salvia et al., 2015).

Nonetheless, interest in communicating product lifetimes to consumers is growing. The European Economic and Social Committee (EESC), an EU consultative body, commissioned a simulation exercise involving consumers in five countries; this predicted that sales of products with a label showing a longer lifespan than similarly priced competing products would typically increase by 14 per cent. Consumers most receptive to lifespan considerations when purchasing were female, aged between 25 and 35 years old and with an above average household income. The report concluded: 'These observations support the notion of minimum lifespan labelling that is binding on manufacturers. A minimum lifespan guarantee could be considered while defining products' conditions of use' (EESC, 2016, p6).

Maintenance and disposal: do users look after their products?

Little research has been undertaken on the care and maintenance practices exhibited by owners, with a few notable exceptions (Gregson et al., 2009; Maycroft, 2009; Laitala et al., 2012; Salvia et al., 2015). More interest has been shown in the condition of products at the point of disposal (e.g. Clarke and Bridgwater, 2012), because such data helps policymakers and waste managers to understand and predict waste streams for specific products and helps marketers to understand and exploit replacement motives.

Appropriate care and maintenance is important, as the performance of products may otherwise deteriorate and their lifetimes be shortened. In the case of washing machines, for example, a regular high temperature 'maintenance wash' to remove bacteria, soap scum and mould growth is recommended by manufacturers. Failure to maintain vacuum cleaners properly can cause failure, as poor suction may signal a blockage and cause the engine to overheat. Furniture may require periodic polishing in order to provide resistance to water or stain damage, while carpets and other floor surfacing should be cleaned regularly to prevent long term damage. Clothing needs to be washed at the right temperature to avoid shrinkage. More generally, stain damage needs to be dealt with appropriately, lubricants applied to moving parts, and so forth.

Whether users undertake maintenance depends on their attitudes to possessions and general cleanliness, the importance they attribute to product lifetimes generally and their emotional attachment to particular items, together with their knowledge, habits and routines. Some do not feel competent or motivated to undertake maintenance. Many are evidently unaware of recommended maintenance procedures, even in the case of 'workhorse products' such as appliances and furniture (Cox, J. et al., 2013). A consumer survey on vacuum cleaners revealed rather negative attitudes to maintenance tasks (Salvia et al., 2015).

In the case of clothing, a survey found that many consumers do not wash clothes at the right temperature and do not feel competent to repair or alter them (WRAP, 2012).

Repair work raises similar issues to general maintenance, with cost often a particular concern (Cooper and Salvia, 2017). Consumers have less control of the situation in the case of faulty goods, however; for example, manufacturers often deter owners from undertaking repairs to electrical items by using proprietary screws or removing warranty cover if repair work has been attempted by the owner. While such practices may be defended by manufacturers on safety grounds, they may also be motivated by a desire for repair work to be undertaken by themselves or an authorized repairer or, perhaps, to favour replacement over repair.

Product failure may bring a mixture of feelings to consumers. When a product is broken beyond repair they may experience disappointment, particularly if the failure was unexpected, but they may also welcome a justification for buying a brand new replacement. The point of failure is often less certain. In the case of products such as clothing, furniture and floor coverings, for example, degradation in quality is gradual. The point at which a consumer becomes dissatisfied and decides to repair or replace such products will vary, and their decisions will depend on the cost of repair relative to replacement. Scott and Weaver (2014) found that retailers and service technicians in the US often advise customers to apply a rule of thumb that products be replaced if the cost of repair is more than half that of purchasing a new item. Technology may play a role: research by McCollough (2007) revealed that consumers in the US were only willing to spend 20 per cent of the cost of a replacement on repairing small electronic items.

As noted earlier, products are increasingly discarded in a functional condition: some are thrown away because they are no longer needed, others because the owner wants a pristine new model or to keep up with fashion or technology. A survey of bulky waste in the UK, primarily furniture, textiles and electrical and electronic equipment, revealed many items to be functional. Among those taken to Household Waste Recycling Centres, 32 per cent were judged re-usable in their current condition and 51 per cent if items requiring slight repair work were included. The proportions were slightly lower for those retrieved through bulky waste collections, 24 per cent of which were immediately re-usable and 40 per cent after slight repair (Clarke and Bridgwater, 2012). Clearly consumers must accept some blame for the throwaway culture; indeed, a European study found that 68 per cent of respondents assigned a 'high to very high' degree of responsibility for product lifespans to users, less than the figure for manufacturers, 80 per cent, but significant nonetheless (EESC, 2016).

Attitudes towards waste affect how people discard products and, specifically, any effort made towards enabling reuse. Decisions on how and where goods are discarded may critically affect reuse potential: some are carelessly dumped, left outdoors in wet weather, or transported with inadequate care. Historically, waste has been regarded as 'rubbish' – perceived as worthless, and 'somebody else's problem' (Crocker, 2016). As householders have increasingly been required to sort their waste for recycling, however, its value as a potential resource has become more apparent. Considerable effort is made by some consumers to ensure that unwanted products are reused wherever possible. Having concluded that fewer discarded products are treated as waste than given away to charity, friends and family or sold, Gregson et al. (2007, p697) criticized the 'throwaway society thesis' – that people are typically carefree towards waste – on the grounds that it 'elevates the contemporary significance of discarding over keeping and preserving.' Indeed, at the other extreme of a throwaway mentality is the resistance to disposal that is manifest in the phenomenon of domestic hoarding (Maycroft, 2009).

The role of producers

Consumer perspectives on product longevity are important, but primary responsibility for the excessive prevalence of short-lived goods is more commonly attributed to producers (e.g. Packard, 1963; Slade, 2006; Bakker et al., 2014b). As consumption grew in the 1950s and 1960s, industry attracted blame for the apparent trend towards shorter product lifetimes. Critics frequently referred to 'planned obsolescence', a deliberate reduction in the useful lifetime of products in order to accelerate replacement cycles, although, significantly, manufacturers in the US themselves expressed concern about the implications of lower quality products for their reputation (Stewart, 1959), ahead of the popular, consumer-oriented debate prompted by publication of *The Waste Makers* (Packard, 1963).

Planned obsolescence was explained by Packard with reference to a decline in the quality of consumer goods ('built-in obsolescence') and styling or other 'superficial' changes intended to encourage people to replace their possessions. The most notorious example of the former has been light bulbs, the lifespan of which was standardized at 1,000 hours for many years by a cartel of manufacturers (Prais, 1974). This case was exceptional, however, being based on a legally dubious arrangement. More generally, a deliberate curtailing of product lifetimes through market-driven incremental reductions in quality has been criticized. In his explanation Packard (1963, p123) cited a director of the US Consumers Union: 'When design is tied to sales rather than product function, as it is increasingly, and when marketing strategy is based on frequent style changes, there are certain almost inevitable results: a tendency to the use of inferior materials; short cuts in the time necessary for sound product development; and a neglect of quality and adequate inspection.' Nearly half a century later, Jackson (2009, p97) argued similarly that the pursuit of economic growth drives innovation such that 'the cycles of creative destruction become ever more frequent. Product lifetimes plummet as durability is designed out of consumer goods and obsolescence is designed in. Quality is sacrificed relentlessly to volume throughput.'

Packard described the second form of obsolescence as 'obsolescence of desirability' or 'psychological obsolescence', noting the effort made by companies to encourage consumers to choose products according to style, fashion and novelty, revealing how designers in the 1950s 'earnestly studied the obsolescence-creating techniques pioneered in the field of clothing and accessories' (Packard, 1963, p73). Whiteley (1987) argued that, prior to Packard's critique in the 1960s, expendability had been positively celebrated by an increasingly fashion-conscious generation. Psychological obsolescence was evident in marketing practices aimed at shaping people's aspirations and expectations, encapsulated in a phrase commonly cited as the first modern use of the term 'planned obsolescence', attributed to industrial designer Brooks Stevens: 'the desire to own something a little newer, a little better, a little sooner than is necessary' (cited in Slade, 2006, p153).

Several decades after Packard's critique, planned obsolescence has re-emerged as a topic of academic discourse (Rivera and Lallmahomed, 2016) and political debate (Valant, 2016), fuelled by a widely-cited historical critique, *Made to Break* (Slade, 2006), and a popular online video, *The Light Bulb Conspiracy* (Dannoritzer et al., 2011). Consumer electronics companies, particularly Apple, have been subject to particular criticism (e.g. Kahney, 2011; Wiens, 2011). Public authorities have responded: in 2015 the French Government passed legislation to penalize companies that intentionally use techniques to reduce the lifespan of products in order to increase replacement rates (Valant, 2016) and the European Commission (2015b) has proposed an independent testing programme to detect planned obsolescence practices and has indicated that, if identified, it will address them.

Manufacturers and retailers face a dilemma: if a company's competitors gradually lower their prices, perhaps by reducing quality, or introduce innovative designs that reflect technological advance or new styles, it is risky for them not to do likewise. Consumers have, to some degree, been complicit, as companies which reduce the lifetime of products only survive if people purchase them. Premium range products, generally designed for lengthy lifetimes, have always been available, albeit at higher prices, but most consumers prefer to purchase cheaper, mass market models in order to spend less and be able to buy additional goods and services. The price of many consumer goods has fallen in real terms: for example, an average washing machine in 2011 cost 72 per cent less than in 1970 (Which?, 2011). Even so, today's premium range washing machines (which are designed to last 20 years) are considered too expensive by the vast majority of consumers, although they are cheaper, in real terms, than the average model sold in 1970.

Any company wanting to produce longer lasting products will need to create brand value based on their durability: for example, unlike most car manufacturers, Volvo has focussed on establishing a reputation for durability in performance rather than style. A range of marketing platforms that are used to differentiate longer lasting products in order to appeal to particular types of customer has been categorized; these include a product's investment value, its association with prestige, and design that allows for flexibility in use (Mackenzie et al., 2010).

New business models

Industrial economies are dominated by companies operating according to linear business models suited to the prevailing 'production-oriented, fast-replacement system' (Stahel and Jackson, 1993), particularly in consumer goods markets (Ellen MacArthur Foundation, 2013b). Researchers have, however, begun to explore how these business models can be reconfigured to fit the needs of a circular economy and, specifically, support the production of longer lasting products such that companies gain the 'potential to maintain control of the flow of materials and products and generate profit from them over time' (Bakker et al., 2014b, p51; Cox, V. et al., 2013; Ellen MacArthur Foundation, 2013a, 2013b, 2014; EEB, 2015). The move to a circular economy requires 'a new way of thinking and doing business', however, which will be challenging because 'companies often encounter great difficulty in changing business models' (Bocken et al., 2016, p312).

Bakker et al. (2014b) have identified five archetypal types of business model that could support increased product longevity: classic long life, hybrid, gap exploiter, access and performance. The first is where a company's primary revenue stream is from sales of high-grade products with a long useful life. In the hybrid model, the price of a durable product may be relatively low because it is used with short-lived consumables which generate a revenue stream, as in the case of computer printers. The gap-exploiter model is used by entrepreneurs who find a new market that enables them to take advantage of left-over value in discarded products. The access model provides product access rather than ownership, as in the case of car sharing schemes, while the performance model delivers product performance rather than the product itself (such as lighting, as distinct from light bulbs).

Other researchers have used case studies to explore the characteristics of companies that currently make products designed for a long life. Bocken and Short (2015), for example, refer to 'sufficiency-driven business models' that focus on influencing consumption, contrasting them with the emphasis on efficiency that is typical of supply-side approaches to industrial sustainability. They provide examples of several companies that make high quality products designed for durability and long term maintenance, such as Patagonia, to demonstrate how a 'sufficiency' ethos can permeate a business through marketing messages promoting product retention and commitment to long term customer relationships.

Revising the business model in order to increase product longevity is likely to require a shift in the 'value proposition' from tangible products to intangible services, such that suppliers offer the utility provided by products over a prolonged period through a new combination (Cooper and Evans, 2000; Oliva and Kallenberg, 2003; Nazzal et al., 2013; Bakker et al., 2014a; Bocken et al., 2014). Currently more common in business-to-business arrangements than consumer goods sectors (Yang et al., 2009), this shift has been described as *servitization* (Vandermerwe and Rada, 1988) and the outcome as a product-service system (Tukker, 2015; Bocken et al., 2014). The extent of change implied varies: in some business models it may merely involve after-sales services that are more substantive than the industry norm. In others, radical change is implied, as in the case of the access model, in which suppliers retain ownership of the product and consumers gain access through systems such as hiring or leasing, and the performance model, in which the user pays a supplier to achieve a specific outcome.

A relatively simple measure that may promote product longevity is the use of guarantees longer than the prevailing norm to signal higher quality design and manufacture to consumers (Eunomia, 2007; Cooper, 2010; Twigg-Flesner, 2010; ERM, 2011; EEB, 2015; Bocken and Short, 2015). This practice is not uncommon for premium range goods: appliance manufacturer Miele, for example, offers parts and labour guarantees for 10 years, though only for its most expensive range. Vacuum cleaner manufacturer VAX offers two or six year guarantees, depending on the price of products. In contrast with traditional one or two year guarantees, the offer of a comprehensive, lengthy guarantee shifts the balance between sale of a product and provision of a service, as the supplier assumes responsibility for the satisfactory functioning of a product over a prolonged period. Many consumers appear to be willing to pay the added costs of this extra service provision (European Commission, 2013a; Knight et al., 2013). Companies may be concerned about potential disputes over whether products with long guarantees have been used with appropriate care, however, and the need for long-term stability in company ownership may prove a further complication.

Another means of achieving such a shift is by promoting hiring (or leasing) as an alternative to ownership; this has been advocated on the basis that it could provide manufacturers with a greater incentive to produce more durable (and reliable) goods because they would be responsible for servicing and replacement costs (ERM, 2011; Ellen MacArthur Foundation, 2013b). While remaining attractive for infrequently used consumer goods (notably dinner jackets and prom dresses), hire has been in long term decline and the companies that have survived, such as Brighthouse, depend on a narrow segment of transient or non-creditworthy customers and have a reputation for high charges (Gibbons, 2012). In some sectors, however, social innovation is reviving the market; there are, for example, a growing number of companies in the UK offering baby equipment (e.g. BabyComes2, TheBabyLoft) and clothing (e.g. GirlMeetsDress, Rentez-vous) for hire.

The implications for product lifetimes of increased hire in consumer goods markets are complex and dependent upon the type of product and its use. There may be opportunities for washing machine manufacturers to make longer lasting models for hire (Ellen MacArthur Foundation, 2013a). On the other hand, products already hired on a short-term basis because they are otherwise unused over long periods, such as DIY-tools, may have shorter lifetimes than purchased items. In the case of vehicles, if increased hire through a growth in car sharing were to result in a smaller but more intensively used stock of cars, replacement cycles may be shortened and, if vehicles were improving in energy efficiency, the consequent benefits would be realized sooner; in this case, the combination of more efficient usage and fewer items being manufactured implies shorter lifetimes but net environmental benefits. By contrast, in the case of consumer electronics subject to technological advance and improved functionality consumers might choose to update hired items with greater frequency, resulting in more discarded items that are functional.

While noting that new business models 'may well undermine or destabilize traditional approaches to business and cause large incumbent firms to fail', Bocken and Short (2015, p59) concluded from their case studies that by redesigning business models carefully 'differentiated value propositions can be developed to appeal to consumers, create competitive advantage and support sufficiency' (ibid., p55). Companies will only consider increasing product lifetimes if they foresee a competitive advantage, however, and this might necessitate changes in market conditions in the form of different cost profiles, consumer preferences or government policy.

Business models reflect the relative cost of the three main factors of production: land (i.e. natural resources), labour and capital. Many scholars and environmental campaigners have long argued for green fiscal reform (reducing taxes on labour and increasing those on energy and materials) as a strategy for greening the economy (Ekins and Speck, 2011) because this should favour longer-lasting products; maintenance, repair and other product life extension activities tend to be labour-intensive compared with manufacturing (Stahel and Reday-Mulvey, 1981; Cooper, 2010). Specific fiscal measures to incentivize the purchase of longer lasting products and reduce the cost of repair relative to replacement include varying the rate of VAT on products according to the length of guarantee and making repair and maintenance work exempt from VAT and employers' national insurance contributions (Cooper, 2010; ERM, 2011; BEUC, 2015; EEB, 2015; RREUSE, 2015). People's purchasing priorities are not determined by price alone, of course, and fiscal reform may not promote a sufficient change in behaviour, but it would at least signal the social benefits of increased product lifetimes to consumers.

Another approach would be to address purchasing preferences through information measures on product lifetimes to enable customers to judge which products offer better value for money (Cooper, 2010; BEUC, 2015; RREUSE, 2015). As noted earlier, a recent study (EESC, 2016) concluded that a label showing a product's anticipated life-span would influence purchasing decisions in favour of products with longer life-spans. Anecdotal evidence suggests that companies may oppose such transparency, however, on the grounds that user behaviour exerts a major influence upon product lifetimes, and are more likely to tolerate lifetime labelling of components than complete products.

The effectiveness of life-span labelling, whether mandatory or voluntary, depends on consumer preference. Another option is legislation requiring minimum product lifetimes, which would provide greater certainty to companies and accelerate change. The Ecodesign Directive offers a means to require minimum standards for certain products and in 2013 was used to require the 'operational motor lifetime' of vacuum cleaners to be a minimum of 500 hours and the hose to be 'still useable after 40,000 oscillations under strain' (European Commission, 2013b). Campaign organizations have proposed a range of other legislative measures to encourage durability and reparability, including a requirement that electrical goods be designed to be disassembled non-destructively without a need for proprietary tools, use of standardized components for parts such as screws, pumps and motors, and greater access to manufacturers' repair manuals (BEUC, 2015; EEB, 2015; RREUSE, 2015).

Implications for the design community

The foregoing analysis of product longevity has significant implications for the design community – and not just those who align their practice with 'sustainable design.' As Bocken et al. (2016, p317) conclude, 'in order to transform the economy from linear to circular, business model and design strategies will need to go hand in hand.' The role of design practitioners is, however, compromised: many are engaged in systems of production and consumption based on rapid replacement cycles and yet, as creative individuals, they instinctively want to see their creations prove durable, loved and cared for. They may be considered victims of a throwaway culture, compromised by the demands of clients who are themselves financially dependent upon the excesses of consumerism (Cooper, 2012).

Bakker et al. (2014b, p15) conclude that, while developing business models may be beyond the expertise of most product designers, design research 'could play a useful role in understanding the factors that influence consumer acceptance of new ownership models and other product service systems.' For example, in the case of a product that is to be leased and refurbished several times during its life, designers have the expertise 'to obtain intimate knowledge of how the product and its parts wear and tear, and of how to decide which parts should last, and which should be replaced, and when.'

Designers also have a role in assessing trade-offs between environmental benefits, perhaps through life cycle analysis (LCA), and estimating the optimal lifespan of products (van Nes and Cramer, 2003, 2005; Kim et al., 2003, 2006; Spitzley et al., 2005; ERM, 2011; Kagawa et al., 2013; Ardente and Mathieux, 2014; Bakker et al., 2014a). For example, while longer replacement cycles for appliances subject to improved energy efficiency may be considered liable to increase carbon emissions, Skelton and Allwood (2013) have argued that optimal life-spans depend on assumptions about future reductions in use-phase emissions. Following an assessment of refrigerators and laptops, Bakker et al. (2014a) concluded that the environmentally optimal lifespan was in each case longer than the current average life-span (20 years and 7 years, respectively, for refrigerators; 14 and 4 years for laptops). Tools already exist to enable designers to improve the environmental performance of products (e.g. Vezzoli and Manzini, 2008).

Forging a society in which products last longer, such that material consumption in industrial nations is reduced without a loss of wellbeing, represents a challenge far greater than designing individual products to be more recyclable or physically durable. Designing for longevity is far more problematic. Longevity is a deeper concept than physical durability, embracing the multitude of variables that determine whether a product's potential lifespan is fully realized. These include the users' beliefs, values, attitudes, habits, routines, knowledge and skills, facilitating conditions such as technical and organizational infrastructure systems (such as access to repair facilities and expertise), and contextual factors such as sociocultural meanings, norms and expectations.

The current prevalence of goods discarded in a functional condition serves to highlight the complexity of the problem and the depth of the challenge facing the design community in seeking solutions to our throwaway culture. Increased product longevity requires of design practitioners an ability to create products that are not merely physically durable but which gain emotional attachment from users (Chapman, 2005; Mugge et al., 2005), and systems of production and consumption that enable product life extension through maintenance, repair, upgrade, adaptation and reuse (van Nes and Cramer, 2005; Nazzal et al., 2013; Salvia et al., 2015).

References

Allwood, J. M. (2014) 'Squaring the circular economy: The role of recycling within a hierarchy of waste management strategies', in Worrell, E. and Reuter, M. A. (eds) *Handbook of Recycling*, Elsevier, Oxford, pp445–477.

Allwood, J. M., Ashby, M. F., Gutowski, T. G. and Worrell, E. (2011) 'Material efficiency: A white paper', *Resources, Conservation and Recycling*, vol 55, pp362–381.

Ardente, F. and Mathieux, F. (2014) 'Environmental assessment of the durability of energy-using products: Method and application', *Journal of Cleaner Production*, vol 74, no 1, pp62–73.

Babbitt, C. W., Kahhat, R., Williams, E. and Babbitt, G. A. (2009) 'Evolution of product lifespan and implications for environmental assessment and management: A case study of personal computers in higher education', *Environmental Science and Technology*, vol 43, no 13, pp5106–5112.

Bakker C., Wang F., Huisman J. and den Hollander M. (2014a) 'Products that go round: Exploring product life extension through design', *Journal of Cleaner Production*, vol 69, pp10–16.

Bakker C., den Hollander M., van Hinte, E. and Zljlstra, Y. (2014b) *Products that Last: Product Design for a Circular Economy*, TU Delft Library, Delft, the Netherlands.

Bayus, B. L. (1988) 'Accelerating the durable replacement cycle with marketing mix variables', *Journal of Production Innovation Management*, vol 5, no 3, pp216–226.

BEUC (2015) *Durable Goods: More Sustainable Products, Better Consumer Rights. Consumer Expectations from the EU's Resource Efficiency and Circular Economy Agenda*, Bureau Européen des Unions de Consommateurs, Brussels, retrieved from www.beuc.eu/publications/beuc–x–2015–069_sma_upa_beuc_position_paper_durable_goods_and_better_legal_guarantees.pdf.

Bocken, N. M. P. and Short, S. W. (2015) 'Towards a sufficiency-driven business model: Experiences and opportunities', *Environmental Innovation and Societal Transitions*, vol 18, pp41–61.

Bocken, N. M. P., Short, S. W., Rana, P. and Evans, S. (2014) 'A literature and practice review to develop sustainable business model archetypes', *Journal of Cleaner Production*, vol 65, pp42–56.

Bocken, N. M. P., de Pauw, I., Bakker, C. and van der Grinten, B. (2016) 'Product design and business model strategies for a circular economy', *Journal of Industrial and Production Engineering*, vol 33, no 5, pp308–320.

Boyle, P. and Lathrop, E. (2008) 'Perceptions of product longevity: Will it keep going and going …?', *Journal of Customer Behaviour*, vol 7, no 3, pp201–213.

Brook Lyndhurst (2011) *Public Understanding of Product Lifetimes and Durability*, report for Department for Environment, Food and Rural Affairs, London, retrieved from http://randd.defra.gov.uk/Default.aspx?Menu=Menu&Module=More&Location=None&Completed=0&ProjectID=17254.

CECED (2015) *Circular Economy Package: The view of home appliance manufacturers, Position Paper: 20/04/2015*, European Committee of Domestic Equipment Manufacturers, Brussels, retrieved from www.ceced.eu/site-ceced/media-resources/Position-Papers/Archive/2015/04/Circular-Economy-Package--The-view-of-home-appliance-manufacturers.html.

Chapman, J. (2005) *Emotionally Durable Design: Objects, Experiences and Empathy*, Earthscan, London.

Clarke, E. and Bridgwater, E. (2012) *Composition of Kerbside and HWRC Bulky Waste*, report by Resource Futures for WRAP, Banbury, retrieved from www.wrap.org.uk/content/study-re-use-potential-household-bulky-waste.

Coats, E. and Benton, D. (2016) *The End of the Upgrade? How O_2 is adapting to a more circular mobile market*, Green Alliance, London, Retrieved from www.green-alliance.org.uk/end_of_the_upgrade.php.

Cooper, T. (1994) *Beyond Recycling: The Longer Life Option,* New Economics Foundation, London.

Cooper, T. (2005) 'Slower consumption: Reflections on product life cycles and the "throwaway society"', *Journal of Industrial Ecology*, vol 9, no 1–2, pp51–67.

Cooper, T. (ed.) (2010) *Longer Lasting Products: Alternatives to the Throwaway Society*, Gower, Farnham.

Cooper, T. (2012) 'Design for Longevity: Obstacles and opportunities posed by new public policy developments', paper presented at Design Research Society Conference, Bangkok, Thailand, 1–4 July.

Cooper, T. and Christer, K. (2010) 'Marketing durability', in Cooper, T. (ed.) *Longer Lasting Products: Alternatives to the Throwaway Society*, Gower, Farnham, pp273–296.

Cooper, T. and Evans, S. (2000) *Products to Services*, Friends of the Earth, London.

Cooper, T. and Salvia, G. (2017) 'Fix it: Barriers to repair and opportunities for change', in Crocker, R. (ed.) *Reuse in an Accelerated World: Mining the Past to Reshape the Future*, Routledge, Abingdon.

Cooper, T., Hill, H., Kininmonth, J., Townsend, K. and Hughes, M. (2013) *Design for Longevity Guidance on Increasing the Active Life of Clothing*, Report by Nottingham Trent University for WRAP, Banbury, retrieved from www.wrap.org.uk/sites/files/wrap/Design%20for%20Longevity%20Report_0.pdf.

Cooper, T., Braithwaite, N., Moreno, M. and Salvia, G. (eds) (2015) *Proceedings, Product Lifetimes and The Environment (PLATE) conference,* Nottingham Trent University, 17–19 June 2015, Nottingham, retrieved from www.ntu.ac.uk/plate_conference/proceedings/index.html.

Cox, J., Griffith, S., Giorgi, S. and King, G. (2013) 'Consumer understanding of product lifetimes', *Resources, Conservation and Recycling*, vol 79, pp21–29.

Cox, V., Boulos, S., Fitzgerald, J., Vinogradova, M. and Buckland T. and Thoung, C. (2013) *Economic Impacts of Resource Efficient Business Models*, report by Ricardo-AEA and Cambridge Econometrics for WRAP, Banbury, retrieved from www.wrap.org.uk/sites/files/wrap/Economic%20impacts%20of%20resource%20efficient%20business%20models%20final%20report.pdf.

Crocker, R. (2016) *Somebody Else's Problem: Consumerism, Sustainability and Design*, Greenleaf, Saltaire.

Curran, T. (2010) 'Extending product life-spans: Household furniture and appliance reuse in the UK', in Cooper, T. (ed.) *Longer Lasting Products: Alternatives to the Throwaway Society,* Gower, Farnham, pp393–415.

Dannoritzer, C., Úbeda I Carulla, J., Barrat, P., Malcolm, M., Sarrado, M. M., Wyss, G., Andrés, M., and Gil, J. P. (2011) *The Light Bulb Conspiracy: The Untold Story of Planned Obsolescence,* Video Project, San Francisco, CA.

Echegaray, F. (2015) Consumers' reactions to product obsolescence in emerging markets: The case of Brazil, *Journal of Cleaner Production*, retrieved from www.sciencedirect.com/science/article/pii/S0959652615012202.

EEB (2015) *Circular Economy Package 2.0: Some Ideas to Complete the Circle*, European Environmental Bureau, March, retrieved from www.eeb.org/index.cfm?LinkServID=1E2E1B48–5056–B741–DB594FD34CE970E9.

EESC (2016) *The Influence of Lifespan Labelling on Consumers*, report by SIRCOME, University of South Brittany and University of South Bohemia, European Economic and Social Committee, Brussels, retrieved from www.eesc.europa.eu/?i=portal.en.publications.38844

Ekins, P. and Speck, S. (eds) (2011) *Environmental Tax Reform (ETR): A Policy for Green Growth*, OUP, Oxford.

Ellen MacArthur Foundation (2013a) *Towards the Circular Economy Volume 1: Economic and Business Rationale for an Accelerated Transition*, Ellen MacArthur Foundation, Cowes, retrieved from www.ellenmacarthurfoundation.org/assets/downloads/publications/Ellen-MacArthur-Foundation-Towards-the-Circular-Economy-vol.1.pdf

Ellen MacArthur Foundation (2013b) *Towards the Circular Economy Volume 2: Opportunities for the Consumer Goods Sector*, Ellen MacArthur Foundation, Cowes, retrieved from www.ellenmacarthurfoundation.org/publications/towards-the-circular-economy-vol-2-opportunities-for-the-consumer-goods-sector

Ellen MacArthur Foundation (2014) *Towards the Circular Economy Volume 3: Accelerating the Scale-Up across Global Supply Chains*, Ellen MacArthur Foundation, Cowes, retrieved from www.ellenmacarthurfoundation.org/assets/downloads/publications/Towards-the-circular-economy-volume–3.pdf

Ellen MacArthur Foundation (2015) *Growth Within: A Circular Economy Vision for a Competitive Europe*, Ellen MacArthur Foundation, Cowes, retrieved from www.ellenmacarthurfoundation.org/assets/downloads/publications/EllenMacArthurFoundation_Growth-Within_July15.pdf

ERM (2011) *Longer Product Lifetimes: Executive summary*. Final Report to Department for Environment, Food and Rural Affairs (Defra), London, retrieved from http://sciencesearch.defra.gov.uk/Default.aspx?Menu=Menu&Module=More&Location=None&Completed=0&ProjectID=17047.

Eunomia (2007) *Household Waste Prevention: Policy Side Research Programme*, final report for Department for Environment, Food and Rural Affairs, London, retrieved from http://sciencesearch.defra.gov.uk/Default.aspx?Menu=Menu&Module=More&Location=None&Completed=0&ProjectID=14681.

European Commission (2013a) *Flash Eurobarometer 367 – Attitudes of Europeans towards Building the Single Market for Green Products*, European Commission, Brussels, retrieved from http://ec.europa.eu/public_opinion/flash/fl_367_en.pdf.

European Commission (2013b) Commission Regulation (EU) no 666/2013 of 8 July 2013 implementing Directive 2009/125/EC of the European Parliament and of the Council with regard to ecodesign requirements for vacuum cleaners, retrieved from http://eur-lex.europa.eu/legal-content/EN/ALL/?uri=CELEX%3A32013R0666.

European Commission (2015a) *Closing the Loop: Commission Adopts Ambitious New Circular Economy Package to Boost Competitiveness, Create Jobs and Generate Sustainable Growth*, European Commission

Press release, Brussels, 2 December, retrieved from http://europa.eu/rapid/press-release_IP-15-6203_en.htm

European Commission (2015b) *Closing the Loop – An EU Action Plan for the Circular Economy*, COM/2015/0614 final, European Commission, Brussels, retrieved from http://eur-lex.europa.eu/legal-content/EN/TXT/?uri=CELEX:52015DC0614

Evans, S. and Cooper, T. (2010) 'Consumer influences on product life spans', in Cooper, T. (ed.) *Longer Lasting Products: Alternatives to the Throwaway Society*, Gower, Farnham, pp319–350.

Fairlie, S. (1992) 'Long distance, short life: Why big business favours recycling', *The Ecologist*, vol 22, no 6, pp276–283.

Gibbons, D. (2012) *Improving Practice in the Rent to Own Market*, report by Centre for Responsible Credit for Church Action on Poverty, retrieved from www.friendsprovidentfoundation.org/wp-content/uploads/2013/03/Church_Action_on_Poverty_-_Improving_Practice_in_the_Rent_to_Own_Market_-_Full_Report.pdf.

Gregson, N., Metcalfe, A. and Crewe, L. (2007) 'Identity, mobility and the throwaway society', *Environment and Planning D*, vol 25, pp682–700.

Gregson, N., Metcalfe, A. and Crewe, L. (2009) 'Practices of Object Maintenance and Repair: How consumers attend to consumer objects within the home', *Journal of Consumer Culture*, vol 9, pp248–272.

Guiltinan, J. (2009) 'Creative destruction and destructive creations: Environmental ethics and planned obsolescence', *Journal of Business Ethics*, vol 89, no 1, pp19–28.

Gutierrez, E., Adenso-Diaz, B., Lozano, S. and Gonzalez-Torre, P. (2011) 'Lifetime of household appliances: Empirical evidence of users behaviour', *Waste Management and Research,* vol 29, no 6, pp622–633.

Han, S., Tyler, D. and Apeagyei, P. (2015) Upcycling as a design strategy for product lifetime optimisation and societal change, in Cooper, T., Braithwaite, N., Moreno, M. and Salvia, G. (eds) (2015) *Proceedings, Product Lifetimes and The Environment (PLATE) Conference,* Nottingham Trent University, 17–19 June 2015, Nottingham, UK, pp130–137, retrieved from www.ntu.ac.uk/plate_conference/proceedings/index.html.

Hennies, L. and Stamminger, R. (2016) 'An empirical survey on the obsolescence of appliances in German households', *Resources, Conservation and Recycling*, vol 112, pp73–82.

HM Government (2013) *Prevention is Better than Cure: The Role of Waste Prevention in Moving to a More Resource Efficient Economy*, December, retrieved from www.gov.uk/government/uploads/system/uploads/attachment_data/file/265022/pb14091-waste-prevention–20131211.pdf.

Jackson, T. (2009) *Prosperity without Growth: Economics for a Finite Planet*, Earthscan, London.

Kagawa, S., Hubacek, K., Nansai, K., Kataoka, M., Managi, S., Suh, S. and Kudoh, Y. (2013) 'Better cars or older cars?: Assessing CO2 emission reduction potential of passenger vehicle replacement programs', *Global Environmental Change*, vol 23, pp1807–1818.

Kahney, L. (2011) Is Apple Guilty of Planned Obsolescence? Retrieved from www.cultofmac.com/77814/is-apple-guilty-of-planned-obsolescence.

Kim, H. C., Keoleian, G. A., Grande, D. E. and Bean, J. C. (2003) 'Life cycle optimization of automobile replacement: Model and application', *Environmental Science and Technology*, vol 37, no 23, pp5407–5413.

Kim, H. C., Keoleian, G. A. and Horie, Y. A. (2006) 'Optimal household refrigerator replacement policy for life cycle energy, greenhouse gas emissions, and cost', *Energy Policy*, vol 34, no 15, pp2310–2323.

King, A. M., Burgess, S. C., Ijomah, W. and McMahon, C. A. (2006) 'Reducing waste: Repair, recondition, remanufacture or recycle?' *Sustainable Development*, vol 14, no 4, pp257–267.

Knight, T., King, G., Herren, S. and Cox, J. (2013) *Electrical and Electronic Product Design: Product lifetime*. Report by Brook Lyndhurst for WRAP, Banbury, retrieved from www.wrap.org.uk/node/18468.

Laitala, K., Klepp, I. G. and Boks, C. (2012) 'Changing laundry habits in Norway', *International Journal of Consumer Studies*, vol 36, no 2, pp228–237.

Langley, E., Durkacz, S. and Tanase, T. (2013) *Clothing Longevity and Measuring Active Use*, report by Ipsos MORI for WRAP, Banbury, retrieved from www.wrap.org.uk/content/clothing-longevity-measuring-active-use.

McCollough, J. (2007) 'The effect of income growth on the mix of purchases between disposable goods and reusable goods', *International Journal of Consumer Studies*, vol 31, no 3, pp213–219.

McDowall, J. (2016) Spain Becomes First EU Country To Set Target For Reuse, *Resource*, 29 April, retrieved from http://resource.co/article/spain-becomes-first-eu-country-set-target-reuse-11038.

Mackenzie, D., Cooper, T. and Garnett, K. (2010) 'Can durability provide a strong marketing platform?', in Cooper, T. (ed.) (2010) *Longer Lasting Products: Alternatives to the Throwaway Society*, Gower, Farnham, pp297–315.

Maycroft, N. (2009) 'Not moving things along: Hoarding, clutter and other ambiguous matter', *Journal of Consumer Behaviour*, vol 8, pp354–364.

Moreno, M., Braithwaite, N. and Cooper, T. (2014) Moving Beyond the Circular Economy, *Going Green: Care Innovation 2014 Conference*, Vienna, Austria, 17–20 November.

Mugge, R., Schoormans, J. P. L. and Schifferstein, H. N. J. (2005) 'Design strategies to postpone consumers' product replacement', *Design Journal*, vol 8, no 2, pp38–48.

Nazzal, D., Batarseh, O., Patzner, J. and Martin, D. R. (2013) 'Product servicing for lifespan extension and sustainable consumption: An optimization approach', *International Journal of Production Economics*, vol 142, no 1, pp105–114.

OECD (2015) *Material Resources, Productivity and the Environment*, OECD Green Growth Studies, OECD, Paris.

Oguchi, M., Murakami, S., Tasaki, T., Daigo, I. and Hashimoto, S. (2010) 'Lifespan of commodities, Part II: Methodologies for estimating lifespan distribution of commodities', *Journal of Industrial Ecology*, vol 14, no 4, pp613–626.

Oliva, R. and Kallenberg, R. (2003) 'Managing the transition from products to services', *International Journal of Service Industry Management*, vol 14, no 2, pp160–172.

Packard, V. (1963) *The Waste Makers*, Pelican, London.

Prais, S. J. (1974) 'The Electric Lamp Monopoly and the Life of Electric Lamps', *Journal of Industrial Economics*, vol 23, no 2, pp153–158.

Prakash, S., Dehoust, G., Gsell, M. and Schleicher, T. (2016) *Einfluss der Nutzungdauer von Produkten auf ihre Umweltwirkung: Schaffung einer Informationsgrundlage und Entwicklung von Strategien gegen 'Obsoleszenz'*, report to the German Federal Environment Agency (in German), retrieved from www.umweltbundesamt.de/sites/default/files/medien/378/publikationen/texte_11_2016_einfluss_der_nutzungsdauer_von_produkten_obsoleszenz.pdf.

Rao, A. R. (2005) 'The quality of price as a quality cue', *Journal of Marketing Research*, vol XLII, pp401–405.

Rivera, J. L. and Lallmahomed, A. (2016) 'Environmental implications of planned obsolescence and product lifetime: A literature review', *International Journal of Sustainable Engineering*, vol 9, no 2, pp119–129.

RREUSE (2015) *Improving Product Reparability: Policy Options at EU Level*, retrieved from www.rreuse.org/wp-content/uploads/Routes-to-Repair-RREUSE-final-report.pdf.

Salvia, G., Cooper, T., Fisher, T., Harmer, L. and Barr, C. (2015) What is broken? Expected lifetime, perception of brokenness and attitude towards maintenance and repair, *Product Lifetimes and the Environment (PLATE) Conference Proceedings*, Nottingham Trent University, Nottingham, 17–19 June, pp342–348.

Schiffman, L. G. and Kanuk, L. L. (2001) *Consumer Behaviour* (2nd edn), Pearson Education, Frenchs Forest, NSW.

Schoon, N., Seath, F. and Jackson L. (2013) *One Planet Living: The Case for Sustainable Consumption and Production in the Post-2015 Development Agenda*, Bioregional, London, retrieved from www.bioregional.com/wp-content/uploads/2014/10/BioRegional-One-Planet-Living-The-case-for-Sustainable-Consumption-and-Production-in-the-Post–2015-Development-Agenda1.pdf.

Scott, K. A. and Weaver, S. T. (2014) 'To repair or not to repair: What is the motivation?', *Journal of Research for Consumers*, vol 26, retrieved from www.jrconsumers.com/Academic_Articles/issue_26/

Scott, K., Barrett, J., Baiocchi, G. and Minx, J. (2009) *Meeting the UK Climate Change Challenge: The Contribution of Resource Efficiency*, report by Stockholm Environment Institute, and University of Durham Business School for WRAP, Banbury, retrieved from www.wrap.org.uk/sites/files/wrap/Final%20Report%20EVA128_SEI%20(1)%20JB%20SC%20JB3.pdf.

Skelton, A. C. H. and Allwood, J. M. (2013) 'Product life trade-offs: What if products fail early?' *Environmental Science and Technology*, vol 47, pp1719–1728.

Slade, G. (2006) *Made to Break: Technology and Obsolescence in America*, Harvard University Press, Cambridge, MA.

Spitzley, D. V., Grande, D. E., Keoleian, G. A. and Kim, H. C. (2005) 'Life cycle optimization of ownership costs and emissions reduction in US vehicle retirement decisions', *Transportation Research Part D: Transport and Environment*, vol 10, no 2, pp161–175.

Stahel, W. (2010) 'Durability, function and performance', in Cooper, T. (ed.) *Longer Lasting Products: Alternatives to the Throwaway Society*, Gower, Farnham, pp157–177.

Stahel, W. R. and Jackson, T. (1993) 'Durability and optimal utilisation: Product-life extension in the service economy', in Jackson, T. (ed.) *Clean Production Strategies*, Lewis, Boca Raton, FL, pp261–294.

Stahel, W. R. and Reday-Mulvey, G. (1981) *Jobs for Tomorrow: The Potential for Substituting Manpower for Energy*, Vantage Press, New York.

Stewart, J. B. (1959) 'Planned obsolescence', *Harvard Business Review*, vol 37, no 5, pp14–174 passim.

Tukker, A. (2015) 'Product services for a resource-efficient and circular economy – a review', *Journal of Cleaner Production*, vol 97, pp76–91.

Twigg-Flesner, C. (2010) 'The law on guarantees and repair work', in Cooper, T. (ed.) *Longer Lasting Products: Alternatives to the Throwaway Society*, Gower, Farnham, pp195–214.

UNEP (United Nations Environment Programme) (2011) *Decoupling Natural Resource Use and Environmental Impacts from Economic Growth*, retrieved from www.unep.org/resourcepanel/decoupling/files/pdf/Decoupling_Report_English.pdf.

Valant, J. (2016) *Planned Obsolescence: Exploring the Issue*, European Parliamentary Research Service, May, retrieved from www.europarl.europa.eu/RegData/etudes/BRIE/2016/581999/EPRS_BRI(2016)581999_EN.pdf.

Van Nes, N. and Cramer, J. (2003) 'Design strategies for the lifetime optimisation of products', *Journal of Sustainable Product Design*, vol 3, no 3–4, pp101–107.

Van Nes, N. and Cramer, J. (2005) 'Influencing product lifetime through product design', *Business Strategy and the Environment*, vol 14, pp286–299.

Vandermerwe, S. and Rada, J. (1988) 'Servitization of business: Adding value by adding services', *European Management Journal*, vol 6, no 4, pp314–324.

Vezzoli, C. and Manzini, E. (2008) *Design for Environmental Sustainability*, Springer, London.

Wang, F., Huisman, J., Stevels, A. and Baldé C. P. (2013) 'Enhancing e-waste estimates: Improving data quality by multivariate input–output analysis', *Waste Management*, vol 33, no 11, pp2397–2407.

Which? (2011) 'Built to last', August, retrieved from www.which.co.uk

Whiteley, N. (1987) 'Toward a throw-away culture: Consumerism, "style obsolescence" and cultural theory in the 1950s and 1960s', *Oxford Art Journal*, vol 10, no 2, pp3–27.

Wiens, K. (2011) Apple's latest 'innovation' is turning planned obsolescence into planned failure, 20 January, retrieved from www.ifixit.com/blog/2011/01/20/apples-latest-innovation-is-turning-planned-obsolescence-into-planned-failure.

Wieser, H. and Troeger, N. (2015) *The Use-time and Obsolescence of Durable Goods in the Age of Acceleration*, report for Austrian Chamber of Labour, Vienna (summary in English), retrieved from www.beuc.eu/documents/files/FC/durablegoods/articles/0515_AK_Austria.pdf.

Wilkinson, R. and Pickett, K. (2009) *The Spirit Level: Why More Equal Societies almost Always Do Better*, Allen Lane, London.

WRAP (2012) *Valuing Our Clothes: The Evidence Base*, Waste and Resources Action Programme, Banbury, retrieved from www.wrap.org.uk/sites/files/wrap/10.7.12%20VOC-%20FINAL.pdf.

Yang, X., Moore, P., Pu, J. and Wong, C. (2009) 'A practical methodology for realizing product service systems for consumer products', *Computers and Industrial Engineering*, vol 56, no 1, pp224–235.

28

HOW ABOUT DINNER?

Concepts and methods in designing for sustainable lifestyles

Annelise de Jong and Ramia Mazé

Abstract

Consumption is increasingly in focus within approaches to sustainable development, with the notion of sustainable consumption raising new issues for design. In designing to reduce the consumption of energy, water and other resources, for example, we need to consider the socio-cultural complexity of consumers' perceptions, actions and routines. Pointing to two such projects in the areas of domestic electricity use and bathing practices, we reflect here upon limitations in concepts and methods common in user centered and sustainable design and, consequently, how we have been further developing our conceptual and methodological frames of reference as design researchers to include these social aspects. We also report on an additional project that draws on these new frames of reference to study *ways of doing cooking* within diverse households, in which we gained insights into how the many resources, products and artefacts involved in food management are deeply embedded in traditions, meanings and aspirations. Issues of environmental sustainability, such as water, energy and waste, are at stake in such design research but, as we argue, so is attention and sensitivity to how these are interwoven in meaningful socio-cultural practices. Through this chapter, we discuss implications of further incorporating approaches to *the social* from other fields into design research and education and vice versa what the social sciences might learn from design for sustainable consumption.

Keywords: sustainability, design, socio-cultural practices, sustainable lifestyles, domestic life

Introduction: design for sustainable consumption

Consumption is increasingly in focus within approaches to sustainable development. Since early framings of sustainability in terms of nature conservation or preservation in the 1970s, discourse on sustainable development has shifted over the last 20 years to focus on sustainable consumption and production (SCP). While the phrase *sustainable consumption* was not much used until the Brundtland report (Brundtland, 1987), it has since become a keystone in declarations and implementations (for example, the 2005 Oslo Declaration, Agenda 21, the Marrakech Process, and UNEP/United Nations Environmental Programme). The shift toward sustainable consumption also implicates design, which is ubiquitous within contexts and practices of consumption. While, historically, design has been employed in service to expanding consumption, bound into economic growth models based on industrial production and mass-consumption, design is increasingly employed towards alternative objectives. It has been evoked in approaches to fostering public debate and changing values (Lorek, 2010), reshaping everyday routines and lifestyles (Vezzoli and Manzini, 2006) and visioning alternative futures (Vergragt, 2010), in which design is located in relation to other disciplines including the social sciences, environmental policy and business innovation. The shift from sustainable production to sustainable consumption in such discourses can be paralleled with a shift in design and design discourse – from a focus on design not only in terms of lifecycles but in terms of how it influences lifestyles, or ways of living.

Indeed, the power of design to affect human behavior is increasingly in focus within design research. Persuasive design, for example, is a growing area of research and practice, aimed at inducing consumers to reflect, act, relate and behave in particular ways. Persuasive designs can take a variety of forms, such as consumer products, information campaigns and computer-based eco-visualizations (some examples in Verbeek and Slob, 2006; Keyson and Jin, 2009; Gustafsson, 2010; DiSalvo et al., 2010; Ehmann et al., 2012). To the extent that such designs have a specifically normative dimension (privileging and determining particular behaviors), critical and ethical dimensions are also increasingly discussed (Mazé, 2007, 2013; Redström, 2006; Strengers, 2011). This has moved design discourse well *beyond the object*, beyond the discrete material qualities, form and function of a particular artefact – the object in design now also includes the roles and meanings of artefacts within processes of use and, even, within longer-term and larger-scale changes in socio-cultural norms (Mazé 2007).

As design for sustainable consumption has been in focus for more than two decades, we have learned a great deal about the challenges of dealing with the social complexity of the consumption context and the limitations of existing approaches. Indeed, eco-efficient and persuasive designs can also produce unanticipated and undesirable behaviors (Verbeek and Slob, 2006). Measurable rebound effects have spurred research that challenges assumptions of rational choice, planned behavior and consumer sovereignty in technology- and economy-centered models of consumption (Power and Mont, 2010). In response, additional concepts and methods have become increasingly relevant for addressing the complex socio-cultural dimensions of design artefacts within longer-term and larger-scale practices of consumption (Kuijer and De Jong, 2011). A range of approaches are developing that combine so-called 'practice theory' from sociology with design, addressing resource-consumptive practices such as commuting, cooking or bathing, bound up with socio-cultural routines and norms around achieving comfort, cleanliness and convenience (Shove, 2003; Shove et al., 2007; Hielscher et al., 2008; Scott et al., 2012; Pierce et al., 2013).

Our work is located within this expanding range of design researchers developing new approaches to sustainable consumption. We argue that a mixed range, or ever-expanding catalog of methods becomes increasingly important for design researchers to engage in sustainable development. While a basic set of existing methods continues to be relevant to design (for example, from user-centered design and applied ethnography), there are also further and less explored potentials. New concepts from the social sciences have become increasingly relevant, and critical engagement with these is necessary to better understand how these complement, challenge or combine with one another in the design researcher's methodological repertoire. In this chapter, we do not present an exhaustive survey or thorough analysis of approaches from the social sciences, but rather, we draw out and develop our interpretations of particular concepts that have been particularly important in our growing body of sustainable design research. While our interest here is particularly concerned with environmental sustainability, the discussion section suggests further implications of the concepts and methods that are more generally applicable to design research and education concerned with consumption.

Methodological approach

Here, we elucidate concepts of socio-cultural practice through the lens of our own practice-based design research projects around consumption practices of electricity use, showering and bathing, cooking and food waste. This chapter is structured as a dialogue between project examples and discussions of key issues that we have drawn from socio-cultural practice theory.

Three projects are described here. Each has a unique context in terms of their research program and structure, funding and sponsorship, location and partners. The projects are highly collaborative and multidisciplinary, and not all authors were involved in all projects. Here, we draw out particular concepts from the projects, which emerged individually within the projects and even more clearly in retrospective discussions between ourselves. This is consistent with *research through design* approaches, in which theories and methods emerge from within specifically situated design research experiments (Koskinen et al., 2011). Like other situated and inventive processes of inquiry (Lury and Wakeford, 2012), such projects do not lend themselves to direct or cross-comparison. Therefore we describe the projects as discrete examples, through which we illustrate, elucidate and elaborate concepts that we have discovered to be highly relevant across multiple examples of our work in this area.

First, we point to two examples that punctuate and motivate the theoretical discussion that is threaded through and built up in this paper. A third example – an explorative study of *ways of doing cooking* – is further elaborated to reflect on and summarize what we consider to be emerging issues for (sustainable) design research. These project examples are described in order to reflect on concepts that have become increasingly relevant for us in reflecting on our past work and directing our future work, and for us to communicate theories and methods from another field into design and design research.

Framing socio-cultural practices and lifestyles

As sustainability implies reconsideration of prevalent human behaviors and social order (for example, resource consumption in the West), it becomes relevant for designers to understand the role of artefacts *beyond the object*, within social contexts and cultures of consumption.

Spaargaren et al. (2006) position a *social practices* approach between socio-psychological perspectives (typically focused on the motives, values and beliefs of individuals) and technological-system perspectives (focused on large-scale regulations and resources). Social practices can be understood as a *unit of analysis* – because research in the behavioral and social sciences can be anchored in a number of disciplines including psychology, sociology, economics and anthropology, though other units of analysis are of course possible. Bracketing interactions between actors and structures, social practices might be understood as the building blocks, or set of socio-culturally situated processes in everyday life, that constitute lifestyles.

Reckwitz (2002) and Schatzki (1996) outline an approach in which practices are the fundamental unit of social existence: 'both social order and individuality ... result from practices' (ibid., p13). Within cultural theory (see Figure 28.3), Reckwitz distinguishes four main tendencies (in which practice theory is one) that differ principally in the location of the social and the unit of analysis. Theories of practice place the social in practices and take practices as the smallest unit of social analysis. The other three types of cultural theory have their main focus on either the human mind (mentalism), discourse (textualism) or communication (intersubjectivism) (see Figure 28.1).

Aligned with a Latourian concern for the *missing masses* in much technology and consumption studies, Shove et al. (2003; Shove et al. 2007) orients practice theory in proximity to the concern of material culture for how products carry meanings, agency and resources for the construction of individual and collective identities. Beyond the study of individual artefacts as carriers of semiotic meaning, she pays attention to the relations among *complexes of stuff*. In contrast to approaches that treat the meaning of products as fixed by design or passively accepted by users, she argues for material culture and social practices as co-evolving. These relations may normalize, to some extent, as habits and routines that embody the values and morals of everyday social or family life. But performing practices takes effort and is therefore purposeful, oriented toward particular ideas about the future, whether this might be about maintenance of the status quo or visions of how things might be different. This opens for understanding the presence and use of products as part of an active construction of meaning on a daily basis.

For our purposes here, we will locate culture as a dimension of practice theory. Thus, our interest is not in terms of the large questions about the origins and formation of ethnic or national cultures, as treated within archeology, but the more micro-anthropological or sociological notions within material culture and practice theory. In material culture, for example, artefacts are understood in terms of the way that they embody and express aspects within the life of an individual, family or social group (such as culture, gender, age, identity, status, etc.). Though related to ways of understanding the self-conscious construction of identity through the purchase and display of consumer products, our interpretation of

SOCIAL THEORY

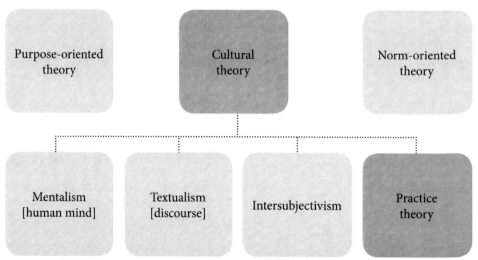

Figure 28.1 The position of practice theory within social theory

Source: based on Reckwitz (2002)

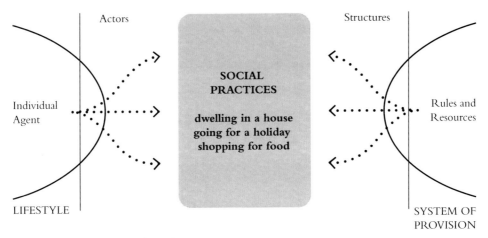

Figure 28.2 Positioning social practices

Source: based on Spaargaren et al. (2006)

practice theory entails a particular interest in the role of products in socio-cultural practices. In this, we understand cultural values and norms as reproduced in everyday life through routines and ordinary *doings* while negotiating complexes of products.

As characterized by Spaargaren et al. (2006; see Figure 28.2), social practices are positioned between socio-psychological perspectives and technological-system perspectives. Between these macro and micro perspectives, social practices may be understood at a range of scales, including households and other social groups (such as co-located or trans-local communities, municipalities, organizations, regions, etc.). At different scales, practices such as cooking and bathing (Kuijer et al., 2013; Scott et al., 2012) travelling and gardening (Spaargaren et al., 2006) can be studied in terms of how they are constituted and how they change.

Reflecting on socio-cultural practices in project examples

Designing for sustainable consumption implies design *beyond the object*, requiring concepts and methods capable of dealing with the complex social and cultural factors interwoven in resource-consumptive practices. This also implies a range of new research questions, in addition to those concerned with form and function, materiality and product language, cognition and usability. We might ask, what is the role of design in complex and ongoing socio-cultural practices? How do we relate to this as design researchers?

These are questions that resonate with our experiences in two previous projects, which we present and reflect upon here to reveal new insights on what we might learn from practice theory in design research. Specifically, we will use these project examples here to explore the role of design, including materials and artefacts, as well as social and cultural actors and groups, in consumption practices. We will also discuss the fresh questions that this retrospective form of critical reflection raised for us; thereby spurring another new project example, which is further elaborated in following sections.

In the first project, presented as *Static!*, we investigated how electricity may be made visible and tangible through the form of domestic artefacts, and how users of such artefacts may thereby reflect upon their energy consumption. In the area of water consumption, as presented secondly in the *Bathing* project, we investigated how the setting, artefacts and ways of bathing are interrelated in households. Central to each project was the development and intervention of new physical artefacts, as well as the study of their effects and roles within sites of consumption. Thus, each project involves multiple methods, ranging from classic qualitative methods of observation and interviews to design methods such as cultural probes (Gaver and Dunne, 1999), experience prototypes (Buchenau and Suri, 2000), co-creation and collaborative analysis (Simonsen and Robertson, 2012).

Project example: Static!

Static! (widely published, including Mazé, 2010; see Figure 28.3) addressed the issue of energy awareness. The research program was crafted along two lines of inquiry: one investigating how electricity could be made more visible and material by design; and the other investigating how such design may induce critical reflection on energy consumption through the objects at hand (Redström, 2010). The first research project was funded by the Swedish Energy Agency to explore the role of design in reducing electricity consumption. It was set up to explore across a number of design, craft, human–computer interaction and social sciences approaches, as evident in the diverse project team and partners. Inspired by results of early cultural probes and interviews, the project team redesigned a series of domestic products (such as curtains, radios, lamps, cables, and radiators) producing a range of product proposals exploring aspects of materiality and visibility. Employing strategies from conceptual and critical design involving the aesthetics of anti-utility or (un)ease-in-use, further experiments involved stimulating reflection, debate and use in various contexts (Mazé and Redström, 2009).

The redesigned artefacts expressed the interdependency between energy, products and actions, which led to the framing of new research questions as to how this would affect use over time. Aspects of use were investigated in various ways, such as including concepts of use as part of the design and craft of the artefacts as well as the study of some artefacts through *domestication* approaches from science and technology studies (Routarinne, 2010; Löfström, 2008), which we see as related in some ways to social practice theories. For example, the Static! Energy Curtain and Static! Erratic Radio were developed conceptually and materially to require active interpretation and interaction on behalf of user. The curtain collects sunlight (through solar panels woven into its surface) for reuse at night (through integrated fiber optics lit by batteries charged during the day). Activating this energy cycle requires a daily choice on behalf of users to draw the curtain open and closed. The basic functionality of the radio, its broadcasting capacity and sound quality, is altered to be dependent upon how much electricity is used by various appliances within a local environment; over-consumption causes the radio to go out of tune.

Prototypes of the curtain and radio were introduced separately into four Finnish households for 3–5 weeks across seasons (Routarinne and Redström, 2007). Methods inspired by domestication attended not only to immediate verbal and physical reactions to the artefact; diverse, unexpected and emergent relations to energy use also surfaced. For example, in one household, introduction of the curtain prompted rearrangement of other furnishings and lighting products as well as profound emotional responses to light, or lack thereof. The radio became the subject of home experiments, in which it was relocated and combined with other materials, while users explored electricity sources and amounts. In addition to how people interpreted and interacted with energy through these artifacts, it became evident that the artefacts prompted reconsideration of larger assemblies of artefacts. As appropriated into the material culture of the home, the study methods exposed how

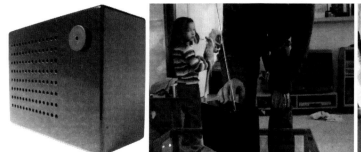

Figure 28.3 Static! Erratic Radio prototype and household study

Sources: radio developed by Anders Ernevi, Samuel Palm and Johan Redström; household study conducted by Sara Routarinne

artefacts changed hands and power relations, how its functionality was repurposed and even cheated, how it prompted self-reflection and rearrangement of pre-existing domestic artefacts.

Roles of material artefacts – stuff – in social practices of consumption

This example illustrates how our concepts and methods in design frame how we pay attention to the social dynamics of use and consumption. In addition to foundational research questions in design around materiality and visibility, the aesthetics of use was also in focus during the conceptualization and craft of artefacts, aspects of which were further examined in the household studies. We might have employed more traditional usability methods for the studies, which typically focus attention on the intelligibility of design or accuracy of use, often with a *unit of analysis* delimited by a particular moment in space and time and by a direct relation between an artefact and a user. Instead, we learned about how the appearance of, and interaction with, artefacts prompts wider and longer processes of negotiation, rearrangement, new artefactual/material combinations and appropriation within family life, the material culture of the home and social practices.

Shove (2003; Shove et al., 2007) discusses how artefacts carry meanings, agency and resources for the construction of individual and collective identities. From our experiences in Static!, we can recognize how concepts such as *aesthetics of use* and our methods of conceptualization, craft, intervention and observation allow us to attend to the interrelation of material artefacts and social practices. These expand the frames of reference typically employed to both practice and study design. Here we move explicitly *beyond the object* but still within the context of things-in-use, in which both materialities and practices may be studied. Our work in Static! is nonetheless irreducible to a consumer-, product-, user- or even eco-centric logic. As in social practice theory, our attention was on how relations among artefacts, people and resources interplay within larger and longer meaning-making processes. Schatzki (1996, p89) articulates the role of artefacts within 'a temporally unfolding and spatially dispersed nexus of doings and sayings'.

Beyond the study of individual products as carriers of semiotic meaning, social practice theory attends to relations among *complexes of stuff*. In contrast to approaches that treat the meaning of artefacts as fixed by design or passively accepted by users, material culture and social practices are understood to co-evolve. Indeed, the household intervention of the Static! curtain and radio prompted extensive reassembly within existing complexes of stuff as well as unexpected activation of emotional reactions, home experiments, and power relations within the family itself. Practice theory argues that relations may normalize, to some extent, as habits and routines that embody the values and morals of everyday social or family life. While initial reception of the Static! radio was by the parents in two of the households (or, more particularly, the male parent) over time, children began to take charge of the radio to play and also to *police* energy consumption in the family. Thus we can understand not only the profound role of material artefacts in reassembling complexes of stuff, but also in the ongoing renegotiation of images or conventions, including the disruption of established head-of-household roles in energy consumption.

In reflecting on this example, we might ask further questions about the expansion of the *unit of analysis*. Beyond individuals and households, we may inquire into more complex dynamics between *stuff, images and skills*, three components of social practices conceptualized in social practice theory and related design research (Shove, 2003; Kuijer and De Jong, 2012; Hielscher et al., 2008). Through the example below, we begin to reflect on implications for larger cultures and *communities of practice* (Wenger, 1998).

Project example: bathing

In a European design project (Bakker et al., 2010), conceptual designs and simple prototypes for more sustainable ways of daily bathing (Kuijer, 2014; Kuijer et al., 2013) were developed and deployed in real-life experiments within homes. Here, we took socio-cultural differences between various European countries in the project (Spain, the Netherlands and Germany) as a starting point for research into sustainable development for living. The aim of the design project was to develop a Living Lab infrastructure, one for each partner country, to be able to perform similar studies in different socio-cultural settings, whilst creating the potential for long-term evaluations. As such, it was geared towards the development of a standard Living Lab home, albeit built with local building materials and technologies, but able to be retrofitted with new prototyped products, services and technologies. We will describe our pilot of bathing practices within residential housing that was started up in the Living Lab project as part of the research agenda. In the pilot, we studied the micro-social, and cross-cultural aspects of the *doings* of bathing. Our aim was to identify and explore the images, values, norms and artefacts associated with bathing rituals, in multiple countries.

Practice theory and human-centered design were two strands of research combined in the pilot project on the practice of bathing (Kuijer and De Jong, 2011). The study started with an analysis of current and past bathing practices, which showed that they are currently highly resource intensive and with a trend to become even more so. Through a combination of secondary research, empirical field observations, self-observation and co-design, we focused on how the *doing* of practices might endure, adapt or decay. Focus was on how people perceive and value their *ways of doing bathing*, and how spaces and artefacts – and changes in these – might support more comfortable and/or more sustainable bathing routines. In this case, a common unit of analysis of bathing practices was framed, and established methods from usability were applied. However, inquiry was pursued in three different countries, Japan, India and the Netherlands, therefore involving very different social, cultural and material practices and norms.

We developed our cultural inquiry into bathing using methods of applied ethnography, in which participants were instructed in self-observation of their bathing routines. In addition, the industry project entailed co-design (Sanders and Stappers, 2008), in which participants were asked to creatively test new bathing concepts that have taken away the continuous flow of water and instead present reservoirs of water. A first non-functioning model was staged to determine if and how this could stimulate new ways of bathing, or bathing performances, using a generative approach to stimulate improvisation through performance (Kuijer et al., 2013). The test included 17 participants of which nine were trained improvisation actors who were all videotaped and analyzed into categorizations of bathing performances. The second iteration involved prototyping in the homes of ten participants, with a variety of households including families, young couple with a baby, and elderly, which were documented with questionnaires and video made by participants themselves. Afterwards they shared their experiences with the designer (Kuijer, 2014), resulting in a new prototype that is currently mounted in a Living Lab test home in Rotterdam.

To illustrate our first attempts to create a better understanding of cultural differences and social groups, we present an example from our previous research, where bathing practices, or ways of doing bathing in the home, were in focus. Bathing is deeply embedded in the routines of everyday life, typically conducted in private spaces with limited social interaction, and largely defined in the very early stages of life (for instance, by copying parental behaviors). As a practice, it is shaped in a historical and cultural context, closely bound to prevailing norms and values within a family, a community and other social groups (Shove et al., 2007). Additionally, however, bathing practices are also conditioned by the utilities and fixtures, proportions and arrangement of space within housing – much housing in places such as The Netherlands and Sweden has extensive building standards and regulations that, consequently, effect bathing practices. This is particularly evident in the experience of people coming from another country – they can experience perceptual and cultural breakdowns within practices that are deeply rooted in embodied experience and socio-cultural norms.

This example illustrates how a common unit of analysis of bathing practices was framed and established methods from usability were applied. However, inquiry was pursued in multiple countries, which opened possibilities for exploring the effects of spaces and artefacts in different socio-cultural practices and contexts, including aspects that are tacit, unspoken and embedded in diverse contexts and cultures. While behavioral accounts, typically orienting towards a psychological basis, may account for differences and change within individuals, a socio-cultural account specifically explores the intersubjective, interpersonal or intercultural, basis for practices. Within social practice theory, this basis is explored in a longer historical (and, potentially, future) trajectory, as well as across cultures, facilitating a rich understanding of change within and across social groups, at a variety of micro/macro levels and temporal scales. This is a wider and deeper basis for understanding practices, which may remediate the overly cognitive and rationalistic bias of behaviorist accounts, which have been insufficient to address undesired or unpredicted change (such as the rebound effect, see Verbeek and Slob, 2006; Power and Mont, 2010).

Practices as unit of analysis and design

Reflecting, retrospectively, through the lens of these examples, we can identify how developing a social practice approach in design, and how expanding design research methods, might suggest a common unit for analysis and for design. Further, we argue that this shared unit might help us to both better understand the role of material artefacts (*stuff*) in consumption practices as well as the role of different actors and socio-cultural groups in changing these practices.

Static!, for example, reveals how the design of material artefacts and intervention methods may serve to reveal routine behaviors and familiar *complexes of stuff* in new ways. Through this, micro-practices of ordinary energy consumption may be questioned, redirected and continually evolved over time as alternative or new ways of doing things at home. To the extent that social practices such as bathing can be studied both in terms of individual actors as well as cultures and communities of practice, we can also begin to understand more complex socio-cultural dynamics among *stuff, images, and skills*. For design research, this allows us to inquire *beyond the object*, in which the specificities of materials and form, function and usability, are integrated into inquiry of the effects of these in the endurance and change of consumption practices, within different spatial-temporal scales.

Just as rethinking the unit allows us to inquire *beyond the object* in design research, it also relocates the focus in consumption research. Previously prevalent approaches within the social sciences have focused on macro-level issues, such as the reproduction of norms and values within cultural groups within society, as well as the aesthetic, symbolic and experiential dimensions of consumer culture. Practice theory draws these micro and macro concerns together, studying the interplay of material and social factors within everyday, ordinary consumption. For example, consumption practices can be examined in terms of changing relations among variables that are intertwined in the achievement of particular everyday practices. Variables include relevant artefacts (material artefacts and resources), the images or conventions that people relate to (such as comfort, cleanliness and convenience, see Shove, 2003), and the knowledge or skills within individuals and social groups. Some social practice and design scholars articulate this more shortly in terms of 'material artifacts, conventions and competences' (Shove et al., 2007, p9) or *stuff-image-skill* (Scott, Bakker and Quist, 2011). Change in such practices, for example in the Bathing project, focused attention on different doings of the same basic bathing practice. In this, our goal was to better understand the meaningful conventions, knowledge and artefacts of specific participants and groups; presenting a more granular perspective on culture than is traditionally framed in consumption studies. It was also our goal for design researchers to think beyond the object and beyond standard assumptions and categories that might be embedded in their subjective experience.

We took this one step further. Beyond those methods adapted from the social sciences, others were critical, such as intervention and co-production, which are more explicitly at home in the field of design research. Expanding the unit of analysis to include analysis not only of existing practices but change in practice due to design, allows us to relate in a new way to one of the important tasks of cultural theory (see Figure 28.1). Cultural theory challenges routinization, for example; the reduction of everyday life to standard, monotonous and mechanical routines. Certainly, a unit of analysis based in practice might result in an endless cataloguing or infinite inventory, without attention to the rich, animated and meaningful aspects of heterogeneity (Highmore, 2002). In our projects, we have focused on heterogeneity both within and across cultures but also on continuities and discontinuities in relation to the agency of design and of actors and groups. In this way, culture cannot be reduced to macro- and slow-moving formulations of ethnicities or nationalities. Instead, it is understood as localized in practices that are deeply rooted and continually performed, reproduced and renegotiated. A shared unit of analysis and design helps to locate a common, or several common, spatial-temporal object(s) for researchers in design and the social sciences. It is a frame that can also highlight differences, spatially across locations, cultures and geographies, and also temporally across practices that may or may not have changed over time.

Co-designing sustainable lifestyles

Through our retrospective reflection on the two project examples (described above), we have developed further research questions that provided the starting point for a new, joint experimental study, which we will discuss in the following section. In this, we are specifically concerned with the dynamics between historical practices, deeply embedded in the present, and future practices of consumption. In relation to such future practices, we set out with methods for exploring the role of design in normative change, or redirection of such practices to specific (more sustainable) ends in selected household practices.

Project example: cooking and food waste studies

The cooking and waste study discussed below is part of our joint work, providing an educational context, but which can also be understood as pilot, or, 'quick-and-dirty' study. Field and design work were primarily carried out by students at Delft University of Technology, under our supervision and according to briefs in which we set out conceptual and methodological frames. An early issue was what kind of frame or focus might constitute *ways of doing* resource-consumptive practices in the home, with possibilities including consuming water and conserving food based on initial household visits. Through discussions, we decided to de-emphasize consumption/conservation *per se* in order to focus on a particular practice – cooking – in which many resources, products, artefacts, people and contexts intersect. Furthermore, cooking is a common and familiar practice, and proximate to activities such as tea/coffee gatherings and dinners, in which outsiders are often welcomed. Thus, we also considered this unit of analysis to have certain advantages for positioning new researchers in the home and for communicating with participants.

Familiar user-centered design research methods, with an ethno-methodological approach, were applied (such as interviews and observations). However, the spatial-temporal unit for applying such methods was expanded in order to capture the development of the practice of food management over time and set within various socio-cultural settings. Our intention was thus to try to understand cooking and waste as they are deeply embedded in present practices that are perhaps not neatly contained within a kitchen, a household or a social group. Experimental methods were also developed that explored alternatives, based on the co-design of cooking and waste practices. Through this, we also set out to explore issues of change and the potential for more sustainable future practices.

Cooking studies: analysis of the practice

An empirical study into cooking practices was carried out over ten weeks based on observations and on-the-spot interviews during the preparation and eating dinner in six households in The Netherlands (De Jong and Mazé, 2010). Participating households were selected to differ in terms of family size, age and country of origin (for example, Iran, Suriname, Vietnam, The Netherlands, and Sweden) with the common variable being the type and standard of the building, apartment and kitchen, although typically based in a Dutch housing type. The results of observations and interviews were analyzed in terms of socio-cultural aspects along the journey from purchase to disposal of food. Despite commonalities in the physical setting including utensils, appliances and apartment layout, the study revealed a wide diversity of practices, causing the researchers to reflect that it is never as simple as 'a kitchen is a kitchen'. For example, the Surinamese home had multiple freezers in the living room for storage, organizing space and practicing doings relevant to cooking. Further insights included the interconnectivity of doing cooking with a range of other associated doings. Cooking proved to constitute and overlap (spatially and temporally) with the buying, preparing and storing of ingredients, preparing and cooking dishes, preparing and storing food that was left over or planned excess. For those that lived alone, food was kept fresh in the fridge, with the expectation that it could be used for an entire dinner the next day. However, for families, leftovers from one dinner were not enough for another, and sometimes leftovers were thrown away. From the observations of people eating in larger groups, such as a household of students and another household in which there was a family gathering over the weekend, food was kept fresh for later occasions than dinner and warmed up in a microwave oven for individuals coming in separately, as in-between snack or lunch.

To map these socio-cultural doings of cooking of different households, pathways to buying, preparing, eating and storing food (waste) were drawn up into a storyboard not with the idea to present a complete overview or an evaluation, but to show the relations, both spatially and temporally, between the different doings (Figure 28.4).

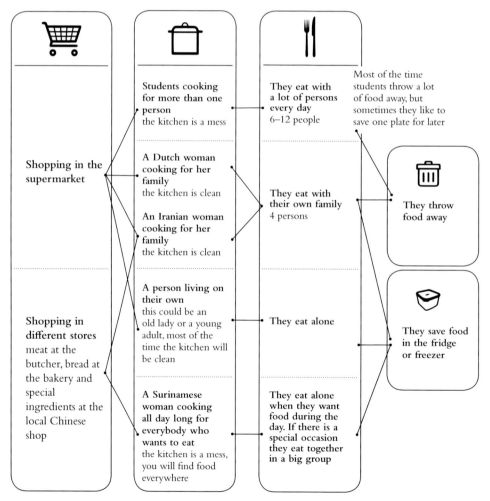

Figure 28.4 Storyboard, documenting cooking practices and socio-cultural 'doings'

Source: study carried out and visualized by Anne Heikamp and Kimberly Hulst

Waste studies: learning and performing different ways of doing

Results from the cooking study were fed into a new follow-up study on waste practices, carried out as the master's thesis of another student (Spengemann, 2011). Starting out with experiments to explore the potential of co-creating alternative cooking practices, the aim was to reduce waste, both in terms of using all parts of ingredients, including those past their prime, those bought in excess, and left-overs.

Different formats were created for engaging, involving and giving participants agency in exploring new food waste practices. Experiments were carried out in the form of a workshop gathering, a dinner game and a community blog with social media tools. The workshop and dinner game were both based on fictitious characters, new recipes and hidden agendas. These elements were introduced to provide in total 11 participants with different, opposing perspectives. The blog was at first open for the student's connections, with 21 people participating at first but, after getting little activity, the blog was restricted to a smaller group. In the blog format, seven participants experimented at home with a set of given tools to compare, try out, reflect and change; exploring their food consumption and waste practices within a more everyday context, over a period of five days.

An important common element of all experiments were so-called Food Challenges. The aim of these challenges was to introduce, confront and guide people into extreme situations (Figure 28.5), such as the instruction 'Don't buy food for a week – live on the food that is stored at your home'. This was introduced as a way to break through current habits of food

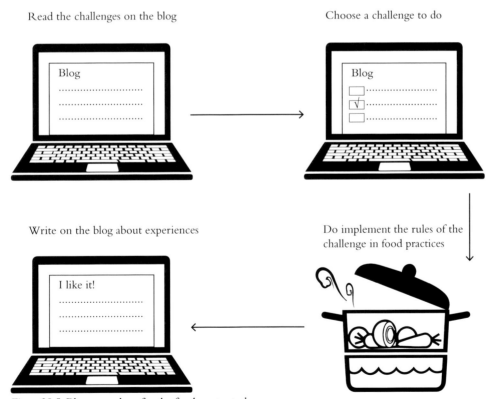

Read the challenges on the blog   Choose a challenge to do

Write on the blog about experiences   Do implement the rules of the challenge in food practices

Figure 28.5 Blog procedure for the food waste study

Source: study carried out and visualized by Pauline Spengemann consumption and to let people actively co-create their own practices (Kuijer and De Jong, 2012). Documentation included video and notes taken of the workshop and dinner-game format. The blog provided documentation in itself.

The goal of the Food Challenges in the Waste study was undeniably normative – the designer is providing tools and rules that steer participants by deliberately placing them in different situations than they might have encountered or chosen themselves. This differentiates the study from the Bathing project, which instead encouraged participants to freely explore new practices. During the study, though possibly unaware of it at the time, participants were uncovering aspects of their own practices by comparing their living situations, routines and beliefs about food waste with the others. Afterwards, they indicated that they had all found their own ways of dealing with their food waste by trying out elements from others and combining those in new ways within their own routines. Here, it also became clear how practices may be socially (re)constructed as well as how they are deeply socially-rooted. Their respective families could react surprised and perhaps suspicious when familiar patterns changed. One of the participants indicated her mother's reaction: 'Oh, and my mom visited and threw away the milk, claiming it had gone sour. I would've used it!'

Afterwards, participants indicated that they continued their own experiments with the food challenges. However, it remained difficult for them to rethink routines in the midst of their everyday lives and settings, where there are obviously certain limits to what can be actually changed, and in which individual action is constrained within larger social systems, norms and environments (as indicated in Spaargaren's model, Figure 28.2). Still, the experiments demonstrated a range of movement and action within constraints, with practical tools and a common community of practice in which participants were able to design their own, as well as some common practices. In addition, these co-designed practices were based on performance and doings (bodily experiences) and not merely imagination and verbalization (Kuijer et al., 2013). In this, design methods developed as interventions directly into everyday practices seemed to offer particular opportunities not only for increasing reflection or changes in thinking, but for alteration of more extensive and enduring activities within the participating group and their families.

A socio-cultural approach to exploring sustainable lifestyles

In this chapter, we have developed interpretations of practice theory in order to discuss the role of design artefacts and methods in the form and practice of everyday life. Sustainability cannot only be about preserving nature, conserving resources or energy efficiency; it involves substantial questions about how people should live their lives. If we recognize the profound role of material culture – and the design of material things – in shaping and changing lifestyles, we can understand sustainability as an issue of *design beyond the object*. As we seek concepts and methods for such design and design research, social practice perspectives are highly relevant in better understanding the role of design in exploring sustainable lifestyles. We list several concepts in such a socio-cultural approach in the next sections.

Starting from material cultures

This is driven by our experiences in previous research, such as the Static! and Bathing projects, which we reflect upon retrospectively here. In these projects, we explored both the rich and meaningful material cultures existing in people's intimate domestic contexts as well as how designed artefacts may be perceived and appropriated. Concepts in these projects, such as *aesthetics of energy use* and *ways of doing bathing*, can be understood in relation to social-cultural practice theories, in which we pay attention to artefactual/material qualities within longer sense-making and meaning-making processes, and the role these play in the renegotiation of conventions relating to sustainability within common socio-cultural groups such as families.

Understanding practices as spatial-temporal unit of analysis

A socio-cultural approach is particularly appropriate to address the more intimate and embodied aspects of lifestyles such as those that are particularly influenced by cultural norms, family tradition, gendered and inter-generational knowledge sharing (Gram-Hanssen, 2006; see also different examples of bathing in Matsuhashi et al., 2009). As we discovered in the Bathing project, social practices approaches attend to such tacit and unconscious forms of knowledge and experience. Design research methods based on verbal expression (such as those in which mentalism or discourse is at the fore) may not elicit such aspects of practice, since these may not be processed on a rational, cognitive or linguistic basis. The specific focus on *doings* locates the deeply rooted basis of practices in actions and performances within socio-material assemblages over time.

Social practice perspectives focus our attention on the roles of design in between individual actors and large-scale systems. In this, design is part of *ways of doing* within socio-cultural groups and at spatial-temporal scales that are larger and longer than the motives, beliefs and actions of individuals (often in focus in socio-psychological and behavioral perspectives).

The frame of the Cooking and Waste study proved to be a good starting point for approaching environmental issues in a holistic way. Direct experience revealed familiar artefacts, but placed in different relations to one another and within different homes, in terms of practices extending (spatially and temporally) beyond typical usability studies. In this way, the study expanded the horizon for understanding beyond the product-centric and even beyond cooking in and of itself; provoking a discussion of the complexity of doings through which people make sense of and live out their everyday lives – alone, in families and in groups. Thus, it seems that we began to approach lifestyles (as built up from socio-cultural practices) in ways that would not have emerged in the same way if water, waste or energy were the sole points of departure.

Experimenting through performances

From our studies, what became evident for us is how *ways of doing* could provide a useful frame for, on one hand, carrying out a focused and, in many ways limited, study, and for, on the other hand, opening up onto a range of wider issues related to socio-cultural and lifestyle issues. Most notably in the Bathing projects the issue of change-agency surfaced, or the role of individual actors and groups, in practices of consumption. In some ways, participants in the pilot could be considered as the object and subject of change, which is rare in user-centered design. Guided by simplified concepts from practice theory in self-observation activities, participants were guided to reflect on their own practices.

Water and energy consumption were at stake in the Static! and Bathing projects but so was the discovery and transformation of people's own and diverse traditions, skills and aspirations. In this case, we understand design as powerful and persuasive but as something that is subject to, and therefore must be sensitive to, socio-cultural practices. While in user-centered design, participants are normally approached as a set of individuals, here, given the emphasis in practice theory on the social construction of practices, we developed an approach stimulating social exchange among participants resulting in the creation of ad-hoc communities (or micro-cultures) for the bathing practice studies. This approach was triggered by the idea in practice theory that novel practices emerge in everyday performance – innovation is seen as an ongoing process of co-construction (Oudshoorn and Pinch, 2003) or co-evolution (Shove et al., 2007). In this perspective, users are not only experts of their own experiences, as argued in co-design (Sleeswijk-Visser et al., 2005), but also designers of novel ways of doing (Scott et al., 2012), and we developed improvisatory role-play methods to extend this potential.

Limitations and implications for design research

Admittedly, this study is limited, based on a small sample, a restricted set of methods and on one visit to each household, without follow-up long-term studies. Our focus was still on, therefore dependent upon, what people are able and willing to say and do. Privacy issues also affected certain situations and interactions. For example, some questions and documentation were sensitive, such as in the Bathing projects and the cooking studies. Certainly, our interpretation of practice theory has focused on *sayings and doings* – perhaps privileging the *what* and *how* of everyday life. Since we are working primarily with qualitative research methods from the social sciences, co-design and some pilot home experiments in these studies, we are still limited in what we can understand about future practices. This casts another light on the problematics, discussed above, of achieving depth (the *why* and *who* that give rise to *sayings and doings*) and of breadth (for example, the generalizability of socio-cultural micro-practices) in this study. Perhaps we might reframe the problem as a question instead:

> If the subject of design research is to understand design artefacts and effects, not only to understand people, how can we understand what is relevant and appropriate in terms of depth?

Design research here is not only about examining artefacts and resources but about how people imagine and learn practices, which are deeply rooted historically, culturally and psychologically, but which are always evolving in relation to changing influences, aspirations and other future-oriented images. This perspective has consequences for thinking and doing (sustainable and user-centered) design. To the extent that we understand the problematics of sustainability to be at stake, not only in design practice but in practices of consumption, these fields suggest the need to expand and deepen how we think of users, or the diversity of those whose lifestyles are influenced by what and how we design. Design materialities and methodologies played important roles in changing ways of lighting, bathing and cooking, for example, but longer and larger social relations are at stake in the practice setting, including issues of gender, cultural difference and power. As experienced with privacy issues in the cooking study, design research might learn not only from the methods of social science but also orientations to issues of subjectivity, positionality and ethics. Diversity and plurality of practices come to the fore in the discussion here – as Highmore (2002, p174) puts it, 'the everyday makes the particularity of lived culture inescapable'. Understanding design as not only concerned with changing the form and function of artefacts, but with the transformation of particular social relations, requires concepts and methods that are sensitive and self-critical.

Social practices, as a shared *unit of analysis and design* in sustainable design, bring design and the social sciences together, as well as technical, cultural, environmental and other disciplines. For design and design research, this means that we cannot only consider individual users, discrete products or user-product interactions isolated in space and time, nor can we only consider materials and resources in sustainable design. As design researchers, thus, we have been arguing here for concepts and methods concerned with social practices in order to reframe how we can analyze and do design. Further, social practice theory treats people as the knowledgeable and capable agents of transitions in practice. This contradicts relegation to mere consumers or users, in which people might be considered only in terms of their purchase and use of products and, typically, in terms of how they make the right or best choices determined by producers and designers, which is a focus in some usability and behavioral approaches. Questioning and changing practices are not only up to design and designers, requiring concepts and methods that are responsive to social agency, including resistance, difference and emergent social formations. Especially when it comes to environmental issues, questioning conventions of production and consumption, and dominant cultures of consumption becomes necessary.

Conclusions

Relating to social practice theory has also entailed a reconsideration of our methods in design. Several of the projects and studies presented here employ methods informed or adapted from the social sciences (such as observation, interviews, comparative and domestication approaches), as well as more mixed or *designerly* methods (such as probes, prototype interventions, improvisatory role-play and co-design). These methods have helped us to work *beyond the object* and in relation to social practices as a unit of analysis and design, in contrast to other social science methods prevalent in design research that are based primarily on verbal expression or that privilege rational, cognitive or linguistic modalities. For example, our focus on *doings* using observation and domestication within different settings located deeply rooted and tacit aspects of practices. Methods in themselves, of course, are not enough. Selecting among them requires knowledge and attention in framing the 'unit' of analysis and design, and sensitivity, capacity and ethical sensitivity in applying the methods.

To take this one step further, we argue that beyond those methods adapted from the social sciences, others were critical such as those that were more mixed or *designerly* (for a discussion of some emerging shared methods; see also Lury and Wakeford, 2012). The particular materialities of Static! prototypes, the co-design modes of making in the Bathing project and the various experiments in the food waste studies, helped us to learn about aspects of those social practices, but they also conditioned perceptions, experiences, material cultures and social formations in several different ways. Through these, we were able to explore and develop foundational knowledge in design craft, aesthetics and methods, as well as explore social research questions perhaps beyond what is typically possible using only mainstream social science methods. For example, interventionist methods using representations and prototypes in the Bathing and food waste studies begin to open up the question of future practices.

In relation to the question of methods, we also experienced certain limits. As long discussed in user-centered and participatory design, starting in present-day lifestyles and established qualitative research methods, it can be difficult to imagine or validate the radical change that many argue environmentalism will require. In our other research projects, and in future work, therefore, we are applying methods from other disciplines and developing new design research methods. For example, in PhD work (Kuijer, 2014), the impact of future artefacts or routines are explored with people in real-life experiments, and in Switch! (Mazé, 2008), futures studies methods are adapted into speculative and participatory design for sustainable development. Related work explores *performative ethnography* (Halse and Clark, 2008), performing future scenarios in collaborative design (Wangel, 2012), and 'context-mapping' (Sleeswijk-Visser et al., 2005), documenting people's dreams about the future – intersections between methods in the social sciences and in design research relevant to alternative ways of approaching sayings and doings.

Even as we ask and explore the various and important things that design research may learn from the social sciences and social practice perspectives, we might also ask questions such as: what can other fields such as the social sciences learn from design? What other concepts and methods might we need for designing sustainable lifestyles? These critical methodological questions underlie our current and future work in the area of sustainable design for everyday life.

Acknowledgments

Static! was a research program at the Interactive Institute funded primarily by the Swedish Energy Agency in 2004–2006. Funding for the European Living Lab project, in which Delft University of Technology participated, was granted by EC no. 212498. We would like to thank our TU Delft students, Anne Heikamp and Kimberly Hulst (cooking study) and Pauline Spengemann (food waste study). Finally, we express our gratitude to the people and families participating in the studies.

References

Bakker, C., Eijk, D. van, Silvester, S. Reitenbach, M., Jong, A. de, Keyson, D. and Scott, K. (2010) 'Understanding and Modelling User Behaviour in Relation to Sustainable Innovations: The LIVING LAB Method', in Horváth, I., Mandorli, F. and Rusák, Z. (eds), in *Proceedings of the Tools and Methods of Competitive Engineering*, Ancona: Università Politecnica delle Marche

Brundtland, G. H. (chairman) (1987) *Our Common Future: The World Commission on Environment and Development*, Oxford: Oxford University Press

Buchenau, M. and Suri, J. F. (2000) 'Experience Prototyping', in *Proceedings of the symposium on Designing Interactive Systems (DIS)*, New York: ACM Press, pp424–433

De Jong, A.M. and Mazé, R. (2010) 'Cultures in Sustainability', in Wever, R. (ed), *Proceedings of European Roundtable of Sustainable Consumption and Production Conference (ERSCP-EMSU)*, Delft: Delft University of Technology

DiSalvo, C., Sengers, P. and Brynjarsdóttir, H. (2010) 'Mapping the Landscape of Sustainable HCI', in *Proceedings of the 28th International Conference on Human Factors in Computing Systems (CHI)*, New York: ACM Press

Ehmann, S., Bohle, S. and Klanten, R. (eds) (2012) *Cause and Effect: Visualizing Sustainability*, Berlin: Gestalten

Gaver, B., Dunne, T. and Pacenti, E. (1999) 'Cultural Probes', *Interactions* vol 6, no 1, pp21–29

Gram-Hanssen, K. (2006) 'Consuming Technologies – Developing Routines', in *Proceedings of Sustainable Consumption and Society, International Working Conference for Social Scientists*, Madison, WI: University of Wisconsin-Madison

Gustafsson, A. (2010) *Positive Persuasion*, Gothenburg: IT University

Halse, J. and Clark, B. (2008) 'Design Rituals and Performative Ethnography', in *Proceedings of the Ethnographic Praxis Industry Conference (EPIC)*, Copenhagen

Hielscher, S., Fisher, T. and Cooper, T. (2008) 'The Return of the Beehives, Brylcreem and Botanical! An Historical Review of Hair Care Practices with a View to Opportunities for Sustainable Design', in *Proceedings of the Design Research Society Conference 'Undisciplined!'*, Sheffield

Highmore, B. (2002) *Everyday Life and Cultural Theory*, New York: Routledge

Keyson, D. and Jin, S. (Eds) (2009) *Designing for Sustainable Living and Working*, Delft: VSSD

Koskinen, I., Zimmerman, J., Binder, T., Redström, J. and Wensveen, S. (2011) *Design Research Through Practice*, Waltham, MA: Morgan Kaufmann

Kuijer, L. (2014). *Implications of Social Practice Theory for Sustainable Design*, Delft: TU Delft

Kuijer, L. and De Jong, A.M. (2011) 'Practice Theory and Human-Centered Design: A Sustainable Bathing Example', in *Proceedings Nordic Design Conference (NORDES)*, Helsinki: Aalto University

Kuijer, L. and De Jong, A.M. (2012) 'Identifying Design Opportunities for Reduced Household Resource Consumption: Exploring Practices of Thermal Comfort', *Journal of Design Research* vol 10, no 1–2, pp67–85

Kuijer, L., De Jong, A., and Van Eijk, D. (2013) 'Practices as a Unit of Design: An Exploration of Theoretical Implications in a Study on Bathing', in Pierce, J., Sengers P., Strengers P. and Bodker S. (eds) TOCHI special issue on Sustainable HCI through everyday practices, *ACM Transactions on Computer-Human Interaction* vol 20, no 4, article 21

Löfström, E. (2008) *Visualisera energi i hushåll: Avdomesticeringen av sociotekniska system och individ- respektive artefaktbunden energianvändning*, Linköping: Linköping University

Lorek, S. (2010) 'Strong Sustainable Consumption and Degrowth', in Wever, R. (Ed), *Proceedings of European Roundtable of Sustainable Consumption and Production Conference (ERSCP-EMSU)*, Delft: Delft University of Technology

Lury, C. and Wakeford, N. (2012) *Inventive Methods*, New York: Routledge

Matsuhashi, N., Kuijer, L. and De Jong, A. (2009) 'A Culture-Inspired Approach to Gaining Insights for Designing Sustainable Practices', in *Proceedings of the Ecodesign Conference*, Japan Society of Mechanical Engineers, Sapporo

Mazé, R. (2007) *Occupying Time: Design, Time, and the Form of Interaction*, Stockholm: Axl Books

Mazé, R. (Ed) (2008) Switch! Energy ecologies in everyday life, *International Journal of Design* vol 2, no 3, pp55–70

Mazé, R. (Ed) (2010) *Static! Designing for Energy Awareness*, Stockholm: Arvinius Förlag

Mazé, R. (2013) 'Who is Sustainable? Querying the Politics of Sustainable Design Practices', in Plöjel, M., Mazé, R., Olausson, L., Redström, J., Zetterlund, C. (eds) *Share This Book: Critical Perspectives and Dialogues about Design and Sustainability*, Stockholm: Axl Books

Mazé, R. and Redström, J. (2009) Difficult Forms: Critical Practices of Design and Research, *Research Design Journal* no 1, vol 1, pp28–39

Oudshoorn, N. and Pinch, T. (2003) *How Users Matter: The Co-construction of Users and Technology*, Cambridge, MA: MIT Press

Pierce, J., Strengers, Y., Sengers, P., and Bødker, S. (Eds) (2013) Introduction to the Special Issue on Sustainable HCI through Everyday Practices, *ACM Transactions on Computer–Human Interaction*, vol 20, no 4, article 20

Power, K., and Mont, O. (2010) 'Dispelling the Myths about Consumption Behavior', in Wever, R. (Ed), *Proceedings of European Roundtable of Sustainable Consumption and Production Conference (ERSCP-EMSU)*, Delft: Delft University of Technology

Reckwitz, A. (2002) 'Toward a Theory of Social Practices: A Development in Culturalist Theorizing', *European Journal of Social Theory*, vol 5, pp243–263

Redström, J. (2006) 'Persuasive Design: Fringes and Foundations', in *Proceedings of the conference on Persuasive Technology for Human Well-Being (PERSUASIVE)*, Berlin: Springer, pp112–122

Redström, J. (2010) Research Frames, in Mazé, R. (ed.) *Static! Designing for Energy Awareness*, Stockholm: Arvinius Förlag, pp15–20

Routarinne, S. (2010) 'Static! At home', in Mazé, R. (ed.) *Static! Designing for Energy Awareness*, Stockholm: Arvinius Förlag, pp103–113

Routarinne, S. and Redström, J. (2007) 'Domestication as Design Intervention', in *Proceedings of the Nordic Design Research conference (NORDES)*, Stockholm: Konstfack

Sanders, E. B.-N. and Stappers, P. J. (2008) 'Co-Creation and the New Landscapes of Design', *CoDesign* vol 4, no 1, pp5–18

Schatzki, T. (1996) *Social Practices*, Cambridge: Cambridge University Press

Scott, K., Bakker, C. and Quist, J. (2012) 'Designing Change by Living Change', *Design Studies* vol 33, no 3, pp279–297

Shove, E. (2003) *Comfort, Cleanliness and Convenience: The Social Organisation of Normality*, Oxford: Berg

Shove, E., Watson, M, Ingram, J. and Hand, M. (2007) *The Design of Everyday Life*, Oxford: Berg

Simonsen, J. and Robertson, T. (eds) (2012) *International Handbook of Participatory Design*, London: Routledge

Sleeswijk-Visser, F., Stappers, P.J., Van der Lught, R. and Sanders, E. B-N. (2005) 'Contextmapping: Experiences from practice', *Codesign* vol 1, no 2, pp119–149

Spaargaren, G., Martens, S., and Beckers, T. (2006) 'Sustainable Technologies and Everyday Life', in Verbeek, P.-P. and Slob, A. (eds), *User Behavior and Technology Development*, Berlin: Springer, pp107–118

Spengemann, P. (2011). *Reducing Food Waste in the Household through Behaviour Change*, Delft: Faculty of Industrial Design Engineering, Delft University of Technology

Strengers, Y. (2011) 'Designing Eco-Feedback Systems for Everyday Life', in *Proceedings of the conference on Human Factors in Computing Systems (CHI)*, New York: ACM Press, pp233–240

Verbeek, P-P. and Slob, A. (2006) *User Behavior and Technology Development*, Berlin: Springer

Vergragt, P. (2010) 'Sustainability Future Visions: Impacts and new strategies', in *Proceedings of the LeNS Conference 'Sustainability in Design: Now!'*, Bangalore, India

Vezzoli, C. and Manzini, E. (2006) 'Design for Sustainable Consumption', in Andersen, M. M. and Tukker, A. (eds), *Perspectives on Radical Changes to Sustainable Consumption and Production, Workshop of the Sustainable Consumption Research Exchange Network*, 20–21 April 2006, Copenhagen, Denmark

Wangel, J. (2012) *Making Futures*, Stockholm: KTH Royal Institute of Technology

Wenger, E. (1998) *Communities of Practice: Learning, Meaning, and Identity*, Cambridge: Cambridge University Press

29

THE SUSTAINABLE
ENERGY FOR ALL
DESIGN SCENARIO

Carlo Vezzoli and Elisa Bacchetti

Abstract

Nowadays, there is a consolidated understanding that sustainable development is not possible without sustainable energy for all. Furthermore, Distributed Renewable Energy (DRE) is seen as key to achieve this aim. The LeNSes project (Learning Network for Sustainable energy systems) fits within this framework, as far as it is aimed at developing and disseminating in African and European higher education institutions a new design discipline: System Design for Sustainable Energy for All (SD4SEA), a design approach where the focus is moved from mere product design for sustainable energies to the wider approach of Sustainable Product-Service Systems (S.PSS) design for sustainable energy for all. This chapter presents the Sustainable Energy for All Design Scenario developed within the LeNSes project. This scenario aims to inspire and inform designers to design within a radically new social, economic and technical system, based on the following research hypothesis: S.PSS are a promising model to DRE in low- and middle-income contexts. The findings have also been produced as a tool, in the form of a set of evocative videos.

Keywords: sustainable scenario, sustainable energy for all, System Design for Sustainable Energy for All, Distributed Renewable Energy, Sustainable Product-Service Systems

Sustainable development is not possible without sustainable energy for all

Nowadays, within the international scientific community dealing with sustainable development, the need for a paradigm shift is often stated, to lead to a new era driven more by democratic and inclusive decentralized or distributed systems based on renewable energies. Though energy is the world's dominant industrial sector, current centralized and non-renewable energy systems are far from being able to take energy to all in a sustainable way. Several authors (Barbero and Pereno, 2013; Colombo et al., 2013; Ki-moon, 2011; Rifkin, 2002, 2011; Vezzoli et al., 2015b; Johansson et al., 2005) have observed that the transition from centralized and non-renewable fossil-fuel resources (oil, coal, etc.) to

Distributed Renewable Energy (DRE) plays a key role in the transition towards sustainable development.

To clarify, DRE generation presents the following environmental, economic and socio-ethical sustainability characteristics:

- *Based on inexhaustible resources*: consequently reducing greenhouse gas emissions and environmental impact for extraction, transformation and distribution.
- *Set up as small-scale generation plants*: consequently reducing economic investment.
- *Easy to install, maintain and manage*: consequently, allowing individuals and local communities to install/manage plants, while fostering democratization of access to resources and enhancing local employment and dissemination of competences.

Based on previous characteristics, DRE generation could be defined as follows:

Small-scale generation plants harnessing renewable energy resources (such as sun, wind, water, biomass and geothermal energy), at or near the point of use, where the users are the producers – whether individuals, small businesses and/or a local community. If the small-scale generation plants are also connected with each other (for example, to share the energy surplus), they become a Renewable Local Energy Network, which may in turn be connected with nearby similar networks.

(Vezzoli et al., 2015a)

Consequently, the extensive usage of distributed generation from renewable resources could lead to a widespread redistribution of power towards single individuals, which is necessary to establish conditions for a more sustainable development (Vezzoli et al., 2014b).

Finally, DRE systems are increasingly seen as a vital catalyst to achieve universal access to energy and thus a wider social and economic development: by enabling education, health and sustainable agriculture, by creating green jobs and by promoting equity (Colombo et al., 2013). Furthermore, the experience gained in developing countries could also contribute to the paradigm shift needed in the energy sector at a global level (ibid.).

SYSTEM STRUCTURE

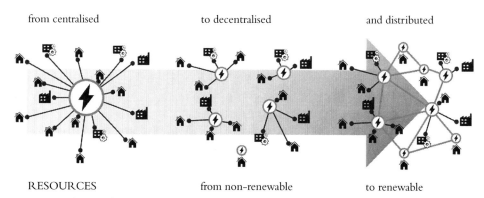

Figure 29.1 The paradigm shift from non-renewable/centralized to renewable/distributed energy generation systems

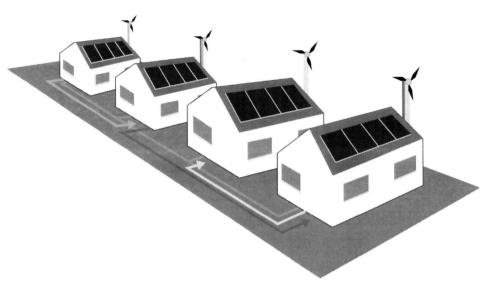

Figure 29.2 A schematic representation of distributed renewable energy generation

This chapter first describes the underpinning research hypothesis proposed by the LeNSes project:

> The Sustainable Product-Service System (S.PSS) model applied to DRE is a promising approach to making sustainable energy accessible to all.[1]

It then describes the scenario developed within this research hypothesis, which consists of four visions. Within this scenario, a new emerging role for designers is introduced, in terms of a new design knowledge base and know-how. Finally, it describes a design support tool (Sustainable Energy for All Design Scenario) that embeds those scenarios in a set of evocative videos;[2] its use has been tested with MSc students in design in a couple of pilot courses in the LeNSes project.

Sustainable Product-Service System applied to Distributed Renewable Energy: a win–win offer model for all

In industrialized contexts, S.PSS have been studied since the end of the 1990s as business models with the potential to decouple the creation of value from the consumption of materials and energy, and thus significantly reduce the environmental load of the life-cycles of current product systems. The most recent definition of S.PSS is 'an offer model providing an integrated mix of products and services that are together able to fulfil a particular customer demand (to deliver a 'unit of satisfaction'), based on innovative interactions between the stakeholders of the value production system (satisfaction system), where the economic and competitive interest of the providers continuously seeks both environmentally and socio-ethically beneficial new solutions (Vezzoli et al., 2014, p71a).

Furthermore, in recent years S.PSS have also begun to be considered for low and middle-income contexts, especially when applied to DRE:

An S.PSS approach may act as a business opportunity to facilitate the diffusion of DRE-based value production systems (satisfaction system) in (all) low and middle-income contexts, because they reduce/cut both the initial (capital) cost of hardware purchasing and the running cost of maintenance, repairing, upgrade, etc., resulting in a key leverage for a sustainable development process aiming at democratizing the access to resources, goods and services.

(Vezzoli et al., 2015c, p6)

Box 29.1 presents a case study to illustrate the research hypothesis. Other case studies[3] also illustrate the validity of the research hypothesis and the following aspects may further clarify the main reasons why S.PSS applied to DRE open new opportunities in low and middle-income contexts:

- Focusing on access rather than (DRE) hardware ownership reduces/avoids initial investment costs (too high for low-income people) so that all can access renewable energy more easily.
- Selling the 'unit of satisfaction' rather than the hardware reduces/avoids unexpected costs for repair and/or maintenance that may lead to the interruption of product use.
- Focusing on a specific context of use leads to the involvement of local rather than global stakeholders, which builds local skills and empowerment.
- Being potentially more labor/relation intensive leads to increased local employment and the diffusion of skills.

Sustainable Energy for All Design Scenario

The Sustainable Energy for All Design Scenario has been developed to show a new picture of a sustainable production and consumption system characterized by a *Sustainable Product-Service System (S.PSS) applied to DRE*, and designed to inspire the design of sustainable energy access systems in low and middle-income contexts.[4]

The scenario is illustrated through four visions framed within two polarity axes. The first axis shows the customer as final user (B2C) at one pole, and as small entrepreneur or small business (B2B) at the other. The second axis sees, at one pole, the offer as a DRE micro-generator (e.g. solar panel system plus its components such as a battery, inverter, etc.) and, at the other pole, as the sum of both the DRE micro-generator and the related energy-using products or equipment (e.g. phone and television sets are energy-using products; woodcutter, sewing machine are equipment).

The four quadrants delineated by the intersection of the two axes identify visions titled as follows:

- Vision 1: Energy for all in daily life.
- Vision 2: Energize your business without initial investment cost.
- Vision 3: 'Pay × use' for your daily life products and energy.
- Vision 4: Start-up your business paying per period for equipment and energy.

Box 29.1 Distributed solar energy and electrical devices as an all-inclusive package, Brazil

Fabio Rosa founded both a for-profit corporation, Agroelectric System of Appropriate Technology (STA) and a not-for profit organization, the Institute for Development of Natural Energy and Sustainability (IDEAAS). Through IDEAAS, Rosa developed an innovative project called The Sun Shines for All (TSSFA) based on a new business model to provide Brazil's rural people with what they needed in terms of energy: energy services, not just solar energy. To that end TSSFA developed a leasing structure whereby customers pay a monthly fee for the use of cost-effective solar energy packages. TSSFA customers sign a three-year service contract but can end the contract at any time by paying the cost of uninstallation. Solar home kits, as TSSFA calls them, include the hardware needed to generate energy, while also providing the installation service and products that use the electricity generated by the solar home system, such as lighting and electrical outlets. All of the tangible inputs are owned by STA and only the service provided by these materials are leased to customers. It is environmentally sustainable because it uses solar energy; it is socio-ethically sustainable because it gives poor people access to useful services; it is economically sustainable because it generates business for TSSFA.

Vision 1: Energy for all in daily life

Quadrant 1 (Figure 29.3) is identified by a business to customer (B2C) offer of a DRE micro-generator. It outlines a vision that has been titled *Energy for all in daily life*, where 'an energy supplier delivers an ownerless DRE system, for daily life activities, to single users and small communities who pay per period/time.'

In this vision the offered DRE micro-generator and its components (e.g. solar panel, wires, storage) are not owned by the customer. This cuts both the initial investment costs and the running costs (e.g. maintenance and repair). Instead, the customer is required to make periodic payments, which are more affordable (for further details see below). This configuration makes energy access economically affordable even in low-middle income contexts so that the quality of life in slums and poor rural areas could be greatly improved, especially in terms of health and security.

The example below shows one possible situation in this vision:

> Max, inhabitant of a rural village, has no access to energy. Therefore he uses an oil lamp for light and he goes to the closest village to charge his phone. If he can have a solar system installed on his roof, guaranteeing secure energy access, he can avoid daily problems, improving his and his family's quality of life.

In the vision, different offers and alternative payment methods can be coupled with the ownerless DRE system to make it more affordable. For example, the DRE system offer could be an all-inclusive package with services such as design, installation, maintenance, repair and substitution, upgrading and end of-life treatments for the DRE micro-generator and its component parts. This is known as a *result-oriented S.PSS*. Alternatively, the offer could provide the necessary information and/or training on the design, installation, maintenance, repair and/or end of-life treatments for the various DRE products and components and the micro-generator (e.g. training course to install/repair the DRE system by the customer). This configuration is a *use-oriented S.PSS*.

The example below shows one possible situation in this vision:

> Max doesn't have to buy the DRE micro-generator and components; he just uses them by paying a fixed amount of money per period. Ownership and related services remain with the energy supplier, who is interested in reducing maintenance and repair needs, improving his own business while reducing the environmental impact.

In terms of payment, DRE systems do not have most of the resource extraction and refinement costs involved in fossil-fuel based systems. Furthermore, when DRE systems are offered as S.PSS, the payment is delinked from mere watt consumption (i.e. the consumers pay only for access to the DRE system and to buy the energy-using product, e.g. mobile phone, TV, etc.). The payment could either be fixed on period (daily/weekly/monthly payments) or on the energy use time of daily life products. Alternatively, it could be based on hybrid modalities.

Since a DRE system is quite complex, it is possible to imagine different stakeholders involved. For example, the energy supplier could be either a multinational energy provider, the local/national public energy supplier, a small or medium size private energy company, a local cooperative of the users themselves or possibly a partnership between some or all of these, depending on the specific context.

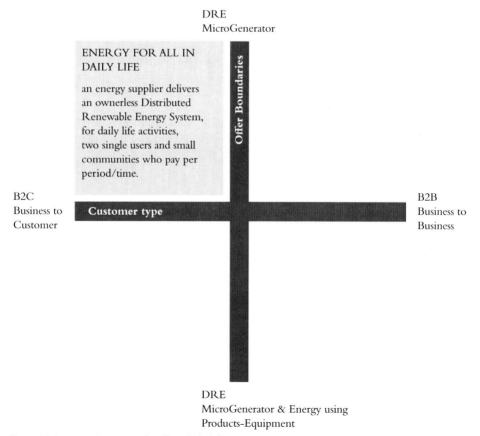

Figure 29.3 Vision 1: Energy for all in daily life

In the rural village without main grid connection, Max receives a phone call from mom at midnight

Now she is in the hospital after an accident

During the conversation the low battery warning appears

And then they lose communication suddenly

Max is so worried about it. He can't do anything

Early next morning he takes the bus and he goes to meet his mom in the hospital

Figure 29.4 Screenshots from the video *Energy for all in daily life* by Korapan Vanitkoopalangkul. Text is given by voice narration

TA-DAAA!!! This is Mark from the energy supplier, he explains that this service has no grid connection, no cost for the system, just pay for the power per period of use

Here you can see what we call a 'micro generator for Distributed Renewable Energy'. He will receive electricity to power products in daily life such as lighting, mobile phone and television and so on

Max is so supervised that he can have it on the roof top

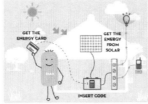
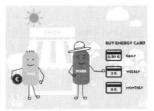

Max paid only for the monthly energy card in the package

Just insert the code from the card, and you can get the energy from solar power

After finishing the credit, he can buy a daily, weekly or monthly energy card at the shop nearby

Figure 29.5 Screenshots from the video *Energy for all in daily life* by Korapan Vanitkoopalangkul. Text is given by voice narration

To summarize, the potential benefits in this vision would be: *reduced transportation* within the system, thanks to local access to distributed and renewable energy; *reduced toxicity* in the energy production and consumption through the use of distributed (locally produced) renewable energy; *optimized system life* for the DRE micro-generator and related components because ownership is retained by the energy supplier whose interest lies in offering a valuable product; *empowered/valorized local resources, favoring/integrating weaker and marginalized strata,* due to the local access to energy that indirectly fosters local empowerment, facilitating/improving the quality of daily life; and, *added value for the customer* in that the package of services (e.g. design, maintenance, training) included in the system offer guarantees the economic feasibility of the system and, consequently, energy access.

Vision 2: Energize your business without initial investment cost

In quadrant 2 (Figure 29.6), identified by a business to business (B2B) offer of a DRE micro-generator, the vision is titled *Energize your business without initial investment cost.* It is a vision where 'an energy supplier delivers an ownerless DRE system to power the equipment of a small entrepreneur, who pays per period/time'.

In this vision, as in the previous one, the ownership of the DRE micro-generator and related components is retained by the energy supplier. This reduces risks for small entrepreneurs (customers, in the vision), who don't have to face any initial investment, except for the purchase of the necessary equipment (e.g. sewing machine for the tailor shop) to start-up or upgrade their small enterprises/companies. In this way, even in low-middle income contexts, a small entrepreneur with stable energy access will be able to guarantee the production/delivery of a predetermined quantity of products/services within a given time, thus satisfying all clients.

The example below shows a possible situation in this vision (many others could be drawn):

> Kate and Tom, tailors in a rural village, have no stable access to energy, so they still use a diesel generator to power their sewing machine. If they can have a solar system installed in their tailor shop, guaranteeing secure energy access, they can guarantee on time delivery and avoid losing clients.

In the vision, the ownerless DRE system provided can be coupled with different offers: the DRE system could be an all-inclusive package with services such as design, installation, maintenance, repair and/or substitution, upgrade and end of-life treatments of the various DRE micro-generators and their components (result-oriented S.PSS); or alternatively, the offer could provide the necessary information and/or training on design, installation, maintenance, repair and/or end of-life treatments for the various components together with the DRE micro-generator and components (use-oriented S.PSS). As for the previous vision, due to the inherent characteristics of renewable energies, the payment for DRE system use is delinked from mere watt consumption, and the small entrepreneurs pay only for access to the DRE system; with a fixed rate on period (daily/weekly/monthly payments) or on the energy use time of work products and equipment.

Due to the variety of small businesses and renewable energies, the stakeholder configuration i.e. multinational energy provider, local/national public energy supplier, small or medium size private energy company, etc. and/or any partnerships between them, could vary.

The example in Figure 29.6 shows a possible situation of this vision (many others could be drawn):

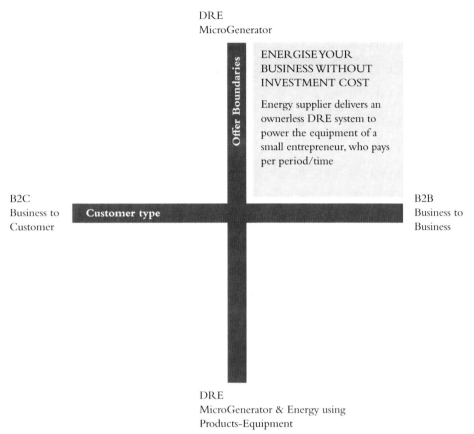

Figure 29.6 Vision 2: Energize your business without investment cost

Kate and Tom don't have to buy the DRE micro-generator and components, but have just to pay a fixed rate per period. Ownership and related services stays with the energy supplier, who is interested in reducing maintenance and repair needs, improving his own business while reducing the environmental impact.

Finally, the benefits of the vision would be: *reduction in the use of resources,* due to reduction in energy consumption from the main grid, which mainly draws on exhaustible resources; *optimized system life* of the DRE micro-generator and related components because ownership is retained by the energy supplier, whose interest it is to take care of installation, maintenance and repairs as efficiently as possible; *Improved employment and working conditions* due to access to a secure source of local energy for production and working activities, thus *favoring and integrating the weaker and marginalized* thanks to the renewable energy support to human effort (e.g. an electric sewing machine instead of a pedal-sewing machine) enabling some categories to continue working; *Profitability and added value for companies,* specifically small entrepreneurs/small businesses who are offered a DRE micro-generator and components without investment and running costs.

Vision 3: 'Pay × use' your daily life products and energy

Quadrant 3 (Figure 29.10) is identified by a business to customer (B2C) offer of a DRE micro-generator (and the related components) plus Energy Using Products. The vision is titled *'Pay × use' your daily life products and energy*, where 'Single users and small communities acquire an ownerless package consisting of a DRE system plus a set of energy using products for daily life, paying for them per use.'

In this vision, as in the previous two, the DRE micro-generator and related components are not owned by the customer. However, unlike the previous visions, the energy using products (e.g. burner, oven, etc.) are included in the ownerless offer. This configuration cuts the initial investment cost of both connection to the main energy grid and purchase of energy using products, as well as the running costs (e.g. maintenance and repair) of the whole DRE system. For example, for many people still using firewood for cooking, energy access could greatly improve their quality of life, while reducing disease caused by toxic emissions from the fire.

The example below shows one possible situation in this vision:

> Mary and Ryan, are a family living in a rural village where cooking with firewood is still the main solution, due to the lack of access to energy. If they can have a solar system installed on their roof, guaranteeing secure energy access, they can reduce health risks, while gaining time no longer needed to collect firewood.

In this vision, even more than in the previous one, we can see the offer as a full ownerless DRE system package, which includes energy using products, and even services such as design, installation, maintenance, repair and substitution, upgrading and end of-life treatments for the whole DRE system (result-oriented S.PSS). Whatever the DRE system configuration, payments may be made either per use (e.g. hours of cooking or number of washing cycles), or fixed and based on period (daily/weekly/monthly payments), or according to hybrid modalities.

In this vision, due to the offer of energy using products, the variety of stakeholders is even greater. For example, the provider could be the energy supplier alone (a multinational energy provider or the local/national public energy supplier), offering both the DRE systems and a set of purchased energy using products, which all remain in its ownership. Alternatively, a partnership between the energy supplier and the producers of the energy using products could be established and both the DRE system and the energy using products remain in their joint ownership. As a further option, a cooperative could be established within the community or group of people that will use the offer in order to retain the ownership of the DRE system and the energy using products.

The example below shows one possible situation in this vision:

> Mary and Ryan can use the common kitchen based in the village to cook, where the energy used comes from the local DRE system. They don't have to buy any component or energy using products in the kitchen, but they pay to cook. Ownership and related services stay with the energy supplier, who is interested in reducing maintenance and repair needs, improving their own business while reducing environmental impact.

To summarize, the potential benefits of this vision would be: *reduced toxicity* and *reduced resource consumption*, substituting firewood and/or charcoal with distributed, locally

Every year many people come to the tailor shop before the New Year festival

In the small village with an unstable main grid, for the tailor shop there is only enough power for one sewing machine

But they have a lot of work to do. If they have another sewing machine, it could help them

But there isn't enough electricity for two sewing machine

Next day, Kate goes to buy fabric in another village. She meets Emma, her friend, they discuss the sewing machine problem

Emma invites Kate to help her shop, Kate asks Emma why she can have 2 sewing machines. Is there enough electricity?

Figure 29.7 Screenshots from the video *Energize your business without investment cost* by Korapan Vanitkoopalangkul. Text is given by voice narration

Emma told that one of them connected with solar system, no need to connect with the main grid

Kate is so surprised!

Just call the energy service company, ask them to connect the system with your machine

  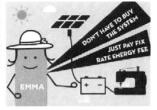

A technician come to check the machine with the service condition document

Basically, installation, maintenance and upgrading is free for this service

Users don't have to apy for the system, they just pay a fixed rate energy fee

Figure 29.8 Screenshots from the video Energize your business without investment cost by Korapan Vanitkoopalangkul. Text is given by voice narration

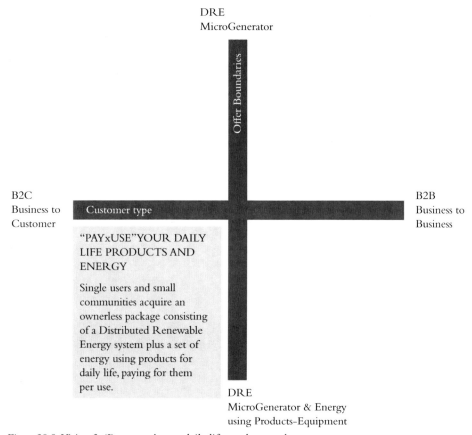

DRE
MicroGenerator

Offer Boundaries

B2C
Business to
Customer

Customer type

B2B
Business to
Business

**"PAYxUSE" YOUR DAILY
LIFE PRODUCTS AND
ENERGY**

Single users and small
communities acquire an
ownerless package consisting
of a Distributed Renewable
Energy system plus a set of
energy using products for
daily life, paying for them
per use.

DRE
MicroGenerator & Energy
using Products-Equipment

Figure 29.9 Vision 3: 'Pay × use' your daily life products and energy

produced renewable energy; *optimized system life*, offering ownerless co-cooking space
and related energy using products, including running services (e.g. maintenance and
upgrading) without additional costs for the user and with supplier interest in offering
valuable products; *increased social cohesion favoring/integrating weaker and marginalized strata*,
the local access to renewable energy in common spaces indirectly fosters local integration
and a sense of community, improving the quality of daily life; the creation of *partnership/
cooperation* among suppliers, facilitating reiteration of the project in other contexts; and,
added value for customers, in fact a package of services (e.g. design, maintenance, training)
is included in the system offer guaranteeing the economic feasibility of the system, and
consequently, of energy access.

In rural area, Mary and Ryan are still using firewood for cooking meals

One day, Ryan got sick

The doctor said is because of the toxic fumes from smoke are burning wood, but Mary needed the fire for cooking meals

Last week, the doctor got a flyer about solar cooker, probably it will be useful

Using solar energy is great idea for cooking, safe and harmless

Figure 29.10 Screenshots from the video *Pay × use* for your daily life products and energy, by Korapan Vanitkoopalangkul. Text is given by voice narration

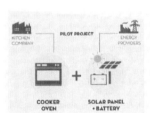  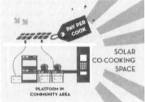

This is a PILOT project, a partnership between kitchen company and energy supplier provides cooker and solar system

Launching 'solar home cooker' as a full package service

And Launching 'solar cooking space' as a platform in community area

Especially you just pay to cook!!

The services are owned by providers, including installation, maintenance by technicians

Figure 29.11 Screenshots from the video *Pay × use* for your daily life products and energy, by Korapan Vanitkoopalangkul. Text is given by voice narration

Vision 4: Start-up your business paying per period for equipment and energy

In quadrant 4 (Figure 29.12), identified by a business to business (B2B) offer of a DRE micro-generator (and the related components) plus equipment, the vision drawn is titled *Start-up your business paying per period for equipment and energy*. It is a vision where: 'a single entrepreneur acquires an ownerless package, consisting of a DRE system plus the equipment to start-up a business.'

In this vision, a small entrepreneur/company (customer, in the vision) receives a full ownerless DRE system package (e.g. carpenter's workshop) composed of a DRE micro-generator and related components and, in this case, the energy using equipment (e.g. circular saw, drill). The ownership of the full-package is retained by the energy supplier or a partnership, cutting the initial investment costs of both connection to the main energy grid (when this is not available) and the purchase of the energy using equipment, as well as the running costs of the whole DRE system. For example, many competent entrepreneurs cannot get a loan from traditional banks. With stable energy access they could increase their business opportunities and working conditions while empowering both the local community, and local economic growth.

The example below shows one possible situation in this vision:

> Ben, carpenter in a big city, wants to move back to his own village to open a carpentry workshop, but no energy access is available. If he can have a solar system installed in his carpentry workshop in the village, guaranteeing secure energy access, he can start his business, offering on time delivery, with the most updated energy using equipment.

In the vision, we can see different options for DRE full-package offers (e.g. a carpenter's shop composed of DRE micro-generator and related components and energy using equipment such as a circular saw and drill); all characterized by the inclusion of services such as design, installation, maintenance, repair and substitution, upgrading and end of-life treatments (result-oriented S.PSS) and/or training courses (use-oriented S.PSS). Consequently, the payment mode may vary in relation to the given offer. Thus, we may see payments made either per use (e.g. hours of carpentry or number of cutting cycles), or fixed and based on period (daily/weekly/monthly payments) or, lastly, based on hybrid modalities.

As in the vision that includes the energy using products, this vision, where energy using equipment is included, there may be various stakeholders in the offer. Two main configurations can be envisioned: at first, the provider could be the energy supplier alone (a multinational energy provider or the local/national public energy supplier), offering both the DRE systems and a set of purchased energy using equipment, which all remain in its ownership. Alternatively, a partnership between the energy supplier and the energy using equipment producers could be established and both the DRE system and the energy using equipment remain in their joint ownership.

The example below shows one possible situation in this vision:

> Ben doesn't have to buy the DRE micro-generator and components or the energy using equipment for his shop. He just pays a fixed rate per period. Ownership and related services stay with the energy supplier who is interested in reducing

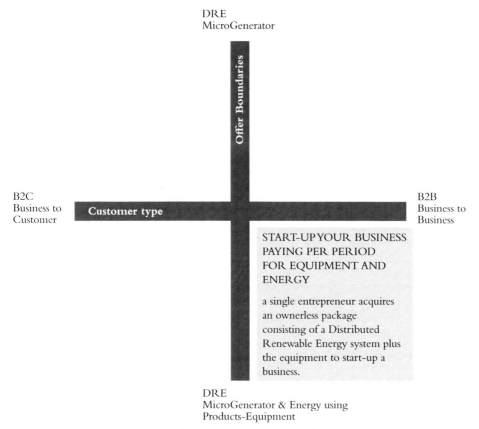

DRE
MicroGenerator

B2C
Business to
Customer

Customer type

Offer Boundaries

B2B
Business to
Business

START-UP YOUR BUSINESS
PAYING PER PERIOD
FOR EQUIPMENT AND
ENERGY

a single entrepreneur acquires
an ownerless package
consisting of a Distributed
Renewable Energy system plus
the equipment to start-up a
business.

DRE
MicroGenerator & Energy using
Products-Equipment

Figure 29.12 Vision 4: 'Start-up your business' paying per period for equipment and energy

maintenance and repair needs, improving their own business while reducing environmental impact.

Finally, the benefits in this vision would be: *reduced resource consumption* offering an ownerless full-package consisting of DRE micro-generator with components and energy using equipment based on distributed, locally produced renewable energy; *optimized system life* offering ownerless working space and related energy using equipment, including running services (e.g. maintenance and upgrade) without additional costs for the entrepreneur/small business and with a vested supplier interest in offering high quality products; *improved employment and working conditions* offering working opportunities to skilled people without initial investment costs; the creation of *partnership/cooperation* among suppliers facilitating the reiteration of the project in other contexts; and, *added value for customers*, in fact a package of services (e.g. design, maintenance, training) is included in the system offer guaranteeing the economic feasibility of the system and consequently energy access.

The Sustainable Design Orienting Scenario development process

After describing the Sustainable Energy for All Design Scenario, this section introduces the process by which it is actually designed. In the first part we describe what is meant in general by Sustainable Design Orienting Scenario (SDOS), its development process and outcomes. In fact, the Sustainable Energy for All Design Scenario is a SDOS that has been developed for the above mentioned set of conditions and aims, and its development process is described in a second paragraph. Finally, the Sustainable Energy for All Design Scenario is described as the tool to be used by designer in the form of a set of evocative videos.

The Sustainable Design Orienting Scenario

The SDOS depicts some possible and promising configurations of partnerships/ interactions among the potential stakeholders of a particular offer system. In this context, socio-cultural, organizational and technological factors are combined to fulfill a particular demand of satisfaction, with a low environmental impact, a high socio-ethical quality and high economic and competitive value. Within a design process, the SDOS can be used for different purposes such as to explore S.PSS opportunities within a specific context, or when proposing sets of possible and potentially sustainable (i.e. economically, environmentally and socio-ethically winning) strategy re-orientations to companies.

An SDOS consists of four visions delineated by the intersection of two axes. Each vision is the result of single ideas collected in clusters (sets of ideas with basic elements in common) and reframed as a schematic narration of promising evolutions in a specific context in relation to sustainability aspects. The scenario composed of those visions constitutes the basis for discussion by which to identify the most promising directions in which to orientate system innovation.

Design process to develop the Sustainable Energy for All Design Scenario

The design process to generate a Sustainable Energy for All Design Scenario has been developed within the LeNSes project, to be used by designers within the new discipline of *System Design for Sustainable Energy for All* (SD4SEA). More precisely, it has been elaborated by the Design and system Innovation for Sustainability (DIS) Research Group[5] in the design department of the *Politecnico di Milano* (one of the partners), along with a master degree thesis.[6]

The Sustainable Energy for All Design Scenario was developed first of all by identifying best practices of S.PSS applied to DRE. Next, by abstraction and generalization, six criteria and an articulated set of guidelines were developed. These were all used in a brainstorming session to generate a multiplicity of ideas of S.PSS applied to DRE.[7] Resulting ideas were then clustered by identifying common elements. Finally, a polarity diagram was drawn, made up of two intersecting axes (two pairs of polarities) displaying four quadrants each identified by two poles, outlining the main characteristics of the visions to be displayed (one vision for each of the four quadrants). These visions together constitute the overall scenario.

 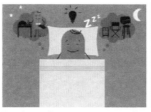 

This is Ben, the local carpenter in the small village, who is very keen to make wood product

Ben has a dream to use a woodworking machine to improve his skills and build a local wood furniture shop

Without financial credit, Ben couldn't get a bank loan for the investment

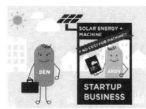 

Finally, he found an event for start up businesses with energy and machine

He didn't understand how the machine and solar panel could work together, probably cost is very high

Figure 29.13 Screenshots from the video *Start-up your business* paying per period for equipment and energy, by Korapan Vanitkoopalangkul. Text is given by voice narration

  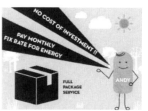

Ben visited the shop to see the real machine with solar power

The woodworking machine comes together with the micro generator of Distributed Renewable Energy

No cost investment, only a monthly fixed rate for energy

Andy explains full service. No cost of machine and solar system, just pay a monthly fixed rate energy cost

You will get everything including full service!

Figure 29.14 Screenshots from the video *Start-up your business* paying per period for equipment and energy, by Korapan Vanitkoopalangkul. Text is given by voice narration

The Sustainable Energy for All Design Scenario as a tool

The Sustainable Energy for All Design Scenario,[8] has been developed as a tool for designers that illustrates some of the possible and promising configurations of S.PSS applied to DRE. In this way, it presents the four visions through a series of interactive videos[9] accessible through a navigator file.

All visions in the Sustainable Energy for All Design Scenario tool are visually presented in one main video, around 90 seconds in duration. It shows a potential narrative story for each vision, highlighting the main advantages and key points of the vision (e.g. stakeholder relations, system ownership). In addition, there are three sub-videos (around 30 seconds each) that highlight the main points of each vision separately: sub-video 1 shows the offer and its payment method; sub-video 2 shows the stakeholders involved and their relations/interactions; and, sub-video 3 shows the sustainability dimensions (environmental, socio-ethical, economic) of the system.[10]

Figures 29.16–29.19 show screenshots from the interactive videos of vision 1, one from each video: main video – the narration; sub-video 1 – the offer and its payment method; sub-video 2 – the stakeholders involved and their relations/interactions; and sub-video 3 – the sustainability dimensions.

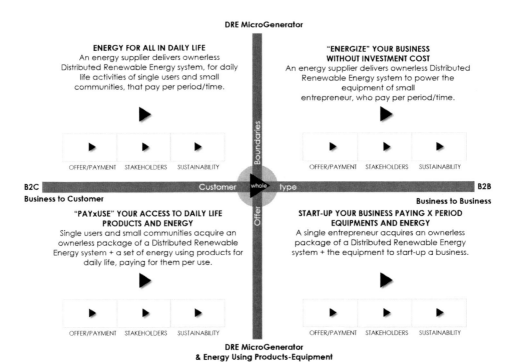

Figure 29.15 Screen shot from the tool: Sustainable Design Orienting Scenario for Sustainable Product-Service System applied to Distributed Renewable Energy

Conclusions

The proposed Sustainable Energy for All Design Scenario offers insights that suggest design options for a radically more sustainable future. At the same time, it calls for a new role, knowledge base and know-how for a new generation of designers (i.e. SD4SEA). This is an emerging discipline promoting a *'stakeholder configuration'* approach, which means designing the interactions of the stakeholders in a particular satisfaction-system, combined with a *'system sustainability and energy 4 all'* approach. The latter means designing stakeholder

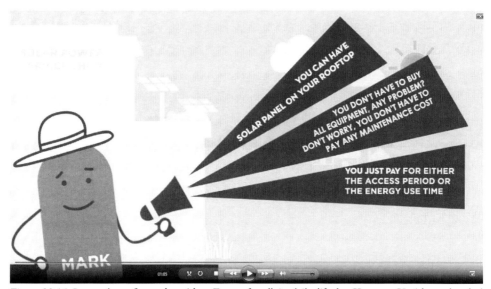

Figure 29.16 Screenshots from the video *Energy for all in daily life*, by Korapan Vanitkoopalangkul (screenshot of main video)

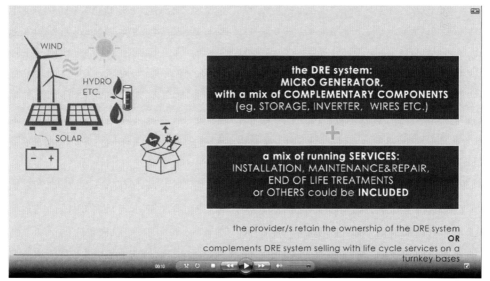

Figure 29.17 Screenshots from the video *Energy for all in daily life*, by Korapan Vanitkoopalangkul (screenshot of sub-video 1)

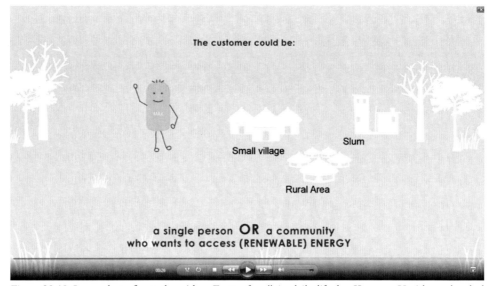

Figure 29.18 Screenshots from the video *Energy for all in daily life*, by Korapan Vanitkoopalangkul (screenshot of sub-video 2)

Figure 29.19 Screenshots from the video *Energy for all in daily life*, by Korapan Vanitkoopalangkul (screenshot of sub-video 3)

interactions (the offer model), which for economic and competitive reasons continuously seek both socio-ethical and environmentally beneficial new solutions that are powered by a DRE system accessible to all.

As part of the LeNSes project, which is currently working to build up a knowledge base and know-how for SD4SEA, some initial, tentative knowledge has been proposed and tested during 4 pilot courses in African HEIs, and will be integrated into the next series of 4 curricular courses in the same HEIs.

Finally, this new set of approaches, tools and skills for designers has started to be considered as an embryonic SD4SEA discipline. This represents a promising contribution to a much-needed key paradigm shift in the energy sector, and many see this as the essential leverage for the transition towards a sustainable society.

Notes

1 Funded by the EU commission, 2013–2016, Edulink II Programme, and coordinated by Carlo Vezzoli of the Politecnico di Milano University (www.lenses.polimi.it).
2 These videos are available for free and in copyleft.
3 See www.lenses.polimi.it/index.php?P=study_cases_select_case.php section case study.
4 The LeNSes project research hypothesis is referred to low and middle-income contexts. Nevertheless, the hypothesis refers even to industrialized contexts; so forth, it can be considered and extended to all contexts.
5 DIS Research Group, Politecnico di Milano, Design Dept., Head Prof. Carlo Vezzoli, researchers Elisa Bacchetti, Emanuela Delfino, Han Shaohua.
6 Master Degree thesis, student Korapan Vanitkoopalangkul (2014), supervised by Prof. Carlo Vezzoli; co-supervised by Francesca Piredda.
7 The SDO Toolkit has been adapted to the new criteria and guidelines and the idea boards of the tools have been used. The tools have been developed by Carlo Vezzoli and Ursula Tischner within the MEPSS EU 5th FP Growth Project.
8 The Sustainable Energy for All Design Scenario is available online in the LeNSes project platform (www.lenses.polimi.it), for free use and download in an open source and copyleft logic, under Creative Commons license.
9 For the purpose of video making, a collaboration with the Imagis Lab (http://imagislab.it/) of the Politecnico di Milano was activated.
10 Sustainability considerations are formulated through the SDO Toolkit – sustainability dimensions and the related criteria. Environmental dimension: system life optimization/transportation-distribution reduction/resources reduction/waste minimization-valorization/conservation/biocompatibility/toxicity reduction; socio-ethical sustainability: improving employment-working conditions/improving equity and justice in relation with stakeholders/enabling responsible-sustainable consumption/favouring-integrating the weak and the marginalized/improving social cohesion/empower-valorize local resources; economic sustainability: market position and competitiveness/profitability-added value for companies/added value for customers/long term business development-risk/partnership-cooperation/macro-economic effect.

References

Barbero, S., Pereno, A. (2013) 'Systemic energy grids: A qualitative approach to smart grids', *Sustainability: The Journal of Record*, vol 6, pp220–226

Colombo, E., Bologna, S., Masera, D. (2013) *Renewable Energy for Unleashing Sustainable Development*, Springer, Berlin

Johansson, A., Kisch, P., Mirata, M. (2005) 'Distributed economies: A new engine for innovation', *Journal of Cleaner Production*, vol 13, pp971–979

Ki-moon, B. (2011) *Sustainable Energy for All: A Vision Statement by Ban Ki-moon, United Nations Secretary-General*, United Nations, New York

Rifkin, J. (2002) *The Hydrogen Economy*, Tarcher, New York

Rifkin, J. (2011) *The Third Industrial Revolution. How Lateral Power Is Transforming Energy, the Economy, and the World*, Palgrave Macmillan, New York

Vezzoli, C., Ceschin, F. (2011) 'The learning network on sustainability: an e-mechanism for the development and diffusion of teaching materials and tools on design for sustainability in an open-source and copy left ethos', *International Journal of Management Education*, vol 5, pp22–43

Vezzoli, C., Kohtala, C., Srinivasan, A., with Diehl, J. C., Moi Fusakul, S., Xin, L. and Sateesh, D. (2014a) *Product-Service System Design for Sustainability*, Greenleaf, London

Vezzoli, C., Delfino, E., Amollo Ambole, L. (2014b) 'System design for sustainable energy for all. A new challenging role for design to foster sustainable development', retrieved from http://dx.doi.org/10-7577/formakademisk.791 (accessed 3 January 2015)

Vezzoli, C., Ceschin, F., Diehl, J. C., Kohtala, C. (2015a) 'New design challenges to widely implement "Sustainable Product Service Systems"', *SV Journal of Cleaner Production*, vol 97, pp1–12

Vezzoli, C., Ceschin, F., Diehl, J. C. (2015b) 'The goal of sustainable energy for all', *SV Journal of Cleaner Production,* vol 97, pp134–136

Vezzoli C., Ceschin F., Diehl J. C., Osanjo, L., M'Rithaa, M., Moalosi, R., Nakazibwe, V. (2015c) 'An African-European network of design universities fostering the goal of sustainable energy for all – An innovative teaching approach based on the combination of Distributed Renewable Energy and design for Sustainable Product-Service Systems', retrieved from http://cedat.mak.ac.ug/news/kidec-2015-more-research-and-solutions-to-design-sources-approaches-and-systems (accessed 23 July 2015)

PART VI

Design futures

The products filling the rooms, cupboards and pockets of our daily lives generate a massive ecological and social burden. Whether the urban space, the building, the glowing television set within or the armchair and slippers pointing at it, designers of things – at all scales – are under increasing pressure to deliver sustainable futures.

Comprising six chapters, this final part draws together previously disconnected scholarship in design ecologies, design futures, social design, design for wellbeing and metadesign. Its contributors collectively develop an argument that shifts economic focus away from anonymous box sales, toward a deeper and more sustained form of user engagement with products, services and experiences; steering our gaze toward an economy where resources are used sustainably through design for longer life, upgrade, re-use and repair; relocating design as an essential driver of social, economic and environmental revolution. Their chapters may be summarized as follows:

30　From good to the greater good – *Anna Pohlmeyer and Pieter Desmet*
　　This chapter shows how material wellbeing – experienced through the ownership of goods – does not necessarily contribute to subjective wellbeing. In contrast, products valued for the activities and experiences they enable can be a profound resource for happiness.
31　Plans and speculated actions: design, behaviour and complexity in sustainable futures – *Dan Lockton and Veronica Ranner*
　　Design that adopts a singular vision of the future does not deal well with the shifting complexities of humanity, culture and society. This chapter explores new ways for design to speculate and plan for sustainability, while embracing this complexity.
32　From product design to relational design: adding 'jeong' to the metadesigner's vocabulary – *John Wood*
　　Reflecting upon designers' roles in an environmentally destructive economy, this chapter notes that design is an integral part of the system needing reform, and calls upon designers to work in more radical, cross-specialist and strategic ways.

33 Products of the open design context – *Paul Micklethwaite*
Open design makes accessible the means of production of our material culture. This chapter considers products in – and of – the open design context, in relation to considerations of sustainability and practices of social and sustainable design.

34 Promoting sustainability through mindful design – *Kristina Niedderer*
This chapter provides an introduction to 'mindful design' and its potential to promote sustainability, and create opportunities for greater reflection and openness to new perspectives in the promotion sustainable product practices and user behaviours.

35 Design for social innovation and new product contexts – *Nicola Morelli*
The role of designers is shifting, from *creators* to *enablers*. To thrive in this expanded role, designers must redefine the conceptual context in which they operate and challenge the assumptions of dominant production and consumption systems.

Much of the work we describe as 'innovation' today is the simple rephrasing of past technologies and their applications. While this rephrasing is inevitable, it is misguided to align the future of product design with these minor tweaks to the status quo. Rather, the future of design must be a more a critical, speculative and dynamic space in which we get to grips with the deep social and ecological implications of our practice; reconnecting us with the essential role of products in cultivating human potential, in socially and ecologically purposeful ways. In this more robust scenario, product design is reinvigorated with a rich culture of critique that directly reinstates it as the central pioneer of positive social, economic and environmental transformation, as opposed to a subservient, end-of-pipe problem-solving agency, as has recently become the custom.

Product designers are essential in this transformational process, due to their innate capacity to imagine a world just beyond our current level of experience, and then formulate (design) plans to realize those imaginings, at scale. Beyond the field of product design, however, there is wider evidence of these practices, and enduring human characteristic, to be found. Whether the selective rearing of high yield livestock, or the genetic modification of a given strain of fungus resistant barley. Through millennia of *striving* to enhance the conditions for life, we have evolved our processes and practices beyond recognition.

Product design is a prospective and exploratory activity that is by its very nature, future-focused. Yet, discussions around futures are always slippery, problematic ones. Despite the evidence base futurologists may refer to, or the insights that underpin their forecasts and speculations, they are informed guesses at best. Design itself can be understood as a propositional practice, which presents alternative interpretations of familiar contexts, and in so doing, shapes parallel realities for users to consider and participate in.

Many futurologists postulate the state of the world 20 years from now, 50 years from now or 100 years from now. Most of us, on the other hand, struggle to describe the world today, exactly as it is, right now. Furthermore, when we talk about futurity, there is a growing preoccupation with emerging technologies, and their commercial potential; a limited discourse in which value and success are measured against an ability to maintain currency with the technological state-of-the-art. Design futures actually have very little to do with these transient, passing moments, and this preoccupation distracts us from the underlying role and purpose of product design as a socially and ecologically transformative activity. Indeed, the future of design is as much to do with rapid manufacture, nanoparticles or advanced robotics, as the future of cooking is to do with the release of higher performance pots and pans.

In a post-awareness-raising era, we must waken from the 100-year spell of a machine-like reality – which promoted fragmentation in our thinking and perception and is inadequate for addressing the complex, interconnected problems of the current age – to reengage the plastic nature of perception, and steer our collective gaze toward a more holistic, expansive vision of an ecological future. The health of our personal and collective mental environment is influenced by the process and product of design. Design is about people. The moment you forget this, you are lost; design loses its meaning, and the made world becomes relegated to a nothing more than a testing ground for emerging technologies. Beyond materials, components, products and spaces, design shapes the human mind, first and foremost. We must look beyond the role of product design as a subordinate solver of disconnected problems, to redefine a more socially and ecologically purposeful definition and understanding of design as a highly connected form of ethical and professional practice.

30

FROM GOOD TO THE GREATER GOOD

Anna Pohlmeyer and Pieter Desmet

Abstract

In this chapter, we outline why and how design can (and cannot) support the sustainable well-being of individuals and communities. Building on findings of well-being researchers, we first address the reasons why material well-being, as experienced through the consumption and ownership of products and goods, does not necessarily contribute to subjective well-being. On the other hand, products that are valued for the activities and experiences that these enable can be a profound resource for happiness. This discussion provides the foundation for an approach to design for well-being that includes three main ingredients: design for pleasure, personal significance and virtue. These ingredients will be detailed in depth and several directions to design for well-being will be introduced, addressing both challenges and opportunities for design theory and practice.

Keywords: design framework, well-being, happiness, experience design, positive design

Introduction

For millennia, design has attempted to improve people's quality of life, and the accelerated technological developments of the last decades have tremendously widened the spectrum of possibilities to do so. Many of us live in a highly designed environment where the majority of our actions are supported and accompanied by products, services and systems designed by humans. In this way, design shapes our lives – from work to leisure, from healthcare and transportation to how we stay connected to the world. This context of design has indisputably made some contribution, making our lives easier and safer as well as providing pleasure, but has it also made our lives more meaningful? In other words: are we *happier* as a result of technological advancement and higher living standards? Unfortunately, empirical data suggests otherwise. For example, while US residents are, materially speaking, much better off than their previous generations (i.e. GNP per capita tripled in the past 50 years), happiness ratings have, on average, essentially remained the same (Diener and Suh, 1997; Easterlin *et al.*, 2010; Helliwell, Layard and Sachs, 2012). This finding, and many other findings like it, not only question the validity of economic growth parameters as indicators for a nation's prosperity, but also the long-term impact of design on people's quality of life and well-being.

Apparently, while designed and purchased with the intention to add value to our daily existence, products and services do not necessarily contribute to our well-being, as is often assumed. Considering that people's quality of life has always been a core value in design theory and practice, it is therefore surprising that design for (psychological) well-being has not been explicitly addressed in the design literature until recently (e.g. Calvo and Peters, 2014; Desmet and Pohlmeyer, 2013; Escobar-Tello, 2011; Hassenzahl *et al.*, 2013). The question of how design can contribute to well-being becomes even more acute when realizing that (next to social inclusion and environmental sustainability) human well-being is a main pillar of sustainable development (Helliwell, Layard and Sachs, 2012). Beyond the ambition to optimize economically sustainable solutions within ecological means, sustainable product design also addresses a more holistic responsibility to design for sustainable societies; thus, including design for well-being and social sustainability. In fact, research has shown (Brown and Kasser, 2005) that sustainable well-being and environmental sustainability are highly compatible as both are derived from intrinsic value orientation (i.e. people who are motivated by values for their own sake such as personal growth, relationships and community involvement in contrast to external incentives such as financial success; Ryan, Huta and Deci, 2008). A society that strives for meaningful experiences and authentic values rather than living in material affluence and driven by short-sighted consumption patterns can combine the three pillars of sustainable development, all at once.

We believe that the design discipline has reached a sufficiently mature theoretical and methodological understanding of how to design simple, as well as pleasurable, solutions in the short term that it is prepared to systematically investigate how to design for long-term impact on people's well-being. We understand design for well-being as the attempt to support people to flourish and to live well. This includes, but also goes beyond, feeling good occasionally (see also Ryan, Huta and Deci, 2008) and, importantly, views people not as consumers but as creators of their own 'good' life. There are many definitions and debates on what constitutes happiness. In our work, we adopt the view that happiness is a combination of experiences of pleasure and purpose (Dolan, 2014), as also aptly put by Lyubomirsky (2007, p32) it is 'the experience of joy, contentment or positive well-being, combined with a sense that one's life is good, meaningful and worthwhile'. The resultant design challenge is, therefore, to create opportunities for people to have pleasurable as well as meaningful experiences supported by design.

This chapter explores the potential and pitfalls of product design to contribute to the sustainable well-being of individuals and communities. Design research on user experiences has moved from a focus on efficiency to pleasure *within* human–product interactions. The next step that we wish to bring forward in this chapter is to support meaningful experiences (in life) *through* human–product interactions. First, we will outline why new activities contribute more to our happiness than new objects, and will argue that objects in turn can be pivotal in mediating activities and experiences. Second, we will describe a design for well-being approach that incorporates the three ingredients of design for pleasure, personal significance and virtue (as previously introduced in Desmet and Pohlmeyer, 2013), and will, in the following, expand on each ingredient separately and in-depth. Third, we will reflect on the framework's integration and implications. A main claim of this chapter is that to design for well-being entails prioritizing indirect effects and intangible values. Opportunities and consequences of this stance for design (processes) will be further discussed.

Why design for experiences

One of the core findings of subjective well-being research is that happiness is much less determined by what we *own* than by what we *do*. In consumer research, this finding has resulted in the well-known 'experience recommendation' (Nicolao, Irwin and Goodman, 2009): if you want to become happier, buy life experiences instead of material items. Numerous studies have shown that doing things (experiential purchases) provides more long-lasting happiness than owning things (material purchases). The experience recommendation seamlessly fits with the 'activity advice' that is voiced in Positive Psychology, which states that to achieve sustainable increases in happiness levels, it is more effective to cultivate favourable, intentional activities than to change one's circumstances (Lyubomirsky, Sheldon and Schkade, 2005). Essentially, both recommendations predict that spending money on activities, like going to a concert, taking a vacation or doing a cooking workshop are better investments in well-being than spending money on a watch, telephone or new shirt.

The underlying mechanism that explains the limited long-term effect on well-being of material objects is called hedonic adaptation: the natural ability of people to adapt to new circumstances (Frederick and Loewenstein, 1999). Hedonic adaptation predicts that no matter how big a circumstantial change is, our happiness will return to a baseline level. So we may be delighted when buying a fancy new smartphone, but this delight fades when we get used to the phone, and it becomes the new reference, the status quo rather than a gain. As a consequence, we require continued increases in material possessions to achieve the same level of well-being. Brickman and Campbell (1971) introduced a treadmill metaphor to describe this effect: people who strive to change their happiness are a bit like rats on a treadmill; they are running and running, but not really getting anywhere. While people eventually adapt to all kinds of changes, hedonic adaptation in relation to buying products (e.g. a bigger house, a more expensive TV screen) has been shown to advance particularly fast (Patterson and Biswas-Diener, 2012). This effect partially explains why it has been repeatedly shown that materialistic people are less happy than people with low materialistic beliefs (Kasser, 2002).

The implication for design seems clear-cut: design for well-being is design that primarily focuses on activities and experiences. After all, the goal of design for well-being as a general field is to have a lasting positive impact on people's lives. This long-term perspective, in line with an emphasis on experiences, challenges prevailing consumption (and design) models.

What that actually means for designers and design processes, however, is less clear-cut because the distinction between experiential and material purchases is not as sharp as it seems. Many products enable gratifying experiences and activities. In fact, Guevarra and Howell (2015) recently showed that buying products that enable experiences (like sports gear and musical instruments) can have a similar well-being effect as buying experiences. This shows that well-being driven design does not require us to abandon material objects, but it does require us to (re)focus our attention on the activities and experiences afforded by these objects. Ergo, if designers only investigate the direct effects of handling a device, the most profound opportunities might be missed. Imagine, for example, playing soccer with your nephew in the backyard on a late summer night. If you reminisce about this experience years later, will you first think of the ball's quality or rather about the fun you had together, the feeling of connectedness, the pride on his face after he scored his first goal? Clearly, the ball is an essential part of this experience (i.e. a resource), but in this case it is not the source of well-being as such. Hence, by acting as a resource that enables or stimulates meaningful or pleasurable activities, design can indirectly affect our well-being. In addition, as symbolic representations design can direct us to positive aspects of our lives or remind us of past meaningful experiences (Pohlmeyer, 2012). These directions open up new design opportunities that require new theories, frameworks and methods to complement those available in traditional interaction design (for an overview, see Jimenez, Pohlmeyer and Desmet, 2015).

Three ingredients to design for well-being

In a previous publication we proposed three main ingredients to design for well-being (i.e. Positive Design): design for pleasure, design for personal significance and design for virtue (Desmet and Pohlmeyer, 2013), as visualized in the framework in Figure 30.1. We proposed that, while each ingredient independently stimulates subjective well-being, the intersection is where people flourish: besides having positive emotions, an individual must also have a sense of meaning, engagement, interest, and purpose in life to truly thrive (Dolan, 2014; Lyubomirsky, 2007; Seligman, 2011; Seligman *et al.*, 2005; Sirgy and Wu, 2009). Consequently, while each of the three design ingredients can serve as a guide in designing for well-being, design for flourishing takes all three into consideration.

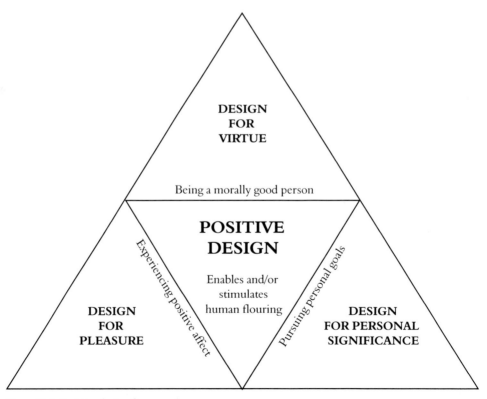

Figure 30.1 Positive design framework

Source: adapted from Desmet and Pohlmeyer (2013)

Design for pleasure

In the introduction to this chapter, we argued that there is more to happiness than 'feeling good'. Our intention was to stress that the importance of positive emotions should not be overestimated. However, it is equally important to not underestimate their contribution to happiness. In fact, positive experiences are a central part of well-being. A life exclusively devoted to personal growth and serving a greater good without experiencing joys in life does not appear fulfilling: lasting happiness is found in a balance of both pleasure and purpose (Dolan, 2014; Lyubomirsky, 2007; Sirgy and Wu, 2009) and in experiences that are beneficial in the present as well as in the future (Ben-Shahar, 2008). There is ample evidence that positive emotions make an independent and direct contribution to well-being (Seligman, 2011). Moreover, they have additional appealing, indirect effects that, in turn, contribute to happiness, such as enhanced creativity, open-mindedness, flexibility and resilience (Fredrickson, 2001; Isen, Daubman and Nowicki, 1987). Hence, design that increases the frequency of conscious experiences of positive emotions and decreases those of negative experiences makes an important contribution to people's well-being. We refer to this contribution as *design for pleasure*.

In the *Oxford English Dictionary*, pleasure is defined as:

> the condition or sensation induced by the experience or anticipation of what is felt to be good or desirable; a feeling of happy satisfaction or enjoyment; delight, gratification. Opposed to pain.

The concept of pleasure is broad because there are many different causes of pleasure (i.e. things that can be considered enjoyable). A person can enjoy the bodily sensations of taking a warm bath, the challenge of an intellectual debate, the time spent with a dear friend or the idea of moving to a new city. Tiger (1992) offered a structure to these broad ideas by distinguishing between four pleasures that differ in terms of underlying causes. They include physio-pleasure (sensual delight), psycho-pleasure (derived from satisfying the intellect), ideo-pleasure (pleasures linked to people's values and ideals), and socio-pleasure (feeling connected to others and/or to society as a whole). Jordan (2000) successfully introduced this model to the design discipline, showing that all four pleasures can be experienced when using a product and that each can be consciously designed for. Not only the causes but also the experiences of pleasure are widely diverse. People can experience a wide range of positive emotions. For instance, Desmet (2012) identified 25 different positive emotions that can be experienced in human–product interactions. These include experiences that appear light and simple, such as joy, surprise and amusement, as well as some that are seen as more complex and substantial, such as pride, love and relief as they connect to deep-seated ideals, achievements and social values. Our point is not to suggest a hierarchy among pleasures, but to emphasize the diversity and profoundness that pleasure can entail.

Products can serve various roles in our pursuit of pleasure. Perhaps the most obvious is that they can be a direct source of pleasure – for what they are, symbolize or represent. One can enjoy the texture of a sweater, the smell of a new book, the craftsmanship of a chair and the innovativeness of an intelligent bracelet. Likewise, one can enjoy the refinement and ease of use of well-designed software and the challenge of playing a computer game. Because sometimes assumed otherwise, we should stress that these pleasures are not necessarily superficial. Surely, some may be considered shallow or frivolous, like the thrill of riding a roller coaster or the pleasure of eating candy. But product pleasures just as much include experiences that are profound and impactful, like the awe experienced at the sight of a Pollock masterpiece or the experience of gratitude for having a pacemaker that enables one to travel. As a second role, products can act as resources for activities that provide pleasure. Here, the individual does not take pleasure in the product itself, but in the activity in which the product is used. A hand-blown wine glass can be enjoyed for its beauty, but it also facilitates an enjoyable social interaction (see also Figure 30.2). Likewise, painting brushes enable inspiring moments of self-expression, and airline services enable adventurous holidays. An interesting additional contribution of design is that it can stimulate people to be more aware of their positive emotions and to savour their experiences. In his seminal work, Maslow (1954, p136) observed that 'self-actualizing people have the wonderful capacity to appreciate again and again, freshly and naively, the basic goods of life, with awe, pleasure, wonder, and even ecstasy, however stale these experiences may have become to others'. Design can stimulate one's capacity for appreciation. Pohlmeyer (2014) explores how design can support people to deliberately pay attention to positive experiences in order to enhance and prolong the positive emotions derived from the event and thereby to delay hedonic adaptation. A wedding guestbook invites people to reminisce about the day many years later, the light of a candle enhances the atmosphere of a romantic dinner and social media platforms allow sharing personal highlights with others. Too often we take things for granted; too soon and hastily we strive for the next new thing. This includes the fascination over the extra space in our new apartment, the pride in our recent accomplishments at work as well as the pleasure of newly acquired products.

Above, we reflected on how products can contribute to well-being by acting as a (re)source for positive experiences. We should mention that design can also contribute by reducing

Figure 30.2 Bits 'n' Bytes by Marije Vogelzang: a low-tech conveyer belt to pass on delicious food (physio-pleasure) and stimulate social interaction (socio-pleasure)

Source: photograph by Fred Ernst

displeasure or negative emotions. Researchers have found the measure of 'affect balance' (i.e. the sum of positive emotions experienced minus the sum of negative emotions experienced) to be more informative than solely positive emotions. It is a matter of relativity – flourishing people experience relatively more positive emotions than negative emotions (Fredrickson and Losada, 2005). Hence, even if someone encounters many positive experiences throughout the day, should these be outweighed by negative experiences, this will have an overall detrimental effect on that person's happiness level. Many design efforts focus on reducing displeasures and negative emotions (e.g. making a chair less uncomfortable and introducing safety devices like helmets). However, negative emotions can be valuable too and are sometimes inevitable. In contrast to the philosophical movement of utilitarianism that seeks a maximization of pleasure and minimization of pain, our understanding of design for well-being takes a more holistic approach by accepting that negative experiences are part of life and should not be abandoned per se. For instance, guilt is an important emotion to indicate moral norms, grief is a manifestation that one cares, and under certain circumstances some fear can even add to enjoyment in creating rich experiences (Fokkinga and Desmet, 2012). Finally, just as negative emotions can be positive in the larger picture, so too, can positive emotions have a negative connotation. For instance, lust and confidence are not positive per se. Think of an abusive situation or of someone who overestimates his competencies, which might lead to risky (for himself) or annoying (for others) behaviour. To determine an emotion's true valence, the situational, social and cultural context, as well as the extent and manner of expression need to be taken into consideration. We call for a sensible and balanced, user-centred design approach that considers contextual factors along with long-term consequences and moral standards.

This section has shown that emotions are a critical part of being human, and of our well-being, and that design for pleasure is a multi-faceted, nuanced endeavour that can contribute to well-being in many ways. Momentary positive emotions alone, however, would draw only a fragmented picture of what it takes for people to truly flourish. In the following sections, we extend our model with the well-being ingredients of personal significance and virtue that add experiences of meaning and purpose in life.

Design for personal significance

People are born with a natural tendency to grow and develop. We all have an innate striving towards actualizing our personal potentials, whatever they might be. As a consequence, we seek out novelty and challenge, explore and learn, exercise and develop our capacities. We often do so by committing to longer-term 'personal goals' that serve as a platform for expressing and developing our desires and deeply held values. These can be all kind of goals, such as getting a diploma, building a miniature city, raising children or mastering the craft of molecular cooking (e.g. for an overview of 135 inter- and intrapersonal goals see Chulef, Read and Walsh, 2001). Personal goals differ between people and may change over time, but the clue is that having (and working towards) them is a profound source of happiness (Lyubomirsky, 2007). They do so for a variety of reasons. First, they provide us with a general sense of purpose and meaning. Second, committing to goals stimulates vitality, gives direction and structure to our daily lives, giving us something to work for. Finally, goals support us in developing our personalities, helping us to connect possible futures and past achievements into a coherent sense of self (Sheldon and Elliot, 1999).

The second ingredient of design for well-being addresses the sense of *personal significance* that is derived from the pursuit and accomplishment of personal goals: design that supports us in living the life that we want to live, doing what we find worth doing and being the person that we want to be. Hence, it moves from a focus on experiencing pleasure in the moment to one of experiencing meaning in the longer term. Before we address how design can contribute in various ways, we should first note that some goals, when achieved, engender more well-being than others. In other words, it matters what goals people select. It has been shown that when people select less favourable goals, they may waste much time and energy trying to approach possible futures that, even if attained, turn out to be empty or even harmful (Kasser, 2002; Sheldon and Kasser, 1999). Goals that have been empirically shown to be particularly beneficial for one's happiness are:

- *approach-oriented* towards something desirable (as opposed to avoiding a negative outcome) (Coats, Janoff-Bulman and Alpert, 1996);
- related to an *activity* rather than to circumstances and possessions as the latter are especially prone to hedonic adaptation (Sheldon and Lyubomirsky, 2006); and
- *intrinsically motivated* (as opposed to external pressure) and express *authentic, deep-seated values* (Ryan *et al.*, 1996; Sheldon and Elliot, 1999).[1]

A person's values are his or her beliefs about what behaviour and end-states are desirable. They transcend specific situations or activities and serve as guiding principles that help us make personal decisions (Schwartz, 1994). Examples of such values include protecting the environment, enjoying life, safety, social power, freedom, tolerance, creativity and tradition. Different people have different values. Yet, as shown above, some are more favourable than others, depending on the underlying motivation. In a similar vein, while acknowledging interpersonal differences, Ryan, Huta and Deci (2008) propose that activities related to the values of personal growth, relationships, community and health are typically profound sources of well-being. Hence, although personal goals are, by definition, personal and thus a matter of subjective preferences, evidence-based recommendations regarding what kind of goals and values to pursue can be additionally taken into consideration to increase the resulting well-being effects.

Having personal goals with a maximum net gain of happiness is not necessarily evident or easy. People may not be aware of their personal values, or these may be obscured by values that are imposed on them by others, media and industry, or they may not know how to formulate goals that reflect their values (Schmuck and Sheldon, 2001). Moreover, even if they commit to favourable goals, it often requires courage to embrace them and willpower to balance conflicting goals and resist the temptations of short-term goals with immediate gratification that endanger longer-term goal attainment (Hofmann *et al.*, 2012; Metcalfe and Mischel, 1999). Equally important is the notion that personal goals are supported (rather than hindered) by external conditions, including educational, economic and social resources (Deci and Ryan, 1985). This means that, even if a personal goal is authentic, when circumstances prevent us from making progress towards attaining the goal, it will be a source of ill-being rather than well-being.

In our pursuit of personal goals, products can serve as resources. For example, musical instruments enable musicians to develop their talent, while running shoes support the development of an athlete's individual running technique and overall performance. Moreover, products can also help us to stay committed to these goals. They can act as reminders for our current goals. Having a piano not only enables us to develop our musical abilities, but having it in the living room makes it a positive reminder of our aspiration to learn how to play the piano. In the case of conflicting goals, products can support to

Figure 30.3 Kitchen Safe by David Krippendorf: a time-locking container, designed to support self-control

Source: www.TheKitchenSafe.com

harmonize goals by moderating and resolving dilemmas, or trigger reflection by the user (Ozkaramanli, Desmet and Özcan, 2015). Studies by Ozkaramanli and colleagues focus on corresponding design strategies (e.g. reducing temptations by introducing barriers or making long-term goals more attractive). For example, a healthy diet stands in contrast to the urge to snack on sweets. Here, a barrier of a jar lock and timer could be added to restrict the user to only indulge in 'bad' habits at a pre-committed time (see Kitchen Safe by David Krippendorf in Figure 30.3).

Products can also lower the threshold to commit to particular goals. A starter kit for molecular cooking, for example, can break down the complexity of the undertaking, opening up the activity to people who previously believed it to be technically beyond them. Design can support motivation, for example, by adding sources of pleasure or by enabling achievement of smaller sub-goals. Complex Lego models are designed to enable children to quickly establish an initial achievement (e.g. building a vehicle) while working to the completion of the larger model (e.g. building a city with many vehicles and other more complex elements). Likewise, online course accountancy, for example, can be designed to include little moments of pleasure that stimulate commitment. A final contribution of products is that they can strengthen our awareness of one's past achievements or of one's progress towards a future goal. Someone may hold on to his worn-out dancing shoes because they serve as a tangible representation of his efforts to become a ballroom dancer (Casais, Mugge and Desmet, 2015). Likewise, trophies and souvenirs can serve as reminders of our past achievements, keeping these vivid by making them touchable and perceptible (Belk, 1988).

Note that enjoyment too can be an authentic personal value, and in that case, people can experience significance from activities that provide pleasure. Moreover, pursuing meaningful goals can be pleasurable in itself (see *ideo-pleasure* in Tiger, 1992). In other words, while pleasure and significance are conceptually different sources of well-being, they can co-exist and strengthen each other.

This section has shown that while design contributes to well-being by playing a role in our pursuit of pleasure ('am I enjoying life?'), it also contributes by playing a role in our pursuit of personal significance ('am I living the life that I want to live?'). We experience a sense of significance when committing to goals that support our personal values. Design can act as a resource for these activities, and it can also symbolize personal values and past achievements.

Design for virtue

To experience momentary pleasures and to live a life in accordance with one's personally significant goals accounts for a great deal of our well-being. This, however, describes a very subjective perspective of what one expects from life; it does not include what one gives back to society, nor does it include a normative stance as to what is right or wrong to expect or how to act in the first place. Does it matter how I reach my goals, and is it at all of importance what kind of person I am? Indeed, the question of morality must not be neglected in a discourse on well-being.

Building on virtue ethics that go back to Aristotle's *Nicomachean Ethics*, but have recently regained attention (e.g. through Alasdair MacIntyre's work *After Virtue*, 2010), the third ingredient of design for well-being is *virtue*. While virtues are also closely connected to values, they are distinct from personal significance in three key aspects:

- virtues are derived from *objective* lists of universally agreed-upon values;
- they have a *moral* stance; and
- they describe what constitutes the good *character* of a person, thus an inherent part of their personality.

In other words, virtues are character traits of a person ('what kind of a person am I?') that are morally valued in religion, philosophy and cultural traditions ('am I behaving honourably?') and advance the good of others as well as of the self. Consequently, to design for virtues not only affects the lives of individuals, but also affects people in interaction and, ultimately, society at large.

One list has been proposed by Peterson and Seligman (2004) who identified six core virtues that emerge across history in the traditions of China (Confucianism and Taoism), South Asia (Buddhism and Hinduism), and the West (Athenian philosophy, Judaism, Christianity and Islam): *wisdom and knowledge, courage, humanity, justice, temperance,* and *transcendence.* While virtues are at the highest level of abstraction, the authors further specify 24 more concrete positive traits[2] that are manifest in a range of behaviours and that define the respective, universal virtues. For example, the virtue of humanity is operationalized with the traits love, kindness and social intelligence. The classification system covers a variety of perspectives: from cognitive (e.g. curiosity), emotional (e.g. bravery), interpersonal (e.g. kindness), and civic (e.g. fairness) to those that protect against excess (e.g. self-regulation) and provide meaning (e.g. gratitude) (Peterson and Seligman, 2004). Many other lists exist and can be consulted. However, due to its overarching nature, detailed description and scientifically based assessment measures, we believe that this list is a valuable entry point for designers.

Aristotle argued that virtues are not a means to happiness, but fulfilling in themselves; happiness is simply a by-product of a virtuous life. As designers, we feel comfortable to make use of this side benefit. In particular, as an important prerequisite for design holds: virtues are not inborn. Instead, they are the result of our upbringing, (social) practices, training, and instruction. This means that they are, although relatively stable once established, in principle capable of change (Peterson and Seligman, 2004) and therefore also malleable through design. Clearly, a person's character itself – just like happiness as such – cannot be designed. However, a person is always situated in a physical and social context, which in turn can be designed.

Design can create enabling (as well as hindering) conditions (Peterson and Seligman, 2004) to trigger, train and establish virtuous behaviours. It starts with the everyday objects, services and buildings that already surround us. These can be designed to support the development and manifestation of virtues by facilitating corresponding practices, offering opportunities of training, supporting decision-making[3] and providing instruction recommendations. This, for example, has been particularly well demonstrated in religions by the design and reverence of artefacts (e.g. bible, prayer beads), rituals (e.g. meditation, fasting during the month of Ramadan), places (e.g. Temple Mount), and the built environment (e.g. synagogue, temple, altar, confessional box) (see de Botton, 2013, for an intriguing review). In the secular world, in contrast, fairly little effort has been put into the design and establishment of virtues in our daily lives. For instance, although schools try to foster the development of children, the primary focus lies on learning intellectual knowledge, skills and abilities, but not on morality and personality. How would a school, a classroom or a curriculum be designed if the learning goals would be social intelligence, humour or modesty? The way a classroom is designed affects how (and what) students learn. Traditionally, a teacher stands in front of a class where he or she presents information while students are expected to take notes individually. The fixation of chair and table arrangements solely to the front in some lecture halls might be efficient in terms of tidiness, but discards the opportunity of interactive learning with peers. In contrast, a recently renovated lecture room at our university (TU Delft) was designed in such a way that students can connect with classmates to the left, right, in front and behind themselves within seconds, allowing them to practise, among others, teamwork, collaboration, and perspective (see Figure 30.4). As mentioned earlier, design will have an effect on consumers and end users whether they want it or not – designers, in turn, have the responsibility to carefully envision and support desirable effects to the best of their knowledge.

Despite the direct advantages of behaving nobly, more than the outcome of virtuous acts it is a person's motive behind these that determine their goodness. In other words, virtues are morally valued, independent of outcome. One can think of multiple ways in which design can accelerate and increase desirable outcomes. Yet, ultimately, the person has to be responsible for the behaviour and outcome in order for it to be a reflection of his or her character and to have a well-being effect for the individual. With regards to environmental sustainability, temperance and related positive traits that protect against excess come to mind. Technology that automatically down-regulates heating and relies on green energy, design that saves on packaging or opts for biodegradable materials and sharing platforms are all valuable, indispensable and effective examples of sustainable design that focus on outcome. Without doubt, these approaches and outcomes are of great value. However, in addition, we would like to point out that in design for well-being that supports the development of a good character a person needs to take responsibility and ownership of actions and needs to make decisions him/herself. Examples of when a person cultivates the virtue of temperance

Figure 30.4 Classroom layouts for individual, teacher-centred learning and teamwork, respectively

(and justice) are when she deliberately chooses fair-trade products or becomes a member of a sharing community, and when she (re)uses her products as long as they are still functioning and not harmful to the environment. Design can help people in making good decisions by, for instance, showing the choice of alternatives or providing feedback that triggers reflection (Jimenez Garcia, 2014; Laschke, Diefenbach and Hassenzahl, 2015), but in order to have a well-being effect products should not make decisions on their user's behalf. The advantage of this perhaps seemingly slow approach in contrast to more efficient, automatic solutions is that once a character is formed, it leads to favourable habits that last in the long run (e.g. to turn the lights off when leaving home) and is fairly stable across situations (e.g. one will also turn the lights off at the office). When a character is formed, it is shown in any kind of interaction – someone who loves to learn will not only show this trait for the upcoming exam that is critical for one's future career goals, but also when visiting a museum or talking to friends. Stability and ownership of desirable decisions and actions safeguard lasting well-being effects and – importantly – release the person from a dependency on the design.

In relation to the Positive Design framework, objectively recommended virtues can certainly also be of personal significance to the extent that these relate to the same values. In particular, while all virtues can contribute to one's well-being, some positive traits have a better personal fit than others. These so-called 'signature strengths' (Peterson and Seligman, 2004) are a person's top strengths: they feel most authentic to a person ('this is the real me'), are intrinsically motivated, and exceptionally fulfilling. They are thus concordant with one's personal interests and values. Research has shown a strong link between signature strengths and well-being (Seligman *et al.*, 2005). One explanation for this link is that strengths support goal attainment (Linley *et al.*, 2010), which in turn also benefits personal significance. Furthermore, as virtues are, by definition, fulfilling in their own right, they themselves can also be a source of pleasure. By putting one's signature strengths to use in a variety of situations and domains, one is most likely to flourish.

In summary, design for virtue can help *initiate* the development of a good character through instructions (e.g. signs for priority seats in a bus), it can provide *enabling conditions to practise* and *internalize* the manifestation of virtues in decision-making and behaviour and provide corresponding *feedback*. However, eventually, as a virtue becomes part of a person's character, such design facilitators will no longer be needed. They can still have a supportive function, but the user acts independently. It is with this view on design as a resource that we hope design can support responsible, active and virtuous citizens to live well in a sustainable society.

Framework integration and implications

Well-being is a complex concept that also necessitates a somewhat more elaborate approach in design. In short, pleasure is about what one enjoys, personal significance is about what one wants and virtues are part of a person's character that is manifested in interactions with the world and considered morally good. The three well-being ingredients all have their unique contribution to well-being that cannot be fully compensated by the other two. As shown in Table 30.1, pleasure, significance and virtue share a number of overlapping attributes, however, in different combinations.

The Positive Design framework integrates different perspectives on the central question of what constitutes happiness and the good life from psychology and philosophy. Its aim is to flesh out those ingredients that are promising and needed when designing for well-being in order to:

Table 30.1 Differences and similarities of well-being ingredients

	Pleasure	*Significance*	*Virtue*
Temporality	in the present	future and past	constant
Focus	emotions	personal values and goals; (life) satisfaction	universal values; morality; character
Experience evoked	pleasure	meaning	meaning
Perspective	subjective	subjective	objective
Related discipline	psychology	psychology	philosophy

1 Understand well-being of people holistically
2 Provide guidance on what (not) to design for
3 Structure the corresponding design process

Each of these components is discussed below.

Understanding well-being of people holistically

A holistic understanding of well-being allows the consideration of short- as well as long-term goals, pleasure as well as meaning and subjective as well as objective standards. A nuanced understanding of pleasure in people's lives, of the diversity of goals, of the impact people have on their surroundings as well as the interplay of all three, equips designers to provide more fitting solutions to stimulate human flourishing than by only addressing one component of well-being. Each ingredient can contribute to one aspect of happiness, but only a balanced life that includes all three perspectives is one in which people flourish. Different designs might have different emphases, the collective of designs, however, should strive for a balance of pleasure, personal significance and virtue. Preferably, all three are combined in one solution. In an earlier publication (Desmet and Pohlmeyer, 2013), we referred to this combination as the sweet spot of Positive Design.

Overlap can evolve on different levels: each ingredient can be combined with one of the other two as well as with both. Activities that reflect our values and connect to personally significant goals are both meaningful and pleasurable. Snowboarding can be a pleasurable sport for someone who finds meaning in being connected to nature and who wants to be physically active. Emotions signal what is important to us – someone who values customs and traditions might get excited when unwrapping the Christmas ornaments to decorate the tree, cheerfully singing along. Positive emotions can also be motivating to commit to goals and values even in the face of difficulty, uncertainty or disappointment. A steep slope is no guarantee for immediate success in the snowboard example; it might take several attempts before one masters this route gracefully. Yet, the anticipation of becoming one with the mountain can provide the motivation not to give up. Positive emotions can be strategically used in the short term to reach a long-term (meaningful) effect. As people might experience that it is difficult to delay gratification (Metcalfe and Mischel, 1999) or to make long-term goals viable in everyday behaviour, design could create pleasurable moments to motivate people to act and thereby implicitly pursue a long-term goal. Furthermore, the expression of virtues can be pleasurable, like bravery in the snowboard example. Although values and virtues can be both intrinsically motivated and therefore not pursued for the sake of positive emotions, these certainly enrich an experience. Finally, virtues can be personally significant and ideally manifested through signature strengths.

Overall, Positive Design is an approach focused on the subjective experience of people paired with universal, moral values as well as evidence-based recommendations.

Providing guidance on what (not) to design for

Most designs intend to improve people's quality of life in one way or another. Positive Design approaches this goal systematically by scrutinizing how design can be relevant to people's psychological well-being. Here, the explicit long-term well-being effect is the key driver in practice as well as in research. Previous work on usability and user experience focused primarily on short-term efficiency, functional effectiveness and the immediate hedonic consequences of human–product interactions. The fundamental mechanisms of information processing and experience are largely applicable for any effect. Thus, they hardly give guidance in terms of what to design, but rather how. For example, the design of input devices and dialogue principles can be used for a games console just as for nuclear weapons. Positive Design is a specialized field that makes use of the fundamentals of interaction design, but always in relation to well-being.

The Positive Design framework holds that in addition to positively addressing pleasure, personal significance and virtue, it is also important that none are violated. This means that a solution should not introduce displeasure or pain that is not in support of an overall pleasurable experience, nor should it infringe someone's values or stimulate feelings of pointlessness, and it should not hinder the development of virtues or encourage vices. If someone derives pleasure from tyrannizing others, it is considered immoral. Consequently, a design supporting such behaviour would not be seen as Positive Design even though pleasure and personal significance are met and might subjectively please this specific user. Hence, although Positive Design is an inherently user-centred approach, it does not imply that users' desires should be supported at all costs.

By incorporating virtues and rejecting violations within the framework, Positive Design is one of the very few models of user experience to include a moral stance, expressing what (not) to design for (value-sensitive design is a notable exception – see Friedman, 1996).

Structuring the corresponding design process

Sooner or later the rather abstract concepts of the framework have to become concrete and actionable in a design process. How can one deliberately design for happiness, and what steps constitute a Positive Design approach? We expect that available user-centred design methods are equally usable for happiness-driven design. As in all user-centred approaches, designs that aim to contribute to user well-being need to be tailored to a defined target group and contextualized accordingly. Yet, something is different in a Positive Design approach, and that is the rank order of priorities. Rather than working one's way up from technical requirements, to interactive elements, to finally experiential consequences, the direction is flipped in Positive Design: the higher goal of pleasurable and/or meaningful experiences is guiding the design process from the start, which results in a metaphorically speaking top-down approach as elaborated in the following.

All products affect how people behave and experience the world, and these effects are both direct (enjoying lightweight hiking shoes) and indirect (enjoying a mountain hike with these shoes) (e.g. Verbeek, 2005). Fokkinga *et al.* (2014) proposed two corresponding 'levels of influence' of the designer. The first level includes everything that happens between the user and the product: how products are perceived, used and experienced. The second level includes all the behaviours and experiences that the product facilitates, enables, leads to, supports or promotes, but in which the product itself is no longer the main focus. Traditionally, design briefs detail requirements for the first level of influence. For example, a brief for a new racing bike can include requirements about ease of storage and cleaning, smoothness of the gears and novelty of appearance. These requirements define the design space for the design's objective properties, such as colour, weight and material. The resulting design is evaluated in terms of this first level, often without considering the wider effects on experience and behaviour, and finally quality of life. In the case of the racing bike, the user may enjoy having racing weekends in the mountains, become increasingly healthy and savour new achievements. These secondary effects can be taken for granted (because it is assumed that this is what racing bikes are about), seen as a bonus (that marketing can capitalize on) or not considered at all. We propose that design for well-being requires us to overturn the chain of events from technical details to interaction effects and finally to the overall effect level, and to instead 'start from the top'. Positive Design requires us to formulate our initial design intentions on the level of resultant, long-term impact. Naturally, for a design to be successful, technical details and direct effects are also vitally important, but if one does not start with determining intentions at the top level, one may never reach it or may introduce features that distract from or contradict the design's essence. This means that design for well-being requires us to first imagine the experiences and activities that will be enabled and facilitated by the product before starting to design the objective properties of a given product. Hence, here function follows experience, and means follow function.

The Positive Design framework has three corners (see Figure 30.1), and each can be taken as the point of departure when formulating design intentions. Which corner to start with and/or prioritize depends on the particular project, including the user group, type of design, the designer and the client. For some products it may be useful to first explore pleasures (e.g. entertainment products), and for others to start with exploring virtues (e.g. products that aim to motivate pro-social interactions) or personal significance (e.g. design for behaviour change). Either way, we propose that in a second instance, the remaining two ingredients need to be considered too, for Positive Design to be achieved.

The key here is that pleasure, personal significance and virtues depend on both the user, and the context of use. Hence, one needs to determine or envision which pleasures, personal goals and virtues are most suitable for the given design project through an inherently user-centred design approach. In addition, objective and evidence-based recommendations from psychology can be consulted to determine which virtues are most fitting (signature strengths) and which goals are most favourable (authentic and intrinsically motivated) to optimally boost long-term well-being.

Conclusion

In his book *Flourish*, Martin Seligman notes that 'the task of positive psychology is to describe, rather than prescribe, what people actually do to get well-being' (Seligman, 2011, p20). Design can be inspired by the resulting insights, but it cannot merely describe – design mediates people's lives (Verbeek, 2005) and will always be prescriptive to a certain extent. This comes as a powerful opportunity to have impact, and, at the same time, comes with the corresponding responsibility.

Positive Design outlines a design future that moves from designing for short-term user satisfaction to long-term human well-being. It combines the vast amount of knowledge developed in user experience design with empirical evidence of positive psychology (i.e. the science of happiness). It aims to give direction on what (not) to design in order to foster sustainable development in terms of human well-being.

At the core, Positive Design is a user-centred design approach. Yet, it requires a reconsideration of existing design principles and approaches. For one, Positive Design takes a holistic approach by incorporating the well-being components of pleasure, personal significance and virtue, which have been detailed in this chapter. We advocate an integration of all three ingredients to stimulate a balance of pleasure and purpose in life and, thereby, human flourishing. Our epistemological approach is a triangulation of perspectives from the user and context itself, paired with objective lists of virtues from philosophy, coupled with evidence-based recommendations from psychology. This complexity affects new demands of analysis and synthesis in the design process.

Furthermore, rather than focusing on the direct impact and material value of a design (as a source), designers should envision the indirect impact of a design (as a resource) by supporting activities and experiences in order to foster well-being. This intended overall effect should be the entry point and leading direction in a design process that all subsequent decisions relate to – a reprioritizing of the design process. Positive Design is thus not simply a label to attach, but a fundamentally new design approach. It is a way to look at the world in relation to design. As it mainly functions as a resource for well-being and emphasizes indirect effects, it is not a niche-approach, but applicable to all domains and technical means (e.g. analogue, digital, product, service) as long as the intended effect can be achieved. Although the design intentions might sound grand, the solutions themselves can address simple interactions and practices in everyday life (e.g. cooking, driving, and even shopping). In other words, looking through a well-being lens can benefit any design for users.

Design for well-being also requires active user involvement. To achieve an increase in people's well-being in the long run, people should not expect to 'be pleased', but rather to engage in activities from which they will derive pleasure and meaning. Users thus need to put effort into the activities and ought to be actively involved in the experience in order to take ownership of its well-being effect. Put differently, one cannot passively consume well-being, and the good life is not about optimizing decisions on behalf of the user and providing favourable circumstances. It is a way of living that design can facilitate, but one that a person has to be responsible for in the end. Consequently, design has to walk the line of supporting the user while safeguarding authenticity of the experience. In this vein, design empowers people to live a life of individual, and ideally collective, well-being.

Positive Design is still a nascent theory and more work needs to be done to refine a structured approach to Positive Design and the specification of design effects. Yet, we believe the framework can already serve designers as a source of inspiration and guidance that stimulates design thinking beyond the direct, short-term impact of the product to truly and lastingly enhance people's quality of life.

Notes

1 Sheldon and Elliot (1999) refer to these goals as being *self-concordant*.
2 Peterson and Seligman (2004, p13) refer to these traits as *character strengths*: 'Character strengths are the psychological ingredients – processes and mechanisms – that define virtues.'
3 I.e. practical wisdom (Schwartz and Sharpe, 2010): the ability to judge what is the right thing to do.

References

Belk, R. (1988) 'Possessions and the extended self', *Journal of Consumer Research*, vol 15, no 2, pp139–168

Ben-Shahar, T. (2008) *Happier: can you learn to be happy?*, McGraw-Hill, Maidenhead

Brickman, P., and Campbell, D. T. (1971) 'Hedonic relativism and planning the good society', in Appley, M. H. (ed.), *Adaptation level theory: a symposium*, Academic Press, New York

Brown, K. W. and Kasser, T. (2005) 'Are psychological and ecological well being compatible? The role of values, mindfulness, and lifestyle', *Social Indicators Research*, vol 74, pp349–368

Calvo, R. and Peters, D. (2014) *Positive computing: technology for wellbeing and human potential*, MIT Press, Cambridge, MA

Casais M., Mugge R. and Desmet P. M. A. (2015) 'Extending product life by introducing symbolic meaning: an exploration of design strategies to support subjective well-being', *Proceedings of 2015 PLATE conference*, Nottingham Trent University, Nottingham, pp44–51

Chulef, A. S., Read, S. J. and Walsh, D. A. (2001) 'A hierarchical taxonomy of human goals', *Motivation and Emotion*, vol 25, pp191–232

Coats, E. J., Janoff-Bulman, R. and Alpert, N. (1996) 'Approach versus avoidance goals: differences in self-evaluation and well-being', *Personality and Social Psychology Bulletin*, vol 22, No 10, pp1057–1067

De Botton, A. (2012) *Religion for atheists*, Penguin Books, London

Deci, E. L. and Ryan, R. M. (1985) *Intrinsic motivation and self-determination in human behavior*, Plenum, New York

Desmet, P. M. A. (2012) 'Faces of product pleasure: 25 positive emotions in human–product interactions', *International Journal of Design*, vol 6, no 2, pp1–29

Desmet, P. M. A. and Pohlmeyer, A. E. (2013) 'Positive design: an introduction to design for subjective well-being', *International Journal of Design*, vol 7, no 3, pp5–19

Diener, E. and Suh, E. (1997) 'Measuring quality of life: economics, social, and subjective indicators', *Social Indicators Research*, vol 40, pp189–216

Dolan, P. (2014) *Happiness by design: change what you do, not what you think*, Hudson Street Press, London

Easterlin, R. A., McVey, L. A., Switek, M., Sawangfa, O. and Smith Zweig, J. (2010) 'The happiness–income paradox revisited', *PNAS*, vol 107, pp22,463–22,468

Escobar-Tello, M. C. (2011) 'Explorations on the relationship between happiness and sustainable design', PhD thesis, Loughborough University, Loughborough

Fokkinga, S. F., and Desmet, P. M. A. (2012) 'Darker shades of joy: the role of negative emotion in rich product experiences', *Design Issues*, vol 28, no 4, pp42–56

Fokkinga, S. F., Hekkert, P., Desmet, P. M. A. and Ozkan-Vieira, E. (2014) 'From product to effect: towards a human-centered model of product impact', *Proceedings of Design Research Society's 2014 Conference*, June 16–19, Umeå, Sweden, retrieved from www.drs2014.org/media/655163/0386-file1.pdf

Frederick, S. and Loewenstein, G. (1999) 'Hedonic adaptation', in Kahneman, D., Diener, E. and Schwarz, N. (eds), *Well-being: The foundations of hedonic psychology*, Russell Sage Foundation, New York, pp302–329

Fredrickson, B. L. (2001) 'The role of positive emotions in positive psychology: the broaden-and-build theory of positive emotions', *American Psychologist*, vol 56, pp218–226

Fredrickson, B. L. and Losada, M. F. (2005) 'Positive affect and the complex dynamics of human flourishing', *American Psychologist*, vol 60, no 7, pp678–686

Friedman, B. (1996) 'Value-sensitive design', *interactions*, November–December, pp16–23

Guevarra, D. A. and Howell, R. T. (2015) 'To have in order to do: exploring the effects of consuming experiential products on well-being', *Journal of Consumer Psychology*, vol 25, no 1, pp28–41

Hassenzahl, M., Eckoldt, K., Diefenbach, S., Laschke, M., Lenz, E. and Kim, J. (2013) 'Designing moments of meaning and pleasure: experience design and happiness', *International Journal of Design*, vol 7, no 3, pp21–31

Helliwell, J. J., Layard, R. and Sachs, J. (eds) (2012) *World happiness report*, The Earth Institute, Columbia University

Hofmann, W., Baumeister, R. F., Förster, G. and Vohs, K. D. (2012) 'Everyday temptations: an experience sampling study of desire, conflict, and self-control', *Journal of Personality and Social Psychology*, vol 102, no 6, pp1318–1335

Isen, A. M., Daubman, K. A. and Nowicki, G. P. (1987) 'Positive affect facilitates creative problem solving', *Journal of Personality and Social Psychology*, vol 52, no 6, pp1122–1131

Jimenez Garcia, J. (2014) 'Beyond the numbers: A user-centered design approach for personal reflective healthcare technologies', PhD thesis, Delft University of Technology, Delft

Jimenez, S., Pohlmeyer, A. E. and Desmet, P. M. A. (2015). *Positive Design Reference Guide*, Delft University of Technology, Delft

Jordan, P. W. (2000) *Designing pleasurable products*, Taylor & Francis, London

Kasser, T. (2002) *The high price of materialism*, MIT Press, Cambridge, MA

Laschke, M., Diefenbach, S. and Hassenzahl, M. (2015) 'Annoying, but in a nice way: an inquiry into the experience of frictional feedback', *International Journal of Design*, vol 9, no 2, pp129–140

Linley, P. A., Nielsen, K. M., Gillett, R. and Biswas-Diener, R. (2010) 'Using signature strengths in pursuit of goals: effects on goal progress, need satisfaction, and well-being, and implications for coaching psychologists', *International Coaching Psychology Review*, vol 5, no 1, pp6–15

Lyubomirsky, S. (2007) *The how of happiness*, Piatkus, London

Lyubomirsky, S., Sheldon, K. M. and Schkade, D. (2005) 'Pursuing happiness: the architecture of sustainable change', *Review of General Psychology*, vol 9, pp111–131

MacIntyre, A. (2010) *After virtue*, 3rd edn, University of Notre Dame Press, Notre Dame, IN

Maslow, A. (1954) *Motivation and personality*, Harper, New York

Metcalfe, J. and Mischel, W. (1999) 'A hot/cool-system analysis of delay of gratification: dynamics of willpower', *Psychological Review*, vol 106, pp3–19

Nicolao, L., Irwin, J. R. and Goodman, J. K. (2009) 'Happiness for sale: do experiential purchases make consumers happier than material purchases?', *Journal of Consumer Research*, vol 36, pp188–198

Ozkaramanli, D., Desmet, P. M. A. and Özcan, E. (2015) 'Beyond resolving dilemmas: three design directions for addressing intrapersonal concern conflicts', *Design Issues*, vol 32, no 3, pp78–91

Patterson, L. and Biswas-Diener, R. (2012) 'Consuming happiness', in Brey, P., Briggle, A. and Spence, E. (eds) *The good life in a technological age*, Routledge, New York, pp147–156

Peterson, C. and Seligman, M. E. (2004) *Character strengths and virtues: a handbook and classification*, Oxford University Press, New York

Pohlmeyer, A. E. (2012) 'Design for happiness', *interfaces*, vol 92, pp8–11

Pohlmeyer, A. E. (2014) 'Enjoying joy: a process-based approach to design for prolonged pleasure', *Proceedings of the 8th Nordic Conference on Human-Computer Interaction (NordiCHI'14)*, ACM Press, New York, pp817–876

Ryan, R. M., Sheldon, K. M., Kasser, T. and Deci, E. L. (1996) 'All goals are not created equal: an organismic perspective on the nature of goals and their regulation', in Gollwitzer, P. M. and Bargh, J. A. (eds) *The psychology of action: linking cognition and motivation to behaviour*, Guilford Press, New York, pp7–26

Ryan, R. M., Huta, V. and Deci, E. L. (2008) 'Living well: a self-determination theory perspective on eudaimonia', *Journal of happiness studies*, vol 9, no 1, pp139–170

Schmuck, P. E. and Sheldon, K. M. (2001) *Life goals and well-being: towards a positive psychology of human striving*, Hogrefe and Huber Publishers, Seattle, WA

Schwartz, B. and Sharpe, K. (2010) *Practical wisdom: the right way to do the right thing*, Riverhead Books, New York

Schwartz, S. H. (1994) 'Are there universal aspects in the structure and contents of human values?', *Journal of Social Issues*, vol 50, no 4, pp19–45

Seligman, M. E. P. (2011) *Flourish*, Free Press, New York

Seligman, M. E. P., Steen, T. A., Park, N. and Peterson, C. (2005) 'Positive psychology progress. Empirical validation of interventions', *American Psychologist*, vol 60, pp410–421

Sheldon, K. M. and Elliot, A. J. (1999) 'Goal striving, need satisfaction, and longitudinal well-being: the self-concordance model', *Journal of Personality and Social Psychology*, vol 76, pp482–497

Sheldon, K. M. and Kasser, T. (1995) 'Coherence and congruence: two aspects of personality integration', *Journal of Personality and Social Psychology*, vol 68, pp531–543

Sheldon, K. M. and Lyubomirsky, S. (2006) 'Achieving sustainable gains in happiness: change your actions, not your circumstances', *Journal of Happiness Studies*, vol 7, no 1, pp55–86

Sirgy, M. J. and Wu, J. (2009) 'The pleasant life, the engaged life, and the meaningful life: what about the balanced life?', *Journal of Happiness Studies*, vol 10, no 2, pp183–196

Tiger, L. (1992) *The pursuit of pleasure*, Little Brown, Boston, MA

Verbeek, P. P. (2005) *What things do: philosophical reflections on technology, agency, and design*, Penn State University Press, Pennsylvania, PA

31

PLANS AND SPECULATED ACTIONS

Design, behaviour and complexity in sustainable futures

Dan Lockton and Veronica Ranner

Abstract

Design and sustainability are enmeshed. Many visions of a sustainable future assume large-scale changes in human behaviour, in tandem with scientific advances. A major component of this is design which relates to people's *actions*: the design of products, services, environments and systems plays an important role in affecting what people do, now and in the future. This has become known, in recent years, as design for behaviour change, behavioural design, or in the case of specific focus on sustainability, design for sustainable behaviour. However, planning anything around human action is bound up with assumptions and – in the case of much work around design for behaviour change – determinism. Design which adopts a singular, linear vision of the future, and future human behaviour, does not deal well with the complexities of humanity, culture and society. How can we 'plan' for sustainability while embracing this complexity? Is it possible to use speculation and reflection to think through some of the potential consequences and side effects? In this chapter, we introduce questions that designers interested in futures, sustainability and people's actions can use to explore speculative approaches to future human behaviour.

Keywords: design, sustainability, futures, behaviour, complexity

Introduction: design, sustainability and human (in)action

> An interventionist is a man struggling to make his model of man come true.
> – *Argyris and Schön, 1974, p28*

Both design and sustainability are about futures – bringing into being a world where humanity and other forms of life will 'flourish on the planet forever' (Ehrenfeld, 2008, p6) or where we can 'go about our daily affairs … [knowing] that our activities as civilized beings are expanding our future options and improving our current situation' (Sterling, 2005, p44). Design might be one of the mechanisms by which much of our current predicament has come about (Papanek, 1971), but perhaps 'the future with a future for "us" can only be reached by design' (Fry, 2015, p8).[1]

Thus, design and sustainability are deeply enmeshed. A major component of this is design which relates to people's *actions*: the design of products, services, environments and systems plays an important role in affecting what people do … now and in the future. What has become known in recent years as design for behaviour change, behavioural design, or in the case of specific focus on sustainability, design for sustainable behaviour (Wever, 2012; Lockton *et al.*, 2008).

While well intentioned, this approach is often centred on quite small changes in current actions, with short timeframes, rather than long-term futures. In this context, different understandings and definitions of 'sustainability', and degrees of ambition for change, complicate the notion: What kind of behaviour? Whose behaviour? What kind of sustainability? What (time) scale of sustainability is applied and whom is it geared towards? Is the intended change in behaviour a reduction in some unsustainable behaviour, or a shift to something very different? Is this sustainability defined solely in anthropocentric terms, or is it framed as something more systemic? These questions are crucial to many of the subjects discussed throughout this book.

Although work in this field is currently commonly framed at the level of everyday interaction with products – using heating or air-conditioning more efficiently, or recycling packaging – at a higher level, large-scale changes in human action are central to many visions of societal transitions to more sustainable futures (Irwin *et al.*, 2015). In many cases, scientific and technological advances would need to go hand-in-hand with people, *en masse*, changing the way they act for potential environmental impact to be achieved, whether through adoption of new everyday practices at home and at work (for example, new diet choices, telecommuting), decisions about capital investment or purchases (for example, installing photovoltaics or home DC networks), or – more fundamentally – changes in assumptions, attitudes, political norms and worldviews (for example, de-emphasizing economic growth).

Design futures as speculated action

More radical visions may require radical changes to the way we act, but may also mean we need to be more attentive to the way we act, and act more carefully, and in a more considered way rather than disruptively. Whatever happens with changes to our food, our energy use, our methods of travel and our everyday ways of life, design is going to be central to public engagement with these issues, but also to the way in which the scientific community – in proposing and developing such changes – considers its impact on society.

Design affects *what* people do, and what people perceive they *can* do. Everything around us that has been, or is being, designed, from the layout of our cities to the infrastructure of our governments to the way our doctor's surgery receptionist welcomes us, in some way influences how we engage with and make use of it, how we make decisions, what is easy and what isn't. It also, over time, affects how we think, and how we understand the world that we're part of, both individually and together as a society.

Design research often also involves consideration of how broader social influences affect what people do, and how people's relations and actions individually and collectively help construct what society, community and culture will be in the future. Whether we consciously take account of it or not, design is enmeshed in an overall system of relationships between objects and between people which may often be invisible (Burckhardt, [1980]2012). The sociological concept of practices as units of analysis (rather than behaviour) – 'the mundane activities that make up most of what people do in their daily lives, such as bathing, cooking, laundering and cleaning … socially shared entities with a certain persistence *over time and space*', as described by Kuijer *et al.* (2013) – can offer a useful analogy for designers in exploring various futures. Not least as by considering the transformation of people's actions in socially and culturally situated contexts above the level of the individual, we may be able to develop a more thorough understanding of design's role for larger, potentially systemic changes.

When we bring together considerations of design, futures and behaviour, we are essentially looking at *speculated actions* in the context of sustainability. With *speculated actions*, we propose to interweave elements of Design for Behaviour Change (DfBC) with elements from Critical Design, more specifically, Speculative Design (SD). This pairing works from our perspective, due to its common shared referent of object-orientedness for interaction. This shared referent supports both surfacing the relata between the two approaches, and also highlighting the troublesome aspects of object-orientedness. Both areas of design take human behaviour as their main subject for exploration, but differ fundamentally in their current approach. DfBC takes an interest in the perspective of *influencing* human behaviour towards change, whereas SD takes it as subject for exploration, towards unfolding the unexpected, the yet unimaginable. One may say, SD takes an approach of both exposing and mapping human behaviours and conditions that have not materialized yet, but are likely to be brought into being. These two approaches may seem incompatible at first glance, but often enough, both the design stances of DfBC and SD have one shared problem in common – their self-referentiality obfuscates the agency of the designer or other decision makers. On a more positive note, we see potential to use both stances as a comparative backdrop for each other. We draw on our own research around design, behaviour and sustainability (Lockton) and experiential speculative futures (Ranner), but take this synthesis in a new direction. In this chapter, we reflect on and explore some of these ideas, taking into account the complexity of systemic change.

This? Plans, assumptions and determinism

Design can be at once a proposition and a statement, the 'This?' and 'This!' in Dilnot's (2015) pithy encapsulation. Tonkinwise (2015, p2) argues that designs are essentially 'criticisms of things about the present. Design criticises (the present) by making (future) alternatives'. Design can be seen as 'a conversation for action … [about] what to conserve and what to change, a conversation about what we value' (Dubberly and Pangaro, 2015, p74), involving 'a process of observing a situation as having some limitations, reflecting on how and why to improve that situation, and acting to improve it.'

By putting into place certain conditions and affordances and not embodying others, design is also a form of *prediction* about the future, along the lines of Brand's (1994) approach to architecture. Like many prophecies, it can become self-fulfilling: design to some extent 'creates' the future which it claims to predict. It is that particular process that we would like to be taken less lightly – when preconceived assumptions are being normalized into predictions, and therefore lend one possible design configuration (of the many that exist) more legitimacy. This is significant, as it determines the following steps of modulation into material making. We inhabit and interact with the results (and in some cases the aftermath) of other people's predictions; we 'live the surprise results of old plans' (Holzer, 1983–1985). We are living in the ruins of other people's visions: and our children will live in the ruins of ours.

Certainly, not all design is planning, 'trying to pin the future down' (Dunne and Raby, 2013, p2) but there is a substantial overlap. Design which aims to evoke or produce changes in human action, on a large or small scale, necessarily involves having models of human behaviour and human nature: assumptions about how and why people will act and change what they do, and how to motivate and persuade them to do things differently. Even probabilistic approaches to futures model a limited set of possibilities; moreover, *all* design is essentially modelling (Alexander, 1964; Ayres, 2007; Dubberly and Pangaro, 2007), and every technology embodies a hypothesis about human behaviour (Greenfield, 2013; Lockton *et al.*, 2012). Designers cannot escape having a model of humans (Froehlich *et al.*, 2010), and they also cannot escape the socio-historical context that had shaped their understanding of possibilities in the first place (Ranner, 2012).

Assumptions about people, how they (will) live, how they (will) make decisions, and what (will) affect their behaviour are integral to the whole programme of design that considers the future. Of course, though, all modelling involves simplification, and so any vision which specifies how design changes what people do will inevitably not capture the complexity of human nature, in a number of ways, whether it is a proposal of what *should* be, a speculation of what *could* be or an assertion of what *will* be. Indeed, any vision that proposes a 'coherent' future where large numbers of people all undergo the same shift in behaviour or practice, and act in the same way, is fundamentally a mismatch for our experience of the variety of human behaviour throughout history. Just as we now have both William Gibson's unevenly distributed pockets of the future (NPR, 1999) alongside – and interacting with – pockets of the past, it is likely that our future will involve the same complexity. It may be, however, that the models in use or espoused by designers (or clients) imply or lead to a singular, linear vision or narrative of the future, thus effectively presupposing it and perhaps, then, bringing it into being.

Variety and complexity

> The ultimate goal of design for behavioural outcomes might be to discover an 'inverse transform' between behavioural and design variables; that is to say, given there is a set of behavioural objectives, it is possible to determine what design characteristics are needed to achieve these objectives.
>
> *– Watson et al.,2015*

The quote from Watson *et al.* highlights one common issue in many treatments of design and behaviour: a top-down determinism (Broady, 1972) modelling people in a way which simply does not match the complexity and interconnectedness of real-life behaviour and practices. People's actions, now and in the future, are deeply enmeshed with social and cultural contexts, power structures, and other people's actions, and more nuanced than any singular vision can ever capture, which highlights the inadequacy of strongly reductive approaches (Lockton, 2012); appealing as these models might be to some engineering mind-sets. While assumptions and issues around modelling people are not necessarily always *explicit* stances taken by designers or researchers, they embody tensions that arise when a new approach touches on areas which have previously been the preserve of other disciplines with different traditions, expectations and aims.

Every discipline which deals with people, however tangentially, has its own models of human behaviour (Gintis, 2007) – assumptions about how people will act, what people are like, and how to get them to do something different (Weinschenk, 2013). Many issues with assumptions in design for behaviour change can be characterized as *deficiencies in inclusion*. This means both the extent to which people who are the targets of the behaviour change are included in the design process for those 'interventions' (this terminology is itself revealing), and the extent to which the diversity and complexity of real people's lives, in a social and cultural context, are reflected and accommodated in the measures proposed and implemented.

Should designers attempt to recognize the diversity and heterogeneity of people, across cultures (e.g. Spencer *et al.*, 2013), across different levels of need and ability, and across situations, 'maintain[ing] the messiness of actual human beings' (Portigal, 2008, p72)? A stance of committing to engaging with the complexity, the variety (Beer, 1974), of real life – rather than simplifying it away – stands in opposition to the notion of designing a perfect 'solution' to a problem, or even, perhaps, the approach of running large randomized controlled trials on behaviour change (e.g. Haynes *et al.*, 2012), without seeking to understand, qualitatively, why the measures work on some people but not others.

People, societies and their actions are diverse, even in the face of attempts to design this away, or treat it as reduced (Scott, 1999). Along these lines, Brynjarsdóttir *et al.* (2012, p947) characterize much design for behaviour change around sustainability as 'a modernist enterprise', focusing both on individuals at the expense of broader social considerations, and on narrowing the broad scope of sustainability into 'the more manageable problem of "resource management"' (ibid., p948).

Much design work around behaviour, nevertheless, employs a kind of 'standardized model of a person', treating humans as if they were predictable, often identical, components with 'failure rates' and 'compliance rates', for example, as seen in some data-based approaches to the Quantified Self and Internet of Things technologies (Fantini van Ditmar and Lockton, 2016). As Greenfield (2013, p37) argues, this perhaps 'willed blindness to … complexity' is found in approaches to future human interaction with the built environment as much as it has often been in the context of information technology (e.g. Suchman, 1987).

When applied to futures, the issue is that, as Dunne (2005) notes, *we may end up behaving in the way the models assumed anyway*, because we are configured by the systems and structures in which we live our lives – a curious form of self-fulfilling determinism which is perhaps best countered by promoting a much more pluralistic approach to visions of the future? A related issue is that the narrative created by initial promoters of a new concept (e.g. the commercial concerns behind much of the 'smart city' hype) can end up shaping and dominating the way in which the concept is taken up in government and other contexts, partly by providing the language and terminology, but also by disseminating scenarios in which members of the public act and live in certain ways, 'marked by an odd sideways tense in which present and future are collapsed, and no distinction is made between the subjunctive mood and the indicative' (Greenfield, 2013, p47). There is clearly value in enabling – and provoking – designers to interrogate, surface and make explicit the assumptions and models of people that they, and other stakeholders, are bringing to a project.

Power and intent

An elephant in the room when discussing design and behaviour more generally, is *power*: the whole phenomenon is centred on the attempt to influence other people's actions, sometimes in an oddly detached way which assumes that the designers (those in power) will not, themselves, be affected by the influence – and so potentially violating Rawls's (1971) *veil of ignorance* principle, ethically. Glanville (1986, p90) puts it in cybernetic terms: 'The idea is that there is a controller who has the power to make the controlled do exactly what the controller wants, without the controller being in any way affected.'

Sometimes this intention to influence is overt; sometimes it's deliberately covert, with the designer's *intent* obfuscated, hidden or simply not explained. Nevertheless, design is always *political*, as Horst Rittel reminded us (Rith and Dubberly, 2006), something Winner (1980, p22) also notes in relation to '*inherently political technologies*, man-made systems that appear to require or to be strongly compatible with particular kinds of political relationships,' with 'politics' referring to 'arrangements of power and authority in human associations as well as the activities that take place within those arrangements.' While researchers such as Tromp *et al.* (2011) and Dorrestijn and Verbeek (2013) have explored and offered more critically informed perspectives on design for behaviour change – in both physical and digital contexts – many of the themes (emerging mainly from science and technology studies (STS) and actor-network theory perspectives) around the agency of nonhuman actors (Latour, 1992), how users are 'configured' (Woolgar, 1991), the 'inscription' of behaviour (Akrich, 1992) and behaviour steering (Jelsma and Knot, 2002) seem to have received scant attention from design and HCI researchers caught up in the instrumental hubbub of trying to change behaviour.

DiSalvo (2012) considers that *revealing hegemony* through design can be a powerful agonistic tactic, as part of what he terms *adversarial design*. There are parallels perhaps with Zinnbauer's (2015) *ambient accountability*, in the sense of making power relations and the 'behind the scenes' stories more explicit. Revealing hegemony could be particularly pertinent where the objects of attention are systems – or proposed systems – where that hegemony includes an aim to influence behaviour. As such, there is an opportunity to use speculative design as part of a process of revealing forms of hegemony in behavioural visions of the future.

Perhaps because of design's general lack of visibility within academic political science discourse, the ethics and politics of designers' power in influencing public behaviour have not been examined in the depth that might be expected. Although critiques have been outlined (by designers) of other designers' work around behaviour, particularly examinations of some of the 'darker' areas (Savičić and Savić, 2013; Nodder, 2013; see also http://darkpatterns.org), there has been little attention paid so far to the ethics and political dimensions of 'behaviour' in a design futures context, particularly questioning the role that designers may play as instruments of other interests, for example in creating the visualizations and scenarios which are used to promote certain visions of future public behaviour.

A basic criticism concerns the ethics of trying to influence behaviour through limiting choice (the euphemistic 'choice editing' – Thorpe, 2010) in the first place (e.g. Perks, 2008) – which directly conflicts with, for example, Heinz von Foerster's (1995) ethical imperative: 'always try to act so as to increase the number of choices'. Sunstein and Thaler (2003) argue in this context, using the example of a cafeteria director choosing how to lay out the items presented to customers. Since in any planning process some decisions will be made which affect behaviour, it is incumbent on designers to consider the impact of these decisions, and try to achieve a 'desirable' behavioural outcome (we might well ask, 'desirable for whom?'). By this argument though, choosing not to think about influencing behaviour is still a decision about influencing behaviour. The decision process should be recorded and made explicit.

Some progress has recently been made around the ethics of design for behaviour change and persuasive technology – for example, Lilley and Wilson (2013), Pettersen and Boks (2008), Gram-Hansen and Gram-Hansen (2013) offer practically applicable perspectives for designers. But these practical perspectives are, necessarily, focused primarily on the here and now, incremental changes to the design of products or interfaces, rather than looking more broadly at the kinds of future humanity wants or needs, on a larger scale.

Speculation and futures: designing the traffic jam

A good science fiction story should be able to predict not the automobile, but the traffic jam.

– Attributed to Frederik Pohl (Lambourne et al., 1990)

While design around behaviour change may involve concealing intent, speculation is often about making intent explicit. By presenting possible worlds, possible futures – the 'This?'/'This!' of Dilnot (2015) – speculative design can be open about its intent(s) and motivations, in terms of opening up design as a conversation for learning, reflecting and, perhaps, deciding together (Dubberly and Pangaro, 2015).

One approach for visions or predictions of 'design futures' is to envision multiple possibilities or scenarios, often using a 'cone of possibilities' approach (Candy, 2010), extrapolating current 'weak signals' into scenarios which can then be designed for – *now*, and multiple 'thens'. However, solely considering this approach to design futures potentially misses the process between now and these multiple 'thens' – the reality, messiness, interconnectedness and complexity of how human, socio-cultural, technological and scientific interaction actually leads from now, to then. And it is this process which designers have agency within, if only they engage with its existence and complexity. Equally, we might consider that any approaches which put a single point for 'now' fundamentally miss the complexity of current society, and of history/histories. Thus, we are never starting from 'now' as if it were a fixed point, because 'now' is itself a varied, complex array of perspectives and backdrops.

Figure 31.1 The Design with Intent toolkit cards

Source: Lockton et al. (2010)

As we have discussed, much current work on design for behaviour change – in a sustainability context as much as in others – embodies, even if not consciously, a singular, modernist vision for future human behaviour (Brynjarsdóttir *et al.*, 2012), predicated on a normative vision of 'streamlined' people acting in predictable, specified ways. In a cybernetic sense, it is inherently about reducing variety (Conant and Ashby, 1970) and attempting either to simplify the complexity of human action, to simply ignore it (the 'willed blindness' of Greenfield, 2013). In drafting a version of *normal*, everything else is automatically treated as defective.

Speculative design approaches, in facilitating a pluralistic treatment of futures, can help to open up, and explore variety and complexity in human behaviour. We cannot predict and plan human behaviour as if people are engineered components, so we can only speculate on actions.

One tentative way of applying this thinking can be to use a series of questions to provoke designers, or other stakeholders, to consider and reflect on the possible ways in which design techniques might affect actions in diverse future scenarios, including effects at both the level of individual behaviour and, supra-individually, wider social practices. Essentially, this is thinking through first- and second-order consequences of design decisions – not just immediate intended effects on behaviour, but the side effects, the 'traffic jams' in Pohl's phrase. The *Design with Intent toolkit* (Lockton *et al.*, 2010; Figure 31.1), introduced here, can be used in conjunction with a series of such questions.

Design with Intent

In 2005, influenced particularly by Winner (1980), Akrich (1992) and Lessig (1999), the first author (Lockton) started a blog called *Architectures of Control in Design*, which sought to examine examples from digital, product and architectural design where systems had (or appeared to have) been intentionally structured to influence people (users) to behave in particular ways. While this was a critical, or at least reflective, endeavour, and gradually informed by STS perspectives (often thanks to readers' suggestions), it evolved into a PhD project (Lockton, 2013) which, on the face of it, inverted this approach, by not only cataloguing design principles (again, digital and physical, and multidisciplinary) inherent in these 'behaviour change' examples, but presenting them in a *design pattern* format which enables them to be *used* as a generative tool for creating new products, services and environments with a behaviour change intent. It can be used as a 'suggestion tool' to help a form of directed brainstorming, or serve as an exploratory, reflective or teaching tool. The toolkit was developed via an iterative, participatory process, running workshops with students and designers throughout its development to understand how it is being used and how to improve its structure and content. The patterns were extracted – and abstracted – from a literature review of treatments of human behaviour in a range of disciplines. Sustainability related examples were a major focus (e.g. Lockton *et al.*, 2013). With some adoption in industry and design education, the *Design with Intent toolkit* – a *method deck* in current 'design thinking' parlance – has perhaps contributed to growing the field it initially aimed to criticize.

However, the pattern format can still afford a valuable interrogative, deconstructive and speculative function for approaches to design and behaviour, primarily through provoking designers to surface – and question – the assumptions they are bringing to a project, and the potential consequences of design decisions. As Figure 31.1 shows, the toolkit cards feature simple example cases which illustrate the application of the particular patterns.

In the toolkit, 101 design patterns for influencing behaviour are described and illustrated, grouped into eight 'lenses' – categories which provide different disciplinary 'worldviews' on behaviour change, challenging designers to think outside the immediate frame of reference suggested by the brief (or the client), and helping with transposing ideas between domains. The lenses – architectural, error proofing, interaction, ludic, perceptual, cognitive, Machiavellian, and security – are not intended to be ontologically rigorous, but primarily a way of triggering multiple viewpoints within a process of ideation. The patterns, phrased as questions, are essentially recurring problem – 'solution' instances, to enable questioning whether a 'new' problem situation might be similar or analogous to one encountered previously elsewhere, even in a different context. This format potentially makes the patterns useful for cross-disciplinary transfer.

Although pragmatic applications of the toolkit are often in the context of quite 'immediate' problems (redesigning an existing product or interaction), there is scope for more speculative application.

Consequence questions: a list

The use of the toolkit in exploring consequences can be enabled, simply, by asking a series of questions about any speculated, proposed, or imagined future behaviour change scenario, and discussing, in a group, the – perhaps disparate – perspectives and ideas triggered by these questions.

One way of doing this is:

1 Starting with some theme or situation seem as problematic, with a sustainability and human behaviour focus.
2 Set a time-frame for possible proposals to address the 'problem'.
3 Use the Design with Intent patterns as inspiration to generate speculative concepts or proposals (as outlined in Lockton *et al.*, 2013, or in any way which works) which potentially match the time-frame chosen.
4 Asking questions, or a subset of them, from the following list – *ethics* (*universality* and *veil of ignorance*), *sustainability* (*boundaries* and *practices*), *complexity* (*futures* and *nuance*), *power* (*agency* and *politics*) and *intent* (*side effects* and *humaneness*) – to provoke discussion.

The list is by no means exhaustive, nor profound; the questions are simply based around the kinds of issues that have been raised in numerous workshops and discussions with students, designers and thinkers. Some questions may be most effective at triggering discussion if one or more participants acts as an advocate (devil's, if necessary), initially at least, for the proposal(s) developed from the toolkit patterns. Some questions may, in the process of considering them, suggest improvements to the concept being discussed, or end up splitting it further into multiple possible variants or directions which satisfy different criteria:

1 Ethics
    a Universality: What would happen if this behaviour became universal, i.e. if *everyone* acted or were influenced in this way? Is that what you intend to happen? Would you say that this 'should become a universal law'? (Kant, [1785]1993) If not, why not? Whose behaviour should be influenced and whose shouldn't? Why?
    b Veil of Ignorance: What are you assuming *your* status would be in the scenario you envision? Is your behaviour going to be affected by the intervention? Would you still support the idea if you didn't know what place you would have in the scenario,

what skills or background you would have, and whether your behaviour was going to be 'changed'? (Drawing on Rawls, 1971.)

2 Sustainability

    a *Boundaries:* If you are working with 'sustainability' in mind, what definition are you using, tacitly or explicitly? In what way will this behaviour change lead to greater sustainability? For whom? Where is the boundary drawn between humans and nature? Is your treatment of sustainability primarily ecological, or does it include a social component? Is the intended change in behaviour a reduction in some unsustainable behaviour, or a shift to something very different?

    b *Practices:* Is this intended to be a short-term change in behaviour, or something longer-term? What level does it frame the problem at? Does it take account of the wider social and cultural context, and the creation or emergence of new practices, or is it about individual people making decisions in isolation?

3 Complexity

    a *Futures:* In what ways does the proposal assume the future will be like the present, or the past, and in what ways will the future be different? What is the *texture* of the future imagined – how 'evenly distributed' is it, in the phrase attributed to William Gibson?

    b *Nuance:* To what extent does the proposal recognize the diversity of the people whose behaviour it seeks to influence? Does it assume particular cultural experience or group membership? How nuanced are the models of people employed? Is it likely that people will experience the design's effects on them this in different ways? Would the proposal enable people to construct their own meanings or understandings, or does it assume that everyone will understand it in the same way?

Figure 31.2 Design students at Carnegie Mellon University trying out an early version of the consequence questions together with the Design with Intent toolkit cards

4 Power

    a *Agency:* How much agency would people have over what they do, in this future vision? Would this proposal give one party, or some parties, an advantage over others? Would it create new power structures, or reinforce existing power structures? Or could it break down existing structures, and give different people agency to change the system? Does it remove or increase the choices available to people?

    b *Politics:* What are the political standpoints, assumptions or worldviews embedded in the proposal?

5 Intent

    a *Side effects:* What could be side effects of the proposal? What new problems might emerge in a scenario where the proposal is implemented? What technological or environmental limits might we reach? What might the new 'behaviour change' issues be in this future society? How might people subvert or avoid influence on their actions?

    b *Humaneness:* Simply, does this design approach 'wish us well'? (Scarry, 1985, p292; Dilnot, 1993, p58)

A hypothetical example

Let us briefly look at a hypothetical application scenario: a group of designers are interested in the question of *changing diets in developed countries towards lower carbon food choices.* They are interested in ways of enacting and maintaining a longer-term change in social norms, perhaps by promoting a vegetarian or vegan diet as new normal or the 'default'. The time frame is 2022–2025 (i.e. starting five years from now), but rather than proposing immediately realistic or implementable proposals, they are going to create speculative ideas to explore what they might lead to. One way to do so could be to use the Design with Intent cards, in a group – they pick three patterns at random and see what ideas they suggest or trigger:

- *Material properties*: Can you use the properties of different materials to make some actions more comfortable than others?
- *Are you sure?* Can you design an extra 'confirmation' step before an action can be performed?
- *Desire for order*: Can you use people's desire for tidiness to influence them to rearrange elements or take actions you want them to?

Based on these provocations, the group arrives at one idea, that is a subdermal implant (perhaps inspired by recent material science research; e.g. Tao *et al.*, 2012; Hwang *et al.* 2012) that people can 'configure' to react to chemicals in certain food types. This configuration could consist of a pleasurable feeling or perhaps an unpleasant 'twinge' when particular foods are encountered in the immediate environment, before they are eaten. This feeling acts as a kind of sensory confirmation step before someone consumes particular food types. Another variant idea could be that the implant causes a visible or tangible pattern (order) or disorder (e.g. a temporary rash) that people prefer to show or feel, or not. Specific Material User Interfaces (Ranner, 2013) could be attuned to show or remind us what was eaten, so as to provide individual learning and reflection on personal health and nutrition (Ranner and Lockton, 2015). Another variant idea could be to further the embeddedness of such implants so as even to enhance the purpose of food detection, perhaps in form of a tongue implant that enables the taste of other foods (meat?) to be simulated while eating non-meat foods.

We, as observers, can dislike the ideas and pick them apart as horrifyingly technocentric, but judging the quality or ethics too prematurely would miss the point of such thought experiment – at least initially. Whatever the ideas may be, the aim would be, for the designers in this scenario, that they intend to change behaviour on a large scale, based on the assumption that these types of implants become widespread. In assuming this vision, what happens if they ask some of the consequence questions? They can go through the questions – ethics (universality and veil of ignorance), sustainability (boundaries and practices), complexity (futures and nuance), power (agency and politics) and intent (side effects and humaneness) in a structured manner – and pick ones that seem most relevant to start with, and then extend to others, or not.

Here, perhaps, side effects might be good to start with: what happens to livestock in this scenario? If most people become vegetarian, does a new subculture emerge of dedicated carnivores? How do they get their meat? Does meat become very expensive or even shift its position in socio-cultural context? Do people become addicted to the pleasurable feeling from the implant? Do these implants and their sensation wear off? Do people who are already vegetarians miss out from not having the implant? Do they end up having it anyway? One can see how asking these kinds of questions leads to further questions.

How these questions spur discussion is likely to depend very much on the speculative ideas and provocations, as well as the participants, involved – and of course there are no right or wrong answers. It may be that these kinds of questions end up dismantling the ideas, or shifting them in a different direction. It may be that they are mostly too negative, too sceptical, focusing on the problematic aspects of behaviour change rather than the potential benefits – in which case, those benefits will need to be argued. Different focuses and levels of knowledge of sustainability will also affect what is considered in more breadth and depth, and what is not.

However, as a starting point for provoking designers, or other stakeholders, to reflect on the possible ways in which people's actions might be affected by design in these future scenarios, and both the level of individual behaviour and wider social and environmental effects, these kinds of questions can offer perspectives which facilitate a more pluralistic treatment of futures and 'design for behaviour change'. Here, the multiplicity of voices becomes the main focus, and variety and contradiction of ideas the advantage – rather than reducing variety, the *polyphony and completeness* of as many ideas as possible is the goal. In suggesting a deepened cross-fertilization between DfBC and SCD, we may also equip designers with a pragmatic process that allows them to address, mediate, and channelize complexity in the design process in a conducive manner.

Conclusions

This is an exploratory chapter: we are not claiming to have solved what cannot be solved, by definition. However, given the importance of design in reaching any kind of sustainable future for humanity, and the importance of human actions within that, it is vital for designers who are engaging in considerations of future behaviour change, to reflect upon, and open up, the field of possible futures rather than concentrating on single, linear, deterministic visions.

Speculative design techniques can help to preserve and learn from more variety and complexity in exploring the future, and the potential side effects, consequences and other dimensions of 'behaviour'. They can also enable designers to explore the messiness and complexity of the process between the 'nows' and the 'thens' – a process which designers potentially have agency within, if only they engage with its existence and complexity.

In this chapter, we have outlined a set of questions around ethics, sustainability, complexity, power and intent which designers interested in futures, sustainability and people's actions can use to explore the consequences of speculative approaches to future human behaviour. If they enable a more pluralistic, more open discussion, about design and behaviour change in a futures context – even if there are no answers – then we have achieved what we set out to do.

Acknowledgements

Thanks to Delfina Fantini van Ditmar and Michael Hohl for their suggestions during the writing of this chapter. Dan would like to acknowledge the Oxford Futures Forum 2014, at which some of these ideas were formed, and to thank Molly Wright Steenson for enabling the consequence questions to be tested with her students. Veronica would like to thank Anthony Dunne for conversations that led to the formation of some of the considerations in this chapter. She would also like to thank Fiorenzo Omenetto for the opportunity to study reverse engineered silk in his laboratory at Tufts University in Boston (MA, USA).

Note

1 These are all quite optimistic views of the future. It is worth contrasting the alternative – one in which humanity does not survive – and reflecting on what it might, in turn, mean for design. For example, Wiener (1954, p40): 'In a very real sense we are shipwrecked passengers on a doomed planet. Yet even in a shipwreck, human decencies and human values do not necessarily vanish, and we must make the most of them. We shall go down, but let it be in a manner to which we may look forward as worthy of our dignity.'

References

Akrich, M. (1992). 'The De-Scription of Technical Objects'. In Bijker, W. and Law, J. (eds) *Shaping Technology/Building Society*, MIT Press, Cambridge, pp205–224.

Alexander, C. (1964). *Notes on the Synthesis of Form*. Harvard University Press, Cambridge, MA.

Argyris, C., and Schön, D. A. (1974). *Theory in Practice: Increasing Professional Effectiveness*. Jossey-Bass, San Francisco, CA.

Ayres, P. (2007). 'The Origin of Modelling', *Kybernetes* vol 36, no 9–10, pp1225–1237.

Beer, S. (1974). *Designing Freedom*. Wiley, London.

Brand, S. (1994). *How Buildings Learn: What Happens After They're Built*. Penguin, New York.

Broady, M. (1972). 'Social Theory in Architectural Design', In Gutman, R. (ed.) *People and Buildings*. Basic Books, New York, pp170–186.

Brynjarsdóttir, H., Håkansson, M., Pierce, J., Baumer, E. P. S., DiSalvo, C., and Sengers, P. (2012). 'Sustainably Unpersuaded: How Persuasion Narrows Our Vision of Sustainability'. *Proceedings of CHI 2012*, Austin, Texas.

Burckhardt, L. ([1980]2012). 'Design is Invisible'. In Fezer, J. and Schmitz, M. (eds) *Lucius Burckhardt Writings: Rethinking Man-made Environments*, Springer, Vienna, pp153–165.

Candy, S. (2010). The Futures of Everyday Life: Politics and the Design of Experiential Scenarios. PhD dissertation, University of Hawaii.

Conant, R. C., and Ashby, W. R. (1970). 'Every Good Regulator of a System Must Be a Model of that System'. *International Journal of Systems Science* vol 1, no 2, pp89–97.

Dilnot, C. (1993). 'The Gift'. *Design Issues* vol 9, no 2, pp51–63.

Dilnot, C. (2015). 'History, Design, Futures: Contending with What We Have Made'. In Fry, T., Dilnot, C. and Stewart, S. C. (eds), *Design and the Question of History*. Bloomsbury, London, pp131–272.

DiSalvo, C. (2012). *Adversarial Design*. MIT Press, Cambridge, MA.

Dorrestijn, S., and Verbeek, P. P. (2013). 'Technology, Wellbeing, and Freedom: The Legacy of Utopian Design'. *International Journal of Design* vol 7, no 3, pp45–56.

Dubberly, H. and Pangaro, P. (2007). 'Cybernetics and Service-Craft: Language for Behavior-Focused Design', *Kybernetes* vol 36, no 9–10, pp1301–1317.

Dubberly, H. and Pangaro, P. (2015). 'Cybernetics and Design: Conversations for Action'. *Cybernetics and Human Knowing* vol 22 no 2/3, pp73–82.

Dunne, A. (2005). *Hertzian Tales*. MIT Press, Cambridge, MA.

Dunne, A. and Raby, F. (2013). *Speculative Everything*. MIT Press, Cambridge, MA.

Ehrenfeld, J.R. (2008). *Sustainability by Design*. Yale University Press, New Haven, CT.

Fantini van Ditmar, D. and Lockton, D. (2016). 'Taking the Code for a Walk'. *Interactions* vol 23, no 1, pp68–71.

Froehlich, J. E., Findlater, L., and Landay, J. A. (2010). 'The Design of Eco-feedback Technology'. *Proceedings of CHI 2010*. ACM, New York.

Fry, T. (2015). 'Whither Design / Whether History'. In Fry, T., Dilnot, C. and Stewart, S. C. (eds) *Design and the Question of History*. Bloomsbury, London, pp1–130.

Gintis, H. (2007). 'A Framework for the Unification of the Behavioral Sciences'. *Behavioral and Brain Sciences*, vol 30, pp1–61.

Glanville, R. (1986). 'The Question of Cybernetics'. Paper presented at Symposium on Architecture, Humanity and Learning, Vienna.

Gram-Hansen, S. B. and Gram-Hansen, L. B. (2013). 'On the Role of Ethics in Persuasive Design'. Paper presented at Ethicomp 2013, Kolding, Denmark.

Greenfield, A. (2013). *Against the Smart City*. Do Projects, London.

Haynes, L., Service, O., Goldacre, B. and Torgerson, D. (2012). *Test, Learn, Adapt: Developing Public Policy with Randomised Controlled Trials*. Cabinet Office, London.

Holzer, J. (1983–1985). 'Survival, Jenny Holzer Style'. Retrieved from www.arthistorysalon.com/?p=452.

Hwang, S.-W., Tao, H., Kim, D.-H., Cheng, H., Song, J.-K., Rill, E., *et al.* (2012). 'A Physically Transient Form of Silicon Electronics'. *Science* vol 337, no 6102, pp1640–1644.

Irwin, T., Kossoff, G., Tonkinwise, C. and Scupelli, P. (2015). *Transition Design 2015: A New Area of Design Research, Practice and Study that Proposes Design-Led Societal Transition toward More Sustainable Futures*. Carnegie Mellon University, Pittsburgh, PA.

Jelsma, J. and Knot, M. (2002). 'Designing Environmentally Efficient Services; a "Script" Approach'. The *Journal of Sustainable Product Design* vol 2, no 3, pp119–130.

Kant, I. ([1785]1993). *Grounding for the Metaphysics of Morals* (trans. J. W. Ellington). Hackett, Indianapolis, IN.

Kuijer, L., de Jong, A. and van Eijk, D. (2013). 'Practices as a Unit of Design: An Exploration of Theoretical Guidelines in a Study on Bathing'. *ACM Transactions on Computer–Human Interaction* vol 20, no 4, article 21.

Lambourne, R. J., Shallis, M. J. and Shortland, M. (1990). *Close Encounters: Science and Science Fiction*. Adam Hilger, Bristol.

Latour, B. (1992). 'Where Are the Missing Masses? The Sociology of a Few Mundane Artifacts'. In: Bijker, W., Law, J. (eds) *Shaping Technology/Building Society*, MIT Press, Cambridge, MA, pp225–258.

Lessig, L. (1999). *Code and Other Laws of Cyberspace*. Basic Books, New York.

Lilley, D. and Wilson, G.T. (2013). 'Integrating Ethics into Design for Sustainable Behaviour'. *Journal of Design Research* vol 11, no 3, pp278–299.

Lockton, D. (2012). 'POSIWID and Determinism in Design for Behaviour Change'. Working paper, Social Science Research Network.

Lockton, D. (2013). 'Design with Intent: A Design Pattern Toolkit for Environmental and Social Behaviour Change'. PhD thesis, Brunel University, London.

Lockton, D., Harrison, D. and Stanton, N. A. (2008). 'Making the User More Efficient: Design for Sustainable Behaviour'. *International Journal of Sustainable Engineering* vol 1, no 1, pp3–8.

Lockton, D., Harrison, D., and Stanton, N. A. (2010). *Design with Intent: 101 Patterns for Influencing Behaviour Through Design v.1.0*. Equifine, Windsor.

Lockton, D., Harrison, D., and Stanton, N. A. (2012). 'Models of the User: Designers' Perspectives on Influencing Sustainable Behaviour'. *Journal of Design Research* vol 10, no 1–2, pp7–27.

Lockton, D., Harrison, D., and Stanton, N. A. (2013). 'Exploring Design Patterns for Sustainable Behaviour'. *The Design Journal* vol 16, no 4, pp431–459.

Nodder, C. (2013). *Evil by Design: Interaction Design to Lead Us into Temptation*. Wiley, New York.

NPR (1999). 'The Science in Science Fiction'. Broadcast 30 November. Retrieved from www.npr.org/templates/story/story.php?storyId=1067220.

Papanek, V. (1971). *Design for the Real World: Human Ecology and Social Change*. New York, Pantheon Books.

Perks, M. (2008). '"Nudging": The Very Antithesis of Choice'. *Spiked Online*, 29 December. Retrieved from www.spiked-online.com/review_of_books/article/6049.

Pettersen, I. N. and Boks, C. (2008). 'The Ethics in Balancing Control and Freedom when Engineering Solutions for Sustainable Behaviour'. *International Journal of Sustainable Engineering* vol 1 no 4, pp287–297.

Portigal, S. (2008). 'True Tales: Persona Non Grata'. *Interactions*, vol 15, no 1, pp72–73.

Ranner, V. (2012). 'From Hardware to Wetware: How Sericulture Could Shift our Manufacturing Attitude in an Age of Biotechnology'. Paper presented at Slow Technology: Critical Reflection and Future Directions, Designing Interactive Systems Conference (DIS 2012), Newcastle, UK.

Ranner, V. (2013). 'UISilk – Towards Interfacing the Body'. In *Proceedings of the Second International Workshop on 'Smart Material Interfaces: Another Step to a Material Future'*, ACM, New York, pp13–18.

Ranner, V. and Lockton, D. (2015) 'Reflective Silk – Behaviour Change through Better Self-Knowledge'. Paper presented at Digital Research in the Humanities and Arts Conference (DRHA 2015), Dublin City University, Ireland.

Rawls, J. (1971). *A Theory of Justice*. Harvard University Press, Cambridge, MA.

Rith, C. and Dubberly, H. (2006). 'Why Horst W.J. Rittel Matters'. *Design Issues* vol 22, no 4, pp1–20.

Savičić G. and Savić, S. (2013). *Unpleasant Design*. GLORIA, Belgrade.

Scarry, E. (1985). *The Body in Pain: The Making and Unmaking of the World*. Oxford University Press, New York.

Scott, J. C. (1999). *Seeing Like A State: How Certain Schemes to Improve the Human Condition Have Failed*. Yale University Press, New Haven, CT.

Spencer, J., Lilley, D. and Porter, C.S. (2013). 'The Opportunities Different Cultural Contexts Create for Sustainable Design'. In *Proceedings of ERSCP-EMSU 2013*, 4–7 June 2013, Istanbul.

Sterling, B. (2005). *Seeing Things*. MIT Press, Cambridge, MA.

Suchman, L. (1987). *Plans and Situated Actions: The Problem of Human-Machine Communication*. Cambridge University Press, New York.

Sunstein, C. and Thaler, R. (2003). 'Libertarian Paternalism is Not an Oxymoron'. Working paper, University of Chicago Law School.

Tao, H., Kainerstorfer, J. M, Siebert, S. M., Pritchard, E. M., Sassaroli, A., Panilaitis, B. J. B., Brenckle, M. A., Amsden, J. J., Levitt, J., Fantini, S., Kaplan, D. L. and Omenetto, F. G. (2012). 'Implantable, Multifunctional, Bioresorbable Optics'. *Proceedings of the National Academy of Sciences* vol 109, no 48, pp19,584–19,589.

Thorpe, A. (2010). 'Design's Role in Sustainable Consumption'. *Design Issues*, vol 26 no 2, pp3–16.

Tonkinwise, C. (2015). 'Just Design: Being Dogmatic about Defining Speculative Critical Design Future Fiction'. Working paper, retrieved from www.academia.edu/15086757/Just_Design_Being_Dogmatic_about_Defining_Speculative_Critical_Design_Fiction_Futures.

Tromp, N., Hekkert, P. and Verbeek, P.-P. (2011). 'Design for Socially Responsible Behavior: A Classification of Influence Based on Intended User Experience'. *Design Issues* vol 27, no 3, pp3–19.

Von Foerster, H. V. (1995). 'Cybernetics and Circularity'. Paper presented at American Society for Cybernetics Annual Conference, Chicago. Retrieved from www.cybsoc.org/heinz.htm.

Watson, J., Clegg, C., Cowell, C., Davies, F., Hughes, C., McCarthy, N., Westbury, P. (eds) (2015). *Built for Living: Understanding Behaviour and the Built Environment through Engineering and Design*. Royal Academy of Engineering, London.

Weinschenk, S. M. (2013). *How To Get People To Do Stuff*. New Riders, Berkeley, CA.

Wever, R. (2012). 'Editorial: Design Research for Sustainable Behaviour'. *Journal of Design Research* vol 10, no 1–2, pp1–6.

Wiener, N. (1954). *The Human Use of Human Beings*. Doubleday, New York.

Winner, L. (1980). 'Do Artifacts Have Politics?' In Winner, L. (ed.) *The Whale and the Reactor: A Search for Limits in an Age of High Technology*. University of Chicago Press, Chicago, IL, pp19–39.

Woolgar, S. (1991). 'Configuring the User: The Case of Usability Trials'. In Law, J. (ed.) *A Sociology of Monsters: Essays on Power, Technology and Domination*, Routledge, London, pp58–102.

Zinnbauer, D. (2015). 'Crowdsourced Corruption Reporting: What Petrified Forests, Street Music, Bath Towels, and the Taxman Can Tell Us about the Prospects for Its Future'. *Policy and Internet* vol 7 no 1, pp1–24.

32

FROM PRODUCT DESIGN TO RELATIONAL DESIGN

Adding 'jeong' to the metadesigner's vocabulary

John Wood

Abstract

As design is a formative part of our environmentally destructive economy, it will need reform. Some alternatives exist in our 'metadesign' framework – a radical, cross-specialist, comprehensive and integrated way of co-managing complex systems. Here, we can learn from ecosystems, as they are exemplars of complexity management. For example, in the living world, 'sexual recombination' weaves new opportunities from existing data and materials. Thus, instead of focusing on the design of individual products, metadesigners might also work towards a multiplicity of innovations and their synergies. Ultimately, this represents a quest to change whole paradigms. This is an ambitious task that would include (re)inventing grammar and vocabulary to invoke new possibilities. In the traditional paradigm of observational drawing, the designer is taught to gaze at, and reflect upon, the (singular) product, thus objectifying it as a pure 'form' that is detached from context. Within the paradigm of product design, the manufacturer would normally have expected to extract new materials in order to replicate new forms, products or devices. A disadvantage of this individuated, object-centred tradition is that it tends to mask unfamiliar synergies that reside in the relations among people and things. This chapter discusses the Korean word 'jeong' as the basis for a more relational framework of practice for metadesigners.

Keywords: jeong, paradigm, relation, synergy, metadesign

Introduction

It is well known that human activities have contributed to a surplus of greenhouse gases that pose a serious threat to future food security, business viability and political stability. In addressing this challenge, many designers tried hard to re-invent their professional practices in order to ensure our survival. Unfortunately, these efforts failed, mainly because of historical and other factors that limited the design profession's ultimate role and reach. Indeed, over the last century, by acting on behalf of a system aimed at achieving economic growth at all costs, designers became unwitting accomplices to a global disaster. Since the 1970s, by helping to foster the insatiable desire to consume, they played an increasingly important role in developing an economy based on rapid throughput and waste. During the same period, 52 per cent of the number of mammals, birds, reptiles, amphibians and fish across the globe have been lost (WWF, 2014) and Indeed, three of nine 'planetary boundaries' are already believed to have been crossed (Rockström, 2015). These are indicators of environmental changes that may prove critical and irreversible. If so, the Earth's 'carrying capacity' would be seriously reduced, thus making life intolerable for many living creatures, including mankind. These problems were not caused by a lack of technological understanding. Indeed, in the last few decades we have witnessed important advances in medicine, building science, food production and nutrition yet, over the same period, we have seen increases in the number of empty homes and paid workers needing food banks. Likewise, the incidence of obesity and diabetes is now a global epidemic. These problems derive from an economic mindset that emphasizes short-term profits (Hutton, 1996), rather than the survival of living species (Leakey and Lewin, 1996). In short, the somewhat limited idea of 'sustainable design' as 'leaner' products or 'greener' services is not enough. In order to help designers to find more comprehensive and integrated alternatives we are developing a methodology for practical and effective action that we call 'metadesign'.

Metadesign

I define metadesign as an emerging framework of practice that will enable designers to change, or to create, behavioural paradigms. This is an ambitious task that cannot be achieved by what we currently understand as 'design'. Paradigms are complex, self-perpetuating systems that are co-sustained by habitual processes that are part of the prevailing social, cultural, economic, aesthetic, psychological, technological and linguistic milieu. As these factors reinforce one another, they fiercely resist change unless they can be addressed in a comprehensive and joined-up way. As this also means identifying simultaneous points of intervention we must devise more comprehensive and radical agenda that includes team-based practices. The ultimate aim of metadesign is to bring about a more ecological and 'synergy-oriented' society to replace the existing 'product-oriented' world of consumption and profits.

The problem with specialization

Governments have experts to advise them of the dangers of biodiversity depletion and climate change, so they know that a radical reform in human behaviour is needed. Yet, even though the most powerful international agencies see the seriousness of climate change as a more serious threat than nuclear war (Schwarz and Randall, 2003), our leaders have failed to act swiftly and appropriately enough. Indeed, politicians and civil servants tend to choose the least effective methods, such as setting targets, taxes and penalties (Meadows, 1999). It is strange that they seldom ask designers to help them to achieve the requisite transformation. Commercial corporations have long valued designers for their ability to inspire lifestyle changes, perhaps because they can appeal more directly to the sensory and emotional aspects of daily life. If governments were to employ metadesigners directly to work on behalf of society as a whole, perhaps daily life would become cheaper and safer. It might, at least, provide a more equal basis from which the corporate world could conduct transactions. Given the rapid evolution of social media technology, such a step might also have radical implications for new forms of 'creative democracy' in the future (Dewey, [1939]1976;

Jones, 1998). While these are possibilities that might, conceivably, have come to pass in the late twentieth century, this has yet to happen. One reason for the delay is that the modern design industry is still a relatively junior profession consisting of quite disparate agencies, methodologies and practices. This helps to explain why social and environmental problems continue to be addressed in a piecemeal, disjointed or incremental way. The problems we face are structural and monolithic, yet the endeavours of designers are dispersed across a growing number of specialisms. We need new and comprehensive solutions that reconcile resource flows, food security, energy needs, clothing, shelter, mobility and communication in a joined-up and synergistic way. Unfortunately, this grand scale of thinking is unlikely to emerge from individual architects, fashion designers or automobile designers. This is not particular to designers. It is common to all specialisms, because practitioners are usually trained to look at problems that match their special knowledge and skills, rather than seeing the bigger picture, beyond their frame of expertise.

Re-designing design

Although 'sustainable design' has yet failed to save the world, I believe that designers have great potential as agents of change, especially if government and business will accept their help. But they may first need to develop more sophisticated, cross-disciplinary team methods that qualify them to work at a strategic level. This may take some time, as the fragmentation of the design profession into many specialisms made it easier for corporations to exploit the creative power of designers without being challenged about the ethics or efficacies of their business thinking. Society may also need to be shown that designing at the wrong levels is an expensive and potentially damaging habit. For example, instead of re-designing cities for local diversity, convenience and accessibility, we try to make transport systems faster and more comfortable for commuters. This means that workers waste huge amounts of time and money sitting in trains, buses and cars. Instead of solving this problem at a logistical level we use the increasingly 'green' claims of car manufacturers to attract rail and bus users back onto the roads. Instead of designing clothing for personal shelter, comfort and the carrying of food or luggage, we make fashion items disposable and attractive. Clearly, the need to design at a more strategic level would need the strong support of governments. The idea of metadesign agencies being managed, or supported centrally may sound rather fanciful in the current political context. However, it is not unthinkable. After all, most professionals in medicine, the civil service and police are paid directly by the State to make things run better. In the 1880s, the UK government saw design as a way to sweeten the shift from a craft-based to an industrialised society. By creating new forms of beauty in electric lamps, telephones, railway trains, automobiles and fashion garments designers made useful objects desirable. However, by the second half of the twentieth century designers had discovered how to create new products and attune them to prevailing tastes and predilections. In emphasizing the rhetorical appeal of products (Buchanan, 1989) they then learned to attune those tastes to the will of the corporations (Forty, 1986). If designers had known how to deliver a more circular, waste-free revenue stream for corporations we might all be in a better place now. Instead, they became the dependable foot soldiers of economic growth.

Multiple temporalities

If metadesigners are to work in more comprehensive and transformative ways, they would benefit from a closer inspection of the relatedness and interdependencies of things. Instead of being commissioned to focus on single products that address single issues or needs, they might also be expected to find what Buckminster Fuller called 'synergies-of-synergies' (Fuller, 1975) that satisfy many criteria and help a diversity of stakeholders in many different ways. Interestingly, challenging the western emphasis on individuality of people and products raises questions about temporality. In particular, it uncovers an important confusion about the nature of time that emerged from the history of western ideas and beliefs. Broadly speaking, after Aristotle, design tended to be conceived as a linear process in which particular products or services are first envisaged, then realized at a later time (Simon, 1969). Aristotle argued that design is a special category of causation in which the 'final cause' of a product was its implied 'future' as envisaged in the act of design. This idea implies that design is a form of management, in the sense that both set out to achieve a desired goal, albeit using different methods (Bauman, 2006). If we were to work within a longer timescale of 'futures', this would encourage designers to take more responsibility for their actions. But this would require them to visualise all the possible ways that consumers might use, or misuse, their designs, once they become ready for use. This is an unrealistic expectation because the future spirals away from us in an unimaginable vortex of possibilities. In Aristotle's terms, the 'cause' of next week's consumer product would be the vision of all the implications contained in one product. This poses a big question about who can, or should, take ultimate responsibility for all of these implications, and this means changing the way we train designers. In evolutionary terms, the timescale of ecosystems is very different from the short-term idea of 'futures' that industry still uses. While, in Aristotle's sense, it is 'caused' by a long-term notion of purpose, it nevertheless offers greater emphasis on the shared pleasures of co-designing in the 'now'. If metadesign can be developed as a collective, co-creative set of practices, then the idea of 'design futures' may, ultimately, give way to the preferred quest for a 'design presence'.

The importance of 'languaging'

Developing metadesign as a way to address big issues, such as bio-diversity losses and climate change, is ambitious. In my view, it means revising many things on many levels, including the way we have learned to think, as designers. This should not mean abandoning our distinctive working ability to re-imagine images and forms, however, it may mean adding more verbal and textual skills to the repertoire. Indeed, the act of naming can work to re-direct, or even to re-design, big systems. In 2002, when we launched the 'Writing-PAD' network and, subsequently, our Journal of Writing in Creative Practice we soon found that many design practitioners have mixed opinions about the usefulness of words. Nonetheless, it has been known for centuries that language pre-determines the belief systems that guide our behaviour (Lakoff and Johnson, 1980). One of our metadesign practices is, therefore, to invent new words, or to use them in new ways (Wood, 2011). For example, Maturana and Varela used the word 'language' (i.e. noun) as a verb to describe how living organisms 'language' their situation in order to survive (Maturana and Varela, 1980). This inspired us to re-think the customary binary distinction between theory and practice. The lack of additional words to bridge this distinction reflects a long-standing schism between the text-oriented tradition of monastic scholarship and the working culture of the medieval crafts guilds (Schön, 1985). This separation seems to be perpetuated in the lack of names that help us to optimize the creative interplay between thoughts and actions (Bohm, 1980). Donald Schön's famous term 'reflection-in-action' is a rare exception (Schön, 1985). However, some writing styles can inspire, or guide, pragmatic actions, just as the making of some artefacts has little use-value, except as critical, satirical or philosophical propositions.

Table 32.1 Revision of the usual distinctions between 'theory' and 'practice'

	'Doing' stuff	*'Knowing' stuff*
Form giving	picturing, sketching or 3D modelling to enable others to do things better	artefacts intended to satirize or criticize without offering usability (e.g. critical design)
Design thinking	idea frameworks that directly help others to improve lifestyles or make things work better (e.g. metadesign)	text (well argued) that explains the truth without having to improve lifestyle/usability (e.g. pure science)

Re-languaging 'sustainability'

The importance of language in shaping the way that its users behave can be exemplified by common confusions regarding the term 'sustainability'. At the time of its inception (Brundtland, 1987), 'sustainable development' seemed to represent the modest claim that the poorest nations should be allowed to develop at a pace and extent that would not compromise the future wellbeing of others. Today, we see it routinely used in cynical and exploitative ways to sell products and to inflate the status of particular brands. Whereas living systems depend on a reciprocal basis of exchange, the verb implied within 'sustainment' does not. It seldom implies a dynamically active (i.e. in grammatical terms, 'transitive') meaning. For example, when we say that something is 'sustainable' we seldom, if ever, ask who, or what, will sustain what. Does 'Nature' sustain us? Can we sustain 'Nature'? The verb 'to sustain' has at least two different senses. It may mean integration (i.e. in a non-temporal, structural or organizational sense) or prolongation (i.e. into the future). Even in this latter sense we seldom specify what we expect to be sustained. For example, fresh food may be kept in a refrigerator, but its freshness cannot be sustained. The idea of 'co-sustaining' ourselves is not a perfect substitute for the idea of creating 'sustainable lifestyles'. However, it reflects the fact that we can design neither the present, nor the future. Even this simplified form of design using Aristotle's model of time contrasts sharply with accepted economic theories and practices of accountancy. Where the reflective nature of design practice tends to invite a precautionary or provisional element, standard accountancy practices seem to 'discount futures' as though they are extraneous to good business (Gollier, 2004).

Metadesigning paradigms

Tacitly, at the pragmatic level, designers are paid to determine the short-term outcome of their work, but are not required to take into account its long-term impact. If this professional role shields them from a personal sense of responsibility for their design's 'futures', this should also be factored into the design of metadesign. In short, we need a comprehensive 'metadesign' approach that works to improve paradigms, rather than focusing just on products and services. Some dislike the word 'paradigm' because they think its use is pretentious. Ironically, the etymology of the word derives from product design and the mass dissemination of similar products. The ancient Greek word 'paradeigma' (παράδειγμα) meant the supreme 'master-version' of a factory product from which 'show copies' were made. The Greeks understood this process as a divine order, in which a succession of copies from the most perfect down to the saleable production copies that were the least perfect. Plato's idea of the 'real' corresponded more closely with a pure topological concept, rather than with any of the more tangible copies (Onians, 1991). From an ecological standpoint, the Platonic idea of a perfect, form-based world has been both seductive and alienating for several thousand years. Today, the proliferation of computer generated 'forms' on flat screens has driven the (Platonic) fetishization of abstract form to new levels. If designers are to think beyond this paradigm they may need to move from a strongly 'product-based' focus to a more relational emphasis that encourages a richer sensory engagement with the living world.

The paradigm as 'system'

In the twentieth century, the Platonic, product-centred notion of 'paradigm' gave way to a more complex definition when linguists began to use it for discussing structures of meaning (e.g. Saussure, 1974). The science historian Thomas Kuhn also used it to describe much more complex factors, including the social pressures, cultural assumptions and political structures that may continue to sustain out of date belief systems (Kuhn, 1962). In this modern sense, we can now describe the whole post-Platonic culture of form-driven design as a 'paradigm'. This is a very important idea for metadesigners, as it raises the question as to whether it is appropriate, practical or even possible to 'design' a paradigm. They can be understood as systems that may include designer friendly entities, such as images and material things. However, they will also include ideas, meanings, assumptions, interests and identities. If the paradigm is well established, most of these component parts will seem to conspire to reinforce one another. They will also have come to seem normal to us. This makes them hard to notice, and even harder to change. Explored on a practical level, the key forces that define paradigms are often the vested interests of influential players and their alliances. In my view, we will need to design greener life support paradigms before we can know which greener products are needed. But this calls for new ways of thinking that will, inevitably, confound some of our beliefs and assumptions. Working with paradigms would, therefore, entail working with, for and alongside communities, in ways that are sensitively self-aware.

The paradigm of invention

A distinctive quality of a paradigm is that it can withstand many small modifications without losing its essential nature. Hence, in the case of language, substituting different adjectives, nouns or verbs in a sentence will not change its grammatical (i.e. 'paradigmatic') structure. This is a useful model, as it means that one might re-design a paradigm, rather than a given exemplar of it. By redesigning the paradigm of invention, for example, one might achieve outcomes that had seemed unthinkable from inside it. Whereas the word 'invention' implies the finding of an individual 'thing', the words 'enterprise' and 'entrepreneurship' are relational, because they involve the management of several things at once (i.e. 'entrepreneurship' literally means 'taking from within or between). In the UK, the (1843) Utility Designs Act offered a massive reduction on patent registration fees. It enabled any inventor with £10 to secure a three-year copyright. This encouraged a plethora of physical contraptions, gadgets and gizmos, rather than cultivating more comprehensive approaches to the biggest problems. While many of today's inventions are likely to take the form of a digital 'app' that does something cool, both modes of invention tend to focus on single, rather than multiple, outcomes or fixes. The paradigm of invention also celebrates the inventor's originality or individuality and connects with the Enlightenment myth of 'genius'. This belief system wrongly implies that great innovation can usually be attributed to a special individual. However, more recently, we now understand ideation as a combinatorial process, whether or not this takes place in different parts of the brain, or between several people (Koestler,

1964). By modifying the paradigm of invention we might, for example, envisage designers working across disparate fields, such as belief systems in language, species diversity or soil types – mainly to achieve a multitude of outcomes for a variety of stakeholders. Creating a new paradigm of collective invention is difficult using western syntax, not only because of the concepts involved, but also because of the need to understand them from within the relations, rather than the active 'players' creating them.

The paradigm of money

Money is one of society's most influential paradigms, largely because it is a tireless and almost invisible catalyst to action. Georg Simmel noted that we attribute value to money, irrespective of its amount. This irrational assumption is what drives bosses and workers alike. For some, the attraction of money is so powerful that seems to be as 'real' as Nature: 'the liveliness of the attached hopes and emotions shine on it with a warmth that lends it a colourful glow' (Simmel, 1900, p. 259). However, where some have challenged the notion of what Richard called the 'illusion of economic growth' (Jackson, 2009) and pointed out that it is ecologically unrealistic (Meadows, Meadows and Randers, 1972). Where the biosphere is ontological, money is merely epistemological. And, whereas ecosystems consist of living creatures, each with a characteristic personality or spirit, currency systems (especially large ones) are profoundly empty of quality. As Georg Simmel put it, the quality of money 'consists exclusively in its quantity' (Simmel, 1900, p. 259). By spending money we acquire things and dispatch them to other places. And, even without touching anything, we act at a distance. Money therefore alienates us from our actions and encourages a dangerous confusion between (ecological) qualities and (economic) quantities. It is important to remind ourselves that large numbers confuse all humans (du Sautoy, 2009), including even the cleverest economists (Kahneman, 2003). What may be clear from this very brief analysis of money systems is that metadesigners will need considerable additional resources in order to make a helpful contribution to the design of economic thinking.

Homogeneity and competition

A key feature of the capitalist system is the pressure on successful businesses to grow in size. Another one is the valorization of competition. If all café owners in one locality were suddenly to become French patisseries or Italian bistros, then their business culture would quickly become more competitive. In this example, however, competition would have derived mainly from a lack of diversity. Arguably, such a situation would be boring for local customers and stressful for the café proprietors. The idea of competition has been favoured by economists for such a long time that we tend to see it as normal. This is also because of the temptation to see the primary source of abundance as quantity, rather than quality. Until now, this idea has made sense in the context of mining, agriculture and money, for example. All of these, in different ways, have confirmed our faith in an ultimate 'economy-of-scale'. Today, however, the future is beginning to look rather different to us. As our non-renewable energy supplies are running down it is easier to see how a more combinatorial culture of design would encourage us to value the differences between locally adjacent things. In short, instead of seeking to scale-up everything in the quest for more of the same thing, we need to cultivate a global 'diversity-of-diversities'. Whereas homogenization and standardization will lead to competitive and fragmented business practices, variety and accessibility can foster a more connected 'synergy-of-synergies'. Diversity increases the potential for new combinations, rather in the way that a chef creates unexpected flavours out of several well-known ingredients. The same principle applies within the business world.

The paradigm of synergy

If we are to devise better practical, cultural, economic and political approaches, designers can help by learning to think in a more relational way. They might start by reflecting upon Buckminster Fuller's idea that the universe is a global 'synergy-of-synergies' (Fuller, 1975). This might require a new way of thinking that is combinatorial, rather than product-centred. While the western fondness for seeing things as tangible, individuated objects has inspired huge scientific achievements in terms of material goods, it has also sustained a somewhat eccentric philosophical belief system. What the Platonic form-centred paradigm hid from us is that amassing larger quantities of the same thing is less useful than cultivating a diversity of different things that might be combined in new and meaningful ways. After all, no product, asset or resource has any meaning or use value on its own. Unfortunately, some people find these ideas frighteningly difficult and there are few clear explanations of synergy (Fuller, 1975; Corning, 2003) and even less practical advice for designers (Magee, 2007; Nieuwenhuijze and Wood, 2006). This may explain why the idea of synergy remains so poorly understood today. Buckminster Fuller described it succinctly as the 'behaviour of whole systems unpredicted by the behaviour of their parts taken separately' (Fuller, 1975). However, it could also be described as a kind of 'free gift' that Nature bestows when existing entities are combined in the right way. However, abundance only emerges when things are combined in a larger context. Once again, we need to learn from the way that ecosystems work. For example, sexual recombination is a hugely important innovation process that creates abundance by juxtaposing existing resources in a way that offers new possibilities. In a relational sense, the 'difference' can be seen as a resource in itself. It challenges the status quo by shifting professional identities and modifying working vernaculars. Indeed, it probably means preparing designers to anticipate change on both practical and conceptual levels at the same time. In order to attain a 'synergy-of-synergies', metadesigners may need to see the world as a 'diversity-of-diversities', from which an abundance of synergies emerge.

Team tools

An affirmative spirit can be crucially important for facilitating individual creativity. For example, if someone convinces themselves that a task is hopeless or impossible, they are unlikely to act. Moreover, it has been found that entrepreneurs have a stronger than average tendency to feel optimistic (Ucbasaran et al., 2010). Many design thinkers appear to make positive assumptions, even though they have an incomplete picture of their destination, or the methods to use (Lawson, 2006). Trevor Bayliss, the inventor, persisted in developing his clockwork radio invention, even though every world expert he consulted told him his idea was impossible (Schroeder, 2002). This kind of problem can easily be further magnified, or multiplied, within co-creative teams, especially when ideas and strategies become entangled with emotions. There can also be a temptation to move from playful co-creativity and to engage, instead, in critical debate that can suffocate the processes of unhampered imagination and creativity (Robinson, 2010). This can be especially true where there is a (western) emphasis on preserving one's individual opinion, or where 'truth' seems more important than synergy. In a team of four, each member shares responsibility for making three of the six relationships work (i.e. at least 50 per cent of the total number). In larger teams, the ratio of impact may be smaller, but the complexities of large groups make them more volatile and difficult to manage. We discovered some of these issues in 1995, when our research team began to look for new synergies in the world around us. We soon realized that our search was ineffective because our team was, itself, less than synergistic. We therefore designed tools that encourage affirmative interdependence. Some of them deliberately appeal to the rational mind, even though this may not be the actual problem. We might, for example, ban words like 'but' or 'no'. We may also remind team members that many of the technological miracles that we take for granted were 'unthinkable' to us until relatively recently. The next step is to ask them to think about their possible blind spots about the 'future possible'. The third step is to form small, heterogeneous teams to locate possibilities that are currently unnoticed. Next, the teams would seek ways to realize these ideas as tangible realities.

The meaning of 'Jeong'

If designers are to work more satisfactorily with complex systems they need to be able to discuss them using appropriate language. In the West, the idea of individuality became increasingly well defined over the last few thousand years, perhaps leading to less well understood notions of collective presence. The Korean word jeong (정) has the same characters in Japanese and Chinese, but carries different overtones in Korean and no adequate equivalent in English. Arguably, jeong can be seen as a synergistic paradigm that straddles the conventional boundaries of verbs and nouns. It is also a complex emotional bond that unifies people in an ineffable sense of collective duty. Some dictionaries translate it as 'feeling, love, sentiment, passion, human nature, sympathy, heart', but this does little justice to how it works. For one reason, it refers to a multiplicity of complex emotional states that are specific to the belief systems and cultural habits of Korea. Notably, jeong is not only significant in terms of its meaning but, also, for the standpoint of its description. Where the southern African word ubuntu suggests a cultural solidarity with common ethical values, jeong more strongly acknowledges the feelings that extend among, and even beyond, the person experiencing them. It may, therefore, be easier to define as (or from within) a feeling, or sense of emotional dependability. Whereas classical scientific thinking inspired an industrial mindset that is rational and reductionist, jeong offers an altogether more complex and emotional framework within which to work. Instead of identifying things objectively (i.e. from an impartial outsider's individual standpoint or perspective), jeong appears to gain its meaning from within a shared field of feelings. Moreover, it seems to be located not only inside our hearts but, also, from outside. In other words, the location of jeong is both within and among individuals. It can be difficult to understand an emotion as being seated outside an individual's heart, yet it may be related to the idea of collective emotion.

Jeong as a synergistic system

Some systems are designed to achieve homogeneity, standardization and quantity instead of diversity, complementarity and quality. In others, a competitive culture may simply reflect a lack of technological capability or ingenuity. This is where economic ideologies become entangled with scientific beliefs. Just as a particular reading of Adam Smith's writings in the eighteenth century encouraged economists to encourage individual greed, so dubious interpretations of early evolutionary theories inspired a strong belief in the economic virtues of competition. However, subsequent evolutionary theories have also shown that symbiosis is a less expensive way to introduce innovation at the ecological level (Margulis, 1998). This seems apparent when mapped out as a cost-benefit hierarchy of organizational viabilities. Table 32.2 (below) shows simplified ecological relations that include two adjacent organisms (P1 and P2) within an ecosystem. Ecologists often map this to depict only two, interdependent players. However, my version privileges the habitat ('Eco') as a 'player'. This is because it is a shared resource upon which all other players are interdependent. The table is intended for use by metadesigners, when planning, setting up and managing relations in a business, or a community context. Some companies work within a narrative in which profit is seen as the organization's ultimate goal. In more realistic terms, survival is always paramount. The survival of a business or species will always depend on the match between its adaptability and the ever-changing conditions of its habitat. Using the language of metadesigners, we might say that an individual's survival depends exclusively on how well it can maintain a correspondence between its internal and external identities (Maturana and Varela, 1980) and its perceived value within the prevailing paradigm (Pimm, 1997). Almost always, this is a co-creative process in which giving is reciprocal to receiving. Indeed, parasitic enterprises where there is receiving without giving are an exception. Again, in developing these ideas it will be helpful to apply aspects of jeong, rather than the western mindset of individual gain, competition and the economy of scale. As the 'tragedy of the commons' hypothesis illustrates (Hardin, 1968), if citizens fail to see the contributory effect of their individual greed, sooner or later their actions will compromise the ecological basis for their survival.

The idea of exploring the Korean word jeong derives from my 2010 visiting professorship at Kyung Hee University in Seoul, South Korea. Other material in this chapter has been extrapolated from research with our think-tank called 'Attainable Utopias' (2002). This led to several years of AHRC and EPSRC funded research that challenged the traditional (Western) focus on 'products' and reflected on methods for auditing and re-designing 'relations'. Before that, I had sought to challenge the way that design tends to be taught at university level. My attempt to seek a new vision of design began in 1989, when introducing a strongly ethics-oriented BA(Hons) Design Programme at Goldsmiths, University of London. This

Table 32.2 Relative benefit/loss chart for different types of coupling

Eco	P1	P2	Coupling	Summary
+	+	+	Mutual	Beneficial for ecosystem and both partners (P1 and P2)
+	+	0	Commensal	Beneficial for ecosystem; P1 benefits without harming P2
+	+	–	Exploitative	Beneficial for ecosystem; P1 benefits at the expense of P2
–	+	0	Amensal	Beneficial for ecosystem; harmful for P1, neutral for P2
+	–	–	Competitive	Beneficial for ecosystem but P1 and P2 both suffer
0	+	+	Mutual	A neutral effect on ecosystem with benefits to both partners
0	+	0	Commensal	A neutral effect on ecosystem; P1 benefits without harming P2
0	+	–	Exploitative	A neutral effect on ecosystem; P1 benefits at the expense of P2
0	–	0	Amensal	A neutral effect on ecosystem; P2 benefits at the expense of P1
0	–	–	Competitive	A neutral effect on ecosystem but P1 and P2 both suffer
0	0	0	Neutral	A neutral effect on ecosystem; a neutral effect for both P1 & P2
–	+	+	Mutual	Harmful for ecosystem but (indefinite) benefits for P1 & P2
–	+	0	Commensal	Harmful for ecosystem; P1 benefits without harming P2
–	+	–	Exploitative	Harmful for ecosystem; P1 benefits at the expense of P2
–	–	0	Amensal	Harmful for ecosystem; harmful for P1, neutral for P2
–	–	–	Competitive	Harmful for ecosystem and a negative impact on P1 and P2

was followed by creation of the Design Futures and Metadesign Master's programme in 1995. In 2016 the department was subsequently ranked as number one in the Guardian's UK universities chart.

Conclusion

This chapter reminds readers that, as the design professions evolved alongside an economic and political mindset that has created much of the problems we face, it therefore calls upon designers to challenge their roles, assumptions and methodologies. In addressing issues of climate change and serious reductions in the Earth's ecological carrying capacity I have therefore adopted an ambitious standpoint by advocating the re-design of design itself. What is needed is a more collective, comprehensive and joined-up approach to life-support systems, based on a better informed and more creative understanding of the biosphere. In seeking an alternative to consumption-based systems of production and disposal I advocate a profound conceptual shift from products to relations. This will have the enormous benefit of shifting attention from making products desirable as possessions to the seeking of synergies on every possible level. As this notion fits awkwardly within the modern Western mindset, I briefly discuss the Korean word 'jeong' because it illustrates meanings and possibilities that can be explored and developed by others.

References

Bauman, Z. (2006) *Design, Ethics and Humanism*, Cumulus Conference, L'Ecole de Design Nantes Atlantique, Nantes, France, 5–17 June. Retrieved from www.cumulusassociation.org/wp-content/uploads/2015/09/WP_Nantes-16_06.pdf

Bohm, D. (1980) *Wholeness and the Implicate Order*. Routledge & Kegan Paul, London.

Brundtland, E. (1987) *Our Common Future*. Oxford University Press, Oxford. Report of the World Commission on Environment and Development. Retrieved from www.un-documents.net/wced-ocf.htm (accessed 18 March 2012).

Buchanan, R. (1989) Declaration by Design: Rhetoric, Argument, and Demonstration in Design Practice. In V. Margolin (ed.), *Design Discourse*. University of Chicago Press, Chicago, IL, pp91–111.

Corning, P. (1983) *The Synergism Hypothesis*. Institute for the Study of Complex Systems, Palo Alto, CA.

Dewey, J. ([1939]1976) Creative Democracy: The Task Before Us. In J. Boydston (ed.), *John Dewey: The Later Works, 1925–1953*, vol. 14. Southern Illinois University Press, Carbondale, IL, pp224–230.

Du Sautoy, M. (2009) The Trillion Dollar Question. *The Guardian*, 25 March. Retrieved from www.theguardian.com/world/2009/mar/25/trillion-dollar-rescue-plan.

Forty, A. (1986) *Objects of Desire: Design and Society, 1750–1980*. Thames & Hudson, London.

Fuller, R. B. (1975) *Synergetics: Explorations in the Geometry Of Thinking* (in collaboration with E. J. Applewhite; introduction and contribution by A. L. Loeb). Macmillan, Basingstoke.

Gollier, C. (2004) *The Economics of Risk and Time*. MIT Press, Cambridge, MA.

Hardin, G. (1968) The Tragedy of the Commons. *Science* vol. 162, no. 3859, pp1243–1248.

Hutton, W. (1996) *The State We're In*. Vintage Books, London.

Jackson, T. (2009) *Prosperity Without Growth: Economics for a Finite Planet*. Earthscan, London.

Jones, J. C. (1998) Creative Democracy, with Extended Footnotes to the Future. *Futures* vol. 30, no. 5, pp475–479.

Kahneman, D. (2003) A Psychological Perspective on Economics. *The American Economic Review* vol. 93, no. 2, pp162–168.

Koestler, A. (1964) *The Act of Creation*. Hutchinson, London.

Kuhn, T. (1962) *The Structure of Scientific Revolutions*. University of Chicago Press, Chicago, IL.

Lakoff, G. and Johnson, M. (1980) *Metaphors We Live By*. University of Chicago Press, Chicago, IL.

Lawson, B. (2006) *How Designers Think: The Design Process Demystified* (4th edn). Elsevier, Oxford.

Leakey, R. and Lewin, R. (1996) *The Sixth Extinction: Biodiversity and Its Survival*. Phoenix, London.

Magee, E. (2007) *Food Synergy: Unleash Hundreds of Powerful Healing Food Combinations to Fight Disease and Live Well*. Rodale, New York.

Margulis, L. (1998) *The Symbiotic Planet: A New Look at Evolution*, Science Masters, New York.

Maturana, H. and Varela, F. (1980) *Autopoiesis and Cognition: The Realisation of the Living*. Boston Studies in Philosophy of Science. Reidel, Boston, MA.

Meadows, D. H. (1999) *Leverage Points: Places to Intervene in a System*. Sustainability Institute, Hartland, VT.

Meadows, D. H., Meadows, D. L., Randers, J., Behrens III, W. W. (1972) *Limits to Growth: A Report for the Club of Rome's Project on the Predicament of Mankind*. Universe Books, New York.

Nieuwenhuijze, O. and Wood, J. (2006) Synergy and Sympoiesis in the Writing of Joint Papers; Anticipation with/in Imagination. *International Journal of Computing Anticipatory Systems* vol. 10, pp87–102.

Onians, J. (1991) Idea and Product: Potter and Philosopher in Classical Athens. *Journal of Design History* vol. 4, no. 2, pp65–73.

Pimm, S. L. (1997) The Value of Everything. *Nature* vol. 387, pp231–232.

Robinson, K. (2010) Changing Education Paradigms. Retrieved from www.youtube.com/watch?v=zDZFcDGpL4U.

Rockström, J. (2015) *Bounding the Planetary Future: Why We Need a Great Transition*. Great Transition Initiative. Retrieved from www.greattransition.org/publication/bounding-the-planetary-future-why-we-need-a-great-transition

Saussure, F. de (1974) *Course in General Linguistics*. Fontana, London.

Schön, D. (1985) *The Design Studio*. RIBA Publications, London.

Schroeder, D. (2002) Ethics from the Top: Top Management and Ethical Business. *Business Ethics: A European Review* vol. 11, no. 3, pp260–267.

Schwartz, P. and Randall, D. (2003) *An Abrupt Climate Change Scenario and Its Implications for United States National Security*. Jet Propulsion Laboratory, California Institute of Technology, Pasadena, CA.

Simmel, G. (1900) *The Philosophy of Money*. Routledge, New York.

Simon, H. A. (1969) *The Sciences of the Artificial* (3rd edn). Massachusetts Institute of Technology, USA

Ucbasaran, D., Westhead, P., Wright, M. and Flores, M. (2010) The Nature of Entrepreneurial Experience, Business Failure and Comparative Optimism. *Journal of Business Venturing* vol. 25, no. 6, pp541–555.

Wood, J. (2011) Languaging Change from Within: Can We Metadesign Biodiversity? *Journal of Science and Innovation* vol. 1, no. 1, pp25–32.

WWF (2014) *Living Planet Report 2014: Summary*. WWF, Gland, Switzerland.

33

PRODUCTS OF THE
OPEN DESIGN CONTEXT

Paul Micklethwaite

Abstract

Open design is commonly seen to derive from the power of the Internet and its associated technologies to distribute the means of producing and reproducing data and content of all kinds – including product designs. Open design connects the generation and transmission of digital content to actual material production and physical embodiment – the making of tangible things. Open design therefore represents an opening-up of the means of production of our material culture – how we make things. This chapter considers products in the open design context more broadly, in relation to considerations of sustainability and practices of social and sustainable design. It takes a broad view of the term 'product'. Object-based designing is not necessarily the optimal way of addressing the 'wicked' problems we face as manifestations of the inherent unsustainability of our existing systems of production and consumption, and our current lifestyles and value systems. The open design context can be seen to extend beyond the current model of the creation of products via an expanded circle of participation, to include the expanded field of design represented by service design and social innovation. This chapter, therefore, considers not simply products *in* the open design context (in the form of new modes of doing product design) but also products *of* the open design context. It uses an expanded idea of *product* which includes any form of designed outcome, physical or non-physical, and an expanded idea of *openness* which goes beyond the internet- and digitally-enabled production of physical objects.

Keywords: open design, sustainable design, social design, products

Open (product) design

Open design is commonly described as the development of physical products through the free sharing of information. As in the free and open source software movements before it, the internet facilitates the sharing of data, allowing other individuals to copy or evolve the original object.

– *Ozorio de Almeida Meroz and Griffin, 2012, p406*

The above definition identifies several key characteristics of open design. It is commonly seen to derive from the power of the Internet and its associated technologies to distribute the means of producing and reproducing data and content of all kinds – including product designs. Open design connects the generation and transmission of digital content to actual material production and physical embodiment – the making of tangible things. Open design represents an opening-up of the means of production of our material culture – how we make things. We have become used to a sense of empowerment as consumers, although this may be largely illusory considering the degree of marketing and media penetration into almost every corner of our public and private lives. Via open design we are now becoming empowered as producers, able to not simply select our preferred product from those made available to us in stores or catalogues, but to go some way in the creation and manufacture of our ideal product. Open product design is closely associated with open manufacture, whereby the subsequent production or making of an object is also delegated to the end user. This is delivered by, for example, local 3D printing, which replaces centralized large-scale industrial product manufacturing. In this way, custom products may be made on-demand by the people who will actually use them. This, in total, is the common model of the open design context, in which product design is no longer the exclusive domain of trained professional designers.

This chapter considers products in the open design context more broadly, in relation to considerations of sustainability and practices of social and sustainable design. It takes a broader view of the term 'product' than is contained in the model of open design given above. An object-based notion of design, as evident in conventional product design, is often at odds with emergent modes of designing such as service design and social innovation. These modes of designing are interdisciplinary by default, and often generate a range of (we hope) integrated design outcomes which may be both material and immaterial, physical and virtual. In these often multi-modal contexts, product design can seem an archaic discipline if it is predicated on a traditional idea of a physical object as its sole or primary design outcome. Object-based designing is not necessarily the optimal way of addressing the 'wicked' problems we face as manifestations of the inherent unsustainability of our existing systems of production and consumption, and our current lifestyles and value systems (Buchanan, 1992). Product-as-solution is often an over-simplistic design strategy, and risks reducing the complexity of an embedded social problem (such as a disabling physical environment) to a solution which only deals with somewhat superficial surface symptoms (for example, medical aids to allow users to perform a currently difficult task). As von Busch (2012, p444) asserts, 'many new designs are bug fixes of old failures. New design *paradigms* seemingly take a leap in a different direction.'

The open design context can be seen to extend beyond the current model of the creation of products via an expanded circle of participation, to include the expanded field of design represented by service design and social innovation. This chapter, therefore, considers not simply products *in* the open design context (in the form of new modes of doing product design) but also products *of* the open design context. It uses an expanded idea of *product* which includes any form of designed outcome, physical or non-physical, and an expanded idea of *openness* which goes beyond the internet- and digitally-enabled production of physical objects.

The open design context

Open product design can be seen as a reaction to the increasingly closed or 'overlocked' design of the product systems presented to us by leading consumer brands such as Apple (von Busch, 2012, pp446–447). These products are physically impenetrable to their users; their much-vaunted ease-of-use (see any Apple advertising campaign) is not based on any user awareness of, or access to, their highly complex and unknowable ways of working. Modern consumer electronic products embody a clear disconnection between how a technology works, and how we use it. We can be an expert user of a smartphone without having any understanding whatsoever of how it delivers the functions with which we are so adept. Digital literacy does not extend to understanding anything about the device with which we interact to perform feats of manual dexterity and mental agility. These products are unintelligible to a large extent because they are inaccessible – we only ever experience their surfaces, and the virtual interfaces which sit on top of the physical operations of the hardware sealed inside their monochrome encasements. As electronics are increasingly added to products which were hitherto passive, mechanical or manually-operated, so we are increasingly locked-out from knowing how our products work. The looming 'Internet of Things' will be constituted by a growing network of physical objects embedded with electronics, software, sensors and network connectivity, enabling them to collect and exchange data on our behalf but without our involvement or knowledge. Far from feeling empowered, we are at risk of becoming increasingly enslaved to our autonomous smart devices and the technological networks which support them.

Fairphone – 'ethical, open and built to last' (www.fairphone.com) – is an example of contemporary industrial product design informed by openness. Fairphone has a number of ambitions:

- Extend the smartphone's longevity, from influencing the lifespan to increasing reparability.
- Consider our true impact while involving all stakeholders in the creation of our products, from users and suppliers to factory workers.
- Create products that make our value chain efforts tangible, from using fairer materials to making transparent our design processes.
- Use the Fairphone hardware as an open platform and give developers the tools to own and create software for the Fairphone 2.
- Empower alternative operating system organizations that match our open standards.

(Fairphone, undated a)

Transparency of production is one form of openness, contrasting with the obscurity of the manufacture of many consumer products (how were they made, by whom and where?). The Fairphone is also designed for openness, as a means of involving users in its continued development: 'We're using open source methods to help us achieve our goals. This includes striving to make our operating system (OS) source code and development environment available for anyone to use, review, modify and improve' (Fairphone, undated b), Fairphone exhibits three types of openness, identified by Ozorio de Almeida Meroz and Griffin (2012, p408): 'open access, open content and open hardware'. The design and production of the Fairphone is conventional in most respects – with the exception of the increased attention paid to social ethics and environmental sustainability (and the openness and transparency about both), and to some extent modular design (allowing users to modify and repair their handsets as required). Openness in terms of active involvement by users relates primarily to the continuing development of the operating system. This is not open design in the sense of the definition given at the beginning of this chapter, yet represents an interesting approach to increasing product longevity by involving users in the refinement of how a product such as a smartphone works at the level of operating software. The Fairphone is presented by its manufacturer as a more ethical and considered smartphone, which is delivered via, and evident in, an increased degree of openness when compared to any of its competitors. It is not a radical departure from the existing smartphone archetype, however. In comparison with the upgradeable phone concept of Stuart Walker,[1] in which the separated components of a phone must be reassembled each time we seek to make a call or use it in some other way, the Fairphone might be considered an example of ecomodernism in that it makes little significant challenge to the existing design language and typology of the phone itself. The Fairphone is also produced in the same factory as other phones, albeit with greater respect for the workers. It is designed with repair and upgradeability in mind, yet the potential for extension of product life is unclear in the case of a product of such fast-paced technological change. In this regard, Walker's phone-in-pieces concept is more open than the Fairphone, and due to the high level of required user engagement, perhaps more likely to attain increased longevity. The upgradeable phone concept embodies the principle that a product is simply a temporary configuration of components and materials. The easier it is to disconnect these and separate them out from the product, the greater the prospect of their continued use beyond the useful life of the product that they constitute. This is an interpretation of open product design which directly serves environmental sustainability, in which a product is considered as a manifestation of an assembly of materials which could easily be used differently. Walker's concept suggests a design strategy which allows the product user to decide when and how to define a product, from elements which are, to some extent, open in their potential configuration.

Open product design represents a form of resistance to the enclosure of technology and the ways in which it is mediated to consumers by corporate bodies focussed primarily on financial profit. In an open design model, a passive consumer is upgraded to an active 'prosumer' who helps to define the functionality and benefits they want, and is perhaps also involved in the creation of an appropriately designed product. This participation is facilitated by the meta-platform that is the internet: 'Open design has emerged as a topic generated by a new logic of thinking: the internet with its rhizomatic creative networks and open software' (von Busch, 2012, p443). The top-down hierarchy of conventional systems of production, whereby products are delivered to consumers as packaged and sealed *fait accompli*, is subverted by a more horizontal structure in which a linear value chain is replaced by a network of actors who together constitute a system of interconnecting nodes, all of which can potentially have influence on each other. The common presumption is that this is all for the better and greater levels of design participation will yield more successfully designed outcomes.

This same ethos of transparency and open participation informs similar recent shifts in other cultural and political domains. As we seemingly enter the era of 'open everything', design can have a role not just in the creation of better products, but in forming the new design context itself. As Otto von Busch tells us in his sceptical consideration of the implications of this new model of dispersed, but perhaps unrewarded, creative labour: 'the open environment proposed by the ideology is still very much under construction, or perhaps in constant reconstruction, in a state of non-linear emergence … a larger societal project being built from the open ideology' (von Busch, 2012, p448). Open product design should therefore be considered within an open design context, or system, which goes beyond how we seek to produce objects. This is the new design paradigm presented by design for social innovation and sustainability (DESIS), and most notably by Manzini (2015). In this emergent cultural mode, design is used to respond to wicked problems and shared social challenges by *diffuse design* (performed by everybody) and *expert design* (performed by those who have been trained as designers), ideally acting in concert. This interaction between expert and non-expert designers is based on new forms of collaboration which open-up design practice to involve everyone affected by, and with an interest in, a problem and its solution. A key characteristic of this new cooperative paradigm is that our interest in a problem, as users or consumers or audiences of design, moves from being passive to being active – we are empowered to co-design the preferred alternative reality that we would like to move towards.

The DESIS agenda unifies two other emergent design agendas – social design and sustainable design. Open design is often presented as a new paradigm which challenges existing conventional 'closed' design. If open design leads us to think of conventional design as 'closed' in comparison, so social design and sustainable design lead us to think of mainstream design as both non-social and non-sustainable, respectively. These two emergent design paradigms are considered here now as they relate to ideas of openness and product design.

Open social design

Social innovation is an emerging mode of practice which seeks to respond creatively to the so-called wicked problems which can seem immune to traditional policy-based approaches and interventions:

> Our interest is in innovations that are social both in their ends and in their means. Specifically, we define social innovations as new ideas (products, services and models) that simultaneously meet social needs and create new social relationships or collaborations. In other words, they are innovations that are both good for society and enhance society's capacity to act.
>
> *(Murray et al., 2010, p3)*

It is hard to distinguish social innovation from social design, in that both are socially-directed and essentially participatory:

> Although all designing can be understood as social, the term 'social design' highlights the concepts and activities enacted within participatory approaches to researching, generating and realising new ways to make change happen towards collective and social ends, rather than predominantly commercial objectives.
>
> *(Armstrong et al., 2014, p15)*

Social innovation may be a design-based practice (when it is done or led by trained or self-styled designers), or a design-related practice (when it is done by others who do not recognize what they do as design). Social innovation is essentially participatory and open in its practice and methods, being in large part defined by its commitment to co-creation and co-design. Social innovation is always open design, in this sense, this openness extending to the common ideal of sharing how it is done and what it produces: 'The methods for social innovation should be a common property, and should evolve through shared learning. Chances of it being successful will increase if we can share our experiences and quickly reflect on what works and what doesn't' (Murray *et al.*, 2010, p9).

Social innovation and social design are not always product-based, however, where product means object. Akin to service design, they often seek to reorganize existing social and material assets for the delivery of greater social value, rather than to add to or remake our material culture via the creation of new products. In this sense, service design can be viewed as the design of a series of touchpoints via which a service (banking, for example) is delivered to a user. Some of these touchpoints are of course likely to be tangible and afford physical interaction (an ATM, for example). The service itself is an intangible, abstract thing we experience via a series of potentially dissociated interactions and create mentally by constructing a mental model of how these interactions perform together to deliver a higher-level goal.

Social design/innovation often addresses behavioural challenges, such as schoolchildren spending their lunch money on fried chicken fast food takeaways at the end of the school day: cheap, quick and sociable, the chicken shop is now part of many schoolkids' lives. Jay Rayner wonders if anyone can wean our children off their favourite fast food' (Rayner, 2013). This phenomenon is part of a larger archetypal wicked problem – growing obesity and poor health in young people living in urban environments in the UK. Fried chicken is a very well-designed product, and the chicken shop is a very well-designed environment in which to make that product available to consumers – an example of extremely effective design directed towards an specific end, albeit an undesirable one. Consumerist design is about giving people what they want, rather than what they perhaps need. What we want may not be very good for us, yet it is what we ask for, seek out and are willing to pay for. The challenge here is not simply to introduce good design where it is lacking – there is already a good deal of very effective, if misdirected, design in evidence in many problematic contexts. Rather, the challenge is to apply design in a way that modifies the current scenario towards a preferred alternative; in this case, 'to work within the current fast food culture to provide a healthy, cheap and tasty alternative to current fast food offerings in low income areas with the long-term aim of reducing the levels of youth obesity' (Stoll et al., 2015, p10). The designed response here was a pilot mobile food outlet serving healthy, affordable meals located near a popular chicken shop. Crucially, the meals offered were familiar and appetizing to the young people being lured away from their familiar fried chicken.

Design agency, Shift, describes what it does as 'product design for social change', and all of its outcomes as 'consumer products'. Stoll et al. (ibid., p1) introduce the healthy fast food project discussed here as embodying 'a new approach to improving the food environment'. This suggests a broader design approach than that of much conventional object-based design, which typically views the physical object as its primary outcome. The physical outcome in the healthy fast food project, the Box Chicken mobile outlet, is the means to the end of serving nutritious, tasty and convenient meals. The *project* outcome – heathier eating habits amongst a young local target audience – is delivered via a broad range of elements which come together in the Box Chicken service. The term 'product' is used by Shift to describe any consumer offering – products, tools, services and experiences. (Stanhope, 2011, p2) There is nothing inherently more open about Shift's product design process than we might expect from any well-executed design project. It is based on thorough and careful analysis of the relevant issues and user behaviours, but then proceeds in a manner recognisable to any product designer.

It is important to note that this is not co-design with the intended audience involved in designing their own outcome, with assistance from trained designers. Openness is more clearly identified as the core operating principle of the online collaborative innovation platform www.openideo.com.

OpenIDEO brings together creative people from all corners of the globe to solve design problems (social design) for social good. The platform is unlike any other: it walks participants through the innovation process in three distinct phases;

it encourages visual contributions; and, it features an automated feedback tool called the Design Quotient. The DQ rewards both the quality and quantity of an individual's contributions. All contributions are valued – even simply applauding the efforts of others.

(Hulme, 2011, p222)

The OpenIDEO platform exploits internet-based technologies to foster remote and often non-real-time collaboration among people who would probably not otherwise have found one another:

In recent years, emerging technologies – from digital video to social networks – have provided completely new means to collaborate. Establishing our own web-based community and hosting challenges online seemed a natural next step.

(Hulme, 2011, p222)

As in the open product design model discussed above, this model of distributed collaboration to address social challenges could not exist without the Internet; at least not in this always-accessible, ultra-responsive form. (It is interesting to consider what a slower, old-tech version of this model would look like, and how workable it might be.) Openness is an ideological stance for OpenIDEO:

OpenIDEO welcomes all creative thinkers. The seasoned designer and the aspiring designer, the dreamer and the analyst, the MBA and the social entrepreneur, the hacker and the strategist, the big ideas guy and the details-oriented girl, the active participant and the curious lurker. No matter what field you work in, what level of experience you have, what country you're from – if you're keen to collaborate on solutions to challenges facing the world today – you're welcome to join us. We've got creative thinkers from many disciplines outside of the design world in our community – from police officers to doctors to social entrepreneurs to high school students and beyond. We believe that diversity is a cornerstone of effective collaboration.

(OpenIDEO, 2014)

The OpenIDEO design process has six phases, in response to published challenges: ideas; feedback; refinement; evaluation; top ideas; and, impact. The process takes several months to move collectively through these phases, representing selection, development and refinement of concepts in response to the published challenge. This process is open in its ethos and methods, with an OpenIDEO team visibly acting on the platform as facilitators of constructive collaboration. Critique of the contributions of others is carefully monitored to ensure that the inclusive spirit of the platform is maintained at all times (some users may find this lack of criticism over-polite, and to the detriment of the optimal development of ideas and concepts posted to the platform). OpenIDEO seemingly represents wide-open participation in its design process; there are limits, however. The most significant barrier to entry is that you must be online to access the platform. The language of OpenIDEO is English, which is widespread but not universal. Even if these two potential barriers are surmounted, participation on the platform probably requires a degree of conceptual familiarity with design as a structured, systematic process. Despite these challenges, OpenIDEO represents the most widely accessible (and therefore, open) example of design as *process*, rather than *outcome*: 'Openness should thus not only be sought in the final product, but rather in the space that is provided in the brainstorm/designing phase to make unexpected things occur' (van der Beek, 2012, p438). This is distinct from design systems, which appear open to user participation, but are actually highly constrained.

> Shopping at IKEA is a fun experience, where the consumer is pushed into creation, through a semi-open model. The website, for example, has the means for every consumer to design their own kitchen through the modular system. Although IKEA is only open within its own system and thus not modular at all, it does, however, give its consumers the feeling that they are the creators of their own home.
>
> *(Bouchez, 2012, p475)*

In this way, it can be seen that the 'feeling' of creation felt by a consumer whose actions are tightly scripted is not open design in a meaningful sense.

OpenIDEO represents an opening-up of designing which extends users' participation beyond consultation to actual generation of outcomes or solutions:

> Open ideology, especially in design, can also be seen as a continuation of the participative track in design, engaging users in the design process to such a degree that they will actually produce the objects themselves. 'Open' then becomes an essential part of co-creation and co-design, where the designer steps back from the drawing table and instead facilitates creative processes among users, rather than coming up with a finished solution.
>
> *(Von Busch, 2012, p451)*

The role of the 'expert' designer is then to develop the means (via a platform such as OpenIDEO, for example) for user participation in this expanded innovation process and, as in the case of OpenIDEO, facilitate the performance of 'diffuse' design (Manzini, 2015). This diffuse designing is not entirely open, however – it is constrained by the conditions set by the designers of the platforms being used. In order to ensure that the outcomes are viable and deliverable, the constraints and conditions for participatory design must be set for the users (van der Beek, 2012, p438). These restrictions may perhaps be adjusted to allow for differing degrees of openness and user determination of the outcomes, but the parameters need to be set by 'expert' designers.

This account of social design (social innovation) illustrates how conventional design might be considered non-social in comparison. Whilst all design has an intended user (this might be considered one defining requirement of design), the inherent openness of social design in being based on the direct participation of users distinguishes it from other modes of designing.

Open sustainable design

A second emergent design paradigm – and the most significant in its implications – is design for sustainability. There is growing evidence that we cannot be very hopeful of the long-term prospects for human flourishing, or even survival, on the Earth. The planetary impacts of the ongoing global Industrial Revolution (what we might reasonably now call the Anthropocene) are being detected and felt with increasing frequency and severity (IPPC, 2014). The design profession that has emerged to serve the unsupportable goals of this era of unsustainability, notably limitless growth, needs reinventing. Open design can be seen as the best response to the seemingly intractable challenge of embedded unsustainability – the ultimate higher-order wicked problem (Laitio, 2011, p192). If the unsustainability of our increasingly globalized system of industrial production and consumption is a manifestation of a closed, top-down worldview, concentrated in increasingly dominant corporate interests, then the bottom-up openness of the New Economy is seen as our best chance of responding (Thackara, 2015). Not all 'sustainable design' is open, in this sense. The eco-design practiced by manufacturers seeking to redirect themselves towards the goal of sustainability is rarely more than eco-modernism, designing for the market in the usual closed way, but with a green façade.

The socially responsive and ecologically aware drives in contemporary design (using Papanek's terms; Papanek, [1971]1984) are unified in the formulation of Design for Social Innovation and Sustainability (Manzini, 2014). DESIS pursues sustainability goals via the application of the ethos and methods of user-participation and co-design. In this regard, the DESIS principles are echoed in those of open design.

> Thus, where once methods of production were highly centralized in large, hierarchical corporations, this data-sharing coupled with new technologies proposes a new decentralized, grassroots, bottom-up production model.
>
> *(Ozorio de Almeida Meroz and Griffin, 2012, p407)*

The open design context, which is characterized by non-traditional interrelations between multiple actors, requires a particular way of doing design.

> The design process needs to be absolutely open to adapt to these a-signifying ruptures. There needs to be a context of continuous feedback and dialogue. A non-hierarchical, interdependent structure means that the designer really needs to stand next to the consumers and be available during the course of the process to jump in for new implications. This requires a new understanding of the role of the designer. The new strategic position of the designer is that of a nonstrategic continual awareness. Designing has become something which is never finished nor can it be done from a distance and has therefore to become ultimately dynamic and reflexive.
>
> *(Van der Beek, 2012, p434)*

This description of an open design process is very similar to the most familiar design process in social design, the Double Diamond, in which an open initial phase of problem exploration is followed by a point of problem definition, and then a phase of development of a proposed problem response (and perhaps, solution). The Double Diamond is characterized throughout by direct engagement with, and focus on, users and audiences; those on whose behalf we are addressing wicked social challenges. It often incorporates co-design as an ethos and method, as a direct attempt to include users in the designing of an appropriate outcome.

The synergy between open design and social/sustainable design is further evident in terms of what we should be designing for. Not only how, but also where, to direct our designing is one of the deepest questions faced by design and designers today. A shift to greater openness in design can serve the greater goal of challenging our current dominant cultural paradigm of unsustainability.

Openness, in short, is more than a commercial and cultural issue. It's a matter of survival. Systemic challenges such as climate change, or resource depletion – these 'problems of moral bankruptcy' – cannot be solved using the same techniques that caused them in the first place. Open research, open governance and open design are preconditions for the continuous, collaborative, social mode of enquiry and action that are needed.

(Thackara, 2011, p44)

Object-based design has been the driver of the consumerist model which we now recognize as being problematic, both in its immediate personal effects and wider long-term collective impacts. As we pursue prosperity without growth we need to decouple our notions of wellbeing and wealth from the production and consumption of goods. Non-object design, such as the design of services or new patterns of behaviour, represents the most likely route to achieving this. This is expressed in the idea of 'circuitry' as a design strategy for sustainability:

The hybrid design fields that are emerging through the combination and fusion of environments, objects and services are becoming increasingly relevant. The focus is shifting from designing products intended for consumption to programming – or 'designing' – processes for networks of people, enterprises and organizations – processes which represent a pool of possible sustainable futures.

(Sikiaridi and Vogelaar, 2012, p483)

These processes for networks to generate their own potential scenarios of sustainable living should probably be as inclusive and open as possible, to maximize their chances of being successful. The wisdom of crowds has long been understood, and can be exploited in 'wiki' design: 'The greatest potential in open design lies in building from incentives ...

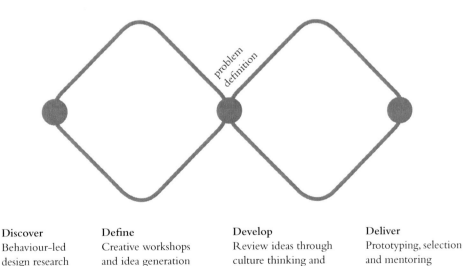

Discover	Define	Develop	Deliver
Behaviour-led design research	Creative workshops and idea generation	Review ideas through culture thinking and design	Prototyping, selection and mentoring

Figure 33.1 The Double Diamond representation of the design process

Source: UK Design Council, 2012

open and peer-to-peer processes have a built-in drive to seek the most sustainable solution' (Laitio, 2011, p193).

We might replace the word 'incentives' here with 'needs'. Thackara (2015) provides a compendium of examples of how communities around the world are creating a new economy from the ground-up, rather than the top-down; we might see openness as an essential ingredient of such enterprises.

The challenges that have appeared on the online innovation platform OpenIDEO in its first five years represent examples of openness in design being directed towards goals of sustainability. The platform exists 'to pursue impact for social good around a variety of global issues' (openideo.com). We might therefore argue that it is inherently concerned with issues of sustainability. The questions posed by OpenIDEO present differing degrees of challenge and complexity: 'How might we establish better recycling habits at home?'; 'How can we manage e-waste and discarded electronics to safeguard human health and protect our environment?'; 'How might urban slum communities become more resilient to the effects of climate change?' The exploration of these questions via this online platform represents an example of 'open and peer-to-peer processes' identified above as being the most promising routes to viable and sustainable outcomes. If the barriers to truly open participation on such platforms can be removed their potential to move from designing for, to designing with, to designing by their intended audiences (those directly affected by and experiencing the challenges posed) will be increased (Suri, 2007).

Conclusion (open-ended)

This chapter initially considered the conventional understanding of open product design. It has argued that this is a limiting conception of the potential for increased openness in design. Just as sustainable product design could be seen as a limiting conception of the potential for increased sustainability in design. A consumer product may be unfairly victimized when it is literally the product of an unsustainable system of production, in which case, how could it be otherwise? Unsustainable consumption behaviour may, equally, be designed-into the object by that same system. What else can we do with a disposable razor or cheap biro pen, other than discard them via our flawed waste collection and recycling infrastructure, or make a clumsy and short-term attempt at reuse?

The best response to an apparently unsustainable product may not be a new alternative eco-product, which delivers the same function and benefit (we hope), whilst doing slightly less harm. Tweaky eco-design does not offer the giant strides towards sustainability that are needed. Rather than victimizing the product in isolation from the system that it is a product *of*, we should address the structural factors which effectively lock-in unsustainability to virtually all examples of product design – certainly those which are manufactured at any significant scale.

Open design is interesting, from a sustainability perspective, not simply because of its potential for innovation in product design, via bespoke or made-to-measure customization. It positions this pursuit of the perfect product in a new open system of design and production, which opposes the mass-production model which leads to over-production and marketing-driven over-consumption of products. If we only make what we need, where and when we need it, we design-out much of the unsustainability embedded in conventional products derived from their over-supply and distribution. We do not, however, address the unsustainability which derives from the constant pursuit of novelty, the newest and the latest. Distributed manufacture and the capability to adapt a product design according to our every whim may actually feed that process, rather than hinder it. We may end up with even more stuff that we soon do not know what to do with.

The exploration of open design in this chapter has hinged on what we mean by the term 'product' and how far we are willing to go beyond object-based or product-as-solution designing and its inherent generation of more physical stuff. The current popular model of open product design addresses the means by which we produce objects, but is still premised on producing evermore objects. The volume of objects in the world could well proliferate if we all individually produce our own perfectly bespoke items, which may be too tailored to us to be of very much use to others. If we use the term *product* to describe any outcome of a design process – objects, tools, services, experiences – then the potential value of the emergent open design context to our pursuit of the goals of sustainability increases massively.

The real value of open design to a collective pursuit of goals of sustainability therefore rests on how open we are in applying its principles. 'The long-term value of open design will depend on the questions it is asked to address.' (Thackara, 2011, p45) In this context, as in all others, we must continue to ask the most fundamental question of design: 'What, in other words, should open designers design?' (ibid.) A turn to openness is challenging to current dominant corporate interests, which are premised on principles of ownership, control and protection. Designers may be equally cautious of ceding ground to other participants in the performance of design. Who pays whom for what, in an open design context, is a question not easily resolved in a commercially driven paradigm. Yet it is a question that we must see beyond if we are to truly and effectively engage with open and sustainable design.

Note

1   See http://stuartwalker.org.uk/designs-1/14-evolving-objects-upgradable-phone-concept

References

Armstrong, L., Bailey, J., Julier, G. and Kimbell, L. (2014) *Social Design Futures: HEI Research and the AHRC*. University of Brighton/Victoria and Albert Museum. Retrieved from mappingsocialdesign. files.wordpress.com/2014/10/social-design-futures-report.pdf.

Bouchez, H. (2012) 'Pimp Your Home: Or Why Design Cannot Remain Exclusive From a Consumer Perspective'. *The Design Journal* vol 15, no 4, pp461–78.

Buchanan, R. (1992) 'Wicked Problems in Design Thinking'. *Design Issues* vol 8, no 2, pp5–21.

Fairphone (undated a) 'Long-Lasting Design'. Retrieved from www.fairphone.com/roadmap/design.

Fairphone (undated b) 'Extending the Life Span of Our Products'. Retrieved from www.fairphone. com/projects/creating-a-developer-friendly-software-environment.

Hulme, T. (2011) 'IDEO & Openideo.com'. In van Abel, B., Klaassen, R., Evers, L. and Troxler, P. (eds) *Open Design Now: How Design Can No Longer Be Exclusive*. Book Industry Services (BIS), Amsterdam, p222.

IPCC (2014) *Climate Change 2014: Synthesis Report. Contribution of Working Groups I, II and III to the Fifth Assessment Report of the Intergovernmental Panel on Climate Change*. IPCC, Geneva, Switzerland.

Laitio, T. (2011) 'From best design to just design'. In van Abel, B., Klaassen, R., Evers, L. and Troxler, P. (eds) *Open Design Now: How Design Can No Longer Be Exclusive*. Book Industry Services (BIS), Amsterdam, pp190–198.

Manzini, E. (2014) 'Making Things Happen: Social Innovation and Design'. *Design Issues* vol 30, no 1, pp57–66.

Manzini, E. (2015) *Design, When Everybody Designs*. MIT Press, Cambridge, MA.

Murray, R., Caulier-Grice, J. and Mulgan, G. (2010) *The Open Book of Social Innovation*. NESTA, London. Retrieved from www.nesta.org.uk/publications/open-book-social-innovation.

OpenIdeo (2014) 'Frequently Asked Questions'. Retrieved from https://challenges.openideo.com/ faq?_ga=1.268332616.794824864.1454840654.

Ozorio de Almeida Meroz, J. and Griffin, R. (2012) 'Construction of a Dutch Idea'. *The Design Journal* vol 15, no 4, pp405–422.

Papanek, V. ([1971]1984) *Design for the Real World: Human Ecology and Social Change* (2nd edn). Thames & Hudson, London.

Rayner, J. (2013) 'Fried Chicken Fix: Afterschool Fast Food'. *The Guardian*, 26 October. Retrieved from www.theguardian.com/lifeandstyle/2013/oct/26/fried-chicken-fast-food-shop-schoolkids.

Sikiaridi, E. and Vogelaar, F. (2012) 'Rebooting (Dutch) Design'. *The Design Journal* vol 15, no 4, pp479–491.

Stanhope, N. (2011) *The Incidental Effect: Exploring New Methods in Behaviour Change*. Shift Design, London. Retrieved from shiftdesign.org.uk/content/uploads/2014/09/Shift-incidental-effect.pdf.

Stoll, N., Collett, K., Brown, D. and Noonan, S. (2015) *Healthy Fast Food: Evaluating a New Approach to Improving the Food Environment. Evaluation Report*. Shift Design, London. Retrieved from shiftdesign.org.uk/content/uploads/2015/11/Shifts-Healthy-Fast-Food-Evaluation_November-2015-V2.pdf.

Suri, J. F. (2007) *Design for People? Design with People? Design by People? Who is Designing Now?* Retrieved from http://designingwithpeople.rca.ac.uk.

Thackara, J. (2011) 'Into the Open'. In van Abel, B., Klaassen, R., Evers, L. and Troxler, P. (eds) *Open Design Now: How Design Can No Longer Be Exclusive*. Book Industry Services, Amsterdam, pp42–45.

Thackara, J. (2015) *How To Thrive In The Next Economy: Designing Tomorrow's World Today*. Thames & Hudson, London.

van der Beek, S. (2012) 'From Representation to Rhizome: Open Design from a Relational Perspective'. *The Design Journal* vol 15, no 4, pp423–441.

von Busch, O. (2012) 'Generation Open: Contested Creativity and Capabilities'. *The Design Journal* vol 15, no 4, pp443–459.

34

PROMOTING SUSTAINABILITY THROUGH MINDFUL DESIGN

Kristina Niedderer

Abstract

In order to promote sustainability, there is a need for attentiveness and responsible action towards the environment, which requires changes in perspectives at the levels of both production and use. This chapter provides an introduction to mindful design and its potential to promote sustainability. Based on an analysis of the concepts of mindfulness and mindful design, the chapter proposes that mindfulness offers a pertinent means of creating openness to new perspectives, that this can be embedded within design and that, through its use, mindful design offers the potential to instil such attitudes in the user to promote sustainable behaviour. The chapter offers a number of examples in support of this proposition, and to consider the ethical stance embedded in mindful design and its relation to the production and use of mindful design.

Keywords: behaviour change, mindful design, mindfulness, responsible design, sustainability

Introduction: the need for mindful behaviour change

Environmental sustainability is perhaps one of the most urgent problems we face today. It affects a broad range of issues, including the world's future habitability and its social and economic prosperity (Committee for Climate Change, 2015; IEA, 2015, p3; IPCC, 2015). Environmental problems tend to be interdependent, complex issues that need to be considered in a holistic way. This means sustainable interventions require changing or adapting economic systems and perspectives as well as social attitudes and behaviours (Stern, P. C., 2000; Stern, N. H., 2006).

Recycling is a prominent example in this regard, which encompasses interventions such as legislation to change behaviour towards resource use, or voluntary commitment by end-users towards preserving resources, or entrepreneurship to develop opportunities for preserving and reclaiming resources that otherwise might go to waste. Such inventions may on the one hand target behaviours of manufacturers to improve product specifications and production patterns for the purpose of reducing energy consumption, waste, CO_2 emissions, and to enable the recyclability of all product parts. On the other hand, they may seek to promote a change in user behaviour towards purchasing sustainable materials/goods and towards recycling them to reduce waste and the need for resource mining and by extension reduce CO_2 emissions.

These goals can be promoted through different ways of reinforcement, which either work as incentives or deterrents, and which are either driven by prescription or voluntary engagement (Lockton, Harrison and Stanton, 2010; Niedderer, 2013). For example, legislation is prescriptive. It can work as a deterrent or incentive using taxes, e.g. higher waste tax can be used to incentivize companies to recycle more and waste less and to reduce new resource use and CO_2 emissions as a means of working towards set targets for the reduction of greenhouse gas emissions (Crown, 2008). Similarly, the charging of a fee for plastic bottles (e.g. in Germany) ensures the re-turn and re-use of energy rich products.

At the other end of the spectrum, there are voluntary initiatives and social pressures, which are dependent on people's commitments to achieve desired goals, such as recycling banks or centres. Successful voluntary initiatives often go hand-in-hand with legislation, such as in an example of the above mentioned re-use schemes where drinks retailers are forced to take back their bottles (whether glass or plastic), and consumers are incentivized to return them to the retailers. In addition such schemes can offer opportunities for enterprise in facilitating novel ways of re-using or recycling the returned materials.

There are two considerations, which can be drawn from this. First, without the combination of legislation, design innovation and voluntary commitment, this system could not work. This shows that attentiveness to all parts of the system is required if sustainability is to be improved, and a sense of responsibility by all concerned to ensure the implementation of any sustainability initiatives. Second, changing a complex system requires a change of perspective to enable a rethinking – and subsequent redesigning – of the system. In the case of recycling, it has required a change from a model of 'cradle to grave' to the 'cradle to cradle' model (Braungart and McDonough, 2010) to establish a system that functions within an equilibrium and that does not exhaust itself.

While leading approaches such as the 'cradle to cradle' model have become increasingly well established, their consequent implementation is far from easy, because it requires attentiveness and responsibility on the part of all concerned as well as an ability and willingness to shift perspectives at the levels of both production and consumption.

This chapter proposes the use of mindfulness, and in particular mindful design, as a way of enabling such attentiveness and responsibility and of enabling a change in perspectives and thinking that is conducive to help implement sustainable change. The chapter first discusses the concept of mindfulness and how this can be embedded in mindful design. It then provides a number of examples to demonstrate its application and affect with regard to sustainable behaviour. The conclusion reflects on the benefits of mindful design as well as its ethical stance with regard to use and production of design.

Relating design and mindfulness

Design, loosely understood here as the act of giving form to all human-made things, may be seen to have an ambiguous relationship with environmental sustainability, because of both its *material* and *functional* nature.

In terms of its *material* nature, on the one hand, (mass- and over-) production of design is the cause of many sustainability problems from resource depletion to rising waste mountains. For example, fashion with its fast cycle through the four seasons causes a lot of unsold garments to be destroyed as waste at the end of each season, or garments that have barely been worn by the user to be discarded to be replaced by the latest fashion. How and how often cloths are being washed is also a large factor (Blackburn, 2009, p3). On the other hand, through sustainable innovation, design can also offer solutions or improvements to existing problems. For example, government backed innovation has led to the development of new, cleaner technologies, such as electric or hydrogen powered cars to reduce CO_2 emissions.

Because of its *functional* nature, design has found its way into all corners of our daily lives. Its ubiquity and functionality entails that it directs and influences our actions mostly without us noticing, leading to adapting our behaviours to it and causing behavioural change at every level (Niedderer, forthcoming). For example, the use of a car will allow us to move more flexibly, perhaps to go to work further away from our home, visit friends, go shopping etc. Unthinkingly, we will surrender to its use where we could perhaps choose another means, such as public transport or cycling, that might potentially be cheaper, more efficient to reach our destination, and more environmentally friendly.

The above examples indicate that the functional nature of design is not neutral and that it requires responsible decision-making on the part of both the designer (and all that are concerned in the production management and process) and the user. The first are required to consider whether and what designs should go into production, whether any design should adhere to the cradle to cradle model, or whether economic gain is the priority. With regard to the latter, Jelsma posits that designers should take moral responsibility for the actions that take place as a result of human interactions with artefacts, intentional or not:

> Artefacts have a co-responsibility for the way action develops and for what results. If we waste energy or produce waste in routine actions such as in household practices, that has to do with the way artefacts guide us.
>
> *(Jelsma, 2006, p222)*

However, Jelsma's view is not offering a complete picture: while the design of any product may be seen as the designer's responsibility, it is in the user's responsibility to decide whether to purchase any product, when and how to use the acquired product and to what end. For example, it is the end-user's decision how often to buy new clothes, how frequently to wash and wear them and how long to keep them. Similarly, it is the user's decision every day whether to walk, use their car or bike, or the train to go to work. Furthermore, the user has the freedom to decide what to do with any product, and often this may not be an intended function at all. For example, a bike can be used for travelling, but connected to a dynamo it can also be used to generate light or electricity, or it could be used to operate a pump, or parts of it could be used to support a tree or as a weapon. The latter uses are not generally envisaged in the design of a bike, but they are no less possible than the first. It is important to acknowledge this freedom of use, and misuse, on the part of the user. Indeed the difficulty to predict users' actions is regularly acknowledged (e.g. Tromp, Hekkert and Verbeek, 2011), and it is important to recognize that there are a number of factors that determine the decision-making process of the user.

The question is how to facilitate intentional sustainable change, and how designers can contribute to it through the products they design? This questions arises if we acknowledge the need for both designers and users to take responsibility for the products they create and their actions with them, but also the difficulty of directing the user's actions.

Generally, design for behaviour change (e.g. Lockton, Harrison and Stanton, 2010; Tromp, Hekkert and Verbeek, 2011) distinguishes different ways of doing so, which can be defined into two pairs of principles to influence human behaviour through design: first,

Table 34.1 Basic design mechanisms for enabling behaviour change

	Positive influence: promoting behaviour	*Negative influence: restricting behaviour*
Physical mechanisms	enabling	constraining
Psychological mechanisms	incentive	deterrent

through physical influence, which can be either enabling or constraining and, second, through psychological influence, which can act as either an incentive or deterrent (see Table 34.1). Barriers at a pavement that will prevent drivers physically from driving onto or parking on the pavement are an example of constraining (or prescriptive) design, while traffic lights work as a psychological deterrent through communicating a legal prohibition of crossing them when they show a red light. Many designs also use a combination of these.

These mechanisms, which can be utilized in designing specific products and their actions, are mainly directed towards the action intended by the designer. This area is fairly well researched by now. Although less well researched, it is no less important to pay attention to the motivation of the user (Lockton, Harrison and Stanton, 2010), which may direct any unintended or aberrant action of the user with a product.

While designers have little chance of foreseeing every possible use or action an end user may have with an object, what they can do is to raise the user's awareness of the possible actions with the object to encourage reflection to encourage responsible action. In other words, designers can create mindfulness of the user's actions with the product and of the consequences these actions have on themselves, on others and on the natural environment.

Mindfulness has been defined in different ways. This research follows the Western psychological tradition of mindfulness (Langer, 1989; Langer and Moldoveanu, 2000a, 2000b) in which mindfulness is understood as the process of creating awareness and attentiveness 'to bring one's full resources to a cognitive task by using multiple perspectives and attending to context, which creates novel ways to consider the relevant information' (Luttrell, Briñol and Petty, 2014, p258).

For example, a person routinely commuting to work by car, when confronted with the proposition to lead a more sustainable lifestyle, if mindful might reconsider how they travel to work, perhaps instead deciding on a combination of walking and taking the train. They might look at the bigger picture seeing that walking will not only reduce CO_2 emissions, but at the same time can increase their exercise and improve their health. In this way, the change in behaviour is seen to provide an opportunity to improve one's lifestyle and responsible behaviour overall. By contrast, a *mindless* person might continue to drive to work, and decide to go to the gym once a week also taking the car, thus adding an extra journey while getting exercise rather less frequently.

However, the state of mindfulness is elusive (Langer, 1989, pp2–9), because it requires breaking through established patterns of experience and preconception (ibid., pp19–42). Traditionally, meditation and education have been used to disrupt these patterns and to open them to (re)inspection to create mindful awareness (ibid., pp81–114; Udall, 1996, p107). However, this makes mindfulness reliant on specific contexts, which are not generally available in everyday life. Design can offer a valuable alternative here, because it is available in everyday contexts. Furthermore, recent studies on computer-supported mindfulness found that appropriate design interventions can significantly surpass the efficacy of traditional mindfulness training (e.g. Chittaro and Vianella, 2013).

In the following section, I will discuss how mindfulness can be embedded within design as 'mindful design' to facilitate mindful sustainable behaviour change.

Mindful design and how it works

In extension of the above definition of mindfulness, mindful design – as the integration of mindfulness into design – refers to a design's quality to enable the awareness and attentiveness of a person (user) towards the product they are interacting with, towards their (physical, social, experiential etc.) environment and towards the consequences of their actions with the product.

Mindful design can be seen as a useful tool to address and promote sustainable behaviour change, because it addresses the four key factors of sustainable behaviour change: *attitude, external context, personal capability* and *habit/routine* (Stern, P. C., 2000, p416).

- *Attitudinal factors*, according to Stern, include norms, beliefs and values.
- *Contextual factors* include interpersonal influences (e.g. persuasion); community expectations and public or interest group pressures; government regulations, policies or other legal and institutional factors; monetary incentives and costs; advertising; and capabilities and constraints in dealing with things or one's environment.
- *Personal capabilities* include the knowledge and skills required for particular actions, general capabilities and resources such as literacy, money, and time; as well as socio-demographic variables such as age, educational attainment, race, social status and power.
- *Habit/routine* is important because 'behavior change often requires breaking old habits and becomes established by creating new ones' (Dahlstrand and Biel, 1997). Habit, in the form of standard operating procedure, is also a key factor in environmentally significant organizational behavior' (Stern, P. C., 2000, p416).

Mindfulness, and by extension mindful design, addresses all four criteria. It draws attention to and induces reflection of one's pre-conceptions, one's own actions including routines and habits, and the external context (Langer, 1989). Mindfulness thus allows (re-)considering one's habits/routines and inherent attitudes in relation to the wider context, and in turn to re-assess one's personal capabilities for change in any given context. In the following, I discuss how mindful design works and how the four factors are practically embedded within it.

Mindful design is based on two key principles, or *stages*. It first needs to create awareness of an action (or use) to be reflected on, and then it needs to direct this awareness towards the content of this action and offer potential alternative perspectives or solutions. The first process is called a 'disruption' the second a 'thematization' (Niedderer, 2007, 2014).

The process of disruption is based on the fact that our attention is drawn to what we are doing if an object does not perform exactly the way we expect it to (i.e. if the expectation or efficiency of the interaction with the object is broken in some way). This process is connected to an object's functionality. Function can be disrupted on either practical or symbolic levels, or both. For example, the disruption of the practical function is used regularly as part of safety features, such as warning notices on computers (e.g. when closing a document without having saved it; see Figure 34.1). The computer briefly disrupts our action through a security banner, which requires an additional action to complete the command (e.g. 'save/don't save/cancel'), thus raising our awareness. Similarly, symbolic function can be used to raise the user's attention, as in the example of the shower tiles where the tiles discolour after about three minutes, reminding the user that they should limit their shower time to save water and energy (Lagerkvist et al., 2012). In this case, there is no physical barrier to prevent the user to continue showering, but the discolouration is a subtle symbolic cue of their detrimental impact on the

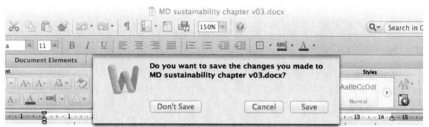

The disruption of function only works when it is accompanied by a second stage, the 'thematisation', which directs the user's attention towards some content for reflection. The thematisation will usually address one (or more) of the key factors elaborated by

Figure 34.1 Safety feature

environment. The cue utilizes the metaphor that showering for too long is damaging the natural environment, symbolized by the disappearing of the decoration on the tiles).

The disruption of function only works when it is accompanied by a second stage, the 'thematization', which directs the user's attention towards some content for reflection. The thematization will usually address one (or more) of the key factors elaborated by Stern (i.e. attitude, external context, or habit/routine), and it must connect with or provide the solution to the disruption. In the case of the safety feature of the computer operating system, the pop-up 'save/don't save/cancel' banner interrupts our routine, and the sentence on the banner and the associated options for resolution constitute the thematization, that is, the sentence explains why the process in question has been interrupted, and it offers different buttons to proceed to the desired solutions. In the case of the shower tiles, where the symbolic function is used, instead of the practical function (showering/water flow) being interrupted, a related feature is interrupted (tile pattern disappears) which holds a clear symbolic meaning related to the practical action.

The availability of different solutions is important, because they offer choice, and choice in turn requires conscious reflection on the different options available (Langer, 1989, p123) leading to mindful reflection. In line with Stern's key factors, this may include a heightened awareness to:

(1) a greater sensitivity to one's environment, (2) more openness to new information, (3) the creation of new categories for structuring perception, and (4) enhanced awareness of multiple perspectives in problem solving.

(Langer and Moldoveanu, 2000a, p2)

However, there will be a practical limit of how many choices can be combined in one object. While adding more choices can increase reflection and thus mindfulness, too many options can make a product potentially confusing to use (Norman, 2002, pxii). Therefore, it is important to maintain a balance between clarity of message and number of choices appropriate to the context of application, if we are to avoid overwhelming users.

In addition to content and choice, the thematization can offer different (levels of) meaning, adding complexity as a way of questioning established concepts. For example, a mindful object might raise reflection on the level of the immediate action, such as the computer safety feature or the shower tile. However, if designed differently, the design of the shower tiles could have further levels of meaning. For example, they could also direct the user's attention to issues of hygiene in that the discolouration could also show stains if not cleaned regularly.

The thematization thus has three 'mechanisms' or 'features' to guide the user's awareness, which comprise *content*, *choice* and *complexity* (Niedderer, 2014, pp348–353; Figure 34.2). These three features need to address one or more of Stern's key factors, including attitude, external context, or habit/routine. In addition, through offering multiple (novel) choices and perspectives, the thematization should offer the user a new outlook on their personal capabilities.

The final point, which is of importance here, is the role of emotions. Mindless behaviour regularly tends to be driven by emotions (Niedderer, 2014, pp354–357). In the case of sustainability, often this may be feelings of comfort. Such feelings may lead us to use the central heating more to feel comfortably warm, take a bath to relax instead of taking a shower, or use a car instead of cycling or walking to avoid extraneous activity. Emotions guide our lives constantly, and often they make us feel incapable (or unwilling) to change accustomed behaviours. They constitute a complex system of 'survival instincts' that influence our judgment without requiring conscious decision-making and guide our physiological, experiential and behavioural activity in response to survival-related problems and opportunities (Keltner and Ekman, 2000, p163). Because they don't require deliberate decision making, they can open the door to mindlessness and promote a singular perspective. For example, an emotional response established as appropriate in one situation may be unthinkingly transferred to a new situation where it might be entirely inappropriate. For example, using one's car for a two-hour journey may be appropriate, but taking it to go to the corner shop which is two minutes away to buy some bread could be considered inappropriate.

While emotions can lead to mindlessness, at the same time they can be used as an incentive to enhance mindful design because it is possible for opposing emotions to cancel each other out (Niedderer, 2014, p356). For example, positive emotions can partially overlay or cancel out negative emotions (Cohn et al., 2009, p8). In the case of the shower tiles, potentially negative feelings about having to curtail one's shower might be offset by the satisfaction of doing something good to protect the environment. In this way, they can be useful to increase perceptions of personal capabilities and thus support the options for personal capabilities and action offered through the thematization.

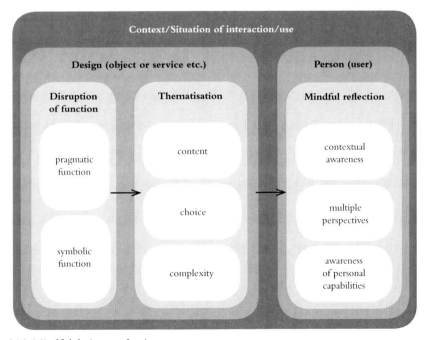

Figure 34.2 Mindful design mechanisms

Designing for mindful sustainability

Having discussed the need for behavioural change, the role of mindfulness in stimulating behaviour change, and how design can enable or support mindful change, this final section will look at the application of mindful design in the context of sustainability.

Over the last two decades, as the spotlight on sustainability has grown and with it the awareness of sustainability, designers have increasingly sought to facilitate behaviour change. By now, a large number of design innovations have emerged with the aim to promote sustainable behaviour. Many of these are focused either on policy, on technological advance, or on service design (e.g. Crocker and Lehmann, 2013; Fuad-Luke, 2009; Bhamra et al., 2011; Dusch, Crilly and Moultrie, 2011). For example, consumer aids to promote sustainable behaviour and consumption in the house include displays to inform about energy or water use, some in form of meter displays, others in form of electrical cords that change colour to alert the user, etc. Yet others include sensor driven devices that switch off light in rooms or heating when not used. What most of these designs have in common is that they either function automatically, or they raise attention, but without the requirement for active reflection and response.

Among the various approaches to sustainable product design, solutions of mindful design have also begun to emerge, some of which will be discussed in the following. Interestingly however, compared to other design areas, such as *safety* or *social design*, there seem to be as yet comparatively few mindful design solutions for sustainability. The following discussion will therefore not only introduce some examples of sustainable mindful design, but also elicit problems and opportunities of mindful design in the context of sustainability, and consider how its use in promoting sustainable behaviour change could be extended. The discussion will focus on three specific areas of sustainable behaviour change: energy and water consumption in the home, energy consumption and CO_2 emissions within personal transport (cars), and issues of waste reduction and recycling.

Sustainable consumption in the home

This first set of examples is concerned with energy and water consumption in the home. Most houses have electricity and water meters, and usually the heating system is controlled with some kind of thermostat to regulate the temperature. There are also novel interventions, such as smart home heating systems, which can be operated remotely and are slowly coming into use (e.g. Egan, 2014), or meters from solar or wind energy home systems, which provide information about the differential between energy generated and energy used (Letrendre and Taylor, 2009). These kinds of interventions are designed to provide information to the user about their energy or water use. They tend to be supported by educational information, but rarely offer direct nudges to the user as in the example of the shower tiles or safety feature discussed above, even though some simple visual and/or audio solutions might be integrated (e.g. drawing the users attention to the temperature, to the duration of heating cycle, etc.).

Another example in the household, which relates to water consumption, is the lavatory cistern, for which countless water saving mechanisms have been developed over the years. Usually, they either feature two buttons, a larger indicating larger water consumption and a smaller one for smaller consumption, or a large flip-button, which when pressed at the lower end releases water and when pressed at the upper end stops the water again. This thinking brings us some way towards mindful design in that it provides choice, but not fully because there is no 'disruption' to raise the user's attention and that would require a deliberate action as in the example of the computer safety feature discussed above. Indeed, the idea underlying the safety feature could be transferred into this context. For example, if there was a single button that, when pressed did not initialize the flush but instead revealed the two-button option, then the first step would aid raising awareness of the choice that followed and therefore promote more conscious decision-making at the second stage. There are many more areas in the house where such mindful design solutions could provide useful reminders for water or energy saving such as washing machines and tumble driers, kettles, ovens and fridges.

Sustainable considerations for personal transport

The second area for discussion is concerned with personal transport. The discussion is divided into two parts; first, the reduction of car use, and second, the reduction of fuel consumption when using a car.

By now, there have been many different attempts at encouraging cycling over driving, using various different means. Urban cycling schemes (e.g. CityBike, 2015) seek to encourage cycling simply through ready access and increased availability (enabling mechanism). Cycling mentor schemes use dedicated cyclists to encourage non-cyclists to take up cycling by joining them and supporting them with route guidance and other forms of constructive input (enabling mechanisms + motivating support; Wunsch et al., 2015). While both examples have found more or less wide reception, they both rely on the prior commitment of the user to use their bike. Therefore, the decision-making moment at home is clearly the most crucial point for deciding which mode of transport to use. One experimental design, which can be classed as mindful design, is addressing this critical point of decision-making. It is predicated on the use of keys to use and lock the car and bike. The design is a 'key-board' on the wall where both keys are kept. In the design, the keys are weighted such that when choosing the car key the bike key will fall off (but not vice versa) to make the user reflect about using their bike while they pick up the bike key (Laschke et al., 2014; Figure 34.3).

Figure 34.3 Keymoment, designed by Matthias Laschke and Marc Hassenzahl

Source: reproduced with permission from Matthias Laschke and Marc Hassenzahl, © 2015

In this design, the practical function and expectation that a key board should safely hold keys is disrupted, and the attention is drawn to a specific content: to the key and its purpose, to cycling, because of the bike key having to be picked up. This actively puts the choice before the user: cycling or driving? The design thus pits personal emotions (comfort of driving) versus social good ('save our earth') combined with more personal effort. In this scenario, reservation (negative emotion) to the latter might be overcome by satisfaction (positive emotion) about oneself in doing something for one's health at the same time.

The authors also consider the question of emotional 'friction' because of the factor of having to pick up the keys from the floor is likely to be annoying to most people. While this is of course intentional, it shows that the 'disruption' has to be chosen and designed very carefully to provide an (emotional) balance between disrupting/attention raising features and their perceived benefits, because it is likely that mindful designs with less intrusive or annoying disruptive features might ensure a longer-lasting use than ones that create too much annoyance. The authors have therefore considered solutions to give the user a 'break', e.g. by putting the keys on top of the board (Figure 34.4). An alternative solution might have been to offer a visual or audio response (e.g. traffic light, or image/message reminder), thus making use of a symbolic disruption instead of a disruption of the practical function.

Beyond influencing the initial decision making process, there is also the option of raising the awareness of the driver of their fuel consumption. While this is less effective than not using one's car, it can still contribute to a more sustainable (and possibly safer) driving style. Modern cars already have a number of mindful features designed into them. However, they usually pertain to the driver safety rather than to fuel consumption or CO_2 emissions. For example, in many cars,[1] a dashboard light will indicate to the driver if they have not yet fastened their seatbelt, and in some it might actually prevent them driving. Another safety feature in modern cars is the dimming of the dashboard controls when the light levels get low to remind the driver that they ought to switch on the car's headlights. This cue is fairly subtle but effective, making the display more difficult to read until the headlights are switched on, at which point the display reverts to its normal brightness. In terms of consumption, while

Figure 34.4 Keymoment – have a break, designed by Matthias Laschke and Marc Hassenzahl

Source: reproduced with permission from Matthias Laschke and Marc Hassenzahl, © 2015

modern cars have display features that can be called up to show average consumption when travelling, there is not yet an equivalent to the above mentioned safety features even though it is easily imaginable that the display could offer a reminder when going beyond a certain level of consumption. Similarly, some cars offer different drive-style features that can be selected, including automatic, sport and economic drive modes. Here the choice feature that could underpin a mindful design feature is already available, but there is no mechanism (disruption) yet to remind the driver upon starting a journey to reflect on which feature to choose. Again, such an alert would be easy enough to add as a feature, and could also contribute positively to the overall experience of driving.

Waste reduction, waste collection and recycling

Besides energy saving measures, the preservation of resources and the reduction of waste are a key issue of product design and manufacture. Over the past three decades or so, legislation, education and voluntary work have contributed to building an extensive system, the consumer facing end of which includes bins for separating out bio-waste, recyclable materials, end-waste, etc., recycling banks, and recycling centres. One of the remaining challenges of this system is the difficulty of consistent voluntary commitment and separation which, if not observed, causes difficulties at the recycling stage leading to inferior produce (EEA, 2005, 2014). In glass recycling for example, this leads to glass cullet where colours are mixed and therefore colour standards cannot be upheld, especially for clear glass, or where there are other contaminants entering the process and which are difficult to remove (WRAP, 2008).

Waste collection and recycling is also a field where mindful design solutions have yet to emerge. Existing solutions such as recycling bins for different materials are clearly useful. However, they suffer from the aforementioned problems of either not being used at all, or of being used at random (Tromp, 2013). Given the importance of these issues, it may be worth considering how powerful examples of mindful design can be transferred into such unexplored product design contexts and scenarios. For example, the mechanism used in the computer safety feature which could be applied to a specific situation or product, such as a recycling bin reminding the user of the eligible content.

Conclusion

This chapter has discussed the urgent need for more sustainable action and behaviour. It has briefly explained the key mechanisms of behaviour change and their application within design, as well as the role and benefit which mindfulness can have in promoting sustainable behaviour change. The chapter has then explained how design can be used to instil mindful behaviour change. It has illustrated the idea of mindful design through a number of examples from sustainable design as well as safety design to explain the transformative role mindful design can play in the development of everyday product design solutions.

The conclusion of this review of mindful design in the context of sustainability is that mindful design is not yet widely recognized. To address this shortcoming, the above discussion has offered some existing mindful design examples and pointed to several areas of sustainability where mindful design could be applied to beneficial effect. There are also some powerful examples emerging with regard to social, health and safety interventions, which could offer further guidance for the development of mindful sustainable design solutions (Niedderer, forthcoming). One of the most striking current examples comes from a crossover of the social and safety context. It is the example of a *traffic junction* in Drachten, the Netherlands (Webster, 2007). This junction had a very high incident rate, which was not improved by further signage. Adopting the shared space model, the traffic planners finally took away all signs, creating a 'shared social space' where each road traffic participant (including pedestrians, cyclists and cars) has equal rights, and which improved the traffic safety of the junction significantly. The design works because the removal of the expected traffic guidance (disruption of expectation) causes individuals to take note of their social context (awareness), and by doing so it requires them to take responsibility for their actions as well as their own safety, thus creating a safer traffic environment overall. This model has by now been transferred to many other crossings in the UK and elsewhere, including junctions in London and Coventry.

One of the reasons why mindful design has not yet been adopted more strongly in the context of sustainability might be because it is strongly predicated on the material nature of design and its production. Like many other sustainable solutions, mindful design solutions inherently take a strong ethical stance. This ethical stance, which acknowledges the need for change and for taking on responsibility, needs to be adopted by designers and manufacturers to promote the development of mindful design solutions. It is my hope that this chapter offers a contribution for all concerned to adopt a sustainable ethical stance.

Note

1 The examples provided here are drawn from an Audi A3 registration in 2015.

References

Bhamra, T. A., Lilley, D. and Tang, T. (2011) 'Design for Sustainable Behaviour: Using Products to Change Consumer Behaviour'. *The Design Journal*, vol 14, no 4, pp427–445.

Blackburn, R. S. (2009) *Sustainable Textiles: Life Cycle and Environmental Impact.* Woodhead Publishing, Sawston.

Braungart, M., and McDonough, W. (2010) *Cradle to Cradle: Remaking the Way We Make Things.* North Point Press, New York.

Chittaro, L. and Vianella, A. (2013) 'Computer-Supported Mindfulness: Evaluation of a Mobile Thought Distancing Application of Naive Meditators'. *International Journal of Human-Computer Studies*, vol 72, pp337–348.

CityBike. (2015) 'Info'. Retrieved from www.citybikeliverpool.co.uk/info.html.

Cohn, M. A., Fredrickson, B. L., Brown, S. L., Mikels, J. A. and Conway A. M. (2009) 'Happiness Unpacked: Positive Emotions Increase Life Satisfaction by Building Resilience'. *Emotion*, vol 9, no 3, pp361–368.

Committee for Climate Change. (2015) *Progress in Preparing for Climate Change: 2015 Report to Parliament.* Committee on Climate Change, London. Retrieved from www.theccc.org.uk/wp-content/uploads/2015/06/6.736_CCC_ASC_Adaptation-Progress-Report_2015_FINAL_WEB_250615_RFS.pdf.

Crocker, R. and Lehman, S. (2013) *Motivating Change: Sustainable Design and Behaviour in the Built Environment.* Routledge, Abingdon.

Crown (2008). *Climate Change Act 2008.* The Stationery Office, London.

Dahlstrand, U. and Biel, A. (1997) 'Pro-environmental Habits: Propensity Levels in Behavioral Change'. *Journal of Applied Social Psychology*, vol 27, pp588–601.

Dusch, B., Crilly, N. and Moultrie, J. (2011) 'From Attitude to Action: The Development of the Cambridge Sustainable Design Tool Kit'. In *Proceedings of CADMC*, University of Cambridge, Cambridge.

EEA (2005) *Effectiveness of Packaging Waste Management Systems in Selected Countries: An EEA Pilot Study.* Office for Official Publications of the European Communities, European Environmental Agency, Luxembourg.

EEA (2014) *Recycling Rates in Europe.* European Environmental Agency, Luxembourg.

Egan, M. (2014) 'Heat Genius Review: Smart Home Heating System Can Save You Money, Will Keep You Warm – and it's Wireless', *TechAdviser*, 27 October. Retrieved from www.pcadvisor.co.uk/review/smart-thermostats/heat-genius-review-3582552.

Fuad-Luke, A. (2009) *Design Activism: Beautiful Strangeness for a Sustainable World*. Earthscan, London.

IEA (2015) *Energy and Climate Change*. International Energy Agency, Paris. Retrieved from www.iea.org/publications/freepublications/publication/WEO2015SpecialReportonEnergyandClimateChange.pdf.

IPCC (2015) *Climate Change 2014: Synthesis Report*. Intergovernmental Panel on Climate Change, Geneva. Retrieved from www.ipcc.ch/pdf/assessment-report/ar5/syr/SYR_AR5_FINAL_full_wcover.pdf.

Jelsma, J. (2006) 'Designing "Moralized" Products'. In Verbeek, P. P. and Slob, A. (eds), *User Behavior and Technology Development: Shaping Sustainable Relations Between Consumers and Technologies*. Springer, Berlin, pp221–223.

Keltner, D. and Ekman, P. (2000) 'Emotion: An Overview'. In Kazdin, A. (ed.) *Encyclopedia of Psychology*. Oxford University Press, London, pp162–167.

Lagerkvist, S., von der Lancken, C., Lindgren, A. and Sävström, K. (2012) *Static! Increasing Energy Awareness: Disappearing-Pattern Tiles*. Interactive Institute, Sweden. Retrieved from http://dru.tii.se/static/disappearing.htm

Langer, E. J. (1989) *Mindfulness*. Addison Wesley Publishing Company, Boston, MA.

Langer, E. J. and Moldoveanu, M. (2000a) 'The Construct of Mindfulness', *Journal of Social Issues*, vol 56, no 1, pp1–9.

Langer, E. J. and Moldoveanu, M. (2000b) 'Mindfulness Research and the Future'. *Journal of Social Issues*, vol 56, no 1, pp129–139.

Laschke, M., Hassenzahl, M., Diefenbach, S. and Schneider, T. (2014) 'Keymoment: Initiating Behavior Change through Friendly Friction'. Paper presented at NordiCHI '14, 26–30 October, Helsinki, Finland.

Letrendre, S. and Taylor, M. (2009) *Residential Photovoltaic Metering and Interconnection Study*. SEPA, Washington, DC. Retrieved from www.solarelectricpower.org/discover-resources/publications-and-media.aspx.

Lockton, D., Harrison, D. and Stanton, N. A. (2010). 'The Design with Intent Method: A Design Tool for Influencing User Behaviour'. *Applied Ergonomics*, vol 41, no 3, pp382–392

Luttrell, A., Briñol P. and Petty, R. E. (2014) 'Mindful Versus Mindless Thinking and Persuasion'. In Ie, A., Ngnoumen, C. T. and Langer, E. (eds) *The Wiley Blackwell Handbook of Mindfulness*, vol 1., Wiley, Chichester, pp258–278.

Niedderer, K. (2007) 'Designing Mindful Interaction: The Category of the Performative Object'. *Design Issues*, vol 23, no 1, pp3–17.

Niedderer, K. (2013) 'Mindful Design as a Driver for Social Behaviour Change'. In *Proceedings of the IASDR Conference 2013*, IASDR, Tokyo, Japan, 26–30 August.

Niedderer, K. (2014) 'Mediating Mindful Social Interactions through Design'. In Ie, A., Ngnoumen, C.T. and Langer, E. (eds) *The Wiley Blackwell Handbook of Mindfulness*, vol 1, Wiley, Chichester, pp345–366

Niedderer, K. (forthcoming) 'Facilitating Behaviour Change through Mindful Design'. In Niedderer, K., Clune, S. and Ludden, G. (eds) *Design for Behaviour Change*. Ashgate, Farnham.

Norman, D. A. (2002) *The Design of Everyday Things*. Basic Books, New York.

Stern, N. H. (2006) *The Economics of Climate Change*. HM Treasury, London.

Stern, P. C. (2000) 'New Environmental Theories: Toward a Coherent Theory of Environmentally Significant Behavior'. *Journal of Social Issues*, vol 56, no 3, pp407–424.

Tromp, N. (2013) 'Social Design: How Products and Services Can Help Us Act in Ways that Benefit Society'. PhD thesis, TU Delft, Delft, The Netherlands.

Tromp, N., Hekkert, P. and Verbeek, P. P. (2011) 'Design for Socially Responsible Behaviour: A Classification of Influence Based on Intended User Experience'. *Design Issues*, vol 27, no 3, pp3–19.

Udall, N. (1996) 'An Investigation into the Heuristics of Mindfulness in Higher Art and Design Education'. PhD thesis, University of Surrey, Guildford.

Webster, C. (2007) 'Property Rights, Public Space and Urban Design'. *The Town Planning Review*, vol 78, no 1, pp81–101.

WRAP (2008) *Refillable Glass Beverage Container Systems in the UK*. Waste and Resources Action Programme, Banbury.

Wunsch, M., Stibe, A., Millonig, A., Seer, S., Dai, S., Schechtner, K. and Chin, R. C. C. (2015) 'What Makes You Bike? Exploring Persuasive Strategies to Encourage Low-Energy Mobility'. In MacTavish, T. and Basapur, S. (eds) *PERSUASIVE 2015*, LNCS 9072, pp53–64.

35

DESIGN FOR SOCIAL INNOVATION AND NEW PRODUCT CONTEXTS

Nicola Morelli

Abstract

Designers have played a key role in the definition of the present production and consumption system, interpreting and addressing social and technological change. In the last decades however, the speed of technological change is increasing, and major environmental, social and economic issues are challenging the way we live, produce and consume material and immaterial resources. The crisis of the existing system also involved all its key actors, including designers, whose role has been crucial in the diffusion of consumption patterns and lifestyles. From being a key resource for the system, designers now risk to become part of the problem. They need to reframe the conceptual context in which they operate, which implies challenging the basic assumptions of the existing production and consumption systems, from the idea of comfort to the dominant function of technology in innovation processes. This chapter proposes that reshaping the production and consumption system is possible by working on different perspectives, which link rapid social changes to the ongoing technological innovation. Those perspectives emphasize new opportunities to use social change and technological innovation to mobilize every creative resource available in our society, including citizens' diffuse design capabilities, tacit knowledge and local knowledge generated by social aggregation. This way of framing the future is also shifting the role of designers from *creators* to *enabler;* therefore designers' *expert* knowledge is becoming a key support for a broad transformation towards a more sustainable system.

Keywords: expert and diffuse design, social innovation, co-creation, innovation platforms

> The world we live today includes problems that cannot be solved with the way of thinking we had when we created them.
>
> – *Albert Einstein*

Introduction

In complex systems, such as the biological and social systems we are living in, change is part of the system's dynamic. The speed of change in this particular historical moment though, seems not to be consistent with the natural speed of biological and social change. This requires our social, technical and natural systems to face new problems and find new solutions that impact on our way of living (i.e. the way we produce what we need and the way we consume what we produce).

The challenge for the whole system is, of course, also a challenge for designers that have played a key role in the development of the existing production and consumption system. So far designers have interpreted and addressed wide social, cultural and technological changes, but, as soon as the present system revealed its limits (such as its limits in managing environmental resources, inability to address economic inequalities among different geographical areas or social inequalities among different groups in the same cities or nations), designers have also been seen as part of the most crucial problems we are facing nowadays. Future sustainability measures require designers to interpret the present changes from different perspectives: the first perspective focuses on transformations in the existing social system; the second perspective focuses on technological changes and the effects this would have for ecological and social sustainability. Social changes are supposed to bring about innovation in the technological system, whereas technological changes that quickly transforming our way of living, could and should be addressed towards preferable and desirable futures. The combination of the two perspectives should bring about a radically new way of producing, organizing and using products, services and technological infrastructures around us.

Why we need a radical change

History has always been a continuous change; however the emergence of several complex problems in our contemporary history can be seen as a clear sign that the transformations in this period are possibly much quicker or more radical than we have previously seen. Inequalities, famines, climate change, migrations, changes in the inner structure of our society are all introducing new challenges that often cannot find solutions in the classic tools of government policies or in market solutions, that means that the products and services we have now are inadequate to address such challenges. The solutions to such problems can only come from a radical perspective change, and this implies substantial innovation processes within the social structure.

The challenges we are facing require designers to have a strong ability to interpret the ongoing transformations and propose valid alternatives to the mainstream development model. This means that we need a new design capability that is informed by a broader view of the existing production and consumption system; a capability to look at the future beyond the limitations of existing paradigms, looking at systemic perspectives that link design and technological opportunities to broader sustainable social changes.

This capability is not necessarily a prerogative of designers. Indeed the capability to devise preferable courses of action that change the existing situation into a preferred one (Simon, 1972) is a characteristic of all human beings. Ezio Manzini (2015) considers this fundamental human capability to be the key to addressing the change needed in this historical moment. The professional designer, argues Manzini, is just a person with some methodological tools that can help and support a diffuse design capability; but the paradigmatic change this system needs right now should come from a wider change in the way people live their everyday lives and plan their futures. However, this does not necessarily mean that such diffuse design capability will address the emerging problems in the right direction.

The world we inhabit today has been shaped by historical, technological and cultural events in which designers have often played a crucial role. Since the Industrial Revolution, in the late 1700s, rapid and radical changes have transformed diverse agricultural societies into more homogeneous industrial economies. Technological advances have radically changed the way we live. Economic systems have supported this change in some parts of the world (the 'Western countries') and communication systems have contributed to the distribution of a new model of development across the globe. The acceleration of changes in the last two centuries has been particularly high, with respect to the previous period.

The lifestyle changes this progress brought about have been interpreted and addressed by designers and design schools the world over. This is particularly so in cases where individuals could interact with industrial companies, relevant economic stakeholders and active social contexts. Designers worked on both the opportunities and challenges disclosed by technological innovation. In this way, they had a crucial role in the shift from mass production to new production platforms and product architectures that produced customizable solutions and addressed smaller target groups. They support the optimization of industrial products and to open up new markets. In the last few decades, designers have also become increasingly employed in the redefinition of public policies and public services.

This development, though, did not come without major challenges: the emerging industrial system was bringing about enormous transformations on social, cultural and natural systems. After the first environmental crisis in the 1970s it became quite clear that the existing development model could not be sustained by the planet's metabolism. Nevertheless, besides few remarkable exceptions, the vast majority of designers did not change their attitudes toward the production system, and paradigm, they were working within. By doing so they became co-responsible for the environmental and social crisis that this model caused.

Designers designed their own trap, and now they need to get out of it. This will only be possible, by looking beyond the limits of the existing paradigm. This means that some of the fundamental points of the existing paradigm should be critically discussed.

The decline of an idea of comfort

The development of the industrial society has seen a progressive shift from the informal to the formal economy (Normann, 2000). This has been possible by introducing new products, services or technologies in our daily life. The washing machine replaced the activity of washing clothes (which was previously a form of social activity in some villages, for example); television replaced family conversations around the fireplace, schools replaced children's education at home and nursing homes are now taking care of our elders that were previously living with their children, and grandchildren in a diverse multigenerational community.

In the prevailing market logic, this shift implies more business opportunities for industrial companies to monetize what are, essentially, fundamental human or social processes. Thus, the nature of the relation between many production systems and their customers is at the heart of our idea of *comfort*. On one hand comfort is a way to *relieve* customers from the many tasks of the everyday life (Manzini, 2005). On the other hand, it may be seen as a scheme for social control that has functionally contributed to the process of modernization (Maldonado and Cullars, 1991). In both cases comfort comes with a cost: it frames people into pre-determined behavioural schemes and makes certain human skills redundant. The collateral effects of comfort are the loss of basic capabilities to repair objects (today they are just replaced, or the repair process is outsourced), to prepare food (today most of our food comes semi-prepared or ready-made, to save our time) and even to find ways to spend our time or to socialize (today entertainment services are keeping us occupied and even dating opportunities are offered as a service). The quantitative and qualitative increase of products and services that provide comfort has made people passive and increasingly dependent on consumer products or commercial services.

The idea of *comfort* proposed by this logic has been progressively disabling people (Manzini, 2005) because it deprives them of the capability to solve problems in the future. What customers now save in physical effort or time will be paid in the future in terms of lost knowledge and skills.

The critic to this idea of comfort leads towards a shift in perspective: from a vision that considers users as problem holders, to a vision that considers users as co-producers. That implies considering people's capabilities (time, practical knowledge and social skills) as a resource to define new solutions. The idea of comfort is: disabling people's *personal resources* (physical skills, knowledge, organizational and entrepreneurial skills, design capabilities) as well as their *social resources* (personal acquaintances, mutual trust, shared experiences that can develop in a social context). Sennett (2012) observes that modern society is de-skilling people in practicing cooperation. If the idea of comfort creates *passive* users (consumers, rather than people) the natural capabilities of individuals to cooperate and find new solutions is significantly undermined.

In fact, the idea of comfort is based on the disaggregation of homogeneous social contexts into *target groups,* with the aim of finding sets of products and services that can better address the needs of each group. The links among the groups become therefore less relevant, together with the social skills that were supporting those links. If social skills are a resource, their progressive regression should be seen as a component of the question of sustainability.

One way for designers to contribute to the restoration of this resource is to consider people as co-designers, and use their personal and social knowledge and skills in the production process. The design process must aim at defining such *enabling ecosystems* (Manzini, 2015), in which the people's resources are more fully empowered. In this scenario, people define their own problems and decide upon the most appropriate solution using the most appropriate commitment of their own personal and social capabilities.

The limits of the technocratic paradigm

The Industrial Revolution brought about a progressive acceleration of technological change. The development and diffusion of new technologies has been accelerated by transport means first, and by information and communication technologies in the last decades. The direction of this change does not look like it is going to slow down. The potential of new technologies is still vast and broad changes in the way technological knowledge is managed are promising newer developments.

Technological changes have deeply influenced our culture(s), and the way we live over the last century to the point that the social perception of technology itself is evolving. The traditional view of technology as a tool for the development of society is gradually being undermined by a newer vision in which technology becomes the substrate and the structure of society itself. From being a simple means, technology is becoming an end; from being a 'neutral' component in our economic and social structure, technology is becoming a diriment, ubiquitous condition. This condition supports whoever adjusts its way of working or living to the mainstream technocratic paradigm, whereas it marginalizes individuals or social groups that do not want (or are unable) to fit in this paradigm.

The technocratic paradigm is often seen as an absolute limitation, where life gradually becomes a surrender to situations conditioned by technology, itself viewed as the principal key to the meaning of existence (Bergoglio, 2015). But the technocratic paradigm is also hiding macroscopic changes that are affecting technological development. One of them concerns the way technological knowledge is owned, managed and exchanged.

The development of a networked society is making technological knowledge widespread and available to a larger group of citizens, which are now able to control and often generate novel and diffuse innovation processes. Such processes may be even faster and more effective than those generated by industrial experts (von Hippel, 2005). The hierarchical control of technological knowledge is showing its limits in front of the networked knowledge of hundreds of thousands of users. This also applies to technological systems. Here centralized systems (e.g. energy production, hardware systems of complex products, software solutions) are competing with diffuse systems, which use natural resources (such as for energy production) or distributed production systems.

Such changes are more visible when the point of view is moved outside the dominant technocratic paradigm, from a perspective that takes into account the relevant social transformation unleashed by technological changes in the last decades. This also points out the ineffectiveness of technological knowledge to address the great challenges of our time, such as the question of sustainability. Scientific and technical change alone cannot solve the systemic problems we are facing, and cannot address the demand for a systemic change towards a more sustainable society. The range of validity of scientific and technological solutions is often restricted to very limited social, natural and economic contexts and – as such – neglects critical connections between disconnected and diverse systemic components.

From products to solutions

Our homes and cities are a composition of objects that have been gradually added to our living environment and are somehow having an 'independent life'. Each object is there because it *serves us* with specific performance, or because it holds valuable references to a universe of meanings that are relevant to us.

We live among those objects, trying to find a balance between our functional and affective needs – that would justify objects and infrastructures around us – and our need to control the vast amounts of material and semantic noise created by this plethora of designed objects.

The dialectic exchange between human beings and the material world around them has acquired a new dimension in the last decades. This has been enabled – in large part – by the development of networks that link people to people, people to objects and even objects to objects. In the mature phase of the network society objects are linked to infrastructures that manage their behaviour, their performance or their status. They are monitored and controlled through sensors and microcomputers, as in the case of home automation or in large networked cities. The possibility to connect everything (as described in the Internet of Things) is based on a networked model to distribute energy sources, knowledge and information processing and even manufacturing processes. This model is opening new perspectives for the replacement of centralized energy sources with a system of distributed, renewable resources, located close to the points of demand (Biggs et al., 2010), large computing capabilities are now made possible by networks of microcomputers that directly link users, networks and the space/objects around them (Ratti, 2013). More recently, the miniaturization of productive units is supporting distributed production and consumption networks, which in turn is activating networks of microenterprises at the local level that are changing the established production system. These new products will possibly be designed and highly customized to local or user-related contexts. The simplification of the production process corresponds to a complexification of the range of possible solutions, involving new forms of organization of services that will use the codified knowledge of manufacturers and local service providers as well as the personal/local knowledge of users. This will possibly push the limits of extreme customization (Morelli and Nielsen, 2007). The design focus will therefore make the shift from the individual product to the personalized and local solutions this distributed system will make possible.

Framing the future

The need for a more sustainable production and consumption system is not limiting the possibilities for developing new solutions, it is in fact expanding them. If the existing paradigm was strongly supported by a continuous and rapid evolution of an industrial/technical system, the scenario of a sustainable production/consumption system could instead start from a change in social attitudes; those two strategic positions highlight two perspectives (see Figure 35.1):

- A first perspective focuses ongoing social changes and highlights different behaviours, emerging patterns and promising initiatives; starting from social changes this perspective is also emphasizing the need for major technical changes.
- A second perspective looks at ongoing technical changes and suggests strategic views that would eventually bring about large social changes.

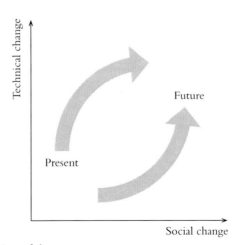

Figure 35.1 Two perspectives of change

The first perspective: social changes create new technological opportunities

The first perspective focuses on the way we live, on the social system and on the cultural basis of our life. A wide range of problems is emerging that needs urgent actions in contemporary societies, from the rise of life expectancy to migration and social inequalities; from the increased incidence of social diseases to the mismatch between GDP and people's actual well-being.

The existing institutional systems do not seem to be able to address these issues. Government structures and public services are often limited by a regulatory framework based on social/economic conditions that are no longer effective, or valid. Furthermore economic crises are undermining local and national governments' capabilities to intervene on such macro-phenomena with adequately planned solutions.

On the other hand, the dominant market-oriented approach fails to assign an exchange value to critical assets, such as natural assets like the cleanliness of the air, or social assets like local communities or cultural heritage, for example. This approach would often fail to recognize the real values that are at stake in the present crisis.

The challenge is to generate a clear disconnect between the way existing systems have been designed, and a new way of looking at existing problems, which mobilizes the widest possible set of resources. This would include individual and social design capabilities, personal experience and forms of tacit, social or local knowledge. Indeed, the new solutions should not just be a reaction to the emerging problems, but rather a meaningful system of feasible ideas based on new social forms and new economic models (Mulgan, 2006).

For these ideas to work, design action must be shared. That means it has to emerge from the action of social groups, citizens and grassroots organizations, rather than arising from the agency of a single designer. Design has to be a *diffuse attitude*, to which *expert designers* should offer their support (Manzini, 2015).

This represents a significant change in designers' social roles that also urges designers to recognize some *signposts* that could orient appropriate design action.

Making things together

Individual capabilities are potentiated by the natural attitude of humans, as social animals, to get together and do things they would not be able to do alone. Collaboration stems from people's capability to join individual resources (knowledge, time, money, skills) in order to do something that is valuable for those who collaborate. Collaboration, observes Sennett (2012) demands a specific expertise, or *techné*, that can be defined as the social skills to listen, to manage the conflict or to grasp critical points in a dialogue with others. Such skills are undermined by the existing socio-technical ecosystem.

Collaboration not only concerns the capability to find shared solutions, but also to define shared problems and identify shared values. An expert cannot *design* collaboration; it should emerge from a social context. However, expert design can emphasize opportunities for doing things together, possibly introducing elements of an ecosystem that support collaboration and co-creation (see Box 35.1). Rather than defining solutions, expert design will support participation, a path that has already been identified in design studies over the last decade, but also a radical shift in the role of design, that flies in the face of the 'expert' mind-set that is prevalent in business today (Sanders, 2008).

The new design challenge is not in the *invention* of new creative solutions, but in the support and amplification of phenomena that are somehow already happening. For many

---

Box 35.1 The Circle initiative (UK)

The need to provide more effective assistance to an ageing population inspired the Circle initiative in UK. At Circle, members can also be helpers, and much of the content and activity is user-generated. The system has a wide network of paid and voluntary helpers that help taking care of members' needs, from climbing a ladder for changing a light bulb, to accompanying someone on a hospital visit, to sorting someone's paper work. Members also take part in a wide range of social activities. Circle team members range in age from their fifties to their nineties and actively participate to the activities of the network (Cottam, 2010).

Box 35.2 Social Street (Italy)

In times of crisis, people often turn to one another for help in solving the problems of everyday life. Usually the help comes from family members or from neighbours, but the dispersive and impersonal environments of contemporary cities often make it hard to find support when needed. This is particularly true for several people that are moving from town to town and are new to a local neighbourhood. This inspired the *social street movement* in Italy. The movement started in 2013 in Bologna and is growing up very quickly. The medium used by the group for socialization is not new, the founder created the first social street using the 'group' feature in Facebook, but the scope of the initiative expanded as soon as the citizens participating to the social street realized its potential. Today the social street movement is spreading in many locations, inspiring people to do more things together.

This, in turn, challenged the existing technological infrastructure used as the communication platform. New platforms (such as *Nextdoor*, *My Neighbourhood* and *Streetlife*) and applications are now being invented that address the need of location-based networks, which link geographical positioning systems (GPS) with several social networking applications.

---

reasons, people are already doing things together, and to do that, they do not necessarily need special technological advancements. In fact, some of these initiatives are challenging the rigidity of existing technological infrastructure and imposing new logical perspectives, even without requesting any major technological change (Box 35.2). Although such initiatives are often self-organized, a strong effort is needed to keep them active and relevant for their large numbers of users.

The *expert designer* contribution to the success of such initiatives consists on understanding and supporting the elements of the ecosystems that feed the relationships between people and other social stakeholders. The design domain includes physical and virtual infrastructures, norms, trust mechanisms and interaction opportunities that would represent the 'glue' for collaboration within such communities (see Box 35.3).

Making things small and scaling them up

Participatory initiatives may represent viable solutions only if they could offer a valid alternative to large, centralized production and consumption systems. This means the success of such initiatives is linked to the solving of an apparent paradox: on the one hand, they have to expand to a scale that is comparable or relevant in respect to centralized production systems; on the other hand, they can only survive if they can keep their specific characteristics, such as strong social ties among participants, small scale, diversity and localization. This paradox is also the main problematic issue for expert designers, and the focus of much research in this context.

Neighbourhood-based social networks are based on the tight link between logical links (shared interests, shared values) and the physical urban space where participants are living. The motivation for these kinds of initiatives is to create forms of collaboration that solve basic problems (taking care of kids, finding ingredients for cooking) or to find social opportunities (organizing a party, knowing local people).

The structures designed to support such initiatives should address the need for *relevance* – making sure that the participants' interest is kept alive – and *trust,* which requires that adequate forms of commitment are put in place, based on physical presence and *abstract systems* mediated by technologies or expert knowledge (Morelli, 2015; Giddens, 1990).[1]

The contribution of expert designers could consist of the identification of catalysts that generate relevance and support trust, such as *active mobs* (Leadbeater and Cottam, 2008) or physical evidences, such as Public Innovation Places (Manzini and Staszowski, 2013). The second aspect of the apparent paradox concerns the scalability of such initiatives in terms of horizontal scaling up – that is, the increase of the participant basis, or vertical scaling up – that implies an institutionalization of the initiatives (Morelli, 2015). A systematic design intervention to ensure reproducibility of such initiatives should take into account the internal social structures, the capabilities and skills that generate relevance and trust and possibly reproduce the overall architecture of the initiatives, rather than simply increasing their size.

In order to support scaling-up processes, expert designers could create (online or offline) platforms – that work as a ground for local collaborative encounters. The scalability of such initiatives depends on the possibility to reproduce the same platform architecture (e.g. Box 35.3; Figure 35.2). In different geographical contexts that means that scalability in this case does not mean the exponential increase of participants but the reproduction of the systemic architecture of an ecosystem. The expansion of social innovation from a local context to wider regional or national or international contexts cannot happen though a *wildfire* expansion but through the multiplication of *nodes*, or *clusters* (Morelli, 2015).

Box 35.3 Life 2.0 (Denmark)

The Life 2.0[2] project aimed at creating an infrastructure that could support elderly people's independent life. An online platform was created, that would link the social skills of community providers to the technical skills of IT providers and the business skills of local business activities. The project identified the many different social stakeholders and the relationships between them. The architecture of the system is reproducible in other locations, as far as the main actors of the ecosystem could be available (Figure 35.2). The platform supporting this project is both virtual – a Website and an iPad application – and physical, as it includes the physical infrastructure community providers are arranging to support elderly people's community.

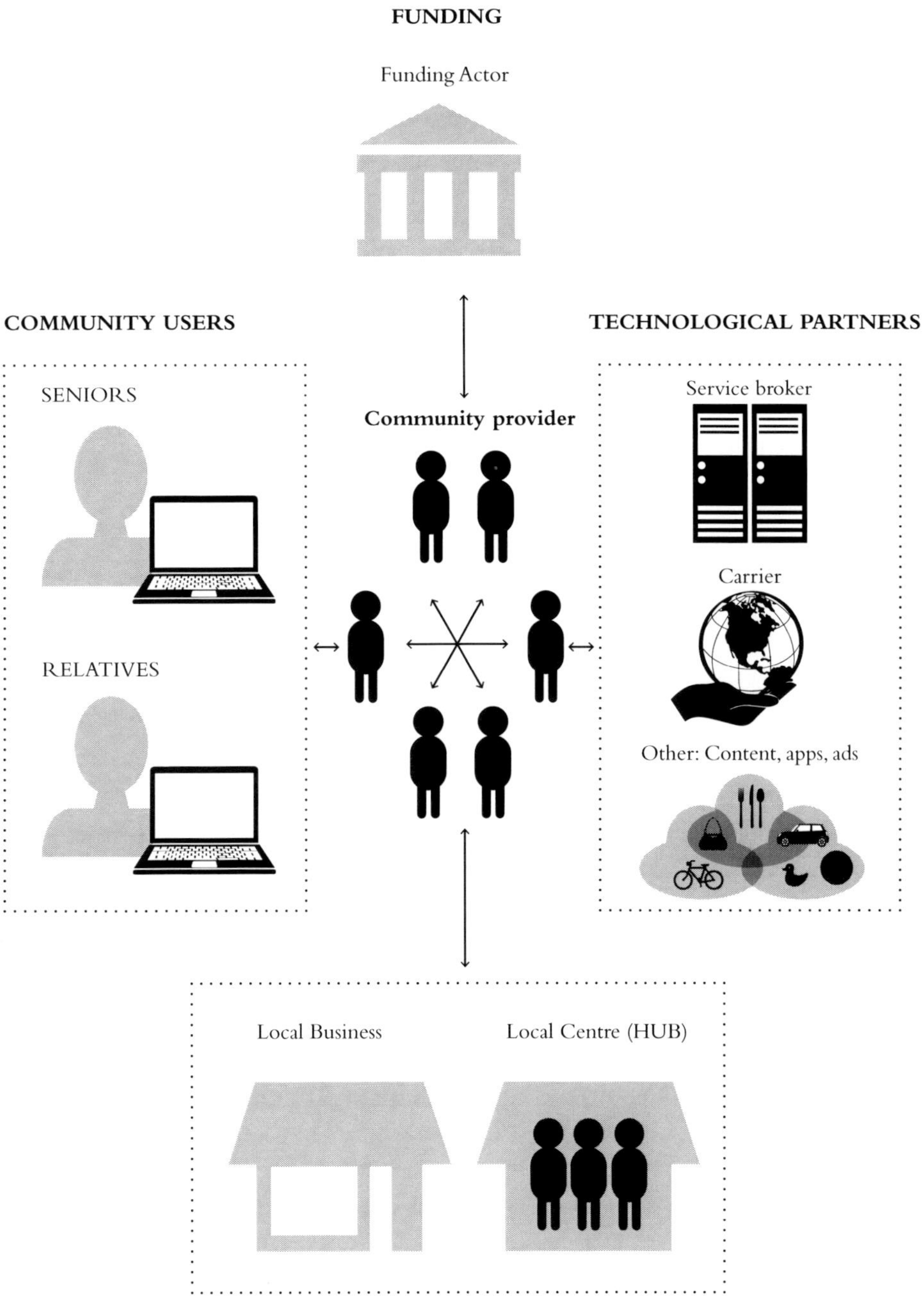

Figure 35.2 The Life 2.0 ecosystem

Sharing infrastructures, products, experiences

The recent economic crisis emphasized a need that had already emerged in the debate on sustainability: the need to shift from private ownership to accessibility, and from a product/ based to a utilization-focused service economy (Stahel, 1997; Rifkin, 2000). Phenomena that were previously considered as social experiments, such as car sharing, co-housing, cooperative movements, are now becoming widely diffused, also because of the economic crisis, which is reducing the access to individual property. Those initiatives are increasing the utilization value of goods, while decreasing the need for individual ownership. A utilization-focused service economy – or *sharing economy* – goes towards a general reduction of the material intensity of our production and consumption system, and a more efficient use of existing resources. Sharing material objects is also connected to sharing time and knowledge, which means creating the conditions for collaboration among citizens, with the motivation of saving money but also improving social links.

Beside the evident economic advantages, sharing and collaborative initiatives are also activating social dynamics that were previously disappearing, because they are based on mutual help, resource sharing and reutilization. Therefore sharing usually reinforces social cohesion, especially for local communities. Several peer-to-peer (P2P) platforms have been designed to support sharing and collaboration. These platforms help manage the risks that malicious or erroneous uses of collaboration undermine trust among the members. The mechanisms of trust are not always the same: while young generations are more confident in mutual feedback mechanisms, older generations that are less used to online communication can only feel safe if more traditional social mechanisms (direct acquaintance, personal meetings) are also in place. This is typically the case with elderly people, as seen in the Life 2.0 case, mentioned above.

The success of the sharing economy, however, can be seen as a typical example in which Design is not necessarily pointing at a desirable future. Some successful sharing platforms for hospitality are jeopardizing the economic solidity of local tourist infrastructures. Likewise, car-sharing platforms are pushing professional taxi drivers out of the market. The critics to this phenomenon emphasize the fact that for-profit platforms have co-opted some of those social phenomena (Schor, 2014), thus transforming them into opportunities for high profits for few companies, that are using a very cheap and precarious workforce, the citizens sharing their time, goods and living spaces (Baker, 2014; Slee, 2014).

Second perspective: technological change creates (desirable) social innovation

A second perspective for a future change is starting from this quick and sometimes inevitable technological change. Such change is not necessarily leading our social system towards desirable directions. The persistent success of dystopian movies and literature on technological nightmares (from *Blade Runner* to *The Matrix*) are possibly a sign of a diffuse fear for the speed of technological change.

When aiming at socially sustainable scenarios, design action could instead seize the opportunities of some relevant technological changes. The following sections will illustrate some of those changes.

Smart cities

Significant investments have been placed to support future Internet technologies, such as smart grids, sensor networks and infrastructure to support transportation, business and environment. The expectation is that *smart cities* will increase cost effectiveness, reduce environmental impact and increase citizens' satisfaction for urban services and infrastructures (Marsh, 2014).

The term *smart city* is nowadays a buzzword to indicate the enormous increase in information content *in* cities, *on* cities and *for* cities.

The rhetoric of smart cities is often linking technological aspects and business-led urban development, but smart cities also raise high expectations about the opportunities of social inclusion and social sustainability, support to creative industries and environmental sustainability (Hollands, 2008; Caragliu et al., 2009).

The rhetoric of technological advancements is often looking at complex solutions, whereas simple solutions are often more effective to address citizens' needs and lead to real behavioural changes and wider scales bottom-up transformations. This is particularly true for some part of society which has limited access to the latest technological innovation or that is culturally or psychological unprepared to seize the opportunities of new technologies, such as elderly people. *Frugal solutions* (i.e. simple ICT solutions) that can activate mutual learning environments and activate open learning mechanisms, would possibly shift the centre of urban innovation processes, from technologies to citizens. Besides the obvious potential for business and technical development, the promise of smart cities is to turn passive citizens in to active participants, able to define their own problems (instead of receiving solutions to pre-defined problems, or non-problems) and actively participate in the designing of new urban systems and services.

The emphasis on human factors have inspired several European projects, including Peripheria[3] and My Neighbourhood.[4] Focusing on the activation and participation of citizens, Life 2.0, activates elderly people through an online platform and a network of physical meeting places. Similarly, Citadel on the move aims at extending the use of open data. Those projects include the definition of technological platforms, but their development is based on citizens' participation and co-creation. Besides supporting technological solutions, designers have been involved in these projects also for developing action kits, and design tools, that could support the practice of participation, even without the direct intervention of expert designers.[5]

Opening-up data for citizens

The concept of *open data* is not new, although its formalization is, and increasing amounts of open data available is catalysing interest in this concept. Large amounts of data are now collected as a result of increased computing capability of the information and communication systems we use throughout our everyday lives. Large parts of the data sets created from our mobile communications, sensors networks, microcomputers, online pages, and social network are openly available to the public. The concept of open data refers to those data sets that are publicly available, so that people, companies and organizations can freely use, reuse or redistribute to support new services. Open data may consist of textual (such as mathematical data, formulae, medical information) or non-textual information (such as maps or images).

So far, few private companies have sized the opportunities offered by this new resource. At the same time public administrations and governments are putting a considerable effort to define standards and create large datasets to make open data publicly available and usable. The 2014 Digital Accountability and Transparency Act (DATA) in the USA aims at improving citizens' ability to track and understand data about public expenditure. In Europe, the *Fiware project*, aims at creating a platform with a large set of API (Application Programming Interfaces) that ease the development of new applications.[6]

The perspective opened by public initiatives is promising, but the availability of those data is not necessarily making sure that they can be widely used to address real social needs. The usability of open data is a critical determinant, together with their availability.

This is not just a technical question, as the rapid growth in the availability of data is turning open data into a new commons (i.e. a new public resource available to citizens). Such resource however is only available to those who know how to make sense of such data. Citizens that cannot access, or do not have the necessary skills to make a meaningful use of, open data are now at risk of experiencing a new form of exclusion.

The strategies to broaden the accessibility and usability of open data should be based on citizens' participation and direct involvement in the definition of the needs and the use of open data for the design of the appropriate solutions. Designers (product or service designers) can support this process of co-creation through the definition of technical or creative tools or innovation platforms that support accessibility and usability of data; furthermore they can have a crucial role in representing (through video sketching, prototypes or experience prototypes) new scenarios in which open data can be used as a relevant resource.

New initiatives are emerging such as the *Open4Citizens*[7] project that seek to involve citizens in hackathon sessions (together with IT experts, public administrators, interest groups and small business) in order to support a true co-design process for the development of new apps. Besides the design of the apps themselves, which is the obvious result, the main outcome of those processes is a wider citizens' awareness of the potential that such initiatives may represent, to change the relation between citizens and power and to generate social innovation.

Exploring new forms of production

Information technology is boosting the do-it-yourself (DIY) culture to a level that is now promising large social changes and shifts. The Internet has unleashed collective creativity of communities that can more effectively exchange free and open knowledge to generate innovation paths that are often threatening traditional industrial production (von Hippel, 2005). The technological and organizational structures of the traditional system are challenged by social aggregations, such as FabLabs or community-led *Maker Spaces* with the potential to offer quick and highly personalized solutions. Networked knowledge, together with cheap and accessible 3D printing facilities, is turning digital fabrication into forms of diffuse production that promise to revolutionize the way production systems are organized today, and in the near future.

As for open data, the rhetoric of technological enthusiasm should not hide some fundamental considerations: although the phenomenon is strongly rooted in social collaboration and open exchange of knowledge, digital fabrication is still far from being accessible to everybody as it requires a form of specialized technical knowledge. Nevertheless, the flourishing of FabLabs and cooperation spaces to support digital fabrication will most possibly create an ecosystem for new forms of networked micro-production initiatives, which will locate production close to the place where things will be needed and used. This will present new opportunities for social innovation and the revitalization of areas previously excluded by industrialization, or where the local economy had been depressed by the relocation of industrial production (Manzini, 2015). Once again, this phenomenon is about a diffuse creativity, which is questioning the assumed role of expert designers in the future development of those new forms of production. Interesting perspectives and capabilities are opening for designers, with the development of ecosystems that facilitate accessibility to this new production infrastructure.

Conclusions

This chapter is an attempt to cast an eye beyond the conceptual limitation of the present production and consumption system, towards a possible and desirable future. Despite Simon's definition of design as a widely diffuse attitude, the design profession has so far survived by pointing out the added value that an expert designer can provide to the existing production system. The perspective of a socially sustainable future challenges this position, because the perspective of a sustainable society seems to be strictly linked with the need to mobilize every creative resource available in our society, including the personal and tacit knowledge every individual uses for solving everyday problems. This resource will be fundamental for a sustainable future.

The context designers have developed so far includes problems that cannot be solved with the mind-set designers have used to create it, and so the challenge of designing a new context may be articulated on different layers.

A first layer concerns the nature and quality of design solutions. It concerns the way such solutions are designed, the capability of expert designers to support enabling ecosystems and adequate solution architectures that activate participatory processes. This means creating *innovation platforms* that mix highly technological tools with frugal tools that more effectively match the technological knowledge of the members of a local community.

A second layer concerns the reproducibility of such solutions. It concerns a revision of the existing scalability mechanisms and the introduction of new forms of scalability.

A third layer concerns the redefinition of the public perception of the design profession as well as the redesign of the existing power structures in which designers have worked, so far. In this sense the perspective shift in the role of the designer, from creator to enabler, goes hand in hand with a radical change in the social role of businesses and other public institutions.

Notes

1 Giddens proposes an accurate analysis of the question of trust in social interactions. He uses the terms of *facework commitments* to indicate trust relationship in circumstances of co-presence and *faceless commitments* to indicate trust relationship based on abstract systems. He was mainly referring to experts (medical practitioners, engineers) we trust for many aspects of our activities. The question of trust became more complex with the emergence of social networks. In the projects reported by trust is an essential glue that keeps together citizens in the same community or communities of *weaker* citizens, such as elderly people. It is not based on an expert knowledge, but rather on the mutual acquaintance of the members of the community.
2 Life 2.0 was a EU funded project aimed at creating a platform of services to support elderly people's independent life. See www.greenprimary.eu.
3 See http://humansmartcities.eu/project/peripheria.
4 See http://my-neighbourhood.eu.
5 See, for instance Marsh (2014).
6 See www.fiware.org.
7 *Open4Citizens* is a EU-funded project aimed at increasing the accessibility of open data to all citizens. At the time of writing this chapter the project was in its early phases.

References

Baker, D. (2014). Don't Buy the 'Sharing Economy' Hype: Airbnb and Uber are Facilitating Rip-offs. *The Guardian*, 27 May. Retrieved from www.theguardian.com/commentisfree/2014/may/27/airbnb-uber-taxes-regulation.

Bergoglio, J. (2015). Laudato Si': Encyclical Letter of the Holy Father Francis, on Care for Our Common Home. Retrieved from http://w2.vatican.va/content/francesco/en/encyclicals/documents/papa-francesco_20150524_enciclica-laudato-si.html.

Biggs, C., Ryan, C. and Wiseman, J. (2010). *Distributed Systems: A Design Model for Sustainable and Resilient Infrastructure*. Melbourne: Victorian Eco-Innovation Lab (VEIL).

Caragliu, A., Del Bo, C. and Mijkamp, P. (2009). Smart Cities in Europe. *3rd Central European Conference in Regional Science (CERS)*, October 7–9, Košice, Slovak Republic.

Cottam, H. (2010). Participatory Systems. *Harvard International Review* vol 31, 50–55.

Giddens, A. (1990). *The Consequences of Modernity*. Cambridge: Polity Press in association with Basil Blackwell.

Hollands, R. G. (2008). Will the Real Smart City Please Stand Up? *City* vol 12, 303–320.

Leadbeater, C. and Cottam, H. (2008). The User Generated State: Public Services 2.0. Retrieved from www.partnerships.org.au/Library/Public_Services_2.0.htm (accessed 6 February 2015).

Maldonado, T. and Cullars, J. (1991). The Idea of Comfort. *Design Issues* vol 8, 35–43.

Manzini, E. (2005). Enabling Solutions for Creative Communities. *Design Matters* vol 10, 64–68.

Manzini, E. (2015). *Design, when Everybody Designs*. Cambridge, MA: MIT Press.

Manzini, E. and Staszowski, E. (2013). *Public and Collaborative: Exploring the Intersection of Design, Social Innovation and Public Policy*. London: DESIS.

Marsh, J. (ed.) (2014). *The Human Smart Cities Cookbook*: Rome: Planum.

Morelli, N. (2015). Challenges in Designing and Scaling Up Community Services. *The Design Journal* vol 18, 269–290.

Morelli, N. and Nielsen, L. M. (2007). Mass Customisation and Highly Individualised Solutions. Stretching Mass Customisation Beyond the Traditional Paradigm of Industrial Production. In F. Piller and M. Tseng (eds), *MCPC 07: The 2007 World Conference on Mass Customisation and Personalisation*, 7–12 October, Boston, MA/Montreal.

Mulgan, G. (2006). *Social Innovation: What It Is, Why It Matters and How It Can Be Accelerated*. Oxford: Saïd Business School.

Normann, R. (2000). *Service Management: Strategy and Leadership in Service Business*. Chichester; Wiley.

Ratti, C. (2013). *Smart City, Smart Citizen*. Milan: Egea.

Rifkin, J. (2000). *The Age of Access: The New Culture of Hypercapitalism, Where All of Life is a Paid-For Experience*. New York: J. P. Tarcher/Putnam.

Sanders, E. (2008). Co-creation and the New Landscapes of Design. *Co-Design* vol 1, 5–18.

Schor, J. (2014). Debating the Sharing Economy. Retrieved from www.greattransition.org/publication/debating-the-sharing-economy-does-the-sharing-economy-build-social-capital (accessed 22 August 2015).

Sennett, R. (2012). *Together: The Rituals, Pleasures, and Politics of Cooperation*. New Haven, CT: Yale University Press.

Simon, H. (1972). Designing Organizations for an Information-Rich World. In M. Greenberger (ed.), *Computers, Communication, and the Public Interest*. Baltimore, MD: Johns Hopkins University Press, 37–72.

Slee, T. (2014) Sharing and Caring. *Jacobin*, 24 January. Retrieved from www.jacobinmag.com/2014/01/sharing-and-caring.

Stahel, W. R. (1997) *The Functional Economy: Cultural and Organisational Change*. Washington, DC: National Academy Press.

Von Hippel, E. (2005). *Democratizing Innovation*. Cambridge, MA: MIT Press.

INDEX

3D Hubs 237
3D printing 152–3, 194, 236–49, 515, 552
3TG 197–205
543 Broadway Chair 210

abstract machines 336–7
accelerated consumerism 251
access-based consumption models 391–2, 398
access economy 352
acrylonitrile butadiene styrene (ABS) 115, 148, 239
active citizens 551
activism 226, 230, 267, 335, 345, 335–48
actor network theory 47, 492
Acute washer 155
additive manufacturing technology 237 *see also* 3D printing
Adidas 123, 232, 272
Advisory Council on Intellectual Property (ACIP) 247
aesthetics of environmentally sensitive products 208
affective diffusion 38
affordances 30, 131, 302, 395
ageing gracefully 34, 119, 181, 193 206–7, 212, 374, 383–5
agents of change 1, 5, 97, 504
agonism 202, 338
Airbnb 160–9, 356
Airbus 242
ancestral hominids 48
animism 8, 41–52
anthropocene 85, 256, 335, 521
anthropological research 332
anthropology 44
anthropomorphism 45

Apple 34, 42 118, 203, 251, 256, 272, 413, 516
applying sustainable design 112–26
Arduino 237
Aristotle 61, 478, 505
Arthritis Foundation 279
ARUP 183
assistive technology devices 273
attachment: emotional 42, 46, 37, 123, 303–11 391–404, 411, 417; object 391–404; product 25–40, 295, 374
Attainable Utopias 511
attitude objects 224
Audi 164
austerity 42
Axis of influence 131, 141

Bacchetti, Elisa 443
Bag Borrow or Steal 162
Baxter, Weston 391
Beck, Ulrich 353
behaviour: sustainable behaviors 127–44, 153, 337; unsustainable behaviours 24, 325–6, 330, 448, 496
behaviour change 527–39; design for behaviour change 117, 319, 487–501, 529; sustainable behaviour change 127, 140, 316; promoting sustainable behaviour change 530–1, 534, 537 *see also* design for sustainable behaviours (DfSB)
behaviour intervention selection axis 135
behavioural design 33, 487–501
Bhamra, Tracy 363
Belk, Russell 160
Benjamin, Yorick 173
biodegradable resin 214
biodiversity 56, 89, 179, 184, 503

bio-semiotics 46, 71
biosphere 173
BMW 164
Boks, Casper 316
Boots 119
bottom-up 25–40, 522, 551
Braiform 115
Brezet's model of innovation 117
Broom 149
Brown, Tim 105
Buddhism 56, 62
Bullus, Anna 228
Busch, Otto von 335
business model innovation 115
business models 405–22 *see also* new business
    models

capitalism 4, 14, 83–96, 163, 353, 356
carbon absorptive forests 98
Carson, Rachel 13
Cartesian 43–50, 76–78
centralized manufacturing 245
Centre of Product Design and Manufacturing,
    Indian Institute of Science, Bangalore 76
change agent 101–11
Chapman, Jonathan 35, 50
cherished 314
Childs, Peter 391
chloroflourocarbons (CFCs) 15
Christianity 62
circular economy 5, 97,174, 194, 352, 359–61;
    and business models 405–22; and design
    practice 115–17; and consumers 374–89; and
    possessions 391–404; and product design
    case study 145–59; and product services
    systems 363–73; and unmaking waste 250–65
circular lifecycle 148–51
Claesson Koivisto Rune 210
Clark, Arthur C. 42
climate change 254
closed loop of production 260
closed loop emotionally valuable e-waste
    recovery 119
Cloud Institute for Sustainability Education
    108
co-creation 370, 396, 428, 518, 521, 540–54
coercive affordances 335
cognitive instruments 29
collaborative: analysis 428; consumption 160–
    72; design 440
commodity culture 79
complexity 487–501
computer-aided design (CAD) 178, 239
computer revolution 168
conflict free smelter programme (CFSP) 200
conflict minerals 2, 193, 197–205
Confucius 62
Conran Design 183

consumption 363–73; conspicuous 26, 127;
    commodity-consumption 80; green 21;
    hyper-consumption 251–2; material 112,
    268, 276, 417 ; patterns of 7, 198, 276, 337,
    470, 527, 540; rates of 8, 360; water 141, 156,
    427, 437, 534; sustainable 118, 121, 165, 222,
    256, 261, 317, 351
conspicuous: production 237; transformation
    227
constructive psychology view of human
    experience 291
consumer: behaviour 374–90, 405–22; durables
    374, 409; studies 4, 97, 387
consumerism 36, 42, 250–61, 407; culture of
    223; excessive 417; green 11–24; modern
    250; paradigm of 338; reductions in 65
consumers' replacement decisions 377
continuous education 112–26
Cooper, Tim 405
Cornwall council 183
corporate sustainability reports (CSR) 102
Council of Industrial Design 14
cradle to cradle 21, 115, 269, 294, 528 ;
    certification 184
cradle to grave 19, 119, 363, 528
creative commons license 162, 247
critical design 489
Crocker, Robert 250
cultural: diversification 70; identity 75; probes
    428; theory 432
culture of consumerism 223
Cupchik, Gerald C. 25
cyclic 173–91

D4S Shelter 176–91
Darwin, Charles 43, 48, 300
David Rockwell's Grand Central Chair 308
Deleuze, Giles and Guattari, Felix 336
Dell, 203
dematerialization 21, 236, 244, 349–58
Democratic Republic of Congo 197–205
democratized production 245
design abacus 117
Design Council UK 18, 120
Designers Accord 103
design for: behaviour change 117, 319,
    487–501, 529; flourishing 472; happiness
    117; personal significance 469–86; pleasure
    469–86; sharing 163; sustainability 160–172,
    316–34; sustainable behaviour (DfSB)
    97, 116, 127–44, 316–34, 488; sustainable
    consumption 423; the circular economy 117,
    174, 359; virtue 469–86
Design for the Real World 14, 102, 175
design framework 469–86
design ingredients tool 289
design-led community engagement 104
design: research 271–81; strategies 127–44

design thinking 97, 101–111, 272, 494, 506 *see also* user centered design
design with intent toolkit 137, 332, 494–9
Desmet, Pieter 469
diffuse attitude 546
diffuse design 521
diffusionism 43
digital accountability and transparency act 552
digital: disruption 237; manufacture 186–88; rights management (DRM) 162
Dilnot, Clive 83
dimensions of behaviour change tool 137
dirty carbon, 117
DiSalvo, Carl 339
distributed renewable energy 443–64
DIY 69, 238; activities 346; culture 552; materials 206–21
Dodd-Frank Act 197–205
domestic life 423–42
double diamond 522
DRE micro-generator 450
Dutch electronic art festival (DEAF) 74

eBay 237
ecocide 42
ecodesign 11–24; directive 408, 416; strategies 115, 316; web 117
eco-effectiveness 21
eco-efficiency 21
eco indicator 99, 117
eco kettle by Brian Hartley 133
eco-modernism 18
Ed Carpenter's shoe for Adidas 232
Edison, Thomas 41
electrical and electronic equipment (EEE) 194, 410
electrical and electronic equipment (EEE) Directive 113
Electrolux 121
electronics industry citizenship coalition (EICC) 200
electronic waste (e-waste) 151
Ellen MacArthur Foundation 115, 364, 406
Ellul, Jacques 69
embodied stories 222–35
emotion and design 271–81
emotional design 34, 287, 298–315
emotional durability 26, 41–50, 187, 193, 343, 359, 374, 393, 401
emotionally durable design 21, 36, 41
empathy 57, 65, 104, 271–81
end-of-life 35, 316–17, 360, 368, 408
end of life collection 115
entrepreneurship 110, 166, 507
Enuf Shower 136
environmental: impact assessment (EIA) 19; improvement 316–334
environmentality 11–24

environmentally conscious design 174
environmental: sustainability 470–486; stewardship 63–5
epistemologies 41
Eternally Yours: Time in Design 207
Eternally Yours: Visions on Product Endurance 206
Etsy 237
European Economic and Social Committee (EESC) 411
European union's eureka programme 19
e-waste 2, 151–52, 239, 354, 524
experience: design 282–97, 298–315, 469–86; frameworks 394
experience prototypes 428
expert and diffuse design 540–54
extended producer responsibility 351

FabLabs 552
Fairphone 202, 377, 516
Fairweather, Adam 227
Fair Trade 110, 480
Fallan, Kjetil 11
Farmer's Market (New Balance shoe) 230
First Things First 102
Fitzpatrick, Colin 197
Flusser, Vilém 336
food miles 230
food waste 210
Forest Stewardship Council (FSC) 106
formal economy 542
Foucault, Michel 14
four threads of experience 284
FreeCycle 162
Fry, Tony 21, 90, 338, 352
Fuller, Richard Buckminster 509
functional obsolescence *see* obsolescence
fused deposition modelling (FDM) 239
future proofing 182
futures 487–501

Gant, Nick 222
Gell, Alfred 42
General Motors 164
Giaccardi, Elisa 206
Giddens, Anthony 17, 553
Global e-Sustainability Initiative (GeSI) 200
globalization 69–82
global recession 357
glulam 178
Go Get 259
Google's Project ARA 152
GrabCAD 237
grassroots design 69–82
Great Depression 33, 269
green: capitalism 87; consumerism 11–24; consumers 16; consumption 21
greening 18, 84
Grimaldi, Silvia 298

G-Star Jeans 232
Guerra, Joseph and Sonrab, Sina 217
guerrilla gardening 343
Gumdrop Bin 228
Gyrecraft 232

hackers 69–82
hacking 335–48
happiness 469–86
Happy Misfit Armchair 210
Hardin, Garrett 13, 511
Hawthorne effect 138
Haydn 302
Hector Serrano's Waterproof Lamp 306
hedonic adaptation 285, 471
Heidegger, Martin 69, 85, 88
Hella Jongerius's Soft Urn 308
heresthetics 340
Herman Miller 119
Hernandez, Richard J. 363
Hinte, Ed van 21, 206
Hiut Denim 117
home energy management systems (HEMS) 131
homeotechnology 81
Hood, Bruce 49
Huelsen, Jannis and Schwabe, Stephan 214
Huissoud, Marlène 214
human-centered design 430 *see also* user-centered
 design
human-centered approach 104
human flourishing 7, 53, 66, 481–4, 521
hybrid economies 166

IDEO 104, 163
iFixit 238
If This Then That (IFTTT) 133
IKEA 120, 255
IKEA effect 394
immaterial culture 267
imperfection 206–21
Industrial Design Society of America 14
industrial PSS (IPSS) 365 *see also* product service
 systems
industrial revolution 168, 542
Ingold, Tim 45–8
innate product sustainability 149
innovation platforms 540–54
insightful procurement 183
Intel 203
International Organization for Standardization
 (ISO) 106
International Tin Research Institute (ITRI) 201
internet of things (IoT) 42, 491, 516, 544
IPR protection 247
Islam 62

jeong 502–513
Jong, Annelise de 423

Jordan, Patrick 284–6, 473
Judaism 62

Karana, Elvin 206
Kasser, Tim 165
Keynes, John Maynard 83
Kirkpatrick, John 21
Kockelkoren, Petran 69
Kropotkin, Peter 86

Latour, Bruno 43, 46, 426
learning 83–96
Lego 148, 286, 477
LeNSes project 443
Leube, Michael 41
Levi's 511 Commuter range 118
Life 2.0 550
life cycle analysis 19, 98, 350, 417
life cycle assessment 173–91, 349
Lilley, Debra 127
living lab 261, 430–40
Lobos, Alex 145
Lockton, Dan 326, 487
Lofthouse, Vicky 112
logic of inversion 48
longevity of a product 298–315
Loughborough University 117
low carbon 173–91
low effort energy demand reduction (LEEDR)
 project 13

maker's bill of rights 240
maker spaces 552
making 83–96
manufacture 363
Manzini, Ezio 541
Marcel Wanders' knotted chair 305
Margolin, Victor 13
Marine Conservation Society 230
Marxism 87, 91–2
Maslow need hierarchy framework 165, 474
material culture 98; literacy 222–35; mediations
 75; memories 222; possessions 165; resilience
 173–91
materialism 160–72, 252
materials experience 206–21
Mazé, Ramia 423
McDonagh, Deana 271
McDonough, Michael and Braungart, William
 21, 42, 528 *see also* cradle-to-cradle
meaning 53–68
meaningful objects 25; possessions 275
mediation 69–82
medium-density fibreboard (MDF) 223
mend and make do 19
Mercedes 164
metadesign 502–13
Micklethwaite, Paul 514

Miele 415
mindful design 527–39
modernism 12, 43
modernization theory 45
Montreal protocol 16
Moore's law 354
Morelli, Nicola 540
Morris, William 86, 340
Mugge, Ruth 374
Mu folding plug 118
multi-situated materials 206–21
Mumford, Lewis 69

Napster 162
narrative 298–315
narrativity 304
Natural Capital 174
naturalistic materialism 53–68
Nest 118
networked society 544
New Balance 230
new business models 273, 364, 391, 414–19
Niedderer, Kristina 527
Nietzsche, Friedrich 54–5
Nike 123
Norman, Donald 32, 50
Norwegian University of Science and
  Technology 317

object-activist 234
object experience 194
obsolescence 250–61, 405–22; absolute 238;
  perceived 62; planned 33, 42, 406; product
  63, 238; psychological 413; relative 238, 254;
  technological 254
On-Edge Lamp 312
open design 514–26
OpenIDEO 519
Organisation for Economic Co-operation and
  Development (OECD) 407
Ortíz Nicolás, Juan Carlos 282
Our Common Future 16

Papanek, Victor 14, 102, 112
paradigm 502–13
pareidolia 49
Park, Miles 236
Parsons School of Design 112
Parupu chair 210
passive users 543
patina 179, 187, 194, 212, 268, 343, 383 *see also*
  ageing gracefully
Pedagogy of the Oppressed 339
peer-to-peer (P2P) 162, 166, 351, 550
Peirce, Charles Sanders 71
performance economies 365 *see also* service
  economy
performative ethnography 440

persuasive: design 424; technology 133
Pesce, Gaetano 210
Peters, Peter 77
Peugeot 164
phenomenology 71
Philips 113, 119, 203, 406
Philips Design 116
philosophy of technology 69
PhoneBlocks 152
Pinterest 122
planned obsolescence *see* obsolescence
platonic 507
plastics: polyethylene terephthalate (PET) 19;
  polylactic acid (PLA) 153, 239; polypropylene
  149
pleasant experiences 282–97
Plessner, Helmuth 69, 74, 79
poetic meaning 299
Pohlmeyer, Anna 469
Politecnico di Milano 458
positive: design 469–86; emotion 298, 378;
  psychology 33, 471, 483; user behaviour 153
possession 391–404
post-awareness-raising era 466
post-industrial economy 83–96
post-materialism 166
post-war mass-consumption 251
practical application 112–26
practice based 173–91
practice theory 426, 430
Pré 177
Priestman Goode 183
principles of behaviour change 316
probe-head 335–348
product: attachment 25–40, 295, 374;
  experience 298–315; lifecycle 145; lifetimes
  405–22; longevity 182, 391, 401, 405–22;
  personalization 382; poetics 222–35; repair
  236–49
product-service systems 12, 119, 174, 259, 349–
  58, 361–73 *see also* sustainable product-service
  systems and new business models
products that last 206
product-user (emotional) relationship 272
prosthetics 242
prosumer 21, 517
prototype schemata and template schemata 302
psycho-animists 35
psychological ownership 391–404
Puma 123
Purity and Danger 256

quantitative unsustainability 349

Raspberry Pi 237
Ranner, Veronica 487
recyclability 146
recycling: banks 528, 537; closed loop 227;

culture of 232; habits 524; recycling rates 146;
   targets for 406; waste facilities 98, 412
Red Dott Awards, The 123
refurbishment 359, 374–90
registration, evaluation, authorization and
   restriction of chemicals (REACH) 197
Regt, Rutger de 210
relation 502–513
RelayRides 164
remaking making 91
remanufacturing 151, 259, 364–71, 374–90
renewable energy 110, 182, 360, 443–64, 508
repairable 1, 240, 260, 360; unrepairable 65, 238,
   259
repairing 91, 187, 236, 255, 377, 397, 412, 446
Repair Café 239
replacement parts 236–49
Reprap project 239
repurpose products 240
research through design 425
resilience thinking 206–9
resource security 406
responsible design 14, 60, 120, 527–39
Restart Project 239
restriction of hazardous substances directive
   (RoHS) 113, 197
re-valuation 222–35
Rognoli, Valentina 206
Rubbish Theory 256
Rubik's cube 286
Ruskin, John 86, 340

Salvation Army 19
Samsung 251
Sandel, Michael 343
Scarry, Elaine 91
Schumacher, E. F. 14, 54
Sculpteo 237
Sea Chair 232
second hand goods 253, 386–87, 391, 397–8
Second World War 15, 19
Securities and Exchange Commission (SEC)
   200
semiotic meaning 426–9
semiotics 70–9, 139, 223, 302
service design 359, 370–1, 514–18, 534, 552
service economy 360–3, 550
Shapeways 237
sharing 160–72; economy 98, 160–7, 349–58,
   550; platforms 167, 247, 479, 550; revolution
   168
Sherin, Aaris 101
SimaPro 177
Simmel, Georg 508
SINTEF (Scandinavian independent research
   organization) 320
six virtues from religion and philosophy 478
smart city 551

social: design 514–26, 534, 546; enterprise
   202, 239; impact 103, 113, 133, 194, 197;
   innovation 117, 359, 540–54; issues cards
   117; justice 335–48; responsibility 65; values
   368, 473
socio-cultural practices 423–42
social practice theory 140, 429–31, 439
speculative and participatory design for
   sustainable development 440
speculative design 489
Spineless Lamps by Frederik Roijé 306
spirituality: forms of 54–6: Japanese 61;
   traditions 60
Stahel, Walter 356, 365
standardization 79
Starck, Philippe 149
Static! 427
Stevenson, Robert Louis 54
stewardship 399
storytelling 110, 383
strategy 101–11
subjective well-being 469–86
supra-functionality 277
surprise 298–315
SusHouse project 358
Sustainable Apparel Coalition 123
sustainable: approaches 11; behaviour 127–44,
   153, 337; design 250–61, 282–97, 514–26;
   emotion 25–40; energy for all 443–64;
   future 20, 50; homes 534; lifestyles 423–42;
   materialism 165; practice 101; product
   development 174; product-service systems
   363, 443–64; scenario 443–64; societies 470;
   thinking 101–11; transport 535
sustainable development: 16, 21 22, 174;
   approaches to 156, 423–440; pillars of 470;
   policies 177, 183, 190; strategic 190
sustainment 83–96
Swedish Energy Agency 428
synergy 502–513
system design for sustainable energy for all
   443–64
systems thinking 145–59

tactical media 81
take back 118, 255, 351, 360, 528
taoism 62
Tamura, Nao 209
Taylor, Damon 11
technical mediation 69
technological obsolescence see obsolescence
technosphere 174
Teenage Engineering 244
Thackara, John 89, 112, 524,
The High Price of Materialism 165
The Waste Makers 269, 413
Thingiverse 237
Thomas Cook 78

throwaway: culture 412, 417; society 269, 409
Tonkinwise, Cameron 349
tool libraries 162, 167, 351
top-down 25–40
Torrey Canyon oil spill 13
trade in 98, 199
tradition 53–68
transient products 59, 65
transitional object 37
transition design 349–58
transparency 106, 516
Transport for London (TfL) 175
triple bottom line (tbl) model 146
Tversky, Amos 29

Uber 160, 356
UK Marine Conservation Society 230
Ultimaker original 3D 240
UN 11, 12, 190; human development index 198; environment programme (UNEP) 15
Underskog by Kristine Bjaadal 212
unilineal evolutionism 41–52
unsustainable 53; design 11; design practices 63
upcycle 42, 190, 232
upgradeability 517
upper palaeolithic period 36
use phase 316–34
user behavior 145–59
user centered: design 127–44, 332; design approach 475, 483; research methods 319; sustainable design 116 *see also* human centered design
user experience 282–97
user needs 271–81
usership 268, 349, 356
utilitarian design 28; values 65
utility designs act 507

values 53–68
Velcro 278
Vermeer, Johannes 29
Vezzoli, Carlo 443
vintage 245, 269
virtuous circularity 222–35
Volkswagen 164

wabi sabi 209
Walker, Stewart 53
washing machine 19, 42, 155, 542
waste electrical and electronic equipment directive (WEEE) 113, 197
waste-making 250–61
waste: Bio 537; food 210; recycling facilities 98, 412; reduction 408, 537; studies 435; streams 411
water footprint 118
wearable technology 272
Web 2.0. 162
weighted ethical matrix 137
well-being 469–86
wicked problems 514
Wilson, Garrath T. 127
Wood, John 502
Woodham, Jonathan 12
workers rights 107
world commission on environment and development (WCED) 16

Xerox 259, 371
xylinum cones 214

Zachrisson Daae, Johannes 316
zero waste 117, 260
zero waste economy 261
Zipcar 160

Taylor & Francis eBooks

Helping you to choose the right eBooks for your Library

Add Routledge titles to your library's digital collection today. Taylor and Francis ebooks contains over 50,000 titles in the Humanities, Social Sciences, Behavioural Sciences, Built Environment and Law.

Choose from a range of subject packages or create your own!

Benefits for you

- » Free MARC records
- » COUNTER-compliant usage statistics
- » Flexible purchase and pricing options
- » All titles DRM-free.

Benefits for your user

- » Off-site, anytime access via Athens or referring URL
- » Print or copy pages or chapters
- » Full content search
- » Bookmark, highlight and annotate text
- » Access to thousands of pages of quality research at the click of a button.

REQUEST YOUR FREE INSTITUTIONAL TRIAL TODAY

Free Trials Available
We offer free trials to qualifying academic, corporate and government customers.

eCollections – Choose from over 30 subject eCollections, including:

Archaeology	Language Learning
Architecture	Law
Asian Studies	Literature
Business & Management	Media & Communication
Classical Studies	Middle East Studies
Construction	Music
Creative & Media Arts	Philosophy
Criminology & Criminal Justice	Planning
Economics	Politics
Education	Psychology & Mental Health
Energy	Religion
Engineering	Security
English Language & Linguistics	Social Work
Environment & Sustainability	Sociology
Geography	Sport
Health Studies	Theatre & Performance
History	Tourism, Hospitality & Events

For more information, pricing enquiries or to order a free trial, please contact your local sales team:
www.tandfebooks.com/page/sales

 Routledge
Taylor & Francis Group

The home of
Routledge books

www.tandfebooks.com